VENICE

ALTA MACADAM

SOMERSET - LONDON

CONTENTS

Ninth edition 2014

Published by Blue Guides Limited, a Somerset Books Company
Winchester House, Deane Gate Avenue, Taunton, Somerset TA1 2UH
www.blueguides.com
'Blue Guide' is a registered trademark.

ISBN 978–1–905131–60–0

A CIP catalogue record of this book is available from the British Library.

Distributed in the United States of America by
W.W. Norton & Company, Inc.
500 Fifth Avenue, New York, NY 10110.

The author and the publishers have made reasonable efforts to ensure the accuracy of all the
information in *Blue Guide Venice*; however, they can accept no responsibility for any loss,
injury or inconvenience sustained by any traveller as a result of information or advice
contained in the guide.

Statement of editorial independence: Blue Guides, their authors and editors,
are prohibited from accepting any payment from any restaurant, hotel, gallery or other
establishment for its inclusion in this guide, or for a more favourable mention than
would otherwise have been made.

Every effort has been made to contact the copyright owners of material reproduced in this
guide. We would be pleased to hear from any copyright owners we have been unable to reach.

Your views on this book would be much appreciated. We welcome not only specific
comments, suggestions or corrections, but any more general views you may have: how
this book enhanced your visit, how it could have been more helpful. Blue Guides authors
and editorial and production team work hard to bring you what we hope are the best-
researched and best-presented cultural guide books in the English language. Please
write to us by email (editorial@blueguides.com), via the comments page on our website
(www.blueguides.com) or at the address given above. We will be happy to acknowledge
useful contributions in the next edition, and to offer a free copy of one of our titles.

Editor-in-chief: Annabel Barber,
with special thanks to Judy Tither and Joseph Kling.

Maps: Dimap Bt.
Floor plans and watercolours: Imre Bába
Architectural line drawings: Michael Mansell RIBA & Gabriella Juhász
Photographs by Annabel Barber, Tom Howells, James Howells
All maps and images © Blue Guides.
Cover: Church of the Redentore, Michael Mansell RIBA & Gabriella Juhász © Blue Guides.

Design by Stephen Reid and Blue Guides
All material prepared for press by Anikó Kuzmich.

Author's acknowledgements: As for all past editions I am first and foremost indebted to
Frances Clarke, who keeps me carefully up to date with all that is going on in Venice. She is a
wonderful friend and I am deeply grateful to her. Laura Corti gave me generous hospitality
on countless visits to the city. Sonia Finzi was kind enough to supply me with many practical
details about all things Venetian. I was also able to call on the wide knowledge of Etta Lisa
Basaldella. I would like to thank Maria Da Villa Urbani of the Procuratoria di San Marco,
who smoothed my path during visits to St Mark's Basilica.

Thanks also to James Christie and Carole Mason, for comments on the previous edition.

Printed in Hungary by Dürer Nyomda Kft., Gyula.

About the author and contributors

ALTA MACADAM is the author of over 40 Blue Guides to Italy. She lives in the hills
above Florence with her husband, the painter Francesco Colacicchi. In the 1970s she
worked for the Photo Library of Alinari and in the following two decades for Harvard
University's Villa I Tatti. She is at present external consultant for New York University
at the photo archive of Villa La Pietra in Florence, and as author of the Blue Guides to
Florence, Rome, Tuscany, Umbria and Central Italy, she travels extensively every year
to revise new editions of the books.

CHARLES FREEMAN (C.F.) is a freelance academic historian with widespread interests
in Italy and the Mediterranean. His *Egypt, Greece and Rome, Civilizations of the Ancient
Mediterranean* (Oxford University Press, 3rd ed. 2014) is widely used as an introductory
textbook to the ancient world and is supported by his *Sites of Antiquity: 50 Sites that
Explain the Classical World* (Blue Guides, 2009). His *The Horses of St Mark's* (Little
Brown, 2004) is a study of the famous horses through their history in Constantinople
and Venice. He is a Fellow of the Royal Society of Arts.

NIGEL MCGILCHRIST (N.McG.) is an art historian who has lived in the Mediterranean—
Italy, Greece and Turkey—for over twenty-five years, working for a period for the Italian
Ministry of Arts and then for six years as Director of the Anglo-Italian Institute in Rome.
He has taught at the University of Rome, for the University of Massachusetts, and was
for seven years Dean of European Studies for a consortium of American universities. He
lectures widely in art and archaeology at museums and institutions in Europe and the
United States and is author of *Blue Guide Greece the Aegean Islands*.

VENICE IN CONTEXT

Highlights of Venice

The most famous sights in Venice—St Mark's Basilica, the Doge's Palace and Rialto Bridge—are, not surprisingly, also the most visited. During daylight hours, except in the depths of winter, these areas can become dramatically overcrowded. Your best weapons are patience, time and tolerance of your fellow human beings. No visit to Venice is complete without entering St Mark's magnificent basilica, glowing with mosaics, or without walking through the seemingly endless, grandly decorated rooms of the Doge's Palace (as well as finding time and a peaceful spot to study and appreciate the marvellous exteriors of these buildings, both of them architectural wonders, and their extraordinary settings, on the vast Piazza San Marco and the open waterfront).

But since Venice is one of the most beautiful and best preserved cities in the world, a walk through any of its narrow streets or quiet squares, or along its lovely little canals, can be as rewarding as a visit to its greatest monuments. Surprisingly swiftly you can get away from the crowds, since they are entirely absent in great swathes of the city. The secluded district of Dorsoduro, for example, is one of the most delightful areas to explore. The island of the Giudecca, with the church of the Redentore, a masterpiece of Palladio, is also a peaceful district seldom visited by tourist groups. On the next-door island of San Giorgio Maggiore is another church by Palladio, with a superb view from its bell-tower.

The excellent public transport system of water-buses provides countless delights, and just sitting on one of these without necessarily going to a specific destination allows you to see the townscape in all its glory from the water, as well as to appreciate its lagoon setting. The trip along the Grand Canal on vaporetto number 1 should certainly not be missed, as this is the only way you can see all of Venice's grandest palace façades. A ride on one of the gondola ferries (*traghetti*) across the Grand Canal is another memorable experience.

Of the numerous churches in the city, two of the finest are the great foundations of the mendicant orders: the huge Dominican church of Santi Giovanni e Paolo, with many funerary monuments to doges, some of them Renaissance masterpieces; and the Franciscan church of the Frari, which has more good funerary monuments as well as paintings by Bellini and Titian. Venice is also one of the best places in Europe to see art *in situ*: paintings and altarpieces still displayed in the buildings for which they were commissioned. Wonderful works by Venice's most famous painters, still in churches all over the city, include many by Bellini, Tiepolo, Tintoretto, Titian and Veronese. The churches of San Zaccaria, Santa Maria Formosa and San Giovanni in Bragora have precious altarpieces by Venetian painters. San Sebastiano is decorated with superb paintings by Veronese; Santa Maria dei Miracoli has exquisite Renaissance carvings by Pietro Lombardo. The Madonna dell'Orto, in a lovely quiet area of the city, contains important works by Tintoretto. La Pietà has a fine 18th–century interior and San Stae has 18th-century paintings.

The best buildings which belonged to the *scuole*, or lay confraternities dedicated to charitable works during the Republic, include the Scuola Grande di San Rocco, with over fifty paintings by Tintoretto, one of the most remarkable pictorial cycles in existence; the Scuola Grande dei Carmini, with beautiful ceiling paintings by Tiepolo; and the Scuola di San Giorgio degli Schiavoni, charmingly decorated with paintings by Vittore Carpaccio.

Museums of great interest include the famous Gallerie dell'Accademia, home to the most important collection of Venetian paintings in the world, with Giovanni Bellini, Titian, Tintoretto and Veronese all well represented. Museo Correr is the city museum, with historical collections and some important paintings, and it is attached to the Museo Archeologico with its ancient Greek and Roman sculpture. The Ca' d'Oro, the most splendid palace on the Grand Canal, has some fine Venetian sculptures; and Ca' Rezzonico, also facing the great waterway, retains its grand 18th-century decorations, including frescoes by Tiepolo. The Peggy Guggenheim collection contains one of the most representative displays of 20th-century art in Europe. The splendid Palazzo Grimani is a fascinating example of a noble residence, its decorations conceived and commissioned by a cultivated and influential family.

Of all the islands in the beautiful Venetian lagoon, the most evocative is Torcello, with its ancient cathedral. Murano is interesting for its glass-works and glass museum, and its Veneto-Byzantine basilica.

A walk through the city in the very early morning provides you with a glimpse of the daily life of the Venetians and just how the city works. At this time it is the sounds of Venice which are the most striking: the voices of the inhabitants with their particular cheerful dialect, the birdsong from the many gardens and terraces, the cry of the seagulls, the noise of the boats transporting provisions and merchandise all over the city. At this time the street-cleaners are also silently at work, using the traditional 'witches' brooms' (since these are still by far the best way of reaching into the cracks of the steps of the bridges). So much goes into preserving the extraordinary atmosphere of Venice, and one is thankful that modern technology has not been allowed to disturb certain details of its way of life.

History of Venice

This race did not seek refuge in these islands for fun, nor were those who joined later moved by chance; necessity taught them to find safety in the most unfavourable lo-cation. Later, however, this turned out to their greatest advantage and made them wise at a time when the whole northern world still lay in darkness; their increas-ing population and wealth were a logical consequence. Houses were crowded closer and closer together, sand and swamp transformed into solid pavement...The place of street and square and promenade was taken by water. In consequence, the Venetian was bound to develop into a new kind of creature, and that is why too, Venice can only be compared to itself.

Goethe, *Italian Journey*, 1786–8

Venice is a city of ambiguities, not least in the way it presents its past. Stung by accusations that it never had a Classical heritage, the city created a legend that it had been founded by refugees from Troy, long before Rome had even been heard of. A more enduring foundation myth is that it began life in the year 421 under the protection of the Virgin Mary, precisely at midday on the Feast of the Annuncia-tion, 25th March, and this is celebrated by reliefs of the Angel Gabriel and Mary both on the façades of St Mark's and on the Rialto Bridge.

In truth, it was probably not until the 6th century that Lombard invaders, sweeping down through the northeast of Italy, forced refugees out onto the scattered islands of the lagoon. There is evidence of settlement on the island of Torcello by 600. In these early years the Byzantine Empire kept control of this corner of Italy, and the popula-tion was ruled from Ravenna by an appointed military official, the *dux*. The islanders gradually consolidated their identity: by the 7th century they had their own bishopric (on Torcello) and when Ravenna itself was overrun by the Lombards in 751, the *dux* be-came the city's doge, a ruler now chosen from within the emerging merchant families.

It was trade with the Islamic East which stimulated the wealth of early Venice. Doc-uments and archaeological evidence (in coins) show increasing numbers of Venetian ships heading east as early as the 8th century to the stable and expanding economies of the Arab world. Slaves from northern Europe appear to have been one export, and gold, spices and relics from the Holy Land the return. The early Venetians, then, were focused on the two great civilisations of the Near East: their Byzantine overlords in Constantinople, and the world of Islam. Wealth grew steadily. The cathedral at Tor-cello is a lone foundation of the 7th century, but there are twelve new churches in the 8th century and 23 in the 9th. In this century too the original patron saint of the city, the Byzantine Theodore, was replaced by the Evangelist St Mark, whose body was reputedly smuggled out of Alexandria in 828 and placed in what was the doge's private chapel; now St Mark's Basilica. The centre of power in Venice began to shift from the islands to the area around St Mark's, and in the 11th century the basilica was rebuilt with domes which echoed the (now vanished) church of the Holy Apostles in Constantinople. Despite the transfer of the city's allegiance to St Mark, the links with the Byzantine Empire remained close, and in 992 Venetians were given special trading privileges in Constantinople in return for recognising continuing Byzantine sovereignty.

Venice was too remote from the East to be truly controlled, however, and by 1082 its independence was recognised. After this, in return for naval help they had given to the Byzantines, the Venetians were allowed to trade freely throughout the Empire. The city vigorously developed its own identity as a stable and effective trading community. The doge had originally been an absolute ruler, but after the year 1000 documents suggest that he was aided by officials, the forerunners of the interlocking councils which were later to run the Republic. In 1144 there is the first mention of Venice as a *comune* (the word used to describe the self-ruled cities of northern Italy), and communal activity was reinforced by the need to defend and sustain Venice's precarious position in the lagoon. The city's government took a leading role in regulating water supplies, reclaiming land and setting out communal space. St Mark's Square, modelled on an imperial forum in Constantinople or the great squares of an Islamic city such as Damascus, showed the ability of the Venetian government to preserve space in a crowded city from the incursions of the wealthy merchant families (no other Italian city of the period had such a large open space). Under the patronage of Doge Sebastiano Ziani (1172–8), the square was extended westwards to reach its present size. The procurators, responsible for the fabric of the basilica and the square itself, were among the most prestigious officials of the city, and they took on added functions in overseeing the welfare of patrician families. Some even used the position as a stepping stone to the dogeship. Meanwhile merchants' palaces were beginning to spread along the Grand Canal. 'While the burghers and barons of the north were building their dark streets and grisly castles of oak and sandstone, the merchants of Venice were covering their palaces with porphyry and gold', as John Ruskin put it. It was this combination of public and private display along the waterfronts which was to make the city appear so glittering to outsiders.

THE FOURTH CRUSADE AND EMERGING PATTERNS OF POWER

The 12th century was a time of increasing tension, as disputes between Venice and Constantinople erupted in self-defeating trade wars. Nothing, however, could have prepared the city for the events of the Fourth Crusade (*see also p. 59*), when under the energetic leadership of Doge Enrico Dandolo, Constantinople was sacked by the crusaders and the Byzantine emperor deposed. Venice trumpeted herself as 'lord of a quarter plus half a quarter of the Roman [i.e. Byzantine] empire'. Large sections of Constantinople, Thrace, the coast of Greece and Crete now passed to Venice, giving her trading posts all the way to the East, with control too of the entrance to the Adriatic. Back in the city, the doges took on the trappings of a Byzantine emperor, appearing to their subjects on the loggia of St Mark's as if they were in the imperial hippodrome of Constantinople. In the reign of Doge Ranier Zeno (1253–68), opulence reached its zenith. St Mark's Square was paved and the doge himself would process around it in rich cloth and jewels. The grand ceremony of the *Sensa*, when the doge went out into the lagoon in the *Bucintoro*, the state barge, and threw a gold ring into the sea to symbolise Venice's 'marriage' to the waters, reached its most elaborate form.

Abroad, however, the newly acquired empire was less stable. Genoa, Venice's most powerful trading rival, allied with Michael Palaeologus and restored him to the Byzantine throne (1261). The Venetian quarter in Constantinople went up in flames. For the next century, Venice and Genoa were engaged in a series of deadly wars, which only ended in 1380, when Venice drove off a Genoese force at Chioggia. There were years of unrest and hunger as other cities disputed Venice's trading routes. In 1310 there was an assassination attempt on Doge Pietro Gradenigo after he had failed in a war against Ferrara. He survived, but a Council of Ten was set up to oversee internal security. Its secretive work and readiness to intrude into every aspect of political and social life gave it an unwholesome reputation. In 1355, Doge Marin Falier even tried to seize power and establish a dictatorship (much as nobles in the mainland cities were doing at the same time). He was overcome, deposed and executed.

These troubles masked a steady consolidation of power in the hands of the nobility at the expense of the doge. The *Serrata* of 1297 restricted government to the noble class and they, sitting on the Great Council, elected the bodies which ruled Venice (*see pp. 94–5*). The consolidation was marked from 1340 by the amalgamating of the private house of the doge, the seat of justice and the meeting halls of the councils into one building, the Doge's Palace, the highest achievement of the Venetian Gothic, the style which was now flamboyantly decorating the residences of the nobility. Venice's confidence is shown in the openness of these buildings to the sun and the sea, a vivid contrast to the enclosed, fortress-like *palazzi* found, for instance, in Florence at this period. The arrival of the mendicant orders, the Dominicans and the Franciscans, saw the fine Gothic churches of Santi Giovanni e Paolo and the Frari (both begun in the 14th century and finished in the 15th) bring a new dimension to the city's religious life, which up to now had centred either on St Mark's or on small parish churches (of which San Giacomo di Rialto is the sole survivor).

The communal identity of the city was strengthened by its use of space, notably St Mark's Square, for ceremonial rituals which displayed the doge, his councillors and its citizens to each other. The anniversary of the arrival of the body of St Mark was celebrated on 31st January. The saint's own feast day was 25th April; and the miraculous recovery of his intact body after a fire destroyed the basilica in the 11th century was commemorated on 25th June. The anniversary of the dedication of the basilica itself followed on 8th October. Gentile Bellini's *Procession of the Relic of the True Cross* (1496; *see p. 143*) shows how the procession on a ceremonial occasion was arranged, so that each participant could look round to see the officials preceding or following him.

For those excluded from political power—all those outside the four or five percent of the population who belonged to noble families—the *Scuole Grandi* provided an alternative source of influence. The *scuole* were in fact charitable institutions, but their officials were given high status within the city. Each year on 26th April, for instance, they paraded their relics (the School of St John the Evangelist had a relic of the True Cross, the centrepiece of the procession shown in Bellini's painting), and then presented candles to the doge, as well as to his leading councillors, to foreign ambassadors and senior members of the clergy. The Venetian statesman Gasparo Contarini, writing in the mid-16th century, argued that such rituals satisfied these men's ambition and cooled any resentment they might feel towards the nobility. Certain non-noble families, making up perhaps another seven per cent of the population, were also granted the status of *cittadino originario*, which allowed privileged access to administrative posts.

All this display and stability depended on commercial prosperity. The Rialto was like a permanent trade fair, where goods were brought from all over the Mediterranean. Spices and precious stuffs, furs, jewels and raw materials for cloth, often from as far afield as India and China, all came through the Byzantine or Islamic states. Metals, finished cloth and, it appears, slaves, were brought from Europe by merchants over the Alps. Venice acted as the entrepôt. Once customs fees had been paid, goods could be reshipped either by Venetian vessels (who were also heading west by the 1320s) or by those merchants, mostly Italian and German, who had been given special trading privileges. The Germans had their own great storehouse and meeting house, the Fondaco dei Tedeschi, across the Rialto Bridge from the main markets; the Turks later had another. There were many more smaller communities—Florentines, Luccans, Slavs, Armenians—who would have their own areas of town and places of worship. The Venetians proved adept at working out credit arrangements, dues and storage facilities, all of which accrued further wealth for the city. Venice was also a centre for embarking to the Holy Land, pilgrims would be taken on a tour of the city's relics before choosing their boat from those assembled along the Riva degli Schiavoni. Bedding could be purchased and then resold on the return.

MAINLAND EXPANSION AND THE FALL OF CONSTANTINOPLE

Up to now Venice's possessions had all been in the East, but in the 14th century it was hotly debated whether she should expand onto the mainland, to secure her own supplies of grain and gain more effective control of the Alpine passes. The Hundred Years War between England and France (1337–1453) heightened the city's insecurity, and the expansionist party gained strength. The city of Treviso, just inland, was, in fact, taken in 1339, but it was not until 1404–05 that a power vacuum left by the fall of the aggressive Gian Galeazzo Visconti in Milan allowed Venice to seize Vicenza, Verona and Padua. In 1420 the acquisition of the Friuli and Udine brought Venetian territory, the *terraferma*, up to the foot of the Alps. Then a famous debate broke out between Doge Tommaso Mocenigo who, as spokesman for 'the party of the sea', presented an idealised version of Venice as a city purely focused on maritime trade, and Francesco Foscari, who succeeded Mocenigo as doge in 1423, and who stood for expansion on land. The wars with rival mainland cities that broke out under Foscari showed just how intractable the mainland was to prove, and it was not until 1454 that a peace treaty with Milan recognised Venice's new Italian possessions.

The immediate effect of the expansion was an economic boom, and the years 1420–

50 could be seen as the highest point of Venice's power. Her trade routes were extensive and well policed; she had defeated her rivals. Her wealth was being ploughed into such opulent palaces as the Ca' d'Oro on the Grand Canal, and the façades of the Ca' Foscari and the palaces of the Giustinian family near the Rialto Bridge reflect the confidence of the age. Venice's population, which like that of the rest of Europe had been devastated by the Black Death in 1349, had recovered to some 100,000 by 1400, and grew steadily to 140,000 by 1500.

Yet just as she seemed more secure, the news came through in 1453 that Constantinople had fallen to the Ottoman Turks. From now on Venice was to be on the defensive in the East. Although Cyprus, a vital staging post for Eastern trade, was taken by Venice in 1489, the Ottomans began to nibble away at other Venetian outposts in the Aegean. In one war Ottoman raids even reached the Adriatic, and the clouds of smoke from the destruction could be seen from the campanile of St Mark's. Meanwhile, in 1498, Portuguese traders had rounded the Cape of Good Hope and reached India, showing that the riches of the East no longer had to come overland, to be sent onwards through the entrepôt of Venice. It was a presage of future economic decline.

SIXTEENTH-CENTURY VENICE

In 1494 the French invaded northern Italy, causing unrest which Venice attempted to exploit by expanding further on the mainland. It was a misguided strategy which succeeded only in uniting the powers of Europe against her. The pope organised the League of Cambrai in opposition, and there followed a humiliating defeat at Agnadello, near Milan, in 1509. Even Venice's 'own' cities closed their gates against her fleeing troops. 'In one battle', wrote Machiavelli, 'the Venetians lost what in eight hundred years they had gained with so much effort.' Although the land was regained, Venice's power and image were irreparably damaged, and when Pope Clement VII presided over a reorganisation of the Italian states in 1530, Venice was not even consulted. Despite the odd success in the next century, notably the Battle of Lepanto in 1571, when Venetian galleys routed the Turkish fleet, there was little to celebrate. Cyprus, in fact, had been lost to the Turks just before Lepanto.

But the Venetians were always adept at manipulating their image, and they concealed their humiliation by presenting themselves as the ideal republic in which everyone lived in harmony. The propagandist for the city was Gasparo Contarini in his *De magistratibus et republica Venetorum* (written in the 1520s but published in 1543). 'Such moderation and proportions characterise this Republic,' he wrote, 'that this city by itself incorporates at once a princely sovereignty, a governance of the nobility, and a rule of citizens so that all appear as equal weights.' Contarini even compared the Venetians with the Greeks under the Roman Empire: defeated perhaps, but still the arbiters of all that was culturally best. There was now some truth in this. While the merchant families of the early 15th century had shown little interest in art, the late 15th and 16th centuries produced Giovanni and Gentile Bellini, Giorgione, Tintoretto, Veronese, and the first artist to achieve a quasi-aristocratic status for his profession, Titian.

Though Contarini's depiction was largely a myth, the endless interaction of foreign merchants made Venice a much more fluid society than most in Europe. Her wealth was also too great to be easily dissipated, and she showed some resilience in creating her own industries. The city had produced only 2,000 lengths of wool in 1500; by the end of the 16th century she was manufacturing between 20,000 and 26,000 lengths annually. After having imported silk workers from Lucca in the 14th century, the industry grew in the 16th century to employ thousands of weavers. Standards, set by the government, were very high, ensuring that Venice's European reputation rested heavily on the quality of her luxury goods. Glass-making, based then as now on Murano, where fires from the furnaces could not spread far, dominated the international market for the whole of the 16th century. Mirrors were a great speciality. Printing was another important industry. The great printer Aldus Manutius had, by his death in 1515, published 55 texts in Greek and 67 in Latin (as against only six in Italian). Thirty-one of the Greek texts were the first printed editions anywhere and confirmed Venice's status as the leading Greek cultural centre in Italy. The major library of Greek manuscripts donated by Cardinal Bessarion in 1468 is still part of the Libreria Marciana (*see p. 81*).

To the outside world, therefore, Venice still appeared a prosperous city, and no expense was spared in further glorifying her surroundings. In 1490, the Torre dell'Orologio, the clock-tower, was built in St Mark's Square, facing directly towards the water so that it would provide a backdrop for important visitors as they landed. The Procuratie, the arcaded buildings on either side of the Piazza, were rebuilt during the 16th century. Most magnificently of all, the architect Jacopo Sansovino was commissioned to design a mint (the Zecca) on the waterfront and a grand library along the western side of the Piazzetta, with its northern facade in St Mark's Square itself. At the base of the Campanile, the city's bell-tower, he built the exquisite Loggetta, where nobles met for discussion before entering the Doge's Palace for formal debate. Likewise, when a fire destroyed much of the Rialto in 1505, it was rebuilt in a programme which culminated in Sansovino's Fabbriche Nuove, the warehouses to the north (started in 1554), and the Rialto Bridge, built in the 1590s to a design by Antonio da Ponte. The *scuole* played their own part, as shown in the great upper chamber of the Scuola Grande di San Rocco, built between 1515 and 1560 and sumptuously decorated by Jacopo Tintoretto. Andrea Palladio's great church of San Giorgio Maggiore was begun in 1565. 'We have always,' proclaimed the Senate in 1535—with justification—'striven to provide this city with most beautiful temples, private buildings and spacious squares, so that from a wild and uncultivated refuge it has grown, been ornamented and constructed, so as to become the most beautiful and illustrious city which at present exists in the world.'

VENICE IN DECLINE

Venice's relationship with the Church was always ambiguous, as is perhaps symbolised by the fact that the city's cathedral was not St Mark's (until 1807), nor any major building in the centre of the city, but San Pietro di Castello, out of the way at its eastern extremity. The Church was not allowed to intrude on the city's economic or political independence. Whatever the Church said about usury, the Venetians justified their high interest rates as 'a Venetian custom', and when the pope forbade any trade with Muslim states in the 1340s it was said that the Venetians complied but placed Islamic-style cresting on the Doge's Palace in protest. In the early 17th century Venice came into direct conflict with the Church. The head of the Servite Order in the city, Pietro Sarpi, a man who was both intellectually brilliant and devout, had criticised the way in which the papacy put its territorial ambitions before the spiritual welfare of its flock. At the same time Venice had shown its supremacy over the Church by trying clerics in secular rather than Church courts. The pope, Paul V, was outraged, and in 1606 he placed Venice under papal interdict. It was a misjudged strategy. The Venetians, urged on by Sarpi, stood firm and expelled the Jesuits, who sided with the papacy. To his embarrassment, Paul found that no one in Europe was willing to support this outdated exercise of papal power and he had to withdraw his interdict. It was an important moment in the reassertion of secular against religious power in Europe.

Nevertheless, from the 17th century onwards, Venice was entering what one of its leading historians, Pompeo Molmenti, called the *decadimento*, the years of decline, which were to end with the extinction of the republic in 1797. The economic vitality of the city was being eroded by the consolidation of the French, English and Dutch mercantile relationships in the Levant and by the rise of Atlantic trade. Even within the Adriatic, Venice faced competition from the expanding Austrian port of Trieste and she had to endure Austria's tightening grip on the land around the *terraferma*. A series of debilitating wars with the Turks saw the loss of Crete, Venice's last major possession in the Mediterranean, in the 1660s. Even though Venice did regain some territory in the Peloponnese in 1680, the increasingly debt-ridden city could not hold it, and it was surrendered back to the Turks in 1718.

By the 18th century Venice was living off its past. It was a city that visitors now came to view, rather than admire for its achievements. 'The English use their powder for their cannon, the French for their mortars, in Venice it is usually damp and if it is dry they use it for fireworks', one visitor remarked. Another, William Beckford, complained how the Venetians 'pass their lives in one perpetual doze'. The playwright Carlo Goldoni's satires on the Venetian aristocracy making fools of themselves in front of their canny servants in their villas on the mainland sum up an age of frivolity and lack of purpose. Coffee house activity became more prominent—in St Mark's Square Florian was founded in 1720, Quadri in 1775. Venice's courtesans were renowned throughout Europe, and Casanova became a symbol of sexual decadence. Outsiders such as the patrician Lombard family of the Rezzonico could now buy their way into the city. (Their palace and its collections give a vivid impression of 18th-century Venice.)

NAPOLEON AND THE EXTINCTION OF THE REPUBLIC

For the sober observer of Enlightenment Europe, Venice was viewed with some derision as a corrupt, and—through the continuing activities of the Council of Ten—despotic state. The radical philosopher Jean-Jacques Rousseau, who spent some time in the city as Secretary to the French Ambassador, called the Council 'a tribunal of blood'. 'Venice sacrifices everything with the single object of giving no offence to other states,' was another scathing observation. The city was no match for the dynamism of the revolutionary French general Napoleon, who swept through Italy in 1796 and 1797. Venice, with no forces with which to confront the invader, grovelled in negotiations and finally succumbed to an ultimatum to install a 'democratic government' or submit to a French assault. The Great Council was summoned for the last time on 12th May 1797, but not even the required quorum of 600 members was reached. Those who did attend voted to replace themselves by a democratic government in the hope of 'preserving the religion, life and property of all these most beloved inhabitants'. Lodovico Manin, the 118th doge, acquiesced in the capitulation, handing his robes to his manservant with the tired words, 'I shall not be needing these again'. Thus, wrote Pierre Daru in his *History of the Venetian Republic* in 1819, 'a republic, famous, long powerful, remarkable for the singularity of its origin, of its site and institutions, has disappeared in our time, under our eyes, in a moment.'

FRENCH AND AUSTRIAN RULE

French talk of democracy proved hollow. The only immediate beneficiaries of the capitulation were the Jews, who were released from their ghetto. A 'Festival of Liberty' was held in St Mark's Square, at which the doge's regalia and the *Libro d'Oro*, the book which contained the official list of nobles, were burned. Napoleon, who did not visit the city himself until 1807, then ordered the burning of the *Bucintoro* and a choice of plunder for himself. The famous Horses of St Mark's (*see p. 67*) were taken to Paris, along with some of the city's finest paintings and most precious manuscripts. The new ruler's pragmatism was then shown by the transferral of Venice to Austria in the Treaty of Campo Formio in October 1797.

In 1805, when the French defeated the Austrians at Austerlitz, Venice came back under French control, and was incorporated into Napoleon's Kingdom of Italy. Some improvements were made, including the Giardini Pubblici, reclaimed from swampland in the east of the city, and the setting up of a cemetery outside the city on the island of San Michele; but the French treatment of Church property was more ruthless. The creation of a palace wing, complete with ballroom, at the western end of St Mark's Square, involved the demolition of one of Venice's most treasured churches, San Gemignano, whose façade by Jacopo Sansovino was a Venetian favourite. Altogether some 50 religious buildings and 40 palaces vanished in these years.

When Napoleon fell in 1815, the persistent efforts of the great Venetian sculptor Canova at the peace negotiations in Paris led to the return of the Horses and some of Venice's other treasures, but the European powers once again placed Venice under direct Austrian rule. The Austrians proved less destructive than the French, but they presided over a city whose spirit had been destroyed. Over 90 percent of the servants employed in the Venetian palaces lost their jobs, and Venice's decline was hastened by the continuing growth of the port of Trieste. It was not until the 1830s that a Venetian bourgeoisie began to re-emerge. In 1846, for the first time in her history, Venice was connected to the mainland, by a railway bridge. While romantics like Gustav von Aschenbach, the narrator of Thomas Mann's *Death in Venice*, might well complain that entering Venice through a station is like entering a palace by the back door, this was the first time the city was truly accessible to a wider public. In the late 1840s the annual number of tourists exceeded the total number of inhabitants (some 120,000) for the first time.

Austrian rule had its advantages (the education system was probably the best in Italy), but no one could deny that the Austrians exploited the Veneto for men and taxes, or that their police became increasingly obsessive about the growth of the 'secret societies' which planned to unite Venice to an Italian nation. With growing economic discontent in the 1840s and the spread of revolutionary fervour throughout Europe in the spring of 1848, Venice was bound to be affected. The hero of the revolution which followed was Daniele Manin, a lawyer imbued with the ideals of the Enlightenment, who declared a new Venetian republic in a speech from a coffee table at Florian's on 24th March. It was a heroic gesture, and the Austrians were forced by rioting crowds to withdraw from the city. For 17 months Venice held out while the Austrian troops took advantage of the failed revolutions elsewhere in Italy to regroup their forces. By the summer of 1849, a bombardment of the city began and famine led to cholera. In August 1849, Manin made a last defiant speech to the Venetians and then fled into exile as the Austrians arrived to reoccupy the city. It is good to note that when Venice eventually became part of the Kingdom of Italy in 1866, Manin's body was brought up the Grand Canal in a procession made up of thousands of gondolas to be buried in the northern exterior arcade of St Mark's.

QUESTIONS FOR THE FUTURE

Venice in the 19th century appeared to be a city in decay, its palaces sliding into the lagoon. The predatory Lord Byron helped to give the city—as Casanova had done before him—a reputation for sexual adventure. Certainly homosexuals were able to live more freely in Venice than in England, and some employed gondoliers who doubled as their lovers. There were many visitors who indulged in the nostalgia of vanished greatness. Writers and composers found solace in the city and even relished the sense of decay. When there was talk of widening or filling in canals for sanitary reasons, it was John Ruskin who pleaded that 'the voice of poetry should be sought in the gloomy canals and picturesque alleys.' Yet the damp and crumbling buildings which he had come to muse over could hardly be left suspended picturesquely on the water's edge, and so a debate began over whether Venice should be preserved and its palaces restored as a museum, or whether it should be modernised in the interests of its permanent inhabitants. The debate over restoration crystallised in the 1860s when the Fondaco dei Turchi (the former storehouse for Turkish merchants), which even Ruskin admitted was 'a ghastly ruin', was rebuilt in an unrecognisable form to save it. Such *lucidatura*, as it was known, was deeply offensive to romantics such as Ruskin, who wished for the preservation even of ancient dirt. 'Off go all the glorious old weather stains, the rich hues of the marble which nature, mighty as she is, has taken ten centuries to bestow,' he complained to his father as he observed a cleaning of St Mark's. He opposed every attempt to create new iron bridges, install gas lighting or make the city more habitable for its citizens. Venice risked becoming the public property of a foreign intelligentsia who would define it as they wished it to be. Local architects such as Camillo Boito (1836–1914), who actually worked to recreate the essence of an ancient building, sometimes by removing later accretions, became furious at the way outsiders portrayed him and others like him as 'barbarians'. When the Campanile collapsed in

1902, there were some—the Futurists, for instance—who argued that now was the time to let Venice sink forever below the lagoon. This time the conservatives triumphed. *Dov' era, com' era* ('Where it was, how it was') was the cry which successfully led to the replacement of the tower exactly as it had been, even if new materials had to be used. It was compromise of a sort which has enabled Venice to continue to present a façade of superb churches and great galleries against a backdrop of upmarket boutiques and opulent hotels for visitors, while its own citizens become strangers in their own town. A population of 184,000 in 1950 has fallen to under 60,000 today, with a comparative collapse in local services. Visitors average 60,000 a day (almost double the number that is thought to be sustainable), meaning that at times they outnumber the permanent inhabitants.

Yet there are far greater dangers to Venice. In November 1966, a massive flood left the city under two metres of water for several days, causing an estimated six billion dollars' worth of damage. It was a dramatic reminder of how vulnerable Venice has become to the very environment which in previous centuries it had used to its advantage. While the 1966 floods reached a record (since records of 1923) of 194cm, there have been floods of 149cm in November 2012 and 143cm in February 2013 (deep enough to affect 60 percent of the city). The Mo.S.E., the barrier that will protect Venice has been years in the building (*see pp. 34–5*).

Today's visitor can still enjoy Venice as a fantasy, even though the ever-increasing numbers of tourists make the core of the city less and less comfortable to visit. And behind the fantasy lie highly challenging conservation issues. What is being preserved and for whom? Have the citizens been sacrificed for the preservation of a tourist playground? Is there a realistic chance of saving the city in any case? If so, is this an Italian or an international problem? It is perhaps unfortunate that an early morning walk through the narrow *calli*, when the light is clear on the lagoon and some of the ancient churches are beginning to open alongside canals where the fruit barges are bringing up their wares, all too easily dispels the fears one must hold in more realistic moments.

Charles Freeman

The Art of Venice

A first sight of Venice is one of the revelations of a lifetime. However much we may know about its construction, it still seems wholly improbable that a city can really be suspended on the water. The water is everywhere, and it has conditioned not only Venice's attitude to the world outside, but also the themes and nature of its paintings. Most important of all has been the determining influence of the water on the materials with which artists could work. Everywhere else in medieval Italy and southern Europe, wall painting was the principal mode of expression in figurative art; but in Venice, the walls of the churches and public buildings, whose foundations stood under water, were unusable for fresco work, since the paintings rapidly perished from salt and damp. Venetian art could only ever truly flourish by the development of new kinds of materials and techniques and supports. And as it turned out, these essentially Venetian developments were to change the course of Western art.

A crucial example of this was the adoption, in the 15th century, of canvas as a support for painting. It happened in Venice not just because its atmosphere was inimical to fresco painting, but because, in the Arsenale, there was the largest manufactory of sailcloth in the world, for fitting out the military and merchant navies of a city who depended entirely on ships for her survival and defence. Though a simple idea, when combined with the revolutionary new techniques of painting in oil which were arriving in Venice at the same time, its consequences were far-reaching.

Venetian painting owes its influence and much of its character to these material considerations. But none of this explains its genius: it owes that principally to two giants of the history of art, Giovanni Bellini and Titian. Neither was a thinker or scientist in the way that, in Florence, Brunelleschi, Leonardo or Michelangelo had been. They were simply master painters; and for this reason the Renaissance in Venice, which comes a whole generation later than it does to Florence, has a completely different nature: not primarily theoretical or intellectual, but practical and visual. As a result, its artistic influence across Europe was greater and more compelling: in fact it all but eclipsed the memory of Florence.

THE ORIGINS OF VENETIAN ART

From its earliest examples, there is a richness at the core of Venetian art, which arises from an intrinsic delight in beautiful materials. Nowhere exemplifies this better than the Basilica of St Mark. It is here, in this extraordinary building, that the story of Venetian art begins. Already by the 12th century, St Mark's had one of the most richly decorated interiors in the Christian world: its floors were made up of hundreds of thousands of cut pieces of precious ancient marble; its walls, inside and out, were clad in ancient jaspers, porphyries, alabasters and polychrome marbles, which the moisture often made more brilliant and translucent; and then there were the mosaic ceilings of coloured glass-flux, and glass with gold leaf overhead. All this was consciously created to vie with the greatest churches of Constantinople. When the passage from Revelation was read, those listening inside the basilica knew that what they saw around them was a glimpse of the New Jerusalem, a deliberate evocation of John's vision of the walls and pavements of heaven (*Revelation 21: 18–21*).

In this same period of the 11th and 12th centuries, the Pala d'Oro, a Byzantine masterpiece of cloisonné enamel, was put up on the main altar of St Mark's. This was one of the defining moments of Venice's early artistic history. Its tiny, icon-like panels, framed in jewels and gold, are certainly a long way from a painting by Bellini; but he and the other great painters of the Venetian Renaissance cannot be properly understood without looking at the Pala d'Oro, because it is here that that same love of the depth and translucence of colour first becomes fully evident.

In the early Middle Ages, the workshops of St Mark's dominated the art of the city: no patrons other than the Church counted for much. The only place in the Venetian lagoon where there was an independent and more commercial flourishing of art was on the island of Murano, where secret techniques for making glass were being perfected. Glass is a versatile medium, which performs remarkable tricks with colour and light. When we look at the works of Bellini and Giorgione and Titian, we should not forget that these artists were working in what was Europe's foremost centre for glass production. Its translucence is there in their works, and it was there in material form also, at the heart of their painting.

In addition to this, and in ever richer variety, were the commodities of Venice's expanding commercial empire. Like ancient Rome before her, Venice looked east for trade, and dominated the market in luxury goods: spices, textiles, dyes, precious stones, metals, and—of greatest importance for the history of art—pigments, colours and resins. On these, Venice soon gained the European monopoly, reserving those of the best quality for herself.

FOURTEENTH- AND FIFTEENTH-CENTURY PAINTING

Early Venetian art was the child of Byzantium. A picture was a sacred object similar to an icon, a focus of devotion, whose painstaking creation by a team of craftsmen partook of the nature of a spiritual exercise. We know the master artists of the mid-14th century often only by their first name: Paolo or Lorenzo, called 'Veneziano', 'from Venice'. At first sight, these early works can seem like many others of the same epoch produced elsewhere; but there is a technical mastery and a management of colour in them that goes beyond that of their contemporaries. There is a deliberate play on different kinds of surface—shiny and opaque, metallic and enamel-like—which would have appeared highly compelling in the low candle-light and wide spaces of a Venetian church interior. Their elaborate Gothic decoration is courtly and refined, quite in contrast to the style of the early Tuscan painters. Vasari had delighted in telling how Giotto was just a country shepherd boy when Cimabue found him doodling on a rock in the Mugello valley: that is very Florentine—a pride in humble, amateur genius. Venice had no fields or shepherds or rocks: it was all city. Artists were formed in urban workshops of considerable sophistication, often with Greek Constantinopolitan masters teaching a method and style of painting whose roots lay in the Hellenistic traditions of the late Roman Empire of the East. This tradition produced devotional paintings in the 14th century, all of which aspired, to a greater or lesser degree, to emulate the exquisite richness of the Pala d'Oro.

The wealth of technical know-how involved in these intricate creations was jealously guarded: it naturally tended to be kept within families, and we therefore see a handful of family workshops emerge in Venice during the 1400s: the Crivelli, the Vivarini and the Bellini. The paintings of all three of these workshops show, in different ways, a new concentration on volume and the sculptural qualities of figures. This is initiated by the first generation, Jacopo Bellini (c. 1400–70/71) and Antonio and Bartolomeo Vivarini. The elegant patterned design, the enamel-like paint surface, and the rich colour are all still there; but the new interest in the solidity of the figures reveals something unusual and important for Venice—that she was, for once, looking over her shoulder at what was happening in the nearby mainland centres of Ferrara and Padua. During the 1440s the great Florentine sculptor Donatello was working in Padua: his powerful influence must have been impossible to ignore. In 1442, Andrea del Castagno, one of the brightest and most modern painters from Florence, came briefly to decorate the church of San Zaccaria in Venice. Their influence is not immediately obvious; it is subtle and cautious, as befitted the natural conservatism of the city. Slowly the soft Gothic flow of early Venetian painting acquires backbone and anatomy, and its figures begin to inhabit a world that has spatial order and coherence.

Notwithstanding the perfect craftsmanship of their work, the Crivelli and Vivarini remain imaginatively in the Gothic world. The works of Carlo Crivelli (1430/5–94/5), in particular, have an arresting and unforgettable personality—an exhilarating combination of purely decorative fantasy and yet a naturalism that takes us completely by surprise. A Madonna and Child, who almost seem carved in stone, stare from their niche at a startlingly realistic horsefly or bluebottle that appears to have alighted on the surface of the painting. This is not mere play, however; Crivelli's masterful paintings, with their wealth of fruit, flowers and fauna, are woven from an intricate web of allegorical allusions, in which the cucumber is made to symbolise the Resurrection of Christ and the infamous bluebottle represents the presence both of evil and, more specifically, the plague. A highly accomplished but very eccentric painter, Crivelli left Venice early, after a period in prison for adultery, and worked for most of his life further south, in the Marche. He always proudly signed himself 'Venetus' nonetheless.

Jacopo Bellini appears instinctively to have looked beyond the imaginative world of this beautiful but old-fashioned style. On his death, he left two sketchbooks containing over 230 drawings, which include fascinating experiments in spatial composition, perspective and architectural design. They are a unique legacy; nothing like them exists for any other Italian artist of the early 15th century. We do not know enough about Jacopo to say where the stimulus for these innovations came from; but their importance, especially for his family, was immense. Jacopo had two sons who were painters,

Gentile (named after Gentile da Fabriano, who came to Venice in 1408 to decorate the Doge's Palace) and Giovanni; he also had a daughter, who married the most talented artist in northern Italy at the time, Andrea Mantegna. The Bellini dynasty was to have a defining influence over the evolution of Venetian art for the next hundred years.

The two brothers had different vocations: Giovanni was to develop an art of wide, international appeal, while Gentile created a genre which was deeply and uniquely Venetian. Something in the solipsistic nature of being an island-city meant that Venice appears never to have tired of celebrating itself, its beauty and its pageantry. Gentile has left us a remarkable documentation of the appearance of the 15th-century city. In 1496, for the Scuola di San Giovanni Evangelista, he contributed the finest paintings to the cycle depicting the story of the relic of the True Cross (now in the Accademia; *see p. 143*); they are simultaneously full of space and detail, of narrative interest and architectural documentation. A decade later, and similar in conception, *The Preaching of St Mark* and *Martyrdom of St Mark in Alexandria* (left unfinished at the time of his death, and now in the Brera Gallery in Milan) both contain fascinating passages of orientalising fantasy—the minarets and turbans and giraffes of an imagined Alexandria—based on drawings made when Gentile worked at the court in Constantinople between 1479 and 1481. Something of Gentile's renown can be gauged by the fact that the Ottoman sultan called him there all the way from Italy. It was at this period that he executed his brilliant portrait of the conqueror, Mehmet II, now in the National Gallery, London.

ARCHITECTURE AND SCULPTURE

This orientalism in Gentile Bellini reflects how much of an eastern taste and aesthetic had already been absorbed by Venice. Domes become moulded and stylised with an oriental profile; the runs of arches and finials along the front of the Doge's Palace or Ca' d'Oro (which was further gilded and coloured) have more in common with the Alhambra than with contemporary architecture in Florence or Rome; the slender *campanili* seem at times like minarets; and the colours and abstract designs of some of the façades would not be out of place in Isfahan or Jaipur. It is in its architecture, more than anything else, that Venice goes so entirely its own way. Once again the water is fundamental to this development, because the delicately varying colours of marble and stone used in a Venetian façade make sense with the rippling surface of the water in front. Furthermore, these elegant façades, which emphasised beauty over fortification, were possible in Venice in a way that was unimaginable in the turbulent world of Florence: the rigorous constitution of the Serene Republic discouraged the inter-family mob rivalries which were a common feature of Florentine history and necessitated the construction of residences as impregnable as the Strozzi and Medici palaces. Nor had Venice any need for defensive walls. The lagoon, with its maze of invisible underwater channels, was the city's perfect defence: in times of danger it was sufficient to pull up the posts that marked these channels and leave the waters to confound any invader. Its unique geography once again allowed Venice to develop architecturally in a way quite different from the other cities of Europe.

The elegant Venetian façade replaced the windowless, fortified exterior necessary in other cities, at the same time dispensing with the interior courtyard, which was necessary as a well of light elsewhere. This saved precious space, and for the palaces themselves it meant that the *piano nobile* could occupy the whole extent of the building's plan. Its grand rooms possessed much greater areas of window than elsewhere, made from the special, clear glass that Venice, alone in Italy, produced. The resulting interiors were light, unencumbered and resplendent. There was no horse-drawn traffic below, and none of the accompanying smells and noise that went with it. The tide washed the lagoon daily; mosquitoes were unable to cover the distance from the mainland out to the islands; in short, Venice became just about the most salubrious city in Europe.

Nor could any city come close to Venice in the calculated grandness of its main approach from the sea. To arrive slowly by ship at the city's ceremonial entrance, the Piazzetta of San Marco, passing the sweep of palaces culminating in the Doge's Palace and the entrance to the Grand Canal, was to be subjected to one of the clearest—and most excitingly beautiful—programmes of aesthetic propaganda anywhere. There was to be no doubt that you were entering one of the world's richest imperial capitals. The south and west fronts of St Mark's which greeted you as you stepped ashore were decorated with marble and sculptural trophies from Rome, from Constantinople, and from many parts of the Mediterranean, mostly captured from Venice's aspiring rivals.

The early architecture of Venice is shrouded in anonymity, but by the 15th century two architects stand out. They were contemporaries, relations and rivals: Mauro Codussi (c. 1440–1504) and Pietro Solari, called 'Lombardo' (c. 1438–1515). Codussi changed the external appearance of Venetian mansions with a new use of materials. He showed how effective the white, Istrian stone, which had previously only been used for details on brick housefronts, could be when used for covering the whole façade, especially if combined with a lower area of rustication, as in his refined Palazzo Corner-Spinelli of 1480—one of Venice's first truly 'Renaissance' palaces. An unforgettable characteristic of his work, which was copied all over the city, was the introduction of a type of marble tracery window, created by surmounting a pair of round-arched windows with an oculus, all within a larger round-arched frame; but a more general love of the rhythmic combination of semi-circles and rectangles lies behind all his creations, recognisable in the upper façade of the church of San Zaccaria (1483) and in the little-visited, but perfect, funerary church of San Michele (1469–78). This was Codussi's first—and perhaps his purest and best—architectural essay: it shows his thoughtful study of Alberti's Malatesta temple at Rimini.

A number of strikingly similar elements are found in one of the loveliest of all Venetian buildings, the church of Santa Maria dei Miracoli (1481–9), whose appearance, as you approach from around the corner of a narrow *calle*, is itself a sort of miracle. It was designed by Pietro Lombardo, who had worked as both sculptor and architect in Padua before settling in Venice. The church has the appearance of a treasure-chest. Both on the outside and the inside, the complex and ingenious architectural details in Istrian stone frame precious marbles and porphyry insets. Yet the form of the building could hardly be simpler. This again invites contrast with Florence, where often complex abstract forms in architecture were paramount, and decoration was reduced to the minimum. In Santa Maria dei Miracoli, Lombardo has transfigured a perfectly elementary form with dignified and beguiling decoration.

Pietro Lombardo had two sons, Tullio (1455–1532) and Antonio (c. 1458–1516); together they formed a family *bottega*. Venice's sculptural tradition had mostly been a decorative adjunct of architecture up until the late 15th century; its outstanding examples were the scenes, carved by Giovanni and Bartolomeo Bon, on the corners of the south and west façades of the Doge's Palace, depicting stories from the Book of Genesis: *Adam and Eve*, and a beautifully concise and unforgettable *Drunkenness of Noah*. The same sculptors had been responsible for the design and sculpture of the magnificent Porta della Carta (1438–43). With the Lombardo family, however, sculpture acquires the status of an independent artform, unfettered from architectural decoration. Tullio in particular was a deeply attentive student of Classical originals; but it takes time in his development for the Classicism to become absorbed into a coherent, Renaissance sculptural language of truly Venetian character. Once it does, the results are of a rare beauty: the delicate portrait relief of two heads, like a piece of Roman funerary sculpture, in the Ca' d'Oro, and the monuments to Doge Andrea Vendramin (d. 1478) and to Doge Giovanni Mocenigo (d. 1485) in the church of Santi Giovanni e Paolo, are exquisite and poised essays in Classicism. Their figures beautifully typify the humanity and freshness of the early Renaissance in Venice.

CARPACCIO AND GIOVANNI BELLINI

Nobody looked more carefully at Venice's array of architecture or at the big narrative paintings of Gentile Bellini than Vittore Carpaccio (c. 1460–1525/26). He watched intently the grand ceremony and pageantry of Venice, as well as its domestic life and interiors. He appropriated them all and fused them into what have become some of the most delightful narrative tableaux in the history of painting. He has the Venetian love of rich textile; the Venetian love of crowds and special occasions; above all the Venetian love of Venice.

Just as with Gentile's paintings, Carpaccio's were largely commissioned for the Venetian *scuole*. These *scuole*, self-governing lay confraternities, were a particularly Venetian phenomenon: they united groups of men of similar profession or craft (surgeons, painters) or ethnic origin (Slavs, Greeks) and their object was to provide material and spiritual succour to their members, as well as to the poor and indigent more generally. They were a middle-class phenomenon, from which patricians were excluded. The surplus of their revenues was used to decorate their meeting houses, which were generally small but fine buildings. Carpaccio's two great painting cycles, the *Lives of St George, St Tryphon and St Augustine* (in the Scuola di San Giorgio degli Schiavoni) and the *Legend of St Ursula* (now in the Accademia; *see p. 144*), have a wide and inexhaustible appeal for their clarity and narrative interest. Carpaccio's scenes have a tendency towards the static; even the 'Massacre of the Eleven Thousand Virgins' from the *Legend of St Ursula* is a curiously un-dramatic scene; he is more in his element with the graceful details of the interior of St Ursula's bedroom or of St Augustine's study, where the tiny, seated dog is a quite unforgettable presence. In both of these interiors there is an unusual, and masterfully evoked, Venetian light, which shows the influence of Giovanni Bellini, Carpaccio's greatest Venetian contemporary.

In Giovanni Bellini we witness the imaginative discovery of light in Italian painting. Where other painters had dallied with it, Bellini firmly grasped its primary importance. No painter in Italy before him was so sensitive to its inflections or understood so well its expressive potential. The only problem for Bellini was how to transfer that sensitivity into paint, because, like his father, he grew up in a world in which painting was done in egg-tempera on a gessoed, wooden panel. As a technique this offered little flexibility: tempera colours are bright and opaque, they dry almost instantaneously and give no possibility for correction or alteration. Bellini fared well in such a milieu nonetheless, because he was instinctively such a master of line, of detail and of the creation of volumes by shade. But during his lifetime—and it may have been through his brother-in-law Mantegna—he came in contact with the new, Flemish method of mixing pigment with walnut oil and a siccative resin, to create hitherto unimagined effects of translucency, depth of colour, and delicacy of shadow. At first hesitant—perhaps just laying transparent oil glazes over dry tempera colour—it is not long before Bellini begins to expand the possibilities of the new medium, always working, however, in the manner in which he had been trained, with precision and in superimposed layers. To look at his exquisite early Madonnas is to realise that the new technique was perfectly adapted for his particular sensibility.

Then, in 1475, at the height of Bellini's maturity as a painter, a little-known genius by the name of Antonello da Messina visited Venice for a year, collaborated with Bellini, and left behind him works which made a deep and lasting impression. Antonello had understood and mastered the Flemish technique of painting in translucent glazes of pigment and varnish, loosened with oil—a method initiated and perfected almost half a century earlier by Van Eyck. The greatest painting Antonello left behind in Venice— the San Cassiano altarpiece, of which only central fragments remain today in the Vienna Kunsthistorisches Museum—created a long echo in Bellini's work and in the works of other contemporaries, Cima da Conegliano and Marco Basaiti, whose great altarpieces are now in the Accademia.

Giovanni Bellini's works are to be found in many churches around the city: there are early, slightly stiff, pieces such as his *Polyptych of St Vincent Ferrer* (1460) in the church of Santi Giovanni e Paolo, and later masterpieces such as the Frari triptych of 1488. Last of all is his sublime *Virgin with Saints*, signed and dated 1505, on the north wall of the church of San Zaccaria, painted in oil. In 1500, Leonardo da Vinci had visited Venice, and it is not wholly fanciful to see some lessons learnt from the Florentine master in this extraordinary picture. As in Bellini's magnificent earlier portrait of Doge Leonardo Loredan (National Gallery, London), this picture represents a mastery of oil technique. It has the stillness and transparency of deep water; the warm colours of Venice, reminiscent of its enamels and its glass; and it shares the almost palpable light of the lagoon. It represents the summit of Venetian art, before the genius of Bellini's pupils was to turn everything on its head.

GIORGIONE, TITIAN AND TINTORETTO
The thunder of Giorgione's famous *Tempesta* announces the coming of a new season in Venetian painting. This tiny and enigmatic picture (now in the Accademia; see p. 149) was not a large, public or religious work like nearly all Venetian painting before:

it was a private commission, for a select and intellectual group, for whom the discussion and debate of its deliberately recondite allegory provided erudite entertainment. Small and intimate though it is, the painting breaks entirely fresh ground: in it, landscape is no longer just a background, it is the emotive purpose of the picture.

Giorgione (c. 1476–1510) was around 40 years younger than Giovanni Bellini, and his life was to be tragically cut short—possibly by the plague—at the age of thirty-five. He instinctively understood the potential of Bellini's achievement with the softer medium of oil, but he did not wish to be bound by Bellini's rather geometric ideas of composition, his patterning of colour, or his adherence to the primacy of line. Giorgione begins to dissolve line in shadow, and to replace pattern with a tonal unity of colour and mood. Slowly and unobtrusively, landscape and its expressive power elbows everything else out of the way: in his *Adoration of the Shepherds* (now in Washington) it is not the miraculous birth, which occupies just one corner of the picture, but the receding landscape all around, which commands our attention. Brilliant colour is vanishing and is replaced by an ever more expressive depth of shadow, as for example in his moving study of the face of an elderly lady (sometimes thought to be his mother), bearing the inscription '*Col Tempo*' ('in time, it shall come to us all'), in the Accademia. How were such rich depths of paint achieved? Not by the addition of more varnish and oil to the pigment, which would risk deadening the colour. Giorgione was adding ground glass (available to him from the factories in Murano) to his pigment preparation—a brilliant development, because it simultaneously did three things. It hastened the drying time of the paint; it gave bulk to the glazes while reducing the amount of oil necessary, thereby cutting the risk of yellowing with time; and it imparted an inner brilliance and depth.

Watching intently all these trials and experiments from the wings, was a young apprentice, Tiziano Vecellio (c. 1485–1576), from the mountains of Cadore above Venice, who was scarcely even in his adolescence. Giovanni Bellini's studio was the Rutherford Laboratory of Venetian painting: Alvise Vivarini, Antonello da Messina, Carpaccio, Sebastiano del Piombo, Vincenzo Catena, Lorenzo Lotto, Marco Basaiti, Giorgione, Titian—virtually every name in Venetian painting of the period passed through it in one capacity or another, and was affected by what was happening there. But it was the last and youngest of these, Titian, who was to transform the nature of painting completely, and in the process turn Venetian art in his age from a local phenomenon into the most influential force in European painting. He was the friend and assistant of Giorgione, and on the latter's death was his artistic heir, completing a number of his unfinished works. But what Titian was to do with the technique of painting makes even Giorgione seem old-fashioned. Every painter mentioned so far was taught to paint—whether in oil or tempera—with what we might call the 'tempera mentality'. This means painting in layers of colour, following a carefully drawn design, on a solid, smooth white gesso base. In the early painters such as Lorenzo Veneziano or Jacopo Bellini, the thin layers of colour were in opaque egg-tempera, while in Giovanni Bellini and Giorgione they were often transparent layers, or 'glazes'. Whatever the medium, though, the process was the same: a bright white base plus drawing plus thin layers of colour, added successively so that they subtly interacted with and modified the layers below, to create exactly the desired effect. A painting was therefore a complex stratified creation: in optical terms, its reflective white gesso base was a mirror which sent the light back to the eye through the layers of interposed colour. Their pictures therefore were back-lit; and the surface smooth and flat.

Titian, although trained in exactly this manner by Giovanni Bellini, dispensed with it almost immediately. He saw that oil paint could have a quite different effect if it did not refract the light from its depth, but reflected it from its surface. He also saw that the surface of a painting had far greater life if it was not flat, but broken and agitated, like the surface of the water on the lagoon—playing with the light rather than absorbing it. Lastly, he abandoned the wooden panel for the ease and texture of stretched canvas, learning to exalt its weave as a living element of the painting. His example was so completely compelling that fresco and egg-tempera painting died an almost immediate death: canvas was adopted all over Europe as a support, and the method of painting with dissolved contours and broken surfaces, using varying heights of impasto (thickness of paint strokes) spread to the corners of the continent. Velázquez, Rubens, Delacroix, Constable, Rembrandt, even the French Impressionists and Cézanne, are heirs in different ways to Titian's emancipation of painting. Furthermore, with pre-prepared oils and lightweight canvas, the artist could sketch in front of nature, giving scope and possibility to a new artform: landscape painting. With the disappearance of the primacy of drawing, and the new living texture of the broken surface instead, the potential for drama and pathos was increased. And, thanks to the ease with which light, rollable canvas could travel, the exchange of images around the continent was a development of comparable importance to the invention of printing.

Titian's active painting career may have spanned over 80 years—more even than his long-lived contemporary Michelangelo. Of the many examples of his work in Venice, two highlight different ends of the fascinating spectrum of his development: his *Assumption of the Virgin* of 1518 in the church of the Frari, and his last work, the unfinished *Pietà* of 1573–5, intended for his own tomb and now in the Accademia. It is a rare joy when a great painting is seen in the place for which it was created. Titian's *Assumption* still occupies the centre of the 14th-century Gothic interior of the Frari like a vision of intense, liquid colour—an unforgettable ruby red, which has the shimmering effect of glass. Only in a painting as great as this is the exhilaration of the miraculous event itself matched by the picture's chromatic vigour and sweeping design. It belongs to another imaginative world from the Pala d'Oro; but its intensity of colour and texture and the play on surface and depth are both similar to it in effect, and quintessentially Venetian. In the same church, by rights, should hang Titian's *Pietà*, painted 60 years later and left unfinished at his death. Here the colour has leached out of Titian's vision, except for a few sickly hues. The weave of the canvas breaks the surface of the paint and the febrile brush-strokes dissolve the contours of everything. Titian's assistant, Palma Giovane, who 'finished' this work after his master's death, described the way Titian worked: 'the last retouching involved his moderating here and there the brightest highlights by rubbing them with his fingers...And so he would proceed...in the last stages...painting more with his fingers than his brushes'.

When rules are abolished, anarchy can swiftly follow. Titian had, in effect, spirited away the design, the reassuring line, and the familiar compactness of a picture's surface. The old certainties of painting were now gone. And into the vacuum rushed that dynamic painter, and curious counterpart to everything Titian stood for: Tintoretto (1519–94). After the sheer technical mastery of Bellini, Giorgione and Titian, it takes time to adjust to the apparent haste of Tintoretto. Where Titian had altered the physical surface of a painting for good, Tintoretto revolutionised its imaginative space. Venetian painting had, up until now, generally disposed the figures of a composition across the vertical plane of the picture: in Tintoretto, that plane swings inwards and back, often diagonally, and we find ourselves watching a drama which takes places in a daringly receding space, as, for example, in the early *Miracle of the Slave* in the Accademia, or the late dramatic *Last Supper* (1594) in the chancel of San Giorgio Maggiore. Tintoretto, according to Boschini, was mostly self-taught, and he learned to achieve these effects by studying foreshortening and the effects of light and shade produced by suspending wax models in specially constructed boxes, which were illuminated from different angles. Sometimes these special effects can disturb with their artificiality, and give rise to the over-rhetorical poses of some of his figures. But in his maturity, as in the famous cycles of the *Life of Christ* (1576–81) and *Life of the Virgin* (1582–7) for the Scuola di San Rocco, his designs acquire a new and mystical power which goes beyond rhetoric. In the latter cycle, his *Flight into Egypt* depicts the Holy Family head-on, as they come forwards out of the picture towards us: it is in this simple, but complete, originality of concept that his greatness lies. There is nothing traditionally Venetian in Tintoretto's light effects. The actual light of this world interested him less than the unworldly luminosity he creates instead. This very unusual illumination, and the broken surface of his paint, were to be important influences on El Greco when he stayed in Venice in the 1560s. The rapid darkening of the oils and varnishes since Tintoretto's time has inevitably altered our perception of his desired effects, and we can only guess at how delicate and dramatic they may have appeared at the time—or even to Ruskin, 300 years later, who was so profoundly moved by them.

FROM PALLADIO TO GUARDI

It is strange that, in this city of ornate and colourful façades, the distilled Classicism of Palladio's architecture should have become so memorable an ingredient of the scene. Facing back across the water to the Gothic fantasy of the Doge's Palace, is Palladio's serene San Giorgio Maggiore, whose façade, made up of interlocking temple fronts in white stone, is everything which the Doge's Palace is not. Still, reposed, unshowy, cerebral and utterly international, it throws into relief everything that came before: it is the perfect counterpoint which the city needed. Andrea Palladio (1508–80) was from Padua, and he only properly settled in Venice in his 63rd year. By rights he does not belong in this survey; and yet his architecture is such an integral part of the city's whole, that it is not possible to omit him. The serenely measured, yet luminous, interiors of San Giorgio Maggiore (begun 1565) and of the church of the Redentore (begun 1577) are amongst the great achievements of Renaissance architecture. They use that same combination of white walls with stone details which had embodied and enhanced the interiors of buildings by Brunelleschi and Michelangelo: yet Palladio's designs appear at once simpler and more universal. His first work in

Venice, the refectory of San Giorgio Maggiore (1560), is already the product of accumulated experience and maturity. The proportions of its spaces have a perceptible, physical effect on the visitor passing through the cadenced progression of ante-rooms and majestic doorways. His is an architecture which profoundly quells human anxiety.

Where Palladio calms, Baldassare Longhena (1604–82), who was much indebted to Palladio's legacy, exhilarates and surprises; where Palladio's idiom was international, Longhena's is, once more, idiosyncratically Venetian. His church of Santa Maria della Salute is Venice's greatest creation of the Baroque era. Like the outlines of St Mark's and the Doge's Palace, its profile stays in the memory long after everything else has receded. Its position at the entrance to the Grand Canal, its unusual octagonal plan, the reassuring weight of its monumental entrance set back from the waterfront, the form of its ballooning domes like wind-filled spinnakers over the prow of the Dogana, and, above all, the unforgettable and luxuriant scrolls of its buttresses with the crown of sculptural figures above them, combine in a piece of consummate architectural theatre. It is the first large-scale octagonal building since Romanesque times—a period when spiritual numerology saw in the number eight a symbol of new life and rebirth. This building was a votive offering, dedicated to the Virgin by the city of Venice in gratitude for salvation after the terrible plague year of 1630: in its unusual eight-sided design, Longhena brilliantly echoes this ancient symbol.

Longhena's work itself marks a moment of renewal for Venetian art. Far from being a period of retreat, the final century of the life of the Republic, before its extinction in 1797, brings an unexpected burst of creativity. Just at the point when it appeared that fresco painting had been dealt a terminal blow by Titian's perfection of oil-on-canvas, and just as it seemed that the city's great 17th-century decorative works, such as those in the Doge's Palace, had lost their way and become irremediably clogged, an artist emerges in Venice who is one of history's greatest ever practitioners of fresco, and who conceives designs for large-scale decorative programmes of a lightness which is positively uplifting. Giambattista Tiepolo (1696–1770) is a phenomenon difficult to account for. Just as the Venetian palette seemed to be getting darker and darker, Tiepolo works exclusively with bright and sunlit colours; just as decorative schemes were becoming more artificial and more crowded with rhetorical figures, Tiepolo purges the situation with his insistence on large areas of space and sky, and the seemingly unaffected naturalness of his narratives. Few other painters embody 'brilliance' better. His mastery of *quadratura* and of complex perspective and foreshortening had no peer in his age: nor had the sheer *élan* of his imaginative ideas, and his simultaneous grasp of every detail within the context of the whole. His ceilings never overwhelm or tire or confuse; they always succeed and they always delight. And for this reason his services were widely sought on the Italian mainland, in Spain and in Germany, to produce works that have since remained among the greatest examples of decorative art in Europe. Many of his finest works are outside Venice; but in Palazzo Labia on the Cannaregio Canal, his visual narrative of *Antony and Cleopatra*—a subject perfectly suited to his imagination—is one of the city's greatest joys.

His exact contemporary, Canaletto (Antonio del Canale, 1697–1768), reached international fame from Venice by a technical mastery of a wholly different kind. In him, as also in the works of his contemporaries Pietro Longhi (1701–85) and Francesco Guardi (1712–93), Venice returned to one of her oldest habits: the description and celebration of her own beauty. This time, however, in these last decades before the end of the Serene Republic, it was to be a description without the glorification of earlier times. Longhi's humorous and delicately painted vignettes of Venetian life were to have little influence outside Venice; but Canaletto's views of the city and its buildings were exported widely, especially to England through the agency of the British Consul, Joseph Smith. Their popularity depended on the outstandingly rendered light and shadow which suffused the ordered spaces he described. He gives remarkable delight to the eye both from a distance and close to. Canaletto came to London between 1746 and 1754: in his views of the city, he performed the remarkable feat of making the banks of the River Thames look as serene and beautiful as the Bacino di San Marco. Stillness is all in Canaletto. The coruscations of light and vibrancy of atmosphere in Guardi's views of the city reveal a diametrically different response to its beauty, a response which was only appreciated many generations later, once European sensibilities had been educated to see things differently by the Impressionists. For Canaletto, the light is the vehicle of his passion for the architecture: for Guardi, the architecture is a necessary receptacle for his passion for the light.

The works of Canaletto and Guardi remind us that so much of Venetian art, indeed so much of the fascination of the city, has always depended upon its unique light—immediately, tangibly different from anywhere else in Italy because of the surrounding water which constantly modifies it. It is this that explains the primacy of the visual sensibility in Venice: we look in vain for internationally great writers, poets, thinkers or scientists. Venice has no Dante or Leonardo or Alberti or Machiavelli; but it produced painters whose universal influence has been incomparable, because of one fundamental lesson they imbibed from the endless modulations of their native light. They instinctively understood how light in painting is the vehicle of human empathy. Bellini and Titian, and the painters who worked near to them, showed for the first time how feeling is evoked and expressed not by idea or narrative or description, but by the drama of light and colour; and Titian above all, with his new and dramatic use of the oil and canvas medium, evolved the technical tools for this revolutionary way of painting. Venice may not have altered the course of intellectual history as Florence so notably did; but there are few painters in 17th-, 18th- and 19th-century Europe who were not profoundly touched by her far-reaching influence.

Nigel McGilchrist

Topography of Venice

Venice stands in a unique position, built on an archipelago of islets or shoals, a few kilometres from the mainland, in a lagoon protected from the open sea by the natural breakwater of the Lido. Seawater enters the lagoon through three channels. The city is supported on piles of pine, driven down about 7.5m to a solid bed of compressed sand and clay, and many of the buildings are built above a foundation course of Istrian limestone which withstands the corrosion of the sea. As long as it is protected from the air, pine is the only wood which hardens with time when exposed to water, becoming almost fossilised.

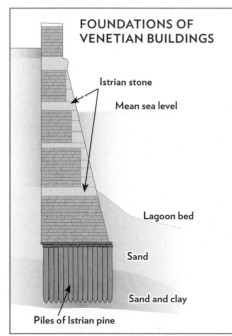

FOUNDATIONS OF VENETIAN BUILDINGS

Istrian stone

Mean sea level

Lagoon bed

Sand

Sand and clay

Piles of Istrian pine

The irregular plan of the city is crossed by some 170 canals, the broadest of which, the Grand Canal, divides the city into two unequal parts. The other canals, called *rii* (*rio* in the singular), with the exception of the wider and straighter Cannaregio Canal, have an average breadth of 3–4m. They are spanned by about 430 bridges, mostly built out of Istrian stone, but some in iron or wood.

The only *piazza* is that of St Mark: there are two *piazzette*, one in front of the Doge's Palace, the other, the Piazzetta Giovanni XXIII, by the north flank of St Mark's Basilica. Any other square in Venice is called a *campo* (or, if very small, a *corte* or *campiello*). The streets, nearly all narrow, are called *calli*; the more important thoroughfares, usually shopping streets, are known as *calle larga*, *ruga* or *salizzada* (the name given to the first paved streets in 1676). A smaller alley is called *caletta* or *ramo*. A street alongside a canal is called a *fondamenta*: a *rio terrà* is a street along the course of a filled-in *rio*. A *riva* is a wharf. A *sottoportego* passes beneath the overhanging upper floor of a building. A *piscina* is a place where a basin of water (*bacino*) connected to a canal formerly existed; and a *sacca* a stretch of water where canals meet. A *lista* is a lane which led up to an ambassador's palace.

THE BUILDINGS OF VENICE

A Venetian palace or important residence is sometimes called Ca' (or Casa) instead of Palazzo. The ground floor of a typical palace has an *androne*, a long hallway opening from the water-gate, with a courtyard behind it, often with a well. The main rooms are on the first floor or *piano nobile*, arranged on either side of the *portego*, a large central oblong hall rising above the ground-floor *androne* and usually lit by tall windows.

CA' REZZONICO: A TYPICAL PALAZZO

Water entrance

Androne

Courtyard

Portego

Courtyard

Land entrance

GROUND FLOOR   FIRST FLOOR

On the upper floors, palaces sometimes have a protruding loggia (*liagò*), and, on the roof, characteristic open wooden balconies called *altane*. Venetian chimneys have a particularly charming shape. In front of the most important palaces, and in particular those on the Grand Canal, wooden *pali* or mooring posts are traditionally painted with the livery colours of their proprietors.

Other important buildings include *scuole*, lay confraternities dedicated to charitable works (and also the name of the buildings which served as their headquarters). A *fondaco* (or *fontego*) was a trading-post, and a *magazzino* (or *magazen*) a warehouse.

Beneath many of the *campi* are cisterns for rain-water, which was collected through grilles in the pavement. Below ground level the water filtered through sand before reaching the central well-shaft, which is crowned with a *vera da pozzo* (well-head), usually made of Istrian stone or Verona marble. Hundreds of these are still to be seen in the city's *campi*, their carvings dating from the Byzantine period to the 19th century.

Almost all the bridges remained without parapets up until the 19th century, when wrought-iron balustrades were added. Also at this time many bridges were rebuilt in iron or cast-iron. The bridges are also used to carry gas and water pipes and electricity cables throughout the city.

Names of the streets and canals are painted in black on a white ground (the signs are known in the Venetian dialect as *nizioleti*; 'little sheets') and they are renewed regularly. Names are now tending to appear in Venetian dialect rather than in Italian (so that the names given in the text can sometimes be slightly different from those to be found *in situ* or on the maps). Houses are numbered consecutively throughout each of the six *sestieri*, the districts into which the city has been divided since the 12th century (San Marco, Castello, Dorsoduro, San Polo, Santa Croce and Cannaregio).

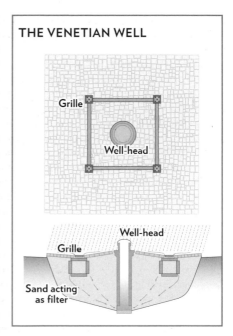

THE VENETIAN WELL

Grille

Well-head

Well-head

Grille

Sand acting as filter

THE VENETIAN LAGOON

The hauntingly beautiful Venetian Lagoon is separated from the open sea by the low, narrow sandbars of the Lido and Pellestrina, which are pierced by three channels: the Porto di Lido, the Porto di Malamocco, and the Porto di Chioggia. A shallow expanse of water, with an average depth of only about a metre and an area of 544km square, it is the largest coastal lagoon in the Mediterranean, and the only one in the world which supports a large town in its centre. On some of the islands, townships and monasteries were established in the Middle Ages, most of which have now diminished in importance, except for Murano, with its glass manufactories. On others, isolation hospitals were built, and after a fire in the Arsenale in 1569, many of the smaller islands were used as forts or stores for gunpowder. The Lido became a famous resort in the early 20th century. The future of some of the islands, abandoned in the 1960s and '70s, is uncertain. There is an excellent service of public *vaporetti* to all the inhabited islands.

The ecology of the lagoon

The survival of the lagoon and Venice itself depends on an extremely delicate ecological balance between the open sea and the enclosed lagoon, and from as early as the 12th century work was being carried out to preserve it. Since the early years of the 16th century, the lagoon has been protected by a board presided over by the Magistrato alle Acque. Canals were dug between the early 16th and the 18th centuries to divert the silt-bearing rivers (notably the Brenta and Bacchiglione, the Piave and Sile) away from the area so that they could flow directly into the sea to the north and south of the lagoon. In the 18th century a great sea wall (the *murazzi*) was constructed at Pellestrina, out of pozzolana and Istrian stone, to control the eroding waters of the Adriatic, and in the 19th and early 20th centuries outer breakwaters were built up at the three entrances. The salt marshes, the extent of which dramatically diminished in the last century, still protect a great number of aquatic species, although marine life is threatened by the increase in seaweed.

Much damage was caused in the 1920s and '30s by the growth of the port of Marghera and by the decision in the 1950s to set up the second largest oil refinery in Italy inside the lagoon itself, only a short distance from Venice. The three sea entrances were deepened to allow tankers into the lagoon, and a channel 12m deep was excavated in the 1960s so that these ships could cross the lagoon from Malamocco, all of which accelerated the process of erosion. The discharge of nitrogen and the creation of dump sites inside the lagoon also caused serious problems. In 2001 ships without a double hull and carrying dangerous cargo were banned from the lagoon. The Marghera refinery is no longer operational, and the future of this huge area is still being discussed.

The natural process of subsidence in the lagoon was increased by the construction of artesian wells for industrial use (drilling has officially been prohibited since the 1970s, but the extraction of liquids or gas in the Adriatic and the lagoon area has not been totally halted). There is a suggestion that a buffer zone of artificial wetlands should be created in order to preserve the lagoon from pollution from the *terraferma*. In Venice itself, the foundations of the buildings and the quays on the main canals are continuously being eroded by the wash or wave damage (*moto ondoso*) caused by motorboats, which continue to exceed the speed limits imposed by the city council.

But on the positive side, in the last few years sea defences have been strengthened, the beaches on the sea at Pellestrina and Cavallino reclaimed, some of the grass-grown shoals which emerge from the lagoon and the mud banks normally awash at high tide reconstructed, the polluted waters cleaned, and the fish-farms in the marshes (where eels, mullet and sea bream are raised) reopened to tidal flow. Maintenance work in the centre of Venice itself has involved the dredging and cleaning of many of the canals and, where possible, the level of the lower-lying *fondamente* has been raised to 1.2m above mean sea level. Additional operations are being studied to guarantee the hydrodynamics necessary to maintain water quality and the ecosystem.

Navigable channels in the lagoon are marked by piles (*bricole*). A particularly good view of the lagoon can be had from the walk around the outside of the walls of the island of Lazzaretto Nuovo (there is also a little observation post in one of the towers). There is a reserve run by the WWF (World Wide Fund for Nature) in the southern part of the lagoon at Alberoni.

ACQUA ALTA AND THE MO.S.E

At present the greatest problem facing Venice is the notable increase in the number of days when the city suffers from *acqua alta* (a flood tide over 80cm above mean sea level). When the tide reaches 110cm, about 12 percent of the city is affected by flooding; exceptional conditions can cause the level of the tide to reach 140cm and in this case 59 percent of the city is under water for a number of hours. At present Piazza San Marco, one of the lowest parts of the city, is flooded many times a year. Details of how the city authorities deal with these emergencies are given on p. 370.

Acqua alta is caused not only by subsidence (there has been a diminution in the height of the land in the lagoon in respect of sea level of about 23cm since the beginning of the 20th century) but also by the gradual rise in the mean sea level and climate change in general.

A project known as Mo.S.E. (*Modulo Sperimentale Elettromeccanico*), first mooted in 1970 and finalised in 1984, has been underway since 2003 to regulate tides of over 110cm by the installation of moveable barriers at the three lagoon entrances, using a system similar to those already functioning in the Netherlands and Britain. At the time of writing, it appeared that the project would not be completed before 2016. Sluice gates, filled with water, are designed to lie on the seabed, and they will be raised (by replacing the water with compressed air) only when a particularly high tide is expected. Each barrier is independent and measures some 20m across, is 18–30m high, and 4–5m thick: to close all three entrances to the lagoon, 78 of these are needed. At the widest Lido entrance (800m) an artificial island has been built in mid-channel to facilitate construction work. Breakwaters have been designed to protect the three entrances to the lagoon, and the depth of the channel at Malamocco will be reduced by two metres in order to inhibit excessive tidal surge.

The barriers will be able to be activated in about 30mins once a high tide is forecast, and will probably remain raised for anything between two and five hours. All three entrances will have locks for use by shipping when the barriers are closed. The gates have been designed to withstand a tide of 3m (the disastrous 1966 flood reached a level of 1.94m) and so take into account the predicted rise in the level of the sea (to a maximum of 60cm). Essential maintenance work to ensure the smooth running of the operation will be carried out by the Consorzio Venezia Nuova, a private consortium of firms, in warehouses in the northern area of the Arsenale. There has been opposition from environmentalists, who are worried about the project's impact on the lagoon ecology, but most experts are hopeful that these measures will be effective in protecting the city and its inhabitants. For further information, see www.salve.it.

Venice in Peril

Since the last edition of *Blue Guide Venice*, progress on the project to complete the Mo.S.E. floodgate system (*see p. 34*) has fallen behind schedule and it seems that the barriers will not be in place before 2016. Serious flooding in December 2010 prompted some experts to reiterate warnings that the system adopted would prove inadequate to control a predicted rise in average tide levels: in fact conditions worsened in December 2012 with high tides repeatedly reaching 1.43m above mean sea level in January 2013. A further loan from the European Investment Bank via Rome has been made available to the Italian government.

The Mo.S.E. project had been directed from the outset by the Consorzio Venezia Nuova, while the construction of the 79 massive steel barriers continues at the shipyards at Monfalcone, near Trieste. The Consortium will supervise the installation of the barriers at the lagoon entrances at Treporti, Malamocco and Lido, and their continual maintenance at monthly intervals, which will entail extracting them from their base for cleaning and greasing.

In 2013 an agreement was reached between the Venice city authority (*Comune*) and the Ministry of Defence awarding jurisdiction over the 48 hectares of the historic Arsenale to the *Comune*. Although no longer an operational naval base, the Marina Militare retains the area to the left of the Rio dell'Arsenale and its study centre holds regular courses for staff and invited specialists in the Library, entered through the monumental gateway surmounted by the rampant lion of St Mark and guarded by the massive seated lion carried off from Piraeus by the Venetian fleet in 1692 and now discovered to bear runes inscribed by Scandinavian guards c. 1040. The Comune will now have to find funds, or sponsors, for the conservation of the main area around the Darsena Grande, where the buildings are leased to the Biennale (*see p. 293*). Venice in Peril has undertaken to update the security of the monumental Armstrong Mitchell Crane, which stands at the edge of the main basin. Made in Newcastle-upon-Tyne in 1886, it was imported to Venice (one of many that Armstrong sold all over the world— Venice is the only survivor) to facilitate mounting guns on Italian warships. With the cessation of military activity in the Arsenale in the 1950s, the crane gradually fell into disrepair and is now in urgent need of funding—estimated in the region of £2million, to preserve its machinery (housed in the octagonal brick base) and to stabilise the iconic hydraulic crane.

Venice in Peril has also confirmed its commitment to preserve the tomb of Canova in the Frari, where the pyramidal brick structure, adorned with lifesize sculptures by Canova's pupils, is seriously suffering from rising damp, causing damage to the surface of the marble. A conservation project has been approved which will involve the temporary removal of each statue group, their conservation, and isolation of the pyramid construction from rising damp. The estimated cost is some €450,000, which the Venice in Peril Committee is hoping to raise. The small working models of this and other major examples of Canova's work are in the collection of the Gallerie dell'Accademia, who intend to devote a room to the sculptor once reconstruction of the galleries is complete (delayed at the time of writing for lack of funds). Nearby at the Archivio di Stato, the former cloister of the Frari, Venice in Peril has been enabled to undertake the restoration of the monumental doorway into the cloister, surmounted by a 7th-century relief of the seated Christ, flanked by two angels, badly blackened but not otherwise damaged or polluted. The project has been most generously funded by a long-term French friend and supporter.

In Cannaregio the church of the Madonna dell'Orto (Venice in Peril's first Venetian conservation project) continues to be a landmark, attracting visitors to an area of Venice that was once rather neglected. Guided by the dedicated community of the Padri Giuseppini who direct the adjacent school, and flanked by the former cloister, now perfectly restored by the Venice in Peril trustee who inherited it, the church serves its lively community while its prestigious Bazzani organ attracts distinguished musicians to give recitals. The campanile of the Madonna dell'Orto (Ruskin's 'last dark sentinel') is also a landmark from the northern lagoon.

Taking the vaporetto from the Fondamente Nuove out towards Murano, Burano and eventually Torcello, the first stop is at San Michele in Isola, the cemetery island (where Venice in Peril restored the Cappella Emiliana) whose soil has become the last resting place of numerous one-time residents or transitional visitors of many nations. Lately recognised by the municipality as a non-profit location of social utility (ONLUS), an international steering committee is trying to raise funds to pay for urgent re-consolidation of the terrain, weakened by persistent wet weather and gales.

By the time this edition of the Blue Guides reaches the bookshelves, there may well be some radical modification to the way the ever-increasing flotillas of large cruise liners are allowed access to the lagoon. The city has witnessed major eruptions of protest against tug-guided monster ships of various lines slowly edging up the Giudecca Canal towards the Stazione Marittima. The incidents in Genoa have greatly stimulated public support for the '*No Grandi Navi*' movement: the Port Authority will probably have to find make some compromise over the channel used, if not ban entry altogether. But the alternative—perhaps providing a shuttle service of smaller but more frequent craft—could provoke a more dangerous phenomenon of *moto ondoso*, depending on the routes indicated. *Vedremo*.

Venice in Peril is, as in the past, immensely grateful to the Blue Guides for their continued indulgence and interest and, as ever, to Alta Macadam for her encyclopaedic knowledge and sympathy.

Frances Clarke,
Dorsoduro 1113, Venice.
www.veniceinperil.org

The Twentieth Century & Beyond

The Biennale art show has kept Venice at the forefront of the contemporary art world ever since it was first held in the city in 1895. The famous exhibition attracts hundreds of thousands of visitors and its extraordinary prestige survives. Indeed, the event has expanded, so that now in alternate years there is the Biennale of contemporary architecture, as well as myriad collateral events devoted to dance, theatre, cinema and music. The pavilions in the Giardini, built to display works from the participating countries, survive as extremely interesting works of architecture (*for more on the Biennale, see p. 293*).

In the early 1930s the civil engineer and architect Eugenio Miozzi carried out some important functional interventions in the city: it was he who designed the Ponte della Libertà, really only a causeway for cars, which for the first time linked Venice to the mainland and is still its only vehicular access. At the same time, at Piazzale Roma, he built the first multi-storey car park (the largest of its time in Europe). Venetians still keep their cars there, although many other car parks have since been built at Tronchetto. Miozzi also rebuilt the iron Scalzi Bridge in stone, for visitors arriving by train, and further down the Grand Canal rebuilt the Accademia Bridge in wood. Much more ambitious were his two buildings on the Lido, the Casinò and Palazzo del Cinema, both in full Fascist style and important examples of their period.

Carlo Scarpa was at work in Venice in the late 1950s and early '60s and two of his works are open to the public: the ground floor and garden of Palazzo Querini-Stampalia and the Olivetti showroom on Piazza San Marco.

In the 1980s and '90s, large housing developments were carried out, often in areas formerly occupied by factories or warehouses. Some of these were designed by well-known Italian architects, including Vittorio Gregotti (in the Saffa area on the Cannaregio Canal) and Giancarlo de Carlo (low-cost housing at Mazzorbo). Venice University's department of architecture (IUAV) converted a former cotton factory in Dorsoduro into lecture halls, and the buildings of the vast slaughterhouse (Macelli) on the Cannaregio Canal were skilfully rehabilitated as premises for the university from the 1990s onwards.

The 21st century has seen some of the most interesting urban interventions, combined with ongoing care for the city's buildings. Funds have been gratefully received from François Pinault for major restoration work on both Palazzo Grassi and the

Punta della Dogana, in return for permission to exhibit part of his vast collection of contemporary art in both buildings. The Japanese architect Tadao Ando created the exhibition space inside the Punta della Dogana, while the 17th-century exterior was left intact. Since the 1990s, the Swiss architect Mario Botta has been at work at Palazzo Querini-Stampalia, radically altering the original aspect of the building (except for the second floor, where the period rooms remain). In 2009 Renzo Piano designed a small room to display some of Emilio Vedova's works at the Magazzini del Sale on the Zattere. A conversion project at the other end of the scale, and with no starchitect involved, is that at no. 792 Calle delle Beccarie off the Cannaregio Canal, where in 2006 the municipality, in collaboration with the Venice in Peril Fund, restored an attractive small building to provide housing for a number of local families. More ambitiously, the old mill built in 1895 on the Giudecca, the Mulino Stucky, has been turned into apartments and a hotel, but its huge exterior, extremely conspicuous from many parts of the city, has been kept exactly as it was.

One of the most successful major restorations of a Venetian palace has been that of the 16th-century Palazzo Grimani in the *sestiere* of Castello, undertaken by the Italian state. It is now a museum and can be visited. Since 2004, the municipality has been quietly at work on the adaptation of the former church and convent of Santi Cosma e Damiano on the Giudecca to provide housing, studios and office space, an exemplary project which hopefully will be imitated elsewhere.

2008 saw the opening of a fourth bridge across the Grand Canal, grandly baptised the 'Ponte della Costituzione' to commemorate the 60th anniversary of the Italian Constitution, but always known as the Calatrava Bridge after its Spanish architect, Santiago Calatrava. Though its design is extremely pleasing, it has been criticised for the problems of stability it is creating at its terminal points on both banks. And instead of opting for a simple ramp to accommodate wheelchairs (as at Ponte delle Guglie in Cannaregio), the bridge is fitted with an exterior cabin lift, but at the time of writing this was still not functioning.

In 2012 the Prada fashion house opened an exhibition space at Palazzo Corner della Regina on the Grand Canal. Also on the Grand Canal, the Fondaco dei Tedeschi, at the foot of the Rialto Bridge, is the subject of renovation plans (*see p. 108*). The fashion designer Pierre Cardin (born in the province of Treviso) had hoped to build a 250-metre 'Palais Lumière' (designed by his nephew) on the edge of the lagoon at Marghera. Containing luxury flats and shops, it would have been the tallest skyscraper in Italy, but the project was abandoned following violent opposition. Other long-term projects still in the pipeline are David Chipperfield's extension to the cemetery of San Michele and a new Palazzo del Cinema on the Lido.

There is no doubt that the conservation work which has been in progress for decades, funded by both the Italian state and international private committees, is of outstanding significance. There is a very real sense that everything possible is being done to preserve Venice and its treasures for future generations, while at the same time the city remains in the vanguard of modern art and architecture.

Venice Food & Drink

The cuisine of Venice is, unsurprisingly, first and foremost a cuisine of the sea. Fish is plentiful and so are shellfish and seafood: from the ubiquitous *vongole*, lagoon clams, to the extreme delicacy of *moeche*, soft-shelled crabs eaten whole. Artichokes thrive in the saline air. They are plentiful and extremely good. Most of the market stalls, and the greengrocers' barges that are moored at a couple of points, sell ready-prepared *fondi di carciofi*, artichoke hearts, in season (late winter and early spring). From the *terraferma* at Treviso comes the delicious curly-leaved *radicchio*. Pasta is a staple, of course: spaghetti, for eating with *vongole*; or bigoli, a thicker type, served with a rich meat ragout. But very typical of Venice, and often served as a vehicle for different kinds of fish paste, is polenta, cut into squares and sometimes char-grilled. More details of all these, and of the dishes traditionally prepared with them, are given below.

FIRST COURSES

Risotto is a favourite Venetian first course. The rice is often cooked with fish (*risotto di pesce*) or with squid in their ink (*risotto nero* or *risotto di seppie*). *Risotto primavera* is a vegetable risotto, while *risi e bisi* is a risotto served in spring cooked with fresh peas, celery and ham. As in the rest of Italy, pasta is served in numerous ways in Venice, the most common being with a seafood dressing (such as *pasta alle vongole*, spaghetti with clams). A winter dish is *pasta e fagioli*, a thick bean soup made from haricot beans and short pasta seasoned with bay leaves and dressed with olive oil. Polenta in Venice is made from a particularly fine-grained maize from the Friuli region and tends to be white, distinct from the yellow polenta popular in the rest of Italy.

A delicate first course, only available in season, is baby grey shrimps (*schie*) served with polenta. Cold hors-d'oeuvres include *sarde in saor*, fried sardines marinated in vinegar and onions, and *granseola*, spider crab. Mussels (*cozze*) in their shells are also often served in Venice: if they are *in bianco* they are lightly cooked with parsley and garlic, whereas *cozze al pomodoro*, with tomato, is a richer, spicier dish.

In summer, raw (cured) ham (*prosciutto crudo*) is particularly good (some of the best comes from San Daniele in Friuli) served with melon or green figs.

SECOND COURSES

Probably the most famous meat dish of Venice is *fegato alla veneziana*, calf's liver thinly sliced and fried with onions. *Carpaccio*, raw beef sliced very thinly, was invented in Venice, it is said by Giuseppe Cipriani, founder of Harry's Bar. He created it for Countess Amalia Nani Mocenigo, who had been advised by her doctor to avoid cooked meat. The name 'Carpaccio' is a reference to the great Venetian painter Vittore Carpaccio, whose characteristic palette of brick red, cream and green is reminiscent of the dish itself: the raw beef, its mayonnaise sauce and the bed of rucola or bitter green salad on which it is served.

The chief speciality of Venetian cooking, however, is fish, which is always the most expensive item on the menu (though unfortunately only about 20 percent is now caught locally and much of it is not caught in the open sea, but is farmed: *di allevamento*). Especially good is *dentice* (dentex) or *orata* (gilthead bream), often best served grilled. The cheapest fish dish is usually *fritto misto*, small fried fish, including octopus, squid, cuttlefish and prawns. Crustaceans include *scampi* (the Venetian word for shrimp), which are often served grilled, or boiled and dressed with olive oil, lemon, salt and pepper. A particularly Venetian dish is *seppie*, cuttlefish (or squid), usually cooked in their own ink and served with polenta. Eel (*anguilla* or *bisato*) is also often served, sometimes grilled or *alla Veneziana*, cooked in lemon with tuna fish, or marinated in oil and vinegar (with a bay leaf) and then fried with wine and tomato. Crab is also a favourite Venetian dish: *granseola* is spider crab served cold in its shell; *molecche* (or *moeche*) are soft-shelled tender baby crabs, stuffed with egg and fried and served hot (they are only available in early spring); *mazzancolle* are Mediterranean prawns. Scallops are called *capesante*, and clams are *caparozzoli* (or *vongole*). *Baccalà* is salt cod: when called *baccalà mantecato* it is cooked in milk, oil and garlic, and blended into a creamy mixture, and when simmered in milk it is called *baccalà alla vicentina*. *Stoccafisso* is unsalted cod. *Sampiero* is John Dory and *coda di rospo* is angler fish (served grilled or baked). *Zuppa di pesce*, fish stew made with a variety of fish, is a meal in itself.

Vegetables which are particularly good in spring include asparagus and artichokes, locally grown on the island of Sant'Erasmo. A vegetable found almost exclusively in Venice and the Veneto is *radicchio rosso*, bitter red chicory usually served grilled.

It is worth spending time (at least looking even if not buying) at the splendid Rialto markets, open every morning except Sunday (and the fish market is closed on Monday), where the local fish and vegetables can be seen in all their splendour.

DESSERTS

Although Venice has numerous cake shops (*pasticcerie*) which sell delicious confectionery, the city is not famous for its desserts. To end your meal, you may be offered a slice of pineapple (*ananas*) or a *sgroppino*, a lemon sorbet with a dash of grappa or vodka. For something more substantial, there is always *tiramisù*, the delectable concoction of mascarpone, sponge fingers and chocolate powder, whose invention is disputed between the Veneto and Tuscany.

A great variety of delicious biscuits are baked in Venice, and sold at cake-shops, bakeries or grocery stores. They include *zaeti*, made partly from cornmeal, and *bussolai buranelli*, ring-shaped biscuits made in Burano (*esse* are similar, only shaped like a letter S). The Venetians are also very fond of simple biscuits (rather similar to rusks) known as *baicoli*, made from wheat flour, sugar, salt and yeast. Fritters (*frittelle*) are often served in bars in winter (especially at Carnival time), flavoured with raisins, pine

nuts or lemon peel. Charming biscuits in the form of St Martin on horseback, decorated with sugar and chocolate, are widely available all over the city around the feast of
San Martino (11th Nov). At this time *cotognata* (or *persegada*), a sweet jelly made from
quinces, is also sold. After Christmas, for Epiphany, *pinsa* is made from cornmeal, fen-
nel seeds, raisins, candied fruit and dried figs.

APERITIFS

A tradition persists in Venice and the Veneto of taking an *ombra* or *ombreta* (usually
before dinner): a glass of white or red wine (or sparkling white wine, Prosecco) in a
bacaro or *osteria* (a selection of these is given on pp. 365–6). The word *ombra* means
shadow, and derives from a stall that once stood in Piazza San Marco in the shade of
the great Campanile and sold wine by the glass. As an alternative to straight wine, light
cocktails are also popular, particularly *spritz*, a typical Venetian aperitif made from
white wine or Prosecco, bitters and soda. The bitters part typically consists of Cam-
pari, Aperol (made with oranges) or Cynar (made with artichokes). The Bellini is a
famous cocktail invented at Harry's Bar, made from Prosecco and fresh peach juice.
All aperitifs are typically served with an array of delicious savoury snacks (*cicchetti*),
a great Venetian speciality, which may include fried fish, cooked or raw vegetables, a
piece of tasty cheese, a creamy mixture of salt cod, olives, *sarde in saor*, amongst many
other possibilities.

WINE

Viticulture in the modern sense of the word has been practised in the Veneto since the
7th century BC. In the Middle Ages the land under vine increased dramatically with
plantations made by the monastic orders, mainly the Benedictines. The wine regions
of Verona, Vicenza and Treviso developed as a result of this. The whole area around
Venice, including the islands of the lagoon (though not the parts facing the open sea)
were all covered in vineyards. Wines are still made on the island of Sant'Erasmo. Look
out for the 'Orto' label. Indigenous grape varieties include Corvina, Garganega, Rab-
oso and Rondinella (grown chiefly around Verona) and Barbera, Riesling Italica and
Renana. Cabernet and all three Pinots (Bianco, Nero and Grigio) are also popular. The
best known wines of the Verona region are Valpolicella, Bardolino (red), Soave (white)
and Amarone and Recioto (*passito*).

Recioto is perhaps the region's most important wine, largely because of the unique
way in which it is made. *Appassimento* is the most characteristic wine-making technique of the Veneto, and involves naturally drying the grapes before pressing, either
on straw or by leaving them to hang and shrivel on the vine. This latter method was
widespread throughout the Mediterranean, from Spain to the Greek islands. One of
the most refined examples of this ancient technique survives in the Veneto, in the hills
that border Verona to the north. The results are the red Amarone (where the wine fer-
ments to dryness) or sweet Recioto (where some residual sugar remains).

The origins of the name Recioto are not documented, though it may derive from a
word denoting the 'ears' of a bunch of grapes: a protruding cluster which catches more
sun and thus develops more sweetness. What is certain is that the wine known to the

ancient Romans as 'Retico' was one and the same. Virgil considered it one of the finest wines known to man, second only to the Neapolitan Falernian. Cassiodorus, minister of the Gothic emperor Theodoric, has left a description of Retico to posterity. Several centuries later, red and white wines from Verona, white Recioto from Vicenza, and Passito from Treviso, were being apostrophised as the Wine of Doges. Among the best such wines made today are Moscato and Passito di Bagnoli, Recioto di Gamberella, Torcolato Breganze and—the two most important—Recioto di Soave and Amarone della Valpolicella.

But there is plenty of excellent table wine available too. In restaurants the house wine (*vino della casa* or *vino sfuso*) varies a great deal, but is normally of a good standard and reasonable price. Wines readily available in Venice include those from the Collio hills in the Friuli region, where white varieties such as Pinot Bianco, Pinot Grigio and Verduzzo are produced, along with Chardonnay. The white wine grape formerly known as Tocai Friulano is now known simply as Friulano or Sauvignon Vert. Its former name, Tocai, was deemed too similar (by an EU ruling) to the name of the famous Hungarian wine region of Tokaj, even though the wines have nothing in common. Another indigenous grape is Terrano, producing an intense wine with an unusual acidic taste.

Picolit is a light dessert wine from the Friuli, which was drunk with enthusiasm during the days of the *Serenissima*, and exported to the courts of Europe in the 18th century (and much appreciated by Goldoni).

Another characteristic wine of the Veneto is the sparkling Prosecco, whose heartlands lie among the hills of Conegliano-Valdobbiadene. Prosecco is a grape variety which has given its name to the wine from which it is made. It is quite a sight hanging on the vine: enormous bunches of huge, round, yellow berries, whose intoxicating, muscat-like scent fills the air at harvest time. Bottled Prosecco comes in two types: the gently fizzing *frizzante*, and the *spumante* bubble-bath. The fresh, playful, approachable character of the grape is present in both. Its qualities of youthfulness and optimism and its low alcohol content make it a drink which can be taken quite harmlessly at any time of the day or night.

THE GUIDE

Sestiere of San Marco

For centuries, this sestiere was the first place any visitor to Venice would set foot, and while today far fewer people arrive by water, it is still the district to which most are first drawn. The magnificent Piazza San Marco is the backdrop for the defining and enduring symbols of the Serenissima: the Basilica of St Mark and the Doge's Palace.

The small *sestiere* of San Marco lies very much at the heart of Venice: it stretches from Piazza San Marco to the Rialto Bridge, cradled in the curve of the Grand Canal and bounded by the narrow *calle* known as the Merceria. It was here that the administrative, financial, commercial, political and cultural centre of Venice developed. Little has changed: this is the area which has Venice's most important monuments, its seat of local government, the Fenice theatre, and the greatest number of ho-

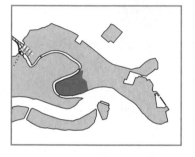

tels and the most expensive restaurants, cafés and shops. It is also in the lowest-lying part of the city and therefore particularly liable to flood. It is always the most crowded part of town, particularly around St Mark's and along the well-trodden route between Piazza San Marco and the Accademia Bridge. There are still secluded quarters, however, many of which are explored at the end of this chapter.

ST MARK'S BASILICA

The Basilica of St Mark is the most important church in Venice and its most splendid building, with superb Byzantine mosaics. It stands high in importance among the churches of Christendom. Founded in 832, its sumptuous architecture retains the original Greek-cross plan derived from the great churches of Constantinople, in particular from the (destroyed) 6th-century church of the Holy Apostles. Its five onion-shaped domes are Islamic in inspiration. This famous shrine has been embellished over the centuries by splendid mosaics, marbles and carvings. It contains outstanding art treasures. Numerous different styles and traditions have been blended in a unique combination of Byzantine and Western art.

Opening times

*Map p. 406, E2. The **basilica** is open to visitors daily 9.45–4.30 or 5; Sun and holidays 2–4.30 or 5. However, the mosaics are only lit for one hour on weekdays, 11.30–12.30, and on Sun and holidays from 2–5. From Easter to the end of October you can book the visit for a small extra fee at www.venetoinside.com.*

*The **Treasury and Pala d'Oro** (the gilded and enamelled high altarpiece) can be seen from 10–4 or 6; Sun and holidays 3–6 (both with a small extra admission charge). The north transept is usually reserved for prayer (entrance by the north door); and services are frequently held in the Chapel of the Madonna of Nicopeia and in the sanctuary on Sundays (on other days Eucharist is celebrated here at 9am), when many of the basilica's treasures and mosaics can be seen to full advantage; attending a service gives an incomparable sense of St Mark's as a functioning place of worship.*

*The **Museo di San Marco**, which houses the original gilded Horses of St Mark's, also includes access to the loggia on the façade and two balconies in the interior. It is open 9.45–4.45 (admission charge).*

Tips on visiting

The basilica must be the most visited building in Venice, and unfortunately the authorities have not yet found a way of coping satisfactorily with the crowds. It sometimes has a rather shabby atmosphere, and the attendants are not always as friendly as they might be. Most of the narthex, which has some of the most important mosaics, has been inaccessible for years. In the interior you are restricted to a 'one-way' route in the nave, thus it is worth paying the small entrance fee to see the magnificent Pala d'Oro, which allows you also to explore the east end of the church. A visit to the Museo di San Marco is highly recommended since you get a remarkable view of the interior from the gallery and come very close to some of the mosaics (as well as enjoying the view of the Piazza from the façade). It is difficult to appreciate fully the beauty of the mosaics unless they are illuminated (for times, see above).

Certain areas of the basilica normally kept closed or reserved for prayer (see p 63), can sometimes be seen by special request at the offices of the Proto of San Marco (the architects in charge of the fabric of the building) inside the basilica; enquire about procedure from one of the uniformed guards.

HISTORY OF ST MARK'S BASILICA

The basilica was formerly the private chapel of the doges and was used throughout the Republic's history for state ceremonies. It replaced San Pietro di Castello as the cathedral of Venice only in 1807.

The first church, built on a Greek-cross plan by Doge Giustiniano Particiaco, was consecrated in 832. Recent investigations of the foundations seem to confirm that they are still those of this first church. The building rests on a wooden platform supported by wooden piles, 50–80cm long, driven down through the sand into the solid lagoon bed of sand and clay some 2.5–3.5m below the present pavement. The church was damaged by fire in a popular rising in 976 against Doge Pietro Candiano IV and restored by Doge Pietro Orseolo I. In 1063, when Doge Domenico Contarini carried out important work to consolidate the building, which had been damaged by movement in the foundations, he decided to add the narthex. At this time he may also have blocked up a number of apertures which had provided light in the interior when he commissioned the first mosaics. Work was continued by Doge Domenico Selvo (1071–84). The church as it stands today was reconsecrated in 1094 when the relics of St Mark were refound (*see box below*) by Doge Vitale Falier. The original brick vaults were at a later stage surmounted on the exterior by false domes built in wood and covered with lead and each topped with an onion-shaped crown.

The mosaic decoration, begun at the end of the 1200s, is the work of centuries. After 1159 the walls were faced with marble from Ravenna, Sicily, Byzantium and the East. After the Fourth Crusade and sack of Constantinople (1204), many of the greatest treasures which now adorn the basilica (including the four Horses) were transported to Venice. The sculptural decoration of the upper façade dates from the end of the 14th and beginning of the 15th centuries. For some 40 years in the 16th century Jacopo Sansovino was *proto* of San Marco, and during this time he carried out important work to consolidate the structure of the building; a task which continues to this day.

> ## THE LEGEND OF ST MARK
>
> According to legend, St Mark the Evangelist anchored off the islands of the Rialto during a voyage from Aquileia to Rome. While he was there, he had a vision of an angel who greeted him with the words *Pax tibi, Marce, evangelista meus. Hic requiescet corpus tuum.* ('Peace be with you, Mark my evangelist. Here will be your resting place.'). This portent was supposed to have been fulfilled in 828, when two Venetian merchants brought the body of St Mark from the port of Alexandria and placed it in charge of Doge Giustiniano Particiaco, who ordered the first church on this site to be built. When this church was damaged by fire in the 10th century, the body of St Mark was lost, only to be miraculously 'rediscovered' by Doge Vitale Falier in 1094. The basilica has numerous depictions in mosaic (both on the façade and in the interior) of the various adventures of the body of St Mark, and it was a favourite subject with Venetian painters, notably Tintoretto. The symbol of St Mark (a winged lion) has been emblematic of Venice since the 9th century. There are numerous stone lions all over the city, although almost every one of them was defaced at the fall of the Republic. The lion of St Mark can still be seen on columns, in *piazze*, or decorating public buildings in many towns which were once subject to the *Serenissima*, in the Veneto and further afield. The saint was invoked as a battle cry ('*Viva San Marco!*') during the Republic, and again in the 19th century during the Venetian struggle against Austrian rule.

MAIN FAÇADE OF ST MARK'S

NB: The lower order of the façade is described here. The upper order, better seen from the loggia (reached from the Museo di San Marco), is described on pp. 68–9.

The sumptuous main façade of St Mark's is in two orders, each of five arches, those below supported by clusters of columns and those above crowned by elaborate Gothic tracery, pinnacles, sculptures and tabernacles. A balcony with water-spouts separates the two orders, and copies of the famous horses stand here. The columns are of different kinds of marble, many from older buildings, and most of them have fine capitals. At the left end of the façade, a huge single column with a fine capital supports three porphyry columns. Between the arches are six bas-reliefs. From left to right: *Hercules Carrying the Erymanthean Boar*, *St George*, *St Demetrius*, the *Virgin Orans*, the *Archangel Gabriel* and *Hercules and the Hydra*. The first is a Roman work; the third was made by a Byzantine craftsman in the late 12th century, and the others are all 13th-century works in the Veneto-Byzantine style. Below the reliefs at either end of the façade, between the columns, are statuettes of water-carriers.

THE DOORWAYS

In the lunettes of the elaborate arches which decorate the five portals are mosaics: the four on either side of the central doorway record the legend of St Mark (*see p. 49*), but only one of these is original.

(1) First doorway: 17th-century mosaic (on a cartoon by Pietro Vecchia) of the *Removal of the Body of St Mark from Alexandria*. The Moorish window has Byzantine reliefs and mosaics.

(2) Second doorway: 17th century mosaic of *Venice Welcoming the Arrival of the Body of St Mark*. 13th-century reliefs above a Gothic window.

(3) Central doorway: Crowned by a mosaic of the *Last Judgement* (1836). Among the columns flanking the doorway, eight are in red porphyry. The three arches have beautiful carvings dating from c. 1240 (first inner arch) to c. 1265 (third outer arch), constituting one of the most important examples of Italian Romanesque carving, showing the influence of Benedetto Antelami, the greatest sculptor of 12th-century Italy. The main outer arch surrounding the mosaic has, on its underside, carvings showing Venetian trades (such as boat-building and fishing), and, on the outer face, *Christ and the Prophets*. The middle arch depicts the months and signs of the zodiac on the soffit and the Virtues and Beatitudes on the outer face. The small-

est arch shows the Earth, the Ocean, and seven pairs of animals on the soffit, and, on the outer face, scenes of daily life from youth to old age. The doors are 6th-century Byzantine. In the lunette, a marble carving of the *Dream of St Mark* by the school of Antelami.

(4) Fourth doorway: Early 18th-century mosaic of *Venice Venerating the Relics of St Mark* by the Roman mosaicist Leopoldo dal Pozzo (based on a cartoon by Sebastiano Ricci). Above the door, a window with Gothic tracery surrounded by fine carvings of Christ and two prophets on a mosaic ground.

(5) Doorway of Sant'Alipio: In the arch above the door, a beautiful mosaic of the *Translation of the Body of St Mark to the Basilica* (1260–70). This is the only original mosaic to have survived on the façade, and is the earliest representation known of the exterior of the basilica (you can see that the Horses are already in place). Beneath it is a fine arched lunette with early 14th-century bas-reliefs of the symbols of the Evangelists and five pretty arches decorated with fretwork, Islamic in style. The architrave above the door is formed by a long 13th-century Venetian bas-relief in the early Christian style. Superb capitals surmount the columns on either side of the door, which is the work of an otherwise unknown master who signs himself 'Magister Bertuccio' and records the date 1300 (he also made the fourth doors).

SOUTH FAÇADE (towards the Doge's Palace)

This continues the design of the main façade. The first doorway **(6)**, blocked by the construction of the Cappella Zen in the 16th century, was formerly one of the main basilica entrances and the first to be seen from the waterfront. The columns are surmounted by two marble griffins (12th–13th century). The second arch **(7)** contains the 14th-century bronze doors of the Baptistery and a Gothic window. The two upper arches are finely decorated; between them and above a small 10th-century door is a Byzantine mosaic of the *Madonna in Prayer* (13th century), in front of which two lamps are lit every night in fulfilment of the vow made by a sea-captain after he had survived a storm at sea. The Gothic sculpture which crowns the arches is partly the work of the Florentine sculptor Niccolò di Pietro Lamberti, who came to work in the city in 1416. The two rectangular walls of the Treasury **(8)** are richly adorned with splendid marbles and fragments of ambones and plutei (9th–11th century). The front of the bench at the foot of the wall bears an inscription of the late 13th century—one of the earliest examples of the Venetian dialect.

At the southwest corner of the façade is the **Pietra del Bando (9)**, a stump of a porphyry column thought to come from Acre (now part of Israel), from which decrees of the Venetian government were proclaimed from 1256 onwards. It was hit when the Campanile collapsed in 1902, but at least it saved the corner of the basilica from serious damage.

The two famous sculptured groups in porphyry known as the *Tetrarchs* **(10)** are thought by some scholars to represent Diocletian and his three co-rulers, and by others the four sons of Constantine. Their symbolic embrace was apparently meant to represent political harmony. Probably Egyptian works of the 4th century, they used to decorate the Philadelpheion in Constantinople.

In front of the baptistery door are two isolated pillars **(11)**, beautifully carved in the 6th century and traditionally thought to have been brought by Lorenzo Tiepolo (later doge) from the church of St Saba in Acre after his victory there over the Genoese in 1256. Excavations in Istanbul, however, have confirmed that they came from the church of St Polyeuctus, built in AD 524.

NORTH FAÇADE (facing Piazzetta Giovanni XXIII)

This was probably the last to be finished, and was splendidly restored in 2005–10. It has a wealth of decoration. Between the arches and in the upper bays are interesting bas-reliefs, including one (between the first two arches) showing the *Flight of Alexander the Great*. He is shown in triumph and as a Byzantine emperor in a chariot pulled by two griffins: the curious iconography includes two little skewered piglets which Alexander holds above the griffins' noses to egg them on in their flight to Heaven (as in donkey and carrot). The story told by the Greeks was that after Alexander had conquered

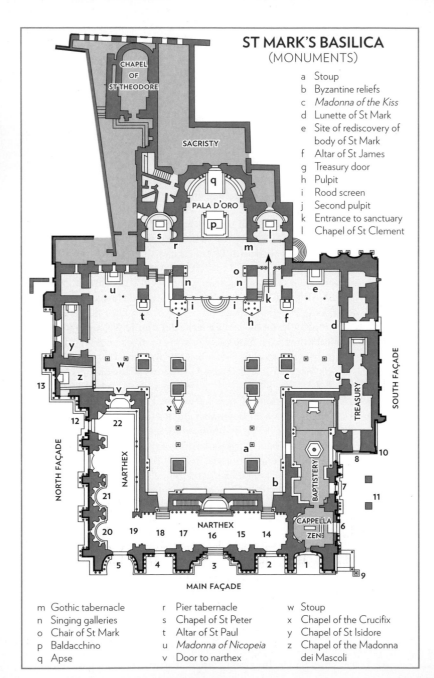

ST MARK'S BASILICA
(MONUMENTS)

a Stoup
b Byzantine reliefs
c *Madonna of the Kiss*
d Lunette of St Mark
e Site of rediscovery of body of St Mark
f Altar of St James
g Treasury door
h Pulpit
i Rood screen
j Second pulpit
k Entrance to sanctuary
l Chapel of St Clement

m Gothic tabernacle
n Singing galleries
o Chair of St Mark
p Baldacchino
q Apse

r Pier tabernacle
s Chapel of St Peter
t Altar of St Paul
u *Madonna of Nicopeia*
v Door to narthex

w Stoup
x Chapel of the Crucifix
y Chapel of St Isidore
z Chapel of the Madonna dei Mascoli

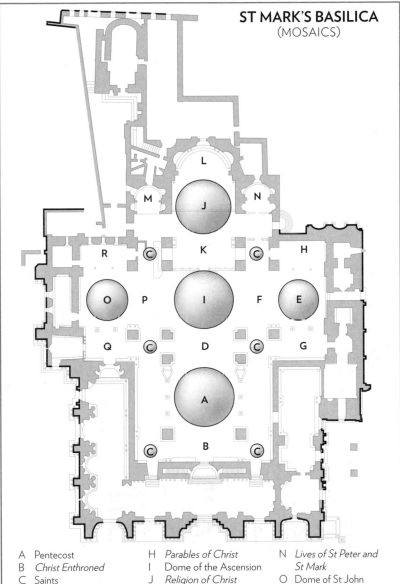

ST MARK'S BASILICA
(MOSAICS)

A Pentecost
B *Christ Enthroned*
C Saints
D Scenes of the Passion
E Dome of St Leonard
F *Life of Christ*
G *Body of St Mark*
H *Parables of Christ*
I Dome of the Ascension
J *Religion of Christ*
K *Life of Christ*
L *Christ Pantocrator*
M *Lives of St Peter and St Mark*
N *Lives of St Peter and St Mark*
O Dome of St John
P *Miracles of Christ*
Q *Life of the Virgin*
R *Miracles of Christ*

almost the entire known world, he decided to attempt to conquer Heaven, too. The last of the four arches, the **Porta dei Fiori (12)**, has beautifully carved 13th-century arches enclosing a *Nativity* scene. The *Sacrifice of Isaac* was probably carved in the 13th century by Nicola Pisano while on a visit to Venice (he is best known for his works in Tuscany). Some of the 13th-century reliefs by Venetian artists in Byzantine style have been removed to the Museo di San Marco and replaced here by casts (including *St John the Evangelist*, *Christ Enthroned*, and a scene of deer in a wood).

The upper part of the façade (as on the south front) has early 15th-century statues by the Tuscan sculptor Niccolò di Pietro Lamberti, and more fine water-carriers thought to be by his son Pietro di Niccolò Lamberti, although these have also been attributed to Jacopo della Quercia. Beyond the Porta dei Fiori the projecting walls of the Mascoli and St Isidore chapels bear Byzantine bas-reliefs including a *Virgin Orans* dating from the 12th century (in a 19th-century tabernacle).

The huge **red marble sarcophagus (13)** contains the body of Daniele Manin, who proclaimed the city's independence from Austrian rule in 1848 (*see p. 123*). Manin died in Paris in 1857 and his body was returned to Venice 20 years later. After lying in state at the foot of the Campanile, his sarcophagus (designed by Luigi Borro) was finally installed here, after two decades of discussion, and even though the Church authorities had refused his burial inside the basilica.

RELIEFS OF THE VIRGIN ORANS

St Mark's Basilica has five reliefs of the Virgin, veiled and haloed, in a frontal pose with both arms raised in a gesture of prayer and the hands held at shoulder level with the palms facing the viewer. These icons, sometimes with the Greek letters ΜΡΘΥ, standing for 'Mother of God', expressed the Virgin's role as intercessor for humankind. Made before 1261, all of them came to Venice from Constantinople, where, with pierced hands, they had been used as fountains of holy water, modelled on a miraculous image (the holes were later blocked up). There are two other similar reliefs in the churches of Santa Maria Mater Domini and San Giovanni Crisostomo.

NARTHEX

The west narthex was probably built c. 1063–72 and it seems that the north side was added at least 100 years later (certainly before 1253), but scholars still debate the exact date of construction. It once provided a fitting vestibule to the basilica, although it is today sadly cluttered with barriers and notices, and now only partly accessible, given the strictly imposed routes for entering and leaving the basilica. The slightly pointed arches, probably the earliest of their kind in Italy, support six small domes. The fine columns of the inner façade were either brought from the East or are fragments of the first basilica. The lower part of the walls is encased in marble; the upper part and the pavement are mosaic. The superb mosaics of the domes and arches show stories from the Old Testament, and are mainly original works of the 13th century.

(14) First bay: Early 13th-century mosaics of the *Story of Genesis* to the *Death of Abel*, spectacularly restored in 2007 (*but this bay was inaccessible at*

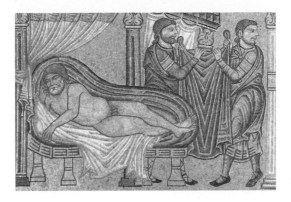

ST MARK'S NARTHEX· MOSAIC OF THE DRUNKENNESS OF NOAH
'And he drank of the wine, and was drunken;
and he was uncovered within his tent. And Shem and Japheth took a garment,
and covered the nakedness of their father; and their faces were backward,
and they saw not their father's nakedness.' *Genesis 9: 21–23*

the time of writing). The 24 episodes are divided into three bands: in the centre of the dome, *Creation of the Sky, Earth and Firmament*; in the middle band, *Creation of the Sun, Moon, Animals and Man*; third band, *Stories of Adam and Eve*. The seven days of Creation each have an increasing number of angels, from one to seven. The carefully worked-out iconographical scheme is thought to have been inspired by the Cotton Bible miniatures (probably late 5th century), once in the collection of Sir Robert Bruce Cotton (1571–1631), whose library is now in the British Museum. In the pendentives are four winged seraphs. The **Door of San Clemente** (protected by outer doors), cast in the East, is traditionally supposed to have been a gift from the Byzantine Emperor Alexius Comnenus. Dating from the second half of the 11th century, it is decorated with 22 plaques with Christ, the Madonna, prophets and

saints (their names in Greek). The Byzantine capitals of the columns flanking it are beautifully decorated with birds.

(15) First arch: Mosaics of the *Story of Noah* and the *Flood*. Here lies Doge Vitale Falier (d. 1096), who consecrated the basilica in 1094 and who was responsible for much of its most beautiful decoration. The tomb, made up of Byzantine fragments, is the oldest surviving funerary monument in the city.

(16) Second bay: In front of the main door, two tiers of niches contain the earliest mosaics in the basilica (c. 1063), doubly precious since they have never had to be restored. They represent the Madonna with the apostles Peter, Paul, James, Andrew, Simon, Thomas, Philip and Bartholomew, with the four Evangelists beneath. The *St Mark in Ecstasy* in the semi-dome was added centuries later in 1545 (on a cartoon attributed to Lorenzo Lotto). Two Byzantine angels stand on the columns flanking the arch.

The great **central door** (protected between two wooden doors) was commissioned in 1113 by Leone da Molino, who was a procurator of St Mark's: it is modelled on the Byzantine door of San Clemente in the first bay. It has 36 plaques with Biblical figures.

The **slab of red Verona marble** with a white marble lozenge in the pavement traditionally marks the spot where the Emperor Frederick Barbarossa was forced to kneel before Pope Alexander III in 1177. This marked a significant moment in the history of Venice's rise to power, since the city had been chosen as the scene for the reconciliation between the Papacy and the Empire (despite the fact that it had at first, under the dogeship of Sebastiano Ziani, joined the Lombard League against Barbarossa).

(17) Second arch: Mosaics of the *Death of Noah* and the *Tower of Babel*. The tomb of the wife of Doge Vitale Michiel (d. 1101) is decorated with plutei and transennae which were carved in the previous century.

(18) Third bay: In the dome and the arch above the door, the mosaics illustrating the *Story of Abraham* date from c. 1230. In the pendentives are four tondi with prophets. In the lunette above the door there is a Byzantine mosaic of *St Peter*.

(19) Third arch: Mosaics of *St Alipio* and *St Simon*, and, in the centre, a tondo with *Justice* (c. 1230).

(20) Fourth bay: The tomb of Doge Bartolomeo Gradenigo (d. 1342) is by a Pisan sculptor. The three-year reign of this doge saw the beginning of the reconstruction of the Doge's Palace and is also remembered for a terrible flood, the consequences of which were thought to have been alleviated by the intervention of St Mark, together with St Nicholas and St George (the famous tale of the fisherman and the ring is illustrated in Paris Bordone's painting now in the Galleria dell'Accademia; *see p. 145*).

The mosaics along this side of the narthex were partly re-made in the 19th century; they portray the *Story of Joseph*, and, in the pendentives, the prophets.

(21) Fifth bay: The tomb of Doge Marin Morosini (d. 1253) has been recomposed but includes a 13th-century relief.

(22) Seventh bay: Mosaics of the *Story of Moses*. The bust of 'Papa Giovanni' (who was Venetian Patriarch when elected Pope John XXIII in 1958) is by Giacomo Manzù, a sculptor well known for his religious subjects.

THE INTERIOR

The glimmering interior of St Mark's is one of the great sights of the Christian world. Five mighty domes cover the Greek cross, alternating with barrel vaults; each of the four arms has vaulted aisles in which the numerous columns with exquisite foliated capitals support a gallery (formerly the matroneum), fronted by a parapet of ancient *plutei* (dating from the 6th–11th centuries). The sanctuary, where the religious and political ceremonies of the Republic were held, is raised above the crypt and separated from the rest of the church by a rood screen. The whole building is encased by Eastern marbles below and splendid mosaics on a gold ground above, illuminated high up by small windows (the rose window in the south transept and the arch opened at the west end are later additions which alter the delicate effect of dim lighting). At the centre of the nave hangs a huge Byzantine chandelier, while red lamps decorate the side chapels.

The splendid 12th-century pavement, which has subsided in places, has a geometric mosaic of antique marble with representations of beasts and birds. Part of it is covered with protective matting. The light in the interior of the church changes constantly; ideally it should be visited at different times of the day, though in high season the crowds make this impossible.

West end: Over the nave rises the great **Dome of the Pentecost (A)**, dating from the early 12th century and probably the first of the five domes to be decorated with mosaics. It shows the *Descent of the Holy Spirit* with the twelve Apostles seated in a circle; the figures in pairs between the little windows represent the *Converted Nations*; and in the pendentives are four huge figures of angels. Lower down above the main door into the narthex is a brightly coloured lunette of ***Christ Enthroned between the Madonna and St Mark* (B)**, a very fine restored 13th-century work. In the barrel vault stretching to the façade (better seen from the gallery in the Museo di San Marco) are scenes of the *Last Judgement*, *Paradise*, the *Apocalypse* and *Vision of St John* dating from the 16th–17th centuries and partly restored in the 19th.

South aisle: Here is a superb frieze of five mosaic rectangles with the elegant single figures of the Madonna and the prophets Isaiah, David, Solomon and Ezekiel (c. 1230; well restored in the 19th century). On the wall above, the splendid large composition of the *Agony in the Garden* is the earliest 13th-century mosaic in the basilica. On either side of the windows, and in the arch above, are scenes from the lives of the Apostles (dated to the end of the 12th and beginning of the 13th century). The simple **stoup (a)** is of Oriental porphyry (the carved base is now in the Museo di San Marco). On the south wall are two **Byzantine reliefs (b)**: *Christ between Mary and St John the Baptist*, and an 11th-century *Virgin Orans*.

The little domes and arches at the piers forming the side aisle (as in the rest of the church: *all marked **C** on the plan*) are beautifully decorated with 13th-century mosaics (mostly of saints), many of them restored or re-worked.

On a corner pier is a bas-relief of the Madonna and Child (known as the ***Madonna of the Kiss* (c)** since it has been worn away by the kisses of the devout), thought to date from the 12th century. The exquisite mosaics on the arch towards the nave also date from the late 12th century and portray **scenes of the Passion (D)**: the *Kiss of Judas*, *Crucifixion*, *Marys at the Tomb* (15th-century copy), *Descent into Limbo*, and the *Incredulity of St Thomas*.

South transept: The **Dome of St Leonard (E)** has just four lone figures of male saints: St Nicholas, St Clement, St Blaise and St Leonard (early 13th century); in the spandrels are four female saints: St Dorothea (13th century), Sts

Erasma and Euphemia (both 15th century), and St Thecla (early 16th century). In the arch towards the nave are very fine mosaic scenes from the **life of Christ (F)** (early 12th century): the *Entry into Jerusalem, Temptations of Christ, Last Supper* and *Washing of the Feet*. The first narrow arch in front of the rose window is decorated with Sts Anthony Abbot, Bernardino of Siena, Vincent Ferrer and Paul the Hermit, good works dating from 1458 (showing Tuscan influence).

On the right wall the mosaic shows prayers for, and the miraculous rediscovery of, the **body of St Mark (G)**, with interesting details of the interior of the basilica. Made in the 13th century (although later restored), it includes a supposed portrait of Doge Vitale Falier, who was present when the body was found in 1094, and a portrait of the mosaicists' contemporary Doge Ranier Zeno, who reigned from 1253–68. In the vault (difficult to see) are 17th-century scenes from the life of the Virgin. The mosaics on the arch above the Altar of the Sacrament show the **parables and miracles of Christ (H)** (late 12th or early 13th century; restored); those on the end wall (scenes from the life of St Leonard) were renewed in the early 17th century from cartoons by Pietro Muttoni.

Above a door which is now kept closed but which was once the main entrance to the church from the Doge's Palace, is a 13th-century mosaic **lunette of St Mark (d)**. The huge Gothic rose window was inserted in the 15th century. The altar in this transept has a tabernacle borne by columns of porphyry and *pavonazzetto*. It is flanked by two bronze candelabra dating from 1527. On the two pilasters are rectangles of fine marble inlay; the one on the left marks the **place where St Mark's body was miraculously rediscovered (e)** on 24th June 1094 (illustrated in the mosaic on the opposite wall). On the wall to the right of the altar is a relief of *St Peter Enthroned* (and two bishop saints in mosaic beneath the arch); to the left of the altar, a Byzantine relief of the *Madonna and Child*. The mosaic pavement here bears early Christian motifs. On the nave pier is the **Altar of St James (f)**, a charming work with beautiful decorative details by Antonio Rizzo. Here is the entrance to the sanctuary and Pala d'Oro (*see k, below*).

Treasury: The little **door (g)** which leads into the treasury has a pretty ogee arch with a 13th-century mosaic of two angels holding a reliquary of the True Cross and a 14th-century statuette of the *Risen Christ*. The treasury (*for admission see p. 48*) contains a rich store of booty from the sack of Constantinople during the Fourth Crusade of 1204 (*see opposite*). Even though many of its most precious possessions were melted down in 1797 on the fall of the Republic, it still retains one of the most important collections in existence of 12th-century Byzantine goldsmiths' work.

In the anteroom is a fine silver statuette of St Mark made in 1804 by a little-known artist, Francesco Francesconi. On the left is the sanctuary, with precious Byzantine reliquaries. Above the altar frontal made of oriental alabaster is a relief of *Christ Among the Apostles*, and, even higher, a tondo of *Christ between Two Angels* (13th century).

On the right is the treasury proper, in a room with exceptionally thick walls thought once to have been a 9th-century tower of the Doge's Palace.

THE FOURTH CRUSADE

In 1201, a band of Frankish knights, led by Geoffrey de Villehardouin, arrived in Venice seeking men and ships to transport them on crusade to the Holy Land. The Great Council acceded to the demand: ships were made ready, and it was decided that the aged doge, Enrico Dandolo, should accompany the crusaders as the leader of the Venetian contingent. But when Villehardouin and his men found themselves unable to pay Venice the amount they had agreed, the crusaders remained stranded in the Adriatic for two years. It was only when envoys arrived from Constantinople asking for help in ousting the usurping emperor, Alexius III, that Venice saw an opportunity to become the saviour of Christendom, and the fleet set sail for Byzantium. The lawful claimant to the throne, Alexius Angelus, son of the deposed emperor Isaac, promised that once he was placed upon his rightful throne the crusaders' passage to the Holy Land would be financed, and—more important still—that he would unite the churches of East and West, placing himself and his bishops at the disposal of the pope. Constantinople was completely unprepared for war, and Alexius III fled. The city elders then freed the deposed Isaac, restoring him to the throne. With the aim of their siege—deposing the usurper—achieved, the crusaders had no further reason to attack. Hostilities ceased, and Alexius Angelus was crowned Alexius IV, as co-emperor. But he could not fulfil the promises he had so rashly made: the imperial coffers were empty, and Isaac had no intention of abjuring his religion. Alexius was also unpopular with his own people. At length a plot by the son-in-law of Alexius III to regain the throne succeeded: Alexius IV was strangled, and a new emperor, Alexius V Ducas, took his place. For Venice this represented a reason to resume the siege, to depose the usurper and murderer, and place a Latin emperor of her own choosing on the throne instead, thus uniting the churches of East and West. Not only this, but Venice would be assured of trade privileges in a Latin Constantinople such as she had never known under the Byzantines. In vain Alexius V sued for peace: in April 1204 the city was besieged and fell, and then was cruelly sacked. Baldwin of Flanders was proclaimed emperor, and Venice apportioned to herself half of the city itself, as well as other strategic territories in the western Aegean and Peloponnese. Many of the priceless treasures of Byzantium were removed to Venice, to adorn St Mark's basilica. For over 50 years, until 1261, when Michael Palaeologus recaptured the throne, there was no Byzantine emperor of the East. Even after the reconquest, the Byzantine empire was much weakened. When it fell to the Ottomans in 1453, Venice struggled to retain her lands in Greece, which eventually also fell to the Turks. She was ultimately the victim of her own success.

Highlights of the treasury's holdings include two elaborate silver-gilt altar frontals (13th and 14th centuries), an Egyptian alabaster vase (500–300 BC), a Roman ampulla in onyx and a Roman lamp in rock crystal. There are four exquisite Byzantine icons (11th–13th centuries), with gilding and enamels, two of them depicting the *Crucifixion* and two of them depicting St Michael Archangel (one of these has the central panel with the Archangel dating from the late 10th century framed by Venetian craftsmen in the 13th century).

Church vessels and plate include beautiful Byzantine chalices and patens

(10th–11th century) in onyx, agate, alabaster and other precious materials. The
remarkable incense burner or coffer in
the shape of a Byzantine garden pavilion
with five domes is a Romanesque-Byz-
antine work from southern Italy (12th–
13th century). There is also a bowl made
of turquoise (a gift in 1472 from the Shah
of Persia), one in alabaster, and one
in rock crystal and enamel, decorated
with Classical figures, which may be a
Corinthian work; and a glass phial with
incised decoration (Saracen, 10th century). The exquisite paten with Christ
blessing, a Byzantine work thought to
date from the 11th century, is richly decorated in oriental alabaster, cloisonné
enamel, gold, silver gilt, rock crystal and
pearls. A rare chalice is known to have
belonged to the 10th-century Byzantine
Emperor Romanos, since his name is
inscribed in blue enamel letters on the
base. It is possibly a reused Roman work
of the 1st century AD, with a Byzantine
silver-gilt mount and cloisonné enamels,
and gold. The chalice with a Eucharistic
inscription made of sardonyx is also a
Byzantine work of the 10th–11th century
in imitation of a Classical work.

Also displayed are the sword of Doge
Francesco Morosini (*see p. 75*), a gift
from Pope Alexander VIII; a Gothic
reliquary casket which belonged to
Charles VIII of France; a lovely gospel
cover in gilded silver (12th century, from
Aquileia); and huge precious gems.

Crossing: The central **Dome of the
Ascension (I)** shows Christ seated on a
rainbow, with the symbols of the Evangelists, the angel, the lion, the bull and
the eagle below Him, as described in the
Vision of St John the Evangelist. Below
them are four figures representing the
rivers of Paradise. It is a brilliant work
of Venetian masters of the late 12th century. Around the Ascension in the centre
are the Virgin and two angels and the
twelve Apostles; between the windows,
the 16 Virtues of Christ.

After his coronation in the sanctuary
the doge traditionally showed himself to
the people from the **polygonal pulpit
(h)**, above which is a 15th-century statue
of the *Madonna and Child* attributed to
Giovanni Bon, father of the more famous
sculptor Bartolomeo. The presbytery is
raised above the crypt on a stylobate of
16 little marble arches at the foot of the
rood screen. The **rood screen (i)**, with
eight columns of dark marble, bears the
great Cross (or rood), a work in silver
and bronze by the otherwise unknown
Venetian Jacopo di Marco Benato
(1394). The very fine marble statues of
the *Virgin*, *St Mark the Evangelist*, and
the *Apostles*, of the same date, are usually considered the masterpiece of the
brothers Jacobello and Pier Paolo dalle
Masegne, who signed them together
(their work is often indistinguishable).
They ran the most productive workshop
in Venice in the last decades of the 14th
and the beginning of the 15th centuries.

The **second pulpit (j)** is really two
pulpits one above the other, supported
by precious marble columns and surrounded by parapets of *verde antico*. It is
crowned by a little oriental cupola. The
fine stairway can be seen from the left
transept. At the spring of the pendentives of the central cupola are four lovely
gilded marble angels (Romanesque
works showing the influence of Antelami). In the pavement is a large rectangle
of veined Greek marble on the site of the
old choir (11th–12th century).

Sanctuary: The **entrance to the sanctuary (k)** is from the south transept beneath a transenna bearing Gothic statues of the Madonna and four female saints. Ahead is the **Chapel of St Clement (l)** with sculptures by the Dalle Masegne brothers. The upper part of the altar is by Antonio Rizzo. Below is a votive relief of saints with the 16th-century doge Andrea Gritti in adoration. Tickets for admission to the sanctuary and Pala d'Oro can be bought here (*for times, see p. 48*). On the side pier is a fine **Gothic tabernacle (m)**. The **singing galleries (n)** have reliefs of the martyrdom and miracles of St Mark, made in 1537–44 by Jacopo Sansovino, who is buried in the baptistery (*see p. 64*). The other works in bronze he made for the sanctuary of the basilica include the four Evangelists on the marble balustrades (c. 1552); the gilded door of the tabernacle in the apse; and the very fine reliefs of the *Entombment* and *Resurrection* on the sacristy door, in the frame of which he included a self-portrait, as well as portraits of Pietro Aretino and Titian.

The sanctuary dome is a superb work of the 12th century showing the **Religion of Christ (J)** as foretold by the prophets with the bust of Christ Emmanuel holding a half-revealed scroll (re-made around 1500), surrounded by the Virgin between Isaiah and Daniel and eleven other prophets. In the spandrels are symbols of the Evangelists. In the arch above the rood-screen are 16th-century mosaics of the **life of Christ (K)** on cartoons by Tintoretto. The mosaic in the apse at the east end is ***Christ Pantocrator (L)***, the ruler of the universe, signed 'Petrus F.' and dated 1506, but copied from its 12th-century prototype. Below, between the windows, are the four patron saints of Venice: St Nicholas, St Peter, St Mark and St Hermagorus, among the earliest mosaics in the basilica (probably completed before 1100). The figures of **St Peter and St Mark (M, N)** are particularly beautiful, and on the arches above the singing galleries to the left and right are mosaic scenes from their lives (early 12th century, some of them restored). The mosaics on the end walls are partly hidden by the organs; they represent more scenes from the lives of these saints, and also of St Clement.

The small marble **chair of St Mark (o)** is on the right, set up on a high podium. This was a gift from the emperor Heraclius to the patriarch of Grado in 630, and was traditionally held to be the throne used by the Evangelist during his preachings in Alexandria. In fact it is a symbolic Egyptian throne made in Alexandria probably in the early 7th century and subsequently decorated by Venetian craftsmen. The organ (1767), made by the famous Venetian organ-maker Gaetano Callido, has been reconstructed.

The **baldacchino (p)** of the high altar is borne by four beautiful columns of eastern alabaster sculpted with scenes from the life of Mary and of Christ which are extremely interesting both from an artistic and from a historical point of view. Incredibly enough, it was for long uncertain whether these were Byzantine works of the early 6th or even 5th century, or Venetian works of around 1250: the most recent scholarship suggests they are, indeed, early Byzantine works. On the side walls are six Gothic statues of saints. The **sarcophagus of St Mark** is preserved beneath the altar. An altarpiece attributed to Michele Giambono has been placed over the altar (covering the back of the Pala d'Oro).

In the central niche of the **apse (q)** are two fine gilded capitals from Orseolo's basilica, and an altar with six precious columns, including two of unusually transparent alabaster, and statues of *St Francis* and *St Bernardino* by Lorenzo Bregno, who was Antonio Rizzo's nephew and was active in the city at the beginning of the 16th century.

Beyond a Gothic **pier tabernacle (r)**, with more sculptures by the Dalle Masegne, is the **Chapel of St Peter (s)**, with a large 14th-century relief of *St Peter* with two small kneeling procurators. The two columns have superb Byzantine capitals.

Pala d'Oro: Behind the high altar is the Pala d'Oro, an altarpiece glowing with gemstones, enamel and old gold, the most precious work of art in the basilica. This is one of the most remarkable works ever produced by medieval gold-smiths, and incorporates some of the finest Byzantine enamels known. The first Pala was ordered in Constantinople by Doge Pietro Orseolo I. Embellished in 1105 (in Constantinople) for Doge Ordelafo Falier, it was enlarged by order of Doge Pietro Ziani in 1209, and finally re-set in 1345 by Gian Paolo Boninsegna, with a new gilded silver frame decorated with busts and embossed patterns.

In the upper part, the Archangel Michael is surrounded by roundels with the busts of 16 saints; on either side are six exquisite enamel scenes: *Entry into Jerusalem, Descent into Limbo, Crucifix-ion, Ascension, Pentecost* and *Dormition of the Virgin* (these last perhaps from the church of the Pantocrator in Constan-tinople). In the centre of the lower part, the Pantocrator (thought to be a 12th-century work also from Constantinople)

is surrounded by 14th-century Venetian panels, with the four Evangelists in the tondi. Above are two rectangles with an-gels, on either side of a lozenge depicting the empty throne prepared for the Last Judgement.

Below the Pantocrator are three niches with the Virgin in prayer flanked by the empress Irene of Byzantium and Doge Ordelafo Falier. In this central lower section there are also two inscrip-tions on gilded plaques recording work on the Pala carried out by the Falier doges in the 12th–13th centuries and by Andrea Dandolo in the 14th century. The other 39 niches in three rows show the standing figures of prophets, apostles and angels with enamels from Constan-tinople.

In the border, the 27 rectangular scenes from the lives of Christ (at the top) and of St Mark (at the two sides) are thought to survive from the Pala of Doge Falier. The precious stones used to deco-rate the work include pearls, sapphires, emeralds, amethysts, rubies and topaz. The enamels have been worked using the cloisonné technique, divided by narrow strips of metal. This is considered one of the most exquisite examples of this art, typical of Byzantine craftsmanship.

North transept: The beautiful **Dome of St John (O)** was decorated in the first half of the 12th century. The Greek cross in the centre is surrounded by stories from the life of St John the Evangelist. On the arch towards the nave are 16th-century mosaics of the **miracles of Christ (P)** on cartoons by Jacopo Tin-toretto, Giuseppe Salviati and Veronese. On the left wall the arch has scenes from the **life of the Virgin (Q)** and the Infant Christ (end of the 12th, beginning of the

13th century). The cycle was continued with the *Story of Susanna* on the west wall in the 16th century (from cartoons by Palma Giovane and Tintoretto).

In the archivolt (better seen from the Museo di San Marco), *Miracles of Christ* (end of the 12th, beginning of 13th century; restored), and, on the end wall, the huge *Tree of Jesse* (from a cartoon by Giuseppe Salviati, 1542). The east wall of the transept has the *Communion of the Apostles* and *Christ at Emmaus* from cartoons by Aliense and Leandro Bassano (1611–17).

On the nave pier is the **Altar of St Paul (t)** by Antonio Rizzo, which matches that of St James (f). The **Chapel of the Madonna of Nicopeia** (**u**; *used for services*) contains a precious icon, the *Virgin Nikopoios*, representing the Virgin enthroned with the blessing Christ Child. This type of icon, with a frontal view of the Child as Redeemer, was known as the 'Victory maker', since it would often be carried by the Byzantine emperor into battle at the head of his army. A similar icon is known to have hung in the apse of Haghia Sophia in Constantinople in 843, but this work, stolen by the Venetians from Constantinople in 1204, was traditionally considered to be the original icon and became the protectress of Venice. It remains the most venerated image in the basilica to this day. Most scholars now consider it to date from the 12th century. It is surrounded by a fine enamelled frame encrusted with jewels. Candelabra dating from 1520 and Byzantine bas-reliefs flank the altar. The arch over the altar has Baroque mosaics of the **miracles of Christ (R)**.

Above the **door to the narthex (v)** is a pretty carved ogee arch with a late 13th-century mosaic. The Greek marble **stoup (w)** has Romanesque carvings. On the nave piers are a *Virgin Orans* made in Constantinople in the 11th–12th century, and a large bas-relief of the Madonna and Child known as the *Madonna 'dello schioppo'* ('of the explosion') because of the gun placed here as an ex-voto.

North aisle: Here is a memorable frieze of five mosaic rectangles with the single figures of a beardless Christ and the prophets Hosea, Joel, Micah and Jeremiah. On the wall and arch above is a depiction of the life of Christ and the Apostles, replaced in 1619–24 from cartoons by Padovanino, Aliense and Palma Giovane. The lovely little **Chapel of the Crucifix (x)** has a pyramidal marble roof surmounted by a huge oriental agate and supported by six columns of precious marble with gilded Byzantine capitals. It contains a painted wood Crucifix thought to have been brought from the East in 1205. Nearer the west door is a stoup made of *bardiglio* marble, streaked with blue and white.

AREAS OF THE BASILICA NORMALLY CLOSED

The chapels described below are closed to regular visitors. Applications to view them must be made to the office of the Proto of San Marco; see p. 48.

The barrel-vaulted **Chapel of St Isidore (y)** was constructed by Doge Andrea Dandolo in 1354–5 and covered by mosaics in a beautiful decorative scheme depicting the history of the saint. The relics of Isidore were brought to Venice from the Greek island of Chios in 1125 (and his head joined them in 1627): the 14th-century tomb with a statue of the saint is attributed to a follower of Marco Romano.

The **Chapel of the Madonna dei Mascoli (z)** is so named because it became the chapel of a confraternity of male worshippers (*maschi*) in 1618. The mosaics (1430–50) on the barrel vault, which depict the life of the Virgin, are one of the most important mosaic cycles of this time. They were carried out under the direction of Michele Giambono, whose style is usually considered to be typical of the International Gothic. Here, however, using cartoons by the famous Tuscan artist Andrea del Castagno and probably also Venice's Jacopo Bellini, he produced one of the earliest examples of Renaissance art in Venice. The *Birth and Presentation of the Virgin* (left wall) bear his signature; on the right wall are the *Visitation* and *Dormition of the Virgin*. Set into the end wall, encased in splendid marbles, is a carved Gothic altar with 15th-century statues by Bartolomeo Bon. On the wall outside the chapel is a Byzantine relief of the *Virgin Orans*.

In the **Baptistery** the mosaics (c. 1343–54) are extremely fine. They illustrate the life of St John the Baptist and the early life of Christ. The delightful scene of the *Banquet of Herod*, above the door into the church, shows the influence of the greatest Venetian painter of the time, Paolo Veneziano. They were carried out for Doge Andrea Dandolo, who is buried here in a Gothic sarcophagus by Giovanni de' Santi. This doge, a friend of Petrarch, took a degree at Padua University and was a famous man

of letters. He was the last doge to be buried in St Mark's, in 1354. The font was designed by Jacopo Sansovino (c. 1545), who is also buried here: he was not only one of the most prominent architects in Venice, but also, as *proto* of St Mark's, looked after the basilica for many years (and carried out a number of sculptural works for the sanctuary). Beneath a huge block of granite (with an ancient inscription), said to have been brought from Tyre in 1126, traces are visible of a rectangular font, for total immersion, with fresco fragments thought to have survived from the earliest church. Near a 13th-century relief of an angel is the sarcophagus of Doge Giovanni Soranzo (d. 1328). The reliefs of the *Baptism of Christ*, and *St George* and *St Theodore* (on horseback) date from the 13th–14th centuries and there are 13th-century fresco fragments on the walls.

The **Cappella Zen** was built largely by Tullio Lombardo in 1504–22, in honour of Cardinal Giovanni Battista Zen, who had left his patrimony to the Republic on the condition that he was buried in the basilica (he died in 1501). Unfortunately, the construction of the chapel blocked up the original entrance to the narthex from the Piazzetta. The very fine doorway into the narthex remains: beneath a 19th-century mosaic of the *Madonna* between two 12th-century archangels are niches with mosaics (early 14th century) alternating with fine statuettes of prophets (by the school of Antelami). The mosaics in the barrel vault dating from the late 13th century (but restored) relate to the life of St Mark. There are some interesting bas-reliefs (11th–13th centuries) and two red marble Romanesque lions, which probably once stood outside the entrance to the basilica. But the chapel is especially remarkable for its bronze sculptures, which include Cardinal Zen's tomb and the altar: these were begun by Alessandro Leopardi and Antonio Lombardo. In 1506 Antonio also made the classical statue of the *Madonna 'of the Shoe'* (so called because when a poor man offered a shoe to the statue, the shoe miraculously turned to gold).

The **crypt** may date in part from the 9th century (although it has recently been suggested that it post-dates the original church). It has an interesting plan with 50 ancient columns. The body of St Mark was placed here in 1094. The pavement dates from the 19th century.

THE MUSIC SCHOOL OF ST MARK'S

The music school of the Doge's Chapel of St Mark, founded in 1403, became famous towards the end of the 15th century, when the first Maestro di Cappella was appointed. These distinguished *maestri* were usually well-known composers who acted as directors of religious music. Music was performed on all state occasions and every day at Vespers. The Flemish choirmaster Adrian Willaert (c. 1490–1562) was appointed Maestro di Cappella in 1527, and remained here until the end of his life. Using the two organs, he experimented with double choirs, and totally changed the performance of music in the basilica. The composer Andrea Gabrieli first became organist in 1564, and then Maestro di Cappella; his more famous nephew Giovanni, also a composer, succeeded him in 1585. Much of their choral and organ music was composed for the basilica, with its unique acoustics and divided choirs (using the two pulpits): for example, *Selva morale* (1641) and *Messa a quattro voci et salmi* (1650). Giovanni's fame attracted the German composer Heinrich Schütz as a pupil in 1609. Claudio Monteverdi directed the music at St Mark's from 1613 until his death in 1643, and wrote some beautiful church music during this period for small groups of solo voices and instruments, to be sung at Vespers. He was followed by Giovanni Rovetta (1596–1668). Monteverdi's pupil Pier Francesco Cavalli (1602–76), who came to Venice from Crema as a chorister, became organist at St Mark's and later followed his master's operatic lead, becoming Maestro di Cappella for the last nine years of his life. From 1748 until 1785 the position was held by Baldassare Galuppi (*see p. 322*).

MUSEO DI SAN MARCO

From a small door to the right of the main west door, very steep narrow stairs lead to the Museo di San Marco and the loggia (*for admission see p. 48*). It is well worth visiting this museum both for its contents (which include the original Horses of St Mark's) and also because it enables you to have a much closer view of the mosaics inside the basilica. There is also access to the loggia on the façade, with a wonderful view of Piazza San Marco.

Beyond models of the basilica at various stages of its construction, there is a display on the technique of mosaic decoration and how mosaics are restored. The gallery above the narthex provides a splendid view of the interior of the basilica. The mosaics directly above include a *Last Judgement* from a cartoon by Tintoretto, Aliense and Maffeo da Verona (1557–1619; restored in the 19th century), and *Paradise*, a Mannerist work of 1628–31, and, on the arch, the *Apocalypse and Vision of St John*, by the Zuccato brothers (1570–89; also restored).

In the area beyond, some of the original 13th- and 14th-century mosaics from the Baptistery and Cappella Zen, detached in 1865, are displayed. The double bass made by Gasparo da Salò was presented in the late 18th century by the Procurators of St Mark's to Domenico Dragonetti when he was a member of the orchestra.

Beyond two short flights of steps is a *Madonna and Child* in gilded terracotta. This was made by Jacopo Sansovino for the Loggetta at the foot of the Campanile, but it was broken when the tower collapsed in 1902. A charming work, it has recently been recomposed from the shattered fragments, although the young St John, to whom the attention of both the Madonna and Child is specially drawn, was damaged irreparably.

Above the north transept, from one of the walkways which encircle the upper part of the basilica, where Jacopo Sansovino inserted iron girders to consolidate the structure, you can see the wonderful mosaic domes at the east end. The nearest is the Dome of St John, which was made in the first half of the 12th century and illustrates the life of the Evangelist. Dating from the end of that century (and subsequently restored) are the four charming scenes of miracles of Christ, including the miraculous draught of fishes, in the archivolt immediately above. On the end wall is a huge mosaic *Tree of Jesse*, made in the 16th century from a cartoon by Giuseppe Salviati. Stairs lead up to a room which displays watercolours and drawings published by Ferdinando Ongania from 1881–93, which provide a fascinating and extremely accurate documentation of every detail of the basilica. It was at that time that it was realised (partly as a result of Ruskin's objections) that restoration work needed to be more carefully monitored. The watercolour by Alberto Prosdocimi of the main façade in 1881 is particularly impressive.

The huge Sala dei Banchetti, once used for state banquets, was purpose-built in 1623 by Bartolomeo Monopola as an annexe to the doge's apartments. The ceiling was frescoed by Jacopo Guarana and Francesco Zanchi. After the fall of the Republic the room was incorporated into the Palazzo Patriarcale. Now filled with an overcrowded display of precious fabrics, it is difficult to appreciate the grandeur of the room. A group of late 15th-century Flemish tapestries which belonged to Cardinal Zen are displayed near some exquisite lace vestments. The magnificent series of ten tapestries depicting the *Passion of Christ*, made around 1420 to cartoons attributed to the Venetian painter Niccolò di Pietro, is the oldest complete series of tapestries to have survived in Italy. Two very early Byzantine embroidered fabrics are also displayed here, one with the *Lamentation over the Dead Christ*, and another with two archangels, probably made in Venice in the early 13th century. The magnificent cover for the Pala d'Oro was painted in 1345 by Paolo Veneziano and his sons Luca and Giovanni. The lion of St Mark was carved in the late 15th century, and used to watch over the organ in the basilica. Four tapestries made for the Medici by Giovanni Rost in 1531 have scenes from the life of St Mark. The five Persian (Isfahan) carpets date from the early 17th century, and were formerly used to adorn (and protect) the pavement of the basilica.

Museo di San Marco: the Horses of St Mark's

Standing in a room with sculptural fragments (including five large 13th-century reliefs which were once on the north façade of the basilica), in a sadly cramped corner, are the four magnificent gilded copper Horses of St Mark's. After their restoration in 1979, the controversial decision was taken to exhibit them here and place replicas on the façade of the basilica.

THE STORY OF THE HORSES OF ST MARK'S

In 1549, Anton Doni, a Florentine living in Venice, noted that of all the many treasures of the city, the finest were the four gilded horses which stood aloft on the loggia of St Mark's. Four horses, always stallions, were in Antiquity a sign of triumph and splendour. From the 7th century BC, the four-horse chariot race was the most prestigious in the Olympics, and such racing eventually became the most exciting spectator sport of the Roman Empire. Yet it was also in a four-horse chariot, a quadriga, that an emperor would parade in a Roman triumph.

The four horses of St Mark's are the only team to survive from the ancient world. They are beautifully crafted; even the 'chestnut', the horny lump on the inner side of the back leg is cast, as are muscles and veins. They came to Venice as part of the plunder of the Fourth Crusade of 1204, and were placed on the loggia some time before 1267, as shown in the mosaic of that date above the Door of Sant'Alipio. The site was a prestigious one. Their position might symbolise the triumph of Venice but it has also been argued, by the art historian Michael Jacoff, that they were intended to represent the Evangelists, drawing the chariot of Christ. It is also possible that they symbolise a hippodrome, as the doges in the 13th century used the loggia as a platform to show themselves to the people, just as emperors did in the hippodrome in Constantinople.

The horses quickly endeared themselves to the Venetians as a symbol of the freedom of their city. When the Genoese threatened Venice from Chioggia in 1379, the Genoese commander promised he would put 'bridles on those unreined horses of yours'. It was perhaps inevitable that Napoleon would include them among the plunder he took from Venice in 1797. In Paris, they were placed on the triumphal Arc du Carrousel, probably precisely the sort of setting for which they had been designed.

The origins of the horses remains mysterious. They have been attributed to almost every great sculptor of the past, including Pheidias and Lysippus. Yet it is their casting in copper which has helped towards a solution. Even though copper, with its high melting point, is more difficult to mould than bronze, it is now known that any sculpture which was to be gilded had to be cast in copper, as bronze reacted badly to the mercury-based gilding method and became blemished. This method of gilding (highly effective, as can be seen by its survival) appeared in the 2nd century AD. By this time no one but an emperor would have commissioned such a symbol of triumph. The most likely candidate is Septimius Severus, who conquered Byzantium in AD 195. It is known that he celebrated his triumphs with arches surmounted by *quadrigae* and that Constantine preserved Septimius' city when he rebuilt it as Constantinople in 330. This may well account for the horses' presence there in 1204. For a fuller account see Charles Freeman, *The Horses of St Mark's* (Little Brown, 2004). C.F.

THE MOSAICS OF ST MARK'S

The mosaics (only lit at certain times; *see p. 48*), which cover a huge area of the basilica, were begun after 1063 by Greek masters who established a workshop of mosaicists in Venice. Their work was badly damaged in a fire in 1106. In the 12th and 13th centuries the Venetian school of mosaicists flourished, much influenced by Byzantine prototypes, and the decoration of the interior was largely completed by 1277. The three main domes in the central part of the church depict the Religion of Christ as foretold by the prophets (in the presbytery), the Ascension (central dome), and Pentecost (in the dome nearest the west door). Similar decorative schemes existed in the 9th-century church of the Holy Apostles in Constantinople, and other Byzantine churches. The mosaics in the Narthex illustrate the Old Testament. The other main mosaic cycles illustrate scenes from the life of the Virgin and the legend of St Mark, and the lives of the saints.

Over the centuries some of the mosaics have had to be repaired or renewed and work continued on them right up until the 20th century, although the original Byzantine and medieval iconographical scheme has been largely preserved. In the 14th and 15th centuries mosaics were added to the baptistery and other chapels, with the help of Tuscan artists including Paolo Uccello and Andrea del Castagno. In the early 16th century many well-known Venetian painters (such as Titian, Giuseppe Salviati, Tintoretto and Palma Giovane) provided cartoons for the mosaicists, including the Zuccato brothers, and the partial replacement of the mosaics took place. From 1715–45 Leopoldo dal Pozzo carried out restoration work and added new mosaics. In 1881 a mosaic laboratory was set up for the restoration of the mosaics. Many of them were cleaned in the 1970s, when a remarkable survey of them was undertaken by Otto Demus. The Museo di San Marco has a small display illustrating mosaic technique and restoration.

Mosaics are composed of tesserae, individual cubes of coloured glass, stone, and enamel set in a plaster bed. The pictorial design was sketched onto the wall beforehand. Early mosaic technique had a limited range of colours, which encouraged a rather non-naturalistic style with attention focused on line and simplified colour definition. Blue was made by adding cobalt; green with copper oxide; and red with copper. Gold and silver were obtained by overlaying the tesserae with a thin layer of glazed metal. In more opulent mosaics, mother-of-pearl was also used, as well as white and grey marble. The tesserae were often set into the plaster at different depths and angles, in order to catch as much light as possible and create a brilliant, sparkling glow. When Tuscan painters were called in, they instead laid the tesserae as smoothly as possible and developed a range of colours that could produce delicate tonal gradations, so that mosaic decoration became, in essence, 'paintings in stone'.

Museo di San Marco: the loggia

From the loggia there is a spectacular view of the piazza, and you can also inspect the Gothic sculpture on the upper part of the façade. The central window is flanked by arches filled in the 17th century with mosaics (*Descent from the Cross, Descent into Hell,*

Resurrection and *Ascension*) designed by Maffeo da Verona. The façade is crowned by fine Gothic sculpture, begun in the early 15th century by the Dalle Masegne brothers and continued by Lombard and Tuscan artists (including Pietro di Niccolò Lamberti, who worked on the central arch, which has the gilded lion of St Mark and is crowned by a statue of the saint). Between the arches are figures of water-carriers by a Lombard master of the 15th century, and the two outer tabernacles contain the *Annunciatory Angel* and the *Virgin Annunciate*, attributed to Jacopo della Quercia. A few other sculptures in Venice, including one on a corner of the Doge's Palace, are sometimes attributed to this great Tuscan sculptor, but there is no work in the city documented by him and we do not even know if he ever came here.

The south-facing loggia overlooks the Piazzetta. Here, at the angle of the balcony (hidden behind the flagstaff), is a red porphyry head—an unexpected 'trophy' to find decorating a sacred place. For long thought to be a contemporary portrait of Justinian II (d. 711), it is now dated even earlier and taken to be a portrait of Justinian I (527–65), the last Roman emperor of the East. Like the Tetrarchs (*see p. 51*), it was probably carried back from Constantinople after the Fourth Crusade in 1204. It still retains an air of mystery and it is fascinating to be able to get face to face with this ancient work of art which portrays a man of great character. For centuries the Venetians knew it by the name of '*Carmagnola*', as they liked to identify it with an unfortunate sea captain called Francesco Bussone, who was thus nicknamed, and whose head had been exposed on the Pietra del Bando below for three days after he was unjustly condemned to death as a traitor in 1432.

THE CAMPANILE & LOGGETTA

Map p. 407, E2. Campanile normally open daily 9 or 9.30–dusk (4.45 in winter, 7 in spring, 9 in summer). The bell-chamber is reached by a lift from the Loggetta.
Over 98.5m high, the **Campanile** was first built in 888–912, and completed in 1156–73. It was later restored, the last time by Bartolomeo Bon the Younger in 1511–14. In 1609 Galileo demonstrated his latest invention, the telescope, to Doge Leonardo Donà, a friend and supporter, from the top of the tower, and even dedicated the instrument to the doge. Repeatedly struck by lightning, in 1793 the Campanile was fitted with a lightning conductor, one of the first in Europe. On 14th July 1902, it collapsed without warning causing little damage (except to the Loggetta) and no human casualties. From the proceeds of a worldwide subscription, an exact reproduction of the original was immediately begun, '*Dov' era e com' era*'—'where it was and as it was'—and opened on 25th April 1912, St Mark's feast day, 1,000 years after it was first completed. At its base instruments record the level of the tides in the lagoon.

The brick tower of the Campanile is surmounted by a bell-chamber with four-light windows of Istrian stone, and a square storey decorated with two winged lions and two figures of Venice beneath the symbol of Justice; the spire at the top is crowned by a golden Archangel Gabriel. Only one of the original five bells (the *marangona*) survived the collapse of the tower; the others were presented by Pius X. During the time of the

Republic the *marangona* rang to signify the start and end of the working day, the *nona* was tolled at noon, the *mezza terza* called the senators to the Doge's Palace, the *trottiera* signalled that the Great Council was in session, and the *maleficio* rang at the time of an execution.

From the top of the Campanile there is a magnificent view of Venice and the lagoon, and (on clear days) of the Euganean Hills and the Alps. Goethe climbed the Campanile on the evening of 30th September 1786 and beheld the sea for the first time.

At the base of the campanile is the **Loggetta**, in red Verona marble, Jacopo Sansovino's first work to be completed in Venice (1537–46), though when it was crushed by the fall of the Campanile in 1902, it had to be restored. It was originally a meeting-place of the *nobili*, or patricians, during sessions of the Great Council (*Maggior Consiglio*) in the Doge's Palace. After 1569, owing to its strategic position, a military guard was posted here when the Council was sitting. Its form is derived from the Roman triumphal arch and its sculptures celebrate the glory of the Republic. Three arches, flanked by twin columns, are surmounted by an ornate attic. White Carrara marble, Istrian stone, and a dark green marble have been used for the decorative details. Between the columns are niches with bronze statues of *Athena*, *Apollo*, *Mercury* and *Peace*, also the work of Jacopo Sansovino. The three reliefs in the attic show Venice (represented by the figure of *Justice*), Crete (represented by *Jupiter*) and Cyprus (represented by *Venus*). The two fine little bronze gates by Antonio Gai were added in 1734.

PIAZZA SAN MARCO

Piazza San Marco (*map p. 407, D2–E2*) is one of the most famous and beautiful squares in the world. Laid out around the two most important buildings in Venice, the Basilica of St Mark and the Doge's Palace, it had more or less reached its present vast dimensions by the 12th century, although it was partly redesigned in the 16th century, when it was enclosed on three sides by the porticoed façades of stately palaces, built as the residence of the Procurators of St Mark's, who looked after the basilica. The colonnades (hung with draped curtains on sunny days) open out towards the east end of the piazza and the fantastic façade of the basilica. On the left, the decorative clock-tower (Torre dell'Orologio) provides an entrance from the piazza to the Merceria, the main pedestrian thoroughfare of the city, which leads to the Rialto.

Called by the Venetians simply 'the Piazza', it is the only square in Venice to be so named, since all the others are termed *campi*. It retains the character Henry James gave it over a century ago: 'It is in the wide vestibule of the square that the polyglot pilgrims gather most densely: Piazza San Marco is the lobby of the opera in the intervals of the performance.' The two most famous cafés in the square are Florian and the Caffè Quadri, both with orchestra podiums, and concerts are provided for clients at the tables outside. The orchestral battles between the two were famous in their day.

The sale of grain to feed the famous pigeons of St Mark has been prohibited since 2008 since the birds cause great damage to Venice's buildings.

In front of the basilica are three tall flagstaffs which, during the great days of the

Venetian Republic, bore the red-and-gold standard with the winged lion of St Mark. Nowadays, on Sundays and holidays, the standard is still flown, but beside the Italian tricolour and the flag of the European Union (and there is a solemn little military ceremony at 9am and at sunset when they are hoisted and lowered). The elaborate bronze pedestals were added in 1505. The pavement of the piazza survives from 1722.

On days when there is an *acqua alta*, the Piazza is one of the first places to be flooded; the duck-boards used on these occasions are usually stacked in readiness (the water first reaches the atrium of the basilica). The problem of flooding in the piazza is known to have existed since at least the 13th century, and there has been a drainage system beneath the pavement for centuries, which helps in part to channel the water away.

PUBLIC CEREMONIES IN PIAZZA SAN MARCO

The Piazza provided a magnificent setting for the sumptuous public ceremonies held throughout Venice's history, the form of which often echoed Byzantine spectacles. These were staged to impress the inhabitants as well as foreign ambassadors and merchants from overseas, and splendid long processions lasting many hours would give a visual sense of the dignified order within the Venetian State. Processions took place on religious festivals (including the Feast of St Mark, Palm Sunday and Corpus Christi), as well as on important occasions such as the arrival of a foreign dignitary, and officials would include the Canons of St Mark's, the Doge, the Council of Ten, the Procurators, and representatives of the *scuole* and religious orders, and they would be accompanied by the musicians and choir of St Mark's. Gentile Bellini's celebrated painting of the *Procession of the Relic of the True Cross* (1496; in the Gallerie dell'Accademia) provides us with one of the most accurate representations of such a ceremony.

PROCURATIE VECCHIE

Along the entire north side of the Piazza run the stately arcades, with three open galleries, of the Procuratie Vecchie, reconstructed after a fire in 1512, probably to a design by the great Renaissance architect Mauro Codussi, who had died a few years earlier, having built numerous important churches and palaces in the city (*see p. 233*). Work was continued under the direction of Bartolomeo Bon and another local architect, Guglielmo dei Grigi, before Jacopo Sansovino added an upper storey, with a hundred arches, in 1532. The building served as the residence and offices of the Procurators of St Mark's who, after the doge, were considered the highest officials in the Republic and were in charge of the building and conservation of the basilica. Besides the doge, they were the only patrician officers of the Republic who were elected for life. By the 13th century they had taken on a role of fundamental importance not only as guardians of the basilica but also as administrators of the conspicuous sums of money given by noble families to St Mark's. Once occupied by the offices of an insurance company and by the magistrates, the building is now mostly empty.

Beneath the portico is the famous **Caffè Quadri**, which, together with the even more famous Florian opposite, is considered the most elegant café in Venice. It was opened in 1775 by Giorgio and Naxina Quadri, and is mentioned countless times in descriptions of the city. It gained a reputation as the 'Austrian café' during the time

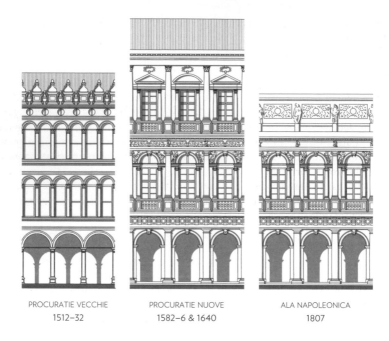

| PROCURATIE VECCHIE | PROCURATIE NUOVE | ALA NAPOLEONICA |
| 1512–32 | 1582–6 & 1640 | 1807 |

when Venice was under Austrian rule. Quadri has pretty Venetian-style decorations in its little rooms, and a tiny bar where you can stand at the counter with a drink. The restaurant, in two lovely rooms upstairs overlooking the Piazza, was opened in 1844 (*see p. 362*).

PROCURATIE NUOVE

The Procuratie Nuove, on the south side of the square, were planned by Jacopo Sansovino to continue the design of his Libreria, which faces the Doge's Palace. Up to the tenth arch from the left they are the work of Vincenzo Scamozzi (1582–6); they were completed by his more famous pupil Baldassare Longhena around 1640. Like the Procuratie Vecchie, they were also a (later) residence of the Procurators, but became a royal palace under Napoleon.

In the portico beneath is the renowned **Caffè Florian**, named after its first proprietor in 1720, Floriano Francesconi. It retains its comfortable old leather-seated benches and chairs around the columns and a charming old-fashioned interior with an intimate atmosphere, decorated in 1858 by the little-known artist Lodovico Cadorin. There is a little bar at the back where you can sit at the counter; light lunches and afternoon tea are also served. It has been famous for over a century as a place where all the illustrious visitors to the city come to enjoy the scene. Even if you don't intend to sit and take a coffee you are made to feel welcome, and can look at the book which tells its history on the stand at the entrance. Florian's was the meeting place of Italian patriots during Austrian rule; during the 1848 uprising in the Piazza the wounded were brought here. Balzac is said to have likened it to a stock exchange, a theatre foyer, a reading room, a club and a confessional.

ALA NAPOLEONICA

The west end of the piazza, between the two Procuratie, was once occupied by the small, centrally-planned church of San Gemignano, with a very fine Istrian stone façade by Jacopo Sansovino. Napoleon (who apparently remained unimpressed by Venice on his one visit in 1807, when he spent only slightly over a week here) had it pulled down in the same year to make space for a suite of grand reception rooms, including a ballroom, forming a wing of the royal palace in the Procuratie Nuove: it came to be known as the Ala Napoleonica. It is the best-known work of Giuseppe Soli, who, in the two lower floors, copied the style of the Procuratie Nuove, but appropriately added a row of Roman emperors, who look down from the top storey.

MUSEO CORRER

Map p. 407, D2 . Open 9–5 or 7. Entrance beneath the Ala Napoleonica. The ticket also includes entrance to the Museo Archeologico and the Libreria Marciana.

From the days of Napoleon the Procuratie Nuove were used as a royal palace by the French and Austrian courts during their occupation of Venice before Italian Unification in 1866. In 1920 they were presented to the city by the Savoy royal family. They are now occupied by the Museo Correr (which illustrates the history of Venice and has a picture gallery) and the Museo Archeologico, which has some masterpieces of Greek and Roman sculpture. These are adjoined by the Libreria Marciana, which preserves its 16th-century painted decorations and houses the city's precious collection of books.

The nucleus of the Correr collection was left to Venice by the wealthy citizen Teodoro Correr (1750–1830), who spent his life collecting works of art that illustrate Venetian history. It was first opened to the public in 1836 in Correr's house on the Grand Canal, but since 1923 it has been housed here. Some of the exhibition space was designed in 1952–60 by Carlo Scarpa. Apart from the historical collections and the picture gallery, you can also visit the ballroom and some of the other 19th-century rooms in the Ala Napoleonica, including a suite of royal apartments.

THE BALLROOM AND ROYAL APARTMENTS

The **Ballroom (2)** was designed by Lorenzo Santi in 1822, and here are displayed a winged Cupid and two-figure group of *Orpheus and Eurydice* by Antonio Canova, Italy's greatest Neoclassical sculptor. A door leads out of the far end into nine rooms of the **Royal Apartments**, occupied by the Austrian Habsburgs in the period leading up to Italian Unification. In particular they record the presence of Princess Elisabeth ('Sissi') of Bavaria, the young bride of Franz Joseph, who stayed here in 1856–7 and again in 1861–2. Some of the reception rooms retain their earlier Neoclassical decora-

THE HISTORICAL COLLECTIONS

tions by Giuseppe Borsato (1830s), designed in honour of Emperor Ferdinand I, as well as even earlier painted ceilings from Napoleon's day (1806–17), while Sissi's private apartments were decorated for her by Giovanni Rossi: the Boudoir, with her favourite flowers—cornflowers and lilies of the valley—is particularly charming with its gilded stuccoes. The rooms are beautifully furnished, and all the wall-hangings have been carefully remade by the famous Venetian fabric company Rubelli.

The last room, decorated by Borsato for Napoleon, linked the apartments to the **public rooms** overlooking the Piazza. The first of these (5) provides an appropriate setting for some more important works by Canova: exquisite small models for a funerary monument (never realised) for Francesco Pesaro, and that of Titian (adapted for use as the sculptor's own tomb in the Frari); a marble statue of *Daedalus and Icarus*; a painting of *Eros and Psyche*, and an unfinished portrait of a portly Venetian antiquarian called Amedeo Svajer, which recalls English paintings of the period. The contemporary furniture includes a French circular table with mythological scenes in Sèvres porcelain. To the left is the **Throne Room (4)**, where there are particularly lovely detached frescoes by Giovanni Carlo Bevilacqua and panels with mythological scenes and dancers, early works by the most famous Italian painter of this period, Francesco Hayez.

THE HISTORICAL COLLECTIONS

These rooms, all of them overlooking the Piazza, display paintings and objects illustrating the history of Venice with particular reference to the doge and officials of the Republic. Only a very few of the most significant pieces are mentioned below.

Room 6: Formal hats worn by the doges are displayed beside a portrait in profile of Doge Francesco Foscari, by the Venetian painter Lazzaro Bastiani, who worked with Gentile Bellini (and must have been influenced by Gentile's portrait of Doge Giovanni Mocenigo, exhibited in the Picture Gallery; *Room 36*). The doge is shown wearing his brocaded *cornu* hat, and his benign features belie an iron character which resulted in numerous military victories (with the help of famous *condottieri* such as Gattamelata and Colleoni) on the Italian mainland over the Visconti of Milan; victories which saw a spectacular expansion of the power of the Republic. This was painted around the time that the Council of Ten decided that Foscari, at the grand old age of 84, should abdicate (1457): as it turned out, an unnecessary step: he died just a week later.

Room 7: The wood engraving by Matteo Pagan of a procession in Piazza San Marco (1559) has been carefully studied by scholars and historians for its illustration of the hierarchy at the doge's court and for the costumes worn by the officials and onlookers. Ballot boxes and instruments used to count votes record the complicated procedures during the election of the doge. Examples of the *promissione ducale* (*see p. 94*) made by the doge as he took office are also exhibited.

Room 11: A complete collection of coins minted in Venice from the 9th century to the fall of the Republic (1797), and the huge standard flown by Doge Domenico Contarini from his galley when he defended Crete for the Republic in the 17th century. The painting of *St Justina with*

Venetian Officials, including treasurers, is a late work by Jacopo Tintoretto, with the help of his son Domenico.

Rooms 12–13: The maritime history of Venice, with models of galleys, navigational instruments, ships' lanterns, plans of the Arsenale, and a portrait painted in 1769 by Alessandro Longhi of a *Capitano da Mar*, the Captain General of the Venetian fleet.

Room 14: The inscribed edict warning against the misuse of the city's waterways is a reminder of the importance of the *Magistrato alle Acque*, which to this day takes care of Venice's public waters. Also here are two globes made in the late 17th century by the Venetian cartographer Vincenzo Coronelli.

Rooms 15–16: The armoury, with armour made in the 16th and 17th centuries and arms dating from the 14th–16th centuries.

Rooms 17–18: Two rooms devoted to Francesco Morosini who, as Captain General of the Venetian fleet, had many victories—most famously his conquest of the Peloponnese (although during the siege of Athens in 1687 he all but reduced the Parthenon to ruins). After such success he was unanimously elected doge in 1688. The finely carved triple lantern and the standard from his galley, Turkish banners and Persian shields he captured during his campaigns, his sword and prayer book (with a hidden dagger), and the *cornu* hat he wore as doge, are all preserved here.

Rooms 19–22: Small Renaissance bronzes from the late 15th–17th centuries by Paduan and Venetian sculptors, including Bartolomeo Bellano, Il Riccio, Jacopo Sansovino and Alessandro Vittoria. At the foot of the stairs is a quaint gilt-wood statue of a seated man in a top hat, a 19th-century copy of one venerated in a temple in Canton (and thought to be an effigy of Marco Polo).

From Room 18 or 19 there is access (with the same ticket) to the Museo Archeologico Nazionale and the Libreria Marciana. If you decide to visit them now, they are described on pp. 79–80; otherwise you can complete the visit to the Correr Museum, and then return to visit the others. The Correr itinerary takes you upstairs to the Picture Gallery at this point, returning to complete the historical collections afterwards.

THE PICTURE GALLERY

The Picture Gallery, or Quadreria, follows a strictly chronological arrangement and provides a good overview of art in Venice up to the late 15th century.

Rooms 25–26: Works by Paolo Veneziano, considered the founder of the Venetian school, and his successor as the leading artist of his day, Lorenzo Veneziano (no relation).

Room 27: Here are a few detached frescoes, interesting as rare examples of the Gothic period in Venice. There is also a charming little statue of Doge Antonio Venier, a portrait carried out during his dogeship in the 1380s or '90s by his contemporary Jacobello dalle Masegne, whom the doge had asked to work on the sculpture for the Basilica of St Mark (including the rood screen). The doge is shown kneeling, and he used to hold a standard—this was probably once part of a statuary group including the lion of St Mark, which may have decorated a lintel in the Doge's Palace.

Rooms 28–29: More Gothic works, with the International Gothic school represented with *Madonnas* by Michele Giambono and Jacobello del Fiore.

Rooms 30–31: Room 30 has an exquisite little *Pietà* by Cosmè Tura, who was the most important painter from Renaissance Ferrara. This is one of his masterpieces, showing not only his entirely original style, but also the influence of painters from Tuscany and northern Europe. The *Profile of a Man* exhibited beside it is also by a Ferrarese painter of the same period, and there are more works by painters from the same school in the next room (Room 31), including another charming portrait of a man in profile by Baldassare Estense, who was court painter in Ferrara. Also displayed here is a beautiful *Madonna and Child*, an early work (c. 1460) signed by the Venetian artist Bartolomeo Vivarini.

Room 32: This is one of the few rooms on this floor of the Procuratie Nuove to have survived from the late 16th century. The wonderful wood engraving of Venice in 1500 by Jacopo de' Barbari is displayed here: it is doubly precious since the six original wood blocks (made out of pear wood) have survived in excellent condition. De' Barbari invented the idea of the perspective view of a city, as seen from above: his work was to influence the long series of maps and views of cities which were produced right up until the 18th century. Very few representations of Venice had been made before this time, and this bird's-eye view, showing in detail how the city appeared in 1500, is of fundamental importance to historians of Venice. It was originally attributed to Dürer, but in the 19th century was recognised as the work of the otherwise little-known De' Barbari, who left Venice for the court of the Habsburg emperor Maximilian I. The engraving survives in three states and was first printed by a German merchant, Anton Kolb (the last time prints were made from these blocks was in the 19th century).

Rooms 33–35: A collection of works by Flemish and German painters, including religious scenes by Pieter Brueghel, Hugo van der Goes and Dieric Bouts. Displayed with them is Antoncllo da Messina's *Pietà*—a very ruined painting (*see below*).

A MASTERPIECE AT THE CORRER

Perhaps the most influential and important painting of the Correr collection is Antonello da Messina's *Pietà*. Antonello can be seen as the godfather of all subsequent Venetian painting. He came from Messina in Sicily: Giorgio Vasari says that he travelled to Flanders to study with Jan van Eyck. This is almost certainly not accurate, but what is true is that Antonello brilliantly absorbed and understood the technical revolution initiated by Flemish painting under the Van Eycks, and was profoundly influenced by its subtle delicacy. In 1474/5 he came to Venice. Though he stayed only a year, he produced a number of works that changed the course of painting in Venice forever, finally wrenching it out of its rich, but backward-looking, Gothic tradition. It was Antonello—either in person or by example—who taught Bellini and his contemporaries a new technique: no longer to paint in tempera (in other words with a fast-drying and opaque mixture of egg-yolk, water and pigment), but to experiment with the new Flemish technique of painting in thin, translucent veils of pigment in an oil and varnish mix. This allowed the bright white preparation of the panel to illuminate the colours from behind, giving an astonishing brilliance to both the strong and the delicate tints. Venetian painting was never to be the same again. And even though this *Pietà* has suffered terribly from overcleaning in past centuries, you can still unmistakably pick out the changing gradations of colour and the naturalism of the light.   N.McG.

Room 36: The *Transfiguration* is a remarkable early work by Giovanni Bellini, painted around 1460, which shows Christ between Moses and Elijah on Mount Tabor, with the apostles Peter, James and John below. The subject matter is particularly interesting as this is probably the first altarpiece of the Transfiguration to have been painted, as the religious festival celebrating the event was only introduced (by Pope Calixtus III) in 1457. The influence of Mantegna and Flemish painters such as Jan van Eyck can be seen here. The *Crucifixion* probably dates from about the same time (the landscape has remarkable depth). Other works by Bellini are a *Pietà* (the two angels as well as Christ

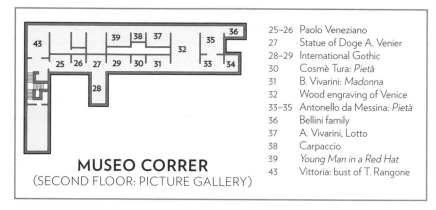

MUSEO CORRER
(SECOND FLOOR: PICTURE GALLERY)

have their mouths memorably open in horrified pain), the *Madonna Frizzoni*, damaged when it was transferred from panel to canvas, and a portrait of a young saint crowned with laurel leaves. The other *Crucifixion* is attributed by some scholars to Giovanni's father, Jacopo. The portrait of Doge Giovanni Mocenigo in profile is by Giovanni's brother Gentile: the doge appears as a homely old man, and he was in fact known for his gentle character. Gentile is thought to have left the portrait unfinished when he was called to Constantinople in 1479 to paint the Sultan's portrait (now in the National Gallery in London). He executed a number of other portraits of the rulers of his day, but is best remembered for his huge historical works for two of Venice's *scuole* (*see pp. 143 and 145*).

Room 37: Here, in its fine original frame, is displayed *St Anthony of Padua*, a delicately painted work showing the emaciated saint 'in the clouds', by Alvise Vivarini, member of the famous family of painters from Murano. Other painters from Venice and the Veneto represented here include Bartolomeo Montagna, whose *St Justina* shows the saint in the guise of a pretty Venetian girl, and Lorenzo Lotto, whose *Madonna*, crowned by two angels, includes a lovely landscape.

Room 38: Here is Vittore Carpaccio's famous painting of *Two Venetian Ladies*, probably painted around 1495 or later. For long thought to represent two courtesans, other critics, including Ruskin, thought it was simply the portrait of a mother and daughter with their pets. It is known to be the lower half of a painting; the other half, depicting hunting scenes in the lagoon, is now owned by the J. Paul Getty Museum in California. Some scholars think the panels decorated two doors of a cupboard. The two patrician ladies, dressed in high fashion, with the bleached blonde hair that was all the rage in their day, are shown deep in contemplation, seated on a roof terrace, a feature of many contemporary Venetian houses. Various symbols may represent allegories of Love (the dove and the orange) and Maternity (the lily and myrtle plants). Carpaccio was one of Venice's greatest painters (*see p. 262*), and another painting by him (*St Peter Martyr*) is also displayed here.

Room 39: The delightful portrait of a *Young Man in a Red Hat*, formerly attributed to Carpaccio, is now thought to be by an unknown Ferrarese artist and dated c. 1490. However, the *Madonna and Child and Young St John*, dating c. 1495, has been attributed to Carpaccio since its restoration in 2001.

Room 43: Bust of Tommaso Rangone, a rich and learned physician, one of several portraits of him in Venice by Alessandro Vittoria.

The Picture Gallery ends here, and stairs lead down to the continuation of the historical collections (see plan on p. 74).

Room 45: The *Bucintoro* (*Bucentaur*) was the gala ship used to transport the doge from his palace to the entrance to the lagoon near San Nicolò al Lido for the ceremonial marriage of Venice with the sea on the *Festa della Sensa* (Ascension Day; *see p. 333*). The lanterns and gilded wood fragments which decorated the last ship were carved in 1729 by the successful Rococo sculptor Antonio Corradini.

Rooms 46–53: Paintings and objects illustrating daily life in Venice during the time of the Republic.

MUSEO ARCHEOLOGICO NAZIONALE

Map p. 407, E2. Entrance from Room 18 or 19 of the Museo Correr (and with the same ticket).

The museum was founded in 1523 from a bequest of Greek and Roman sculptures made to the Republic by Cardinal Domenico Grimani; in 1593 his grandson Giovanni Grimani, Patriarch of Aquileia, donated more of his collection from Palazzo Grimani (*see p. 272*). The collection includes three Gallic warriors found on Grimani property in Rome near the Quirinal Hill, copies of a group presented by Attalus of Pergamon to Athens; the precious Grimani Altar with Bacchic scenes (1st century BC); Roman copies of Greek works including the *kore* known as the *Abbondanza Grimani*, an Attic original of c. 420 BC; and a fine series of female statues of 5th and 4th centuries BC, including *Hera* and *Athena*. Roman busts include a famous bust in bronze thought to be of the emperor Vitellius, a particularly fine Roman portrait of the early 2nd century AD. Two Roman bronze statuettes dating from the 1st–3rd centuries AD were found in the 20th century in the lagoon near Malamocco.

The so-called *Zulian Cameo* of Jupiter, from Ephesus, is variously dated to two centuries before Christ or two centuries after. There is a head of a Hellenistic princess in rock crystal; and two heads of Jupiter, one of them the *Chalcedon Cameo* (Pergamene art, 3rd century BC).

Early Christian pieces include a 5th-century Byzantine reliquary casket in ivory found near Pula, Istria and an 11th-century Byzantine ivory plaque of Sts John the Evangelist and Paul.

Among the earliest works are some bronzes from 1700 BC and pre-Roman material, including Villanovan and Corinthian vases. The Correr Collection includes Greek and

Roman heads and torsos; a black Romano-Egyptian head; and a small Roman mosaic of a harbour scene (4th century AD).

LIBRERIA MARCIANA

Entered from the Museo Correr and the Museo Archeologico, with the same ticket. Shown on the plan on p. 74.

The famous Library of St Mark is also known as the Libreria Sansoviniana, after Jacopo Sansovino, who designed it in 1537 and provided it with a splendid façade on the Piazzetta (*described on p. 82*). The magnificent Great Hall and Vestibule are open to the public. Today the library contains about one million volumes and 13,500 manuscripts (many of them Greek), and is also housed in the adjoining building of the Zecca, again designed by Sansovino.

GREAT HALL

The walls and ceiling of the Great Hall (the reading room) are magnificently decorated. The 21 ceiling medallions with allegorical paintings (completed in 1557) are the work of seven Venetian Mannerist artists, who each painted three tondi (*a handlist is lent to visitors*). Both Sansovino and Titian advised the procurators on the choice of artists, but Paolo Veronese is today by far the most famous of the group (his works are those in the second row from the window end).

In 1562–72 the same artists then went on to decorate the walls with paintings of philosophers: on the end wall by the desk are two by Jacopo Tintoretto; on the right wall are four more by Tintoretto and two by Lo Schiavone; on the far wall, on either side of the door into the vestibule, are two by Paolo Veronese. The floor was moved here from the Scuola Grande della Misericordia in 1815. The cases usually display photocopies of some of the library's holdings.

VESTIBULE

The Vestibule or Anteroom, connected to the Great Hall by a monumental doorway, has a ceiling decorated in the 16th century with remarkable *quadratura* by the little-known Cristoforo Rosa, who had also been commissioned to paint the central panel of the *Allegory of Wisdom*; in the end this was executed by Titian himself, and although one of his least known works, it is painted with a delightful freshness of touch. In 1587 Cardinal Domenico Grimani arranged a public gallery of some 200 pieces of statuary on the walls of this room, and this has been partially reconstructed, also with the use of casts. It is a fascinating illustration of how great archaeological collections used to be displayed. The monumental staircase (which leads down to the original entrance on the Piazzetta) has a splendid stuccoed vault by Alessandro Vittoria.

Displayed here since its recent restoration is a celebrated world map dating from around 1450, over 40 years before the discovery of America, drawn by Fra' Mauro, a monk in the monastery on the island of San Michele. It is annotated with some 3,000 inscriptions which illustrate the geographical knowledge of the period, as well as Classical references and descriptions by travellers including Marco Polo. It is one of the library's most precious possessions.

BOOKS IN VENICE

Petrarch gave his books to Venice in 1362, but it was not until Cardinal Bessarion presented his extremely important collection of Greek and Latin manuscripts in 1468 that the library was formally founded. Bessarion (1389–1472), an Armenian born in Trebizond (in modern Turkey), accompanied Emperor John VII Palaeologus to the Council of Florence in 1439 as the Orthodox Archbishop of Nicaea. The council failed to unite the churches of East and West, but Bessarion remained in Italy and made his mark both as a Humanist scholar and a churchman (his fame was such that he was even considered seriously as a candidate to succeed Nicholas V as pope in 1455).

Pietro Bembo (famous as one of the speakers in Castiglione's *Courtier*) was librarian here and became the official historian of the Venetian Republic in 1530. An erudite Venetian humanist, Bembo had collaborated closely with the celebrated printer Aldus Manutius, who opened the Aldine Press in Venice in 1494. The press became famous for its publication of the Greek classics as well as works by Petrarch and Dante. It has been estimated that about a quarter of the 1,821 books published in Europe between 1495 and 1497 issued from Venetian presses. Bembo, who used both Latin and Italian in his writings and was a great scholar of Greek philosophy, acted as secretary to Leo X and was then created a cardinal in 1539 by Paul III, and it was he who was instrumental in finally persuading the doge to commission a fitting building for the Bessarion collection from his friend Sansovino.

The most precious works which today belong to the library include a late 14th-century *Divina Commedia* with illuminations; evangelistaries dating back to the 9th century; a Byzantine book cover with *Christ Pantocrator* and the *Virgin Orans,* dating from the late 10th or early 11th century and decorated with silver-gilt, gold cloisonné enamel, gems and pearls; the exquisite *Grimani Breviary*, illuminated by Flemish artists of c. 1500; a map of Tunis by Hadji Mehemed (c. 1560); Marco Polo's will; navigational charts; and a manuscript in Petrarch's hand.

PIAZZETTA DI SAN MARCO

The Piazzetta (*map p. 407, E2*), with the Doge's Palace on the left and the Libreria Marciana on the right as you face the water, is an extension of Piazza San Marco from St Mark's to the waterfront: this was the entrance to the city in the days of the Republic, when the ships carrying ambassadors and foreign dignitaries would dock here and the visitor would at once be confronted with Venice's most magnificent buildings.

Near the water's edge are two huge monolithic granite columns brought back to Venice from the ill-fated expedition to Constantinople by Doge Vitale Michiel II (*see p. 254*) and erected here at the end of the 12th century. One bears a winged lion, adapted as the symbol of St Mark. It is thought to be a Hellenistic work (4th–3rd century BC) and may have come from a tomb in Cilicia or Tarsus. The other column is crowned with a copy of a statue of the first patron saint of Venice, the Greek soldier St Theodore, and his dragon (the original is now in the courtyard of the Doge's Palace).

A scaffold used to be set up between the columns for executions; and as paintings by Canaletto and others show, there used to be numerous market stalls and booths here until they were ordered to be removed by Jacopo Sansovino when, as a procurator of St Mark's, he was in charge of the Piazza.

FAÇADE OF THE LIBRERIA MARCIANA

NB: The Great Hall and Vestibule can be visited from Museo Correr; see p. 80.
The façade of the Libreria Marciana, opposite the Doge's Palace, is the masterpiece of Jacopo Sansovino, hence the library's other name, Libreria Sansoviniana.

JACOPO SANSOVINO

The Tuscan architect and sculptor Jacopo Sansovino (1486–1570) left Rome for Venice in 1527 at the age of 41. Rome had just suffered its infamous sack by the troops of the Holy Roman Emperor Charles V; Sansovino's invitation came from Doge Andrea Gritti, who later became a close friend. In the 1530s he was appointed *proto*, or chief architect in charge of the fabric of St Mark's and the Piazza, and redesigned the Piazzetta, isolating the Campanile (and designing the Loggetta at its foot) and building the library. He helped to introduce a new Classical style of architecture into the city, based on his knowledge of Roman buildings; his library was considered by Palladio to be the most beautiful building since the days of Antiquity.

By the time of Sansovino's death at the age of 84 he had built the Zecca (Mint), the Fabbriche Nuove at the Rialto on the Grand Canal, the churches of San Francesco della Vigna, San Martino and San Giuliano, and Palazzo Dolfin and Palazzo Corner, both on the Grand Canal. His son Francesco wrote a remarkable guide to the city in 1581 called *Venetia città nobilissima et singolare*.

Begun in 1537, the library is built of Istrian stone, its ornate grand design derived from Classical Roman architecture, with a Doric ground floor, and an Ionic *piano nobile* with an elaborate frieze beneath a balustrade crowned by obelisks and statues of gods and heroes, executed by Sansovino's collaborators including Alessandro Vittoria, Tiziano Minio, Tommaso Lombardo and Danese Cattaneo, as well as the Florentine Bartolomeo Ammannati, who came to Venice to work with Sansovino early in his career, before he became famous as an architect and sculptor in his native city. After Sansovino's death in 1570 it fell to Vincenzo Scamozzi to finish the building (between 1588 and 1591), having already successfully completed the Procuratie Nuove to Sansovino's design. A versatile architect, born in Vicenza, Scamozzi is known for his numerous fine buildings in the Veneto. He also collaborated with Palladio, wrote a treatise on architecture, and even planned the cathedral of Salzburg. In the first years of the 17th century he was still at work in Venice, at the churches of San Lazzaro dei Mendicanti, San Salvatore and the Tolentini, and he built Palazzo Contarini degli Scrigni on the Grand Canal. He is also remembered as the master of the most famous Venetian architect of the 17th century, Baldassare Longhena.

THE WATERFRONT

The quay on the busy waterfront is called the **Molo**. Until 1846, when the railway line connected the mainland to Venice, this would have been a visitor's first view of the city—and it must have created an amazing impression indeed. Opposite it stands the island of San Giorgio Maggiore with its fine Palladian church. On the neighbouring Giudecca, two other Palladian façades can be seen, of the Zitelle and Redentore churches. Nearer at hand is the promontory known as the Punta della Dogana with the Pinault Foundation and the church of the Salute.

The severe, rusticated Doric **Zecca** or Mint (now part of the Libreria Marciana) was Jacopo Sansovino's first commission in Venice, begun in 1536. On the site of the 13th-century mint, he provided large windows on the *piano nobile* for the furnaces and arches on the ground floor for shops (the top floor was not part of his original design). The first golden ducat was issued in 1284, and at the height of the Republic the Venetian *zecchini* were used as currency throughout the world.

The public gardens known as the **Giardini Reali** take their name from the former Palazzo Reale in the Procuratie Nuove which backs onto them. They were laid out c. 1814 after the demolition of a splendid huge Gothic building which contained the Republican granaries (but which blocked the royal family's view of the basin of San Marco). They are decorated with two small Neoclassical buildings designed by Lorenzo Santi, one of which, formerly a coffee-house, is now used as a tourist information office. Across the bridge is the building which was once the seat of the Magistrato della Farina, the magistrates in charge of the distribution of bread and flour to the citizens of the Republic from the granaries (it is now the Port Authority office). By the San Marco landing-stage is **Harry's Bar**, which, since it was opened in the 1920s by Giuseppe Cipriani, has been famous for its international clientèle. All the notable, wealthy visitors to Venice in the 20th century came here to be seen and talked about—and it is perhaps particularly associated with the flamboyant figures of Ernest Hemingway, Orson Welles and Truman Capote. Inside, the bar was intentionally placed right at the entrance so that more timid clients could immediately find a place to 'lean on'. It continues to flourish, under the direction of Giuseppe's son Arrigo, as the city's most celebrated restaurant and cocktail bar. It has an inconspicuous entrance on Calle Vallaresso, and it is a 'national monument', meaning that its original furnishings will be preserved intact.

THE DOGE'S PALACE

This magnificent palace, built for the doges, is one of Venice's most famous buildings, with a remarkable Gothic exterior. Formerly the official residence of the doges and the chief magistrates, it was founded on this site in the 9th century, when they moved from Malamocco. The present building dates from the 14th century, and the two façades overlooking the Bacino di San Marco and the Piazzetta are wonderful examples of florid Gothic architecture. In the vast interior, the decoration of the numerous rooms used by the governing bodies of the Republic, by Venetian painters of the 16th–17th centuries (after fires in 1574 and 1577), survives intact. To study with care the pictorial and historical significance of these paintings, which cover both the walls and ceilings, requires several hours, but they give a vivid idea of the glory of Venice at the height of her power.

Opening times and tips for visiting

Map p. 407, E2. Open 1 April–31 Oct 9–6 (closes at 7); 1 Nov–31 March 9–5 (closes at 6). The building can be extremely cold in winter. Although very well kept, it is often crowded with tour groups (except for the Museo dell'Opera on the ground floor). The fascinating 'Itinerari Segreti', tours of the 'secret' rooms used by the administrators of the Republic, take place daily in English at 9.45, 10.45, and 11.35, by appointment at the ticket office; you can also book in advance. Only 25 people are allowed on each tour. For information and booking, T: 041 4273089 or www.visitmuve.com.

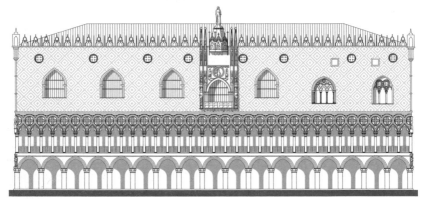

DOGE'S PALACE: WATERFRONT FAÇADE

HISTORY OF THE BUILDING

The palace was begun in the 9th century and was rebuilt in the 12th under Doge Sebastiano Ziani, but was then almost totally destroyed by fire. In 1340 a large sum of money was voted by the Great Council to build a room big enough to contain its 1,212 members. Inaugurated in 1419, it had windows on the Bacino di San Marco and extended as far as the seventh column of the portico on the Piazzetta. Shortly afterwards, in 1422, with the financial aid of Doge Tommaso Mocenigo, the Great Council decided to demolish part of the 12th-century law courts on this site in order to extend the façade towards the Basilica of St Mark in exactly the same style and using the same building materials. It is thought that the building was constructed under the direction of officials of the Republic by a group of master masons, including Filippo Calendario, but the exact role of this obscure figure (whose name is not connected with certainty to any other building work) is still not clear. All that is known is that he was beheaded in 1355, together with Doge Marin Falier, because he had supported the Doge in his conspiracy against the State, but sources as early as the 15th century connect his name to the Doge's Palace.

DOGE'S PALACE: WATERFRONT FAÇADE
Detail from the column capital showing the Deadly Sins and
the personification of Vanity.

After another conflagration in 1483, Antonio Rizzo began the main interior façade and the Scala dei Giganti, and the work was continued by Pietro Lombardo, Giorgio Spavento and Scarpagnino. Although it was again twice damaged by fire in the 1570s, it was decided to restore rather than rebuild it, under the direction of Antonio da Ponte. Paintings glorifying Venetian history were commissioned for the ceilings and walls of the main rooms. The courtyard and façade overlooking the Rio di Palazzo were completed in the 17th century (following Rizzo's original design) by Bartolomeo Monopola.

THE WATERFRONT FAÇADE

The main façade is a superb Gothic work begun around 1340. Each arcade of the portico supports two arches of the upper loggia, decorated with quatrefoil roundels. This in turn is surmounted by a massive wall 12.5m high with a delicate lozenge pattern in white Istrian stone and pink Verona marble. Marble ornamental crenellations crown the façade. The windows belong to the immense Sala del Maggior Consiglio, the hall of the Great Council. In the centre is a balconied window built in 1404 by Pier Paolo di Jacopo dalle Masegne and crowned by a statue of Venice as *Justice* by Alessandro Vittoria. The other statues which decorated the window were removed and restored in 2006 and are now displayed inside the palace (Room 32).

High reliefs inspired by Old Testament subjects adorn the three external corners of the building. They would have been seen by the Venetians as statements of the importance of the Christian faith. On the corner nearest to Rio di Palazzo, the relief depicts the ***Drunkenness of Noah* (A)** and, in the loggia above, the Archangel Raphael. On the corner nearest the Piazzetta are ***Adam and Eve* (B)** plucking figs from a tree which sprouts leaves to cover their nakedness, with the Archangel Michael above. The level of today's pavement is higher than the original, so that the bases of the portico columns

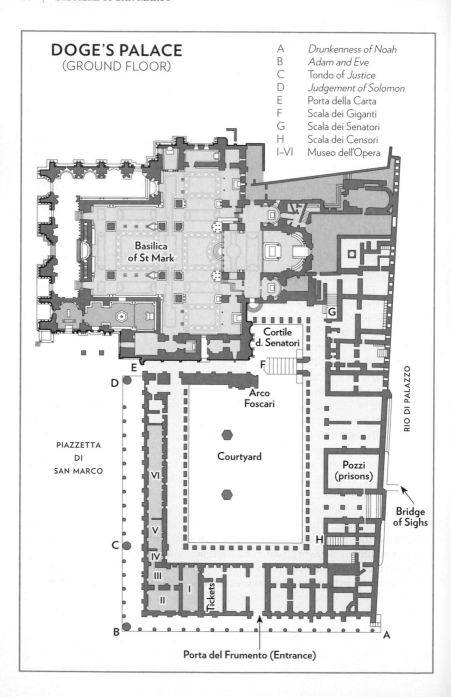

DOGE'S PALACE
(GROUND FLOOR)

A   *Drunkenness of Noah*
B   *Adam and Eve*
C   Tondo of *Justice*
D   *Judgement of Solomon*
E   Porta della Carta
F   Scala dei Giganti
G   Scala dei Senatori
H   Scala dei Censori
I–VI   Museo dell'Opera

Basilica
of St Mark

Cortile
d. Senatori

Arco
Foscari

PIAZZETTA
DI
SAN MARCO

Courtyard

Pozzi
(prisons)

RIO DI PALAZZO

Bridge
of Sighs

Tickets

Porta del Frumento (Entrance)

are now covered, altering the proportion of the lower façade (the columns seem somewhat stumpy).

The beautiful column capitals are superb examples of medieval carving dating from 1340–55. It is well worth taking time to study them on the comfortable benches beneath the porticoes. In a complicated series of allegories, they represent the virtues of wise government and the importance of justice. The exceptionally fine capital on the corner nearest to the Piazzetta, together with seven others from this side of the building, are good copies of 1884–7. The originals are in the Museo dell'Opera (*see p. 88*).

THE PIAZZETTA FAÇADE

The original 14th-century building reached as far as the seventh column of the portico, above which is a tondo showing the crowned figure of *Justice* **(C)**, the personification of Venice, sitting on a throne guarded by two lions with two Vices trampled underfoot and the sea full of fish below. The first six capitals of the ground-level portico were carved at the same time as those facing the water, in 1340–55 (three of them were replaced by copies in 1876–84). They represent sculptors, animals with their prey, craftsmen, astrology and foreign nations. The seventh one beneath the tondo of *Justice*, which is slightly bigger than the others, has scenes of death and courtly love. The last twelve capitals (two replaced in the 19th century) were carved when the palace was enlarged in 1424 and are mostly copies of the earlier ones on the main façade. The most interesting is the last one, nearest the basilica, showing Justice surrounded by famous legislators and wise men. This bears the signature of two Florentine sculptors, Pietro di Niccolò Lamberti and Giovanni di Martino da Fiesole, who also worked together on the tomb of Doge Tommaso Mocenigo in Santi Giovanni e Paolo (and Lamberti had worked with his father Niccolò on the sculpture on the façade of the Basilica of St Mark). On the corner above is a high relief illustrating the *Judgement of Solomon* **(D)**, with the Archangel Gabriel in the loggia above, beautiful works attributed by some scholars to the famous Tuscan sculptor Jacopo della Quercia (c. 1410; *but see p. 69*).

Following the extension of the palace as far as the basilica, the **Porta della Carta (E)** was added, in 1438–43. In the centre is a balconied window (1538) similar to that on the front of the building. The Porta della Carta, thought to owe its name to the state archives or *cartae* (papers) which used to be kept near here, is an extremely graceful gateway in the florid Gothic style, one of the most important works by Bartolomeo Bon and his family workshop, which was extremely active in Venice in the mid-15th century. Bartolomeo was born in Venice and in his architecture and sculpture successfully combines elements from northern sculptors with the influence of the more classical Tuscan Renaissance. He worked on the Ca d'Oro (and carved the magnificent well-head there) and produced sculptures for the exteriors and portals of a number of churches in the city (including Santi Giovanni e Paolo and the Frari). The Porta della Carta bears his signature on the architrave (original now in the Museo dell'Opera), and the crowning figure of *Venice*, symbolised by Justice, is attributed to his hand. He also probably carved the original statues of Doge Francesco Foscari kneeling before the lion of St Mark, which were destroyed by Napoleon's troops in 1797 but were replaced here with excellent reproductions in 1885 (the head of the doge survived French mutilation and can be seen in the Museo dell'Opera). The name of the sculptor who carved the very fine statues of *Temperance, Fortitude, Prudence* and *Charity* is unknown.

THE RIO FAÇADE AND BRIDGE OF SIGHS

The fine Renaissance **east façade** on Rio di Palazzo, built of Istrian stone, can be admired from Ponte della Paglia or Ponte della Canonica, which cross Rio di Palazzo. Begun by Antonio Rizzo (*see p. 90*), it was continued by the Lombardo family, by Scarpagnino, and finally completed in the 17th century by Bartolomeo Monopola.

The Ponte della Paglia, a bridge of Istrian stone, was first constructed in 1360. It was widened in 1844 when the pretty balustrade of little columns with sculpted pine cones was added. Low down on the arch (only visible from the waterfront) is a tabernacle with a relief of the Madonna and two gondolas, dating from 1583. Here can be seen the famous **Bridge of Sighs** (*Ponte dei Sospiri*), an elegant little flying bridge in Istrian stone, one of very few works by Antonio Contino (1600). It was constructed for the passage of the Inquisitors of State between the prisons and the law courts, and only received its popular name in the 19th century when the idea of the 'sighing' prisoners on their way to trial fired the imagination of the Romantics.

INTERIOR OF THE DOGE'S PALACE: MUSEO DELL'OPERA

The entrance to the palace is through the Porta del Frumento at the centre of the main façade. The door gets its name, *frumento* (wheat), from the offices here which used to be occupied by the government officials responsible for the distribution of grain.

On the ground floor, in rooms which were once used as prisons, the Museo dell'Opera displays the original capitals and columns from the exterior portico (mostly dating from 1340–55; restored). These six rooms are hardly ever visited by groups, so they are one of the most peaceful areas of the palace. Diagrams show where each capital was on the façade.

Room I: Six 14th-century capitals from the waterfront façade. They show Solomon and wise men (personifying the Liberal Arts); birds with their prey; heads of men from different latitudes (each is shown with markedly different features and hats, but since the capital is without inscriptions it is difficult to identify them: one apparently represents a Tartar and another, with a turban, a Moor); kings of the ancient world and Roman emperors: Titus, Trajan, King Priam of Troy, Nebuchadnezzar, Alexander the Great, King Darius of the Persians, Julius Caesar and Augustus (holding a globe with the inscription *Mondo di pace*); heads of women of various ages in different costumes and head-dresses; and other heads including a soldier in armour decorated with two Crosses, and so usually identified as a crusader, and another capital showing children (sometimes thought to represent a crusader's family).

Room II: Four 14th-century capitals from the Piazzetta façade. One of them illustrates the months: March is represented by a figure playing a musical instrument; June is shown with cherries; September by a young man crushing grapes; December by the butchering of a pig. The other months are shown in pairs. Another capital has the heads of animals with their prey. The third shows sculptors carving blocks of stone or sculpting figures, including the four patron saints (identified by their haloes and crowns) of the Scuola dei Tagliapietra, stonemasons, and their four disciples. The fourth capital shows craftsmen at work (a stonemason, a blacksmith, a notary, a peasant, a surveyor, a carpenter, a cobbler and a goldsmith).

Room III: The magnificent capital from the Piazzzetta/waterfront corner of the palace, which depicts the *Creation of Adam* with the planets and signs of the zodiac, is displayed here. It was greatly admired by Ruskin. Larger than the other capitals, it represents the focal point of the carefully worked-out narrative scheme which told the history of the universe and the history of man. The *Creation of Adam* shows God the Father seated on a throne and Adam as a boy. Saturn, depicted as an old man with a beard, is shown sitting on Capricorn (a goat) holding Aquarius (a jug). Jupiter, wearing a doctorial head-dress, is seated on Sagittarius (a centaur with a bow and arrow) and he indicates the sign of Pisces. Mars, a warrior in armour, is seated on Aries with Scorpio on his left. The Sun, personified by a young boy with rays around his head, is seated on Leo and he holds a disc carved with a face. Venus, holding a mirror, is seated on Taurus and holds the sign of Libra (the scales). Mercury, in a toga holding an open book, is shown between Virgo and Gemini (the twins). On the last side, the Moon, represented by a girl in a boat holding a crescent moon, is shown with Cancer. The movement in the sea and the girl's clothes symbolise the moon's influence on tides and winds.

Also here are two 14th-century capitals, one decorated with baskets of fruit and the other with allegories of the Seven Deadly Sins and Vanity (the deadly sins—Lust, Greed, Pride, Anger, Avarice, Envy, and Sloth—are all represented by female figures except for Pride).

Rooms IV–V: The massive wall of the old palace can be seen in Room IV, and in Room V, stonework from the tracery on the upper loggia.

Room VI: Splendid 14th–15th-century capitals from the upper portico, some with traces of gilding and paint. They are decorated with a great variety of motifs including foliage, flowers, shells, musicians, nuns, female heads, the lion of St Mark, animals, children, griffins, eagles and warriors. The marble head of Doge Francesco Foscari is the only part of the original relief of the doge kneeling before the lion of St Mark on the Porta della Carta to have survived destruction in 1797. It is attributed to Antonio Bregno or Bartolomeo Bon; the original architrave of the Porta della Carta, with Bartolomeo Bon's signature, is also here. The bust of Doge Cristoforo Moro used to be part of a group in the courtyard, also destroyed in 1797.

COURTYARD AND SCALA DEI GIGANTI

Three sides of the courtyard belong to the Doge's Palace, while the flank of St Mark's (the Chapel of the Doge) rises above the fourth. After the fire in 1483, it was Antonio Rizzo who designed the magnificent east façade, which has four storeys with a double

row of porticoes and numerous windows. The carved decoration is extremely beautiful and is partly the work of the Lombardo family (*see p. 280*). At this time Doge Marco
Barbarigo also commissioned Rizzo to design the ceremonial **Scala dei Giganti (F)**,
as a setting for the doge's coronation ceremony (which up to then had not been held in
public). Built of Istrian limestone, it is famous for its exquisitely-carved reliefs. On the
wide landing at the top, the doge was crowned (over a white skull cap) with the jew-
elled and peaked *cornu*, modelled on a Byzantine head-dress and always an important
symbol of his position (an example can be seen in the Museo Correr). The giant statues
of Neptune and Mars (the *giganti* of the stairway's name) symbolise the maritime and
terrestrial might of the Republic. They are late works (c. 1554) by Jacopo Sansovino,
added in order to diminish the figure of the doge during his coronation.

ANTONIO RIZZO

Not much is known about Rizzo's early life, although his presence is documented in
Venice from 1457. His first works include the sculpted altars of St James and St Paul
in St Mark's. From 1483 he was appointed chief architect of the Doge's Palace and it
is in the courtyard that we see his extraordinary skills both as architect and sculptor:
he designed the two façades of its eastern wing and the Scala dei Giganti, and worked
on the Arco Foscari, carving for it marble statues of *Adam* and *Eve* (replaced by
copies; the originals are in the palace; *Room 24*), which are his most beautiful works.
His contribution to the diffusion of the classical Renaissance style in Venice was
fundamental, and in these two figures we also see the influence of northern European
art, in particular (in the figure of Eve) of Dürer, who was in Venice at that time. The
classical figure of Adam is one of the most remarkable nude figures produced in
Renaissance Venice. Rizzo also designed and carved the tomb of Doge Niccolò Tron
in the Frari, one of the very best Renaissance tombs in the city. There are others
sculptures attributed to him on the exterior or inside Venetian churches (the Madonna
dell'Orto, Sant'Elena, the Salute), but these are undocumented works, and some
scholars believe them to be by his more famous contemporary Pietro Lombardo. Rizzo
remains a somewhat shadowy figure, perhaps less famous than he deserves to be.

The right-hand end of the façade was finished by Scarpagnino in the 16th century, when
the two **well-heads** were made by Nicolò de' Conti and Alfonso Alberghetti, both gun-
smiths. They are superb Mannerist works, possibly designed by Sansovino, and the only
bronze well-heads in Venice. The lower storeys of the south and west sides were completed in Rizzo's style by Bartolomeo Monopola in the 17th century. Monopola also built
the Baroque façade on the side nearest the basilica, incorporating a clock and the side of
the **Arco Foscari**, a triumphal arch facing the Scala dei Giganti. It was begun in the 15th
century by the Bon family and completed by Antonio Bregno and Antonio Rizzo. On
the side facing the main courtyard is a statue of the *condottiere* Francesco Maria I della
Rovere, Duke of Urbino, the only work in Venice by the Florentine sculptor Giovanni
Bandini (1587), and (right) a page-boy attributed to Antonio Rizzo (both are copies;
originals inside the palace; *Room 24*). The main front of the arch bears mid-15th century
statues and bronze copies of two fine marble statues of *Adam* and *Eve* by Rizzo.

THE DOGE'S APARTMENTS (Primo Piano Nobile; *plan below*)
From the courtyard, the Scala dei Censori leads up to the inner loggia. From here the
Scala d'Oro (1), built in 1558–9 to Sansovino's design and decorated with gilded stuc-
coes (using 24-carat gold) by Alessandro Vittoria, continues up to the first floor (Primo
Piano Nobile) and the Doge's Apartments, reconstructed after a fire in 1483.

Room 5 (Sala degli Scarlatti): This
first room was the Robing Room (it takes
its name from the scarlet robes worn by
the ducal counsellors). It was decorated
in the first years of the 16th century with
a beautiful gilded ceiling, and boasts a
fine chimneypiece by Tullio and Antonio
Lombardo. Over the door is an interesting bas-relief by their father, Pietro, of

*Doge Leonardo Loredan at the Feet of the
Virgin.* Many scholars consider this one
of Pietro's very best reliefs. Opposite is a
Madonna in coloured stucco (attributed
to Antonio Rizzo).

Room 6 (Sala dello Scudo): This was
where the doge's guards were stationed,
and it is named from the shield which

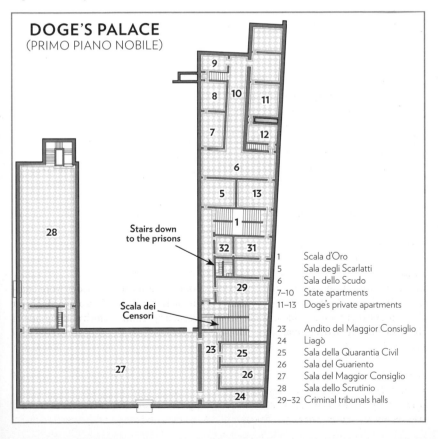

DOGE'S PALACE
(PRIMO PIANO NOBILE)

Stairs down
to the prisons

Scala dei
Censori

1	Scala d'Oro
5	Sala degli Scarlatti
6	Sala dello Scudo
7–10	State apartments
11–13	Doge's private apartments
23	Andito del Maggior Consiglio
24	Liagò
25	Sala della Quarantia Civil
26	Sala del Guariento
27	Sala del Maggior Consiglio
28	Sala dello Scrutinio
29–32	Criminal tribunals halls

was displayed here showing the arms of the doge who was in office. The walls are covered with maps and charts (16th century, but repainted in 1762), and two globes are kept here.

Room 7 (Sala Grimani): This has another chimneypiece by Tullio and Antonio Lombardo. The ceiling (which bears the arms of Marino Grimani, doge from 1595–1605) is decorated with rosettes, above a frieze by Andrea Vicentino. Four charming paintings of the winged lion of St Mark, the famous symbol of Venice, are displayed here. The two opposite the fireplace are by Donato Veneziano (with two saints and a view of Venice). Vittore Carpaccio's painting of 1516 shows the lion between the sea and the *terraferma*, and has a very accurate view of the Doge's Palace and the Campanile and the domes of St Mark's in the background, as well as a group of galleons setting sail from the Arsenale.

Room 8 (Sala Erizzo): The room has a good ceiling and a fine chimneypiece (with the arms of Doge Francesco Erizzo, 1631–46). Three paintings attributed to Girolamo Bassano (son of the more famous painter Jacopo) are hung here.

Room 9 (Sala degli Stucchi): Named after the stuccoes carried out in the late 16th and early 17th centuries. The apse of St Mark's can be seen from here.

Room 10 (Sala dei Filosofi): So called since for a time it housed the paintings of philosophers by Tintoretto and Veronese now in the Libreria Marciana (*see p. 80*). A doorway leads to the staircase used by the doge to reach the state council rooms directly from his living quarters. Above the door on the inside is a fresco of *St Christopher*, painted in three days in 1524 by Titian. There is a view of the Bacino di San Marco at his feet.

Rooms 11–13: These were the private rooms of the doge. Beyond the **Sala Corner** (Room 11), with a fine gilded ceiling, is the **Sala dei Ritratti** (Room 12), with a good fireplace by Antonio and Tullio Lombardo. The painted lunette displayed here of the *Dead Christ between the Madonna and St John the Evangelist* (and two kneeling saints) is almost certainly by Giovanni Bellini. Beyond the Sala dello Scudo is the **Sala degli Scudieri** (Room 13; named after the doge's private guards). The two large paintings of doges are by Domenico Tintoretto, son of the great Jacopo.

SECONDO PIANO NOBILE (*plan opposite*)

The Scala d'Oro continues up to a series of grand state rooms, restored after fire damage in 1574 and 1577, when a series of paintings glorifying Venice and her history was commissioned from the leading artists of the day, on a scheme carefully worked out to include the most important military and naval victories of the Republic as well as allegories of wise government and scenes of significant events in the reigns of certain doges.

Room 15 (Atrio Quadrato): The fine wooden ceiling has a painting by Tintoretto of *Justice presenting the Sword and the Scales to Doge Girolamo Priuli.*

Room 16 (Sala delle Quattro Porte): Named after its four doors, this was the magnificent waiting-room where ambassadors and heads of state would attend their turn to be received by officials of the Republic or by the doge himself. It was also the room through which Venetian patricians would pass to and fro on their way to meetings of the most powerful organs of the State (the *Collegio*, Senate and Council of Ten) and so its grandeur and allegorical decorations exulting the power of the Republic took on special significance. It was designed by Palladio after the 1574 fire, although the building work was carried out under the direction of the *proto* in charge of the palace at the time, Giovanni Antonio Rusconi. The very fine stucco work is by a little-known artist from Cremona, Giovanni Cambi, his only work in the city. The four doors are elaborately decorated with allegorical statues, some by Alessandro Vittoria.

The ceiling frescoes by Tintoretto have unfortunately been spoilt over the centuries by restoration: the central rectangle depicts Jupiter presenting the territories on the Adriatic to Venice, and the two tondi show Venice surrounded by the Virtues, and Juno offering Venice a peacock and a shaft of lightning symbolising her grandeur. In the ovals are illustrations of Venetian territories on the Italian mainland. On the entrance wall (by the window) is Giovanni Contarini's *Doge Marino Grimani before the Madonna and Saints*: Grimani was the doge in office from 1595–1605, at the time this room was decorated. On the long wall is an earlier painting, commissioned from Titian by Francesco Venier in 1555: *Antonio Grimani Kneeling before the Faith* (Antonio was a predecessor of Marino Grimani, and a member of the same family). The painting escaped damage in the fire since it was unfinished and was still in the painter's studio

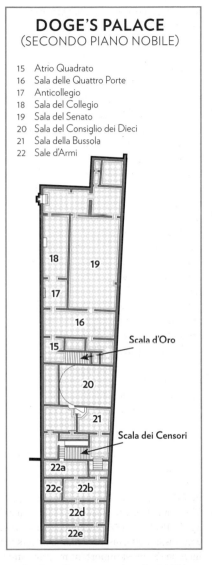

DOGE'S PALACE
(SECONDO PIANO NOBILE)

15 Atrio Quadrato
16 Sala delle Quattro Porte
17 Anticollegio
18 Sala del Collegio
19 Sala del Senato
20 Sala del Consiglio dei Dieci
21 Sala della Bussola
22 Sale d'Armi

at the time. It was completed c. 1600 by Titian's nephew Marco Vecellio. The parts attributed to Titian's own hand are the figure of St Mark, the helmeted warrior, and the view of the Bacino. On the opposite wall are two paintings—one by the Caliari brothers Carletto and Gabriele (Paolo Veronese's sons) and the other by their contemporary Andrea Vi-

centino. (The paintings at the other end of the room are described below since they cannot be viewed from here.)

DOGES AND THEIR COUNCILS

'Though in appearance he seemeth of great estate, yet indeed his power is but small. He keepeth no house, liveth privately, and is in so much servitude that I have heard some of the Venetians themselves call him an honourable slave.' This is how a 16th-century English visitor saw the Doge of Venice. Yet, to the outside world, the doge personified the grandeur of the Republic. On great ceremonial occasions, such as the feast of the Marriage to the Sea every Ascension Day, he would process in splendour across the lagoon in the *Bucintoro*. He was the focus of every major ritual, whether this was the reception of a foreign ambassador or visiting royalty, or the ancient religious celebrations in St Mark's and the square outside it.

Yet, remarkably for Europe at this time, the doges could for centuries only be appointed through election. In the 13th century the pretence was that the appointment was by popular acclaim. 'This is your doge if it pleases you' was the ritual formula by which a new incumbent was presented to the citizens from the loggia of St Mark's. After 1268, the election was through an intricate procedure conducted by the nobility, and certainly from then on the doge's powers became increasingly restricted. On assuming office, he had to make a *promissione ducale*, which was a solemn vow that he would obey certain rules which constrained his authority. He could not leave Venice without authorisation, nor could he open state letters in private or meet foreign ambassadors unless councillors were present. Much of government took place outside his control, and was conducted by the Great Council, or *Maggior Consiglio*. The *Serrata del Maggior Consiglio*, literally the 'locking' of the Great Council, in 1297, restricted membership to those families who had already sat on the council. These 'patricians' included both nobles and merchants, and they inherited the right to sit on the council for life on reaching the age of 25. This signified the introduction of an oligarchic form of government. At the beginning of the 16th century the members were formally registered at their baptism in the *Libro d'Oro* ('Golden Book'). The size of the council varied over the years; the greatest number it reached was 1,700. Clearly such a large body was too cumbersome to conduct power on a day-to-day basis, but it met once a week, on Sundays, and appointed many of the city's magistrates. Increasingly its power was delegated to a Senate, of which the leading state magistrates were members *ex officio*. The Senate, which met three or four times a week, expanded its original duties of jurisdiction in commerce and navigation to include all matters of international affairs, diplomacy and defence. Eventually it had 230 members. The Senate in its turn appointed (for the first time in 1380) a smaller committee, the *Collegio*, a group of 26 counsellors presided over by the doge, which met almost every day to deal with everyday affairs. Major executive decisions were taken by a still smaller council, the *Signoria* of ten members, all of whom were also members of the *Collegio*. Separate from all these organs was the Council of Ten, set up in 1310, at first as a temporary measure, but then permanently, which was given the task of supervising internal security. It soon became notorious for its secret operations and its readiness to intrude into all matters of business. All these councils met in the Doge's Palace.

It is just this proliferation of councils that helps explain the power the doge might exercise. Invariably by the time of his election he was a man of great experience. Giacomo Tiepolo, elected doge in 1229, for instance, had been governor of Crete and had served as the *podestà* (chief magistrate) in Constantinople after the Fourth Crusade, so he knew Venice's international concerns as few others. One of the objections made against the candidate Francesco Foscari, successful in the election of 1423, was that he was only fifty years old. Furthermore, a doge remained in power until death—unless forced to abdicate—while most other posts lasted only a year. Behind the façade of oligarchical rule, a shrewd doge could manipulate his smaller councils with their changing membership to his advantage. Leonardo Loredan (immortalised in Giovanni Bellini's famous portrait), doge between 1501 and 1521, and Andrea Gritti, doge between 1523 and 1538, make the point. It is noted that it was in Loredan and Gritti's reign that the major rebuilding around St Mark's Square took place, and this suggests a consistent guiding hand behind the scenes.

Although the government of Venice appeared undemocratic, it proved impressively stable in comparison to the faction-ridden cities of the rest of northern Italy. The gradual loss of colonies to the Ottoman Empire, wars on the *terraferma*, and the long economic decline were all absorbed without revolution. Yet by the 18th century the system appeared increasingly archaic and lacking in inner vitality. The Council of Ten was seen as repressive, and it was this image of decay from the centre that Napoleon was able to exploit when he forced the Republic to dissolve itself in 1797. Even so, the readiness with which it caved in to his demands made an ignominious end of so many centuries of greatness.

The election of a doge

The procedure given below is that as established in 1268, in order to prevent manipulation of the result by the more powerful candidates and their families:

1) Thirty men are chosen by lot from the Great Council;
2) Nine of the thirty are selected, again by lot;
3) These nine nominate forty electors, reduced by further lots to nine;
4) This second group of nine chooses forty-one electors;
5) Eleven of the forty-one are chosen by lot and select a further forty-one;
6) These forty-one electors make the final decision. C.F.

Room 17 (Anticollegio): This waiting-room served as a vestibule to the Sala del Collegio. It has a 16th-century ceiling with a ruined fresco by Veronese, but it is the paintings on the walls which are of the greatest interest. Opposite the window is Veronese's very fine *Rape of Europa* next to *Jacob's Return to Canaan* by Jacopo Bassano. On the other walls are four paintings by Tintoretto, among his best works in the palace: *Vulcan's Forge, Mercury and the Graces, Bacchus and Ariadne* and *Minerva Dismissing Mars*. The fireplace by Vincenzo Scamozzi has a relief of the *Forge of Vulcan*, an early work by Tiziano Aspetti and Girolamo Campagna.

Room 18 (Sala del Collegio): It was here that the doge and the *Collegio*, or cabinet, deliberated and received ambassadors. The *Collegio*, whose 26 members were known as *savii* ('savants'), included the doge himself, six councillors (one for each *sestiere* of the city) and the three judges of the criminal tribunals. The room is a treasure house of art and its decorations, carried out from 1575–81, survive almost intact, including the original rostrum and benches. The ceiling, by the little-known Francesco Bello, the finest in the palace, is doubly precious because of its wonderful paintings by Veronese. The most remarkable is that in the centre at the farther end: *Justice and Peace Offering the Sword, the Scales and the Olive-branch to Triumphant Venice*. The other panels have allegorical figures of Mars and Neptune, Faith and Religion.

The painting over the entrance, showing *Doge Andrea Gritti before the Virgin*, is by Tintoretto, while above the throne Veronese painted *Doge Sebastiano Venier Offering Thanks to Christ for the Victory of Lepanto*. Facing the fireplace (another work by Campagna) are three more magnificent paintings by Tintoretto: *Marriage of St Catherine, Doge Niccolò da Ponte Invoking the Virgin*, and *Doge Alvise Mocenigo Adoring Christ*.

Room 19 (Sala del Senato): This was where the Senate, or legislative body of the Republic, sat. The senators were also called *pregadi* because, when elected, they were formally 'begged' or 'invited' by the doge to take up their role. Their number was increased from 60 to 120, and they were elected from among the patricians by the Great Council, holding office for just one year. At the centre of the political life of the Republic, they also nominated magistrates, ambassadors, bishops and the patriarch. They treated with foreign courts, and only they could take the grave decision to declare war.

Designed by Antonio da Ponte, the room has a fine ceiling (1581), with *Venice Exalted among the Gods* by Tintoretto in the central panel. Tintoretto also painted the *Descent from the Cross*, with doges Pietro Lando and Marcantonio Trevisan in adoration, over the throne. The prolific painter Palma Giovane, who carried out some of his best works for the Doge's Palace but was overshadowed by his contemporaries Veronese and Tintoretto, painted the three works on the left wall: *Venice Receiving the Homage of Subject Cities Presented by Doge Francesco Venier, Doge Pasquale Cicogna in Prayer*, and an *Allegory of the League of Cambrai*, as well as *Doges Lorenzo and Girolamo Priuli Praying to Christ* on the end wall. Tintoretto painted *Doge Pietro Loredan Praying to the Virgin*, also on the left wall.

Room 16 (Sala delle Quattro Porte; further end): Here is exhibited (on an easel) Giambattista Tiepolo's great painting of *Venice Receiving the Homage of Neptune* (it has been removed from above the windows so that it is easier to see, and replaced there by a photograph). This is the only painting by Tiepolo in the palace, and it was commissioned around 1756 to substitute a painting by Tintoretto which had deteriorated. An allegory of the Venetian state, it shows a splendid female figure personifying Venice, wearing the ducal ermine robe and dominating both the submissive figure of Neptune, who offers her a cornucopia full of gold, pearls and coral, and the tame lion of St Mark. This is Tiepolo's only painting which alludes directly to the glory of the Venetian state, although the air of slightly decadent opulence portrayed seems perhaps to foreshadow the end (it was painted only 40 years before the fall of the Republic).

The paintings on the walls include *Venice under Gattamelata Conquering* *Verona* by Giovanni Contarini, and *Doge Marino Grimani Receiving Gifts from Persian Ambassadors* by Veronese's son Gabriele Caliari. This last records the visit of a delegation headed by Fethi Bey from Shah 'Abbas the Great of Persia in 1603, which remained memorable because of the richness of the fabrics and carpets (clearly depicted here) presented to the doge.

Room 20 (Sala del Consiglio dei Dieci): A corridor (with a view of the top of the façade of San Zaccaria) leads into the room that was the seat of the Council of Ten. This body was appointed after the rebellion in 1310 of Bajamonte Tiepolo against Doge Pietro Gradenigo (*see below*).

BAJAMONTE TIEPOLO'S CONSPIRACY

After the famous *Serrata del Maggior Consiglio* in 1297, which restricted those eligible for election to the Great Council and effectively changed the nature of the government of the Republic from a 'democracy' to an oligarchy, a serious rebellion was organised, in 1310, against the doge responsible (Pietro Gradenigo). This was led by Bajamonte Tiepolo with the aid of some members of the wealthy Querini family and Badoero Badoer, at the head of a fleet in the lagoon. They planned to join forces in Piazza San Marco to storm the Doge's Palace from three directions, and the story is told that as Tiepolo and his horsemen rode from the Rialto into the Piazza, his standard-bearer was killed by a mortar (as in pestle and mortar) which an old lady who was watching the scene let fall (apparently by accident) from a window-sill (*see also p. 105*). This contretemps discouraged the conspirators from proceeding; although unlike Querini, who was killed in a street battle, and Badoer, who was captured and condemned to death, Tiepolo managed to escape and take refuge in his house across the Grand Canal, holding out until he had won the concession of an unusually brief exile of just four years as punishment for his misconduct. Although the uprising was quickly put down, the Great Council set up a special tribunal to investigate the conspiracy, and this body survived as the dreaded Council of Ten, which from that time onwards was on the look out to try offenders of similar crimes against the State. To this day historians discuss the significance of the Tiepolo rebellion, uncertain if the motives behind it were, indeed, to save the government of the Republic from becoming too remote from the people, or whether merely personal interests were at stake, since it is probably significant that all the leaders were from important Venetian families.

As a court which tried political crimes, the Council of Ten became a notoriously severe organ of government, particularly efficient in times of crisis. It was this council which ordered the execution of Doge Marin Falier in 1355, because he had tried to turn his elective office into a despotic seigniory. Judges held office for one year only, and were ineligible for re-election in the succeeding year.

The ceiling contains more paintings by Veronese, notably, in the far right-hand corner (as you stand with your back to the windows), an *Old Man in Eastern Costume with a Young Woman*. The panel by him in the centre of the left-hand side, showing *Juno Offering Gifts to Venice*, was seized by Napoleon and taken to Brussels in 1797, and only returned to Venice in 1920—the original of the oval ceiling painting (*Jupiter Fulminating the Vices*), which was removed to Paris by Napoleon in the same year, was never returned (it is now in the Louvre). On the right wall (facing the entrance): *The Meeting between Pope Alexander III and Doge Ziani*, by the brothers Francesco and Leandro Bassano; on the end wall: *Adoration of the Magi* by Aliense; and on the left wall: *Pope Clement VII and the Emperor Charles V* by Marco Vecellio, painted in 1529 to celebrate the peace declared between pope and emperor at Bologna.

Room 21 (Sala della Bussola): The room takes its name from the walnut-wood screen which gives access to the Sala dei Tre Capi and the prisons. The original ceiling painting by Veronese of *St Mark in Glory Crowning the Theological Virtues* was stolen by Napoleon and is now in the Louvre. On the right of the farther door is a *Bocca di Leone*

(or 'mouth of truth'), a box in which denunciations were placed (posted from the outside). From the end of the 16th or beginning of the 17th century, a number of these were installed in various rooms of the palace (before then the practice had been to drop notes on the floor or to give them to foreigners to deliver). The box could only be opened in the presence of all three head magistrates (*tre capi*) of the Council of Ten. There were notoriously severe punishments for false denunciations, and they were disregarded if anonymous. There are more wall paintings here by Vecellio and Aliense. On the right is the Sala dei Tre Capi del Consiglio dei Dieci, only open on the guided *Itinerari Segreti* (*see p. 102*).

Room 22 (Sale d'Armi del Consiglio dei Dieci): From the landing outside the Sala della Bussola is the approach upstairs (right) to the Sale d'Armi del Consiglio dei Dieci, the Council of Ten's private armoury, in which the state arms and armour were stored until the fall of the Republic. **Room 22a** displays a suit of armour traditionally supposed to have belonged to the *condottiere* and protector of the Venetian Republic, Gattamelata; and one belonging to a page, found on the field of Marignano (1515). In a case is a display of 16th–17th-century helmets (northern Italian); a unique visored helmet of the 14th century, shaped like a bird's beak and made of a single piece; and tournament armour (c. 1510–20). A long case contains swords (the earliest dating from the 15th century), and halberds made by Giovanni Maria Bergamini (Venice, c. 1620–5). Cross-bows are hung on the walls.

The huge Turkish standard on the

ceiling of **Room 22b** is a trophy from the Battle of Lepanto. In a niche is a suit of armour which belonged to Henri IV of France, presented by him to the *Serenissima* in 1603. This was apparently a gift to Venice in gratitude for her support of the king in his far-sighted plan (after he had issued the Edict of Nantes in 1598 in an attempt to end the civil wars of religion in France) to establish some sort of universal Christian republic in Europe. However, hopes of this vanished when he was assassinated in 1610. Displayed here are lances, swords, falchions (short, sickle-shaped swords), suits of armour, Persian arms, horses' battle frontlets (15th–16th century) and painted shields.

Room 22c was formerly a prison reserved for important prisoners. It has another fine display of shields and swords. **Room 22d**, with the bust of Doge Morosini, has a superb collection of swords, lances and shields beautifully displayed in old show-cases. In the centre are two early quick-firing guns, one with 20 barrels, the other with a revolver mechanism, a fuse-case holding 106 fuses made of perforated and embossed copper, signed by Giovanni Antonio Comino, and a culverin (an early type of cannon) complete with its carriage and fittings (?German, 16th century). The lantern belonged to a dismantled Turkish galleon. **Room 22e** has a superb view of the Bacino and island of San Giorgio Maggiore. In the cases are 16th–17th-century pistols; muskets and arquebuses; various instruments of torture and a 16th-century cuirass (breastplate).

PRIMO PIANO NOBILE: SOUTH AND WEST WINGS (*plan on p. 91*)

Room 23 (Andito del Maggior Consiglio): This is the corridor where the patricians would gather during intervals in the session of the Great Council. It has a good 16th-century ceiling and works by Tintoretto's son, Domenico.

Room 24 (Liagò): In this veranda are exhibited three statues removed from the Arco Foscari in the courtyard: *Adam* and *Eve*, the masterpieces of Antonio Rizzo (c. 1470), and *Francesco Maria I della Rovere*, Duke of Urbino and a *condottiere* who served the Venetian Republic, by Giovanni Bandini.

Room 25 (Sala della Quarantia Civil Vecchia): The tribunal of 40 members met here to try civil cases. A fragment of mural painting has been revealed behind the panelling.

Room 26 (Sala del Guariento): The remains of the huge fresco of the *Coronation of the Virgin* by Guariento (1365–7) used to adorn the Sala del Maggior Consiglio. Guariento had been chosen for this exceptionally important commission since he was considered the best artist at work in the Veneto at the time. He is today known almost exclusively for his works in Padua. This famous fresco, ruined by the fire of 1577, was discovered in 1903 beneath Tintoretto's painting. It is one of the very earliest painted works to have survived in the palace.

Room 27 (Sala del Maggior Consiglio): This vast hall was the seat of the governing body of the Republic. It was first built on this scale in 1340, and was large enough to hold the entire assembly of Venetian patricians. Here laws were ratified and the highest officials of the Republic were elected.

The size of the hall is exceptional: it is 52m long, 24m wide and 11m high. There is a fine view from the balcony over the Bacino di San Marco. The 14th–15th-century frescoes by leading artists of the time, and the magnificent ceiling, were all destroyed in the disastrous fire of 1577, but the following year the best-known Venetian artists of the day were commissioned to begin the work of replacing them with painted panels—a task which was only completed in 1595. On the entrance wall is Domenico Tintoretto's *Paradise*, carried out with the help of assistants between 1588 and 1592. It is a painting crowded with figures on a huge scale (7m by 24m), and is Domenico's most important work. The commission originally went to his father, the celebrated Jacopo, but because of his advanced age, was executed by Domenico.

The magnificent ceiling, its wonderful gilding restored in 2010, is divided into 35 compartments, but the most important paintings are in the three central panels. Nearest the throne is *Venice Surrounded by Gods and Crowned by Victory* (*Apotheosis of Venice*), a masterpiece of light and colour by Veronese (painted just before he died in 1588). The central panel, *Venice Surrounded by Gods Gives an Olive-branch to Doge Niccolò da Ponte,* is by Jacopo Tintoretto. At the far end is *Venice Welcoming the Conquered Nations around her Throne* by Palma Giovane, who here takes a worthy place beside his two far more famous and skilled contemporaries. These three artists also worked on some of the large historical canvases around the walls, recording important events in the history of the Republic: on the wall towards the courtyard the 12th-century battles between Church and Empire, culminating in peace proclaimed by Venice in 1175, are commemorated. A notable example is *The Meeting in Venice between Barbarossa and Pope Alexander III in 1177*. On the wall towards the Bacino are the events of the Fourth Crusade of 1204, including Domenico Tintoretto's *Capture and Sack of Constantinople*. On the wall opposite the throne, Veronese's *Triumph of Doge Contarini after the Battle of Chioggia* commemorates the Venetian victory over the Genoese in 1380. Other Venetian artists who had also worked in other rooms of the palace (including the Caliari brothers, the Bassano, Andrea Vicentino, Federico Zuccari, Giulio del Moro and Aliense) collaborated on these series.

The frieze of the first 76 doges (from Obelario degli Antenori, c. 804, to Francesco Venier, d. 1556) begins in the middle of the wall overlooking the courtyard and runs left to right. It is also the work of Domenico Tintoretto and assistants. The space blacked in on the wall opposite the *Paradise* takes the place of the portrait of Marin Falier: an inscription records his execution for treason in 1355 after his famous conspiracy against the State. The frieze is continued in the Sala dello Scrutinio.

Room 28 (Sala dello Scrutinio): The last door on the right admits to the **Sala della Quarantia Civil Nuova**, used by the high court of 40 magistrates, set up in 1492 to act in civil cases for Venetian citizens in the new territories on the *terraferma*. The **Sala dello Scrutinio** itself was used after 1532 to record the votes cast in the Sala del Maggior Consiglio for the new doge and other officials. On the walls are paintings carried out between 1578 and 1615 of victorious Venetian battles throughout the history of the Republic, including the *Battle of Lepanto* by Andrea Vicentino. The *Last Judgement* is by Palma Giovane. The triumphal arch was erected by Antonio Gaspari in 1694, in honour of Francesco Morosini. In the corridor outside there are two plaques: one records Daniele Manin's resistance to the Austrians in 1849 and the other the plebiscite of 1866, when the inhabitants of Venice (together with those of the Veneto and Mantua) voted overwhelmingly in favour of joining the Kingdom of Italy.

Rooms 29–32: A small door to the left of the throne in the Sala del Maggior Consiglio leads out to the Scala dei Censori and a loggia overlooking the courtyard and into the **Sala del Quarantia Criminale** (Room 29), seat of a criminal tribunal. The **Sala al Magistrato alle Legge** (Room 31) has two Flemish works in a totally different style from the paintings in the rest of the palace: *Hell* by Herri met de Bles (who was known in Italy, where he worked at the end of his life, as 'Il Civetta', since his works always include an owl, *civetta*) and the *Derision of Christ* (or *Ecce Homo*) by Quentin Metsys, which is known to have been in Venice by the end of the 16th century and has been kept in the palace since 1664. From the adjoining room **(32)**, which has nine recently restored statues from the balcony on the waterfront façade, stairs lead down to a prison corridor.

THE PRISONS

The prisons are entered across the famous **Bridge of Sighs** *(see p. 88). There is a choice of two itineraries: the one on the right is shorter and passes a few cells before returning across the bridge. Otherwise you can continue downstairs to visit the 'new' prisons.*
The new prisons were built to replace the old ones (known as the '*Pozzi*'), 18 dark dungeons on the two lowest storeys of the palace, which were reserved for the most dangerous criminals. Even the lowest of them, however, was above ground level and they were less terrible than many other medieval prisons.

The new prisons, with their façade on Riva degli Schiavoni, were begun by Giovanni Antonio Rusconi (1560), continued by Antonio da Ponte (1589) and completed by Antonio and Tommaso Contino (1614). A labyrinth of corridors passes numerous prison cells to emerge in a grim courtyard with a well surrounded by barred windows. On the opposite side of the courtyard, stairs lead back up to a room with a display of Venetian ceramics found in the 20th century (many of them during excavations in the 1990s) from various periods (those from San Lorenzo date from the 9th century; those from San Francesco del Deserto from the 14th century, and those found when the Campanile of St Mark's collapsed from the 15th century). Beyond a series of more corridors and cells (some with graffiti made by the prisoners) the Bridge of Sighs is recrossed.

ROOMS USED BY MINOR OFFICIALS

The exit from the Doge's Palace is through some rooms of the **Avogaria** on the mezzanine floor, used by a branch of the judiciary elected as public prosecutors in criminal trials, and who functioned as supervisors during council meetings to safeguard the principle of legality. The **Sala dei Censori** has portraits by Domenico Tintoretto of censors (an office instituted in 1517 to protect the state's public institutions and control electoral procedures). The **Sala dei Notai** has similar portraits of advocates and notaries by Leandro Bassano.

The **Sala dello Scrigno** was where the 'Golden Book' (*Libro d'Oro*) was kept, which registered the baptism of all patricians to provide a record of those eligible as members of the Great Council. The officials who were responsible for recruiting the oarsmen needed to man Venice's warships deliberated in the **Sala della Milizia da Mar**. They were first called to office in 1571 to fit out the great fleet which set sail for the Battle of Lepanto. As it turned out, this great sea battle was the last in history to be fought with galleys manned by oarsmen.

The exit is down the Scala dei Senatori (*plan on p. 86*), which descends to the Cortile dei Senatori, a charming Renaissance work by Spavento and Scarpagnino beside the Scala dei Giganti. From here there is a fine view of the exterior of St Mark's, with the old brickwork visible. The original statue of St Theodore with his dragon, which was set up on one of the columns in the Piazzetta in 1329, is kept beneath the portico. The head is a Hellenistic portrait, the torso is Roman and dates from the period of Hadrian, and the arms, legs, shield and dragon were made by an early 14th-century Venetian sculptor.

THE *ITINERARI SEGRETI*

Literally 'secret tours', these are guided tours of the lesser-known parts of the palace. They last about 1hr and are highly recommended for the unique insight they give into the way the Republic was run (for admission, see p. 84). NB: Order of visit sometimes varies. From the Atrio Quadrato (Room 15; *plan on p. 93*) a door gives access to the tiny administrative offices used by the bureaucrats of the Republic. These were constructed in wood (also for warmth), making optimum use of the space available. Often two floors have been created in one storey of the building.

The **Ducal Chancellery** is particularly well lit since this was where documents were transcribed. It retains its original 18th-century furnishings and is decorated with the coats of arms of all the Chancellors from 1268 onwards. The Grand Chancellor was responsible for keeping all the government records and registering the decisions made by the various councils of state. He was elected for life from the middle classes (he could not be a patrician) and he held an extremely important position within the hierarchy of state officials.

The area of the law courts and judiciary offices of the Council of Ten includes the macabre **Torture Room** (with the four cells for prisoners who had to wait their turn), apparently used at night-time when the neighbouring offices were not in use. The room reserved for the three leading magistrates of the Council of Ten (the **Sala dei Tre Capi del Consiglio dei Dieci**) is, by contrast, highly decorated. The chimney-piece is by Jacopo Sansovino with statues by Danese Cattaneo and Pietro da Salò, and the ceiling paintings are by Paolo Veronese and Giovanni Battista Zelotti. It also has a lovely floor. The *Pietà*, derived from Antonello da Messina's *Pietà* in the Museo Correr (*see p. 77*), is by the great painter's nephew Antonello da Saliba. The little **Sala dei Tre**

Inquisitori was used by the three members of the special commission of inquiry used by the Council of Ten. These officials also examined the conduct of each doge after his death. The ceiling has a painting (in excellent condition) of the *Return of the Prodigal Son* by Jacopo Tintoretto. A *Madonna and Child* by Boccaccio Boccaccino has been hung here.

The tour also takes in the seven prison cells called the ***Piombi***, the 'Leads', so named because of their position beneath the roof. They were built in wood, and have been reconstructed. Prisoners were only kept here for brief periods. One of them was Casanova, and his cell is shown. Giacomo Casanova was arrested in 1755 and sentenced to five years' imprisonment. The charges against him concerned his lifestyle: he was accused of being a mason, a gambler and a cheat, of frequenting people from every walk of life, of practising alchemy and magic, of showing little respect for Christians, and of writing irreverent and satirical verse and reading it in public. He escaped in 1756, with his fellow inmate, Father Marino Balbi, via the roof. His colourful description of the miseries he suffered here and his courageous escape in *Storia della mia fuga dalle prigioni della Repubblica di Venezia che si chiamono Piombi* ('Story of my Flight from the Prisons of the Venetian Republic which are called the Leads') was published in 1788 and widely acclaimed throughout Europe. The writer Silvio Pellico (1789–1854) later described his much grimmer experiences, during his imprisonment here by the Austrians in 1822, in *Le Mie Prigioni*. He was also held at the monastery of San Michele in Isola before being sent to the Spielberg, a notorious prison near Brünn (modern Brno).

The remarkable structure of the great **roof of the Sala del Maggior Consiglio**, built with huge wooden beams in 1577, can also be seen here.

ON AND AROUND PIAZZETTA GIOVANNI XXIII

Piazzetta Giovanni XXIII (*map p. 407, E2*), to the left of St Mark's, is named after Angelo Roncalli, a native of the Veneto, who was Patriarch of Venice when elected to the Holy See in 1958. Greatly loved and respected (and always known simply as 'Papa Giovanni'), he was beatified in the year 2000. The centre of the little square was designed by Andrea Tirali in 1724, when he installed the well-head and the two chubby little lion cubs (carved out of red Verona marble around this time by Giovanni Bonazza), which are now rather worn since they are just the right size to be ridden by children. Palazzo Patriarcale was built in 1834–43 by Lorenzo Santi, Venice's most successful Neoclassical architect. The façade of the deconsecrated church of San Basso, by Longhena, dates from 1675.

TORRE DELL'OROLOGIO
Map p. 407, E2. Daily guided visits but only by appointment at the Museo Correr or Doge's Palace, or T: 8480 82000; www.torreorologio.visitmuve.it. Ticket includes admission to Museo Correr. During the tour, along a series of very narrow stairs, you can see the various clock mechanisms in the little rooms where the clocksmiths lived up until 1998. From the terrace there is a wonderful view of St Mark's and the Piazza.

The Torre dell'Orologio was designed by Mauro Codussi, although the two wings, added in 1505 perhaps by Pietro Lombardo, were heightened in the mid-18th century. The tower was built to house a remarkable clock constructed in 1493–9 by the celebrated Rainieri clockmakers from Reggio Emilia, and which was acclaimed at the time as the most complex astronomical clock in existence. It was modified in 1757 by the famous clockmaker Bartolomeo Ferracina (who also supplied the Doge's Palace with three clocks). The great **clock-face** shows the hours in Roman numerals (the hand of the clock is in the form of the sun); a moveable inner ring, brightly decorated with gilding and blue enamel, shows the signs of the zodiac and their constellations; and in the centre, on a dark blue sky filled with stars, is the earth with the moon, half gilded and half dark: as the moon turns, its various phases are recorded. Above the clock is a **tabernacle with the figure of the Madonna**. Originally, every hour, figures of the Magi, accompanied by an angel, came out of the side doors and processed and bowed before her (the existing statues which you can see during the tour inside date from 1755). This now only happens during Ascension week and at Epiphany, because in 1858 two small drums which display the hour in Roman numerals and the minutes in Arabic numerals were inserted into the little doors (and lit from behind by gas lamps), to make the time easier to read from the Piazza below, especially at night (these have to be temporarily removed when the 'procession' is reactivated).

Above the lion of St Mark, against an enamelled bronze background, hangs a great **bell** cast in 1497, which is struck every hour by two giant mechanical figures in bronze, made at the same time. Because of their colour, they have always been known as the *Mori* (Moors), but were in fact probably intended to represent Cain and Abel. In addition, another mechanism with two hammers strikes the bell 132 times at midday and midnight (the number represents the sum of the preceding eleven hours).

There is another, simpler clock-face on the other side of the tower overlooking the Merceria, where the hours are shown in Roman numerals and the hand is in the form of the sun fixed to a central 'sun' decorated with the lion of St Mark.

The complicated mechanism of the entire clock was modified in 1753 (when the wooden processional figures were remade) and again in 1866. Its various parts were dismantled in 1999 and restoration of the building was finally completed in 2006.

MUSEUM OF DIOCESAN ART

Calle di Canonica leads to Rio di Palazzo, across which rises the façade of the 16th-century Palazzo Trevisan-Cappello, with good marble inlay. The *rio* marks the boundary between the *sestieri* of San Marco and Castello. On the other side of the *rio*, at the end of the short *fondamenta*, is the entrance (at no. 4312) to the **Museum of Diocesan Art** (*map p. 407, E2; open 10–5.30 except Mon*) and the tiny **Cloister of Sant'Apollonia**. Dating from the early 14th century, it is the only Romanesque cloister in the city, and it retains its original brick paving. Sculptural fragments from the basilica (some dating from the 9th–11th centuries) are displayed here. The museum contains a collection of vestments, missals, Church plate, Crucifixes and reliquaries, as well as paintings and sculpture from Venetian churches either closed permanently or temporarily unable to provide safe-keeping for their treasures.

ALONG THE MERCERIA TO THE RIALTO

The Merceria, a narrow *calle* (*map p. 407, E2–D1*), called *Marziaria* in Venetian dialect, is the shortest route from Piazza San Marco to the Rialto. Its name comes from *merce* ('goods'), since from earliest days most of the city's shops were concentrated here. As the busiest thoroughfare of the city, it is always crowded with both Venetians and tourists. On its winding course it changes name five times: Merceria dell'Orologio, Merceria di San Zulian,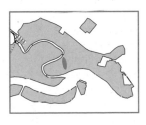
Merceria del Capitello, Merceria di San Salvador and Merceria Due Aprile; and passes some interesting churches, notably San Giuliano, with a fine 16th-century façade and interior, and San Salvatore, with a Renaissance interior and two paintings by Titian

To get to the Merceria, take the passage under the Torre dell'Orologio. Just beyond the arch, above the Sottoportego del Cappello on the left, a relief of an old woman at a window was set up in 1841 to record a fatal incident during Bajamonte Tiepolo's rebellion against the Venetian Republic (*see p. 97*).

SAN GIULIANO
Map p. 407, E1. Open 8.45–12 & 4–6.30.
This church, usually called San Zulian, at the first bend in the Merceria, was rebuilt in 1553 by Jacopo Sansovino and completed after his death by Alessandro Vittoria. The dedication is to Julian the Hospitaller, a legendary saint popular in the Middle Ages but who remains something of a mystery, even though he was the patron of boatmen. The façade, well-suited to this unusually cramped site, bears a seated bronze statue, attributed to Vittoria, of Tommaso Rangone, a wealthy physician and scholar from Ravenna who paid for the rebuilding of the church and who is buried in the chancel. Between the columns on the façade are inscriptions in Greek and Hebrew praising Rangone's munificence and learning.

The charming interior has a simple rectangular plan with two side chapels flanking the sanctuary. The ceiling (1585) has a painting of *St Julian in Glory* by Palma Giovane and assistants. The statues of *St Catherine of Alexandria* and *Daniel* on the third south altar are also by Alessandro Vittoria. In 1582 a much less well-known contemporary of Vittoria's, Francesco Smeraldi, carried out the good stuccoes in the vault of the chapel of the Scuola del Santissimo Sacramento (left of the sanctuary)—this belonged to the confraternity whose main concern was the burial of the dead. On the altar is a relief of the *Pietà* by Girolamo Campagna, who was active in Venice at the same time as Vittoria. The high altar was erected in 1667 by Giuseppe Sardi: it encloses a *Coronation of the Virgin with three Saints* by Girolamo da Santacroce, painted more than a century earlier. On the sanctuary walls hang two huge paintings by Antonio Zanchi, who died in the early 18th century: he also painted the *Assumption* on the second south altar.

Other paintings in the church include a *Pietà*, with three saints below, by Veronese (first south altar); *St Jerome* by Leandro Bassano (between the two south altars); and a *Madonna Enthroned with Saints* by Boccaccio Boccaccino (first north altar). The painting on the west wall (right of the door) by Sante Peranda shows St Roch curing the plague-stricken in one of the isolation hospitals (*lazzaretti*) which existed in the Venetian lagoon. The organ is one of the first works by the great organ-maker from the Veneto, Gaetano Callido (1764).

RIDOTTO VENIER

The Merceria continues across Ponte dei Barettari, one of the widest in the city, re-built in 1771 with an Istrian stone balustrade. To the right beneath the portico is the entrance to the Ridotto (or Casino) Venier, famous in the 18th century—when it was the home of Elena, wife of the Procurator Federico Venier—as the meeting place of elegant Venetian society. The delightful small rooms preserve their original stuccoes and painted decoration intact. Now the seat of the Associazione Italo-Francese, the rooms can be visited on request (*Mon–Fri 9–1 & 3–6; ring at no. 4939*).

SAN SALVATORE

Map p. 407, D1. Open 9–12 & 3 or 4–6.30; Sun and holidays 4–6.30.
Campo San Salvatore was laid out in the mid-17th century, when the former Scuola di San Teodoro was given its façade by Giuseppe Sardi. The column outside the church commemorates Daniele Manin's defence of Venice against Austrian rule in 1848–9 (*see p. 123*).

The church itself (also called San Salvador) was rebuilt in the early 16th century and the Baroque façade was added in 1663, also following a design by Giuseppe Sardi. The plan of the interior, with its five domes and barrel vaults, is one of the best examples in Venice of the way in which the problems of light and construction were solved at the height of the Renaissance. It is the combined work of Giorgio Spavento, also known for his work on the Doge's Palace and the Fondaco dei Tedeschi, and Tullio Lombardo, who took over after Spavento's death in 1509. Vincenzo Scamozzi carefully completed the building at the end of the century.

The church contains two splendid works by Titian—probably both painted in the 1560s: a beautiful *Annunciation* on the third south altar (the altar itself is to a design by Sansovino) and a *Transfiguration* over the high altar. In the former, the Madonna's unusual gesture is apparently derived from a Greek relief which Titian had seen in Venice in the Grimani collection, but it is the majestic figure of the annunciatory angel which dominates the scene. The silver reredos which formerly covered Titian's *Trans-figuration* is only shown at Christmas, Easter and around 6 August; it is a masterpiece of Venetian goldsmiths' work of the 14th century. To make it easy to transport, it was made so that the silver-gilt panels could be folded up; the upper and lower rows of sculpture are later additions.

Sansovino also designed the organ, and its doors were painted by Titian's brother, Francesco Vecellio. One of the doors has another representation of the *Transfigura-tion*. It was probably also Francesco who had the original idea of decorating the sacristy (*sometimes shown on request*) with a delicate pattern of flowers and birds, very unusual for Venice. Here is kept a Renaissance Crucifix found a few years ago in the bell-tower.

The statue of the *Madonna and Child* on the second south altar is by Girolamo Campagna, who sculpted the busts on the adjacent huge monument by Giulio del Moro (1602) to Andrea Dolfin, who was a procurator of St Mark's.

Next to the altar with Titian's *Annunciation* is the funerary monument of Doge Francesco Venier (d. 1556). He is shown lying in gilded robes beneath a lunette of the *Pietà* (where he is also present). The two statues of *Hope* and *Charity* were sculpted by Sansovino, when almost 80 years old (the *Hope* is especially beautiful). The grand monument is resplendent with coloured marbles, and even a mottled slab was chosen to bear the inscription. This doge, although apparently a learned man, is chiefly remembered for his tomb here, since he had an uneventful reign of just two years.

The tomb of Doge Venier's successors, the brothers Lorenzo and Girolamo Priuli, is in the north aisle —a dark classical monument by the little-known architect Cesare Franco. Also in this aisle is a statue of *St Jerome* on the second altar by Tommaso Lombardo, and left of the side door (beneath the organ) is a statuette of the same saint with his lion by Danese Cattaneo (1530). The two statues of *St Roch* and *St Sebastian* on the last altar are by Alessandro Vittoria.

In the chapel to the left of the sanctuary, the *Supper at Emmaus* was commissioned by Girolamo Priuli, whose portrait is included (shown in black sitting next to Christ). It is thought that the drawing is by Giovanni Bellini (who made another painting of the same subject) but it was probably painted by his workshop.

In the south transept, by the little-known architect Bernardino Contino, is the tomb of Caterina Cornaro (or Corner), who died in 1510. Born in Venice, she was married to the king of Cyprus, and as his widow she inherited the island in 1474. The Republic persuaded her to cede her kingdom to Venice in 1489, and in return they presented her with the town of Asolo in the Veneto, where she presided over a court frequented by artists and men of learning, including Pietro Bembo.

CAMPO SAN BARTOLOMEO

Campo San Bartolomeo (*map p. 402, B3–B4*) stands at the crossroads of the city and is usually very crowded. The statue of Goldoni, the dramatist of Venetian life, in a tricorn hat and flowing frock coat, is by Antonio dal Zotto (1883).

In a hidden corner of the *campo* (entered on Salizzada Pio X), close to the Rialto Bridge, is **San Bartolomeo** (called by the Venetians San Bortolo), the church which served the German community in Venice, frequented by the merchants and once the seat of the Scuola dei Tedeschi. Dürer painted his famous *Madonna of the Rosary* for the church when he was in the city in 1506 (it includes his own portrait and those of his contemporaries). He made two visits to Venice, the first in 1494–5 and the second in 1505–7, and on both occasions he was given lodgings in the Fondaco and made his living by selling his engravings. From his letters we know that he was struck by the great respect shown to him and other artists in city at that time, and his works of the period clearly show the influence of Paolo Veneziano and Giovanni Bellini. When the church was renovated in 1610, Dürer's altarpiece was sold, and is now in the National Gallery of Prague. The church was rebuilt in 1723. Today is usually kept locked. There is an amusing grotesque mascaron at the foot of its campanile.

In the *salizzada* behind the Goldoni statue is the venerable old warehouse known as the Fondaco (or Fontego) dei Tedeschi.

MERCHANTS OF VENICE AND THE FONDACO DEI TEDESCHI

The most important trading post and warehouse on the Grand Canal, the Fondaco dei Tedeschi, was first built in 1225. It was leased by the Venetian Republic to foreign (literally 'German') merchants. By the mid-13th century the Germans, Austrians, Bohemians, Hungarians and Flemish all had their warehouses, shops, offices and lodgings here. Goods arriving from the East, including gold, silver, spices and silk, would all be deposited here, ideally placed as it was on the waterfront and in the central Rialto market area, where banking transactions also took place. Built largely of wood, and illuminated with candles and heated with open fires, it was constantly exposed to the danger of fire. We know it had to be rebuilt in 1341 when it was given two floors and provided with 56 rooms, and that it was enlarged at the end of the same century and again in 1423. It burnt to the ground in 1505, but was immediately rebuilt by Giorgio Spavento and completed by Scarpagnino (possibly with the help of Girolamo Tedesco, himself a German): Giorgione was commissioned to fresco the Grand Canal façade and Titian the side façade (on Calle del Fontego): the frescoes have entirely disappeared, although fragments survive in the Ca' d'Oro and Gallerie dell'Accademia. The design of the 16th-century building survives in the present structure, with its square central court and ground-floor portico, and the two upper floors with open loggias. Many of the 80 or so lodgings as well as the meeting rooms were splendidly furnished, and shops on the ground floor opened directly out onto the streets. Throughout its history no arms were ever allowed inside the building.

In the 19th and early 20th centuries it was much altered and restored, and in 1939, after a further restoration had replaced the wooden beams with reinforced concrete, it became a post office. In 2008 it was sold to the Benetton fashion house, amid considerable opposition both at home and abroad, and mixed reactions to architect Rem Koolhaas's radical plans, which include the addition of a glass floor beneath the roof (which will eliminate the courtyard); the creation of a sunken roof terrace; and the insertion of an escalator. Whatever the outcome, it seems that the Fondaco is at least destined to fulfil a commercial function once more.

The **Ponte dell'Olio** (rebuilt in 1899), with its marble columns and iron balustrade, marks the boundary between the *sestieri* of San Marco and Cannaregio.

PIAZZA SAN MARCO TO CAMPO SANTO STEFANO

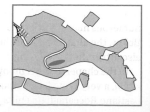

Leaving Piazza San Marco from the end opposite the basilica (beneath the Ala Napoleonica), you join a busy main thoroughfare. Turn left down Calle Vallaresso, which leads to the San Marco landing-stage past Harry's Bar (*see p. 362*). At no. 1332, with tall windows on the *piano nobile*, is the Ridotto.

THE RIDOTTO

Map p. 407, D2.
Now part of the Hotel Monaco Grand Canal, the building was once a famous gambling house, opened with the approval of the Council of Ten in 1638 and where ladies were also welcome. It was in an annexe (or *ridotto*) of Marco Dandolo's house, attached to the private theatre of San Moisè (*see below*). There were two 'sitting out' rooms where savouries and wine as well as coffee, hot chocolate and tea were served, and ten gaming rooms where the croupier was always a patrician. If you were not a nobleman you had to be masked. Francesco Guardi's painting, which shows the crowded interior around 1745, is preserved in Room 17 of Ca' Rezzonico. Although the Ridotto was enlarged in 1768 and another gambling house opened next to the San Cassian theatre, both were closed by order of the Great Council in 1774 in an attempt to heal the decadence in Venetian society. Nevertheless, gambling continued in private houses throughout the city (such as the Ridotto Venier), and Venice today has one of the few official casinos in Italy.

SAN MOISÈ

Map p. 407, D2. Open 9.30–12 & 3–6.30.
The church of San Moisè, dedicated to the prophet Moses, was built in 1668 by the brother of the priest, Alessandro Tremignon. The Baroque façade has an abundance of sculpture (the camels are particularly striking) but the design is over-elaborate and the overall effect unpleasing.

One of the white marble paving stones just inside the entrance has an inscription which marks the grave—transferred from the church of San Gemignano in 1808—of the Scottish financier John Law, a speculator who recognised the advantages in credit operations and paper currency, and had the idea of a national bank, but who was bankrupted after the failure of his 'Mississippi Scheme' and spent his old age in Venice, where he died in 1729.

The interior of the church is interesting for its 17th- and 18th-century paintings. On either side of the organ (by Gaetano Callido, 1801) are two dramatic 18th-century works: a *Crucifixion* by Girolamo Brusaferro and the *Stoning of St Stephen* by Sante Piatti. The altarpieces on the south side date from the 17th century: the *Adoration of the Magi* is by Giuseppe Diamantini and the *Invention of the True Cross* by Pietro Liberi. An extraordinary sculpted altarpiece fills the apse: this was installed in the early 18th century by Heinrich Meyring and shows *Moses Receiving the Tablets of the Law*. The numerous huge figures are arranged in front of a brown rock symbolising Mount Sinai. Below, the altar has a more successful marble relief of the *Worship of the Golden Calf*, also attributed to Meyring.

In the chapel to the right of the sanctuary there is a bronze altar frontal of the *Deposition*, a very crowded composition but technically extremely fine, by Niccolò and Sebastiano Roccatagliata (1633), restored in 2012.

Rio San Moisè is used as a mooring for gondolas, and the little *campiello* here has a good late 14th- or early 15th-century well-head with the Norman shields of the Pesaro family. The Bauer Hotel was built in 1949–54.

The broad **Calle Larga XXII Marzo**, whose name records the date of Manin's rebellion in 1848 (*see p. 123*), was widened in 1880 and is one of Venice's most important shopping streets. The tallest building is the Chamber of Commerce, with an Art Deco façade by the architect and engineer Camillo Puglisi Allegra: it was one of the first buildings in Venice to be constructed with a concrete base to support a load-bearing structure. The friezes and ornaments all have marine themes. On the opposite side, **Calle e Corte del Teatro San Moisè** recall the name of a theatre (demolished in the early 20th century) where Claudio Monteverdi's *Arianna* was performed at the inauguration in 1639. Goethe came here in 1786 and was unimpressed. 'The performance was bereft of ideas and was booed almost all the way through. But one or two of the dancers received rapturous applause. The girls seemed to think it their duty to display their comely bodies to the entire house.' In 1810 the young Rossini produced his first opera (*Cambiale di Matrimonio*) here and in 1896 the Lumière brothers gave their first film projection, using the cine camera they had invented in 1893.

The last *calle* on the left leads to a hotel in the Corte dei Due Pozzi, named after its two well-heads which have probably been here since the 14th century.

SANTA MARIA DEL GIGLIO
Map p. 406, C3. Open Mon–Sat 10–5; Chorus Pass.
This church is dedicated to the Madonna of the Lily ('*giglio*'). It is also known as Santa Maria Zobenigo, deriving from Jubanico, the name of a family who lived in this district before the 12th century. The façade, one of the best examples of the Venetian Baroque style, was built in Istrian stone and Carrara marble by Giuseppe Sardi in 1678–81 as a monument to the Barbaro family, who paid for the rebuilding of the church. It bears portraits of them by Juste le Court. In its unceasing battle against self-aggrandisement and the cult of heroes, the Republic didn't allow commemorative statues of its citizens to be erected, so wealthy families would sometimes donate money to churches and have statues of themselves installed as donors. The relief plans of Zara (Zadar), Candia (Herakleion), Padua, Rome, Corfu and Spalato (Split) record the victories of various members of the family in the service of the Republic.

GIUSEPPE SARDI
Sardi (1624–99) was born in Venice, where his father Antonio (from Ticino) was recognised as a skilled stonemason. Father and son worked together in the 1650s and '60s on the façades of the Scuola di San Teodoro and San Salvatore, and on the oval spiral staircase in the Ospedaletto. Giuseppe became a friend of the great architect Baldassare Longhena, and in 1683 he succeeded him as a procurator of St Mark's. Apart from the façade of Santa Maria del Giglio, usually considered his best work, he also built that of the Scalzi and San Lazzaro dei Mendicanti (following a design by his father). Baroque monuments by him are to be found in San Lazzaro dei Mendicanti and the Madonna dell'Orto, and he also built the high altar for San Pantalon.

SANTA MARIA DEL GIGLIO
Relief map of Corfu town, which became a Venetian
possession in 1401.

In the light interior, the 17th–18th-century paintings above the cornice of the nave and on the ceiling include works by Antonio Zanchi. You are allowed to go behind the high altar to see the two paintings of the four Evangelists in the sanctuary (beneath the organ), early works by Tintoretto made for the organ doors of the previous church and paid for by the procurator Giulio Contarini. Tintoretto also painted the altarpiece (unfortunately damaged during restoration) in the third north chapel showing *Christ with Sts Justina and Francesco da Paola*. This is an ex-voto commissioned by Francesco Duodo, commander of the Venetian fleet at the Battle of Lepanto in 1571, who was buried here in 1592. The fine 18th-century high altar has sculptures by Heinrich Meyring.

The evocative Cappella Molin, which displays the contents of the treasury, is especially interesting for the beautiful painting of the *Madonna and Child with the Young St John*. This is attributed by some scholars to Rubens, and certainly shows his influence (the great Flemish painter is known to have stopped in Venice in 1600 on his way to the court of Vincenzo Gonzaga in Mantua, on the first of many trips to Italy).

The sacristy (*only open on weekdays 10–11.30*) is a little 17th-century room with 16th- and 17th-century paintings.

The *campo* has a Verona marble well-head which may date from as early as the 14th century. On the Grand Canal there is a busy *traghetto* station beside the 15th-century Palazzo Pisani, occupied by the luxury **Hotel Gritti** (*see p. 355*). John and Effie Ruskin stayed here in 1851, the year that *The Stones of Venice* was published.

RUSKIN IN VENICE

The art critic John Ruskin (1819–1900) visited Venice for the first time in 1835. He had been inspired by the poems of Samuel Rogers, who had recreated in verse the dramatic story of Enrico Dandolo and the Fourth Crusade. Venice gave Ruskin a cause, an outlet for his aesthetic yearnings. Exploring the mass of surviving architecture, much of it in decay in what was by then an impoverished city, he was drawn irresistibly to the glories of the Venetian Gothic. While his wife Effie enjoyed tea parties and the attentions of Austrian officers, he spent hour after hour copying ornaments and tracery, in what became an obsession to record the city before, as he believed must happen, it vanished for ever.

For Ruskin, Gothic art was not enjoyable for itself; it was important because it brought out the creativity of the individual artisan, who had had the freedom to create his own interpretations of style. 'As long as the Gothic and other fine architecture existed, the love of Nature, which was an essential and peculiar feature of Christianity, found expression and food.' For Ruskin the Venetian Gothic and Venice's greatness as a Republic were inseparable. He argued that Venice's decline had begun in the 1420s (a view which there is some historical evidence to support), precisely as its art began to abandon the Gothic for the Renaissance.

The Stones of Venice was published between 1851 and 1853. The first volume deals with what Ruskin saw as the role of Christianity in 'colouring and spiritualising Roman or Heathen architecture'. It is also remarkable for its recognition of the influence of the Arab world on early Venetian architecture. ('The Venetians deserve especial note as the only European people who appear to have sympathised fully with the great instinct of the Eastern Races.') The second and third volumes are full of the drawings of arches and windows that he used to make his argument for the superiority of the style. He deplored the coming of the Renaissance: while 'the Gothic architecture of Venice had arisen out of, and indicated in all its features, a state of pure national faith, and of domestic virtue,' Venice's Renaissance architecture 'had arisen out of, and in all its features indicated, a state of concealed national infidelity, and of domestic corruption.' In his 'Index' of Venetian buildings he did not even include Sansovino's Loggetta, seen by most as one of the most charming pieces of Venetian architecture. Palladio aroused particular scorn for his cold formality.

Ruskin can be criticised for an obsessively romantic view, and for wanting to preserve Venice as if in aspic, even down to the marks on ancient marble (as he said of Palazzo Foscari, 'the beauty of it is in the cracks and the stains'); but no one did more to revive serious study in the Gothic. When the young Marcel Proust came across Ruskin's works on the French Gothic, it set him off to Venice to see 'the embodiment of Ruskin's ideas of domestic architecture in palaces that are crumbling, but which are still rose-coloured and still standing.'   C.F.

SAN MAURIZIO

From Santa Maria del Giglio a *calle* (signposted Accademia) leads across two bridges, the first one in the form of a particularly high semi-arch in order that boats can pass beneath it. Looking right from the second bridge you have a view of the pretty Ponte de la Malvasia Vecchia (1858), with a wrought-iron parapet decorated with marine monsters. The *calle* ends in the *campo* with the Neoclassical façade of the church of **San Maurizio** (*map p. 406, B2; closed to worship; there is a display of musical instruments inside; concerts are often held here*), begun in 1806 by Giovanni Antonio Selva and Antonio Diedo. The hexagonal well-head outside is dated 1521 and is decorated with the titular saint and festoons. The leaning brick campanile, which can be seen behind, belongs to Santo Stefano. Calle del Dose da Ponte leads down to a tiny *fondamenta* on the Grand Canal.

Calle del Piovan leads past the little building which used to house the **Scuola degli Albanesi** (1531), the meeting-place of the Albanian community established in this area by the end of the 15th century. There are Lombardesque reliefs on the façade. A bridge crosses the **Rio Santissimo**, named after the Host because it runs beneath the apse of Santo Stefano, which was supported on an arch over the water when it was extended in the 15th century. You can see a low bridge, surmounted by two windows, which once connected two wings of its convent.

SANTO STEFANO AND ITS CAMPO

The huge Campo Santo Stefano (or Campo Morosini; *map p. 406, B2–B3*) is one of the pleasantest squares in the city. The statue (by Francesco Barzaghi) of Niccolò Tommaseo (1802–74) was erected shortly after his death. He was an eminent man of letters who attacked the censorship laws imposed by the Austrians. He was arrested with Daniele Manin in 1848 and they were both exiled the following year.

The palaces in Campo Santo Stefano

The largest palace is the 17th-century **Palazzo Morosini** (no. 2802–3) which has a rusticated ground floor and a grand side entrance decorated with battle trophies. This was the home of Francesco Morosini, the admiral famous for his victory over the Turks in the Peloponnese (*see p. 75*) and who served as doge from 1688–94. It faces the long **Palazzo Loredan** (no. 2945), whose Gothic structure was remodelled after 1536 by Scarpagnino. The Palladian façade on the north end was added by Giovanni Grapiglia. Since 1891 it has been occupied by the Istituto Veneto di Scienze, Lettere ed Arti, an academy of arts and sciences founded by Ferdinand I of Austria in 1838, which has an important library. The Institute also owns **Palazzo Cavalli-Franchetti**, remodelled in the 17th century, behind its large garden protected by railings. It was owned by Archduke Frederick of Austria in 1840, and after his death in 1847 by the Comte de Chambord (heir to Charles X), who lived here until 1866. He entrusted Giambattista Meduna to restore it and create the garden on the Grand Canal. In 1878 the palace was acquired by Baron Raimondo Franchetti, and it remained in the Franchetti family until 1922. In this period it was remodelled in medieval style by Camillo Boito, including the neo-Gothic façade and new wing and interior staircase. At the same time the pesudo-Gothic well-head was set up in the courtyard (which you can see through the gate). Exhibitions and lectures are held here, and it has a pleasant café.

The corner of the *campo* behind Palazzo Cavalli-Franchetti is filled by the imposing **Palazzo Pisani**, which since the beginning of the 20th century has housed the Conservatory of Music, named after the composer Benedetto Marcello (1686–1739; *see p. 224*). This remarkable building, one of the largest private palaces in Venice, perhaps on a design by Vincenzo Scamozzi (1599), was continued in 1728 by Girolamo Frigimelica Roberti, an architect from Padua. They each built one of the two interior courtyards, and Frigimelica added the huge open-arched loggia to connect them. The palace, with its fine stuccoes and painted ceilings by pupils of Tiepolo including Guarana, can be seen on guided tours by appointment. Concerts (*for information, see amici.conservatorio@conseve.it, or T: 041 522 5604*) are given in the spring and summer either in the courtyard or the huge ballroom, a remarkable neo-Palladian 'Egyptian' room, built a few years before Lord Burlington's Chiswick House. We know that the Earl, then still Richard Boyle, visited Venice in the 1720s, where he had his portrait painted.

The church of Santo Stefano
Map p. 406, B2. Open Mon–Sat 8–7; museum 10–5 with Chorus Pass.
The early Gothic church of Santo Stefano was rebuilt in the 14th century and altered in the 15th. The brick façade bears a portal in the florid Gothic style. The lovely light Gothic interior, with three apses, has tall columns alternately of Greek and red Verona marble. The wonderful tricuspid wooden roof is thought to have been built by Fra' Giovanni, known as 'degli Eremitani', since he was the architect of the church of the Eremitani in Padua. It is in the form of a ship's keel and is a vivid demonstration of the skill of Venetian carpenters, who for centuries supplied the Republic with seaworthy ships for her great fleet.

In the pavement at the beginning of the nave is the imposing sepulchral seal, the largest in Venice, of Francesco Morosini (whose palace stands in the *campo* outside; *see above*): this was cast by Filippo Parodi, who had also made the bust for the triumphal arch erected in his honour in the Doge's Palace. Above the west door is the funerary monument of a general, Domenico Contarini (not the doge of the same name), erected in 1650 and including an anachronistic wooden equestrian statue which makes Contarini look slightly ridiculous. The largest monument on the west wall is that of Giacomo Surian, a physician and philosopher, erected in 1493. The sarcophagus is born by two griffins, and the fine Renaissance elements are derived from Pietro Lombardo.

On the walls of the sanctuary are two 15th-century carved marble screens, fine Renaissance works, with statues in niches by Giovanni Buora. The two bronze candelabra are by Alessandro Vittoria.

The **museum** is arranged in the sacristy and adjacent cloister (*entered off the south aisle*). The *Last Supper* by Tintoretto is displayed opposite his *Prayer in the Garden*. Here the typical chiaroscuro effects he uses are dramatically seen: light glimmers only on the bald heads of the disciples, and on the edges of the leaves and grass stems ethereally illuminated. A strange dog is sketched on the steps of the *Last Supper*. Over the altar is a *Crucifixion* by Giuseppe Angeli flanked by two saints in Gothic frames by Bartolomeo Vivarini. Above is a huge painting of the *Martyrdom of St Stephen*, left unfinished around 1630 by Sante Peranda.

In the tiny cloister, where the well-head has a snake (or dragon) biting its tail, are displayed some beautiful sculptures. The earliest are two wood statuettes of *St Andrew*

SANTO STEFANO
Canova's funerary monument to his first patron,
Giovanni Falier.

and *St Jerome* by a master from Strasbourg who worked on the Frari choir stalls, and marble statuettes (c. 1395) of *St John the Baptist* and *St Anthony of Padua* by Jacobello and Pier Paolo dalle Masegne. The sculptures by Pietro Lombardo and assistants include *St Andrew* and *St Jerome* from the Corbelli altar in the church, where the statue of *St Nicholas of Tolentino* by him is still *in situ*. The two statuettes from the stoups of the church are also kept here: *St John the Baptist* by Giovanni Maria Mosca, and an allegorical statue of *Wisdom* attributed to Giovanni Buora. The funerary stele of Giovanni Falier is by Antonio Canova (1808)—Falier was the artist's first patron. There is a very fine high relief of a young saint by Pietro's son Tullio.

Campo Sant'Angelo

Opposite the façade of Santo Stefano, Calle del Pestrin leads past an unusual raised *campo* to a doorway, decorated with two putti holding a shield with the emblem of the Lezze family beneath an angel, which leads into the charming little **Corte de le Pizzocchere**. The late-15th century well-head bears two very worn Lezze shields and rosettes. The Lezze used to live in this quiet corner of Venice, and they let tertiary nuns of the Augustinian order (known as *Pizzocchere*) stay in some property they owned.

Leading west from Santo Stefano, a wide bridge with a beautiful wrought-iron balustrade (beside another fine bridge in Istrian stone) leads to **Campo Sant'Angelo** (*map* *p. 406, B2*). The former convent of Santo Stefano (now a tax office) fills one side of it, its door surmounted by a lunette with a 15th-century relief of St Augustine and monks. There is a view of the fine tower of Santo Stefano—the most oblique of the many leaning towers of Venice—and the vault supporting the east end of the church can also be seen here above a canal. The little church of **Sant'Angelo degli Zoppi** (or the Oratorio dell'Annunziata) contains a large wooden Crucifix (16th century) surrounded with ex-votos and a 17th-century *Annunciation* attributed to Antonio Triva. It was used by a confraternity (of the *Zoppi*, or 'lame'), which offered assistance to disabled sailors. Outside by the kiosk, the well-head, which dates from just before 1500, has a scene of the *Annunciation*. Among the fine palaces here is the Gothic **Palazzo Duodo** (no. 3584), once the Tre Stelle inn, in which the composer Domenico Cimarosa died in 1801. It faces the Gothic Palazzo Gritti (no. 3832).

SAN VITALE
Map p. 406, B3. Open 9.30–6; used for concerts.
The church, known in Venetian as San Vidal, was founded in the 11th century and rebuilt in the 12th with a characteristic campanile incorporating an antique Roman inscription.

The monumental façade by Andrea Tirali dates from 1734–7. The interior, decorated in 1696, has a high altarpiece of *San Vitale*, shown on a splendid grey charger, painted by Carpaccio and signed and dated 1514. Vitale (or Vitalis of Milan) is shown here with Sts James, John the Baptist and George, and a female saint thought to represent his wife, St Valeria. On the balcony above are St Andrew and St Peter with Vitale and Valeria's children Gervase and Protase being entertained by a little nude putto. Despite his triumphant appearance here, Vitale, once believed to have been a soldier in the army of Nero, is now thought never to have existed and his cultus was suppressed in 1969. The altarpiece of the *Archangel Raphael, St Louis Gonzaga and St Anthony of Padua* on the third south altar is by Giovanni Battista Piazzetta, and that on the second north altar (the *Crucifix and Apostles*) by a pupil of his, Giulia Lama, one of the few women painters known to have worked in Venice. The *Immacolata*, with a dragon at her feet, on the third north altar, is by Sebastiano Ricci.

BETWEEN THE ACCADEMIA BRIDGE & PALAZZO GRASSI

At the foot of the Accademia Bridge is Campo San Vidal (*map p. 406, B3*), with a 16th-century well-head. It features in Canaletto's famous painting *The Stonemason's Yard* (now in the National Gallery, London), painted c. 1727, which depicts the view from here looking across the Grand Canal to the buildings of Santa Maria della Carità (now the Gallerie dell'Accademia). Today there

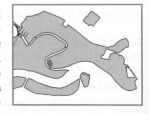

is a little garden and gondola stand here, and it is always busy with people hurrying to and from the Accademia Bridge. Yet very close by there are peaceful little corners.

Cross the *rio* into Calle Giustinian, which skirts the huge bare wall of **Palazzo Giustiniani-Lolin** to end by its grand façade by Longhena with huge mascarons right on the Grand Canal. It was standard practice for the owners of palaces to pay only for the public façade to be decorated. The building is now owned by a music study centre. At the other end of the *calle*, take Calle del Frutarol left. The next *calle*, Vetturi (or Falier), ends at steps directly down to the Grand Canal by the charming 15th-century Gothic **Palazzetto Falier**, with a little garden and two projecting *logge* (or *liagò*), rare survivals of what used to be a characteristic feature of Venetian houses. Here a plaque records the writer William Dean Howells (1837–1920), who was US consul in Venice from 1861–5. In his *Venetian Life* (1866) he records his 'dear little balcony' here, where he lived with his wife Elinor Mead. His novel *A Fearful Responsibility* describes the period in which he lived in Venice under Austrian rule.

Calle del Frutarol continues across a *rio* and turns into Calle Malipiero, which emerges by the flank of the church of **San Samuele**, in front of a well and a side chapel which has a charming statuette of the *Madonna and Child* over its door. The church (*closed to worship; sometimes used for concerts and lectures*) preserves its lovely old 12th-century campanile. A plaque on a house records the death here in 1948 of the Venetian composer Ermanno Wolf-Ferrari. Campo San Samuele, with a few young trees and wooden benches, opens onto the Grand Canal and there is a *traghetto* across to San Barnaba, as well as a vaporetto landing-stage and a good view of Ca' Rezzonico on the opposite bank. The well-head bears very worn shields of officials of the Republic.

PALAZZO GRASSI (FRANÇOIS PINAULT FOUNDATION)
Map p. 406, A2. Open 10–7 except Tues.
This imposing palace was built by Giorgio Massari in 1748 for Angelo Grassi, son of Paolo, who had contributed a huge sum of money to support the Venetian war against the Turks in the Peloponnese and whose family was one of the richest in Venice by the end of the century. When it was bought in 1984 by the Fiat organisation, it was radically restored (partly by Gae Aulenti) as a cultural centre, and important exhibitions were held here in the 1980s and 1990s. It was then sold to François Pinault, a wealthy French collector (and owner, among other businesses, of Christie's and the fashion houses of Gucci and Yves Saint Laurent), who had the Japanese architect Tadao Ando redesign the interior before it was re-opened in 2006. Changing exhibitions here show works mostly from Pinault's own huge collection of contemporary art. The only decorations which survive from the 18th century are on the grand staircase: the frescoes with carnival scenes are attributed to Alessandro Longhi.

Beside the façade of Palazzo Grassi, **Calle de le Carrozze** leads past the small raised theatre in its garden, which has been restored by the Pinault foundation. On the house at no. 3220 there is a relief of *St George and the Dragon* and Byzantine roundels of animals and birds. It is worth exploring **Calle and Corte Lezze** on the left, a very peaceful cul-de-sac with simple little houses in good condition with typical chimney pots and roof terraces, and several pretty gardens behind walls. The *calle* ends in Salizzada San Samuele beside the **ex-Scuola dei Mureri** (or *Muratori*, builders) which has an oblong relief high up on the façade carved with instruments of the trade (a hammer, trowel and mason's level). Its (damaged) name survives on the lintel above the doorway. The lovely simple house at no. 3337 bears a plaque recording that the great Venetian painter Veronese died here in 1588. The *piano nobile* has beautiful carved marble windows with reliefs and a simple little balcony. The Verona marble well-head outside survives from the early 14th century.

Ramo de la Piscina leads out of the far end of the *salizzada* into the curiously shaped **Piscina San Samuele**, its wide, oblong space unique in Venice. Keep left and Calle del Traghetto (or di Ca' Garzoni) leads down to a *traghetto* over the Grand Canal; or you can cross the bridge and follow the *rio* to Corte de l'Albero with the Sant'Angelo vaporetto landing stage.

LA FENICE & MUSEO FORTUNY

LA FENICE

Map p. 406, C2. The theatre can be visited daily 9.30–6 with an audio guide in English. For further information see www.festfenice.com.

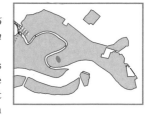

La Fenice is one of the most important opera houses in Italy. It received its name, meaning 'Phoenix' (the mythical bird which rose from the flames), because it replaces a theatre destroyed by fire: San Benedetto—then one of seven theatres in Venice—which burned down in 1773. The fine Neoclassical building was commissioned by the Venier family from Giovanni Antonio Selva in 1786 and inaugurated in 1792 with *I Giuochi d'Agrigento* by Giovanni Paisiello. It was the first theatre in the city to be provided with a small *campo* (the other theatres were more or less hidden away so as not to attract the attention of the authorities). It was also given a water-gate to allow easy access for the scenery, performers and the public. When the theatre had to be rebuilt after a fire in 1836, it was designed on the same lines by Giambattista Meduna, and was again restored in 1854.

Another fire in 1996, caused by arson, destroyed eighty percent of the building, leaving only the walls of the auditorium and part of the foyer standing. The immediate decision was taken to rebuild a replica, which opened in 2004. The only modifications made were the pastel green colour (instead of beige) of the walls of the boxes, the wooden floor in the stalls (beneath which an up-to-date air conditioning and heating system was installed), the moveable orchestra podium, and an electronic system for scene changes. There are also three new rehearsal rooms (posthumous works by the architect Aldo Rossi, who died in 1997), one of which has a reproduction of Palladio's Basilica in Vicenza, and more off-stage space for the performers. The theatre today has a seating capacity of 1,076.

OPERA AT LA FENICE

La Fenice is famous in the history of operatic art. Domenico Cimarosa's *Gli Orazi e i Curiazi* was performed here in 1796 (the composer died in exile in Venice in 1801). The première of Rossini's *Tancredi* took place here in 1813, and many of Verdi's operas had their opening nights at the Fenice: *Rigoletto* was received with great enthusiasm in 1851, but *La Traviata*, which was written for the Fenice, had a disastrous reception in 1853. Verdi subsequently altered its happy ending to a tragic one, but it was the original opera (in the Venetian version) that was chosen to be performed in November 2004 at the reopening of the theatre. Other historic performances included Bellini's *I Capuleti e i Montecchi* (1830) and works by Donizetti and Wagner (including *Rienzi* in 1874).

In the 20th century Stravinsky's *The Rake's Progress* (1951) and Benjamin Britten's *The Turn of the Screw* both had their first nights here. Britten also composed *Curlew River* (1964) and much of *The Prodigal Son* (1968) during stays in Venice. The first Italian performance of *Intolleranza*, by the Venetian composer Luigi Nono (1924–90), was given here in 1961. Other composers whose works had first performances here include Gian Francesco Malipiero, Alban Berg, Prokofiev, Luciano Berio and Paul Hindemith.

The Fenice also became the centre of the political life of the city after the fall of the Republic in 1797. Verdi became a symbol in the struggle against the Austrians, who in 1851 attempted to censor his *Rigoletto*. From 1859–66 the theatre was closed by popular request, as a demonstration of the gloom felt under foreign dominion. When Verdi's name was acclaimed at performances, it was understood to signify support for the Italian king: the letters of his name were an acronym for 'Vittorio Emanuele Re d'Italia'. The theatre was privately owned up until 1935, and in order to make ends meet, it was also used for balls or for the game of *tombola* (It was for this reason that the clock was installed above the stage).

Tour of the theatre

In the foyer the reconstruction work has been carefully integrated (in a slightly different colour) with the decorations which survived the fire. Upstairs, in the corridor outside the boxes, is the interesting original wooden model of the theatre made by Selva himself. The grand Royal Box was first built for Napoleon in 1807. You can also visit the stalls when rehearsals are not in progress. The reception rooms include a billiard room and a ballroom as well as a café.

SAN LUCA

Map p. 406, C1.

The church of San Luca contains a damaged high altarpiece by Veronese and (on the first south altar) a 15th-century high relief of the *Madonna and Child Enthroned*, in terracotta. The famous writer Pietro Aretino was buried here in 1556. Known as 'the scourge of princes', he enjoyed poking fun at the rulers of his day, who came to fear his sharp tongue and outspoken manner. He had a scurrilous reputation: self styled as 'a gift to courtesans', he is said to have lived in Venice with numerous concubines. He is also remembered as the great friend and protector of Titian, who painted the writer's portrait several times (the most famous of which is now in the Uffizi in Florence). Edward Hutton, in his 1922 biography of Aretino, declared: 'He was a monster, it is true: to deny that is to belittle him: but above all he was a man of his day, perhaps the most free and complete expression of the age in which he lived—the 16th century. That, and his enormous ability, together with the fact that he founded the modern Press and used the hitherto unsuspected weapon of publicity with an incomparable appreciation of its power, are his chief claims upon our notice.'

In the *campo*, the building at no. 4038 bears a very unusual pointed brick archway bearing a pair of peacocks.

MUSEO FORTUNY

Map p. 406, C2–B2. Open Tues–Sun 10–6; T: 041 520 0995. Exhibitions are frequently held here.

The 15th-century Palazzo Pesaro degli Orfei, with a magnificent Gothic exterior, was, from 1930, the home of the Spanish painter Mariano Fortuny (1871–1949), who designed the famous Fortuny fabrics here. His gorgeous silks and velvets were derived from ancient Venetian designs, and he set up a factory on the Giudecca (near the Mulino Stucky; *see p. 311*), which is still in operation. He was also a pioneer in costume design, stage sets and lighting for the theatre. The house was left to the city in 1956 by Fortuny's widow. His huge atelier on the first floor has a remarkable *fin de siècle* atmosphere and is filled with curios. The walls are lined with the beautiful fabrics he designed and the lamps he invented for stage lighting are still here. Paintings include a self-portrait of 1890 and portraits of Henriette Nigrin, whom he married in 1924, painted between 1909 and 1930. A case displays portrait busts of his family by the Neapolitan sculptor Vincenzo Gemito.

Off the atelier a room displays paintings by Fortuny's father (including a copy from Goya) and a huge terracotta portrait bust of him by Gemito. In another room are hung photographs taken by Fortuny in 1907 with an Eastman Kodak panoramic camera, as well as photos of the palace in the 1890s (the museum owns some 11,000 negatives). The original model for an extraordinary theatre designed by Fortuny, together with Gabriele d'Annunzio and Lucien Hesse, in 1912 has recently been restored and is on display.

On the ground floor there is a colourful plexiglass door designed by Francesco Candeloro (2010) at the water-gate, and you can sit in peace in the lovely old courtyard, which has an old wooden staircase and loggia, and a venerable wisteria which climbs all the way up the building.

A WALK THROUGH SAN MARCO

This guided walk explores a number of peaceful little courtyards, some with particularly interesting well-heads, and includes a detour to see the outside stair of the famous Palazzo Contarini del Bovolo, as well as memorials to the hero Manin, and the pretty Campo San Fantin.

ON THE NORTH SIDE OF PIAZZA SAN Marco, beneath the portico of the Procuratie Vecchie, at no. 101, is the attractive little **Olivetti showroom** (where the earliest Olivetti typewriters are on show), designed on two levels in 1957 by the Venetian architect Carlo Scarpa with an ingenious staircase and mosaic floor. You can appreciate his typical careful choice of materials including teak, marble, stucco and bevelled glass. Since 2011 it has been owned by the FAI foundation which aims to safeguard Italy's artistic heritage (*open April–Oct 11–6.30, winter 11– 4.30; closed Mon*).

Sottoportego del Cavaletto skirts the interesting side of the building and from the bridge there is a view left of the **Bacino Orseolo**, named after Doge Pietro Orseolo II, who founded a hospice for pilgrims here in 977: today it is usually filled with tourists brought here to board their gondolas. The circular pool is overlooked by Venice's Hard Rock Café.

Continue through Campo San Gallo and take Calle San Gallo right to **Calle dei Fabbri**, a long thoroughfare busy with tourists and lined with souvenir shops (it is used as a route from San Marco to the Rialto). Just to the left is Rio Terrà delle Colonne, with Venchi, specialists in chocolate. If you follow the Rio Terrà to the right, with its portico of wooden eaves and square

stone columns, you come to the lovely old Sottoportego degli Armeni, beneath which is the inconspicuous entrance to the little church of **Santa Croce degli Armeni**, dating from 1496 but rebuilt in the 17th century (*service in Armenian on last Sun of the month at 10.30*). The Armenian community in Venice lived in this charming district from the late 12th century onwards, and they were allowed to build a small *fondaco* on the Rio dei Ferai (from which the little cupola with a lantern and small bell-tower can be seen).

Return to Calle dei Fabbri and continue towards the Rialto, ducking right down Calle Gregolina at the end of which, in a secluded courtyard, there is another view of the campanile of Santa Croce degli Armeni and a delightful, unusual well-head (c. 1475) decorated with carved designs of knotted ropes and wicker-work.

Return to Calle dei Fabbri and cross Ponte delle Pignate, continue past Calle del Gambaro with its wood and marble eaves (it ends on a *rio*), and (some way further on) past several bookshops, including the Goldoni at no. 4742, and a few food shops. Go left into Calle San Luca, which leads into **Campo San Luca**, overlooked (from the façade of Ca' Bortoluzzi-Grillo) by a curiously sombre *Madonna* made in 1913. Calle dei Fuseri leads south out of the *campo*. Take it, and then the first right, Calle

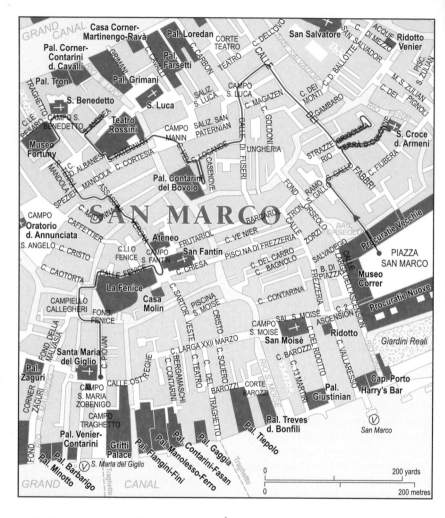

delle Locande (or de la Vida), past **Ramo de le Case Nove**, which is one of the few *calli* which has been left abandoned (showing just how much work is needed to preserve the Venice we enjoy today).

The next *calle*, also on the left, leads to a court from which you can see the celebrated external spiral staircase and loggia of **Palazzo Contarini del Bovolo**. The name *bovolo* means 'snail

shell', recalling the remarkable design of the staircase, which was erected by a local master mason called Giovanni Candi (c. 1499), otherwise unknown. Eight well-heads from various places in the city are preserved in the picturesque little garden: one dating from the 16th century is carved with a stylised design of both the leaves and berries of the laurel tree.

At the end of Calle Locande is **Campo Manin**, strangely modern and urban-looking, and un-Venetian. It was created in 1870 after the campanile and church of San Paternian had been demolished, and a monument by Luigi Borro was set up to commemorate Daniele Manin, whose family house was here (the red palace on the *rio*, which bears a plaque). A diagram in the pavement shows the piazza and church before the 19th-century alterations. The disappointing bank building was erected in 1964 by Pier Luigi Nervi and Angelo Scattolin (it is better inside).

DANIELE MANIN AND HIS REVOLUTION

Daniele Manin was a Venetian lawyer, Jewish by descent on his father's side. When his paternal grandparents converted to Catholicism, they had assumed the name of their sponsor, a brother of Lodovico Manin, who was later to become Venice's last doge. Daniele is remembered as leader of a glorious, if short-lived, republic after his successful rebellion against the Austrians, who had ruled Venice since 1815. Fearing his popularity, the Austrians had him imprisoned in 1848, but the same year, after an almost bloodless revolution, he became president of a new provisional government. Through his prudent leadership and his insistence on order he managed to remain in power for almost a year, holding out against a ruthless Austrian siege, during which the city was subjected to the first air-raid in history, when bombs were dropped from balloons by means of pre-set fuses (they luckily caused very little damage as they either burst or were blown away by the wind). Manin was forced to surrender to the Habsburg power in August 1849, and was sent with his family into exile: he died in poverty in Paris in 1857, aged 53. Perhaps because of his lack of charisma—small of stature as he was, often suffering from poor health, and devoted above all to his family—he and his revolution immediately went down in history as of little significance to the Italian Risorgimento compared with the exploits of his more famous contemporaries Mazzini and Garibaldi. It is only recently that his role began to be recognised. He was a particularly courageous and upright figure, dedicated to a cause which he believed to be noble and right. The Venetians themselves saw to it that he had a fitting tomb at St Mark's (*see p. 54*), and, besides the *campo* that bears his name, he is also commemorated in the name of the Calle Larga XXII Marzo, the date of his revolution.

From the northwest corner of Campo Manin, take Ponte San Paternian and continue along a *calle*, turning right to skirt the huge Teatro Rossini (now a cinema) and then turn right into Calle di Sant'Andrea, which leads to **Corte Sant'Andrea** with a graceful Gothic well-head and a charming relief dating from 1356 of St Andrew between two kneeling monks. Retracing your steps, turn right into the little Campo San Benedetto, which has its pavement raised around its well-head. The church is closed to worship but here is the splendid main façade of the grand 15th-century Palazzo Pesaro degli Orfei, now the seat of the **Museo Fortuny** (*for visitor information and details, see p. 120. The museum has a particularly pleasant courtyard where you can sit and relax*).

charming Renaissance church of San Fantin (*closed to worship*), probably by Scarpagnino (1507–49). It has a beautiful domed sanctuary and apse, attributed to Jacopo Sansovino (1549–63). The **Ateneo Veneto** has occupied the Scuola di San Fantin since 1811 (*used for conferences; for admission see info@ateneoveneto.org or T: 041 522 4459*). It has an Istrian stone façade by collaborators of Alessandro Vittoria, and contains paintings by Paolo Veronese and his school, and a bronze portrait bust of Tommaso Rangone by Alessandro Vittoria. Rangone was a wealthy physician and this is one of at least three portraits of him by Vittoria in this *sestiere*. There is a bust in the Museo Correr and another likeness, a seated bronze statue, surmounting the entrance to the church of San Giuliano (San Zulian).

The well-head sitting on top of a high base has a mill-wheel, the emblem of the Molin family; the well-head in front of the Fenice (which is sunk into the pavement) has shields and a rampant lion and cabbage leaves at the corners, while the one hidden amongst the tables of the *trattoria* is a simple cylinder with coats of arms.

The mill-wheel of the Molin is repeated in a beautiful relief (which includes a blessing angel and two dragons with knotted tails spitting fire at each other) on the brick wall of the **Casa Molin** in Corte San Gaetano opposite the left side of the Fenice. The palace is in very good condition, with a lovely Gothic outside stair, pretty lanterns and Byzantine roundels. High up on a wing of the palace which adjoins the Fenice is another large relief of birds and a Cross.

From here, take Calle de la Fenice

From Campo San Benedetto, take Calle and Ramo Orfei past a little hotel into the wide **Rio Terrà de la Mandola**. Here an arch leads into the old Corte Barbarigo, with its 15th-century well-head. Cross Calle de la Mandola, which has a few local shops (there is a view right of Campo Sant'Angelo; *described on p. 115*). Straight ahead, you join Rio Terrà dei Assassini (which has a second-hand bookshop) and then turn right into Calle de la Verona. On the left a very low passageway leads into the Corte Balbi (or Morosini) beneath an old palace with wooden eaves. Beyond a bridge (note the mascaron on the palace here), the *calle* continues past the side of the Ateneo Veneto to emerge in **Campo San Fantin**.

The *campo*, which boasts a marble rather than a painted nameplate, has three very imposing buildings: the famous Fenice Theatre (*see p. 118*), the Ateneo Veneto, and the along the right flank of the famous theatre. In **Campiello della Fenice** a small building (now part of a hotel) records, once again, the hero Manin (*see above*), specifically Venice's investiture in him of unlimited powers to resist the Austrians 'at all costs'. A marble lion looks down from the terrace and bronze cannon and cannon balls flank the door, and even a window frame is made from cannon. Another inscription celebrates the Venetians themselves and their heroic resistance in 1849, and (in the *campo*) a plaque recounts the valour of the honest citizens of Venice during the First World War.

The *calle* continues past several side entrances to the upper circles of the Fenice. In Corte del Tagliapietra on the right, a lovely simple well-head on a circular base can be seen. The *calle* brings you out onto a *rio*. Skirt it along the lovely *sottoportego* supported by old columns (and with a mosaic *St Christopher*) in full view of a beautiful small Gothic palace on the water, well seen also from the *fondamenta* across the bridge. Keep left for the Campiello dei Callegheri ,which has another pretty well-head with two shields and a bizarre mascaron over the door at no. 2569.

Cross Ponte Storto. From Fondamenta Fenice there is a good view of the Fenice with its water-gate and circular tower (which encloses a staircase) and the bridge which leads over to it and which has recently been renamed after Maria Callas, who often sang here between 1947 and 1954.

Calle Piovan leads directly south to Campo Santa Maria Zobenigo, which has the church of Santa Maria del Giglio (*described on p 110*) as well as a vaporetto landing-stage and *traghetto* across the Grand Canal.

RIALTO BRIDGE
Detail of the Angel Gabriel by Agostino Rubini (16th century).

The Grand Canal

The Grand Canal, over 3km long, is the main thoroughfare of Venice. This splendid waterway, winding like an inverted S through the city, is filled with every kind of boat, from water-buses (vaporetti) to motorboats, barges, sandoli propelled by oars, and gondolas. It is lined on either side with a continuous row of beautiful old buildings, including more than 100 palaces, the most important of which date from the 13th to the 17th centuries. The canal follows the old course of a branch of the Brenta as far as the Rialto,

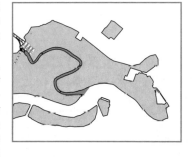

This chapter follows the Grand Canal as it is seen and appreciated from the water: the right bank is followed from San Marco to the railway station, and the opposite bank from the station back to San Marco. The comfortable vaporetto no. 1 travels slowly along the Canal, giving time to enjoy the magnificent scene, as well as the constant activity of the many types of boat on the water. It also provides an insight into the everyday life of the Venetians: from the extremely courteous and efficient sailors who run the water-buses to the local passengers, who stand out for their elegant dress and their quickened pace the moment they set foot on the bank.

ARCHITECTURE ON THE GRAND CANAL

The architectural styles of the palaces usually betray their date. The earliest, dating from the 13th century and known as 'Veneto-Byzantine', still have narrow, rounded, stilted arches at water level and similar windows on the first floors, their shape copied from Byzantine buildings in the East. These façades are sometimes decorated with carved paterae, also typical of Constantinople. Unfortunately some of these venerable buildings were over-restored in the 19th century. As the round arches become more pointed, so the buildings take on a Gothic appearance and, as Ruskin noted with great precision, there are numerous varieties of these Gothic shapes in the windows of Venetian palaces. Venetian Gothic, one of the most characteristic styles to be found on *palazzi* all over the city, lasted throughout the 14th and for most of the 15th centuries,

| VENETO-BYZANTINE | VENETIAN GOTHIC | SANSOVINIAN 'ROMAN' STYLE |
| 1200s | 14TH–15TH CENTURIES | FROM MID-16TH CENTURY |

and there are many delightful examples of this style in the palaces lining the Grand Canal (although very seldom do we know the name of the architect). In the late 15th century a few palace fronts were covered with very fine marble decorations. At the beginning of the 16th century it was Mauro Codussi who grasped the advantages of using Istrian stone to create monumental façades, and from then on the grandest palaces were constructed in this white stone which makes them ever more prominent. In the mid-16th century Jacopo Sansovino introduced an innovative style which he had learnt in Rome and which was to be copied frequently in later centuries. In the 17th century Longhena built some of the last great palaces on the Grand Canal, as well as the wonderful church of the Salute, at the point where this great waterway enters the basin of St Mark's.

FROM SAN MARCO TO FERROVIA (RIGHT BANK)

SAN ZACCARIA LANDING-STAGE

From Riva degli Schiavoni, the *vaporetti* always steer right out into the Bacino di San Marco to avoid disturbing the gondolas moored at the water's edge (and now protected by a floating barrage). From the water there is a wonderful view of the city's most famous stretch of waterfront, which was the entrance to Venice in Republican days.

SAN MARCO LANDING-STAGE

At the entrance to the Grand Canal, between the Hotel Monaco and the Hotel Bauer, is the splendid 15th-century Gothic **Palazzo Giustinian**, which now houses the Biennale headquarters. In the 19th century it was the Hotel Europa: among its illustrious guests were Verdi, Ruskin and Proust. Turner stayed here on his last two visits to the city in 1833 and 1840. He saw Venice for the first time in 1819, but even though none of his stays exceeded more than a few weeks he made hundreds of paintings, watercolours and sketches of the city (many of which he reworked when he returned to England). His portrayal of the water and light of Venice, infused with a unique sense of irreality, informed people's image of Venice for generations. It is perhaps above all his watercolours which provide the most accurate and sensitive picture of his time here. Not surprisingly, perhaps, since he lodged at the Europa, many of his views are of the Salute church across the water.

Across Rio di San Moisè is the plain Classical façade of the 17th-century **Palazzo Treves de' Bonfili**, attributed to Bartolomeo Monopola. **Palazzo Tiepolo** (also 17th century) is now occupied by the Europa and Regina Hotel. There follows **Palazzo Gaggia**, with its tall chimney pots, formerly Ca' Alvisi, where Browning often stayed (*see pp. 180–1*), and next to the 15th-century Palazzo Contarini is the exquisite tiny **Palazzo Contarini-Fasan**, of the same date, with lovely stone balconies with wheel tracery. Its unusual slim form is explained by the fact that it was once a tower, and a chain used to be suspended from the building and stretched across to this bank of the canal in order to close it in times of danger.

Palazzo Manolesso-Ferro (also 15th-century Gothic) has been converted into offices for the Veneto Region. **Palazzo Flangini-Fini** dates from much later (1688) and is attributed to Alessandro Tremignon. Beyond the *rio* is the 15th-century Palazzo Pisani, now the **Gritti Palace**, one of Venice's most famous luxury hotels, with a delightful terrace restaurant on the canal.

SANTA MARIA DEL GIGLIO LANDING-STAGE

The 17th-century **Palazzo Venier-Contarini** is by the landing-stage. Across the *rio*, another 17th-century palace, the **Palazzo Barbarigo**, adjoins the 15th-century Gothic **Palazzo Minotto**, which has a delightful medley of balconies and a little wooden terrace. In 1744 when Pietro Barbarigo lived here he commissioned Giambattista Tiepolo to paint two rooms of the palace: an oval fresco of *Time discovering Truth* survives here, and the others can be seen in Ca' Rezzonico, where they were taken in 1936 (*see p. 171*). Next rises the huge **Palazzo Corner**, also called Ca' Grande, a dignified edifice in the full Renaissance style commissioned from Jacopo Sansovino in 1537 by the Corner family just five years after their Gothic palace on this site had been destroyed by fire. Building began in 1545. Above the rusticated ground floor, with steps leading down into the water, are the Ionic and Corinthian upper storeys, with double columns flanking typical Venetian windows. It is now occupied by the Prefecture. Behind the little garden can be glimpsed the **Casetta delle Rose**, where Canova had his studio and where the martial poet Gabriele d'Annunzio lived during the First World War. Eleonora Duse (who was from Chioggia, where her parents were involved in the theatre) lived here during her affair with d'Annunzio. She was admired for her talent as an actress by both Bernard Shaw and Anton Chekhov.

Beyond a narrow *rio* are the two **Palazzi Barbaro**, one 17th-century and the other 15th-century Gothic, decorated with marbles and carvings. Purchased by the Curtis family in 1885, Henry James often stayed here (*see p. 177*).

Across the *rio* is **Palazzo Cavalli-Franchetti**, a sumptuous building with a garden (on the site of a *squero*), restored in 1878 in neo-medieval style for Baron Franchetti (it now belongs to the Istituto Veneto; *see p. 113*). Behind it rises the ancient brick campanile of San Vitale.

The wooden **Ponte dell'Accademia** was built in 1932–3 by Eugenio Miozzi to replace an elaborate iron bridge designed by an Englishman, Alfred Neville, in 1854. The present structure, partly in iron, is an exact replica (made in 1986) of Miozzi's original. Beyond Casa Civran-Badoer, with a small garden, stands **Palazzo Giustiniani-Lolin** (marked by its two pinnacles), an early work by Longhena (1623). Next comes the 15th-century Gothic **Palazzetto Falier**, with two protruding *logge* (or *liagò*). Across the *rio* is a plain palace which has one corner on the water rusticated in bright white diamond-shaped blocks of Istrian stone: this is the **Ca' del Duca**, begun in the mid-15th century but never completed. In 1457 Andrea Cornaro commissioned Bartolomeo Bon to build a grand palace here which was to be entirely faced with Istrian stone, but just a few years later the site was sold to Francesco Sforza, the Duke of Milan (hence its name), but he also withdrew from the project, so that ever since it has been left as it was, with just one corner faced with Istrian stone. Steps lead down to the water where an archway leads into a pretty little *campo*.

Beyond is the lovely garden, with statuary, of **Palazzo Cappello-Malipiero**, rebuilt in 1622. On the other side of Campo di San Samuele, the 12th-century campanile of the church can be seen (*NB: The San Samuele landing-stage is not used by vaporetto no. 1*). Here is the vast 18th- century **Palazzo Grassi** (*see p. 117*). It was one of the last important palaces to be built on the Grand Canal and the design of the façade is derived from earlier palaces on the waterway including Sansovino's Ca' Grande. Beyond a narrow *calle* is the 17th-century **Palazzo Moro-Lin**, with a long balcony above the portico on the waterfront. **Palazzo Contarini delle Figure** is a graceful 16th-century Lombardesque building (in poor condition) by Scarpagnino, decorated with heraldic trophies and marbles. It is thought to have been named after the two figures (difficult to see) beneath the balcony.

There is now a wonderful view, after the sharp bend of the *Volta del Canal*, as the waterway straightens out for the last 800m or so all the way up to the Rialto Bridge. This stretch of the canal provided the setting for the regattas held at Carnival time during the days of the Republic, and Canaletto painted this view several times (but from the other side of the Canal).

The four **Palazzi Mocenigo** consist of two palaces on either side of a long double façade, with blue awnings at some of the windows. The blue and white posts (or *pali*) in the water in front of the palace show the livery or *divisa* of their proprietors (as elsewhere on the Canal). When the Mocenigo had Giordano Bruno to stay with them here, they betrayed him to the Inquisition and he was sent under escort to Rome, where he was forced to endure a trial which lasted seven long years before being burned alive as a heretic. Bruno was a Neoplatonist philosopher, who as a Dominican and ordained priest had come into conflict with the Church authorities in 1592. A plaque on the third palace records Lord Byron's residence here from 1816–19, when he lived in grand style with a staff of 14, as well as a menagerie of two monkeys, a fox and two mastiffs. During this time he began *Don Juan* and wrote *Beppo*, a work in Italian prose style about Venetian life and manners.

Palazzo Mocenigo is adjoined by the 16th-century **Palazzo Corner-Gheltof**. By the San Tomà *traghetto* stands an old one-storey house, perhaps the simplest building on the entire Canal. Next comes the 15th-century **Palazzo Garzoni** (now owned by Venice University), with two putti high up on the façade.

SANT'ANGELO LANDING-STAGE

As the boat pulls out, **Palazzo Lando-Corner-Spinelli** can be seen (now owned by the famous Rubelli fabric company). By Mauro Codussi (1490–1510), it is a particularly successful Renaissance palace, with a rusticated ground floor, two-light windows, and attractive balconies. Beyond two more *rii* is the buff-coloured **Palazzo Benzon**, which in the time of the Countess Marina Benzon in the early 19th century was the rendezvous of Venetian fashionable society: Byron, Thomas Moore and Canova all came here to pay their respects to the hostess. Next to the 16th-century **Palazzo Martinengo**, with two coats of arms (the façade once had frescoes by Pordenone), are Palazzo and Palazzetto Tron (15th century, but later restored). On Rio di San Luca stands **Palazzo Corner-Contarini dei Cavalli**, an elegant Gothic work of c. 1450 with two coats of arms and a fine central six-light window.

Across the *rio* rises **Palazzo Grimani**, a masterpiece designed by Sanmicheli just before his death in 1559 and built by Gian Giacomo dei Grigi. Still in very good condition, it has a balcony across the whole length of the façade, beneath which are tall Corinthian pilasters. The two upper stories also have very refined decoration. It is now the seat of the Court of Appeal. Next to the rust-coloured façade (decorated with marbles) of the Casa Corner-Valmarana is the **Casa Corner-Martinengo-Ravà**. It was formerly owned by the Morosini family, who received distinguished visitors here in the 16th–17th century, including Paolo Sarpi (a fierce opponent of Church involvement in politics; *see p. 236*) and the astronomer Galileo. In the 19th century it became a well-known hotel, and the novelist James Fenimore Cooper stayed here in 1838.

The 13th-century Veneto-Byzantine Palazzi Farsetti and Loredan are occupied by the Town Hall. **Palazzo Farsetti**, built by Doge Enrico Dandolo (who sanctioned the sack of Constantinople in 1204), was much restored in the 19th century. **Palazzo Loredan** has a double row of arches on two stories and reliefs of *Venice* and *Justice* beneath little Gothic canopies, and bears the arms of the distinguished Corner family. Elena Corner Piscopia (1646–84), who lived here, was the first woman to receive a degree (in philosophy from Padua University in 1678). In the middle of the next group of houses is the tiny Gothic **Palazzetto Dandolo**, with an exceptional number of windows.

RIALTO LANDING-STAGE

Just beyond the landing-stage is Ponte Manin (on the site of a bridge built in stone before the 15th century by the Dolfin family) across Rio di San Salvador. The large rust-coloured **Palazzo Bembo** was the probable birthplace of the scholar Pietro Bembo (1470–1547; *see p. 81*). Across the *rio* stands the classical white façade of **Palazzo Dolfin-Manin**, by Jacopo Sansovino, begun in 1538 for a Venetian merchant, Zuanne Dolfin. It incorporates the Doric, Ionic and Corinthian orders and has a frieze of lions' heads beneath the cornice. Its water-gate is on the side *rio*, so the palace could be extended across the *fondamenta* (and the portico was provided for pedestrians).

The 16th-century **Rialto Bridge**, lined with shops, is a famous Venetian landmark, the successor to many bridges over the Grand Canal at this point (*described on pp. 185–6*). From this side you can see the two 16th-century reliefs of the *Annunciation* by Agostino Rubini (Venice's patron saints Mark and Theodore are on the other side). Just beyond the bridge is the **Fondaco dei Tedeschi**, the former trading house of merchants from Germany and Central Europe (*see p. 108*).

In the next group of houses, in a tiny *campo* with its well on the canal, can be seen one of the oldest private palaces to have survived in Venice, the 13th-century **Ca' Lion** with its outside stair. Beyond Rio San Giovanni Crisostomo are three small palaces and then **Ca' da Mosto**, a venerable 13th-century Veneto-Byzantine building. Just three arches remain on the water level of its ancient arcade, and the windows on the floor above still have stilted arches, but their more pointed shapes show the influence of the Gothic style. This was the birthplace of Alvise da Mosto (1432–88), discoverer of the Cape Verde Islands, and from the later 15th century right up until the 18th it was a famous inn, called the Albergo del Leon Bianco.

Across Rio dei Santi Apostoli stands **Palazzo Mangilli-Valmarana**, which was restored in classical style by Antonio Visentini for his friend Joseph Smith (*see p. 331*), who purchased it in 1740. The name of the adjoining **Palazzo Michiel dal Brusà** is a reminder of the great fire of 1774 (*brusà* meaning burnt) which destroyed the previous Gothic palace on this site. The **Palazzo Michiel dalle Colonne** has a tall columned portico (remodelled by Antonio Gaspari in the 17th century).

Just before the busy *traghetto* station (which serves the Rialto markets), in Campo Santa Sofia, is **Palazzo Foscari** (a fine 15th-century window has colourful marble columns). On the other side of the *campo* is the 14th-century red-painted **Palazzo Morosini-Sagredo** (now a hotel) with a pretty balconied Gothic window and a variety of windows on its partly Byzantine façade, and a little terrace on the water. It is adjoined by the 15th-century Gothic brick **Palazzo Pesaro-Ravà**.

CA' D'ORO LANDING-STAGE

The façade of the early 15th-century **Ca' d'Oro** has the most extravagantly beautiful Gothic decorations of all the palaces on the Grand Canal, and the left side of the building seems to have more apertures than wall space. The portico on the water preserves elements of the previous Veneto-Byzantine Palazzo Zeno on this site, but on the level above, the two wide loggias have extraordinarily fine, delicate tracery. The roof is hidden behind a frieze of marble finials and even the corners of the building are disguised by thin twisted columns. It is one of the few palaces on the Canal which is asymmetrical: the right-hand side, even though also beautifully decorated, is in a different style. The palace was built between 1420 and 1434 for a procurator of St Mark's, Marino Contarini, and is the work of the little-known Matteo Raverti from Lombardy (with collaborators), but it is known that Giovanni and Bartolomeo Bon also worked here. It received its name (the 'Golden House') since the sculptural details were highlighted in polychrome and gilding by a French painter: this has now completely disappeared but the wonderful colour of the stonework and the way it reflects the water is still memorable. The interior of the palace is open as one of the city's great museums (*see p. 225*).

Beyond the green façade of the 18th-century **Palazzo Duodo** (with two statues at water-level and two busts higher up on the façade), now also part of the Ca' d'Oro museum, is the 16th-century **Palazzo Fontana**, where in 1693 Carlo Rezzonico was born: he was elected Pope Clement XIII in 1758. Across Rio di San Felice is a house with a garden with pine trees, then **Palazzo Contarini-Pisani**, with a plain 17th-century façade above a portico; **Palazzo Boldù** (also 17th century, with a rusticated ground floor); and **Palazzo da Lezze**, with its little court on the canal. Across the *rio* stands the handsome **Palazzo Gussoni-Grimani della Vida**, attributed to Sanmicheli (1548–56), formerly decorated with frescoes by Tintoretto. The English ambassador Sir Henry Wotton (*see p. 211*) lived here in the early 17th century, and Rawdon Brown (*see p. 197*) from 1852 until his death in 1883.

There follow two 17th-century palaces, and, on Rio della Maddalena, the 16th-century **Palazzo Barbarigo**, which has almost lost the 16th-century frescoes on its façade. Across the *rio* are the 17th-century Palazzi Molin and Emo on the bend of the canal, and then **Palazzo Soranzo**, with a fine façade probably by Tullio Lombardo's son Sante, with six decorative emblems. **Palazzo Erizzo alla Maddalena** is a red 15th-century Gothic building with a good window. This is adjoined by **Palazzo Marcello** (rebuilt in the 18th century and now owned by the state). It was the birthplace in 1686 of the composer Benedetto Marcello (*see p. 224*). When standing at a window of this palace he heard the wonderful voice of a young girl, Rosanna Scalfi, as she sat singing in a gondola. He went down to meet her and they fell in love; she became his pupil and secret wife (since noblemen were forbidden to marry beneath their class).

The imposing building beyond its garden behind railings (and later wing) is **Palazzo Vendramin-Calergi**, probably Mauro Codussi's last work, and regarded by many as his finest, built in the first decade of the 16th century for Andrea Loredan. The façade is a masterpiece of Renaissance architecture, in Istrian stone and marble with Corinthian columns and pilasters dividing the three storeys beneath a Classical cornice with a finely carved frieze. A characteristic feature are the two-light windows beneath an oculus set within a larger rounded arch. In 1599 the palace passed to the Calergi family (who called in Vincenzo Scamozzi to enlarge it with a wing on the garden side), and in 1738 it came into the possession of the Vendramin. A marble plaque on the waterfront records Wagner, with a profile and inscription supplied by Gabriele d'Annunzio: the great composer rented an apartment here (which can be visited; *see p. 235*) where he died in 1883. Since 1970 the palace has been the winter home of Venice's Casinò.

Beyond the *rio*, **Casa Gatti-Casazza**, with a roof garden (the typical Venetian *altana*), was restored in the 18th-century style.

SAN MARCUOLA LANDING-STAGE

This landing stage is in front of the unfinished façade of the church of the same name. On the other side of a garden is **Palazzo Martinengo-Mandelli**, reconstructed in the 18th century. There follow several 17th-century palaces, including Palazzo Correr-Contarini. Soon the Cannaregio Canal, the second largest in Venice, diverges right. Beyond the church of San Geremia is the little Scuola dei Morti (rebuilt after 1849), and the stone façade of **Palazzo Flangini**, left unfinished by Giuseppe Sardi (c. 1682). Just before the bridge is the long **Palazzo Soranzo-Calbo-Crotta**, a 15th-century building enlarged and altered in later centuries. The bridge which serves the railway station, which replaced an iron bridge of 1858, was built in 1932–4 by Eugenio Miozzi.

FERROVIA LANDING-STAGE

Just before the landing-stage is the Baroque façade of the church of the Scalzi by Giuseppe Sardi. The harmony of the Grand Canal was left undisturbed when the **railway station** was built in 1955: the simple long, low building in Istrian stone is sensibly set back from the waterfront, but provides a very fine view from its steps. Beyond it rise the huge offices of the state railways, built around the same time, but rather more obtrusive. The Ponte della Costituzione, always known as the **Calatrava Bridge** after its architect (*described on p. 220*) was opened in 2008 and provides a useful link between the railway station and Piazzale Roma, the terminus of the road from the mainland (with a multi-storey garage, another work by Eugenio Miozzi, also built in the 1930s). The last landing-stage is at Piazzale Roma.

FROM PIAZZALE ROMA TO SAN MARCO
(RIGHT BANK)

PIAZZALE ROMA LANDING-STAGE

Soon after passing under the **Calatrava Bridge** (*see p. 220*), the boat passes the mouth of the Rio Nuovo, a canal cut in 1933 as a short route from the station to Piazza San Marco. Beyond the Giardino Papadopoli (public gardens), the next important building is the 18th-century church of **San Simeone Piccolo**, with a lofty green dome and Corinthian portico. Just before the station bridge is **Palazzo Foscari-Contarini**, a Renaissance building. Beyond Rio Marin there follows a group of simple palaces before the landing-stage of Riva de Biasio.

RIVA DI BIASIO LANDING-STAGE

On the corner of the next *rio*, just beyond a garden, stands the 15th-century Gothic **Palazzo Giovannelli**. The **Casa Correr**, which has a plain façade, was the home of Teodoro Correr, whose collection forms part of the Museo Correr. The **Fondaco dei**

Turchi is an important Veneto-Byzantine palace (12th–13th century) which from 1621–1838 was the warehouse of the Turkish merchants. It was virtually rebuilt in 1869, much to the distress of Ruskin (*see p. 218*). It is now the seat of the Natural History Museum. Beneath the portico can be seen several sarcophagi; one is that of Doge Marin Falier, beheaded for treason in 1355 (*see p. 11*).

Across the *rio* is the plain brick façade of the **Granaries of the Republic**. This 15th-century battlemented edifice bears a relief of the lion of St Mark (a modern replacement of one destroyed at the fall of the Republic). **Palazzo Belloni-Battagià** was built by Baldassare Longhena in 1647–63 for Girolamo Belloni, whose coat of arms, with a star and crescent motif, appears on the façade. The fine water-gate is flanked by iron grilles. Across the *rio* stand Palazzo Tron (1590) and Palazzo Duodo (Gothic). Beyond a garden is the 13th-century **Palazzo Priuli-Bon**. Above remains of its four Veneto-Byzantine arches on the ground floor are five later Gothic windows set in a stone frame.

SAN STAE LANDING-STAGE

The boat stops in front of the **church of San Stae**, with a very fine façade (c. 1709) by Domenico Rossi. In the *campo* is the little 18th-century *scuola* which belonged to the goldsmiths. After the Palazzo Foscarini-Giovannelli (17th century), across the *rio*, stands **Ca' Pesaro**, a splendid Baroque palace by Baldassare Longhena, the grandest of a number in the city built for the famous Pesaro family. It was begun in 1658. It has a double water-gate with carved heads as the keystones flanked by allegorical figures representing rivers. These are only some of the numerous sculptures which decorate the entire façade, from monsters, to cherubs, to sea creatures, to trophies. An equally elaborate side façade (at a slightly different height) by Gaspari extends all the way along the *rio* on the left. The palace now houses the Museum of Modern Art and the Oriental Museum.

Beyond two smaller palaces rises **Palazzo Corner della Regina** by Domenico Rossi (1724; his design for the façade of San Stae was much more successful). It was restored by the Prada Foundation in 2012 and is open for exhibitions. A plaque on **Casa Bragadin-Favretto** records the studio here of the painter Giacomo Favretto, who died in 1887 and some of whose typical Venetian scenes can be seen in the Ca' Pesaro collection. Beyond two more palaces is the Gothic **Palazzo Morosini-Brandolin**, with a row of quatrefoil windows on the upper storey. A bridge connects Fondamenta dell'Olio with the **Pescheria** (*described on p. 205*), the neo-Gothic fish market. Here begins the **Rialto Market**, always busy in the mornings with Venetians who come here to buy fruit and vegetables from the stalls on the waterfront, and meat and other groceries from the shops nearby. The long porticoed market buildings which follow the curve of the Canal were rebuilt in the 16th century.

RIALTO MERCATO LANDING-STAGE

At the foot of the Rialto Bridge is the ornate Renaissance façade, restored in 1523–5 by Guglielmo dei Grigi (Il Bergamasco), of **Palazzo dei Camerlenghi**, which was once the seat of the Lords of the Exchequer. The name of the *fondamenta* here—Fondamenta dei Prigioni—is a reminder that the ground floor of the palace was conveniently used as a prison.

The boat passes beneath the **Rialto Bridge** (*described on pp. 185–6*). The reliefs of *St Mark* and *St Theodore* are by Tiziano Aspetti. At its foot (and partly concealed by it) is **Palazzo dei Dieci Savi**, a building of the early 16th-century by Scarpagnino, used by the financial ministers of the Republic. A tondo bears a (remade) lion of St Mark, and on the corner stands a figure of *Justice* (late 16th century). Fondamenta del Vin runs in front of a picturesque row of houses. At the end, behind a garden with two tall cypresses, is the rust-coloured façade of **Palazzo Ravà**, a successful neo-Gothic building (1906) thought to occupy the site of the palace of the patriarchs of Grado.

SAN SILVESTRO LANDING-STAGE
Beside the San Silvestro landing-stage is **Palazzo Barzizza**, which bears remarkable traces of 12th-century Veneto-Byzantine carvings on its façade. The terrace is full of plants and there is a tiny garden on the water. **Palazzo Businello** (formerly Giustinian), on the corner of Rio dei Meloni, was rebuilt in the 17th century but also preserves some Veneto-Byzantine elements. On the opposite corner stands **Palazzo Coccina-Tiepolo-Papadopoli**, with its two obelisks. This is a work built in the best Renaissance tradition by Gian Giacomo dei Grigi in the early 1560s. Beyond the garden is **Palazzo Donà**, with a fine 12th–13th-century window. This is adjoined by the smaller **Palazzo Donà della Madonnetta**, named after a 15th-century relief of the *Madonna and Child* set into the façade. It has an interesting arched window with good capitals and paterae. Across the *rio* stands **Palazzo Bernardo**, with a lovely Gothic façade (c. 1442) especially notable for the tracery on the upper *piano nobile*. The smaller **Palazzo Grimani** (now Sorlini) has an Istrian stone façade decorated with marbles. It is an elegant Lombardesque building of the early 16th century.

Beyond, on the corner of Rio San Polo, is the plain façade of **Palazzo Cappello-Layard**. Its second name was acquired after it was purchased in 1883 by Austen Henry Layard (*see p. 179*). He and his wife entertained lavishly here and all the illustrious visitors to Venice in their time would be invited to the palace, including the crowned heads of Europe. Across the *rio* stands **Palazzo Barbarigo della Terrazza**, dating from 1569, which is named after its spacious balconied terrace on the Grand Canal (now used by the German Institute). Next comes **Palazzo Pisani della Moretta**, with graceful quatrefoil roundels above its Gothic windows. It has a fine 18th-century interior (but is not normally open to the public). Beyond the 16th-century Palazzo Tiepolo is the smaller 15th-century Palazzo Tiepoletto. There follow two smaller houses and the rust-coloured Palazzo Giustinian-Persico, a 16th-century building. Palazzo Civran-Grimani, on the corner of the *rio*, dates from the 17th century.

SAN TOMÀ LANDING-STAGE
Just before the Rio di Ca' Foscari rises the grand **Palazzo Balbi** by Alessandro Vittoria (1582–90). Here typical Venetian windows provide light for the central *porteghi* on the two upper floors, but the broken pediments above the side windows and the two elaborate cartouches are all in full Baroque style (which is also evident in the two

bizarre obelisks sitting on the rooftop). The palace is used by the regional government of the Veneto. Next to it, on the *rio*, is the plain brick façade (but with two handsome large chimneys) of the **Fondazione Angelo Masieri**, an international study centre for students of architecture. In 1953 Frank Lloyd Wright, then in his eighties, designed a small palace to be built here in memory of Angelo Masieri, a young student who was killed in a fatal accident when visiting Wright's famous house in Pennsylvania, but planning permission was refused. In 1968 Carlo Scarpa was allowed to remodel the interior. At the *Volta del Canal*, the point where the waterway bends sharply to the left, stands the beautifully proportioned **Ca' Foscari**, a grand residence built in the mid 15th century for Francesco Foscari, when almost 80 years old after 34 years as doge. It is one of the great Gothic palaces in Venice, with notable tracery, fine marble columns, and a frieze of putti bearing the Foscari arms. It is now the seat of Venice University, always named after this palace, and famous for its business school (*its courtyard and interior is described on p. 176*. It is adjoined by the slightly lower but very beautiful long double façade (by Bartolomeo Bon) of the **Palazzi Giustinian dei Vescovi**, which dates from the same period and is also partly owned by the University. Wagner wrote the second act of Tristan here in 1858–9.

After two small palaces rises **Ca' Rezzonico**, a superb building begun around 1667 by Longhena, his most successful secular work, but left incomplete at his death. The façade has extremely pleasing proportions and is not over decorated. You would never know that the top storey was only built some hundred years later by the very skilled architect Giorgio Massari, presumably following Longhena's design. It now houses the city's 18th-century museum. The lowest window on the left-hand corner (by the wooden bridge) belongs to the apartment where Robert Browning died in 1889 (*see pp. 175–6*).

CA' REZZONICO LANDING-STAGE

Behind the landing-stage is the 17th-century Lombardesque **Palazzo Contarini-Michiel**. **Palazzetto di Madame Stern** is a reproduction of a Venetian Gothic palace (using some original medieval pieces), built in 1909–12 by Giuseppe Berti with a garden on the canal. It is named after the wife of the Austrian musician Giulio Stern and is now a hotel. Beyond the plain façade of Palazzo Moro stands **Palazzo dell'Ambasciatore**, so named because it was the Austrian embassy in the 18th century. It is a Gothic building of the 15th century with two shield-bearing pages, fine Lombard works by the school of Antonio Rizzo.

Beyond Rio San Trovaso is **Palazzo Contarini-Corfù**, a 15th-century Gothic building with varicoloured marbles, and, next to it, **Palazzo Contarini degli Scrigni**, built in 1609 by Vincenzo Scamozzi, with a huge mascaron above its water-gate.

ACCADEMIA LANDING-STAGE

At the far end of the *campo* can be seen the 18th-century façade (by Giorgio Massari) of the **Scuola della Carità** beside the bare flank (with Gothic windows) of the former church of **Santa Maria della Carità**, both now housing the famous Accademia picture galleries, and in the process of radical restoration.

Beyond the Accademia Bridge (*described on p. 130*), is **Palazzo Contarini dal Zaffo** (Polignac), a graceful Lombardesque building with fine marble roundels and a garden. **Palazzo Molin-Balbi-Valier** has a handsome ground floor. The 16th-century corner building on Rio San Vio, **Palazzo Loredan-Cini**, is sometimes open to the public (*see p. 177*). Beyond is the pretty Campo San Vio, planted with trees, named after a church demolished in 1813, but the site since 1892 of the Anglican church of St George. After the *campo* is **Palazzo Barbarigo**, with a harshly-coloured 19th-century mosaic façade by Giulio Carlini. Next door is the 15th-century Gothic **Palazzo da Mula**, painted by Monet in 1908–9 (his painting is now in the National Gallery of Washington). The portrait painter and miniaturist Rosalba Carriera died in 1757 in the red **Casa Biondetti**.

The 18th-century **Palazzo Venier dei Leoni**, with its frieze of lions' heads at water level, never progressed beyond the ground floor. It was purchased by Peggy Guggenheim in 1949 and now houses her collection of modern art (*see p. 152*).

Beyond is **Ca' Dario**, whose outside walls incline noticeably. This is a charming building, highly decorated with motifs taken from Classical, Byzantine and Gothic architecture, and with numerous delightful chimney pots. It was built in 1487 and faced with a profusion of varicoloured marbles and porphyry in roundels in all shapes and sizes. It is an interesting example of a palace built not by a nobleman, but by a successful civil servant, Giovanni Dario, who served the Republic as Secretary to the Senate in Albania and Constantinople, negotiating peace with Sultan Mehmet II (whose portrait Gentile Bellini painted) in 1479, and at last retiring permanently to Venice at the age of 75. Despite its exceptionally pretty exterior, over the centuries the house has come to have a reputation for bringing bad luck to its owners, since a number of them have died here in unusual circumstances, including Dario's own daughter, Marietta. It was owned by the historian Rawdon Brown (*see p. 197*) from 1838 to 1842. Next to it is the 15th-century Palazzo Barbaro (Wolkoff).

Palazzo Salviati was built in 1924 by Giovanni dall'Olivo as the headquarters of the Salviati glasshouse (founded in 1866), as the bright mosaic on its façade proclaims. Sir Henry Layard (*see p. 179*) helped Antonio Salviati revive the Venetian art of glass and mosaic and became the principal shareholder of the Venice & Murano Glass and Mosaic Co. Ltd. This firm, apart from carrying out important repair and maintenance work on the mosaics of St Mark's, also made the mosaics for the Wolsey chapel at Windsor and decorations for the Albert Memorial and Westminster Abbey in London. The Salviati glass company, based in Murano, is still one of the most important in Venice.

Palazzo Orio-Semitecolo has fine Gothic windows. This was where Henry James' close friend, the writer Constance Fenimore Woolson, committed suicide in 1894. James (who is thought to have taken her as a model for his 'Miss Tita' in *The Aspern Papers*) came here after the tragedy to sort out her belongings, and, at her express wish, attempted to sink her clothes in the lagoon.

The last big palace on this side of the Canal is **Palazzo Genovese**, a successful imitation of the Gothic style built in 1892. It is now the Hotel Centurion Palace. Beside it are the low buildings of the **ex-abbey of San Gregorio**, with a delightful water-gate crowned by a large relief of the saint.

SALUTE LANDING-STAGE

A marble pavement opens out before the magnificent church of **Santa Maria della Salute** (*described on p. 154*), a masterpiece of Baroque architecture by Longhena. The **Dogana**, the ex-customs house, has a handsome long low 17th-century façade which extends to the end of the promontory. It was beautifully restored a few years ago by the Japanese architect Tadao Ando for the François Pinault Foundation and is open for contemporary art exhibitions (*see p. 157*).

MARK TWAIN ON THE GRAND CANAL

'In a few minutes we swept gracefully out into the Grand Canal, and under the mellow moonlight the Venice of poetry and romance stood revealed. Right from the water's edge rose long lines of stately palaces of marble; gondolas were gliding swiftly hither and thither and disappearing suddenly through unsuspected gates and alleys; ponderous stone bridges threw their shadows athwart the glittering waves. There was life and motion everywhere, and yet everywhere there was a hush, a stealthy sort of stillness, that was suggestive of secret enterprises of bravoes and of lovers; and clad half in moonbeams and half in mysterious shadows, the grim old mansions of the Republic seemed to have an expression about them of having an eye out for just such enterprises as these at that same moment. Music came floating over the waters—Venice was complete.'   From *The Innocents Abroad* (1869)

INCURABILI (SEAT OF THE ACCADEMIA DI BELLE ARTI)
Detail of the façade.

Sestiere of Dorsoduro

Dorsoduro is the district on the 'quiet side' of the Grand Canal, well away from the confusion around Piazza San Marco. Indeed, even if only separated by a few metres of water, it has a totally different atmosphere, and its quiet campi and little canals, often with a fondamenta on each side, are amongst the most picturesque in the city.

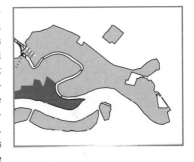

Dorsoduro is principally a residential district, with shops concentrated only in certain small parts. To the south it looks over the Giudecca Canal, and here the wide and sunny Zattere promenade is one of the most congenial spots in Venice. All areas of the *sestiere* lend themselves to exploration, and some of the best and most reasonably-priced restaurants, cafés and hotels are to be found here. There are also two great museums: Venice's most important gallery of paintings, the Gallerie dell'Accademia; and the museum of the 18th century in the splendid Ca' Rezzonico. The Peggy Guggenheim collection of modern art claims to be the most visited museum in the city. The great church of the Salute crowns Dorsoduro's easternmost tip.

GALLERIE DELL' ACCADEMIA

Map p. 409, E3. Open 8.15–7.15, Mon 8.15–2.

The Gallerie dell'Accademia is one of the most important art galleries in Italy, containing masterpieces by Giovanni Bellini, Carpaccio, Titian, Tintoretto, Veronese and Giambattista Tiepolo. The galleries occupy the former church and convent of Santa Maria della Carità, its Gothic doorway surrounded by large reliefs dating from 1377. The convent was occupied by an order of Augustinian canons until its suppression by Napoleon. The adjoining Scuola Grande della Carità, founded in 1260 (with a Baroque façade by Giorgio Massari), was the oldest of the six *scuole grandi* (*see p. 278*) in Venice. Two of its rooms, with some of their original decorations, can still be seen. Palladio added a fine oval spiral staircase and long corridor, which both survive, but most of his work in the *Scuola* was later destroyed by fire.

The collection was first opened to the public in 1817, and includes numerous works from suppressed or demolished churches. Less than half the collection is at present on view, but work has been underway since 2005 to double the exhibition space, now that the Accademia di Belle Arti, which occupied part of the building, has moved to the Zattere. In 2012 the British architect David Chipperfield was entrusted with some parts of the project. The display, still in the old rooms, is therefore subject to constant change and a number of rooms are usually closed. The arrangement will only take its final shape as work nears completion: the description below covers the masterpieces, in roughly chronological order.

EARLY VENETIAN PAINTERS

The earliest works in the collection are traditionally exhibited in the **former chapter house of the Scuola della Carità**, which has a superb gilded wooden ceiling carved in 1461–84 by Marco Cozzi, otherwise known for his skill in producing choir stalls (to be seen in the Frari and some other Venetian churches). It has a painting of the *Holy Father* attributed to Pier Maria Pennacchi.

There are two fine works by **Paolo Veneziano**: a splendid polyptych of the *Coronation of the Virgin*, flanked by stories from the lives of Christ and St Francis, and a *Virgin and Child with Donors*. Born in the last years of the 13th century, Paolo was the first truly Venetian painter: though his works show the influence of Byzantine art (it is thought that he may even have visited Constantinople), they also provide a prelude to the great Venetian school of painting.

Lorenzo Veneziano, who was no relation to Paolo but who succeeded him as an important artistic personality in Venice in the mid-14th century, is also well represented by a large polyptych with the *Annunciation* in the central panel and the tiny kneeling figure of the donor, Domenico Lion, surrounded by saints and prophets. His masterly use of colour is also evident in the later *Annunciation with Saints*, signed and dated 1371.

Another important artist who was at work later in the century is **Niccolò di Pietro**, whose *Virgin Enthroned with Donor* is signed and dated 1394 (with the addition of the address of his studio at the foot of Ponte del Paradiso; *map p. 402, C4*). The late 14th-century polyptych of the *Apocalypse* by **Jacobello Alberegno** is particularly interesting for its iconography.

FIFTEENTH-CENTURY WORKS

Venetian art of the early 15th century is well illustrated by artists working in the International Gothic style. **Jacobello del Fiore**'s triptych of *Justice and the Archangels* was commissioned for a law court in the Doge's Palace in 1421 and shows Venice personified as Justice. The *Coronation of the Virgin* by the same artist shows the Madonna in Paradise surrounded by a huge crowd of saints and angels. The *Madonna della Misericordia*, with St John the Baptist and St John the Evangelist, is also by Jacobello, and *St James the Great between Four Saints* (the '*St James Altarpiece*') is a late work (c. 1450) by **Giambono**. There is also a *Coronation of the Virgin* by him and early 15th-century works by **Antonio Vivarini**.

WORKS FROM THE *SCUOLE*

The Accademia galleries are housed in a building that was once itself a *scuola*, and it is appropriate, perhaps, that works of art removed from several of the other dismembered institutions of the old Republic should now be housed here.

True Cross cycle painted for the Scuola di San Giovanni Evangelista

This charming cycle of paintings (end of the 15th and beginning of the 16th centuries), relate to miracles associated with a relic of the True Cross which was given to the Scuola di San Giovanni Evangelista by Filippo de' Masseri on his return from Jerusalem in 1369. It is still preserved there today (*see p. 204*). The paintings are particularly remarkable for their depiction of Venice, including the old Rialto Bridge and the brightly-painted Gothic palace façades, and also give a vivid picture of 16th-century Venetian dress. Originally there were nine canvases, but today only eight remain:

(1) Offering of the Relic to the Members of the Scuola di San Giovanni Evangelista. The relic had been a gift from the patriarch of Constantinople to Filippo de' Masseri, an officer of state in Cyprus. In this painting Lazzaro Bastiani shows de' Masseri formally handing the relic to the chief guardian of the *Scuola*.

(2) Healing of Pietro de' Ludovici, by Gentile Bellini. In a richly-marbled chapel, Pietro is seen receiving a candle which has been kept close to the sacred relic, the touch of which heals him.

(3) Healing of the Daughter of Benvegnudo. The miraculous healing powers of the relic are again shown, this time by Giovanni Mansueti. He depicts a Venetian *palazzo* of the greatest wealth, filled with richly-dressed citizens, all celebrating the miracle of the relic.

(4) Miracle of the Cross at San Lio. Mansueti shows the moment when the relic, which was being carried at the funeral of a member of the *Scuola* who disparaged it during his lifetime, had become too heavy to carry and could not be got across the bridge. Mansueti not only shows us the moment of the miracle with the funeral procession, with the attendant brothers of the confraternity in great detail, but also the women and children of Venice, drawn to the windows and balconies. Life also goes on, with a man carrying produce on his head, while another appears to chase a cat across the rooftops.

(5) Procession of the Relic in Piazza San Marco. The brothers of the confraternity are bearing the relic around Piazza San Marco, when a merchant, whose son is dying at home in Brescia, falls to his knees in veneration of it. Miraculously, his son immediately recovers. Gentile Bellini shows the Piazza in great detail. St Mark's is immediately recognisable, its mosaics glittering in the sunshine, with the Porta della Carta and the Doge's Palace on its right. To the left of the painting we can still recognise the Procuratie Vecchie as a one-storey building, though the Torre dell'Orologio has yet to be built. On the right of the painting, at the base of the Campanile, we can see the buildings which preceded

Sansovino's Procuratie Nuove. Bellini also documents the brick paving of the square, which remained until Andrea Tirali repaved it in 1722.

(6) Miraculous Saving of a Child Fallen from a Roof. Benedetto Diana portrays the story of the recovery of a young boy who had fallen from the top storey of a house. He shows the typical interior courtyard of a 15th-century Venetian *palazzo*, with its stone staircase; the fall from a great height onto the stone flags is chillingly easy to imagine.

(7) Miracle of the Relic at San Lorenzo. While being carried in procession to the church of San Lorenzo, the relic fell into the canal as the bridge was crossed. The inevitable Venetian onlookers dived into the murky waters to rescue it; we can see people floating face down, trying to locate it underwater, and a Moor is seen standing on a wooden platform on the right of the painting, ready to throw himself into the canal. It evaded the grasp of everyone except for Andrea Vendramin, the chief guardian of the *Scuola*. Gentile Bellini also incorporated contemporary characters in the scene—Caterina Cornaro, Queen of Cyprus, for example, is seen kneeling on the stage on the left, while Gentile and his brother Giovanni are portrayed kneeling on the right.

(8) Cure of a Lunatic by the Patriarch of Grado. Carpaccio depicts Francesco Querini, Patriarch of Grado, performing a miracle with the aid of the relic. The miracle takes place quite discreetly on the loggia of the house on the left, but we can clearly see the old wooden Rialto Bridge. Carpaccio's eye catches everyday details: thickets of chimney pots, fluttering washing and the ever-curious Venetian onlookers.

Works painted for the Scuola di Sant'Orsola

Carpaccio's famous *Legend of St Ursula* (1490–6) is a delightful cycle of nine paintings, with charming details and a remarkably Venetian atmosphere. The story is told as follows:

(1) The Ambassadors from England Arrive at the Court of King Maurus of Brittany, to ask for the hand of his daughter, Ursula, in marriage to the son (Hereus) of their king, Conon. Ursula is shown on the right of the painting counting out on her fingers the conditions of her agreement to the proposal (a delay of three years for her and ten maids of honour, each with 1,000 companions, to make a pilgrimage to Rome; and the conversion of Hereus to Christianity).

(2) Dismissal of the Ambassadors. The envoys return with Ursula's answer.

(3) Return of the Ambassadors. King Conon looks less than happy with the stipulated conditions.

(4) Hereus meets Ursula, and Ursula leaves for Rome. Everyone is wearing their finest clothes, sitting on sumptuous carpets, while banners and flags fly and trumpeters play, but Ursula's mother is seen weeping at her departure. We can see Carpaccio's signature on the central flagpole, while the golden-haired nobleman on the left holds a scroll identifying Nicolò Loredan as one of the probable donors of the cycle. This scene, as the previous one, appears to be set in Venice, with people looking on from windows, balconies and bridges. Throughout the cycle there are hints at the architecture of Venetian buildings such as the Arsenale.

(5) Dream of St Ursula. An angel foretells her martyrdom, signified by the dark-coloured palm leaf he holds. In the room where Ursula sleeps in a double bed, the bridegroom's side as yet untouched, we can see from the golden light accompanying the angel, charming domestic details such as her three-legged stool and travelling bookcase, her book still open on the table along with an hourglass, her slippers neatly by the bed and her little dog curled up at its foot.

(6) Ursula, with Hereus and the Eleven Thousand Virgins, meets Pope Cyriac at Rome. The official in red is thought to be Ermolao Barbaro, Venetian ambassador to the Vatican and who wrote a book on diplomacy. There is a prominent view of Castel Sant'Angelo.

(7) The Pilgrims and the Pope reach Cologne. They find the city besieged by the Huns—the pope and Ursula can be seen leaning out of the boat to talk to the man on shore.

(8) Martyrdom of the Pilgrims. Ursula, refusing to marry a Hun, calmly waits for the arrow of the central archer, while behind her all is chaos and bloodshed. On the right, separated by a column again bearing what is thought to be the Loredan arms, the funeral of St Ursula takes place.

(9) Apotheosis of St Ursula and her Eleven Thousand Virgins. God the Father looks down in benediction on St Ursula, mounted on a podium of palms of martyrdom, and surrounded by the eleven thousand.

Works painted for the Scuola Grande di San Marco

The large canvases from the Sala dell'Albergo of the Scuola Grande di San Marco illustrate scenes from the life of St Mark. The works were commissioned in 1492, first from Gentile and Giovanni Bellini and then after their death from Giovanni Mansueti (who had worked in Gentile's studio). When he died in about 1527, Paris Bordone and Palma Vecchio were chosen to complete the cycle. *The Martyrdom of St Mark* (the saint is shown at the bottom of the painting, but in an insignificant scene in comparison with the splendid crowd) is by Giovanni Bellini (finished after his death in 1516 by Vittore Belliniano), and the *Miracle of St Mark Healing the Cobbler Anianus* is by Giovanni Mansueti, who also painted the *Episodes from the Life of St Mark*. The two later works are *St Mark in a Storm at Sea* by Palma Vecchio, with the help of Paris Bordone, who painted *The Fisherman Presents St Mark's Ring to the Doge*, which has a fine architectural background. This illustrates the popular legend that Venice was saved from a terrible flood in 1340 by the intervention of St Mark, St Nicholas and St George. The three saints asked a fisherman to transport them across the lagoon, for which St Mark thanked him by presenting him with a ring which he told him to give to Doge Gradenigo as proof of their presence. Some 40 years later, in 1562–6, Tintoretto painted four masterpieces for the chapter hall of the *Scuola* illustrating miracles related to St Mark. They are now displayed in the Accademia, and all of them show the painter's remarkable imagination. The *Transport of the Body of St Mark* illustrates the story of the Venetian merchants who stole the saint's body from Alexandria in 828 and took it to Venice. The splendid camel adds an exotic Arab element to the setting and the extraordinary ephemeral ghost-like figures and spectral buildings in the background conjure up a miraculous atmosphere. The nude figure of St Mark is painted with great skill. *The Miracle of the Slave* is another dramatic scene, in which the saint descends in flight from above our heads while the astonished crowd observes the nude figure of the slave who has just been freed from his shackles. The painter's remarkable technique can be examined in the few brush-strokes, which indicate with an extraordinary freshness of touch the details of the hatchet and splinters of wood and severed ropes in the foreground. These two works were paid for by the wealthy scholar Tommaso Rangone (*see p. 124*), whose portrait can be seen at the extreme left, and, in the first work, beside the camel. In *St Mark Saves the Saracen,* a tempest at sea rages while the saint effortlessly lifts the handsome figure of the Saracen out of a sinking boat to safety. *The Dream of St Mark* shows a night scene on board ship with St Mark (who dreams of the angel in the sky) and his three companions warmly wrapped up in blankets, mere blocks of colour. The spreading, luminous wings of the angel light up a busy quayside scene in the background. This is arguably one of Tintoretto's most innovative works.

THE FORMER CHURCH AND SCUOLA DELLA CARITÀ

The large **church of the Carità** was built in 1441–52, with a fine wooden roof. In 1811, after the order of canons who served it had been dissolved, it was divided into two floors by Giovanni Antonio Selva. Today in the central polygonal apse are displayed four early triptychs painted for this church and attributed to Giovanni Bellini and his *bottega*. The four kneeling sculptured angels date from the 15th century. In the left apse is the full-figure effigy in profile of the Blessed Lorenzo Giustinian, signed by Gentile Bellini. It was painted in '*tempera magra*' on very thin canvas and was probably designed as a processional standard (it was already damaged by water in the 18th century; *for Giustinian's story, see pp. 296–7*). The panels of *St Matthew* and *John the Baptist* are by Alvise Vivarini. On the window wall is a polyptych of the *Nativity*, flanked by eight saints, by Bartolomeo Vivarini; *St Clare* by Alvise Vivarini, a superb work, portraying the saint as a stern, uncompromising, highly intelligent woman; and *Sts Jerome and Augustine* and *Sts Peter and Paul* by Carlo Crivelli.

The former **Sala dell'Albergo** of the Scuola della Carità (with benches and a very fine carved 15th-century ceiling, with polychrome and gilding) houses Titian's wonderful *Presentation of the Virgin,* painted in 1534–9 for its present position. The solitary figure of the child Mary is charmingly graceful, and the distant view of the mountains is a reminder of the artist's alpine home. The details such as the man dressed in red above at the window, and the old woman seated at the foot of the steps beside her basket of eggs, are particularly beautiful, as well as the two splendid female figures in the centre of the picture observing Mary. Leaning out of the window above Mary is Titian himself in self-portrait, with his wife behind him.

The large triptych of the *Madonna Enthroned between Doctors of the Church* by Antonio Vivarini and his brother-in-law Giovanni d'Alemagna was also painted (in 1446) for this room, although it was formerly on the wall in front of the *Presentation* (it was moved when the door was opened and steps installed in 1811 by Giovanni Antonio Selva). It is a magnificent work and one of the first in Venice to be painted on canvas.

The exquisite Byzantine reliquary of Cardinal Bessarion was made in the 14th–15th century (nearby is displayed a painting of c. 1540 showing the cardinal holding this very reliquary).

THE GOLDEN AGE: LATE FIFTEENTH AND SIXTEENTH CENTURIES

This was the period of Venice's economic boom, corresponding with her territorial expansion onto the Italian mainland and later, with her victories over the Turks. The collection here is exceptionally rich in exquisite small paintings and altarpieces that provide one of the most vivid insights into Venetian art at its height, with superb works by the following masters:

Marco Basaiti (active 1496–1530): Perhaps of Greek or Albanian origin, Basaiti was probably born in Venice and is thought to have trained in the *bottega* of Alvise Vivarini. His *Calling of the Sons of Zebedee* (1510) has a remarkably intense atmosphere and the two brothers, the apostles James and John, indicate clearly their willingness to devote their lives to Christ; the scene is filled with men fishing.

Giovanni Bellini (c.1433–1516): Bellini is the greatest Venetian master of the 15th century, son of the painter Jacopo Bellini (also represented here). Throughout his long life he continued to exert a profound influence on Venetian painting. He was an innovator whose works reveal all the qualities of the Venetian Renaissance, and in 1482 he was made official painter of the Republic. His brother Gentile was also a very good painter: he produced some of the scenes in the cycle of the True Cross (*see p. 143*).

Some of Giovanni's best paintings can be seen at the Accademia: the *San Giobbe Altarpiece*, which depicts the Madonna enthroned with St Job and other saints, is a very beautiful work, with the magisterial figure of the Madonna holding the Child looking towards the future, beneath a golden apse decorated with a mosaic of six-winged seraphim, which recalls the Basilica of St Mark. The Classical details of the throne and architecture are also exquisitely painted and were repeated in the architecture of the altar itself in San Giobbe (*see p. 240*). The St Sebastian is a superb nude figure study, and at the foot of the throne are three delightful angels playing musical instruments. The Latin inscription reads: 'Hail Virgin, flower of undefiled modesty'. Probably painted in 1478, it had a profound influence on Bellini's contemporaries, as can be seen from altarpieces of similar date (also in the Accademia) by Carpaccio and Cima da Conegliano.

Bellini is especially noted for his beautiful small paintings of Madonnas, more than 80 of which survive by his hand or by one of the many pupils who worked in his important *bottega*. Here at the Accademia are the *Madonna and Child between Sts Catherine and Mary Magdalene*, against a dark background with remarkable light effects on the head of each figure; and the early *Virgin and Child* showing the half-length figure of the Madonna with exquisitely painted hands, holding the standing Child who is playing with his Mother's left thumb, and holding up his right hand in a gesture of benediction. The *Madonna Enthroned with the Sleeping Child* is one of Bellini's most moving works: the Virgin's hands are clasped in prayer and the abandoned figure of the Child, with one arm hanging limply down, has echoes of the figure of the dead Christ in a *Pietà*. The *Madonna degli Alberetti*, named after the two unusual trees, is arguably the most beautiful of all his Madonnas, with an extraordinary expressive energy in the movement of the Virgin's head with her eyes downcast, but turned towards the Child. The *Madonna of the Red Cherubs* receives its name from the red cherubim in the sky (painted thus to symbolise ardent love; the Virgin and Child gaze adoringly into one another's eyes). Again the Virgin's hands are superbly painted and the tender beauty of the Madonna contrasts with the chubby, curly-haired Child, who is shown in a far from idealised portrait.

Bellini's *Pietà* (*Pietà Donà delle Rose*), in a landscape with depictions of Vicenza and Ravenna in the background, shows the influence of German Gothic sculptures of the same subject.

Vittore Carpaccio (c.1460–1525/6): Though certainly influenced by Giovanni Bellini, Carpaccio's approachable, waggish style is something entirely his own. Most famous of all his works in the Accademia is his cycle of the legend of St Ursula (*see p. 144*). The *Ten Thousand Martyrs on Mount Ararat* (interesting for its complex iconography) and *Presentation of Christ in the Temple*, with three charming little angels, were both painted towards the end of the painter's life.

Cima da Conegliano (c.1459–1518): Born in Conegliano in the foothills of the Venetian Dolomites, Cima studied—so Vasari tells us—under Bellini. And certainly his style owes much to him. Three works here in the Accademia are particularly fine: a *Madonna and Child with Saints* (restored in 2006), the *Incredulity of St Thomas*, and the *Madonna of the Orange Tree*, a lovely painting with delightful botanical details.

Giorgione (c.1476–1510): Giorgio da Castelfranco, born in the town of that name in the Venetian hinterland, became known as Giorgione ('great George') as his fame as a painter increased. Very little is known about his life and very few paintings can be attributed with certainty to his hand, but he has always been one of the best known Venetian artists. A pupil of Giovanni Bellini and influenced by Flemish and Dutch masters, he had an innovative technique of painting on canvas, applying a rich *impasto* and a broad range of colours. He was particularly interested in landscape, as can be seen in his late masterpiece *La Tempesta* (*see opposite*) and in the other paintings he produced for his private patrons in Venice, which are diffused with an air of mystery and an atmosphere derived from the spirit of Venetian Humanism. Apart from the *Tempesta*, the Accademia possesses a fresco of a female nude by him dating from 1508 and detached from the Fondaco dei Tedeschi, as well as the famous *Old Woman*. Giorgione died young (of the plague) in 1510, and some of his works, including, in the past, *Old Woman*, have also been attributed to Titian. *Old Woman* is now dated a few years after the *Tempesta* and probably preserves its original frame. Like the *Tempesta*, it once belonged to Gabriele Vendramin. It seems to be an allegory of old age rather than a real portrait (it was for long taken to be Giorgione's mother), although again it has received various interpretations. It was damaged in 1881 when it was transferred to a new canvas support. Scholars have recognised the influence of Dürer, as well as of Carpaccio and Leonardo da Vinci. The woman's scroll reads '*Col Tempo*'—'with time', though the old lady's eyes still burn bright and penetrating in her wizened face.

LA TEMPESTA

The famous *Tempesta* is thought to date from around 1506, and is known to have been the property of the patrician Gabriele Vendramin by 1530. Even though it is one of the few paintings attributed with certainty to Giorgione, it is a work which scholars still have difficulty in interpreting: it is not known whether the subject is meant to be an allegory, or the depiction of a legend or biblical story. In this work the influence of northern painters as well as Carpaccio can be detected. It was greatly admired by Byron when he saw it in the Manfrin collection, and it was acquired by the Italian state in 1932. The atmosphere of the painting is immediately comprehensible: an impending storm—in fact, this is one of the first 'mood' paintings in Western art. But who is the young man with the wooden staff? Or the half-naked woman breast-feeding a child? Why are the broken columns positioned where they are, as if centre-stage? The explanations are many and often unconvincing, and the matter is further complicated by the fact that X-ray examination reveals that Giorgione also changed the picture's plan and altered the dramatis personae. The key to the work may in fact be Francesco Colonna's poem *The Dream of Polyphilus*, published by the famous Venetian printer Aldus Manutius (*see p. 188*) in 1499, which contains a description of Venus feeding Love while the poet-shepherd Polyphilus looks on and the sky becomes heavy with thunderclouds. Whatever the correct reading—and some have argued there is no reading at all—*La Tempesta* remains one of the most forceful images in the history of painting. The air of mystery is underscored by the colours—from the soft greens of the grass to the pale nude against the white cloak and the silvery light of the towers and city walls, which seem to glow beneath the dark sky. A dramatic and visionary scene, in poetic contrast with the apparent indifference of the figures occupying it.

Landscape, which was once no more than a decorative motif in the back corner of a painting, has suddenly stepped out of the shadows and become the protagonist. *La Tempesta* is not figures in a landscape, it is a landscape with figures: the first modern landscape painting.

Andrea Mantegna (1431–1506): Born in Padua, where he produced his first important works, Mantegna then came to Venice where he married Bellini's sister. Only two works by his hand remain in the city (one here and the other in the Ca' d'Oro; *see p. 226*). He moved to Mantua as court painter to the Gonzaga in 1460. His *St George*, with the dragon slumped at his feet (1459), is a beautifully painted work.

Lorenzo Lotto (1480–1556): Vasari tells us that Lotto trained in Venice, but his career took him far and wide in Italy and only a handful of his works are to be found here, including the exceptional portrait known as *Gentleman in his Study*, painted around 1530. The sitter has a striking pallor, as if he were not well, and the lizard, rose petals and book all have symbolic meaning (fleeting life, disappointed love).

Palma Vecchio (c.1480–1528): A follower of Titian. The *Holy Family with Saints* is one of his best works, left unfinished at his death in 1528. It is now thought that Titian completed the head of St Catherine and the landscape in the background.

Titian (c.1485–1576): The collection includes a *St John the Baptist* and a moving *Pietà*, one of his last works, painted the year before his death, when Venice was devastated by a plague (which eventually killed the painter). The muted tones produce a strikingly dramatic and tragic effect, and the kneeling figure of the old man disguised as St Jerome is a self-portrait. The much discussed symbolic significance of the painting seems to be Death and Salvation. (*For more on Titian and his style see pp. 26 and 195.*)

Bonifacio de' Pitati (1487–c.1557): Sometimes called Bonifacio Veronese, because he was probably born in Verona, he came to Venice around 1515 and enjoyed great success at the head of a productive workshop. Although there are a number of works by him in the Accademia, only a few others remain in Venice (in the churches of Santo Stefano, the Angelo Raffaele, Santa Maria Mater Domini and Sant'Alvise). He was greatly influenced by Palma Vecchio and Titian, but then developed a Mannerist style of his own, using vibrant colours and monumental compositions for his numerous narrative paintings. Although they never reach the level of the greatest Venetian masters, his works are interesting for their Venetian associations. *God the Father above Piazza San Marco* provides a detailed documentation of the Piazza in the 1540s, including Sansovino's recently completed Loggetta at the foot of the Campanile. The *Madonna 'dei Sartori'* (the Virgin with Sts Omobono and Barbara), painted for the tailors' confraternity, shows their patron saint in Venetian garb and the scissors, symbol of the *scuola*, at the foot of the throne. This is the only work known to be signed and dated (1533) by this artist. *Dives and Lazarus the Beggar* is probably his best work: the scene is set in a villa in the Veneto.

Tintoretto (1519–94): The Accademia contains a number of very fine works by this great artist: *Creation of the Animals* (the seas teem with fish and the sky is full of birds); the *Temptation of Adam and Eve*; and *Cain and Abel*; and four famous paintings commissioned by the Scuola Grande di San Marco (*see p. 145*). Other works include a *Crucifixion* and the *Madonna dei Camerlenghi*, commissioned by the treasurers of the Republic, who are shown dominating the scene, magnificently robed, followed by their secretaries bearing gifts for the Madonna against the setting sun. It is obvious that the artist paid much less attention to the Madonna and Child than to the crowded scene around her throne. (*For more on Tintoretto's life and artistic style, see pp. 28 and 199.*)

Veronese (1528–88): Veronese's life and art are described on p. 163. Dominating one of the rooms here is the huge painting of *Christ in the House of Levi* (1573), a splendid Venetian banquet scene framed in a Palladian loggia; the man in the foreground against the pillar on the left is said to be the painter himself. Some 50 figures animate the scene, with everyone busy enjoying themselves, dressed in splendid, colourful costumes, and including servants, clowns and dogs. In the background are extravagant buildings against a twilight sky. It was the secular character of this painting that brought Veronese into conflict with the Inquisition, and the name had to be changed from 'The Last Supper' to 'Christ in the House of Levi' before it was allowed to be hung in the refectory of Santi Giovanni e Paolo.

Ceiling paintings include *Venice Receiving the Homage of Hercules and Ceres* (from the Doge's Palace) and *St Francis Receiving the Stigmata* (from a church ceiling). Other works include a *Madonna and Child with Saints*, painted around 1564 for the church of San Zaccaria; the *Battle of Lepanto*, painted shortly after the battle itself in 1571, probably as an ex-voto for a Venetian who had taken part in this celebrated defeat of the Turks at the hand of a Christian fleet; the *Mystic Marriage of St Catherine* (c. 1575); an *Annunciation*, with beautiful architectural details inspired by a church in Vicenza completed by Palladio in 1578, the year this was painted; and a late *Crucifixion*.

Non-Venetian artists of the 16th century: The exquisite *Portrait of a Young Man* by Hans Memling was painted around 1480 but is of unknown provenance. There is a *Madonna and Child* by the Ferrarese painter Cosmè Tura (also named the *Virgin of the Zodiac* from the astrological symbols to left and right of the Virgin, though largely faded on the right). The two goldfinches perched on bunches of grapes above are prophetic symbols of the Passion. *St Jerome in the Desert* is by Piero della Francesca, with a kneeling donor and a view of Borgo San Sepolcro, the painter's Tuscan birthplace, in the background. Piero's signature is on the tree trunk which supports the Crucifix, but this exquisite little painting is damaged since the green pigment has turned brown.

Later 16th-century artists born outside Venice but with strong connections with the Venetian school, include Leandro Bassano (*Resurrection of Lazarus*), Bernardo Strozzi (portrait of the Procurator Grimani and *Supper in the House of Simon*) and Pordenone (*St Lorenzo Giustinian and Saints*). The collection also includes paintings by Domenico Fetti (notably *David* and *Meditation*), Annibale Carracci and Johann Liss.

THE EIGHTEENTH CENTURY

Works by **Giambattista Tiepolo** include a ruined frieze with the *Miracle of the Brazen Serpent*, fresco fragments from the Scalzi, and the circular *Exaltation of the True Cross*. There are also landscapes, bacchanals and hunting scenes by Francesco Zuccarelli, Giuseppe Zais and Marco Ricci, nephew of the more famous painter Sebastiano Ricci. The well-known *Fortune-teller*, by **Giovanni Battista Piazzetta**, is an ambiguous piece, notable for the knowing, worldly expression of the blowsy central figure.

There are *capricci* by **Canaletto** and **Francesco Guardi**, and a view of Venice (*Rio dei Mendicanti and the Scuola di San Marco*) by Canaletto's brilliant nephew **Bernardo Bellotto**, and typical Venetian interior scenes by **Pietro Longhi**.

THE PEGGY GUGGENHEIM COLLECTION

Map p. 409, F3. Open 10–6 daily except Tues. Entrance at no. 704 Fondamenta Venier or no. 701 Calle San Cristoforo. Café-restaurant.

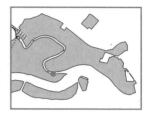

The collection provides one of the most representative displays of modern art (after 1910) in Europe. It is housed in Palazzo Venier dei Leoni on the Grand Canal, which was the residence of Peggy Guggenheim from 1949 until her death in 1979. The palace was begun in 1749 by Lorenzo Boschetti, but only the ground floor was ever built. The building is surrounded by a luxuriant garden redesigned by Giorgio Bellavitis in 1983.

A new wing, opened in 1993, includes a sculpture garden and galleries for temporary exhibitions. The permanent collection, which is frequently changed round, is very well labelled, also in English.

PEGGY GUGGENHEIM

Peggy Guggenheim (1898–1979) was the flamboyant daughter of one of the seven Guggenheim brothers who became rich at the end of the 19th century: their fortune came from copper mines. Peggy's father, Benjamin Guggenheim, was drowned on the SS *Titanic* in April 1912. Though born in New York, Peggy spent most of her life in Europe. In 1939 she decided to create a contemporary art museum in London with the help of the art critic Herbert Read. Her plans were frustrated by the Second World War, and she returned to New York to open (in 1942) a sensational museum-gallery called Art of This Century. Here, up until 1947, she exhibited European works from her own collection as well as giving exhibitions to then-unknown American artists—Jackson Pollock among them. Her patronage helped to launch the careers of several of the artists who were later to form the New York school of Abstract Expressionism. Her first husband was the American collage artist Laurence Vail, and her second the Surrealist Max Ernst.

Her own collection made its European début at the first post-war Venice Biennale (1948) in the otherwise empty Greek pavilion. In 1949 she bought Palazzo Venier dei Leoni (from the heirs of Doris, Viscountess Castlerosse), where she lived for the rest of her life. Here, in 1951, she founded her contemporary art museum and opened it every summer to visitors. Today the collection is owned and operated by the New York Foundation named after one of her uncles, Solomon R. Guggenheim, who founded the famous museum in New York.

In the **Nasher Sculpture Garden** there is a Byzantine-style bishop's throne and sculptures by Arp, Moore, Giacometti and Max Ernst, as well as works loaned from the Nasher Sculpture Center, Dallas. In the corner, beyond the gazebo, an inscription on the wall marks the spot where Peggy Guggenheim's ashes are preserved, next to the place where her pet dogs were buried.

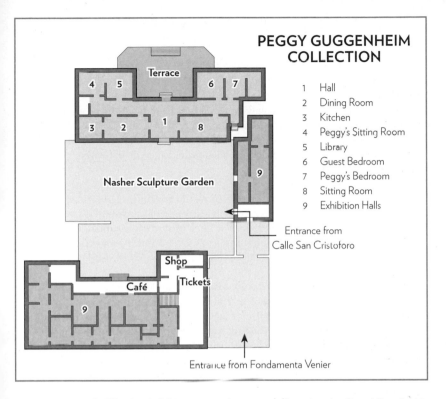

The entrance hall leads straight out onto the **terrace** fronting the Grand Canal with its frieze of colossal lions' heads at water level. Here is Marino Marini's equestrian statue *Angel of the City* and the bright red *Cow* by Alexander Calder, installed in 2012 (from the Schulhof collection).

Interesting photographs in the various rooms of the house where the collection is exhibited illustrate its appearance in Peggy Guggenheim's day.

THE PAINTINGS

Important Cubist paintings include works by Picasso (*The Poet, The Studio*), Braque (*The Clarinet*), Léger (*Men in the City*), Duchamp, Gris, Gleizes, Metzinger and Delaunay. Early Italian Modernism is represented by Futurist paintings by Giacomo Balla and Severini as well as a sculpture by Umberto Boccioni (*Dynamism of a Speeding Horse* and *Houses*) and Metaphysical paintings by Giorgio de Chirico (*The Red Tower*, a typical work, with a darkened, threatening foreground. The equestrian statue on the right of the canvas throws another sinister shadow in front of the mysterious red tower). Works by Kupka, Kandinsky (*Landscape with Red Spot*), Mondrian, Van Doesburg, Malevich, Pevsner, Lissitzky and Hélion represent European Abstraction and non-Objective art in the period from 1910 to the 1930s. Works by Arp, Picabia,

Schwitters and Ernst belong to the Dada movement, while elements of fantasy in works by Chagall (*Rain*) and Klee (*Magic Garden*) relate these artists to Surrealism, which is particularly well represented: Ernst (*The Kiss, Attirement of the Bride* and *Anti-Pope*), Miró (*Dutch Interior II* and *Seated Woman II*), Magritte (*Empire of Light*), Delvaux, Dalí (*Birth of Liquid Desires*), Tanguy, Cornell, Brauner, Matta and others. Peggy Guggenheim's support of young American artists in the 1940s is manifest in the paintings by Jackson Pollock (*Moon Woman, Circumcision* and *Alchemy*, among others) and early works by Motherwell, Still, Rothko and Baziotes. There is also an important painting by Gorky. Post-war European art is represented by Dubuffet, Vedova, Appel, Jorn, Alechinsky, Bacon, Davie, Fontana, Nicholson, Tancredi and Bacci.

THE SCULPTURES

The sculpture collection includes two bronzes by Brancusi (*Maiastra* and *Bird in Space*). Alberto Giacometti is represented by early Surrealist works (*Woman with her Throat Cut* and *Walking Woman*) as well as later works (*Piazza* and '*Leoni' Woman*). There are also works by Pevsner and González (*Cactus Man*). Two mobiles and a silver bedhead (made on commission for Peggy Guggenheim) are by Alexander Calder.

There are also works from the **Gianni Mattioli Collection**, one of the last great private collections of early 20th-century Italian art, exhibited here on long-term loan. Six early paintings by Giorgio Morandi include his first masterpiece, *Bottles and a Fruit Bowl*. There are paintings by Modigliani (*Frank Haviland*) and exponents of the Metaphysical school (Carlo Carrà and Mario Sironi). The collection is dominated by Italian Futurism, with works by Boccioni (*Materia* and *Dynamism of a Cyclist*), Gino Severini (*Blue Dancer*), Balla (*Mercury Passing before the Sun*), Carrà (*Interventionist Demonstration*), Luigi Russolo, Ardengo Soffici and Fortunato Depero.

In 2012 the **Hannelore B. and Randolph Schulhof Collection** was left to the museum. It was begun in the late 1940s with works from the US as well as Europe, and includes paintings from the 1950s and 1960s by Jasper Johns, Alexander Calder, Andy Warhol, Afro, Lucio Fontana, Cy Twombly and Jean Dubuffet.

SANTA MARIA DELLA SALUTE

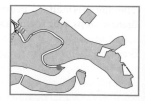

Map p. 406, C3. Open 9–12 & 3–5.30 (6.30 in summer). Sacristy open 3–5.30 and when possible also 10–12, unless Mass is being held.

At the easternmost tip of Dorsoduro, at the beginning of the Grand Canal, stands the famous church of Santa Maria della Salute. It was built in 1631–81 in thanksgiving for the deliverance from the plague of 1630–1, which had left some thirty percent of the city's population dead (46,000 people). It is a beautiful octagonal church, the masterpiece of Baldassare Longhena, and the most important edifice built in Venice in the 17th century. The water is reflected on its bright surface, built partly of Istrian stone and partly of *marmorino* (brick covered with marble dust). It rests on more than a million piles of oak, larch and elm. A unique building, and particularly well adapted to its impressive site at the entrance to the city, it dominates the view of the Grand Canal from the lagoon. The doge visited the Salute annually on 21st November in a procession across a pontoon of boats from San Marco: this Venetian festival is still celebrated every year on the same date. Crowds throng to the church to receive a votive candle. On this occasion a *Madonna and Child* attributed to Gentile Bellini is exhibited behind the high altar.

SANTA MARIA DELLA SALUTE

The church is built on a central plan with six lateral façades; you enter by a monumental flight of steps. Huge volutes surmounted by statues support the drum of the fine dome crowned by a lantern; a smaller cupola covers the east end. The sculptural decoration is attributed to Juste le Court (who also carried out important work in the interior) as well as to other, less well known, sculptors of the time, including Michele Ongaro and Tommaso Ruer.

The dome, sanctuary and aisle
The high **dome**, its drum pierced by large windows, sheds a beautiful light on the

central area of the church, which has a circular aisle (enhanced when the central door is open onto the Grand Canal). The polychrome marble floor is extremely fine.

In the **sanctuary**, much more dimly lit, the arch has four ancient Roman columns. Beneath a second dome is the high altar, on which is a 12th–13th-century Byzantine icon of the *Madonna and Child* (the *Mesopanditissa*) brought from the cathedral of Herakleion in Crete by Francesco Morosini in 1669. The altar is crowned with a remarkable sculptural group (1670) of the *Virgin Casting out the Plague* by Juste le Court, unfortunately rather too small for its setting. It shows a kneeling figure representing Venice interceding with the Virgin and Child, and an ugly female figure, an allegory of the plague, being frightened away with the help of cherubim. Flanking the group are *St Mark* and *St Lorenzo Giustinian*, both patron saints of Venice. The superb bronze paschal candelabrum was made in 1570 by the little-known artist Andrea Bresciano, a friend of Alessandro Vittoria.

In the **circular aisle** are three fine altarpieces of the life of the Virgin by Luca Giordano and an *Annunciation* by another 17th-century painter, Pietro Liberi. The *Pentecost* by Titian is usually dated around 1555 (but the two apostles in the foreground may be by assistants). Beneath it, a beautiful 15th-century Flemish tapestry of the Pentecost serves as an altar frontal, with charming landscapes of exquisite workmanship. Here is the entrance to the sacristy.

The sacristy
The Great Sacristy (*for opening times, see above*) has an important collection of works of art. On the wall opposite the entrance, the *Wedding at Cana* is a splendid work by Jacopo Tintoretto, with very beautiful light effects. Over the altar is hung an early work by Titian showing *St Mark Enthroned between Sts Cosmas and Damian and Sts Roch and Sebastian*. This was a votive painting for the liberation of Venice from the plague (probably that of 1510), and was commissioned by the monastery of Santo Spirito in Isola and moved to the Salute by the order of the Senate in 1656. It shows St Mark (representing Venice) enthroned above and between the two doctor saints (Cosmas and Damian) and the two saints traditionally associated with the plague, St Roch and St Sebastian. Also by Titian and also from Santo Spirito are the paintings on the ceiling in remarkable perspective: *Cain and Abel, Sacrifice of Isaac, David and Goliath* (this last was badly damaged by fire in 2010 but was very well restored in 2012), and eight tondi of the Evangelists and Doctors of the Church. High up to the left of the sanctuary is a votive painting by Padovanino of the Madonna with angels holding a model of the Salute.

Next to the church is the huge **Seminario Patriarcale**, the patriarchal seminary (the Bishop of Venice is officially styled 'Patriarch', one of only five Catholic bishops to enjoy this honour). Some of the seminary buildings have recently been restored to house the Studium Cattolicum, a university where public lectures are sometimes held. More extensive renovations, which involve the rehousing of the famous library and the Manfrediniana Picture Gallery (*at present closed*), have been under way for many years.

PUNTA DELLA DOGANA
(FRANÇOIS PINAULT FOUNDATION)

Map p. 407, D3. Open 10–6 except Tues; combined ticket available with Palazzo Grassi.

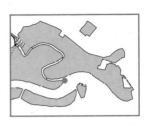

The promontory known as the Punta della Dogana was formerly the site of the *Dogana da Mar,* the customs house for goods arriving in Venice by sea. The building was given its attractive low Doric façade in 1682 by Giuseppe Benoni, the only work in Venice by this engineer, who advised Longhena on the static problems he faced when building the huge church of the Salute. After some decades of abandon, the Dogana was acquired by the municipality, who have leased it for 30 years to the French businessman and collector François Pinault, who owns Palazzo Grassi and who has been made an Honorary Citizen of Venice. It was magnificently restored for Pinault (and the foundations strengthened) by the Japanese architect Tadao Ando. As in Palazzo Grassi, exhibitions are held here of part of Pinault's vast collection of contemporary art and it has become an important venue for exhibitions during the Biennale. Ando preserved the exterior intact with the only addition of iron grilles at the windows and doorways, modelled on Carlo Scarpa's work at the Olivetti showroom in Piazza San Marco. At the entrance is a colossal bronze statue, *Vater Staat* by Thomas Schütte (2010).

THE ZATTERE & SAN TROVASO DISTRICT

Map p. 409, E4–D3.

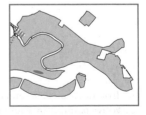

The Fondamenta delle Zattere, the wide, sun-washed quay which skirts the Giudecca Canal, was first paved in 1520. It is named after the cargo boats (*zattere,* literally 'rafts'), which used to pull in and unload here.

The busiest, most lively section of the Zattere begins at the point where Rio di San Vio flows into the Giudecca Canal. Here, side by side, stand two very well-known hotels (*described on pp. 353–4*): the Seguso and the Calcina. The latter is where Ruskin stayed in 1877, on almost the last of his many visits to the city while he was at work on *St Mark's Rest.*

Behind this section of the Zattere opens **Campo Sant'Agnese** (*map p. 409, E3*), with a few trees and oleanders. By the side flank of the church of the Gesuati, where a *rio* (since covered over) went under the church, there is an arch protected by a sculpted dog with floppy ears (the plaque close by records the installation of an aqueduct here in 1838). Above is a beautiful relief of Christ in *pietà* supported by two angels (c. 1480), restored in 2007 by the Venice in Peril Fund.

ZATTERE
Stone posting box for complaints
about the district health service.

The *campo* has a well-head with two garlands and a very worn relief of *St Agnes* dating from 1520. The church of Sant'Agnese (*usually only open for Sunday services*) was founded in the 10th century and is interesting for its simple basilican plan. It contains paintings by the little-known Venetian artist Lattanzio Querena (d. 1853).

THE CHURCHES OF THE GESUATI AND VISITAZIONE

On the Zattere, the church of the **Gesuati** (Santa Maria del Rosario; *map p. 409, D3, open Mon–Sat 10–5; Chorus Pass*), built by Giorgio Massari (1726–43), has a façade which echoes Venice's Palladian churches but on a much less grand scale. The steps are a popular place for people to sit and enjoy the last of the sun. The Rococo interior, with a single nave, has a remarkably successful design, with the dark high altar lit from behind. It has two very fine works by Giambattista Tiepolo: the *Institution of the Rosary*, frescoed on the ceiling in 1737–9, and the *Virgin in Glory with Sts Rosa, Catherine of Siena and Agnes of Montepulciano* (1739) on the first south altar. Two other 18th-century altarpieces also have trios of saints: that on the first north altar by Sebastiano Ricci, and that on the third south altar by Giovanni Battista Piazzetta. On the third north altar the *Crucifixion*, with a beautifully composed group of mourning women at the foot of the Cross, is by Jacopo Tintoretto (c. 1570). The statues and reliefs in the nave are by Giovanni Maria Morleiter, and there is a polychrome wood Crucifix dating from the 15th century in a little chapel on the north side. The elaborate tabernacle on the high altar is encased in lapis lazuli and has precious marble columns.

Outside the church, the Zattere is busy with several vaporetto stops. At the side entrance to the Centro Culturale Don Orione Artigianelli, a former convent with two cloisters, now a very simple but pleasant hotel (*main entrance on Campo Sant'Agnese*), you will see a worried face carved in marble: this is a **bocca di leone**, an official 'post box' with its mouth open ready to receive complaints about the local health service. It dates from the days of the Republic. Next door is the Renaissance church of **Santa Maria della Visitazione** (*often closed*), with a handsome Lombardesque façade and portal (1494–1524). It contains a charming wooden roof filled with 58 panels of saints and prophets and a central tondo of the *Visitation* painted in the 16th century by a Tuscan or northern Italian artist. In the pretty sanctuary are four large painted tondi of the Evangelists (showing the influence of the Florentine art of Andrea del Castagno) and in the choir hangs a *Pentecost* by Padovanino.

At the far west end of the Zattere is the **Stazione Marittima**, opened in 1880 to coincide with the arrival of the railway: its warehouses were accessible from the Giudecca Canal. It is now used mostly by cruise ships and a new car park is planned (an annual boat show is also held here).

SQUERO DI SAN TROVASO

The Squero di San Trovaso (*map p. 409, D3*) is a picturesque little boatyard dating from the 17th century, though it has been altered and restored over time. The living quarters on the upper floor have a long wooden balcony usually decorated with plants. It was in yards such as this (another survives nearby in Rio della Avogaria) that the great Venetian fleet of warships and merchant ships was built before the end of the 15th century; after that date, boat-building was concentrated in the Arsenale. This *squero* now specialises in the construction and repair of gondolas.

THE GONDOLA

The famous gondolas of Venice are of ancient origin and peculiar build, and retain the form they had assumed by the 18th century. They have been painted black since 1562, when it was decided this was an effective way to minimise rivalry between noble Venetian families, each of which had its private gondola. A wooden shelter, or *felze*, used to protect passengers in bad weather. Although some 11m long, gondolas are particularly light and easy to manoeuvre by a single standing oarsman with just one oar. The asymmetrical shape compensates for the weight of the oarsman and the fact that the boat is rowed only at one side. Gondolas are able to transport a great number of passengers in respect of their weight and size. They are constructed with 280 pieces of seven different types of wood, and have a peculiarly shaped crutch (*forcola*), sculpted out of walnut, where the oar rests (it can be angled in three different positions). Another feature is the long prow: known as the *ferro*, it has six 'teeth' representing the six *sestieri*, and a seventh on the other side for the Giudecca. Until relatively recently, gondoliers operated as a closed guild, with the trade passed down from father to son. In 2009 the first ever female gondolier was granted a licence. There is an association for the protection of gondolas: Ente Gondola; www.gondolavenezia.it. (*For more on gondolas and for details about the excellent gondola ferries (traghetti) across the Grand Canal, see p. 350.*)

At the foot of the first bridge over the Rio San Trovaso, by the 15th-century Palazzo Nani, is a famous *bàcaro*, one of the most popular in the area, officially named **Schiavi** after the family of the former proprietor, but known to Venetians as the Bottegon ('the shop'). Now run by Schiavi's three sons, it has a delightful Venetian atmosphere: there is no seating, but when it is sunny, clients stand on the pavement outside and balance their glasses on the canal parapet. It is also a good place to buy a bottle of wine, and is especially frequented for its great variety of delicious *cicchetti*, made and served by the former owner's widow.

THE CHURCH OF SAN TROVASO

Map p. 409, D3. Open 8.30–11 & 2.30–5.30; closed Sun.

The church of San Trovaso, founded in 731 or 931, was once one of the most important churches in Venice. It was dedicated to Sts Gervase and Protase (Santi Gervasio e Protasio), but its name is always concatenated to San Trovaso. The relics of St Chrysogonus were preserved here: after his beheading in Aquileia under Diocletian, these were taken to Zara (modern Zadar) in Dalmatia, but during the Fourth Crusade in 1204 they were seized by the Venetians. However, in 1240 they were given back to Zara and only returned to Italy in the 16th century, not to Venice but to the church of San Crisogono in Rome. San Trovaso had to be reconstructed the year after it collapsed in 1584, and the architect appears to have been a pupil of Palladio. It is unusual in having two similar façades. The peaceful *campo* in front of the main façade is occupied by a raised cistern around its well-head. You can see the four drains for rainwater, situated slightly lower than the well-head so that water runs into them (*see p. 33 for a diagram of a Venetian well*).

Interior of San Trovaso

The interior is rich in works of art. The altarpieces in the north chapels are by Palma Giovane, including (third altar) *Birth of the Virgin*, a very well composed painting. In the chapel to the left of the sanctuary, the *Temptation of St Anthony*, by Tintoretto (c. 1577), was commissioned by Antonio Milledonne, a wealthy citizen who took an active part in government administration and who is shown here in the guise of the saint. The charming decorative painting of St Chrysogonus on horseback, by Michele Giambono (in a 17th-century frame), comes from the earlier church. Although painted in the 15th century, it shows a flowery archaic Gothic style.

The adjacent chapel of the Scuola del Santissimo Sacramento (which survived when the rest of the church collapsed in 1584) preserves its furnishings, including four little lamps (kept permanently alight), a gilded tabernacle, and an altar of Carrara marble. The universal symbol of the chalice and Host appears in many of the carvings. This is one of many such chapels in Venetian parish churches founded during the Counter-Reformation and dedicated to the Eucharist. Their founders tended to be from the lower artisan classes, and their activities were controlled by the Church rather than the Council of Ten (who oversaw the building activities of the other *scuole* in the city). Such chapels are often decorated with paintings by Tintoretto, as is this one. On the right wall is a *Last Supper*, one of a number of paintings of this subject by him still in

SAN TROVASO
Altar of the guild of shipwrights (*squeraioli*).

Venice. In this version, there is a sense of ambiguity: it is not obvious who Judas is, but there are hints. There is an urgency to the scene, with the chair knocked over, disciples leaning towards Jesus wanting to know who is to betray Him, and one member of the party grabbing more wine. As in so many of Tintoretto's canvases, ethereal, wraith-like figures populate the background; but in this work it is the details that fascinate the most. The painting of the *Washing of the Feet* opposite is a copy of a painting by Tintoretto formerly here but bought by the National Gallery in London in 1882.

The two paintings in the sanctuary (*Adoration of the Magi* and *Expulsion from the Temple*) are by Tintoretto's son Domenico. Over the south door is the *Wedding at Cana*, signed by Andrea Vicentino. In the Cappella Clary, to the right of the door, the altar bears a lovely, very low bas-relief in Greek marble of angels holding signs of the Passion or playing musical instruments. One of the most interesting products of the Venetian Renaissance, it is thought to date from c. 1470, but is of unknown provenance and by an unknown master, named the Maestro di San Trovaso after this relief (he is sometimes identified by scholars with Antonio Rizzo, Pietro Lombardo, Agostino di Duccio or even Donatello). The organ is by Callido (1765).

WESTERN DORSODURO & SAN SEBASTIANO

Rio di Ognissanti (*map p. 408, C3*), crossed by two handsome 18th-century bridges, leads through the *sestiere*. Near its eastern end, on the side opposite the *fondamenta*, rises **Ca' Michiel**, unusual in its design since it has two protruding wings: it was famous for its garden in the 16th century. Ponte Trevisan (1772, redesigned in 1861) crosses the particularly pretty Rio degli Eremite, where small boats are usually moored, lined on either side by *fondamente*. The little **church of the Eremite** dates from 1694 (*admission on request at the convent of the Canossian nuns next door, who also run a simple hotel*). It contains two marble altars with 17th-century sculptures by Tommaso Ruer and Antonio Corradini, a ceiling paintings by Niccolò Bambini, and an unusual early 15th-century polychrome wood relief of the *Madonna della Misericordia*.

Fondamenta Ognissanti continues through a very peaceful district, with a good view back of the dome and twin towers of the Gesuati. The **church of Ognissanti** (All Saints) was founded in the 15th century but rebuilt in the 16th, when the campanile was erected with its onion-shaped dome. A house on the opposite side of the canal is decorated with sculpted heads, and another has a characteristic *altana* on the roof, and a relief of the lion of St Mark and more lions' heads supporting the balcony (as well as an ancient carved human head). The boatyard (*squero*) on Rio dell'Avogaria has belonged to the Tramontin, a family of boat-builders, since 1809.

Calle della Chiesa continues, to emerge on Rio di San Sebastiano, with a little group of shops.

SAN SEBASTIANO

Map p. 408, B2. Open Mon–Sat 10–5; Chorus Pass.

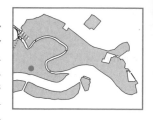

The church of San Sebastiano was rebuilt after 1506 by Scarpagnino. The interior was decorated in 1555–70 by the great Venetian painter Paolo Veronese. He lived in the neighbouring *salizzada*, so this was his parish church (where he is also buried), and it is perhaps here that his great artistic skill can best be understood. Together with Fra' Bernardo Torlioni, the cultivated prior of the church (who was, like Veronese, from Verona), he worked out the complicated iconographical scheme, which includes allegories of the triumph of Faith over Heresy, with frequent references also to the plague and to the life of the titular saint, Sebastian.

In the three central panels of the beautiful **ceiling** (restored in 2010 by Save Venice Inc.), with its elaborate wooden framework, Veronese painted scenes from the life of Esther, the 'fair and beautiful' orphan who 'obtained favour in the sight of all them that looked upon her', so much so that the Persian king Ahasuerus, after banishing his wife Vashti, decided to make her his queen. Esther's subsequent famous defence of the Jewish people, saving them from massacre ('For how can I endure to see the evil that shall come unto my people?'), and her cousin Mordechai the Jew's unselfish protection of the king from danger, are described in the Old Testament Book of Esther. The scene nearest the door depicts the grim expulsion of Vashti; the central scene shows the joyful crowning of the beautiful Esther by Ahasuerus (with a conspicuous white dog seated beneath the throne); and the far scene depicts the triumph of Mordechai, whom the grateful king ordered to be honoured with a procession through the streets of the city, dressed in royal apparel with the king's own crown, and mounted on horseback. This scene is dominated by Mordechai's splendid grey charger next to a dark horse in attendance—both of them with their hooves raised as they seem to prance down to us out of the ceiling, while the crowds wave Mordechai on from the top of a huge marble palace. The smaller panels have putti, flowers and garlands of fruit, and four monochrome roundels with *Hope*, *Charity*, *Faith* and *Justice*.

PAOLO VERONESE

Paolo Caliari (1528–88), the son of a stonemason, was known as Veronese since he was born in Verona, where he learnt his skills. He moved to Venice in 1555 where he soon became celebrated: besides his splendid works here in San Sebastiano, he was commissioned to paint many works for the Doge's Palace and Venice's churches, and today beautiful paintings by him can be seen all over the city. Although a devout Catholic, he was particularly interested in secular subjects, and his elegant, colourful figures are often sumptuously dressed. He frequently included painted architectural elements in his works and collaborated with Palladio at the Villa Barbaro in Maser (he is also famous for the splendid decorations he carried out in numerous other villas in the Veneto). The atmosphere in his works is usually serene, in contrast to the more dramatic scenes produced by his contemporary Tintoretto. He naturally influenced a great many artists, including Giambattista Tiepolo.

In the **spandrels above the nave arches**, Veronese frescoed the Apostles. Around the very top of the walls are the prophets and sibyls, between twisted columns. The **barco**, or monks' choir, has been closed indefinitely: it has frescoes which illustrate the legend of St Sebastian, the Roman centurion who was martyred for his faith. On the **sanctuary arch** are more prophets and sibyls, and in the spandrels, the *Annunciation*. Veronese also painted the three works in the **sanctuary**: the *Madonna and Child with St Sebastian* over the altar (also designed by him); *St Sebastian Encourages Sts Mark and Marcellian to Martyrdom*; and the *Second Martyrdom of St Sebastian* (when he was beaten to death). Above the two side paintings, flanking the round windows, are the Evangelists.

The two altarpieces in the **third south and north chapels** are also by Veronese. One depicts the *Crucifixion* and the other, a small painting, the *Madonna and St Catherine*, with the friar Michele Spaventi (who lived in the convent). This latter chapel also has fine sculpture by Alessandro Vittoria (including a bust of Marcantonio Grimani, and statuettes of *St Mark* and *St Anthony Abbot*).

The two doors of the **organ** (constructed in 1558) were also painted (inside and out) by Veronese—the outer doors show the *Presentation of Christ in the Temple* in a grand architectural setting. Beneath the organ is the door into the **sacristy**, where the panelled and painted ceiling is one of Veronese's earliest works in all Venice (1555). Since the ceiling is so low, his skill can be studied in greater detail. The central scene of the *Coronation of the Virgin* shows the Madonna as little more than a young girl beside the handsome young Christ (offering support to the elderly God the Father) revealed by two cherubs who hold back the clouds. The ovals with the four Evangelists (identified by their symbols) are depicted with ingenious perspective, but the artist's immaturity is perhaps revealed here as it is not clear to us just where each of the saints is directing his gaze. The other tiny scenes have stories from the Old Testament. The sacristy is a very well preserved room, with a lovely old marble floor and wooden benches and paintings round the walls, the best of which is perhaps the *Resurrection* by Veronese's much less well-known contemporary Antonio Palma.

Other works of interest in the church include **St Nicholas of Bari**, painted for the altar beneath the gallery in 1563 by Titian when he was in his mid-seventies—one wonders if the great artist may have felt like or even resembled the genial elderly saint he depicted here. The huge tomb of Archbishop Livio Podocattaro of Cyprus (d. 1555) is by Jacopo Sansovino.

Veronese's brother Benedetto helped him in the frescoed decoration on the smaller panels in the church ceiling. He died ten years after Paolo: the **pavement tomb of both Veronese brothers** is at the entrance to the Lando Chapel to the left of the choir (*closed at the time of writing*; its rare majolica faïence pavement, with no less than 384 tiles thought to date from around 1510, was removed for restoration in 1993–2001 and has yet to be returned). Paolo was simply commemorated in the 17th century with a bust on the wall close by, beside the organ.

Behind the church are two *campi*, one of which has a **well-head in Istrian stone**, dated 1349. The year before, a merchant called Marco Arian had died of plague. Believing that the outbreak could have been caused by contaminated water, he left funds in his will for the construction of a well to provide fresh water for the district.

THE CHURCH OF SANT'ANGELO RAFFAELE
Map p. 408, B2. Open 10–12 & 3–5.30, Sun 9–12.

Tucked away in Campo dell'Angelo Raffaele, in a very quiet, little-visited corner of the city, is the church of Sant'Angelo Raffaele, dedicated to the Archangel Raphael, who has always been particularly venerated (together with the Archangel Gabriel) in Eastern liturgy and whose name means 'God heals'. He is one of just three named archangels in scripture (the third being Michael). The church has numerous depictions, in both sculpture and painting, of the archangel accompanying Tobias (usually seen holding a fish and with a little dog trotting behind him, as for example on the old well-head outside the south façade), whose story is told in the Apocrypha in the Book of Tobias (or Tobit). Tobias was sent on a journey to recover a debt and was accompanied by a fellow traveller, whose real identity as the Archangel Raphael was only revealed to him after the successful outcome of his mission. The fish turned out to be miraculous and its entrails helped cure an old man of his blindness. Interestingly enough, the dog who accompanies Tobias is considered a positive attribute, whereas all the other dogs mentioned in the Old Testament represent or are associated with evil.

Over the main entrance is a 16th-century sculptured *Archangel Raphael* with Tobias and his dog, and there are statues of the *Redeemer* with saints and angels on the tympanum. On the east end is another relief of Raphael, which also records the date of the church's consecration (1193).

The interior was designed on a Greek-cross plan when it was reconstructed in 1618 by Francesco Contino. The organ loft bears a series of little paintings by Antonio Guardi, brother of the more famous painter Francesco (*coin-operated light essential*), setting the story of Tobias and the Archangel in 18th-century Venice: the elegantly-dressed figures seem to have very little to do with the sacred atmosphere of a church. On the west wall are two paintings of the *Last Supper*, one by Bonifacio de' Pitati (Bonifacio Veronese) to the left of the door as you face it, and the other, painted about a century later, by Alvise dal Friso (right of the door). The altar on the north side dedicated to the archangel has a lovely wooden statue of *Raphael with Tobias*, and 18th-century gilded wood candelabra. Above the side door there is an unusual high relief dating from the late 16th century of a female figure holding a staff, with kneeling figures and a dragon. This is usually thought to represent St Martha (with her distaff), although it may simply be the portrait of a mother abbess symbolically overcoming the devil, shown surrounded by her nuns. There is a pretty marble tabernacle in the chapel of the sacrament, to the left of the sanctuary; the carved and gilded wood ensigns preserved here were made in the 18th and 19th centuries to be carried in procession by members of the Scuola del Santissimo. There is another pretty little tabernacle in the sanctuary (unfortunately radically restored in 1772 by the Foscarini) and on the wall behind, yet another painting of Raphael and Tobias, this one dating from 1772, by Michelangelo Morleiter. The fresco of the other famous archangel, Michael, shown overcoming the Devil on the ceiling of the nave, is by Francesco Fontebasso, who also frescoed the baptistery off the sanctuary (*shown on request*). The pulpit was made in 1687 but its carvings and reliefs, in medieval style, appear to be a replica of a 14th-century work.

Outside the church, a bridge leads over the *rio*, where a 19th-century tabernacle houses a wooden Crucifix which may date from the 14th century (restored in 2005 by the Venice in Peril Fund). From here, Fondamenta Barbarigo leads through an area traditionally inhabited by fishermen and sailors towards the lovely little church of San Nicolò dei Mendicoli.

SAN NICOLÒ DEI MENDICOLI

Map p. 408, A2. Open 10–12 & 3–5.30, Sun 10-12.

Founded in the 7th century, though subsequently rebuilt and restored, this church has a well-preserved detached 12th-century campanile and a little 15th-century porch (*entrance on the north side*). The charming interior retains its 12th-century Veneto-Byzantine plan, with fine columns (the capitals were replaced in the 14th century). It is rather dark, and the coin-operated light is helpful. In the nave, the interesting gilded wooden sculptural decoration of the Apostles (similar to that in the Carmini) was added in the late 16th century, and the fine series of paintings was commissioned in 1553 from Alvise dal Friso and other pupils of Paolo Veronese. In the apse is a delightful wooden statue of the titular saint by an unknown sculptor influenced by Bartolomeo Bon. The tondo of *St Nicholas in Glory* in the ceiling was painted in the late 16th century by Francesco Montemezzano: the *Miracles of St Nicholas*, on either side, are by his contemporary, Leonardo Corona. The first north altar has a statue of St Martha with a snarling mastiff-dragon beside her. The organ loft is decorated with scenes from her life.

On the far side of the canal to the west of San Nicolò, a former cotton factory has been converted into lecture halls by the faculty of architecture at Venice University (IUAV). On its roof, conspicuous from the Giudecca Canal, is a sculpture (huge wooden wings) by Massimo Scolari (1991).

Fondamenta delle Terese leads east past the disused church of **Le Terese** (*map p. 408, A2*), completed in 1688 to a design by Andrea Cominelli, and its ex-convent, recently restored for IUAV around the cloister. On the opposite side of the *rio* is the **Casa dei Sette Camini** (named after its seven chimney pots): during its restoration by the Venice municipality, the foundations were carefully raised and it now provides housing for several Venetian families. Close by, at the corner of Calle Riello, is an attractive small palace which was beautifully converted in 2004 into a comfortable little family-run hotel called Tiziano (*see p. 354*)—one of the most successful of numerous such conversions which have taken place in the past few years.

Corte Maggiore (or Mazor) leads down to Fondamenta Barbarigo, which continues left past the church of the Angelo Raffaele (*see p. 164*) into Fondamenta Briati. Nearly opposite the junction with Rio di San Sebastiano is the Gothic **Palazzo Arian-Cicogna** (no. 2376; now a school; *map p. 408, B2*), with a very beautiful six-light window decorated above with a double row of superimposed quatrefoils with fine tracery showing the influence of Eastern architecture. This is particularly interesting since it is known to pre-date the Gothic decoration on the exterior of Doge's Palace. The fine courtyard has an outside stair. Beyond a small group of shops are two handsome old palaces, one (no. 2535) with rounded windows, and the other, next door, with trefoil windows, newly restored. The building crowned with busts and set back from the *fondamenta* is part of the faculty of letters of Venice University. An ancient statue, now headless, and a fat little lion of St Mark perched on a Doric column can be seen in the garden. On the opposite side of the canal is the huge **Palazzo Zenobio**, one of the largest private palaces in Venice, owned by the Armenian community. The early Baroque interior (*not usually open to the public*), designed by Antonio Gaspari, contains landscape frescoes and ceiling paintings by Luca Carnevalis, Gregorio Lazzarini and Giambattista Tiepolo. In the garden is a pavilion in Palladian style by Tommaso Temanza (1773).

CAMPO SANTA MARGHERITA & DISTRICT

Campo di Santa Margherita (*map p. 408, C2–C1*) is spacious and lively, surrounded by simple low houses, some of them dating from the 14th–15th centuries. It is one of the most pleasant squares in the city, always full of local families and their children, who come here to pass the time of day or visit the little daily market (which has three fish stalls in the mornings). It has a miscellany of shops and cafés with tables outside—sedate cafés by day 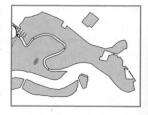 and lively bars at night. The one called simply Caffè in the middle of the west side of the *campo*, with a sign painted bright red, still retains its charming interior and vintage coffee machine. Delightfully old-fashioned, with cordial proprietors, it is one of the cheapest places to sit and have a coffee in all Venice. At the north end of the *campo*, an old house and the stump of a campanile bear interesting sculptural fragments from the former church of Santa Margherita, whose decayed façade is nearby. The little building isolated in the middle of the *campo* is the **Scuola dei Varotari**, where the tanners met: it bears a worn relief dating from 1501 of the Virgin amidst the brothers of the *scuola*.

SANTA MARIA DEI CARMINI

Map p. 408, C2. Open 7.30–12 & 2.30–7.
The church of Santa Maria dei Carmini (or del Carmelo) has a 16th-century brick façade attributed to Sebastiano Mariani da Lugano, with statues by Giovanni Buora. The side entrance has a fine Romanesque exterior porch decorated on one side with Byzantine Greek marble paterae dating from the 11th and 12th centuries (restored in 2006).

The most striking feature of the spacious basilican interior is the gilded wooden sculptural decoration in the nave, similar, though on a larger scale, to that in San Nicolò dei Mendicoli. Above it runs a frieze of 17th–18th-century paintings. The singing-galleries are decorated with paintings by Andrea Schiavone.

On the west wall is a monument to Jacopo Foscarini (d. 1602) by the school of Sansovino. Foscarini was a procurator of St Mark's and took an active part in the government of the Republic, but just failed to become doge. On the north wall near the west door is a vast canvas by Padovanino.

By the side door, on the second altar in the north aisle, the painting of *St Nicholas in Glory with St John the Baptist and St Lucy,* by Lorenzo Lotto, was commissioned for the church in 1529 (and is still in its original Istrian stone frame). This is one of Lotto's masterpieces, with a remarkable coastal landscape beneath, showing the influence of northern painters. Using a bird's eye perspective, it illustrates St Nicholas' protection of navigators and his help in times of famine and pestilence. On the wall beside it is a charming small painting of the *Holy Family* by Paolo Veronese, originally from the church of San Barnaba. In front of the third north altar is a small bronze plaque (c. 1474) with an exquisite relief of the *Deposition*, the only work in Venice by the great Sienese artist of the Renaissance (sculptor, architect and painter) Francesco di Giorgio Martini. It includes portraits (right) of his famous patron Federico da Montefeltro, for whom he worked in Urbino, and of his duchess Battista Sforza.

On the second altar on the south side is a beautiful painting of the *Nativity* by Cima da Conegliano (c. 1509). The lovely vault above the third altar is frescoed by Sebastiano Ricci: the two bronze angel-candelabra on the balustrade are by Girolamo Campagna, and on either side of the altar are statues by (right) Antonio Corradini and (left) Giuseppe Torretti. Also on the south side, on the altar of the guild of fishmongers (carved with a fish and a pelican), is a *Presentation of Christ in the Temple* by Tintoretto.

Above the sanctuary entrance hangs a 14th-century gilded wood Crucifix, and on its walls are four large paintings by Palma Giovane (1613), Gaspare Diziani (1749) and Marco Vicentino (1613).

SCUOLA GRANDE DEI CARMINI

Map p. 408, C2. Open every day 10–5 or 6.

The *Scuola* was founded in 1597. The building, of 1668, is attributed to Baldassare Longhena. In the delightful interior, the 18th-century decoration of the chapel on the ground floor includes monochrome paintings by Niccolò Bambini and an altarpiece by Sante Piatti. An elaborate double staircase, to a design by Longhena with early 18th-century stucco decoration, leads to the upper floor.

The *salone* was also probably designed by Longhena and built by his pupil Antonio Gaspari. The nine superb paintings in the ceiling (1739–49) are among the masterpieces of Giambattista Tiepolo, with allegories of the Virtues around the central *Virgin in Glory* (the *Apparition of the Madonna of Mt Carmel to the Blessed Simon Stock*). The scenes illustrate the legend of the English hermit Simon, who is supposed to have lived in the hollow trunk of an oak tree (hence, perhaps, his name 'stock', meaning 'stump'), before becoming the sixth general of the Carmelite Order in 1247. The frescoes were carried out to celebrate the popular credence of the time that the Madonna herself had presented him with the scapular (the two small squares of woven cloth fastened together by strings which were worn over the shoulder by the Carmelites), which then became his attribute. Though picturesque, this legend is now recognised as a 17th-century invention. Nevertheless, Tiepolo skilfully incorporates the scapular numerous times in the ceiling—mostly as a plaything for the host of delightful putti and angels.

GIAMBATTISTA TIEPOLO

Tiepolo (1696–1770) was the most important fresco painter in Venice in the 18th century. He received many important commissions from the Venetian aristocracy and the Church, and was famous both in Italy and abroad. His Rococo decorative style, with numerous charming details, was particularly well suited to ceilings, and had a great influence on European painting, making Venice a centre of European art. A follower of Veronese, he worked in numerous palaces and churches in Venice, and in villas in the Veneto, as well as in Germany and Madrid (where he died). In 1719 he married Cecilia Guardi, sister of the painter Francesco. Tiepolo's son, Gian Domenico worked with him, and later developed his own style to depict delightful scenes of Venetian social life, many of which can also be seen in Venice.

On the walls are works by Antonio Zanchi and Gregorio Lazzarini. In the Sala dell'Albergo is a good ceiling painting of the *Assumption* by Padovanino, and around the walls, 17th-century paintings including works by Antonio Balestra. The Sala dell'Archivio was decorated in 1748 by Giustino Menescardi. By the door into the Sala dell'Albergo, the painting of *Judith and Holofernes* was added by Giovanni Battista Piazzetta.

SAN PANTALON

Map p. 409, D1. Open 10–7, Sun 9–12.

A bridge (redesigned by Eugenio Miozzi in 1932) leads out of the north side of Campo

Santa Margherita, over the Rio Nuovo and into Campo San Pantalon, with the bare unfinished façade of the church of the same name. In the interior, the nave roof is covered by a huge painting (1680–1704) on canvas by Gian Antonio Fumiani (he also decorated some of the vaults in the side chapels and the painting on the east wall). He was killed in a fall from the scaffolding at the end of the work and is buried in the church. The painting describes, in remarkable perspective, events in the life of the titular saint, and his martyrdom under Diocletian. It is a spectacular feat of *trompe l'oeil*; the eye is drawn up into the seemingly endless heavens, where flailing limbs and clashing wings accompany the martyrdom and apotheosis of the saint.

The treasures of the church are kept in the chapel to the left of the high altar (*entered on the left; you are asked to make a small contribution to the lighting*). Here there is an elaborately carved Gothic tabernacle; paintings of the *Madonna and Child* and four stories from the life of the Virgin by Paolo Veneziano; and a delightful *Coronation of the Virgin*, crowded with saints and prophets, by Giovanni d'Alemagna and Antonio Vivarini (1444). The four Evangelists seated in the foreground are identified by their emblems, and behind them all the other inhabitants of Paradise are shown in serried ranks. There is a high relief on the altar frontal of the *Marys at the Sepulchre* and a crowned statuette of the *Madonna and Child* in a niche dating from the late 14th century.

St Pantaleon is depicted healing a child in an altarpiece by Veronese in the second south chapel (*coin-operated light*), which contains the saint's relics. The painting was commissioned by the parish priest in 1587 for the high altar. The present high altar and tabernacle were designed by Giuseppe Sardi in 1668–71. On a pedestal on the north side (beneath the pulpit) there is an early 16th-century marble bust of the Redeemer, attributed to Cristoforo Solari. Most of the sculptures and paintings in the side chapels date from the 18th century (and include works by Pietro Baratta, Gregorio Lazzarini, Alessandro Longhi, Jacopo and Vincenzo Guarana, Niccolò Bambini and Giovanni Bonazza).

On the right of the church façade, the **Campiello de Ca'Angaran** has a remarkable large sculpted roundel of a Byzantine emperor dating from the late 12th century. Behind the church, off Calle della Scuola, **Calle dei Preti** preserves a venerable 13th-century well-head, one of the very few pre-Gothic ones to survive in the city.

PONTE DEI PUGNI AND SAN BARNABA

From the south side of Campo Santa Margherita, the wide Rio Terrà Canal leads to the peaceful Rio di San Barnaba, crossed by the **Ponte dei Pugni** (*map p. 408, C2*). The bridge was rebuilt in the mid-19th century. Its white marble footprints recall the traditional fist-fights which took place in the 14th–18th centuries (when the bridge was without a parapet) between two rival factions of the city, the '*Nicolotti*' from San Nicolò dei Mendicoli in Dorsoduro, and the '*Castellani*' from San Pietro di Castello. From the bridge, the 17th-century campanile of the church of the Carmini is conspicuous to the right, and that of San Barnaba, dating from the 14th century, to the left. A greengrocer's barge is always moored in the *rio* here.

In the lively **Campo San Barnaba** (*map p. 409, D2*) is the church of the same name, rebuilt modestly in the 18th century, at a time when funds were in short supply as this part of town was home to the '*Barnabotti*', noblemen fallen on hard times who subsisted on state charity in boarding houses here. The name of the restaurant and pizzeria Casin dei Nobili (just under the archway at the back of the *campo*) recalls them. Though the church of San Barnaba retains many of its ecclesiastical furnishings, it is now used as a private exhibition space.

CA' REZZONICO

Map p. 409, D2. Open 10–5 except Tues. The palace has a landing-stage on the Grand Canal (vaporetto no. 1), from which a bridge leads directly to its water entrance. Its land entrance is reached by Fondamenta Rezzonico along Rio San Barnaba. The collection is extremely well labelled, also in English.

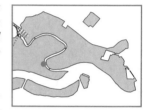

Ca' Rezzonico is one of the most important 17th–18th-century palaces in Venice, with a monumental façade on the Grand Canal. It was begun by Baldassare Longhena c. 1667, and then modified (and the upper storey added) by Giorgio Massari for the Rezzonico family soon after they bought it in 1751, a few years before Carlo Rezzonico became Pope Clement XIII. They also commissioned its splendid frescoed ceilings from Giambattista Tiepolo,

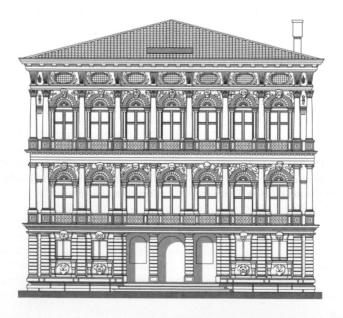

Giovanni Battista Crosato, Gaspare Diziani and Jacopo Guarana. The last member of the Rezzonico family died in 1810, and the palace changed hands frequently in the 19th century, when both Whistler and Sargent had studios here. In 1888 it was purchased by Robert Browning's son, Pen, and the great poet died here on 12th December 1889.

First opened to the public in 1936, it now houses the Museo del Settecento Veneziano, the city's collection of 18th-century art, displayed in rooms decorated in the most sumptuous 18th-century style.

GROUND FLOOR

Behind a pretty fountain (enjoyed by some huge goldfish), the garden was redesigned in the 20th century by Giorgio Bellavitis with a pergola and box hedges (it has numerous benches which are pleasant places to rest). Off the fine *androne* and courtyard is the grand staircase by Giorgio Massari (one of the putti representing *Winter* on the banister is signed by Juste le Court).

FIRST FLOOR

Room 1 (Ballroom): The chandeliers are 18th century and the elaborate frescoes are by Giovanni Battista Crosato and Pietro Visconti. There are some vase-stands and colossal statues of Ethiopian warriors with white glass eyes, part of a set of furniture carved by Andrea Brustolon (*see Room 11*).

Room 2: The splendid ceiling fresco is an allegory of the marriage of Ludovico Rezzonico and Faustina Savorgnan in 1758, painted the same year by Giambattista Tiepolo, one of his last works carried out in Venice, with the help of his son Gian Domenico (the *quadratura* is by Gerolamo Mengozzi-Colonna). The portrait of Francesco Falier as *Procurator da Mar* is by Bernardino Castelli (1786). There is a little **chapel (3)** off this room.

Room 4: Pastels and miniatures by Rosalba Carriera, and a portrait of Cecilia Guardi, Giambattista Tiepolo's wife, painted by their son Lorenzo in 1757. When she sat for this portrait she was already an elderly woman, but she is bedecked with magnificent jewels. The ceiling painting of the *Triumph of Poetry* is by Gaspare Diziani (1757).

Room 5: The room has an 18th-century lacquer-work door and 17th-century Flemish tapestries. The *Allegory of Virtue* on the ceiling is by Jacopo Guarana.

Room 6 (Throne Room): This sumptuous room overlooks the Grand Canal. The ceiling painting of the *Allegory of Merit* is by Giambattista Tiepolo. An elaborate frame (c. 1730) surrounds the portrait of Pietro Barbarigo by Bernardino Castelli. The furniture is attributed to Antonio Corradini.

Room 7: The very fine painting on the ceiling depicting *Nobility and Virtue Overcoming Ignorance* was painted by Giambattista Tiepolo in 1745 for Palazzo Barbarigo on the Grand Canal and moved here in 1936. The page holding

FIRST FLOOR

6 5 4 2
3
12
1
7 9 10 11
8

CA' REZZONICO

1 Ballroom
3 Chapel
6 Throne Room
9 Library
11 Brustolon Room
12 Portego

SECOND FLOOR

18 19 20 21
13
17 15 14 14
16 14 14 14

13 Portego
14 Frescoes by Gian Domenico Tiepolo
17 Guardi Room
18 Longhi Room
19 Green Lacquer Room
21 Bedroom and Boudoir

the train of 'Nobility' is thought to be a portrait of Tiepolo's son Giuseppe Maria, who became a priest.

Passageway (8): Here are some small wood sculptures by Brustolon (the *Magdalene* and an equestrian statue of Marcus Aurelius).

Room 9 (Library): In the 17th-century bookcases are displayed 18th-century *bozzetti* in clay and terracotta by Giovanni Maria Morleiter.

Room 10: Here is a large painting by Gregorio Lazzarini, and one by Antonio Molinari. On the ceiling are five paintings in pretty oval frames by Francesco Maffei from Vicenza.

Room 11: The remarkable furniture is part of a 40-piece set carved out of ebony and boxwood before 1706 for the Venier family palace by Andrea Brustolon. It includes armchairs and vase-stands made for Pietro Venier's collection of Chinese porcelain. The most celebrated piece is the vase-stand with Hercules and Moors. The colossal statues displayed in the Ballroom are also part of this set. Brustolon was the most important wood sculptor at work in the Veneto in the Baroque period. Born in Belluno, most of his works are still in buildings near that town. Other carvings by him can be seen in one of the synagogues in the Ghetto, in Palazzetto Bru Zane, and in the sacristies of the Redentore and the Frari. A terracotta *bozzetto* by him of the *Death of St Francesco Saverio* (1723) is at present exhibited in the Ca' d'Oro. On the ceiling are more paintings by Maffei, and a beautiful Murano chandelier (c. 1730).

Room 12 (Portego): Decorated with 18th-century busts, and with two atlantes by Alessandro Vittoria.

SECOND FLOOR

Room 13 (Portego): Arranged as a picture gallery, this displays the most important paintings in the collection: a contrived landscape incorporating some Roman monuments by Luca Carnevalis; a large historical canvas with the *Death of Darius* by Giovanni Battista Piazzetta (and works by his pupil Giuseppe Angeli); landscapes by Giuseppe Zais, and works by Giovanni Antonio Guardi and Gian Antonio Pellegrini. The two Venetian views by Canaletto are early works dating from the 1720s: they were acquired in 1983 and are the only views of Venice by Canaletto owned by the city (although there are also a few of his paintings in the Gallerie dell'Accademia).

CANALETTO AND THE *VEDUTISTI*

Giovanni Antonio Canal, always known as Canaletto, was born into an old Venetian family in 1697. On his first trip to London in 1746 he carried with him a letter of introduction from his most important patron, Consul Smith, who lived in Venice (*see p. 331*). His fame and thriving market in England was due entirely to Smith, who in the mid-1720s had already commissioned six paintings of Piazza San Marco and the Piazzetta from Canaletto and went on to purchase no fewer than 50 of his paintings (as well as 143 drawings). The business arrangement between the two endured throughout Canaletto's life, and Smith then sold all of his Canalettos to George III, so that today the best collection of his work is in the British royal collections.

The artist also worked in London for around ten years, producing many splendid views of the city and the Thames. Influenced by the views and *capricci*, or imaginary scenes, invented by Luca Carnevalis, he produced many *vedute* of his native city, which came to symbolise its appearance for decades (and are still considered by many to represent the essence of Venice). He was to influence generations of British landscape painters and watercolourists and, through his nephew and most brilliant pupil, Bernardo Bellotto (who worked as court painter in Dresden), his influence extended to the northern European schools as well. A Venetian view by Bellotto can be seen in the Gallerie dell'Accademia. Canaletto was an excellent draughtsman and may have used a camera obscura as an aid to accuracy (his only complete sketchbook survives in the Accademia, although it is not usually on view). He also made a set of very fine etchings and dedicated them to Consul Smith.

Francesco Guardi, born in Venice in 1712 into a family of painters, became a highly successful painter of Venetian *vedute* and *capricci*, a typical 18th-century genre, many of which he painted for British aristocrats. His delightful paintings also record ceremonies in Venice and villas in the Veneto. After his death in 1793 he was forgotten and only rediscovered in France in the mid-19th century. Guardi's work is better represented in his native city than that of Canaletto.

Room 14: This charming series of rooms was created in 1936 in an attempt to reconstruct the frescoed rooms of the simple little Villa di Zianigo, near Mira in the Veneto. This had been purchased by Giambattista Tiepolo in the 1750s, and decorated with frescoes by his son, Gian Domenico, who inherited the property. In 1906 the frescoes were detached and sold to a Venetian antiquarian and then purchased by the state. In the first room there is a scene from Tasso's *Gerusalemme Liberata*, with Rinaldo taking leave of Armida in her enchanted garden. The oval in the ceiling has a hawk swooping on a flock of sparrows. A tiny room has a brightly painted parrot and a frescoed statue of *Abundance* in a niche. Beyond is a room with a delightful scene called the *New World*, one of the last of the series to be carried out in 1791. It shows a crowd of onlookers, with a splendid miscellany of hats: seen exclusively from behind (with none of their faces visible), they are waiting to see a magic lantern show at a fairground. Opposite are two satirical scenes of court life (the *Promenade à Trois*, showing a lady out walking with her husband and lover; and the *Minuet*). Other rooms have carnival scenes with Pulcinella (the Punch of 17th-century Neapolitan comedy) and acrobats (also on the ceiling). The chapel has suitable grisaille frescoes. The last two rooms, also in grisaille, have amusing satyrs.

Room 15: An 18th-century interior is reproduced here, with an early 18th-century spinet and painted cupboards which contain a display of 18th-century porcelain from the Cozzi manufactory of Venice as well as Meissen and Sèvres ware.

Rooms 16–17: A passageway (Room 16) with a rosary-maker's signboard by Francesco Guardi and small paintings by Guardi, Pietro Longhi and Giuseppe Zais, as well as an elaborate torch-holder in Murano glass, leads down to Room 17, which has two well-known paintings by Francesco Guardi: the *Sala del Ridotto* and the *Parlatorio delle Monache*, delightful Venetian interior scenes. The first shows the famous gambling house called the Ridotto (*see p. 109*), and the second the visitors' room at the Convent of San Zaccaria, famous for its laxity and for the high living of its aristocratic inmates.

Room 18 (Longhi Room): The painting on the ceiling is by Giambattista Tiepolo (*Zephyr and Flora*, an early work which comes from Ca' Pesaro). The room is especially interesting for its series of 34 small genre paintings by Pietro Longhi, with contemporary scenes of Venetian life (including one with a rhinoceros). Between the windows on the Grand Canal, *The Painter's Studio* shows Longhi at work. The life-size portrait of Francesco Guardi is also by Longhi.

Room 19 (Green Lacquer Room): The chinoiserie in this room includes fine lacquer furniture. The ceiling fresco of *The Triumph of Diana* by Gian Antonio Guardi was moved from another palace.

Room 20: Three more frescoes (*Minerva*, *Venus* and *Apollo*) on the walls by Gian Antonio Guardi, were also removed from another palace.

Room 21: This is a charming (reconstructed) bedroom with an alcove (with a *Madonna* by Rosalba Carriera above it) and a fine bureau. It has an adjoining closet and boudoir, with graceful 18th-century stucco decoration, and a ceiling fresco by Jacopo Guarana.

THIRD FLOOR

This is really an attic, with low ceilings, and its 13 rooms are used to house the huge collection of paintings left to the city in the 20th century by Egidio Martini, displayed more or less chronologically. Some of the most important works are in the first room (round to the left; with an intriguing view of the bend in the Grand Canal), with Bonifacio Veronese (Bonifacio de' Pitati), Bachiacca, Alvise Vivarini (the *Redeemer*) and Benedetto Licinio (portrait of a lady with her son) well represented. There are also paintings by Guercino (*The Philosopher*), landscapes by Marco Ricci, and Venetian views by Ippolito Caffi, Emma Ciardi and Antonio Mancini. Amongst 18th-century works are some by Rosalba Carriera and *Boy with a Flute* by Giovanni Battista Piazzetta. You can also see a faithful reconstruction of an 18th-century pharmacy on this floor.

THE MESTROVICH COLLECTION AND BROWNING ROOMS

On the ground floor, off the *androne*, a short flight of stairs leads up to the little mezzanine apartment, occupied at the end of his life by Robert Browning. The choice little collection, in just two rooms, of the art historian Ferruccio Mestrovich is displayed here. The Mestrovich family escaped to Venice in 1945, together with some 340,000 other refugees from Zara (Zadar) in Dalmatia, after it was destroyed by Allied bombs in support of Tito in the Second World War. In gratitude Mestrovich bequeathed his collection to the city. In the first room there is a tiny *Ecce Homo*, signed and dated 1499 by Cima da Conegliano; a lovely *Madonna and Child with Four Saints* (and a seascape in the background) by Bonifacio Veronese; a *Deposition* (in the presence of the two donors) by Jacopo Tintoretto; and two spandrels with the *Annunciation* by Carpaccio's son Benedetto. In the second room there is a very striking painting of the *Redeemer* by Benedetto Diana (there is a similar work by him in the National Gallery in London). In quite a different spirit is Francesco Guardi's delightful *Madonna and Child*, showing them both fully dressed for carnival, complete with crowns and hung with pearls: this very unusual painting was clearly inspired by the numerous popular statues of Madonnas dressed in Venetian costume in the city's churches. The portraits (in fine frames) include works by Jacopo Amigoni, Alessandro Longhi and Jacopo Tintoretto. *St Jerome Meditating on the Crucifix* is by the Bolognese painter Ubaldo Gandolfi (1728–81). The charming painted gameboard dates from the 18th century and was used for gambling, in a game similar to the present-day roulette.

The corner room on this mezzanine floor, which has a window on the Grand Canal and one on Rio San Barnaba, retains its decorations from Browning's time, when he stayed here in 1889 as an old man and widower with his son Pen. Pen had purchased the entire palace a few years earlier thanks to the wealth of his wife, Fanny Coddington. The great poet died here in the same year, and his coffin lay in state in the *portego* (just inside the water-gate) before being taken by gondola to the cemetery of San Michele to await his ceremonial burial in Poets' Corner in Westminster Abbey.

If you leave the palace by its water-gate on the Grand Canal and take the little wooden bridge across Rio di San Barnaba, by a window of Browning's apartment decorated with a lion and mascaron you can see the plaque which records 'Roberto's' death with the famous lines from his 'De Gustibus':

Open my heart and you will see
Graved inside of it, 'Italy'.

CA' FOSCARI

It is worth following the Calle de le Boteghe across Ponte San Barnaba (reconstructed in 1873 with an elegant iron balustrade) and then the *calli* (usually busy with students) which lead on to Campiello dei Squelini (*map p. 409, D2*), just out of which is the land entrance to Ca' Foscari, the seat of Venice University (*for a description of the superb Gothic façade on the Grand Canal, see p. 137*). The lovely entrance portal in Istrian stone bears the Foscari coat of arms. You can enter the very spacious courtyard with its 15th-century crenellated wall and a well protected by wisteria, and see the adjoining courtyard of the Gothic Palazzo Giustinian dei Vescovi, also occupied by the university. It has a very fine well-head and an outside staircase attributed to Bartolomeo Bon, which was partly remade on the initiative of the beautiful Lady Helen Vincent (painted by Sargent) when she lived on the second floor of the palace in 1902. The university was founded in 1868 and was the first in Italy dedicated to Economics. The Business School is still highly regarded, as is the Department of Linguistics, instituted in 1954. The interior can be visited on a guided tour (*to book, www.unive.it/visita*), of interest particularly for the ex-Aula Magna, designed by Carlo Scarpa in 1936 (his earliest work), which he modified 20 years later.

A WALK THROUGH DORSODURO

This walk covers the small area of Dorsoduro at its easternmost tip near the great Salute church, exploring a few of its quietest and most picturesque canals and campi before emerging on the Fondamenta delle Zattere, with its cafés and restaurants and its wonderful views of the wide Giudecca Canal.

THE WALK BEGINS AT THE FOOT OF THE Accademia Bridge. Squeezed into the waterfront corner of Rio Terrà Foscarini is a pleasant little bar with its lintel engraved with the words *Fortitudo Mea Deus*: God is my Strength. It makes a good place for a fortifying coffee or Prosecco before beginning the walk; alternatively, around the corner to the left, in Calle Nuova Sant'Agnese, there is the delightful old-fashioned bar Da Gino (on the right; corner of Piscina Venier), which serves very good snacks, reasonably priced, and retains a special Venetian atmosphere.

Calle Nuova Sant'Agnese leads down to the lovely Rio di San Vio. At no. 864 on the left, just before the bridge, is **Palazzo Loredan-Cini**, the former home of Vittorio Cini (*see p. 302*). In 1984 Cini's daughter Yana (1924–89) donated two of its floors to the Fondazione Giorgio Cini to house the Vittorio Cini Collection of Tuscan paintings and decorative arts (*closed at the time of writing but usually open Sept–Oct and March–June 10–1 & 2–6 except Mon; T: 041 521 0755*). Amongst the early masterpieces are a *Maestà* of c. 1315 by the Maestro di Badia a Isola. There is a beautiful *Madonna and Child with Two Angels*, one of the best works of Piero di Cosimo, and a superb unfinished double portrait (1524) of two friends by Pontormo.

Cross the bridge now into **Campo San Vio**, which opens directly onto the Grand Canal. It has several trees, a large well and flagstaff, and a pleasant bench on the waterfront. Across the Grand Canal to the left, on the near side of the narrow Rio dell'Orso, you can see the 15th-century **Palazzo Barbaro**, decorated with marble roundels. It was purchased in 1885 by the wealthy Bostonians Daniel and Ariana Curtis, and here they lived a life of luxury, entertaining on a grand scale. Henry James clearly took the palace as a model for the Palazzo Leporelli, where Milly Theale stayed in *The Wings of the Dove*. In 1892 the collector Isabella Stewart Gardner (who set herself the goal of amassing works of great art to exhibit in her native America, to educate the tastes of her young country) rented the palace from the Curtises and also had James to stay. He was to return in 1899 and again in 1907. The interior of the museum which Isabella Stewart Gardner opened in 1903 at the Fenway in Boston is partly modelled on Palazzo Barbaro. James McNeill Whistler was in Venice between 1879 and 1880, and was a frequent guest here when he had a studio on the upper floor of Ca' Rezzonico. The famous set of etchings he produced while in the city provide a wonderful document of the atmosphere of Venice, both by day and by night: he described it as an 'amazing city of palaces...really a fairy land—

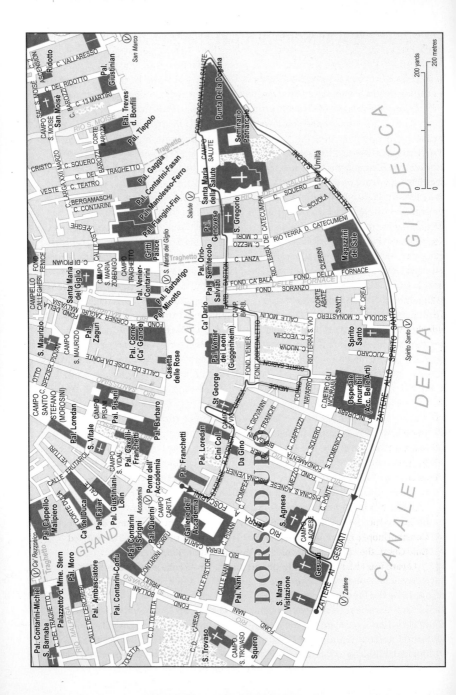

created one would think especially for the painter'. As in his works depicting Paris and London, he ignored the best-known buildings and typical views made popular by his predecessors, and concentrated his attention instead on the texture of the marble and brick surfaces, the ever-changing light, and the distinctive 'floating' quality of the city, which he sought in the remoter districts and smaller canals crossed by their little bridges. The Curtis family also offered hospitality to John Singer Sargent, who also had a studio at Ca' Rezzonico and whose work in Venice was clearly influenced by Whistler. While staying with the Curtises in 1899 he painted their family portrait in the drawing room (now at the Royal Academy in London). In 1908, the elderly Claude Monet came to Venice for the first time on the invitation of the Curtises. He remained many months, finding the atmosphere of the city 'Impressionism in stone'. He returned the following year, and his exhibition of Venetian works in 1912 enjoyed enormous success. Palazzo Barbaro is still partly owned by the Curtis family; their historic family library on the top floor was carefully restored a few years ago.

The unassuming building on the east side of the *campo* is the **Anglican church of St George** (*Sunday worship at 10.30*). It was once the showroom of the Venice & Murano Glass and Mosaic Company (*see p. 138*) but was given to the English community in Venice in 1892 by Sir Henry Layard. The stained-glass windows, made in 1904 by the Whitefriars Glass Company, each have the memorial coat of arms of a distinguished member of the British community in Venice (including Sir Henry Wotton, Layard and his wife, Browning, Ruskin and Horatio Brown). The tombstone of consul Joseph Smith (*see p. 332*) was brought here from the cemetery on the Lido in 1974.

SIR HENRY LAYARD

In 1883, with the help of Rawdon Brown, Sir Henry Layard (1817–94) purchased Palazzo Cappello on the Grand Canal (now Palazzo Cappello-Layard; *see p. 136*). By the time he came to live in Venice, he was already famous as an archaeologist, having discovered Nineveh in the 1840s during eleven years' residence in the Middle East, from where he sent back to the British Museum the great bas-reliefs which are still the main treasures of their Assyrian department. When he returned to England he entered politics as a Liberal MP. In 1877 Disraeli appointed him ambassador to Constantinople, and he was knighted for his diplomatic skills. In 1869 he married Enid Guest, then only 25 years old, and they moved to Venice in 1883.

Layard was also a scholar of Italian art and an astute collector: visitors to Ca' Cappello were shown paintings by Carpaccio, Cima da Conegliano and Giovanni Bellini, as well as Gentile Bellini's famous portrait of Sultan Mehmet II. These, together with a bequest of some 70 other works, were left by him to the National Gallery in London. Enid, who outlived Henry, continued to preside over the Anglo-American community until her death in 1912, and is remembered for the hospital for foreign sailors she founded on the Giudecca as well as for her performances on the guitar. The Anglican church contains a prayer desk donated by her.

Take the narrow Calle della Chiesa past the Anglican church. It ends, by a little shop which sells hand-made clothes made of beautiful fabrics, at the **Rio delle Torreselle**, which you cross on the Ponte del Formager (aptly named because there is a cheese shop on the *fondamenta*). Past the simple little old-style restaurant (Ai Gondolieri), continue along the peaceful *fondamenta* for a short distance and then turn into a passageway with old herring-bone paving, which leads into **Calle delle Mende**, a street of typical little Venetian houses. At Salizzada del Forno, go left, passing Calle del Forno, another pretty little court with simple houses. Around the corner on Rio Terrà San Vio, there is a statuette of *Christ at the Column* on the corner of a house, with the date 1681. Take **Corte del Sabion** left, with its well and *ghisa* fountain. Above the wall can be seen a garden with cedars of Lebanon and wisteria. An archway with a marble tympanum adorned with a relief of the Madonna protecting two members of a confraternity on its outer face leads back onto the *rio*. Continue along the miniature *fondamenta* to the right (past the Peggy Guggenheim Collection on the opposite bank), and follow it round to the intimate **Campiello Barbaro**, with low trees and a little garden beside a fountain with running water, and an old-world antique shop. The busier Calle Barbaro continues to Ponte San Gregorio, which dates from 1772 and has a 19th-century iron balustrade equipped with an iron flagstaff holder. It crosses the lovely **Rio delle Fornace**, which connects the Grand Canal with the canal of the Giudecca. It is particularly charming since it has *fondamente* on either side of the water. Its name recalls the brick ovens (furnaces) which were formerly here.

The *calle* continues past a number of small art galleries and jewellers, and a passageway on the left which leads to a *traghetto* across the Grand Canal. You emerge on a *campo* dominated by the Gothic façade of the **church of San Gregorio** (*closed*) and with a magnificent 15th-century well-head decorated with acanthus leaves and roses. Palazzo Genovese on the Grand Canal here has been rather over-restored as the Hotel Centurion Palace. Just before the tunnel beneath the former monastic buildings of San Gregorio is the entrance (at no. 172) to the charming **cloister** (you can usually see it through the glass door), open when used for exhibitions in conjunction with the Biennale. The tunnel emerges at a bridge beside the fine triple apse of San Gregorio, built in 1342.

A wide marble pavement leads around the splendid church of the Salute (*described on p. 154*). The magnificent view across the Grand Canal takes in one of its most beautiful palaces, the tiny 15th-century **Palazzo Contarini-Fasan** (with wheel-motif balconies), popularly known as the Casa di Desdemona from the legend that it once belonged to the wife of Othello. Next to it (towards San Marco), with its tall chimney pots, is **Palazzo Gaggia**. This was once known as Ca' Alvisi, and it became the residence of Mrs Katharine de Kay Bronson and her daughter Edith in 1876. Mrs Bronson was famous in Venice for her generous hospitality to visitors from England and America, as well as the material help she gave to the children of gondoliers and her interest in the Venetian dialect.

After Elizabeth Barrett's death in 1878, Robert Browning and his sister would come almost every year to stay at Ca' Alvisi or in the adjoining guest-house. Browning also greatly enjoyed visiting Mrs Bronson at the little town of Asolo in the Veneto (his *Asolando* is dedicated to her). Another illustrious guest (in 1887) was Henry James. When Edith married Cosimo Rucellai she went to live in Florence in the Palazzo Rucellai, still owned by her descendants.

The promontory here is the **Punta della Dogana**, once home to the customs house of the Republic, which is now occupied by the Pinault Foundation exhibition space (*described on p. 157*). On the *fondamenta* outside it, there is a *traghetto* station and a little wooden hut which houses instruments to measure the tides. At the tip of the promontory is a delightful little 17th-century turret (look upwards) with two telamones supporting a golden globe on which is balanced a weather-vane depicting Fortune. A 19th-century lamp post stands at the promontory tip. It was repositioned here in 2013, following the removal of US sculptor Charles Ray's marble statue of a boy holding a frog. The statue had been the subject of a number of jibes from Venetians, leading in turn to taunts about Venetian philistinism in the face of contemporary art. More serious than this was the security problem, since a guard had to be posted permanently behind the statue when it was not protected in its perspex box.

The superb view embraces the whole Bacino di San Marco. The promontory divides the Grand Canal from the wide Giudecca Canal, busy with boats of all shapes and sizes, including gigantic cruise ships, and the car ferries which ply to and from the Lido.

Once you have rounded the tip, you find yourself on the **Fondamenta delle Zattere**, which takes its name the barges (*zattere*, literally 'rafts'), which used to unload their cargoes into the warehouses along the quay. In centuries past there were also brickworks and boat-building yards in the area. On the island of the Giudecca directly opposite is Palladio's splendid façade of the Redentore.

Passing another little wooden hut on the water's edge with gauges for measuring the tides, you skirt the long garden wall of the Seminario Patriacale. Cross Ponte dell'Umiltà. Further on, the wide **Rio Terrà dei Catecumeni** opens out onto a characteristic Venetian court with a single row of young trees and two houses above a low portico. The school here succeeds an institution founded in 1571 for the conversion of slaves and prisoners of war to Christianity. The huge **Magazzini del Sale** were the salt warehouses from the time when the salt monopoly was one of the richest resources of the Republic (11th–15th centuries). The exterior was reconstructed in a Neoclassical style around 1835. Part of the splendid 15th-century interior is sometimes opened for exhibitions in connection with the Biennale, and boat-houses and a nautical club owned by the Bucintoro society of rowers (founded in 1882) occupy the rest of the building. The last door gives access to a little museum space designed in 2009 by Renzo Piano dedicated to the works of Emilio Vedova (1919–2006).

The impressive brick wall of the warehouse complex lines the pretty

Rio delle Fornace (de la Fornasa). The simple house on the other side of the canal has a little hanging garden with a statue of the *Madonna*, holding the Child out to greet us (protected by a green 'umbrella'), and the wall is decorated with Byzantine relief panels of animals and birds.

Turn right to follow the *fondamenta* along the *rio* and then take the first *calle* on the right, **Calle Querini**, where a plaque at no. 252 records Ezra Pound (*'Titano della poesia'*) on the little house where he died in 1972, in this secluded corner of the city. The famous poet (b. 1885) published his first book of verse in Venice in 1908 at his own expense: *A Lume Spento* (at the Antonini printing press in Cannaregio, with a print run of just 100 copies). In May 1945 he was seized by Partisans in southern Italy at a villa in Rapallo owned by his companion, the violinist Olga Rudge, and he was handed over to the American command who accused him of treason for his Fascist sympathies and his wartime broadcasts to America in favour of Mussolini. He was held in solitary confinement in Pisa, and in the same year transferred to America where he was interned in a psychiatric hospital in Washington from which he was only released in 1958. He lived the last years of his life in Venice with Olga Rudge in this little house (the 'Hidden Nest'), and she lived on here after Pound's death, dying at the age of 101 in 1996 (the bell still bears her family name).

The Zattere next passes the church of the **Spirito Santo** (*often closed*), founded in 1483, with a Renaissance façade. The interior, remodelled in the 18th century, contains works by Giovanni Buonconsiglio and Palma Giovane, and in the upper nuns' chapel, an 18th-century cycle of paintings of the Mysteries of the Rosary, including an *Assumption* by Francesco Fontebasso. On either side of the church are the former Scuola del Spirito Santo, founded in 1506, with a façade by Alessandro Tremignon (1680); and a famous (but disappointing) residential building of 1958 by Ignazio Gardella.

Continue along the Zattere. You soon pass a huge Classical building by Antonio da Ponte (with a fine colossal stone head on either end of its façade). This was once one of the four main hospitals of the city, that of the **Incurabili**. It was opened in 1522 by Gaetano da Thiene, and in 1537 the founder of the Jesuit order, Ignatius Loyola, was a visitor here. At the end of the 16th century the orphanage attached to the hospital became famous for its girls' choir (along the lines of the Pietà and the Ospedaletto; *see p. 287*); in 1567 Jacopo Sansovino designed an oval church in the courtyard, particularly adapted to concerts (but this was demolished in 1831). The building later became an institute for children, and has recently been restored as the seat of the Accademia di Belle Arti. Founded in 1750, the Accademia's first director was Giovanni Battista Piazzetta; he was succeeded by Giambattista Tiepolo. The door is usually open so that you can see the cloister, but otherwise the entire building has been radically restored as classrooms and administrative offices.

On the corner of Campiello Incurabili, the **green house (no. 560)** with a good 19th-century *St George and the Dragon* relief was purchased in 1883 by Horatio Brown, who lived here for the rest of his life (he died in 1926). Brown was the best-known British resident in Venice of his day, and continued Rawdon Brown's remarkable work in the State Archives (*see p. 197*), bringing out five more volumes of the *Calendar* on Anglo-Venetian relations. (Although they share a name, the two Browns were not related.) Horatio's *Life on the Lagoons*, written here, is dedicated to 'my gondolier' Antonio Salin, and contains an interesting history of the gondola, 'the most perfect carriage in the world'. His two-volume *Studies in Venetian History* provides a fascinating survey of the Republic. He notes that, 'In no other state have we so little about personal details of its great men: Venice demanded and secured the effacement of the individual...the state was everything, the individual nothing.' He produced a detailed analysis of the 'government machinery' of 'one of the most rigid and enduring constitutions that the world has ever seen'. He is also extremely perceptive about the Byzantine influence on Venice, and he identified what he felt to be the most important characteristic of the famous Venetian merchants, who were known throughout the world: that they were usually both the owner and the carrier of their goods, while the commercial policy of the Republic was to accumulate merchandise in the city for distribution so that foreign traders were forced to come to the city to carry out their business activities.

Beyond the bridge the Zattere agli Incurabili follows a garden wall decorated with statues (behind which can be seen a large pine tree and group of ilexes). A **plaque** here recalls the Russian poet Joseph Brodsky (1940–96) and his love of Venice.

The next bridge leads across Rio San Vio. Here the Zattere becomes suddenly more animated, and there are plenty of places to rest and relax, have a coffee or an ice cream (*the churches on this stretch of the Zattere are described on p. 158*). There are also comfortable benches a little further on, where the *fondamenta* widens out beyond Rio di San Trovaso.

SAN TOMÀ
Detail of the healing of Anianus on the Scuola dei Calegheri (1478).

Sestiere of San Polo

The sestiere of San Polo takes its name from the church of San Polo, which sits in one of the largest—and most 'Venetian'—campi in Venice, far away from the crowds, and used by local children as a playground. Goldoni lived close by, and his charming little house can be visited. The district also includes the lively area at the western foot of the Rialto Bridge, with its busy markets where Venetians still come to do their food shopping. There are numerous grocers' shops and bakeries in the calli close by, as well as some of the best bacari in town. Close together at the western limit of the sestiere are the famous church of the Frari, filled with Venetian masterpieces of sculpture and painting, and the Scuola Grande di San Rocco, where the walls and ceilings are covered with superb works by Tintoretto.

The Rialto (*rivo alto*, 'high bank') is thought to have been one of the first parts of the city to be settled, because it was one of the highest points and the best protected. It is still the most crowded area, just as it must have been in the days of the Republic, when it was the commercial centre of the city, attracting merchants, bankers, brokers and traders of all kinds: 'Now, what news on the Rialto?' (*The Merchant of Venice*, Act III, Scene I). The famous bridge—even though it is not particularly attractive and occupies an unusually cramped space—is Venice's most celebrated landmark.

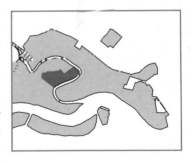

THE RIALTO & ITS MARKETS

The Rialto Bridge stands at the topographical centre of the city (*map p. 411, F2*), linking the *sestieri* of San Polo and San Marco. A bridge has existed at this point since the earliest days of Venice's history, and it remained the only bridge across the Grand Canal throughout the Republic. A bridge of boats was replaced by a wooden bridge in the mid-13th century, but this was destroyed in 1310 by supporters of Bajamonte Tiepolo after their retreat from Piazza San Marco and the failure of their rebellion against the

Venetian state (*see p. 97*). The next bridge collapsed in 1444 under the weight of a large crowd and was rebuilt on a larger scale and as a drawbridge. We have a detailed picture of this bridge in Carpaccio's painting of the *Cure of a Lunatic by the Patriarch of Grado*, commissioned by the Scuola di San Giovanni Evangelista and now in the Gallerie dell'Accademia. In 1524 it was decided to rebuild the bridge in stone and designs were submitted by famous architects including Palladio, Sansovino, Vignola and possibly also Michelangelo, but finally in 1588 the little-known Antonio da Ponte won the commission and the bridge was completed by 1591. Its single arch, 48m in span and 7.5m high, carries a thoroughfare divided into three lanes by two rows of shops.

The Rialto is still famous for its excellent market, open in the mornings, where a great variety of fresh fish, fruit and vegetables can be found at fair prices. Markets were first established here in 1097. The porticoed **Fabbriche Vecchie** di Rialto was reconstructed by Scarpagnino along the lines of the medieval buildings after a disastrous fire in 1514. The long arcaded **Fabbriche Nuove** di Rialto, a serviceable market building which follows the curve of the Grand Canal, was begun by Jacopo Sansovino in 1554. It is now used by the Assize Court.

TWO CHURCHES AT THE RIALTO

Scarpagnino's porticoes extend around Campo San Giacomo, where, amidst the stalls and barrows, is a crouching figure known as the *Gobbo di Rialto*, made in the 16th century by Pietro da Salò: it supports a flight of steps leading to a rostrum of Egyptian granite from which the laws of the Republic were proclaimed.

Across the *campo* is the little church of **San Giacomo di Rialto** (San Giacometto; *map p. 411, F2; open 9.30–7*), once thought to have been founded in the year 421, though first documented in 1152 and so probably dating from that century. It is preceded by a Gothic entrance portico; above is a large clock of 1410. On the exterior of its apse is a 12th-century inscription exhorting merchants to honesty. The domed Greek-cross plan, derived from Byzantine models but on a tiny scale, was faithfully preserved in the rebuilding of 1601. The interior retains its six reused ancient Greek marble columns with finely carved 11th-century Corinthian capitals and pulvins, also in Greek marble. Over the high altar are statues of *St James* and angels by Alessandro Vittoria (1602), and on the right an *Annunciation* by Titian's nephew, Marco Vecellio.

At the end of Ruga degli Orefici (where the goldsmiths had their workshops), in the broad Ruga Vecchia San Giovanni (left), an archway on the left forms the inconspicuous entrance to **San Giovanni Elemosinario** (*map p. 411, F2; open Mon–Sat 10–5; Chorus Pass*), the first church to be built in the Rialto area (mentioned as early as 1051). After the Rialto fire of 1514 it was rebuilt by Scarpagnino in 1527–9, though it still has its campanile of 1398–1410. In the Greek-cross interior, the high altarpiece of *St John the Almsgiver* was painted for the church by Titian (c. 1545). On the left wall there is a painting by the great painter's nephew, Marco Vecellio, which shows the interior of the church in a scene of Doge Leonardo Donà receiving the Holy Water from the parish priest. In the chapel to the right of the sanctuary there is a lovely altarpiece of *Sts Catherine, Sebastian and Roch*, by Pordenone, who also carried out the frescoes on the dome, discovered under a thin layer of plaster in 1985. The church also contains late

16th-century works in the sanctuary by Leonardo Corona, whose crowded compositions show the influence of Tintoretto, even though he never reached the heights of his master: his works produce an effect which is nearly always over-dramatic, with fussy details detracting from the central theme. However, Corona still had a successful career in Venice and was even invited to contribute to the vast decorative scheme to glorify the Republic in the Sala del Maggior Consiglio in the Doge's Palace. Some of his works are also derived from Palma Giovane, who is well represented here in a lunette (at the end of the south side) of *St Roch Healing the Plague-stricken*. Another lunette (attributed to Domenico Tintoretto) on the west wall (right of the door) shows Doge Marino Grimani and Dogaressa Morosina Morosini in the illustrious company of God the Father, with members of a confraternity. The organ was made by Pietro Nacchini in 1749. In the left aisle is displayed a curious stone relief of the *Nativity* or *Birth of St John*, which includes a huge ox. It was found during recent restoration work behind the font.

CAMPO SAN POLO

The peaceful Campo San Polo (*map p. 411, D3*) is one of the largest and most attractive squares in the city. Its shape makes it a favourite playground for children and a few isolated trees provide shade for the benches. You can also sit on the steps around the well-head, which is the largest in Venice and dates from 1838 (the prostrate lion of St Mark represented the governors during the Austrian occupation: instead of sitting upright, the lion

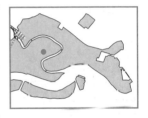

is reclining in an attitude of submission, with his open book). Among the interesting medley of palaces which follow the curved side of the *campo* (once bordered by a canal, as can be seen from the paving) is the grand rust-coloured Palazzo Soranzo (no. 2169–2171), with splendid marble windows and portals. Adjoining it, on the other side of the Sottoportego Cavalli, is the well-proportioned Baroque Palazzo Tiepolo, attributed to Giorgio Massari.

THE CHURCH OF SAN POLO
Map p. 411, D3. Open Mon–Sat 10–5; Chorus Pass.
The church bears interesting **reliefs** (the earliest dating from the 13th century) on the exterior of the east end. The **south doorway** (*used as the entrance*) is a fine Gothic work with leaves and spiral columns attributed to Bartolomeo Bon, with two angels holding an inscription and crowned (on the roof) by the half-figure of St Paul. The isolated **campanile** (1362) has two fine Romanesque lions carved at its base.

The interior, with a ship's keel roof, was altered in 1804 by Davide Rossi and given a Neoclassical arcade. On the left of the west door, **Jacopo Tintoretto's *Last Supper*** is one of the best of his many paintings of this subject. On the left side of the south entrance door is a worn sculptural fragment of the *Nativity*, probably dating from the 16th century. Hanging from the sanctuary arch is a fragment of an early 15th-century

Venetian Crucifix, and in the sanctuary are paintings by Palma Giovane and two bronze statues by Alessandro Vittoria.

At the west end, beneath the organ by Gaetano Callido (1763), is the entrance to the **Oratory of the Crucifix**. The wonderful series of paintings here, illustrating the Stations of the Cross, was carried out in 1749 by Gian Domenico Tiepolo. They are all the same size, relatively small and rectangular, and they portray Christ's Passion in a superb Venetian setting and with a background of the Alps: the biblical figures are accompanied by turbanned orientals in brightly-coloured robes, and elegantly-dressed ladies, probably including portraits of some of the artist's contemporaries. The sequence begins on the right wall, with Christ condemned to death—as in the subsequent scenes, the diminutive figure of Christ (here shown on a balcony, exposed to the crowd) takes second place to the colourful surrounding scene. In the third scene there is an elderly and portly Arab in a turban, splendidly dressed in yellow (the colour chosen for many of the main protagonists in the later scenes), who looks on as Christ falls beneath the weight of the Cross. In Christ's encounter with the Holy Women (the eighth panel), the ladies have gorgeous damascened costumes and have even brought along their well-dressed children to be 'presented'. These are thought to be portraits of the painter's own family. The eleventh scene, showing Christ being nailed to the Cross, is one of the most beautiful, and the artist's attention is at last fully focused on the very finely drawn nude figure of Christ. The last scene, showing Christ placed in the tomb, provides a final dramatic note, as it is dominated by the white sarcophagus and winding sheet stained with blood, with the head of the Dead Christ only just visible. Gian Domenico also painted the four paintings of scenes from the lives of saints in the sanctuary, and the glory of angels and *Resurrection* in the ceiling.

THE ALDINE PRESS AND PALAZZO CORNER-MOCENIGO

North of Campo San Polo, on Rio Terrà Secondo (*map p. 411, D2*), a small Gothic palace (no. 2311) is the traditional site of the **Aldine Press**, set up in 1490 by the Roman scholar and celebrated printer Aldus Manutius on his arrival in Venice in the same year. The press became famous for its publication of the Greek classics. Manutius designed the Italic type in 1501. Numerous other presses were set up in the city in quick succession; it has been estimated that during the 16th century three new books were printed in Venice every week. Manutius' work was carried on by his son and grandson.

The *salizzada* past the south door of San Polo leads to the pretty Ponte San Polo (1775), from where Sanmicheli's main façade of **Palazzo Corner-Mocenigo** (begun after 1545; *map p. 411, D3*) can be seen on the canal (look right). In an apartment here, the scurrilous Frederick Rolfe spent the last years of his life. Having already published his best-known novel, *Hadrian VII*, he arrived in Venice in 1908 and, calling himself Baron Corvo, came to be known and feared as an outspoken eccentric. In his autobiographical *The Desire and Pursuit of the Whole*—not published until 1934, long after his death, to avoid libel actions—he took a keen delight in insulting his contemporaries. His conduct earned him a terrible reputation, and he was many times reduced to near destitution. A.J.A. Symons attempted to solve the mystery of his life in *The Quest for Corvo*, published in the same year.

CASA GOLDONI & SAN TOMÀ

CASA GOLDONI

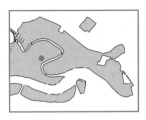

Map p. 411, D3. Open 10–3.30 or 4.30 except Wed; entrance beyond the courtyard.

The house at no. 2793 Calle dei Nomboli, officially Palazzo Centani (15th century), is more usually known as the Casa Goldoni, for it is here that the playwright Carlo Goldoni (1707–93) was born (he subsequently lived at various addresses in the city and died in poverty in Paris). His comedies give a vivid idea of social life in 18th-century Venice. Not only did he satirise the old Venetian aristocracy, but he described with brilliance the ordinary people of the city. He marked an important stage in the development of theatrical production, which hitherto had been dominated by improvised drama by professional masked actors, known as the *Commedia dell'Arte*. The house has a picturesque Gothic courtyard with a charming staircase and a pretty well-head dating from the 15th century. A map here pinpoints the places associated with Goldoni in Venice and the position of its various theatres, fifteen of which were in operation in Goldoni's day. In the interior you can visit just three rooms, at present evocatively furnished with stage sets and costumes from some of his plays. There is an 18th-century puppet theatre and display of puppets. Two portraits of Goldoni are thought to be by Antonio Longhi. On the upper floor there is an important library and archive of manuscripts and letters, open to students.

CAMPO SAN TOMÀ

Campiello San Tomà leads into the larger *campo* of the same name (*map p. 410, C3*). The **church**, which rises at one end of it, has been closed for restoration for many years. The 15th-century **Scuola dei Calegheri** at the other end (now used as a library) once belonged to the city's guild of cobblers and shoemakers. The exterior bears a *Madonna della Misericordia* and a charming relief of *St Mark Healing the Cobbler Anianus*, attributed to Pietro Lombardo or Antonio Rizzo (1478) and decorated at the bottom with stylised shoes. Legend tells that when St Mark arrived in Alexandria, one of his shoes needed mending and the cobbler Anianus was called in to help. While the shoemaker was at work with his awl, he cut his hand with the blade, and swore to the 'only God'. Mark interpreted this as a miraculous sign, and healed the cut (by mixing a little of his saliva with the earth) declaring 'let him be healed in the name of God'. When Anianus saw the power of Mark's faith, he was converted to Christianity, receiving his baptism from Mark himself. As the first Christian in Alexandria, Anianus succeeded Mark as bishop of the city. He is always portrayed in a turban to denote his 'heathen' origins, and as a reminder that the episode takes place in Alexandria. At his death he was buried in a church named after him in Alexandria, but his body—like that of St Mark—was brought to Venice. Anianus's relics arrived in the city in 1288, and he was declared a saint.

SANTA MARIA GLORIOSA DEI FRARI

Map p. 410, C3. Open Mon–Sat 9–5.30; Chorus Pass.
Santa Maria Gloriosa dei Frari, commonly known as
'the Frari', is the church of the mendicant order of
Friars Minor, or Franciscans and is dedicated to the
Assumption of the Virgin. In size it rivals the church of
the other mendicant order, the Dominican foundation
of Santi Giovanni e Paolo. It contains numerous masterpieces of painting and sculpture, including Titian's huge

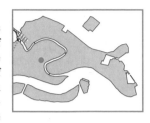

Assumption, as well as his *Pala Pesaro*, and, in the sacristy, one of Giovanni Bellini's
most beautiful works. The church also has numerous important doges' tombs, a statue
by Donatello, and a 15th-century choir.

The original Franciscan church was founded c. 1250, and the present brick Gothic
church was begun c. 1330 but not finished until after 1443. The majestic campanile
(the tallest in the city after St Mark's) dates from the second half of the 14th century.
On the severe west front, the Gothic doorway has sculptures attributed to Alessandro
Vittoria (the *Risen Christ*) and the workshop of Bartolomeo Bon. The other doorways
have sculptures of *St Peter* and a fine 15th-century relief of the *Madonna and Child*
with angels.

SANTA MARIA GLORIOSA DEI FRARI

A Ritual Choir

B Sanctuary
  1) Tomb of Doge Niccolò Tron
  2) Tomb of Doge Francesco Foscari
  3) Crucifix

C North Choir Chapels
  4) Chapel of the Franciscan Saints
  5) Chapel of St Michael
  6) Milanesi Chapel
  7) Corner Chapel

D South Choir Chapels
  8) Chapel of St John the Baptist
     (sculpture by Donatello)
  9) Chapel of the Sacrament
  10) Bernardo Chapel

E South Transept
  11) Tomb of Paolo Savelli
  12) Tomb of Admiral Benedetto Pesaro
  13) Sarcophagus of 'Beato Pacifico'
  14) Monument to Jacopo Marcello

F Sacristy
  15) Triptych by Bellini
  16) *Deposition*
  17) Lavabo
  18) Tabernacle by Tullio Lombardo
  19) Reliquary showcase
  20) Clock

G Chapter House

H South Aisle
  21) Altarpiece by Palma Giovane
  22) Altarpiece by Giuseppe Salviati
  23) *St Jerome* by Vittoria
  24) Monument to Titian

I North Aisle
  25) Emiliani Chapel
  26) Monument to Jacopo Pesaro
  27) *Pala Pesaro*
  28) Mausoleum of Giovanni Pesaro
  29) Mausoleum of Canova
  30) Altar of the Crucifix
  31) Stoup

J West Wall
  32) Tomb of Pietro Bernardo
  33) Monument to Alvise Pasqualigo

INTERIOR OF THE FRARI

The huge interior, some 90m long, is cruciform with an aisled nave of eight bays joined by wooden tie-beams. Titian's magnificent *Assumption* in the apse, at its most impressive when seen from the main west door, is framed by the arch of the monks' choir.

(A) Ritual choir: The ritual choir extends into the nave as in many cathedrals in England and France, but it is rare to see this in Italian churches. The lovely **choir-screen** (1475), by Bartolomeo Bon and Pietro Lombardo, is faced with Carrara marble and decorated with Istrian stone figures of saints and prophets in relief; above are ten apostles and a *Crucifixion between the Virgin and St John the Evangelist*, with angels as lecterns. The three tiers of magnificent **choir stalls** were carved by Marco Cozzi (1468) and have beautifully detailed intarsia decoration by Lorenzo and Cristoforo Canozzi.

(B) Sanctuary: The apse is lit by fine stained-glass windows and is filled with **Titian's *Assumption*** (1518), the largest altarpiece in Venice, celebrated among his masterpieces for its dramatic movement and its amazing colouring. One of the most memorable figures is that of the apostle dressed in red, seen from behind with his arms outstretched towards the Virgin, thus linking her and the cloud of putti to the ground (while one of the little feet of the lowest putto gracefully almost touches the head of another apostle). The Virgin's gesture suggests she is shocked into immobility as she leaves behind earthly matters and prepares herself to meet God the Father, who appears above as a somewhat menacing figure painted in very dark colours against the golden sky of Heaven.

The **tomb of Doge Niccolò Tron (1)** (d. 1473) is a perfectly proportioned monument by Antonio Rizzo. The doge, in office for just two uneventful years, was exceptionally tall and always wore a beard: he is first shown (on the lowest level) in a life-like portrait standing between two beautiful statues of *Faith* and *Charity*. Above is an inscription recounting his exploits and then his effigy on a sarcophagus guarded by the *Virtues*. At the top are five niches with more allegorical figures, which also appear in the frame amongst pages holding the doge's emblem. It is less easy to find religious elements: the lone figure of the *Risen Christ* in the lunette at the very top with the Annunciatory Angel and Virgin on either side. The great variety of precious marbles and the gilding on the details adds to the splendour of this great tomb, recognised as one of the most sublime examples of Renaissance funerary art in Venice.

Opposite is the fine **tomb of Francesco Foscari (2)**, who died in 1457 after 34 glorious years as doge (*see p. 75*). He is shown asleep beneath a beautifully-executed canopy, with statues representing *Power*, *Wisdom* and *Justice*—the virtues of a pious ruler. The late Gothic mausoleum may be the work of Niccolò di Giovanni Fiorentino.

By the high altar (which dates from 1516) is a painted 13th-century **Crucifix (3)** attributed to an artist named from this work the 'Master of the Frari Crucifix', probably of the Tuscan school.

(C) North choir chapels: The **Chapel of the Franciscan Saints (4)** has a *Madonna and Saints* by Bernardino Licinio. In the **Chapel of St Michael (5)**, on the right wall, is the tomb (perhaps by Lorenzo Bregno) of Melchiorre Trevisan (d. 1500), a Venetian commander who donated the reliquary of the Holy Blood to the church (it had been taken from Constantinople in 1480).

The lovely altarpiece of *St Ambrose and Eight Saints* in the **Milanesi Chapel (6)** was begun by Alvise Vivarini (1503) and finished by Marco Basaiti. A plain slab on the floor here marks the grave of the great composer Claudio Monteverdi, who directed the music at St Mark's for the last 30 years of his life (he died in 1643). The date of birth given here is incorrect: we know that he was in fact born in 1567.

The **Corner Chapel (7)** contains the tomb of Federico Corner, an unusual but graceful work (of Tuscan provenance) with an angel in a niche holding an inscription recording Corner's (rather unholy) generosity in paying for the war against the Genoese at Chioggia. The font bears a marble statue of *St John*, exquisitely carved by Jacopo Sansovino (1554). On the altar, in a fine frame, is a painting with superb colouring by Bartolomeo Vivarini (1474) of *St Mark Enthroned*, with four other saints. The stained glass dates from the 15th century. In 1990 some interesting and rare frescoes dating from around 1361 were discovered between the vault of the chapel and the roof, as illustrated on panels displayed here.

(D) South choir chapels: The **Chapel of St John the Baptist (8)** contains an altar erected in 1436 by Florentines resident in the city. They commissioned for it a statue of their patron saint, John the Baptist, by no less a sculptor than Donatello. The first documented work in the Veneto by the greatest sculptor of the Florentine Renaissance, signed and dated 1438, it still stands here—easy to miss at the centre of a tabernacle decorated with other gilded polychrome wood statues by unknown minor artists. It was Donatello's first statue to be made in wood (he may also have chosen this medium knowing that it would make it easier to transport it here from Florence), and is a superb work which has similarities with his later and much more famous *Mary Magdalene*, now in the Museo dell'Opera del Duomo in Florence.

In the **Chapel of the Sacrament (9)** are two Gothic funerary monuments, one of which commemorates the Florentine ambassador Duccio degli Uberti (d. 1336). The **Bernardo Chapel (10)** has a brightly-painted altarpiece by Bartolomeo Vivarini (1482), still in its magnificent original frame.

(E) South transept: The **tomb of Paolo Savelli (11)**, a Roman *condottiere*, dates from around 1406 and was the first in Venice to include an equestrian statue. It is also thought to be a Tuscan work, and shows both Gothic and Renaissance elements. The statues on the marble sarcophagus have been attributed to the great Sienese master Jacopo della Quercia.

Over the door to the sacristy is the fine **tomb of Admiral Benedetto Pesaro (12)**, by Lorenzo Bregno. Pesaro died in Corfu in 1503. His tomb has interesting reliefs with battleships and fortresses illustrating his victories over the Turks. The statue of *Mars* is by Baccio da Montelupo (1537), and is the only work in Venice by this Tuscan artist, who was both a sculptor and architect. The **sarcophagus of 'Beato Pacifico' (13)** (Scipione Bon, a friar of the church who is thought to have supervised part of the building work), beneath an elaborate canopy in a florid Gothic style of 1437, is ascribed to the Tuscan artists Nanni di Bartolo and Michele da Firenze, who also worked in Venice on the exterior sculpture of St Mark's and the Doge's Palace.

The **monument to Jacopo Marcello (14)**, who was killed in battle in 1484 at the head of the Venetian fleet during an encounter with the Turks at Gallipoli, does not follow the usual form of niches and statues but has an oval frame and three free-standing statues at the top of a double sarcophagus. Formerly thought to be the work of Pietro Lombardo, it has recently been attributed to his contemporary, also from Lombardy, Giovanni Buora. The worn fresco high up of the hero's triumph is by a 15th-century artist of the school of Mantegna.

(F) Sacristy: This is a delightful, peaceful room and in the apse, still in the original frame made for it by Jacopo da Faenza, is the splendid **triptych by Giovanni Bellini (15)**, painted for the chapel in 1488. It shows the *Madonna and Child between Sts Nicholas of Bari, Peter, Mark and Benedict*. 'Jewel-like' is an over-used phrase to describe Bellini's Madonnas, but it can aptly be used here. Seeing it is like looking into a shrine. The Virgin, dressed in a glorious blue robe, sits beneath a golden dome, perhaps a reference to the gold-ground mosaics in the Basilica of St Mark. Ruskin justly considered this the greatest work in Venice by Bellini: 'the only artist who appears to me to have united, in equal and magnificent measures, justness of drawing, nobleness of colouring, and perfect manliness of treatment with the purest religious feeling'. It was commissioned in memory of Franceschina Pesaro, who died in 1478 and is buried here, by her three sons (one of them, Benedetto, is buried in the church; *see 12, above*). The four saints were chosen since they bear the names of Franceschina's husband and sons.

The late 16th-century painting of the ***Deposition* (16)** is by Niccolò Frangipane. The Lombardesque **lavabo (17)** has two sphinxes and a classical frieze with lovely coloured marble inlay. Tullio Lombardo made the exquisite little marble **tabernacle (18)**. There is an incredibly elaborate 17th-century **reliquary showcase (19)** by Cabianca and Brustolon, and opposite, an exquisitely carved wooden **clock-face (20)** with allegories of Time, the work of Francesco Pianta (17th century).

(G) Chapter house: Opposite the windows (outside which can be seen the huge Palladian cloister with its elaborate well-head) is the sarcophagus (with a relief of the *Death of the Virgin*) of Doge Francesco Dandolo, and above it a precious lunette, signed and dated 1339 by the first great Venetian painter, Paolo Veneziano. It shows Doge Francesco Dandolo and his wife Elizabeth being presented to the Virgin by Sts Francis and Elizabeth. It is thought to be the earliest doge's portrait drawn from life to have survived.

(H) South aisle: Two painted 16th-century **altarpieces by Palma Giovane (21) and Giuseppe Salviati (22)** flank an altar with a **statue of *St Jerome* (23)**, one of Alessandro Vittoria's best works. The huge Carrara marble **monument to Titian (24)** is raised above the place where Venice's greatest painter is traditionally believed to have been buried. The (somewhat ponderous) monument, bearing a relief of Titian's own high altarpiece of the *Assumption*, was commissioned by the Austrian emperor Ferdinand I from Luigi Zandomeneghi and his son Pietro in 1843, and completed in 1852.

TITIAN

Titian (Tiziano Vecellio; c.1485–1576) succeeded Giovanni Bellini as the most important painter in Venice, and was one of the greatest Italian painters of all time. He was painting at a time when Venice flourished and was at the height of her power. The *Assumption*, commissioned by the Franciscans in 1516, is an early work showing the influence of Raphael and Michelangelo. It had such success with the Venetians that Titian very soon became the favourite portrait painter of the nobility, and he was appointed official painter of the Republic in 1517. This meant that among other duties, he had to paint the portrait of every doge on taking office (since he lived so long he painted no less than six of them: from Antonio Grimani in 1523 to Francesco Venier in 1554). His other masterpiece in the Frari, the *Pala Pesaro* (1526), includes excellent portraits of the Pesaro family. Although there are numerous paintings by Titian in Venice, he also worked for the most important Italian courts, as well as for the papacy, the Habsburg emperors, and Philip II of Spain.

(I) North aisle: The **Emiliani Chapel (24)** has a marble altarpiece with ten statues in niches by the school of Jacobello dalle Masegne (15th century), and the tomb of Bishop Miani, with five similar statues. Near the **monument to Bishop Jacopo Pesaro (25)**, who died in 1547, with a fine effigy, is Titian's ***Madonna di Ca' Pesaro (26)*** (the *Pala Pesaro*). It was commissioned by Bishop Jacopo in 1519, but only completed in 1526. A marvel of composition and colour, it shows the Madonna and Child with saints above members of the Pesaro family (the boy looking directly out at the viewer is Jacopo's nephew and heir, Leonardo). The Bishop is to the left, and his brother to the right, both kneeling in rather static poses. Pesaro led the Venetian fleet in a victory against the Turks in 1502, when he reconquered the Greek island of Santa Maura (now Lefkas): he was in the service of the Borgia pope Alexander VI, whose arms are shown on the magnificent crimson standard held up by a soldier who turns to his captive Turk. The Bishop had already commissioned another kneeling portrait of himself from Titian (now in Antwerp), where he is shown being presented by the pope to St Peter, and the magnificent figure of St Peter also takes pride of place in the *Pala Pesaro*. Titian's great and daring invention here of placing the Madonna at one side of the painting rather than in the traditional central position adds a triangular form to the composition, and the scene is overshadowed by two mighty columns rising to the sky.

FRARI
Detail of the mausoleum of Canova.

The Madonna herself is particularly beautiful, and the Christ Child almost steps off her lap as He plays with her veil. The two putti above the cloud, mischievously playing with a Cross, are painted with the same extraordinary freedom of touch.

The huge **mausoleum of Doge Giovanni Pesaro (27)**, who died in 1659, is a bizarre Baroque work and one of the most elaborate funerary monuments in Venice. It is attributed to Baldassare Longhena, with sculptures by the German artist Melchior Berthel. By any standards it is an extraordinary piece of funerary sculpture. The colossal Moors, by Berthel, are said to represent prisoners taken during struggles against the Ottomans in Crete. Pesaro himself sits high up, seeming to address anyone who will listen, beneath a tasselled baldacchino of red marble, while two long-necked monsters support his sarcophagus. The inscriptions in huge embossed lettering read: *Vixit anno LXX* (Lived 70 years), *Devixit anno MDCLIX* (Died in the year 1659); *Hic revixit anno MDCLXIX* (Here he lived again in the year 1669); i.e. the year the monument was erected.

The **mausoleum of Canova (28)**, the great Neoclassical sculptor, was erected by his pupils (including Luigi Zandomeneghi) in 1827, and reproduces Canova's own design for monuments to Titian (never realised because of lack of funds; the model is preserved in the Museo Correr) and to Maria Christina, Archduchess of Austria and eldest sister of Marie Antoinette, in the Augustinerkirche in Vienna. It adopts the most ancient form of sepulchral monument, the pyramid, also used in numerous other funerary chapels, including that of the Chigi in Santa Maria del Popolo in Rome. The weeping lion of St Mark beside a winged figure representing the Genius of Canova guards the half-open door of the pyramid in which the artist's heart lies on an urn; his body was buried in his home town, Possagno. On the other side, female mourners representing the Arts approach the tomb in a funerary procession. Above the entrance two angels hold up a profile of Canova framed by a snake eating its tail—a symbol of immortality.

The **Altar of the Crucifix (29)**, designed by Longhena, has sculptures by Juste le Court. The holy water stoup bears a statuette of *St Anthony of Padua* (1609) forming a pair with the opposite **stoup (30)**, which has a bronze statuette of *St Agnes* by Girolamo Campagna.

(J) West wall: The **tomb of the senator Pietro Bernardo (31)**, d. 1538, is thought to be a late work by Tullio Lombardo; the **monument to the procurator Alvise Pasqualigo (32)**, who died ten years earlier, is attributed to Lorenzo Bregno.

The church organs are by Gaetano Callido (1795) and Giovanni Battista Piaggia (1732).

ARCHIVIO DI STATO

The extensive adjoining conventual buildings, with the Palladian cloister and another in the style of Sansovino, restructured c. 1815–20 by Lorenzo Santi, contain the Archivio di Stato (State Archives). Among the most famous state archives in the world, they fill some 300 rooms and provide a remarkable record of the Venetian Republic. Throughout the history of the *Serenissima*, the dispatches sent home from Venetian ambassadors and their final reports at the end of their terms of office offer extraordinary insights into the life of the times.

It was here that the English scholar and historian Rawdon Brown spent many years of research, his particular area of study being the documentation which related to England: in 1862 the Master of the Rolls, on behalf of the British government, formally appointed him to carry out this task. He published the reports made by the Great Council from 1496 to 1533, and nine volumes of a *Calendar*, being a record of the papers he found tracing Anglo-Venetian relations in the period from 1202 to 1509 (31 more were to be published over a period of more than 50 years after his death). A plaque in the building records the meticulous work of this 'English gentleman', but it is only recently that the value of the contribution he made to the history of Venice and England has been fully recognised. He saw much of John and Effie Ruskin on their visits to Venice, and Ruskin came to depend on Brown's deep knowledge of Venice and all things Venetian. He was also a collector and enjoyed rowing his *sandolo* out to the Lido every day for a swim. He died while still at work and is buried in the cemetery of San Michele.

In front of the church of the Frari, Ponte dei Frari, with a marble balustrade of 1858, crosses to the Fondamenta dei Frari, with the charming little **Caffè dei Frari**, popular as a place of refreshment. Gondoliers haunt the *rio* here.

SCUOLA GRANDE DI SAN ROCCO

Map p. 410, C3. Open 9.30–5.30.
The *Scuola* of the Confraternity of San Rocco (St Roch), founded in 1478, is famous for its paintings by Jacopo Tintoretto. St Roch was born in Montpellier in 1295. He caught the plague when he came to Italy to help cure victims of the disease, and retired alone to a wood where he was miraculously saved by an angel. He was particularly venerated in Venice in the 15th century, when the

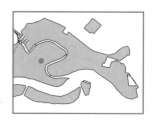

Scuola di San Rocco was founded and his relics were brought to the church. Members of the confraternity offered their services, especially during the frequent plagues which broke out in the city, the worst of which (after the Black Death of 1348) occurred in 1575–7 and 1630. After the plague of 1576, St Roch was declared a patron saint of the city and the doge made a pilgrimage to the church and *Scuola* every year on his feast day (16th August; still celebrated here). Canaletto was the first painter to record this event in a splendid large painting carried out around 1735 (now in the National Gallery in London). There are paintings of St Roch and plague victims in the *Scuola* and in the church beside it (St Roch is usually depicted as a young man with a sore on his leg).

The *Scuola* building was begun in 1515 by Bartolomeo Bon and finished in 1549 by Scarpagnino, who added the elegant main façade, which is usually considered his masterpiece. The less imposing canal façade is also by him. This was the last *scuola* to be founded in the city, and it is the one which has survived the best. The interior is exceptionally well preserved in all its decorative details, but is famous above all for over 50 paintings by Tintoretto, who here produced one of the most remarkable pictorial cycles in existence.

In 1564 a competition was held for the decoration of the building. Tintoretto was the winner, having entered a finished work (rather than a preparatory sketch) of *St Roch in Glory*, which he had already installed in the Sala dell'Albergo. A year later he was elected a brother of the confraternity, and spent the next 23 years working on the paintings (largely without the help of collaborators). In return he received a modest pension from the brotherhood. When Ruskin saw the *Scuola* in 1845 he commented, 'As for painting, I think I didn't know what it was until today', and his visit inspired him to pursue his study of the city and her art.

SCUOLA DI SAN ROCCO: GROUND FLOOR

In the entrance passageway is a statue of *St Roch* by Giovanni Buora (c. 1494). The columned hall, where religious ceremonies were held, was the last to be painted by Tintoretto (1582–7). The superb cycle of paintings illustrates the life of the Virgin and the individual works are on a more intimate scale than those on the floor above, with charming details and splendid landscapes. The *Circumcision* appears to have been painted partly by the *bottega* of Tintoretto and by his son Domenico. The last painting,

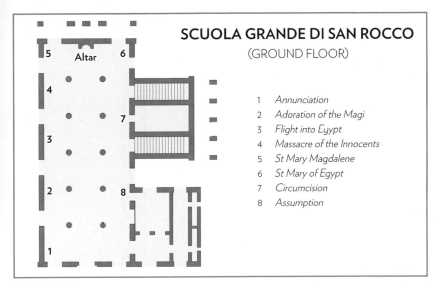

SCUOLA GRANDE DI SAN ROCCO
(GROUND FLOOR)

1 *Annunciation*
2 *Adoration of the Magi*
3 *Flight into Egypt*
4 *Massacre of the Innocents*
5 *St Mary Magdalene*
6 *St Mary of Egypt*
7 *Circumcision*
8 *Assumption*

the *Assumption*, has suffered from poor restorations in the past. The statue of *St Roch* on the altar is by Girolamo Campagna (1587).

TINTORETTO

Jacopo Robusti (c.1519–94), born in Venice, was called Tintoretto because his family were *tintori* (dyers). Throughout his long life (he died at the age of about 75) he worked exclusively in Venice, producing a remarkable number of superb paintings in the *scuole* and churches, commissioned from him by the Venetian middle classes, as well as official works for the Doge's Palace. He was one of the most daring painters who ever lived, and his creative fervour was without parallel. His output was enormous, and evidently he had an extraordinary capacity for work. Unlike Titian, he seems to have given little consideration to his earnings, but was instead intent on grasping every possible occasion to exert his skills as a painter. A member of several *scuole*, he married Faustina Episcopi, the daughter of the *guardian grande* of the Scuola di San Marco; they had eight children. Tintoretto was deeply religious, and his highly dramatic scenes, often in humble settings and always infused with a spiritual content, were given added intensity by his wonderful use of light, producing intense contrasts between the illuminated areas and those in shadow. Although he worked for a brief period with Titian, little is known about where he learnt his skills: he was already well established as an artist by the age of 20. His style of painting was transmitted to his large *bottega* as well as to his son Domenico, who also produced a great many paintings for Venetian buildings.

SCUOLA DI SAN ROCCO: UPPER FLOOR

The grand staircase is by Scarpagnino (1544–46). Its two huge paintings by Antonio

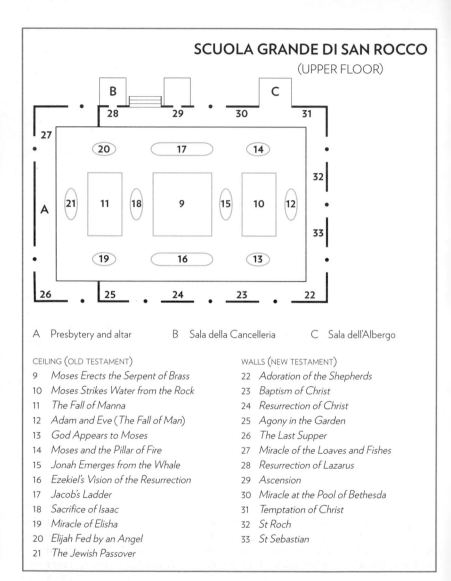

SCUOLA GRANDE DI SAN ROCCO
(UPPER FLOOR)

A   Presbytery and altar   B   Sala della Cancelleria   C   Sala dell'Albergo

CEILING (OLD TESTAMENT)
9   Moses Erects the Serpent of Brass
10 Moses Strikes Water from the Rock
11 The Fall of Manna
12 Adam and Eve (The Fall of Man)
13 God Appears to Moses
14 Moses and the Pillar of Fire
15 Jonah Emerges from the Whale
16 Ezekiel's Vision of the Resurrection
17 Jacob's Ladder
18 Sacrifice of Isaac
19 Miracle of Elisha
20 Elijah Fed by an Angel
21 The Jewish Passover

WALLS (NEW TESTAMENT)
22 Adoration of the Shepherds
23 Baptism of Christ
24 Resurrection of Christ
25 Agony in the Garden
26 The Last Supper
27 Miracle of the Loaves and Fishes
28 Resurrection of Lazarus
29 Ascension
30 Miracle at the Pool of Bethesda
31 Temptation of Christ
32 St Roch
33 St Sebastian

Zanchi (right; 1666) and Pietro Negri (left; 1673) commemorate the end of the plague of 1630. The horror of the suffering it caused is depicted with great realism.

Main hall: the chapter house
The huge chapter house, used for meetings and services, is a splendid hall by Scarpagnino, still dimly lit by the processional lanterns which were used by the

Scuola in the 18th century. It is entirely covered by wonderful paintings by Tintoretto, carried out between 1576 and 1581, with Old Testament subjects on the ceiling and New Testament subjects on the walls. They were chosen in a careful iconographical scheme related to the teaching of St Roch and his efforts to relieve thirst, hunger and sickness. The huge central painting on the ceiling shows Moses erecting the brazen serpent to save those bitten by fiery snakes sent by God as a punishment. The subjects of the other remarkable paintings are shown on the plan. The eight smaller panels in chiaroscuro are replacements by Giuseppe Angeli (1777) of works by Tintoretto. Angeli also restored the painting of the *Miracle of Elisha*. The painting of the *Miracle at the Pool of Bethesda* has been damaged by poor restorations.

On the altar is the *Vision of St Roch*, painted by Tintoretto with the help of his son Domenico. The late 17th-century carved wooden benches, by Francesco Pianta il Giovane, incorporate bizarre figures including (near the altar) a caricature of Tintoretto and a self-portrait.

Presbytery and altar

The carved wooden reliefs on the walls of the **presbytery (A)**, of the life of St Roch, are by Giovanni Marchiori. The two statues on the altar, of *St John the Baptist* and *St Sebastian*, are late works by Girolamo Campagna. The *Annunciation* by Titian was acquired by the *Scuola* in 1555 and the *Visitation* is by Tintoretto. *Christ Carrying the Cross* is a greatly venerated painting, considered to be miraculous, which hung in the church of San Rocco from about 1510 until 1955. Painted c. 1508 and now in poor condition, its attribution has been discussed interminably by art historians, who have vacillated over the decades between Titian and Giorgione: today most of them seem to agree that it is the work of Giorgione rather than a late work by Titian. The *Christ in Pietà*, formerly thought to be an early work by Titian, is also now generally attributed to the circle of Giorgione.

Sala della Cancelleria and Sala dell'Albergo

The charming little **Sala della Cancelleria (B)** preserves its original 18th-century furnishings, and displayed here is a *Portrait of a Man* by Tintoretto, once considered to be a self-portrait.

The **Sala dell'Albergo (C)**, once used for committee meetings by the brethren of the *Scuola*, was the first room to be decorated by Tintoretto (1564–7). On the carved and gilded ceiling is his winning competition entry, *St Roch in Glory* (clearly painted in a hurry) and 20 smaller panels with heads of putti, the Four Seasons, allegories of the *Scuole Grandi* of Venice, and the Cardinal Virtues. The vast *Crucifixion* is generally considered to be the painter's masterpiece. On the opposite wall are *Christ before Pilate*, the *Crowning with Thorns* and *The Way to Calvary*. Here also is displayed a fragment of a frieze from the ceiling of three apples, showing Tintoretto's remarkable painting technique.

At the foot of the stairs leading to the top of the building are displayed **two paintings by Giambattista Tiepolo**, acquired by the *Scuola* in 1785: *Hagar and Ishmael*

Comforted by an Angel, and *Abraham Visited by an Angel*. At the top of the stairs you can visit the **Sala del Tesoro**, where the precious treasury is preserved in old wooden cupboards with intricate locks. The earliest pieces are kept in the first cupboard on the left and include a tiny portable altar dating from around 1430. There are numerous 16th-century chalices. The central cupboard has a vast array of reliquaries dating mostly from the 17th and 18th centuries. Displayed on their own are two early 16th-century processional Crosses.

Also displayed in the *Scuola* is part of a collection of Islamic, Hispano-Moresque and European **majolica and porcelain**, left to the *Scuola* in the 1960s.

THE CHURCH OF SAN ROCCO

Map p. 410, C3. Open 9.30–5.30.

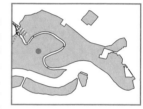

The church of San Rocco was designed by Bartolomeo Bon in 1489 but almost entirely rebuilt in 1725. The late Baroque façade was added in 1765–71 and is the best known work of Bernardino Maccaruzzi. The church contains a number of **paintings by Jacopo Tintoretto**, carried out before he began work on his spectacular cycle of paintings in the *Scuola* next door. The earliest of these, and the finest, is on the right wall of the sanctuary: *St Roch Curing Victims of the Plague*. Painted in 1549 when Tintoretto was 31 years old, it was the first Venetian painting to show the saint inside an isolation hospital such as those which operated in the lagoon during the dreaded outbreaks of pestilence. Tintoretto's other three paintings on the sanctuary walls illustrate episodes in the saint's life. The two paintings on the west wall (including an *Annunciation*) and the two larger paintings on the south side (including the *Pool of Bethesda*) are also by Tintoretto.

It is evident that the young Tintoretto was influenced by Pordenone, who came to the city in 1528 and frescoed the putti in the sanctuary to flank the marble high altar of this church. He also carried out the powerful painting, in a dynamic Mannerist style, of *St Martin* (on horseback) and *St Christopher* (once a cupboard door but now on the upper wall of the north side). Pordenone's name comes from his birthplace in the Friuli, where he painted most of his works, although others are to be seen in the Veneto. In Venice itself he frescoed some palace façades as well as the cupola of San Giovanni Elemosinario near the Rialto. Sebastiano Ricci, another successful artist from the Veneto, who spent his last years in Venice in the early 18th century (*see p. 237*), painted the *Miracle of San Francesco da Paola* for the first altar on the south side (and also the altarpiece on the opposite altar on the north side).

The lovely high altar is in the form of an arch decorated with early 16th-century statues of saints (including *St Roch* on the sarcophagus) by Giovanni Maria Mosca and the *Virgin* and *Annunciatory Angel* by Bartolomeo di Francesco Bergamasco. The carved dossals are attributed to Giovanni Marchiori, who also carved the statues flanking the west door (*David with the Head of Goliath* and *St Cecilia*) in 1743.

PALAZZETTO BRU ZANE & THE SCUOLA GRANDE DI SAN GIOVANNI EVANGELISTA

PALAZZETTO BRU ZANE

Map p. 410, C2. Guided tours are given before concerts and, at the time of writing, in English on Thur at 3.30. T: 041 521005, www.bru-zane.com.

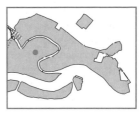

From the north side of the secluded Campo San Stin (*map p. 410, C2*), characteristic of a quiet Venetian square (the church of St Stephen was demolished in the early 19th century but the saint is recorded, together with St Barbara and St James, on the well-head dating from 1508), a passageway, Sottoportego di San Rocco, leads to Campiello del Forner, with the garden wall of the **Palazzetto Bru Zane** (*entrance at no. 2368*), built as a library in 1697 by Antonio Gaspari in the garden of Palazzo Zane, attributed to the *bottega* of Baldassare Longhena in 1682 and now the premises of a school, the Istituto Tecnico Livio Sanudo. The Palazzetto was restored in 2009 as the Centre de Musique Romantique Française and concerts of music by 19th-century French composers are given here almost every day (and there is a festival in autumn). There is a lovely little garden courtyard. In the interior, Andrea Brustolon made the wood balustrade which overlooks the ballroom on two floors, which has a pretty frescoed ceiling recently attributed to Sebastiano Ricci (who also probably painted the ceiling on the grand staircase).

Calle dell'Olio leads left out of Campiello del Forner to reach the courtyard in front of the Scuola Grande di San Giovanni Evangelista.

SCUOLA GRANDE DI SAN GIOVANNI EVANGELISTA

Map p. 410, C2. Only open when not in use for conferences and events. Concerts are often held here. For information, T: 041 718234, www.scuolasangiovanni.it.

This is the headquarters of one of the six chief confraternities in Venice, founded in 1261. The first court has a beautiful marble screen and portal by Pietro Lombardo (1481). The eagle, symbol of St John the Evangelist, recurs frequently in its sculptural decoration. In the second court is the wall of the *Scuola* (right), with Gothic windows, dating from 1454. The relief shows the brothers of the confraternity kneeling in front of St John the Evangelist and the inscription below (a copy of the original is preserved inside) records the acquisition of this site in 1349 for the *Scuola*, which then moved from the church of San Giovanni Evangelista across the way (where by 1301, under the protection of the Badoer family, it had its own chapel). Ahead is an entrance to the *Scuola* supplied by Mauro Codussi in 1512; the double windows above are typical of the work of this architect.

The *Scuola*

The handsome **ground-floor hall** has a fine row of columns with Gothic capitals (decorated with the kneeling figures of members of the confraternity) and sculpture including a 14th-century relief of *St Martin*, with Doge Andrea Contarini and a monk. The chief glory of the interior is the wonderful **double staircase**, a work of great skill and elegance by Mauro Codussi (1498). It leads up to the splendid main *Salone*, transformed in 1727–57 by Giorgio Massari, who designed the magnificent marble pavement, and decorated the walls with a 16th-century cycle of paintings. The **Oratorio della Croce** has a delightful colourful terrazzo floor and 18th-century decorations. Here is kept an exquisite reliquary (only shown in a procession on 14th September) in gilded silver, rock crystal and precious stones, made in the 15th century by Venetian goldsmiths to preserve a relic of the True Cross given by the Patriarch of Constantinople to Filippo de' Masseri, an officer of state in Cyprus in 1366 who in turn donated it to the *Scuola* three years later (the famous cycle of paintings illustrating the history and miracle of this celebrated relic, by Gentile Bellini, Vittore Carpaccio and others, was painted for this *Scuola* and is now in the Accademia (*see p. 143*).

The church of San Giovanni Evangelista

This church (*usually closed*) contains an organ built by Giovanni Battista Piaggia (1760) in an organ case designed by Giorgio Massari, and paintings in the sanctuary by Jacopo Marieschi (*Last Supper*) and Domenico Tintoretto (*Crucifixion*).

CAMPO SANT'APONAL & SAN SILVESTRO

The busy **Campo Sant'Aponal** (*map p. 411, E3*) has eight *calli* leading into it and a lovely well-head. The deconsecrated church of Sant'Aponal (Sant'Apollinare), founded in the 11th century, was rebuilt four centuries later. On the Gothic façade, above a round window, is a badly worn relief of the Crucifix (14th century); below, in a tabernacle, are reliefs of the *Crucifixion* and episodes from the life of Christ (1294).

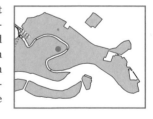

Calle del Luganegher leads from here directly to the peaceful **Campo San Silvestro** (*map p. 411, E3*), where the fine brick campanile has a stone bas-relief. The church of San Silvestro (*closed for restoration at the time of writing*) has a façade completed in 1909, and a Neoclassical interior by Lorenzo Santi. On the right side, the first altar has a *Baptism of Christ* by Jacopo Tintoretto, and the second altar a *Holy Family* by Johann Carl Loth. On the first altar on the left side is a good painting by Girolamo da Santacroce, particularly interesting since it shows the English martyr St Thomas Becket enthroned.

Opposite the church is **Palazzo Valier** (no. 1022), with an Ionic columned doorway, where the great painter Giorgione died in 1510.

Sottoportego del Traghetto leads down to the *fondamenta* along the Grand Canal (with a vaporetto landing-stage).

A WALK THROUGH SAN POLO

This walk begins at the Rialto Mercato vaporetto landing-stage beside the lively fruit and vegetable market. It takes in the church of San Cassiano, with three paintings by Tintoretto; the birthplace of the beautiful Bianca Cappello, who married into the Medici family; and the notorious Ponte delle Tette.

THE ARCADED HALL OF THE NEO-GOTHIC **Pescheria** was built in 1907 by Cesare Laurenti: there has been a fish market here since the 14th century. It is well worth a visit in the mornings (except Mon) just to see the great variety of fresh fish for sale (when the sun is up the heavy red curtains protect the day's catch from the heat). The tops of the columns are carved with all sorts of sea creatures and fishing boats. On the exterior towards the Grand Canal there is a tondo with a painted terracotta relief of Pietro Aretino, who lived nearby (*see p. 119*).

Behind the fish market, a bridge leads over to the peaceful Fondamenta de l'Ogio (or Olio), where there is a mooring for small boats. The Ca' d'Oro on the opposite side of the Grand Canal can be seen in all its glory from here. At the far end of the *fondamenta*, take the narrow **Calle del Campaniel**, which has a view of the bell-tower of San Cassiano. The first turning on the right, Calle de Ca Michiel, leads to a *corte* with an old wooden stair and veranda and a *sottoportego* which leads out to the Rio di San Cassiano. Off it, Calle del Teatro Vecchio leads through an iron gate with a relief of two curious animals above it, one of them a camel (if the gate is open, you can go through into the secluded Corte del Teatro Vecchio, which has a 13th-century well-head in pastel

pink marble decorated with primitive amphorae).

Back on Calle del Campaniel, continue past the foot of the splendid 13th-century campanile of San Cassiano and into the busier Campo San Cassiano, with the flank of the church and a pretty well-head. The **church of San Cassiano** (*open 9–12 & 5.30–6.45*) is thought to have been founded as early as the 10th century but was rebuilt in the 17th century. In the sanctuary are three remarkable **paintings by Tintoretto**: the *Crucifixion*, the *Resurrection*, and the *Descent into Limbo*. All three paintings are extremely unusual for their iconography: the *Crucifixion* is particularly memorable, and unlike any other painting of this subject. The tragic atmosphere of the picture is heightened by the menacing sky and line of soldiers with their spears on the low horizon, and the abandoned pink robe at the foot of the Cross. The dramatic scene of the *Descent into Limbo* includes the nude figure of Eve and a splendid angel flying away. In the *Resurrection*, the figures of the patron saints of the church, St Cassian and St Cecilia, appear, as well as charming putti, two of them holding wreaths of lilies. The altar front was carved by Heinrich Meyring in 1696. In the dark chapel to the right of the high altar, the *Visitation* (with a portrait in a tondo beneath of a member of the confraternity of the Scuola della Visitazione), the *Annunciation to St Zacharias* and the *Birth of St John* are all by Leandro Bassano. Next to the sacristy in the north aisle is a charming chapel

(*automatic light*) which preserves its decorations of 1746.

Directly in front of the church is a bridge leading into Calle dei Morti, which in turn leads into Calle della

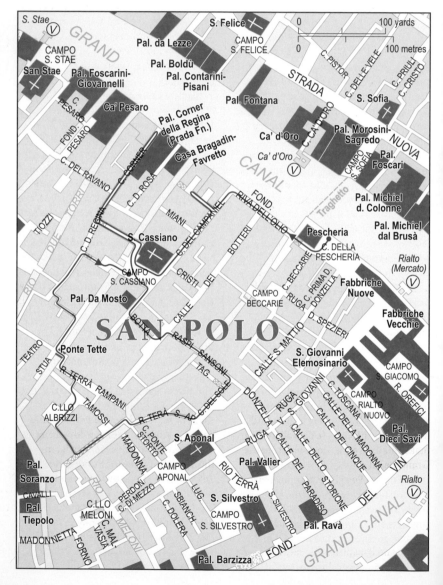

Regina. Turn right and follow it to the Grand Canal at the end: on your right is the land-entrance of the 18th-century **Palazzo Corner della Regina**, which stands on the site of the birthplace of Caterina Cornaro, Queen of Cyprus (1454–1510; *see p. 107*). Since 2011 the palace has been leased to the Prada Foundation. This famous Italian fashion house has restored it and opened it for exhibitions (some of which include part of its own contemporary art collection). The interior has 18th-century paintings and stuccoes and an ingenious staircase.

Retrace your steps to Campo San Cassiano and cross it diagonally to leave by Calle de Ca' Muti (or Ca' Baglioni), past a vast palace owned by the Da Mosto family, after which you turn left into Calle de la Bota, which brings you into the wide Calle dei Botteri. Cross it diagonally into Calle de Ca' Raspi, which leads over Ponte Raspi into Campo dei Sansoni. Calle del Sol (or Sole) leads down to the **Campiello del Sole**, off which there are a number of *calli* and the picturesque Sottoportego del Tagliapiera, with its two columns and another arch onto a *rio*. From the *campiello* there is a view of the Romanesque bell-tower of Sant'Aponal, and at the end of it, Rio Terrà Sant'Aponal leads right: it was created in 1844 when a *rio* was covered over and a number of bridges were demolished to make this area easier to reach from the Grand Canal.

Just across Ponte Storto is the palace (no. 1280) which was the **birthplace of Bianca Cappello**, in around 1560. It is decorated with two busts of Romans, and two reliefs of lions' heads amidst foliage and Byzantine paterae. The beautiful 'daughter of the Republic' fled to Florence at the age of 15, in order to marry a humble clerk, against her parents' will. The marriage was not a success, but meanwhile she had attracted the notice of Grand Duke Francesco I de' Medici. After a long liaison (and following the convenient death of her husband), Bianca married him in 1578, just two months after the death (in childbirth) of his unloved first wife. The Jacobean playwright Thomas Middleton adapted the story of their lives as the plot for his *Women Beware Women*.

Fondamenta and Sottoportego del Banco Salviati lead along a lovely peaceful *rio*. Its name changes to Sottoportego Tamossi, from which the incredibly narrow **Calle Stretta** leads into the spacious Campiello Albrizzi, which has a relief of the lion of St Mark and a lovely old palace with several trios of chimney pots. Calle Albrizzi leads out of the *campo* to Rio Terrà delle Carampane. Its name recalls the Ca' Rampana, which in the 16th century was rented by prostitutes from the Rampana family. Turn left, past the excellent Antiche Carampane restaurant (*see p. 363*), and then right, onto a *rio* which is crossed by the tiny **Ponte delle Tette**, a bridge so named because topless prostitutes used to solicit here in Republican days. The walkway on the further bank is called Fondamenta della Stua, after one of the numerous 'bath houses' which used to exist in the city. After crossing Ponte delle Tette, turn right along the *fondamenta*, then left under the *sottoportego*. Calle della Regina brings you back, under a *sottoportego*, into Campo San Cassiano, from where you can quickly get back to the Rialto. Caffè del Doge serves good coffee (*see p. 367*).

FONDACO DEI TURCHI
Detail of the waterfront façade, with the inscription 'Alere Flammam' (Feed the Flame).

Sestiere of Santa Croce

This district is home to the elaborate Baroque church of San Stae and the little-visited San Simeone Grande, both opening onto the Grand Canal. Between them, in a particularly quiet area, is another little church, San Giovanni Decollato, with early frescoes in a lovely 12th-century interior. The splendid Ca' Pesaro houses the Gallery of Modern Art and Palazzo Mocenigo is a late 17th-century patrician residence.

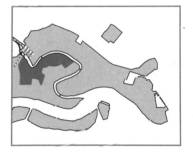

The *sestiere* of Santa Croce grew up around a large monastery and church dedicated to the Holy Cross, in what was once a quiet and remote part of the city. It retains the monastery's name despite the fact that it was demolished in 1810 and only a single column remains. These days this *sestiere* is an area of tiny, quiet back-streets and 19th- and 20th-century housing, with the most interesting buildings on, or close to, the Grand Canal.

SAN STAE

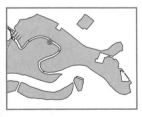

Map p. 411, D1. Open Mon–Sat 10–5; Chorus Pass.
The little Campo San Stae, with its 18th-century well-head, opens out onto the Grand Canal. Here the church of San Stae (Sant'Eustachio) presents a splendid façade to the waterfront. It is the work of Domenico Rossi, who began his career as a designer of pyrotechnical extravaganzas. He later turned to architecture, with considerable success. The temple-like design, with its columns and pediment, owes much to Palladio, though the decorations, with numerous statues and reliefs, are Baroque rather than Classical in style. The church was financed in 1710 by Doge Alvise II Mocenigo, a descendant of the doge who presided over the victory of Lepanto (since that time, all Mocenigo doges have been named Alvise); the Mocenigo family vault is in the floor of the church, and their family palace is just around the corner (*see p. 211*).

The bright white and grey interior is particularly interesting because it contains only 18th-century paintings. Those in the sanctuary, illustrating the lives of the twelve Apostles, were commissioned from the most important artists of the day and include on the left wall (bottom row, the painting nearest to the nave) Giambattista Tiepolo's dramatic *Martyrdom of St Bartholomew*, painted when the artist was only 26; and (next to it, bottom row, central painting) Sebastiano Ricci's *St Peter Freed from Prison*. On the opposite wall (bottom row, nearest to the altar) is the *Martyrdom of St James* by Giovanni Battista Piazzetta.

Niccolò Bambini painted the *Madonna in Glory and Saints* in the first chapel on the right side, and in the third chapel on the left side there is a sculpted Crucifix by Giuseppe Torretti, who also carved (in a totally different style) the bust of Sebastiano Foscarini in the family funerary monument (lowest bust on the right wall).

In the sacristy is a scene by Giovanni Battista Pittoni showing Trajan ordering St Eustace (Sant'Eustachio; San Stae) to worship the pagan idols. The organ above the west door is by Gaetano Callido (1772).

Beside the church is the charming little **Scuola dei Battiloro e Tiraoro** (Confraternity of Goldsmiths), attributed to Giacomo Gaspari (1711). There is a wonderful view from here across the Grand Canal. To the left stands Codussi's magnificent 16th-century Palazzo Vendramin-Calergi (*described on p. 234*). On the corner of a *rio* to the right is another 16th-century palace, **Palazzo Gussoni Grimani**, attributed to Sanmicheli. It was here that Sir Henry Wotton resided in 1619–21.

SIR HENRY WOTTON

Wotton (1568–1639) was a poet and art collector (with a particular interest in drawings by Palladio), and one of the most cultivated Englishmen of his time. He had a profound knowledge of Italy and the Italian language, and his famous letters provide a vivid picture of 17th-century Venetian society.

In a letter dated 1622 from Venice ('this watery seat'), he remarks: 'We are newly here out of our Carnival. Never was there in the licensing of public masks a more indulgent decemvirate [Council of Ten], never fewer mischiefs and acts of private revenge; as if restrained passions were indeed the most dangerous. Now, after these anniversary follies have had their course and perhaps their use likewise, in diverting men from talking of greater matters, we begin to discourse in every corner of our new league...'

He was sent to Venice three times as ambassador by James I but on one occasion he was dismissed by the king for his contention that an ambassador was an honest man sent abroad to lie for the good of his country. He was a friend of Fra' Paolo Sarpi, and gave Venice the support of the English king in the Republic's famous quarrel with the pope in 1606 (*see p. 15*). At the end of his life he was Provost of Eton and went fishing with Izaak Walton. He was probably the first person to recognise great qualities in the writings of Milton, and the poet asked him for his advice before starting out on a journey to Italy.

On this side of the canal, just across the *rio*, is Palazzo Foscarini Giovannelli, where Doge Marco Foscarini was born in 1695. He possessed the most important private library in Venice, confiscated from his descendants by the Austrian government in 1799 and most of it taken to the Imperial Library in Vienna.

The Salizzada di San Stae leads away from the Grand Canal towards Palazzo Mocenigo, passing the church's brick campanile with a 13th-century stone angel at its base, and several fine (but dilapidated) palaces, including (no. 1988) a 13th-century building.

MUSEO DI PALAZZO MOCENIGO

Map p. 411, D1. Open April–Oct 10–5, except Mon; Nov–March 10–4, except Mon. Entrance at no. 1992 Salizzada di San Stae.
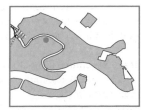
The palace was left to the city of Venice in 1954 by the last descendant of this branch of the distinguished Mocenigo family (who provided the Republic with no fewer than seven doges). It is an interesting example of a late 17th-century patrician Venetian residence, although

it is not as well kept as it might be. There are usually displays in some of the rooms of 18th-century costumes (the palace houses a study centre devoted to costumes and fabrics from the 16th century up to the 1950s).

From the atrium, with 18th-century benches and busts, the staircase leads up to the *primo piano nobile*. The rooms have good furniture (17th–19th centuries), chandeliers from Murano and Venetian mirrors, and some of the 18th-century ceilings, with delicate decorations in stucco, have frescoes attributed to Jacopo Guarana and Giambattista Canal. The *portego* has a fine double doorway dating from the early 18th century, and the most famous members of the Mocenigo family are depicted in the frieze and paintings above the doors. The five larger portraits between the doors include one of Charles II of England. In the red drawing-room, the portrait of a Contarini procurator has a carved frame with elaborate allegories of the Contarini family, attributed to Antonio Corradini. The green sitting room has historical scenes of events in Mocenigo history, attributed to Antonio Stom. On the other side of the *portego* is a room with four monochrome allegories of the Four Seasons by Giambattista Canal, and two huge historical canvases, also by Stom.

At the time of writing a **Museum of Perfume** was set to be opened here by the Vidal family, to illustrate the history of fragrances based on the *Secreti Nobilissimi dell'Arte Profumatoria*, published in Venice in 1555.

SANTA MARIA MATER DOMINI

Map p. 411, D2. Irregular opening hours; always closed at weekends.

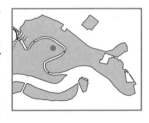

Tucked away in a peaceful corner of the city is the church of Santa Maria Mater Domini, Holy Mary Mother of God. The lovely domed interior, where the clean lines of the Renaissance architectural features are emphasised in dark grey stone, has intimate proportions with Diocletian windows, and an uncluttered sanctuary. The church was probably built following a design provided by Giovanni Buora (1502–40).

The church contains some very fine works by the High Renaissance Venetian sculptor Lorenzo Bregno, including the lovely first south altar (1524), which bears three marble figures of saints in a niche designed in perfect perspective and a relief of *God the Father* in the lunette above. It is thought that Antonio Minello may have helped him in this work. Bregno probably also carved the pretty altar on the right of the sanctuary, and the two statuettes of *St Mark* and *St John* on the altar to the left of the sanctuary are certainly by his hand. In the left aisle is a 13th-century Byzantine marble bas-relief of the *Virgin Orans*, and in the apse a Tuscan high relief in gilded terracotta of the *Madonna and Child*. The richly-coloured painting of the *Martyrdom of St Christina* (second south altar; 1520), with a charming group of angels holding onto the millstone tied around Christina's neck, is by Vincenzo Catena, a follower of Bellini, and the *Transfiguration* (first north chapel) is by his contemporary, Francesco

Bissolo. The copy of a 16th-century *Last Supper* by Bonifacio Veronese forms a pair with Jacopo Tintoretto's very fine *Invention of the Cross* (both are in their original frames).

The *campo* outside the church, with a fine well-head, has several good palaces. At the end opposite the *rio*, Palazzetto Viaro (no. 2120) has a distinguished row of tall trefoil windows (14th century) and a relief of a lion (almost obliterated). Number 2173 has ogee windows with, above, a frieze of Byzantine crosses and paterae. Opposite, no. 2177 has a quatrefoil decoration (almost completely ruined).

CA' PESARO:
GALLERIA INTERNAZIONALE D'ARTE MODERNA
& MUSEO ORIENTALE

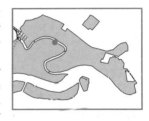

Map p. 411, E1. The palace and its two museums are open 10–5 (10–4 in winter) with the same ticket. Exhibitions are held twice a year on the second floor. There is a pleasant café with tables by the water-gate on the Grand Canal. This great Baroque palace, built for the Pesaro family by Baldassare Longhena, has a splendid façade on the Grand Canal. It was begun in 1658 for Giovanni Pesaro, when he was elected doge. He died the following year (his magnificent tomb in the Frari is also by Longhena) and work was continued by his nephew Leonardo; but by the time both he and Longhena died in 1682, only the ground floor had been completed. The palace was eventually finished by Longhena's pupil Antonio Gaspari. When the last member of the family died in 1830, all the contents were sold at auction in London. Conservation work on the building has recently been completed. Today it houses (mainly on the first floor) Venice's Gallery of Modern Art, founded in 1897. The collection has been put together over the years with the financial help of associations and private citizens in Venice, as well as through donations by the artists themselves. Many of the works purchased were first exhibited at the Biennale. The top floor houses the superb Museo Orientale (although for years there have been plans to rehouse it elsewhere).

GROUND FLOOR
The very fine 17th-century courtyard has an elaborate Renaissance well-head made by Sansovino for the courtyard of the Zecca but moved here in 1905, with an *Apollo* by Danese Cattaneo. In the splendid *androne*, which stretches to a portico at the water-gate on the Grand Canal, four 20th-century Italian sculptures are exhibited: a bronze *Eve* by Francesco Messina; two works by Alberto Viani; and *The Cardinal* by Giacomo Manzù. The prelate sits, swathed in his huge cope, with one hand just visible through the opening.

FIRST FLOOR

The collection comprises Venetian and non-Venetian works from the mid-19th century to the 1930s. The Macchiaioli School of Tuscan *plein-air* painters is well represented and there are a number of fine works from the Novecento and by exponents of the Futurist movement—the collection provides a good 'who's who' introduction to the era. Works from the early Biennale shows include paintings by Klimt and Chagall.

19th-century Venetian works:

Ippolito Caffi, who studied at the Venice Academy and was the last of the great Venetian *vedutisti*, is well represented with views of Venice and Rome (as well as Athens and Cairo). He was in Venice during the revolutionary period in 1849, and took up the role of official artist to record the events. He later enlisted as a sailor in the Italian navy, and drowned while in service when his ship was sunk off the Dalmatian coast in 1866. His atmospheric paintings include *Snow and Fog on the Grand Canal* and *Fair on the Quayside near San Marco*. Other typical Venetian scenes are by Guglielmo Ciardi, his contemporary Giacomo Favretto (his portrait of the Guidini family dates from 1873) and Luigi Nono (he painted the dramatic scene of two abandoned orphans at a Venetian church door in 1903).

Non-Venetian works of the late 19th century:

The Macchiaioli School, active in Tuscany before 1864 and whose members took their inspiration directly from nature, is well represented with Telemaco Signorini's famous *Asylum Interior*, painted in Florence, and by his landscape entitled *November*. The scene showing a dramatic accident during a battle is by the best-known painter of this school, Giovanni Fattori.

Giuseppe de Nittis lived in Paris (where, in 1874, he participated in an exhibition of the Impressionists) and

his pastel portrait of a lady shows how much he was influenced by his French contemporaries. Giacomo Balla, better known in his later period as a Futurist, painted the portrait of a member of the Pesaro family in 1901.

The sculptures by Medardo Rosso constitute the most important collection of his work in Italy: they were donated to the gallery in 1914. His original style, immediately recognisable, produces a fusion of figure with atmosphere in an attempt to abolish borders. He was especially skilled in modelling wax, and spent long periods in both Venice and Paris.

Works from the earliest Biennale art exhibitions:

Exhibited in the former *salone* are works shown at Biennale shows from 1895 up to the 1930s. The two most important works here are by Gustav Klimt and Marc Chagall. Klimt's *Salome* (or *Judith II*) was painted in 1909 (and acquired by the gallery soon afterwards). This great Viennese Secessionist painter had no success when he exhibited at the third Biennale in Venice in 1899, but he was given his own room at the Biennale of 1910. This famous painting (a sequel to his *Judith I*, dating from 1901 and now in Vienna) shows the influence of Oriental and Japanese art (Klimt also designed the frame). The *Rabbi* by Chagall is one of a number of his explicitly Jewish paintings, and was exhibited in his

Russian homeland when he returned there from Paris in 1914. It entered this collection in the late 1920s.

Sculptures by Adolfo Wildt: Room III is devoted to the Italian sculptor Adolfo Wildt (1868–1931), whose Symbolist works are always characterised by smooth and shiny marble surfaces. The works here were donated to the museum by his descendants in 1990.

The De Lisi Bequest: The display includes works by many painters who were members of the Novecento artistic movement, which had one of its very first joint exhibitions at the Venice Biennale of 1924. Major figures well represented here include Felice Casorati, Mario Sironi, Giorgio Morandi, Filippo de Pisis and Giorgio de Chirico. Generally in opposition to the avant-garde movements of the time, the Novecento artists promoted the values of form, and studied with renewed interest the great art produced in Italy in the 14th and 15th centuries, in particular that of Piero della Francesca. They were unanimous in their admiration of Cézanne. There are also paintings by Carlo Carrà, who went through a Futurist and Metaphysical period, and works by 20th-century foreign artists including Tanguy and Kandinsky.

Futurism to the 1950s: The collection includes paintings by Umberto Boccioni, pupil of the great Futurist Giacomo Balla, sculptures by Arturo Martini, and paintings (notably *Le Signorine*) by Felice Casorati. A representative display of Italian art of the 1920s and 1930s includes works by Antonio Donghi (*Woman at the Café*) and Lorenzo Viani.

Italian art of the 1950s, both abstract and figurative, includes works by Filippo de Pisis, in his characteristic light, sketchy style. Notable examples of 20th-century Venetian art are works by Virgilio Guidi—who enjoyed great success at the Biennale of 1924—and his contemporary Bruno Saetti.

SECOND FLOOR
Exhibitions are held here, and there are also plaster sculptures by Rodin of two of his most famous works: *The Burghers of Calais* and *The Thinker*.

TOP FLOOR: MUSEO ORIENTALE
This excellent museum, extremely well kept, would benefit greatly from more exhibition space: housed here since 1925, there have been plans for decades to move it elsewhere. The huge collection (numbering some 30,000 objects) includes paintings, sculpture, arms and armour, lacquer-work, bronzes, ivory (recently restored and redisplayed), jade, musical instruments, decorative arts, fabrics and costumes. It was Prince Henry of Bourbon, Count of Bardi, who collected these objects and artworks during a journey through China, Indonesia and Japan in 1887–9, and they were acquired by the Italian government at the end of the First World War. It constitutes one of the most important collections in Europe of Japanese art of the Edo period (1600–1868), especially interesting for its paintings. Chinese, Siamese and Javanese art are also well represented, and there is a fine Khmer figure of Buddha from Cambodia, dating from the 12th century. The 18th-century twelve-panel Chinese

SAN GIOVANNI DECOLLATO
Worn relief of the head of St John the Baptist.

lacquer screen in Coromandel style, with hunting scenes depicted in inlaid mother-of-pearl and tortoiseshell, was restored in 2007 by the Venice in Peril Fund. The display of precious kimonos is changed every few months.

SAN GIACOMO DELL'ORIO & SAN GIOVANNI DECOLLATO

SAN GIACOMO DELL'ORIO

Map p. 410, C2. Open Mon–Sat 10–5; Chorus Pass.
Of ancient foundation, the church was rebuilt in 1225 (the tall campanile survives from this time) and altered in 1532. The interior contains massive low Byzantine columns (12th–13th century), one (in the south transept) of *verde antico* and one (behind the pulpit) with a pretty flowered capital. There is a beautiful 14th-century

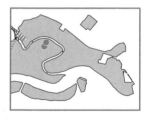

wooden ship's keel roof. The huge stoup in Greek marble was probably used as a font. In the south transept you can also see the old wall of the church with interesting fragments embedded in it (the *Virgin Orans* dates from the 13th century).

In the sanctuary hangs a Crucifix attributed to Paolo Veneziano (c. 1350), and on the east wall is a *Madonna and Four Saints* by Lorenzo Lotto (1546). On the left pier, the charming statuette of the *Virgin Annunciate*, just risen from her elegant chair and holding a spindle, was made by a Venetian sculptor in the mid-13th century. In the lovely chapel to the right of the sanctuary, the dome was frescoed by Jacopo Guarana and the four tondi of the Evangelists in the pendentives were painted by Padovanino. There is a domed tabernacle in precious marbles on the altar.

The paintings in the charming little New Sacristy (at the end of the south side) include works by Francesco Bassano: above a finely carved wood fragment, his *St John the Baptist Preaching* incorporates portraits of Bassano's family and Titian (on the extreme left wearing a red hat). The Old Sacristy (on the north side), with good wood panelling, is entirely decorated with a cycle of paintings celebrating the mystery of the Eucharist by Palma Giovane (1575–81), one of the best works by this extremely prolific painter (he also painted the stories from the life of St Lawrence in the north transept and the *Miracle of the Loaves and Fishes* in the south aisle). Outside the door into the sacristy is a good painting, *Sts Sebastian, Roch and Lawrence*, by Giovanni Buonconsiglio.

From a corner of the *campo* to the south of the church, **Ponte dell'Anatomia** leads directly to a courtyard of the same name, which recalls the site of an anatomical theatre built here in 1671. A small passageway links the *corte* to the little Campiello delle Strope, where there is a lovely old well-head decorated with rosettes and a carved head.

SAN GIOVANNI DECOLLATO
Map p. 410, C1. Open Mon, Tues, Thur 10–12; used by the Russian Orthodox community for services on Sat and Sun.
The church of San Giovanni Decollato (San Zan Degolà; 'St John the Beheaded') was founded in the early 11th century by the Venier family. A relief fragment of the Baptist's severed head has been built into the side wall. The basilican interior has Greek marble columns and Byzantine capitals and a lovely ship's keel roof. In the left apse chapel are 13th-century fresco fragments (remarkable because the damp lagoon climate makes fresco rare in Venice) of *St Helen* and the heads of four saints, and an *Annunciation*, as well as a frescoed vault with symbols of the Evangelists and a 17th-century carved Crucifix. In the right apse chapel there is a charming late 14th-century fragment of *St Michael Archangel*, trampling the demon underfoot: notice the fearsome face incorporated into his armour: this was discovered behind the marble altarpiece which has been moved to the side wall.

FONDACO DEI TURCHI:
NATURAL HISTORY MUSEUM

Map p. 411, D1. Open 9–5, summer 10–6; Sat and Sun 10–6; closed Mon. Entrance through a little garden on Fondamenta dei Turchi.
The large Fondaco dei Turchi was once one of the most important 13th-century palaces in the city. In 1381 it was given to the Dukes of Ferrara, and here, as their guests, stayed John Palaeologus, the Byzantine Emperor, in 1438, and the epic poet Torquato Tasso in 1562. From

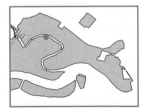

FONDACO DEI TURCHI
Patera of bird and fish from the land façade.

1621–1838 it served as the warehouse of the Turkish merchants, hence its name. In 1869, however, it was virtually rebuilt for the municipality by Federico Berchet—to the consternation of Ruskin, who saw it in the process of its radical 'restoration' when he was in Venice, and volubly deplored what he saw: '...its walls rent with a thousand chasms, are filled and refilled with fresh brickwork, and the seams and hollows are choked with clay and whitewash, oozing and trickling over the marble.'

Today the great palace is home to the Natural History Museum, which offers an engaging mixture of superb modern display (though the labelling is only in Italian) and old-fashioned showcases of stuffed creatures, shells and anatomical models. The first room exhibits the skeleton of a dinosaur, called an Ouranosaurus, over 3.5m high and 7m long, which was found, along with a giant crocodile nearly 12m long, in the Sahara in Niger in 1973. Both date from the Cretaceous period, the last age of the dinosaurs (144–65 million years ago). A fascinating film documents its discovery. There is also a section dedicated to fossils and palaeontology and another illustrating both the extraordinary collections made by Venetian explorers and the history of collecting for scientific research. The last section concentrates on the great variety of life forms on our planet, and a tiny aquarium on the ground floor has tanks with a few sad fish from the lagoon. On the stairs down to the exit you can see a medieval canoe made from a single oak trunk, found on the bed of the lagoon in 1893.

In the courtyard there is an 11th-century square well-head, the most interesting example remaining in Venice from the Veneto-Byzantine period.

WESTERN SANTA CROCE

SAN SIMEONE GRANDE
Map p. 410, B1. Open 8–12 & 5–7.
Also known as San Simeone Profeta, this church sits in a pretty little *campo* which

opens directly onto the Grand Canal. The low interior
has a wide nave with antique columns and statues above
the arcade. In the chapel to the left of the sanctuary is
a remarkable effigy of St Simeon, with an inscription of
1317 giving it as the work of Marco Romano. St Simeon
the Prophet was an aged man of Jerusalem, who had
been told that he would not die before beholding Christ.
On seeing the infant in Bethlehem, he lifted the Child
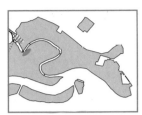
in his arms and pronounced the words now known as the *Nunc Dimittis*: 'Lord, now
lettest thy servant depart in peace...For mine eyes have seen thy salvation.' (*Luke 2:
25–35*). This powerful sculpture, with extremely skilfully executed drapery, hair and
beard, is a very unusual work, the only one signed and dated by Marco Romano, a
Sienese sculptor who worked in Tuscany, Cremona and Venice in the first two decades
of the 14th century. It had an important influence on contemporary Venetian sculptors, but in the past some scholars doubted the authenticity of the early date. Other
14th-century sculptures in the church include (south aisle) a figure of *St Valentine*, a
relief of *St Simeon and an Abbot*, a carved angel (above an arch), and (beneath the portico outside), a large relief of a saint. On the north wall, near the main door, is a large
painting of the *Last Supper* by Jacopo Tintoretto. Over the high altar is a *Presentation
in the Temple* by Palma Giovane.

RIO MARIN AND SAN SIMEONE PICCOLO

On Rio Marin (with an excellent café) stands the grand 18th-century **Palazzo
Gradenigo** (*map p. 410, B2*), decorated with female heads on the two *piani nobili*. On the
other side of its large garden is the smaller, buff-coloured **Palazzo Soranzo-Cappello**,
dating from the previous century, with two rows of balconies and a tympanum on the
top floor. Its lovely garden at the back can usually also be seen through the doorway.
In the 19th century this was the residence of the American writer Constance Fletcher,
a friend of Henry James; in 1887 the great writer took the palace as the setting for his
wonderful short story *The Aspern Papers*.

Further west, on the Grand Canal, is the church of **San Simeone Piccolo** (*map p.
410, B2*), which stands on a high stylobate with a pronaos of Corinthian columns, and
has a very conspicuous tall green dome. Built it in 1718–38 on a circular plan loosely
derived from the Pantheon in Rome, it is the best work of the late Baroque Venetian
sculptor and architect Giovanni Scalfarotto. It is in fact larger than San Simeone
Grande, but the names do not refer to size: San Simeone Piccolo is dedicated to the
Apostle Simon, while San Simeone Grande is named after Simeon the Prophet.

GIARDINO PAPADOPOLI AND PIAZZALE ROMA

Lying to the west of Rio dei Tolentini is the **Giardino Papadopoli** (*map p. 410, A2*),
a public garden which was laid out on the site of the church and monastery of Santa
Croce (after which the *sestiere* takes its name) following their demolition in 1810.
Though once important enough to give its name to an entire district of the city, only
one solitary granite column (with a lovely 11th-century capital) survives from the

buildings, inserted into the garden wall. Further west, across the wide Rio Nuovo, is **Piazzale Roma** (*map p. 410, A2–A3*), the original terminus of the road from the mainland constructed by Eugenio Miozzi in the 1930s. Miozzi also provided Venice's first multi-storey car park here. There are now other roads which lead to more car parks (at Tronchetto) which diverge from the causeway before reaching this point. Piazzale Roma is the site of Venice's bus station.

A handsome new bridge was opened across the Grand Canal here in 2008, to connect the car park and bus terminus with the railway station. Officially called the Ponte della Costituzione, it is always known as the **Calatrava Bridge**, from the name of the architect who designed it, Santiago Calatrava, who specialises in bridges. It is a huge steel span of over 80m, with a walkway built partly of glass and partly of Istrian stone with a bronze handrail. It is used by up to 20,000 people a day and is pleasing and graceful to look at. This has not prevented it from being strongly criticised, partly for the time it took to build and for the notable increase in its cost from the original estimate, as well as for its rather treacherous walkway (it seems that the risers are too shallow for the hurried steps of the Venetians), but above all for stability problems.

SAN NICOLA DA TOLENTINO
Map p. 410, B3. Open 8–12 & 4–6.
From Giardino Papadopoli, Fondamenta del Monastero follows the Rio dei Tolentini to a bridge which leads into the *campo* in front of the imposing church of San Nicola da Tolentino, usually simply called 'I Tolentini'. Its façade, by Andrea Tirali (1706–14), is an unexpected sight: approached by steps, it is a classical temple front, complete with pediment and Corinthian columns (although the actual brick west end of the church can still be seen behind as it is higher: the plan to mask it was never carried out).

The monastic order of the Theatines, founded in Rome in 1524, escaped to Venice three years later with their spiritual leader, Gaetano da Thiene, after the Sack of Rome, knowing that Venice had supported Pope Clement VII rather than the Emperor Charles V, who was responsible for the sack. They built this church a few decades afterwards, on the site of an oratory dedicated to St Nicholas of Tolentino, which dedication they retained. The classical interior by Vincenzo Scamozzi (1591–1602) recalls Palladian models, despite the heavy decorations added in the 17th century. The cupola was demolished in the 18th century—only the drum remains. The tabernacle in the sanctuary, by Baldassare Longhena, has sculptures by Juste le Court (the two angels in the north transept are early works by the same artist). The tomb here of the patriarch Giovanni Francesco Morosini (d. 1678) is by Filippo Parodi. The painting of the *Annunciation* is by Luca Giordano. The organ was made by Nacchini in 1754.

In the first chapel on the south side are charming paintings by Padovanino with scenes from the life of St Andrea Avellino, helped by angels as he crosses a river and falls from his horse. The altarpiece by Sante Peranda shows the death of the saint. In the second chapel are three works by Camillo Procaccini, illustrating the life of St Charles Borromeo. In the third chapel, which has another altarpiece by Sante Peranda, the *Banquet of Herod* and *Beheading of St John the Baptist* are thought to be by Bonifacio Veronese. The south transept is the burial place of three doges from the Corner family, incorporating no fewer than twelve busts of other members of the clan and a relief showing Caterina Cornaro (the Italianised form of Corner) giving the crown of Cyprus to Doge Agostino Barbarigo. The altarpiece of the *Virgin in Glory* is by Palma Giovane and the *Ecstasy of St Francis* over the side door by Gerolamo Forabosco. There is also the pavement tomb of Paolo Renier, who was doge from 1779–89.

In the north transept are two important works of the Baroque period: above one of the doors, the painting of *St Lawrence Distributing Alms* by Bernardo Strozzi, and, close by, *St Jerome Visited by an Angel* by Johann Liss. On the north side are more works by Sante Peranda, and the third chapel has stories of St Cecilia and other saints by Palma Giovane.

The convent of the church is now used by the University of Venice.

PREN
DELIBER
ESSECVTORI CONTPO LA
VALVNQVE EBREO OD EBREA DO
LSIVOGLIA PRETESTO NEI GHE
RI D'ALCVNO DELLI EBREI O D
E GALERA, FRVSTA, BERLINÆ ET
IGVARDO ALLA QVALITÀ DEL DEL
SGRESSORI, SI FORMERANNO PR
NELLA SOLITA CASSELLA E I
RIGOROSAMENTE PVNITI
AGLIA DI DVCATI CENTO I
IL REO.
IATO E SCOLPITO IN PIETRA N
A D'OGNVNO PER LA SVA
RASSOLVTA VOLONTÀ DI L
IN OGNI SVA PARTE VBBI
04

SOTTOPORTEGO DEL GHETTO
Inscription of 1704 listing rules of conduct for converted Jews.

Sestiere of Cannaregio

This, the most northerly of the sestieri, takes its name from the Canal Regio, or Royal Canal, once the main route into Venice from the mainland.

T he Canale di Cannaregio today has a little row of shops and a few cafés and *trattorie* before it reaches the area with the lovely church of San Giobbe. Cannaregio is also the site of the old Jewish Ghetto of Venice; as well as of the Ca' d'Oro, perhaps the most beautiful of all the palaces on the Grand Canal; and of the church of the Madonna dell'Orto in the remote north. Another unexpected delight is the little church of the Madonna dei Miracoli.

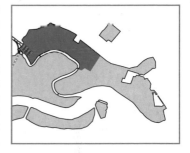

ON & AROUND STRADA NUOVA

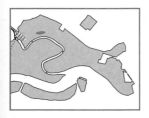

The **Strada Nuova** (*map p. 402, A2–B2*), opened in 1871, was the first of thankfully very few 19th-century interventions in the townscape (thankfully, because none was very successful). Yet though its dimensions—as can be seen at a glance on any map—are alien to the historic city (it is the only *strada* or 'street' in Venice), it is always busy and lively: Venetians come here to shop, and for tourists it is one of the most direct routes from the station to the Rialto and St Mark's. It has a great variety of simple shops selling clothes and hardware as well as food, and its bustling atmosphere provides a genuine glimpse into straightforward day-to-day Venetian life, with no pretensions to elegance.

More or less in the middle of Strada Nuova, hidden behind the housefronts, is the **church of Santa Sofia** (no. 4191; *open 9–12*), with a squat brick campanile. The light interior contains four statues of saints (on the west wall and on the high altar) by Antonio Rizzo. Many Venetians pop in here for a moment during the morning shop, and numerous candles are lit in front of the greatly venerated Crucifix against the first nave column on the right. Apparently dating from the 15th century, with the Evangelists in the terminals (the bottom one has recently been remade), it is rare to see such a precious work of art still serving as a devotional image. Benedetto Marcello (1686–1739) wrote numerous compositions for this church. He also wrote some 500 secular vocal works, and music for recorders, keyboard, cello and violin. In 1720 he published anonymously the *Teatro alla Moda*, a satire on Venetian opera at the Teatro di Sant'Angelo, where his rival Vivaldi was director of music. His most famous work is *L'estro poetico armonico* (1724–27), based on the liturgical music he had heard in the Ghetto. As a patrician, he became a member of the Great Council in 1707, and was elected to the *Quarantia* tribunal in 1716. He lived at Palazzo Marcello on the Grand Canal (*see p. 133*).

Campo Santa Sofia with its Neoclassical well-head (1785) opens out onto the Grand Canal, with a busy *traghetto* ferrying passengers to and from the Rialto markets.

SAN FELICE AND PALAZZO GIOVANNELLI

At the western end of the Strada Nuova, a bridge leads over to Campo San Felice, where the **church of San Felice** was founded in the 10th century (*map p. 402, A2; open 9–12 & 4–7*). It was restored in 1276 and rebuilt after 1531. Above the west door on the *rio*, which has a pretty *fondamenta*, is a carved 14th-century angel. On the altar to the right of the sanctuary, there is a painting by Tintoretto of *St Demetrius* (dressed in shining armour with a maroon cloak and leggings and holding a red banner) together with the donor of the painting, against a mysterious backdrop of lightly sketched Classical ruins and mountain scenery.

Across a further bridge there is a view (right) of the splendid 15th-century façade (with ingenious corner windows) of **Palazzo Giovannelli**. This was a gift from the Republic to the *condottiere* Francesco Maria della Rovere, Duke of Urbino (for his services to Venice) in 1538. It later became the property of Prince Giovannelli, whose famous art collection included Giorgione's *Tempesta* (now in the Gallerie dell'Accademia; *see p. 149*).

SANTI APOSTOLI

At the east end of the Strada Nuova, at the entrance to the pleasant Campo Santi Apostoli, is the ex-**Scuola dell'Angelo Custode** (now the Lutheran Evangelical Church), with a façade by Andrea Tirali (1714). Opposite is the church of **Santi Apostoli** (*map p. 402, B2; open 10–12 & 3.30–7.30*), much rebuilt, with a tall campanile of 1672 and the pretty domed exterior of the Cappella Corner. In the unusually wide interior, the ceiling paintings date from 1748. The Cappella Corner on the south side is an interesting late 15th-century work attributed to Mauro Codussi, with the tombs of Marco and Giorgio Corner by the Lombardo family, including Tullio. The *Communion of St Lucy*, painted by Giambattista Tiepolo around 1748, was later placed on the altar. In the chapel to the right of the sanctuary are the remains of frescoes showing Byzantine influence (a *Deposition* and an *Entombment*), a rare survival in Venice from the early 14th century. The lovely marble relief of the head of St Sebastian is by Tullio Lombardo. In the chapel to the left of the sanctuary is a high relief of the *Madonna and Child*, a charming 15th-century work attributed to Niccolò di Pietro Lamberti, and a painting of the *Guardian Angel* by Francesco Maffei.

Opposite the church, a bridge from the *campo* crosses a *rio* to a *calle* which leads under the portico of **Palazzo Falier**, a Veneto-Byzantine palace (now a hotel) dating from the end of the 13th century—a characteristic merchant's house of the period. It is traditionally thought to have been the home of Doge Marin Falier, executed in 1355 for treason by order of the Council of Ten. In the *calle* a huge stone has a long inscription set up in the 18th century by the Bakers' Guild, forbidding the making or selling of bread in the city by anyone who was not a guild member.

CA' D'ORO

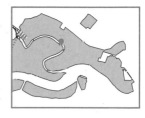

Map p. 402, A2. Open 8.15–7.15, Mon 8.15–2. Entrance in Calle della Ca' d'Oro, which leads from the landing-stage on the Grand Canal. The rooms are not numbered in situ, but the numbering below follows the plans given here.

The Ca' d'Oro is famous for its extraordinarily elaborate 15th-century Gothic façade on the Grand Canal (*described on p. 132*). The palace was carefully restored by Baron Giorgio Franchetti in 1894, and he presented it to the state in 1916, together with his very fine collection of Venetian sculpture and small

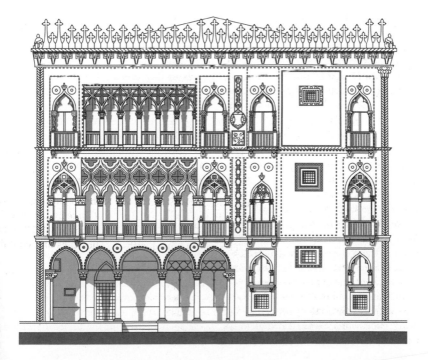

bronzes (15th and early 16th century), and numerous important paintings (including a masterpiece by Mantegna), all of which have been on public view here since 1927. One of the most important museums in the city, it also houses some detached frescoes and a large collection of ceramics. The views of the Grand Canal from the palace windows and the two *liagò* are superb. The collection is very well displayed in modernised rooms, and there are ample places to sit.

GROUND FLOOR

Beyond the ticket office is a charming little entrance court with a 15th-century well. Adjoining is the lovely *androne* (*closed in winter*), through which the house was approached from the canal. The Greek marble columns have beautiful Veneto-Byzantine and Romanesque capitals. The outside staircase, which had been demolished in the mid-19th century, was carefully rebuilt by Franchetti, who also laid the very fine mosaic pavement in opus sectile and had the walls sumptuously decorated in marble. The splendid well-head in red Verona limestone was carved by Bartolomeo Bon (1427) and is decorated with figures of *Charity*, *Justice* and *Fortitude*. It is this important sculptor's first known work and was sold and taken to Paris in the late 19th century but Franchetti managed to buy it back and return it here.

FIRST FLOOR

Anteroom (1): A miscellany of sculptural fragments made in the Veneto, some dating from the Byzantine period, and others from the 14th and 15th centuries, as well as a seated terracotta statue of the *Madonna* by Andrea Briosco (Il Riccio). Non-Venetian works include alabaster scenes of English workmanship illustrating the life of St Catherine, dating from the 16th century. The polyptych of the *Passion* is by Antonio Vivarini and his workshop.

Alcove (2): Franchetti created this little chapel (and brought its richly decorated 15th-century ceiling from another building) to house the most precious piece in his collection, the *St Sebastian* by Mantegna, one of the last works by this famous painter of the Veneto school. It dates from the year of his death, 1506, when it was recorded in the painter's studio. It then apparently came into the possession of Pietro Bembo, who kept it in his home in Padua, and it was purchased in 1807 by the Gradenigo family. A very fragile painting (tempera on very thin canvas), it was beautifully restored in 2007. A Latin inscription ('only divine things are lasting: the rest is smoke [which gets blown away]') is attached to the delicate candle set on the ground, still smoking since it has just been blown out. There are two other paintings of this same saint by Mantegna (one in the Louvre and the other in the Kunsthistorisches Museum in Vienna): here, pierced by numerous arrows and also with sores from the plague, Sebastian's mouth has dropped open in suffering. Although Mantegna was Giovanni Bellini's brother-in-law and was very well known in his lifetime, he is today represented in Venice by just one other small painting in the Accademia. He spent much of his life working for

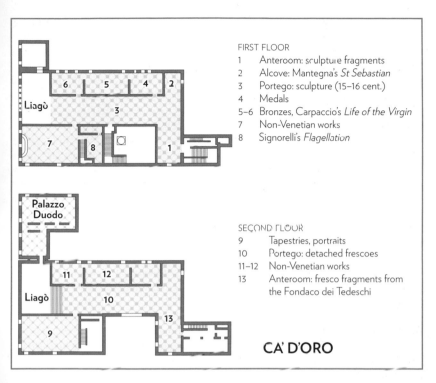

FIRST FLOOR
1. Anteroom: sculpture fragments
2. Alcove: Mantegna's *St Sebastian*
3. Portego: sculpture (15–16 cent.)
4. Medals
5–6. Bronzes, Carpaccio's *Life of the Virgin*
7. Non-Venetian works
8. Signorelli's *Flagellation*

SECOND FLOOR
9. Tapestries, portraits
10. Portego: detached frescoes
11–12. Non-Venetian works
13. Anteroom: fresco fragments from the Fondaco dei Tedeschi

CA' D'ORO

the court of Mantua, where he painted the celebrated Camera degli Sposi. He is one of the best-known Italian painters of the Renaissance, and many important museums outside Italy contain very fine examples of his work.

Portego (3): A characteristic feature of the *piano nobile* of Venetian palaces, extending the entire length of the building and opening onto the *liagò* on the Grand Canal. Here is displayed a superb collection of Venetian sculpture dating from the late 15th and early 16th century, the period when the greatest works were produced in the city. It was the Lombardo family who introduced a new elegant Renaissance style of sculpture to Venice, and Tullio

Lombardo is splendidly represented with his famous double portrait bust of a young couple. The marble relief of the *Madonna and Child* is attributed to Tullio's father, Pietro. Antonio Rizzo came to Venice around the same time as Pietro and it is thought that the female statuette called *Rhetoric* (but perhaps representing an angel) is by his hand. Andrea Briosco (called 'Il Riccio'), from Padua, was one of the most original sculptors of the early Renaissance, and some of his very best bronze reliefs, made for the Venetian church of Santa Maria dei Servi, can be seen here: *St Martin and the Beggar*, four scenes of the legend of the True Cross, and a door of a tabernacle. His contemporary Vittore Gambello made the two battle scenes displayed close by for the same church. The charming bust of a boy (perhaps a member of the Gonzaga family), displayed on a pedestal, is attributed to Gian Cristoforo Romano.

In the early 16th century Giovanni Maria Mosca was at work in the city, and his is the marble relief of the *Death of Portia*. The life-like marble bust of a parish priest of San Gemignano called Matteo dai Letti (d. 1523) is attributed to his contemporary Bartolomeo di Francesco Bergamasco. The marble lunette of the Madonna kissing the Child is by Jacopo Sansovino. The bronze andirons with *Venus and Adonis* are later 16th-century works by Girolamo Campagna.

Room 4: In the case is displayed a superb bronze statuette of *Apollo* by the artist nicknamed 'Antico' since he produced such very fine Classical works that they were sometimes confused with ancient Roman statues. Antico came from Mantua, where he also worked at the Gonzaga court. There is a case of Renaissance medals—double-sided small medallions in bronze, famous for their exquisite workmanship—which were usually cast to celebrate rulers, military leaders, Humanists, important buildings or events. Modelled on Roman coins, they often have a portrait head in profile. There are superb examples by Antico, and especially by the

most skilled medallist of all, Antonio Pisanello, from Verona, who is known to have worked in Venice from 1415–20. Others are by Gentile Bellini, Vittore Gambello, Leone Leoni and Matteo de' Pasti. There are a number of paintings of the Madonna around the walls, including works by Michele Giambono.

Rooms 5–6: More small bronzes, mostly Paduan and Florentine works, are exhibited here. The three painted scenes from the life of the Virgin by Carpaccio once decorated the Scuola degli Albanesi. There are also andirons by Roccatagliata; two 16th-century tondi in bronze with portraits of Agostino Angeli da Pesaro and his son, the scientist Girolamo; and a striking bronze bust of Giampietro Mantova Benavides (d. 1520), by an unknown Paduan sculptor, based on his death mask.

You can walk out onto the *liagò* to enjoy the sensational view of the Grand Canal.

Room 7: Here are displayed non-Venetian paintings of the 14th–16th centuries, including a *Madonna in Adoration of the Child* by Raffaellino del Garbo.

Room 8: The exquisite tiny painting of the *Flagellation* is by Luca Signorelli. There is a 15th-century carved wooden staircase here.

SECOND FLOOR

Room 9: This large room is hung with 16th-century Flemish tapestries. Here is displayed Jacopo Tintoretto's portrait of the procurator Nicolò Priuli. Other procurators (Giovanni Donà,

Marino Grimani and Domenico Duodo) are commemorated with busts by Alessandro Vittoria, although his bust of Benedetto Manzini, the parish priest of San Gemignano, is the most striking of these portraits. A painting of *Venus* now generally attributed to Titian (but which has not always been considered by the master's hand, and which has part of the right side missing), is displayed near a *Sleeping Venus and Cupid* by Paris Bordone. There is a very fine portrait of an unknown gentleman, thought to have been painted by Van Dyck when he was in Genoa between 1622 and 1627.

Portego (10): Some detached and very damaged but beautiful frescoes from the cloister of Santo Stefano by Pordenone (c. 1532: *Expulsion from Paradise, Christ Appearing to Mary Magdalene,* and *Christ and the Samaritan*). Among the frescoes attributed to Domenico Campagnola, the three figures in niches of *Hope, Temperance* and *Charity,* and nudes and putti, are particularly interesting.

Room 11: German, Dutch and Flemish paintings including works attributed to Antonis Mor, Jan van Scorel, and the circle of Dürer. The *Crucifixion* (with a view of Jerusalem in the background),

attributed to a collaborator or follower of Jan van Eyck, was painted some time after 1430 and is known to have been in the Veneto by the mid-15th century.

Room 12: *Jonah and the Whale* by Paul Brill, *The Alchemist* (1668) by Jan Steen, and a *Sleeping Woman* by Gabriel Metsu.

Anteroom (13): Interesting fragments of frescoes by Giorgione and Titian from the façade of the Fondaco dei Tedeschi, including a female nude by Giorgione, and, by Titian, two fragments with a battle between giants and monsters (from a frieze along the side façade), and the figure of *Judith* (or ?*Justice*). The terracotta models (*bozzetti*) are by Giacomo Piazzetta and Stefano Maderno. The great sculptor Gian Lorenzo Bernini is represented with a model for his famous fountain in Piazza Navona in Rome, and two marble busts of Venetian cardinals from the Valier family. The two views of the Piazzetta and Molo are generally attributed to Francesco Guardi.

PALAZZO DUODO

From the lovely second-floor *liagò* you can visit two rooms in Palazzo Duodo, which adjoins the Ca' d'Oro on the Grand Canal. They contain a well-displayed collection of ceramics from the lagoon (those from Malamocco are particularly interesting). From the corner window there is a superb view down the Grand Canal.

SANTA MARIA DEI MIRACOLI

Map p. 402, C3. Open Mon–Sat 10–5; Chorus Pass.
This church, on its tiny secluded *campo*, is an exquisite Renaissance work by Pietro Lombardo (1481–9), sumptuously decorated with splendid marble inlay both inside and out. It is thought that many of the classical details may be derived from the Palace of Diocletian in

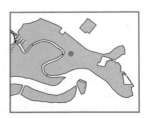

Split, which Pietro is known to have visited on a journey to Dalmatia. The church was built on this confined site, with its north side set directly on the water, because there was a shrine here in the 15th century with a painting of the *Madonna*, held to be miraculous. In fact, in front of the façade of the church, off Calle Castelli, is the Corte de le Muneghe, where, beyond the gate and under the lovely old portico, you can see where the tabernacle was which used to house the image of the Virgin, painted for the Amadi family who lived here, before miracles were associated with it and it was given a more honoured place in the church, which was built especially for it.

Santa Maria dei Miracoli is one of the few churches in Venice where you can see all four external walls. It has a single, unusually tall, nave, a barrel-vaulted roof, high domed apse and tiny attached campanile. It is divided into two orders, with pilasters below and a blind arcade above. A great variety of marble, including pavonazzetto, red Verona, white Carrara and cipollino, was used in the elegant polychrome inlay in geometric designs. The exquisite carved friezes are decorated with shields, helmets, arms, griffins and marine creatures, as well as Classical motifs. At the top of the facade is a semicircular gable which follows the curve of the roof and is decorated with a rose window, smaller oculi, and marble tondi. In the lunette above the door is a 16th-century *Madonna*.

INTERIOR OF SANTA MARIA DEI MIRACOLI

The decoration of the interior is as beautiful as the exterior, with the walls entirely lined with patterned marble panels in pairs (so that the veins match). These are rust-coloured on the lower walls, while above two classical string courses carved in stone, the upper walls have yellow and grey-toned marbles. In the raised choir and domed apse the sculptural decoration, carried out by Tullio Lombardo and his father Pietro, becomes much more elaborate. The lovely marble balustrade has half-length figures of saints and the *Annunciation*, and the pilasters together with their bases and capitals are exquisitely carved. On the east wall is a Cross made from green and purple porphyry. On the high altar is a charming *Madonna* (1409), the sacred image for which the church was built, by the little-known painter Niccolò di Pietro Paradisi. It is the only example of painting in the church apart from the nave vault, which is adorned with 50 panels bearing heads of prophets and saints painted by Pier Maria Pennacchi (1528), and that of the nuns' choir at the west end (also supported by beautifully carved pilasters).

Calle Castelli leads east from the church and emerges on Fondamenta Sanudo (named after the famous 16th-century diarist Marino Sanudo or Sanuto). To the left is the fine Gothic doorway of **Ca' Soranzo Van Axel** (or Palazzo Venier-Sanudo-Van Axel), with Gothic and Veneto-Byzantine elements on its two canal façades. One of the most important late Gothic palaces in the city, it was built for Marco and Agostino Soranzo in 1479, with two courtyards, both with outside stairs. In 1652 it became the property of wealthy Flemish merchants called Van Axel after they had formally been allowed to become Venetian patricians, one of the very few non-Venetian families to achieve this distinction. The palace remained in the family until 1919 when it was sold to the antique dealer Dino Barozzi, who restored it and lived here until 1943, using the two courtyards to display his important lapidary collection.

Behind the church, a bridge leads into Campiello Santa Maria Nova, where **Palazzo Bembo-Boldù**, with tall Gothic windows, bears a curious relief in a niche of a bearded figure holding a solar disc. The church of **San Canciano**, of ancient foundation, was rebuilt in the 18th century. Across Rio Santi Apostoli, **Campiello della Cason** is where Agnello Particiaco lived as doge in 811–27.

THE AREA WHERE MARCO POLO LIVED

From Campo Santa Marina (*map p. 402, C3*), where a high archway connects the symmetrical wings of a former palace, Sottoportego and Calle Scaletta lead to Ponte Marco Polo. On the far side is the side entrance to the **Teatro Malibran** (*map p. 402, B3*), the successor to the theatre of San Giovanni Crisostomo, built in 1677 and the largest and most famous theatre in Europe for music in the 17th and early 18th centuries. In 1707 two operas by Alessandro Scarlatti were put on here, and in 1709 Handel's *Agrippina* had

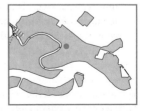

its première (in the presence of the composer); it was a major success. After restoration, the theatre was reopened in 1819 with Rossini's *La Gazza Ladra*. In 1835 Maria Malibran, the gifted Spanish mezzo-soprano, sang here in Bellini's *Sonnambula* in 1835, the year before her death (aged only 28, following a fall from her horse); the theatre was subsequently named after her. It is still known for its concerts.

A *sottoportego* leads into two courtyards. They bear Marco Polo's nickname, 'Milion', earned because his contemporaries thought he always talked in 'millions' and exaggerated his description of his travels in the East. The **Corte Seconda del Milion** is surrounded by ancient houses which bear 12th–15th-century elements, and a beautiful Byzantine arch (possibly a survival from the 12th century), richly carved with animals and birds.

MARCO POLO

Marco Polo (1254–1324) came from a merchant family; his father was one of three brothers who travelled regularly to the East. Marco accompanied his father and uncle in 1271 on a four-year overland journey from Trebizond on the Black Sea through Persia, Tibet and the Gobi Desert to Peking. He was employed for 17 years at the court of the Mongol ruler Kublai Khan, grandson of Genghis Khan, and was sent as envoy throughout the Empire from Siberia to southern India and Japan. He returned to Venice by sea along the coast of China and India. In 1298 he was taken prisoner by the Genoese at the Battle of Cursola, and during a year's imprisonment he dictated to a fellow prisoner, Rustichello da Pisa, a superb description of the world he had seen on his travels. This was probably the first description of Asia ever to reach the West, and remained the most accurate for many centuries. His book was well known throughout Europe during the Middle Ages.

SAN GIOVANNI CRISOSTOMO

Map p. 402, B3. Open 7.30–7.30.

This striking pink and white church almost fills its small *campo*. It was rebuilt after serious damage by fire and is dedicated to St John Chrysostom, a 4th-century preacher who became famous as Patriarch of Constantinople and for his revision of the Greek liturgy. A book which supposedly belonged to him was brought to Venice from Constantinople as a holy relic to be preserved in St Mark's. Built between 1497 and 1504, the church is a masterpiece of Venetian Renaissance architecture and the last work of Mauro Codussi.

The interior of the church is much visited by worshippers, especially since it became the Santuario della Madonna delle Grazie in 1977, dedicated to the highly venerated marble bust of the *Madonna delle Grazie* on the south side. The Greek-cross plan is of Byzantine inspiration. The superb high altarpiece of *St John Chrysostom with Six Saints* (1510–11), with the titular saint writing in his book for all to see and read, is by Sebastiano del Piombo. Above the south side door are four small paintings from the old organ, attributed to Girolamo da Santacroce: the present organ above the west door has its four doors painted by Giovanni Mansueti. The first south altarpiece of *Sts Christopher, Jerome and Louis of Toulouse* is a beautiful (late) painting by Giovanni

SAN GIOVANNI CRISOSTOMO
Relief of the *Coronation of the Virgin*, by Tullio Lombardo.

Bellini (*coin-operated light*). St Jerome relaxes on his rock, reading, while St Louis is dressed in magnificent clerical robes. St Christopher carrying the Child, however, is less memorable than Bellini's figure of the same saint in the polyptych painted for the church of Santi Giovanni e Paolo. The *Death of St Joseph* above the second south altar is by Johann Carl Loth.

The second north altar bears a classical bas-relief of the *Coronation of the Virgin* by Tullio Lombardo, and (above) a Veneto-Byzantine relief of the *Virgin Orans*. The first altar has a very unusual painting of *St Anthony of Padua* by a follower of Vivarini.

MAURO CODUSSI

Codussi (c.1440–1504), born near Bergamo, was extremely important for introducing the Renaissance style to Venice in the late 15th century, and he designed numerous buildings in the city. He worked at the Scuola Grande di San Marco, and that of San Giovanni Evangelista, and made grand staircases part of the design of both buildings. Palazzo Vendramin-Calergi on the Grand Canal is usually considered his masterpiece, and he is also the architect of Palazzo Corner-Spinelli, lower down the same left bank of Venice's main thoroughfare. Codussi also worked in Piazza San Marco on the Torre dell'Orologio, and provided the design for the reconstruction of the Procuratie Vecchie. He revived the use of centralised church plans, as can be seen in his lovely interiors, both here at San Giovanni Crisostomo and at Santa Maria Formosa. He produced the beautiful façade of San Michele in Isola, finished that of San Zaccaria, and designed the distinctive campanile of San Pietro in Castello. His classical style (and frequent use of the Corinthian order) owes much to Leon Battista Alberti, with whom he worked on the Tempio Malatestiano in Rimini.

In the *campo* outside the church, the 15th-century well-head with four lions' heads is in a transitional style from Gothic to Renaissance. From the Salizzada San Giovanni Crisostomo, it is worth taking Calle della Stua left (just before the bridge over Rio Santi Apostoli) to Corte and Sottoportego del Remer, beyond which is Campiello del Remer which opens on to the Grand Canal and has a rectangular 13th-century well-head in red marble. Here is the ancient **Ca' Lion** (or Palazzo Lion-Morosini), a rare survival of a typical old merchant house with its own courtyard which had storehouses on the ground floor and an outside stair giving access to the living quarters on the floor above. It still has a Byzantine arch between two two-light windows on the main floor, where the stair is supported on Gothic arches (although the lower flight of steps on the other side of the building has unfortunately been partly reconstructed).

SAN MARCUOLA TO RIO DELLA MISERICORDIA

SAN MARCUOLA
Map p. 401, D3. Open 8.30–12 & 5–7, except Sun; entrance usually from the east end.
Facing the Grand Canal, and with a vaporetto land-ing-stage in its *campo*, is the church of San Marcuola, or Santi Ermagora e Fortunato, by Giorgio Massari (1728–36), with an unfinished façade. The interior has some unusual paintings around the two facing pulpits, 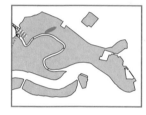 including the *Christ Child Blessing between Sts Catherine and Andrew* and the *Head of Christ* between two male portraits, thought to be by pupils of Titian (perhaps Francesco Vecellio). On the left chancel wall is a *Last Supper*, a good early work (1547) by Tintoretto, which has a more intimate atmosphere than some of the other paintings by him of this favourite subject (even two women and a baby are present). On the right wall is a copy made in the 17th century of Tintoretto's *Washing of the Feet*; the original is now in Newcastle-upon-Tyne, England, and is almost identical to another painting by Tintoretto in the Prado, Madrid. The church also contains paintings—on the ceiling, in the presbytery, on the high altar and in the 18th-century sacristy—by Francesco Migliori, a little-known 18th-century Venetian artist. The statues in the church are by Giovanni Maria Morleiter and assistants. The Callido organ dates from 1775.

The façade of the **Scuola del Cristo**, founded in 1644, survives behind the church, where the well-head is dated 1713 and has three small lions' heads and shields of officials of the Republic, and an inscription states that the water is for the exclusive use of the poor. Any one of the *calli* here leads up to **Rio Terrà San Leonardo** (*map p. 401, D3*), where there is a good daily street market.

PALAZZO VENDRAMIN-CALERGI
Palazzo Vendramin-Calergi (no. 2079; *map p. 401, D3*), with a fine 11th-century Byzantine well-head in its land-entrance courtyard, is the winter home of the Casinò

(the superb façade on the Grand Canal is by Mauro Codussi; *described on p. 233*). The palace was purchased from the Vendramin-Calergi by Maria Carolina, Duchess of Berry, in 1844, who had Giambattista Meduna restore it (and install heating). Her nephew Prince Henry of Bourbon-Parma, Count of Bardi, resided here when not travelling in China, Indonesia and Japan where he amassed his extraordinary collection of Oriental art, which became Venice's Museo Orientale (*see p. 215*). In 1882 Wagner rented from him a very large apartment (with some 20 rooms) on the mezzanine floor and in a wing overlooking the garden.

WAGNER IN VENICE

Richard Wagner, famous for his reform of opera, but also one of the most controversial figures in the history of music, came to Venice many times after his first visit in 1858, when he stayed at the Palazzo Giustinian on the Grand Canal and wrote the second act of *Tristan*. He found that the stillness of the city provided him with the peace he needed to compose. Just after his last and perhaps his greatest opera, *Parsifal*, was staged in 1882, he returned to winter in Venice with his wife Cosima (Franz Liszt's daughter) and their children, staying in Palazzo Vendramin-Calergi where they were visited by Liszt. But the great composer, already in poor health, died suddenly here of a heart attack on 13th February 1883. A special train was sent from Bavaria to Venice so that his family could accompany his coffin back to Bayreuth, where he is buried in the town where the *Ring Cycle* was first performed in 1876.

The Richard Wagner Association of Venice was given three of these rooms by the city of Venice in 1995, including the room in which the composer died. Although none of the original furnishings survive from Wagner's time, the rooms are now arranged as a small museum, with an important library, scores, programmes, autograph letters, and works of art relating to Wagner and his music, donated to the Association in 2003 by Josef Lienhart (*visits by appointment Tues and Sat mornings and Thur afternoons; T: 041 276 0407*). The Association also organises an annual programme of concerts dedicated to Wagner.

Calle Larga Vendramin leads up to **Rio Terrà della Maddalena**, now a crowded shopping street. Just to the left (before the bridge over the Rio di San Marcuola) is a pretty little courtyard (overlooked by a hotel) called the **Volto Santo**, where silk merchants from Lucca came to live and set up their *scuola* after 1398. The name comes from the ancient carved figure of Christ in the cathedral of Lucca, and images representing it survive here on the early 15th-century well-head as well as on the inside of the entrance arch. There are also other sculptural fragments on the houses, including the lion of St Mark and Byzantine roundels.

In the other direction, the little **Campo della Maddalena** has a fine well-head in the form of a Lombardesque capital decorated with poppies, made in the late 15th or early 16th century. The quaint old houses here have tall chimney pots. Palazzo Magno has a Gothic lunette over its doorway. The small round domed **church of the Maddalena** (*map p. 401, E3*) is attractively sited on its canal. A Neoclassical building by Tommaso Temanza (c. 1760), it is closed to worship.

SANTA FOSCA

In Campo Santa Fosca stands the fine, long 15th-century façade of Palazzo Correr (no. 2217) and a **monument to Fra' Paolo Sarpi**, commissioned from Emilio Marsili in 1892. Sarpi (1552–1623) was a Servite friar who became a great scientist (Galileo considered him his master) and historian (his history of the Council of Trent is of fundamental importance). But he is best remembered as the defender of the independence of the Venetian state against papal interference, advocating that the temporal power of secular rulers should remain separate from that of the Roman Church. In a famous dispute between Doge Leonardo Donà and Pope Paul V over the rights of temporal rulers, the pope, though he placed Venice under an interdict in 1606/7, was forced to give way, thanks largely to the able defence of the city's cause by Sarpi. His friend, the English ambassador Sir Henry Wotton (*see p. 211*), who was quick to support him in his conflict with the Jesuits and the pope, declared, 'for learning, I think I may justly call him the most deep and general scholar of the world...His power of speech consisteth rather in the soundness of reason than in any other natural ability'. Sarpi is buried in the church of San Michele in Isola.

The **church of Santa Fosca** (*map p. 401, E3; open Thur and Sun 9.30–11.30*) was founded in the 13th century, and the domed brick campanile was reconstructed after damage in 1410. The church was rebuilt in 1679, and restored in 1741 when the façade was constructed. It contains (over the door on the north side) a damaged *Holy Family* (with a donor) by Domenico Tintoretto, and (on the altar on the right of the sanctuary) a fine Byzantine painting of the *Pietà and Two Saints*.

From the bridge which leads across Rio di Santa Fosca, there is a good view (to the right) of the noble Renaissance façade of **Palazzo Vendramin** on Fondamenta del Forner. The view to the left takes in the 17th-century Palazzo Diedo, attributed to Andrea Tirali, and across another canal, the **ex-convent and church of Santa Maria dei Servi**, founded in 1318 and consecrated in 1491, and once one of the most important Gothic buildings in Venice. Most of it was destroyed in 1812 and only a Gothic doorway and a 15th-century statue of the *Madonna* on the wall survive.

SAN MARCILIANO

Map p. 401, E3–F3. Open 4–7, Sun and holidays 8–1.
In the church of San Marciliano (or San Marziale), high up in the vault, are circular paintings in pretty gilded frames, which are among the best works of Sebastiano Ricci. On the second south altar is *St Marcilian and Two Saints*, an over-restored painting by Tintoretto, and on either side of the chancel, the *Annunciatory Angel* and *Virgin Annunciate* by his son, Domenico. There is a lovely 15th-century wooden statue of the seated *Madonna and Child* on the second north altar. In the sanctuary there is a huge golden globe with the *Resurrection of Christ*, and the four side altars have twisted yellow columns.

The *campo* outside the church, with its early 15th-century well-head with a relief of the titular saint, is on the lovely Rio della Misericordia, described in the walk on p. 246.

SEBASTIANO RICCI

Born in Belluno in the Veneto, Ricci (1659–1734) was considered the most important Venetian artist of his day. During his long career, he worked all over Italy and travelled widely to commissions abroad, including Vienna (Karlskirche, Schönbrunn) and London, where he narrowly lost a competition to fresco the dome of St Paul's, and where his patrons included Lord Burlington (works by Ricci are still to be seen in the earl's London residence, now the Royal Academy). Ricci was also a brilliant draughtsman, and in Venice enjoyed the patronage of Consul Smith (*see p. 331*): the series of biblical scenes he made for him is now in Hampton Court, London. He reinterpreted Veronese in a dazzling, colourful style which was to lift early 18th-century Venetian painting out of its doldrums and steer it on a new course, towards the brilliance of Tiepolo. Apart from those in San Marciliano, there are still a number of ceiling paintings by Ricci in Venice (in the Palazzo Querini-Stampalia, the Seminario Patriarcale and Palazzetto Bru Zane) and altarpieces in San Vitale, the Gesuati, San Rocco, San Stae and San Giorgio Maggiore. He was devoted to his nephew Marco, another very skilled painter, who produced many landscapes and *capricci*, and the two of them often collaborated. Marco, who was also promoted by Consul Smith, is also well known for his works in tempera, his etchings, and his designs for scenery (including sets for the London opera). Sebastiano and Marco shared an apartment in the Procuratie Vecchie in Piazza San Marco, although Marco predeceased his uncle by four years.

Sebastiano is famous as much for the scandals in his private life as for his art. He had a great appetite for other men's wives, and his liaisons often brought him into trouble. His intemperate eating, drinking and womanising eventually took their toll. He suffered acutely from gallstones, and died on the operating table in 1734.

THE CANNAREGIO CANAL

The Cannaregio Canal (*map p. 400, C3–A2*), after which this *sestiere* is named, is the widest waterway in Venice apart from the Grand Canal, and has peaceful *fondamente* on both sides. The stone **Ponte delle Guglie** (1580; restored 1777) has a pretty balustrade, and mascarons on the arch. In 1987 a ramp for the disabled was carefully incorporated into the design of the steps. Here is an entrance to the **Parco Savorgnan**, public gardens 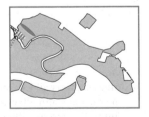 with a children's playground, with two more entrances from Calle Riello and Campo San Geremia.

SAN GEREMIA AND PALAZZO LABIA

On Campo San Geremia stands the **church of San Geremia** (*map p. 400, C3; open 8.30–12 & 4–6.30*), a somewhat clumsy building by Carlo Corbellini (1753–60), although its fine campanile is among the oldest in Venice. The interior (*entrance by* *the south door*) is more successful, though it is very cluttered with mementoes of St Lucy. When the body of St Lucy (martyred in Syracuse in Sicily in 304) was stolen from Constantinople in 1204 by Venetian crusaders, the church of Santa Lucia was built for it (later redesigned by Palladio). When this church was demolished (in 1863) to make way for the railway station (which was named after the saint), Lucy's body was moved here and can still be seen in her chapel (she has a sculpted head, but her skeletal hands and feet protrude from her bright red robe). A portrait of her by Palma Giovane is preserved with relics and church vestments in a room where souvenirs are sold. Palma also painted *St Magnus Crowning Venice* on the second south altar.

Palazzo Labia (*map p. 400, C3*) has a façade in the *campo* by Alessandro (or Paolo) Tremignon (completed c. 1750). The main façade on the Cannaregio Canal dates from the previous century and is by Andrea Cominelli. The huge building has long been the regional headquarters of RAI, the Italian radio and television corporation, but it is due to move to the *terraferma* and the *palazzo*'s future use is uncertain. In the ballroom, the *trompe l'oeil* frescoes by Gerolamo Mengozzi-Colonna provide a setting for Giambattista Tiepolo's splendid frescoes of *Antony and Cleopatra*, amongst his Venetian masterpieces (*normally viewable by appointment, but undergoing restoration at the time of writing*).

THE SCALZI

Map p. 400, B4. Open 7–11.45 & 4–6.45.
The church of the Scalzi, built for the Discalced (Barefoot) Carmelites, is a fine Baroque building by Longhena (1670–80). The Carrara marble façade is by Giuseppe Sardi (1672–80). The impressive dark Baroque interior is profusely decorated with marbles and sculptures, and a huge elaborate tabernacle fills the apse. This is the work of the Carmelite friar Giuseppe Pozzo, who took over work on the interior decoration after Longhena retired from the project. Notice the monk peeping out from between the columns of the high altar. When the ceiling fresco by Giambattista Tiepolo was destroyed by a bomb in 1915, the Venetian painter Ettore Tito was called in to replace it with a painting of the *Council of Ephesus*. Two other vault frescoes painted for the church by Tiepolo survive, albeit in a damaged state (*St Teresa in Glory* in the second south chapel, and the *Agony in the Garden* in the first north chapel).

In the chapel on the south side dedicated to St Teresa of Avila, founder of the Discalced Carmelite order, are large scenes from her life by Niccolò Bambini, and a sculpted altarpiece of her ecstasy by Lazzaro Baldi or Heinrich Meyring (clearly showing the influence of Bernini's famous work of the same subject in the church of Santa Maria della Vittoria, Rome). In the pavement is the tomb slab of Doge Carlo Ruzzini (d. 1735). In the third chapel is a statue of the *Redeemer* by Melchior Berthel and a vault fresco by Pietro Liberi.

The second north chapel was the burial place of Lodovico Manin, the last doge of Venice (d. 1797), who paid for the chapel's elaborate Baroque decoration. The sculpture of the *Holy Family* is by Giuseppe Torretti, and the vault fresco by Louis Dorigny. Two enormous turquoise-blue glass candlesticks made in Murano in the early 18th century have been placed here. In the adjoining chapel there is a bas-relief of *Christ Carrying the Cross* by Giovanni Maria Morleiter and an 18th-century wax *Ecce Homo*. The manual organ by B. Sona dates from 1802.

The **Ponte degli Scalzi**, rebuilt in 1934 from Eugenio Miozzi's design, crosses the Grand Canal here. The **Santa Lucia railway station** was built on the site of the former church of St Lucy (*see San Geremia above*). It is a Rationalist-style building from the 1950s.

ALONG THE CANNAREGIO CANAL

Fondamenta Savorgnan leads along the Cannaregio Canal past the huge **Palazzo Manfrin** (no. 342), built in 1735 by Andrea Tirali. Next, at no. 349, is **Palazzo Savorgnan** (*map p. 400, C3*), built c. 1663 to a design by Giuseppe Sardi. The fine garden façade behind can be seen from the public gardens here. In Calle Riello the terraced houses date from 1547.

Beyond the terracotta-coloured 15th-century Palazzo Testa (no. 468) is the entrance to a large housing development, next to an area formerly occupied by a factory (Saffa), where disappointing, rather claustrophobic buildings designed by Vittorio Gregotti were erected in the 1990s. On the other side of the canal (no. 967) is **Palazzo Surian**, almost certainly by Giuseppe Sardi. This was once the French Embassy and the young Jean-Jacques Rousseau was Secretary here in 1743–4, before he became famous as a political philosopher, educationist and essayist. A central figure of French Illuminism, his egalitarian writings were to inspire many thinkers, including Kant and Marx, and his political thought had a deep influence on post-Revolutionary France.

Further on, the canal is crossed by **Ponte dei Tre Archi**, designed in 1688 by Andrea Tirali (the brick parapet was added in the 18th century). Beyond it, the *fondamenta* continues to the edge of the lagoon past the huge **Macelli**, a slaughterhouse built in 1832 by Giuseppe Salvadori. It was one of the largest in Italy after its extension in 1915, and only ceased to function in 1972. Since 1990 it has been restored as premises for part of the University of Venice. The old brick buildings have been carefully preserved and the alterations made in red steel, in one of the most successful conservative restorations yet carried out here. Another exemplary restoration project, if on a much simpler and smaller scale, can be seen close by at no. 792 in **Calle delle Beccarie**, where in 2006 the municipality, in collaboration with the Venice in Peril Fund, restored an attractive small building to provide housing for a number of local families. On the opposite side of the canal, on the Sacca di San Girolamo overlooking the lagoon, new municipal housing was built in 1987–90.

SAN GIOBBE

Map p. 400, A2. Open Mon–Sat 10–5.

In a secluded *campo* on an eponymous *rio*, a few steps from the Cannaregio Canal, is the church of San Giobbe (St Job), built after 1450 by Antonio Gambello and enlarged by Pietro Lombardo, who was responsible (with assistants) for the fine doorway (the three statues are now exhibited in the sacristy). In the lunette is a relief of *St Francis and St Job*, the latter being the Old Testament prophet to whom the church is dedicated. It is more usual in the Eastern than the Western church to find dedications to prophets, but Venice has two, the other being the church of San Moisè in the *sestiere* of San Marco, dedicated to Moses. San Giobbe's Gothic campanile can be seen from the courtyard, which was once part of the convent which adjoined the church, and which preserves an attractive portico next to a pleasant little garden.

Interior of San Giobbe

The interior is one of the earliest examples of a Franciscan Observant church plan; a single nave without aisles, with the monks' choir behind the presbytery. A carved triumphal arch flanked by two smaller semicircular chapels precedes the beautiful domed **sanctuary**, with sculpted roundels, a masterpiece of Renaissance architecture and carving by Pietro Lombardo and assistants. It was built above the huge pavement tomb of Doge Cristoforo Moro when he died in 1471 (buried here with his wife Cristina Sanudo). The tomb is simply decorated with beautifully carved blackberries (*mori*; the family emblem) around the short inscription, and is devoid of all religious references. The doge is shown in a portrait which, most unusually, has been allowed to be hung on the right wall. He was the founder of the church, which he dedicated to his friend, St Bernardino of Siena, who stayed in the convent in 1443. He is also portrayed in a contemporary terracotta bust attributed to Bartolomeo Bellano, which was left to the church by the doge (and can now be seen in the sacristy). Behind the altar extends the long choir, with 16th-century wood stalls.

The **ante-sacristy** was part of a late 14th-century oratory, and has a painting of the *Nativity* by Girolamo Savoldo. The **sacristy** has a 16th-century wooden ceiling and a charming little triptych of the *Annunciation between Sts Michael and Anthony* by Antonio Vivarini and Giovanni d'Alemagna (1440–50). Three statuettes from the main portal of the church are exhibited here. At the other end of the room is a small painting in a very beautiful frame of the *Marriage of St Catherine* by Andrea Previtali.

South side: the second altar has a painting of the *Vision of God to Job* by Lattanzio Querena, in a beautiful marble frame which belonged to Giovanni Bellini's famous altarpiece, removed from here in the early 19th century and now in the Gallerie dell'Accademia (*see p. 147*). The monument to the French ambassador René d'Argenson by Claude Perrault (1651) is composed of black and white marble supported by two bizarre crowned lions and with a fat putto above the sarcophagus. The fourth altarpiece is by Paris Bordone (*Three Saints*).

North side: the two chapels at the beginning of the north side are beautifully decorated: in the first is a statue of *St Luke* by Lorenzo Bregno; the second (Cappella Martini) was built by Tuscan artists in the early 1470s for a family of silk-workers from Lucca. The vault is lined with majolica tiles and contains five pretty della Robbian roundels in glazed terracotta, thought to be the work of Andrea, the most famous member (with his uncle Luca) of this remarkable family of Florentine sculptors. The marble altar with statuettes of *St John the Baptist* and other saints is by a follower of Antonio Rossellino; the relief of the *Madonna and Child* is missing, since it is now in the Fogg Museum in North America. The Stations of the Cross in the third chapel are attributed to Antonio Zucchi.

THE GHETTO

Map pp. 400, C2–401, D2. Admission to the museum in the campo of the Ghetto Nuovo 10–4.30 or 5.30, Fri 10–sunset; closed Sat and Jewish holidays; T: 041 715 359. Tickets available for the tour, in English and Italian, of the museum and (normally three) synagogues.

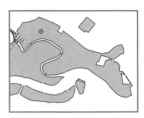

The word 'ghetto' is derived from the Venetian word *geto*, indicating the place where metal was cast: there was an iron foundry here for making cannons until 1390, when it was transferred to the Arsenale. Although Jews from the East, northern Europe, Spain and Portugal had been coming to Venice for short periods (in which they were sometimes tolerated and sometimes expelled), it was not until 1516 that the Great Council permitted Jews to live permanently in Venice, but compelled them to inhabit only this area. A curfew was enforced by guards, who had to be paid for by the Jews themselves. The word ghetto was subsequently used for segregated Jewish communities in other cities all over Europe. The first settlement was on the island of Ghetto Nuovo (named after a 'new' foundry); in 1541 it expanded to Ghetto Vecchio (the site of an 'old' foundry), and in 1633 to Ghetto Nuovissimo. It is estimated that as many as 5,000 Jews lived here in the 16th–17th centuries. Just four wells supplied them with water (the wells in the rest of the city were barred to them). Not until 1797 were Jews allowed (by Napoleon) to leave the district and live in other parts of the city, but the Ghetto was only definitively opened in 1866. There are now some 500 Jewish residents in Venice, only about 30 of whom have chosen to live in the Ghetto, but there are still a number of shops here which sell Jewish objects as well as good bakeries and grocery stores especially frequented by the Jewish community. The five main synagogues (*scuole* or *schole*) remain here, two of them still in use. Built for the first time in the 15th century, in their own distinctive architectural styles, they are named after the various different communities who erected them as meeting places and places of worship. The Jewish cemetery is on the Lido (*see p. 330*).

CAMPIELLO DELLE SCUOLE

At the beginning of Sottoportego del Ghetto (*map p. 400, C3*) are signs of the **gate** which closed the entrance at night. The dark *calle* leads past a **stone embedded in the wall** (on no. 1131 on the left), inscribed in 1704 with a long list of rules for 'converted' Jews who wished to return to the Ghetto. Beyond several carpenters' shops is Campiello delle Scuole with its two synagogues (on upper floors), still usually used for services, and a tall house with numerous windows, typical of this area (families were crowded into small flats with low ceilings). To the left as you enter the square, with an inconspicuous exterior, is the **Scuola Spagnola**, founded c. 1585 as the Scuola Ponentina, with an interior probably rebuilt by Longhena c. 1655. This is the largest of the Venetian synagogues. It has a fine elliptical women's gallery. The **Scuola Levantina** opposite, probably founded around the same time and with a fine exterior,

GHETTO NUOVO
Inscribed sign above the door of a famous old pawn shop.

was erected by pupils of Longhena. The elaborate wood carving of the ceiling and pulpit is by Andrea Brustolon.

GHETTO NUOVO

Ponte di Ghetto Vecchio leads over to the island of Ghetto Nuovo (*map p. 400, C2*), the oldest area of the Ghetto, where large buildings were erected in the mid-15th century by a Venetian merchant around a huge courtyard with three wells. The *campo* (on the site of that courtyard), still with the three wells and with a scattering of trees and benches, is now partly surrounded by tall 17th-century houses with numerous windows: some have as many as seven floors. Here, on the upper floors, are three more synagogues: above a 19th-century portico of four columns is the **Scuola Italiana** (1575); it has a cupola and five windows recalling the Pentateuch. The interior dates mostly from 1739, but also has elements from other periods, from the early 17th to the mid-19th centuries. In the far corner of the *campo* is the **Scuola Canton** (1531), with its tiny wooden cupola just visible. This is the synagogue generally used by the Jewish community in Venice today. Its name may be derived from its corner position, or from the name of a family (Cantono des Juif). It was connected by a passageway with the Scuola Italiana. The **Scuola Grande Tedesca**, the oldest synagogue in Venice (1528), is entered by a 19th-century staircase above the Jewish Museum (no. 2902b), founded by Vittorio Fano in the early 20th century, which has a well-labelled display of Jewish treasures (mostly 17th–18th century). The **museum** has a café and well-stocked bookshop (*for admission see p. 241*).

On a wall opposite the museum, **bronze memorial reliefs** were set up in 1985 in honour of Jewish war victims, many of whom were deported to concentration camps in Germany; another memorial dates from 1993: both are by the Lithuanian-born artist Arbit Blatas. A hospice for the poor was founded here in 1890. It later became an old people's home and is now a simple hotel, with a garden of pomegranates. At no. 2912, under a portico, is the site of a pawn shop, known as the **Banco Rosso**. This was one of three such shops here run by the Jews, along with banking and exchange offices and the offices of money-lenders, all of which were busy during the day with Venetian clients. A passageway (where the doors which closed the Ghetto at night once stood) leads into the **Ghetto Nuovissimo**, added in 1633, with more tall houses.

An iron bridge (guarded by two old sentry boxes) with decorative wrought-iron railings (1865–6) leads out of the Ghetto to Fondamenta degli Ormesini.

MADONNA DELL'ORTO

Map p. 401, E2. Open Mon–Sat 10–5. The campo and adjoining area are described in the guided walk on p. 246. The church of the Madonna dell'Orto was the parish church of Jacopo Tintoretto, who is buried here. It contains some of his most important works. The first church on this site, dedicated to St Christopher, was founded around 1350 by Fra' Tiberio da Parma, general of the Umiliati order of Benedictines. After 1377 it became 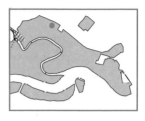 known as the Madonna dell'Orto from a miraculous statue of the *Madonna and Child*, which had been abandoned in a nearby orchard (and is still kept in the church).

The façade is a fine example of 15th-century Venetian Gothic, with good tracery in the windows, and statues thought to be by some of the most important sculptors working in the city at that time, but which still await definitive attributions. In order of date they include: the Apostles in the niches (attributed to the Dalle Masegne brothers), the *Madonna* and *Annunciatory Angel* flanking the doorway (attributed as early works to Antonio Rizzo), and *St Christopher* above (once attributed, as a late work, to Bartolomeo Bon, but now usually thought to be by the workshop of Niccolò di Giovanni Fiorentino). The campanile (1503), with its onion-shaped cupola, is a conspicuous feature of the skyline when seen from the lagoon towards Murano.

INTERIOR OF THE MADONNA DELL'ORTO

The nave and aisles of the spare interior are divided by columns of striped Turkish marble, and the semicircular apse is vaulted. The organ is by Pietro Bazzani (1878).

Choir and apse: The space is adorned by two magnificent huge paintings by Jacopo Tintoretto, the *Last Judgement* and *Making of the Golden Calf*. Standing fourteen and a half metres high and nearly 6m wide, they were probably painted *in situ* around 1562–4 (they fit the Gothic vault of the ceiling). Apart from the paintings for the Scuola Grande di San Rocco, these were considered Tintoretto's most important commissions, and we know that he donated them as a gift to his parish church.

Flanking an *Annunciation* by Palma Giovane are the *Vision of the Cross to St Peter* and the *Beheading of St Paul*, also by Tintoretto, who painted the five *Virtues* in the vault, except for *Faith* in the centre, which was added in the 17th century.

South aisle: On the wall beside the fourth altar is another famous work by Jacopo Tintoretto: the *Presentation of the Virgin in the Temple*. The inclusion of a grand staircase recalls Titian's painting of the same subject executed some 20 years earlier for the Scuola della Carità (now the Accademia; *see p. 146*), although the risers of the steps in this painting are decorated in gold leaf. As so often in Tintoretto's works it is not the subject of the painting which receives most of his attention but rather the bystanders, and in this case the mother in the foreground who has just arrived in time to indicate the figure of Mary to her daughter (who seems to be around the same age). The two other mothers on the steps appear to be absorbed with their own children and quite indifferent to Mary.

The Cavazza family monument, erected in 1657, is richly decorated with polychrome marbles by Giuseppe Sardi, and commemorates in particular Girolamo Cavazza (1588–1681), a diplomat in the service of the Republic. On the first altar, still in its original frame, is *St John the Baptist and Four Saints*, a masterpiece by Cima da Conegliano painted around 1493. In the distance you can see the castle of Conegliano, the artist's home.

The colossal **stone statue of the Madonna and Child** which gave the church its name, carved in the 14th century by Giovanni de' Santi (radically restored), is kept in a devotional side chapel off the end of the south aisle.

Chapel on the right of the choir: A modest slab marks Jacopo Tintoretto's resting-place. A plaque on the wall on the left records Sir Ashley Clarke (1903–94), a former British Ambassador to Italy, who became an honorary citizen of Venice. He was founder of the Venice in Peril Fund, which has restored numerous monuments all over the city, including, in 1968–70, the fabric, sculptures and paintings of this church—the first Venetian building to be comprehensively restored after the flood of November 1966. This British private committee continues to contribute fundamental help to the city by financing restoration projects and the scientific investigations necessary before these can be initiated.

North aisle: The first chapel, an elegant Renaissance work, was completed for the Valier in 1526 by Andrea and Antonio Buora and has a cupola and a semicircular apse. The charming sculpted tabernacle over the altar has remained sadly empty since 1993, when the very beautiful *Madonna*, painted by Giovanni Bellini around 1478, was stolen. On the wall of the second chapel Titian's *Tobias and the Archangel* from the church of San Marciliano has been hung since its restoration. The praying figure on the left is St John the Baptist (*for the story of Tobias, see p. 164*). The Contarini are duly recorded in their chapel (the fourth), with a series of family busts, one (centre left) by Danese Cattaneo and another (centre right) by Alessandro Vittoria. Over this altar is another notable work by Jacopo Tintoretto, *St Agnes Raising Licinius*. At the top of the aisle a narrow brick passage leads to the Sir Ashley Clarke Treasury, housed in a little barrel-vaulted room with massive walls which supports the base of the campanile. It displays liturgical objects in an arrangement intended to illustrate their uses rather than their artistic value. These include vestments, monstrances, reliquaries, processional crosses and vessels for use at Mass. Among them are a precious chalice and reliquary both dating from 15th century.

A WALK THROUGH CANNAREGIO

This walk covers a very quiet residential area of the city, characterised by its three parallel canals with single fondamente, from the remote church of Sant'Alvise to the Baroque church of the Gesuiti, which has an important altarpiece by Titian. Between them is the beautiful church of the Madonna dell'Orto, which contains wonderful paintings by Tintoretto, who lived close by.

THE WALK BEGINS JUST NORTH OF the Ghetto, on the **Fondamenta degli Ormesini**, which runs along the Rio della Misericordia, the first of the district's three parallel canals. By Sottoportego Alberagno, no. 2737 is a tiny bar (without a sign; *closed Mon*) seemingly in the back parlour of a delightfully chatty Venetian lady, where you can start out with an excellent and reasonably-priced coffee (especially recommended, since you will meet no more cafés along the way). The *fondamenta* has a number of pleasant small local shops, again the only ones you pass. Also here is a simple, family-run *trattoria* of good value, the Antica Mola, much beloved by Venetians (also with tables outside in a garden; *see p. 359*).

Calle Malvasia leads to **Rio della Sensa**, a quieter and even prettier canal. Calle del Capitello (or 'Capitolo') leads on up to another bridge, across which is one of the most remote parts of the city: since it is virtually an island with just two bridges connecting it to the rest of the city, it has a vaporetto landing-stage on the lagoon. Here a small *campo* surrounds the **church of Sant'Alvise**, with its attractive little *scuola*, reconstructed in 1608. The church dates from the late 14th century. On its Gothic brick façade is an early 15th-century

Tuscan statue of the titular saint, St Louis of Toulouse, in his bishop's mitre. Louis (Alvise in Venetian) was the son of the King of Naples, Charles II of Anjou, and became a Franciscan and then Bishop of Toulouse. He was canonised in 1317. The church interior (*open Mon–Sat 10–5; Chorus Pass; entrance through the side door*) has a 17th-century frescoed ceiling. Near the nuns' choir on the west wall are eight charming little 16th-century tempera paintings with pretty landscapes, apparently by different artists, showing the influence of Lazzaro Bastiani and Carpaccio. The subjects are *Rachel at the Well*, the *Finding of Joseph*, the *Golden Calf*, *Joshua Taking Jericho*, *Solomon and the Queen of Sheba*, the *Colossus with Feet of Clay*, the *Archangel Raphael with Tobias* and the *Poverty of Job*. On the south altar is a seated 16th-century polychrome wood statue of *St Alvise* and two marble statuettes of *St John the Baptist* and *St Anthony*, perhaps early works by Girolamo Campagna.

Giambattista Tiepolo painted the three superb huge paintings of the *Passion*, probably towards the end of the 1730s. It is thought they were donated to the church by Alvise Corner, son of Doge Giovanni Corner, one of Tiepolo's earliest patrons. They were intended to form a huge triptych, but are now unfortunately displayed separately: the

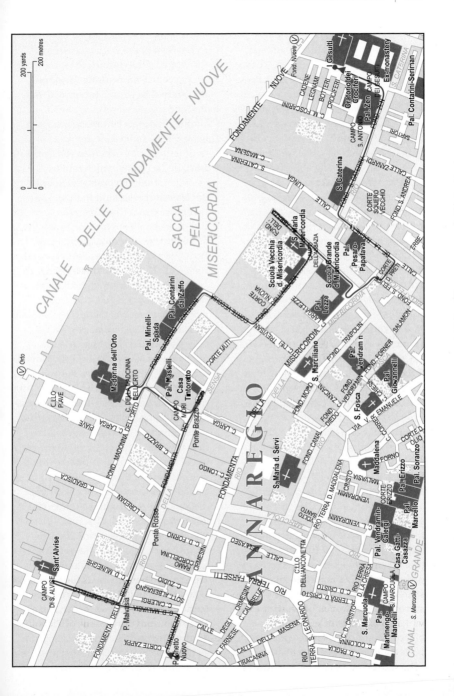

Crown of Thorns and *Flagellation* are on the right wall, and the magnificent central *Calvary* is hung on a wall of the sanctuary. The suffering of Christ is portrayed with extraordinary realism and pathos. The pulpit is surrounded by paintings from the old organ doors by Bonifacio Veronese.

Return now along Calle del Capitello to Rio della Sensa, and follow it left along the pretty *fondamenta*. Close to **Ponte de la Malvasia** is a house with a double façade on either side of a *calle* connected by an arch. A palace on this side (no. 3291) has a relief of *St George and the Dragon*. From Ponte Rosso, there is a view straight down a canal out to the lagoon, and the *fondamenta* continues past a hotel, recently opened, and opposite a ship repair yard. From the next bridge, Ponte Brazzo, you can see the façade of the Madonna dell Orto.

Campo dei Mori has three quaint statues of Moors, popularly supposed to be the Levantine merchants of the Mastelli family, whose palace is close by (*see below*). Further along the *fondamenta*, a plaque at no. 3399 marks the charming **house where Jacopo Tintoretto lived** from 1574 until his death in 1594. Incorporated into the façade, along with several other ancient sculptural fragments, is a quaint turbanned figure, similar to those in Campo dei Mori. This one is called Alfani, his huge turban made from the capital of a column. He stands on a pedestal made in the 15th century in the style of an ancient Roman altar.

Return to Campo dei Mori and take the *calle* that leads out of it, Calle dei Mori (don't miss the Gothic portal at no. 3381 which leads into a little garden with a portico with eccentric columns

and a well), crossing another canal (with a view right of the statues crowning the façade of the Gesuiti) to reach the peaceful **Campo della Madonna dell'Orto**. The church (*open Mon–Sat 10–5; Chorus Pass*) was the parish church of Jacopo Tintoretto, who is buried here, and it contains some of his most important works (*described on p. 243*). In the *campo*, which retains its old paving in stone and brick, the **Scuola dei Mercanti** was built in 1570, and the relief dates from that time.

(On the Fondamenta Madonna dell'Orto is the Boscolo Grand Hotel dei Dogi (*see p. 352*), whose garden extends right up to the lagoon. It was perhaps designed by Giuseppe Jappelli in the early 19th century.)

The walk continues along Fondamenta Gasparo Contarini. On the opposite side of the canal is the fine **Palazzo Mastelli**, also called 'del Cammello', since it bears a charming relief of a man leading a camel (a reminder that Venetian merchants brought merchandise, and in particular spices, from the East by caravan), and then the double façade of a simple low house with symmetrical chimneys and water-gates. On this side is Palazzo Minelli-Spada with two obelisks, and the long façade of **Palazzo Contarini dal Zaffo** (no. 3539). This was built in 1530 for Cardinal Gasparo Contarini (1483–1542), who was also a scholar and diplomat and was well known in his time for the witty literary meetings he organised in the Casinò 'degli Spiriti' in the huge garden of this palace overlooking the lagoon. Here Pietro Aretino, Jacopo Sansovino and Titian were among his guests. Restored at the beginning of the 20th century by the French garden designer Ferdinand Bac, it partly survives, and can be seen through the convent, called the Casa Cardinal Piazza, used partly as a conference centre and as a simple hotel.

The *fondamenta* ends at the **Sacca della Misericordia**, which opens onto the lagoon and which is used as a mooring for private boats. There is a good view of the island of San Michele, with its dark cypresses and church façade, and of the larger island of Murano, with its lighthouse and bell-towers. A bridge leads to Corte Vecchia, which continues to Fondamenta dell'Abbazia, back on Rio della Sensa. Follow it left. The **Corte Nuova**, where there is a pretty little garden, is entered by a fine Gothic archway with reliefs of the *Madonna della Misericordia* and saints. Here were the almshouses built in 1506 by the adjoining Scuola Vecchia della Misericordia and at the same time the portico along the canal was added under the huge building of the *scuola*.

The *fondamenta* ends in **Campo dell'Abbazia**, which preserves its old pavement and 14th-century well-head with two kneeling brethren of the confraternity holding the emblem of the *scuola*. The worn Gothic façade of the **Scuola Vecchia della Misericordia**, founded in 1308 (and restored in the 15th century), stands next to the façade (1659) of the deconsecrated church of Santa Maria della Misericordia. On the wall is a precious 14th-century relief of the *Virgin Orans*, Byzantine in style. In 1589, when the *scuola* moved to the Scuola Grande nearby (*see below*), Domenico Tintoretto was allowed to use the huge upper floor to paint his canvas of *Paradise* for the Doge's Palace (it is used today as a restoration laboratory).

If you follow the narrow *fondamenta* here towards the lagoon, it ends at a gate into Venice's only nursery, called the **'Laguna Fiorita'** (*open Mon–Fri 8.30–12.30 & 2.30–5, Sat 8.30–12.30*), in a walled garden behind the abbey buildings and beside its ancient campanile. It is a delightful friendly place to explore, with a number of greenhouses, and a very fine collection of plants particularly adapted to the lagoon climate.

In the other direction a wooden bridge crosses the *rio* to a *fondamenta* where a little shrine has reliefs of the *Madonna della Misericordia* protecting two friars, and apparently providing them with two ships laden to the gunwales with supplies. It is set into the massive walls of the **Scuola Grande della Misericordia**, begun in 1532 by Jacopo Sansovino (to replace the Scuola Vecchia) but left incomplete at his death because of lack of funds (and a subsequent project designed by Palladio in the 1570s was never carried out). The huge façade, which was to have been faced with marble, remains unfinished in brick. The building does, however, have a splendidly designed lower hall, with numerous columns. Since the fall of the Republic it has been occupied by a military store, an archive, builders' yard, and even a sports centre, and endless discussions continue to this day about how it could best be used (at present it is empty and ignominiously hired out for parties). On the *rio* opposite you can see the brick wall of an overgrown garden on the site of Palazzo Antelini, which was demolished in the late 18th century. Continue past the *scuola* towards the bridge. Around the corner to the right, on the Fondamenta della Misericordia, is the large **Palazzo Lezze**, by Longhena (1654).

Cross the bridge, which leads across the wide canal into Ramo della Misericordia, which in turn leads to the Rio San Felice, here crossed by a private bridge with no parapet: most of the stone bridges in the city were originally built without parapets, but this is the only one to have so survived. Take the bridge beside it, which leads across the little canal to a dark passageway which continues through Corte dei Preti to Calle de la Racheta; follow it left past a couple of little walled gardens. One of the grandest buildings in the *calle*, **Palazzo Pesaro-Papafava** (no. 3764) became the premises of the University of Warwick in 2006 (the University has run a Venice course for 40 years). Just beyond, also on the left, is the **Sottoportego Molin**, with a very worn angel holding a heraldic device above the archway and lovely carved wooden eaves. At the end, a bridge leads across to the Fondamenta Santa Caterina, with the flank of the church of **Santa Caterina**, now deconsecrated and used as a store; the ship's keel roof, destroyed by fire in 1977, has been rebuilt. Part of the convent is used as a state school, and there is a large walled garden here. Fondamenta Zen continues along the attractive Rio di Santa Caterina in another peaceful area of the city past the huge **Palazzo Zen** (nos 4922–4924) with its balconies (in poor repair) designed by Francesco Zen (d. 1538). The Zen family included Nicolò and Antonio, famous seafarers in the early 15th century.

Across the canal, in the Salizzada Seriman, is the fine 15th-century **Palazzo Contarini-Seriman** (no. 4851), now a convent school. The interior (*admission sometimes on request*) contains a staircase with a fresco by the school of Giambattista Tiepolo and a lovely stuccoed alcove.

In the long, stark **Campo dei Gesuiti** is the huge ex-monastery of the Gesuiti, once used as barracks: work is finally under way to transform it into students' lodgings. Opposite, with four tall chimneys, is a little chapel known as the **Oratorio dei Crociferi** (*open only by appointment; T: 041 271 9012, info@scalabovolo.org*). The adjoining hospital was founded in the mid-12th century for crusaders, and received generous help from Doge Ranier Zeno in 1268: in the 14th century it became a hospice for women. The chapel, dating from 1582, with a relief of the *Madonna and Child Enthroned* over the main door, contains an interesting cycle of paintings by Palma Giovane (1583–92), illustrating the history of the hospital, and considered among the best works of this very prolific painter.

The monumental Baroque façade by Giovanni Battista Fattoretto of the **church of the Gesuiti** (Santa Maria Assunta; *open 10–12 & 3.30–5.30*) was rebuilt for the Jesuits in 1714–29 by Domenico Rossi. The highly elaborate Baroque interior has decorative grey and white marble intarsia imitating wall hangings. The frescoes on the ceiling of the nave are by Francesco Fontebasso. When the floor of Istrian stone and green marble was restored a few years ago, a Byzantine bas-relief was found beneath it: this is now displayed in the nave near the West door and represents the victory of Virtue over Vice (symbolised by an eagle killing a rabbit).

On the first north altar is a splendid

painting of the *Martyrdom of St Lawrence*, commissioned from Titian in 1548 by Lorenzo Massolo to decorate his tomb in the church. Finished in the following decade, Titian seems to have been inspired by the temples he had just seen on a trip to Rome for the architectural details in the background of the work, which is remarkable above all for its setting at night. The martyrdom of this Roman saint, traditionally supposed to have been roasted alive on a gridiron in 258, has always been a favourite subject amongst painters and sculptors, and Titian himself painted another similar version of the same subject in later years for Philip II of Spain. It still hangs in the church of the Escorial. Many of the details in the background of this huge painting have been revealed since its restoration in 2012.

The entire west wall is covered by the Lezze monument, the architecture of which is attributed to Jacopo Sansovino (the central bust at the very top, of Priamo Da Lezze, is by Alessandro Vittoria). The first south altarpiece of the *Guardian Angel* is by Palma Giovane. On the second south altar is a sculpture of *St Barbara* by Giovanni Maria Morleiter. On the four piers of the dome are statues of archangels by Giuseppe Torretti; the two tondi in the crossing and in the sanctuary are by Louis Dorigny. The fantastic huge 18th-century high altar, with its barley-sugar columns, is by Fra' Giuseppe Pozzo, who also worked on the Scalzi. In the chapel to the right of the sanctuary is a painting of *St Francis Xavier*, by Pietro Liberi. Over the door into the sacristy, the monument to Doge Pasquale Cicogna has a fine effigy by Girolamo Campagna. You can visit the sacristy where Palma Giovane carried out the entire pictorial decoration, in celebration of the Eucharist, in 1589–90. In the north transept, the *Assumption* is an early work by Tintoretto, with some lovely details in the foreground.

A *salizzada* leads out onto the long **Fondamente Nuove**, which follows the waterfront along the northern lagoon. There are various landing-stages, well indicated, where you can take a vaporetto around the eastern limits of the city past the Arsenale and Sant'Elena and Giardini back to the Riva near San Marco.

NB: If you choose to walk along the Fondamente Nuove, cross the bridge over the wide Rio dei Gesuiti, and take Calle della Croce right until you come to Calle Larga dei Botteri (*map p. 402, C2*), where at no. 5113 a simple inscription on the garden wall records the **last residence of Titian**, where he died of the plague in 1576, aged almost 90.

CAMPO DI SANTI GIOVANNI E PAOLO
Detail of the equestrian monument to Bartolomeo Colleoni, by Andrea Verrocchio (1490).

Sestiere of Castello

Castello, the largest sestiere in the city, occupies the area east of San Marco and Cannaregio. Its name is thought to come from an 8th-century fortress on the island of San Pietro, which is also where—as legend tells us—St Mark found shelter during a storm and his association with Venice began.

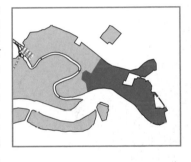

C astello was for centuries the religious centre of the city, with San Pietro di Castello the cathedral of Venice until 1807. Castello was also the maritime heart of the Republic, with the shipyards of the Arsenale from which her trading and naval fleets set sail. The area boasts some superb treasures: the magnificent church of Santi Giovanni e Paolo, that of San Zaccaria, and Carpaccio's delightful cycle of paintings in the little Scuola di San Giorgio degli Schiavoni. Beyond the Arsenale, away from the crush of tourists and souvenir stalls, Castello becomes an area where life goes on untrammelled by visitors, with washing strung out across the canals, and the delightful Via Garibaldi with its local shops and market stalls.

RIVA DEGLI SCHIAVONI

Map p. 404, A2–B2.
Riva degli Schiavoni is a wide, busy quay on the Bacino di San Marco. Often overcrowded around its first few bridges, it becomes an increasingly attractive promenade as it approaches the Arsenale canal. It was called 'Schiavoni' from the inhabitants of *Schiavonia* (Dalmatia), because the waterfront here was often used as a mooring for the trading vessels from Dalmatia and other Slavonic ports.

The **Hotel Danieli** was named after its first owner, a Swiss called Joseph da Niel, who opened it in 1822. It has always been one of Venice's most famous luxury-class hotels (*see p. 352*), and still retains its revolving door and an atmosphere from the days when it was patronised by great writers, musicians and artists, including George Sand and her lover Alfred de Musset, Charles Dickens, Ruskin, Wagner, Debussy and Proust. It occupies the neo-Gothic Palazzo Dandolo, with an ugly extension built in 1948. It was near here that Doge Vitale Michiel II was killed in 1172 as he tried to escape from the Doge's Palace to San Zaccaria. After a successful reign he became suddenly unpopular because of diplomatic failures with Constantinople and his decision not to take the Venetian fleet into battle. By the time he decided to recall the ships from Greece, many of the crew had contracted the plague. After his assassin had been brought to trial and executed, the house on this site was razed to the ground and a decree was issued that no stone building should ever be built on the spot. This was, amazingly enough, observed right up until the 20th century.

Across Ponte del Vin (with pretty colonnades) towers a **monument to Vittorio Emanuele II**, first King of Italy, a typical rhetorical work by the Roman sculptor Ettore Ferrari (1887), showing the king on his prancing charger, holding his sword on high, with snarling lions around the base, one biting through the chains which shackle him. Ferrari erected a number of bronze monuments to Italy's heroes, but this is his only work in Venice. At a house on the quay here (no. 4161) Henry James finished *The Portrait of a Lady* in 1881, during one of the earliest of his many visits to the city—'Straight across, before my windows, rose the great pink mass of San Giorgio Maggiore...Asked what may be the leading colour in the Venetian concert, we should inveterately say Pink...It is a faint, shimmering, airy, watery pink; the bright sea-light seems to flush with it and the pale whiteish-green of lagoon and canal to drink it in'.

LA PIETÀ

Map p. 404, A2. Open 10–12 & 3–5, Sat and Sun 10–5. Concerts are held regularly.
Beyond Rio dei Greci (the bridge, with a stone balustrade was first built in the 14th century) is the grand 18th-century façade by Giorgio Massari (only completed in 1906) of the church of La Pietà, or Santa Maria della Visitazione. The small entrance fee goes to the institute of the Pietà, an orphanage and hospital (*ospedale*) founded in 1346 and famous for its musical orphans (*see p. 287*), which today is still dedicated to the care of children (*entrance from a calle behind the church*).

The bright interior was sumptuously rebuilt in the present oval plan (particularly suitable for musical performances) by Giorgio Massari (1745–60), with galleries for choir and musicians and an oblong vestibule. The contemporary decorations remain intact, with a fine ceiling fresco of the *Triumph of Faith* by Giambattista Tiepolo (1755), and a high altarpiece by Giovanni Battista Piazzetta. The other 18th-century altarpieces include one by Domenico Maggiotto and another by Piazzetta's pupil Giuseppe Angeli. The 18th-century organ was built by Pietro Nacchini. The singing galleries above and a small museum dedicated to Vivaldi can be seen on guided tours by previous appointment (*www.pietavenezia.org*). The very fine painting of the *Supper in the House of Simon* by Alessandro Buonvicino, usually called Moretto da Brescia (1548), can only be seen on the tour as it is high up behind a grille at the west end. Moretto is known to have worked for a time in Venice under Titian, but this is the only painting which survives by him in the city; most of his works are in his native town of Brescia.

Beyond the next bridge, with a stone balustrade (rebuilt in 1871), a plaque on no. 4145 records **Petrarch's house**. The great humanist and poet came to Venice in 1362 to escape the plague in Padua, and lived here with his daughter and her family until 1367. In 1363 he invited his close friend Giovanni Boccaccio to come up from Florence to stay with him here for three months, a few years after he had completed his famous *Decameron*. The house was given to Petrarch by the Republic in return for his promise to leave his library to the city of Venice.

ANTONIO VIVALDI

Vivaldi (1678–1741), son of a barber and violinist, taught at the Pietà on and off for most of his life. He was violin-master in 1704–18, and concert-master in 1735–8, and many of his best compositions were written for the hospital, including numerous concertos which were first performed here. Vivaldi took orders in 1703, but obtained permission not to serve as a priest, apparently because of ill-health. Goldoni, who praised him as a violinist but not as a composer, relates that he was nicknamed '*Il Prete Rosso*' (the red priest), either because of his red hair or from the red robes worn at La Pietà. Vivaldi also wrote some 50 operas and directed the opera house of Sant'Angelo in Venice from 1713–39. The *Quattro Stagioni* (*Four Seasons*) was published in Amsterdam in 1725. He travelled extensively in Italy and Europe, but died in poverty in Vienna, and was forgotten until he was 'rediscovered' in the late 19th century (even though Bach had transcribed many of his concertos for keyboard).

SAN ZACCARIA

Map p. 404, A1. Open 10–12 & 4–6, Sun and holidays only 1 6.

The church is dedicated to Zacharias, the father of St John the Baptist, whose relics are preserved here. It was founded in the 9th century, at the same period as the Basilica of St Mark, and by the same doge, Giustiniano Particiaco.

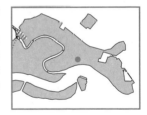

THE *CAMPO* AND CONVENT OF SAN ZACCARIA

The Benedictine convent was one of the most richly endowed in the city. Today's *campo* was once part of the convent and still has just two narrow entrances, one from the Riva, and the other from Campo San Provolo, which preserves its beautiful Gothic portal (the outer face has a large 15th-century marble relief of the *Madonna and Child between St John the Baptist and St Mark*, crowned by the half-figure of St Zacharias). On the right of the church the brick wall of part of the earlier church survives, and the doorway which led into the fashionable nuns' *colloquio*: 'In the last century, especially, the nuns and monks led a pleasant life. You may see in the old pictures of Pietro Longhi and his school how, at the aristocratic and fashionable convent of San Zaccaria, the lady nuns received their friends and acquaintances of this world in the ante-room where the dames and their cavaliers flirted and drank coffee, and the gentlemen coquetted with the brides of heaven through their grated windows.' (W.D. Howells, *Venetian Life*, 1866). Behind the little garden with two elms and architectural fragments you can see the ancient brick campanile. The 16th-century portico on the left of the church used to give access to the nuns' cemetery. The lovely late 15th-century well-head with cherubim and amphorae is in good condition: it was placed here in the 20th century after it had been confiscated from an antique dealer who had tried to sell it (thus avoiding the sad fate of numerous other Venetian well-heads, which left the city in the late 19th and early 20th centuries). The convent was suppressed in the 19th century and the buildings, which include two large Renaissance cloisters, are now occupied by a police station.

The doge would make an annual visit to the convent at Eastertide in gratitude for the donation to the *Signoria* of part of the convent orchard in the 12th century, so that Piazza San Marco could be enlarged. During this ceremony he would be presented with the ducal cap (or *cornu*). No fewer than eight doges of the early Republic were buried in the first church.

THE CHURCH FAÇADE
The very beautiful façade (restored in 2007), which extends above the nave roof, was begun by the little-known Antonio Gambello in 1458 but only the lowest storey on either side of the doorway had been completed by his death in 1481. It has beautiful

rectangular panels of red and grey marble, with veined grey marble set into panels with carvings of cupids and garlands surrounding roundels of prophets. The doorway has delicately carved pilasters and in the yellow marble lunette there is a precious porphyry disc. The superb upper stories in Istrian stone, with their blind arcading with scallop shells, pilasters, columns and windows, were designed by the important Renaissance architect Mauro Codussi. The façade is crowned with a lunette and a statue of the *Redeemer*, and angels carrying instruments of the Passion.

THE CHURCH INTERIOR

The elegant interior, designed by Gambello and completed by Codussi (who added the dome), has a high aisled nave; the columns on fine raised bases have good capitals. The multiple apse with an ambulatory and coronet of chapels lit by long windows, typical of northern European Gothic architecture, is unique in Venice. The aisle walls are entirely covered with 17th–18th-century paintings. The beautiful second south altarpiece, **Giovanni Bellini's *Madonna Enthroned and Four Saints***, is one of the artist's greatest works, signed and dated 1505. It is the last of a series of altarpieces with similar subjects he painted for the churches of Venice, which included the triptych still in the Frari and that painted for San Giobbe, now in the Gallerie dell'Accademia. The architectural setting is Classical, but incorporates an apse mosaic which recalls the interior of St Mark's. The monumental figures of St Peter, St Catherine, St Lucy and St Jerome are enveloped in a remarkable atmosphere of calm, while the angel plays a melody at the foot of the throne. When Napoleon removed it to the Louvre, it was transferred from its original panels onto canvas.

At the end of the north aisle is the **monument to Alessandro Vittoria** (1528–1608), with a self-portrait bust made in 1595 (other remarkable portrait busts which this important sculptor and architect made of his Venetian contemporaries can be seen in the Ca' d'Oro). Vittoria is buried beneath the black tombstone in the sanctuary, carved by him with his name and the date 1605, although he actually died three years later. He also carved statuettes of the *Baptist* and of *St Zacharias* for the holy water stoups, although the *Baptist* was damaged some years ago and is now covered, and the other is a copy of the original. His statue of the patron saint is on the façade.

The chapels

Off the south aisle is the entrance (*very small fee*) to the peaceful chapels of St Anthanasius and St Tarasius. The **Chapel of St Athanasius** contains carved 15th-century wooden stalls by Francesco Cozzi and his brother Marco. There is an interesting little collection of paintings here, which includes (over the altar) an early work by Jacopo Tintoretto, the *Birth of St John the Baptist*. Graceful handmaidens are hard at work comforting the babe and the mother. A bird is drinking at the copper bowl prominent in the foreground, and there is a glory of angels in the sky, while the father, Zacharias, looks on at the side (possibly a self-portrait). Above the entrance door there is a small *Crucifixion* attributed to Van Dyck. To the right of the altar, *Flight into Egypt* by Gian Domenico Tiepolo. On the right wall, the *Madonna and Saints* traditionally attributed to Palma Vecchio has, since its restoration in 2007 by the Venice in Peril

Fund, been attributed to Marco Basaiti. Beneath the pavement a fragment of an earlier pavement has recently been revealed—with beautiful marble inlay in a circular design reminiscent of the floor of St Mark's. The five gilded chairs here (three of them dating from the 17th century) were used for the annual visit of the doge. Beyond, a small room has a charming, old-fashioned display of the **church treasury**.

The waterlogged 10th-century **crypt**, with three aisles divided by low columns, can be visited on a brick walkway: it is, amazingly enough, the only building in the city permanently flooded by water and is a remarkable sight.

The adjoining **Chapel of St Tarasius** has a predella recently attributed to Paolo Veneziano, painted some hundred years before the three fine altar paintings by Antonio Vivarini and his brother-in-law Giovanni d'Alemagna (executed in 1443), all of them with extraordinarily ornate gilded Gothic frames. The central polyptych incorporates an earlier *Madonna and Child and Two Saints*, signed by a certain 'Stefano from the parish of Sant'Agnese' in 1385. These polyptychs are typical of the florid late Gothic style of these painters from Murano, totally at odds with the new Renaissance art produced just the year before, which can be seen above in the fan vault (the early 15th-century chancel of the previous church). These frescoes by Andrea del Castagno and the less well-known Francesco da Faenza (signed and dated 1442; damaged) are one of the earliest-known works in Venice by the Tuscan Renaissance painters who were called to the city to work on the mosaics of St Mark's. Also here are two 15th-century wood statues of *St Benedict* and *St Zacharias*, and a fragment of mosaic pavement thought to date from the 12th century (glass in the floor reveals another fragment which may survive from the earliest church).

SAN GIOVANNI IN BRAGORA

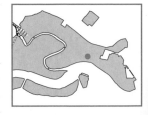

Campo Bandiera e Moro (*map p. 404, B2*) is named after three naval officers (two of them, the Bandiera brothers, lived here) who rebelled against Austrian rule and were executed by the Austrians in 1844. It has a few benches and two well-heads, and a handsome Gothic palace (now a hotel). The church of San Giovanni in Bragora (*open 9–11 & 3.30–5, Sun 9.30–12*), founded possibly as early as the 9th century, was rebuilt in 1475. Dedicated to St John the Baptist, it is not known why it was called 'in Bragora'; the name may derive from a word in Venetian dialect referring either to the marshy terrain here, or to a market-place, or even to the fishing which took place nearby. Outside the church is a little 18th-century building, the Scoletta della Bragora, which used to house a confraternity.

INTERIOR OF SAN GIOVANNI IN BRAGORA

Antonio Vivaldi, who was born in a house in the *campo*, was baptised in the lovely 15th-century font in 1678 (his touching baptismal certificate, also translated into English, hangs here). The church is particularly rich in works of art. In the sanctuary a great marble frame encloses the *Baptism of Christ*, one of the most beautiful works in Venice by **Cima da Conegliano**, painted in 1494. The figure of the Baptist is silhouetted against the evening sky as the fading light illuminates the river Jordan, which flows through a landscape reminiscent of the Veneto. Above, yellow, green, red and blue cherubim ride on a circle of clouds. Cima, a deeply religious painter, was born at Conegliano, in the Veneto, and many of his works can still be seen in that region, but he is also well represented in Venice with other superb altarpieces in the Carmini, Madonna dell'Orto and the Gallerie dell'Accademia. He painted another work for this church eight years later (now hanging to the right of the sacristy door), of *Constantine and St Helen and the Finding of the True Cross*.

It is known that **Alvise Vivarini** was Cima's master, so it is interesting to see a number of paintings by this artist also in the church, including his *Risen Christ* (to the left of the above work), and in particular his small *Head of the Redeemer*, in the north aisle, which might even have provided the model for Cima's Christ in the *Baptism*. Alvise's skill in painting landscapes can also be seen in his otherwise damaged *Madonna and Child*, also in the north aisle. Alvise came from a Venetian family of painters: he was the son of Antonio and the nephew of Bartolomeo, who painted the triptych in the south aisle of the *Madonna Enthroned between Sts John the Baptist and Andrew*, which is signed and dated 1478 and shows his skill in the use of bright colours, in particular the Madonna's striking red-and-black dress.

At the beginning of the south aisle is a wood Crucifix carved in 1491 by a sculptor known as Leonardo Tedesco (his generic last name—'German'—suggests he may have come from northern Europe); the painting and gilding was carried out by Leonardo Boldrini, a little-known artist who was born in Murano. These artists worked together again in the second chapel in this aisle, which is dedicated to St John the Almsgiver, whose relics had been brought to the church from Alexandria in 1247. They made a new sarcophagus for the relics, the front of which, with an effigy of the saint, survives here. (The polychrome terracotta *Pietà* group in the chapel next door was once also attributed to Leonardo Tedesco, but is now thought to be by another German master, since it is typical of northern European works of this subject.) The St John chapel was redecorated in the 18th century, when Jacopo Marieschi provided the altarpiece showing *St John Dispensing Alms* and the lunette illustrating the arrival in Venice of his relics. Marieschi is a typical Venetian painter of this period, whose works can also be seen in a few other churches in the city.

The church preserves two **Byzantine *Madonnas*** (over the side door and over the sacristy door). The latter, dating from the 12th or 13th century, is a very beautiful relief, which still has its polychrome decoration. In the second north chapel, there are three works in the Byzantine style which were carried out at least three centuries later by artists from Crete, who set up a very successful workshop in Venice producing numerous such works for Venetian clients.

On the Baroque high altar are two statues of saints by Heinrich Meyring (c. 1688), and on the sanctuary walls are 16th-century works by Palma Giovane (*Washing of the Feet*—he also painted the *Christ before Caiaphas* on the west wall) and Paris Bordone (*Last Supper*).

You can see the side of the church by taking Calle del Dose back towards Riva degli Schiavoni and following the first *calle* on the left into **Campiello del Piovan**, which has benches beneath its linden trees and no fewer than three well-heads. The one closest to the side of the church (beside a single cypress tree) is square and has a relief of the *Baptist* and two inscriptions reminding the neighbours that its water was for ecclesiastical use only.

THE GREEK DISTRICT

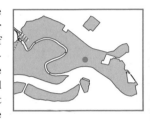

Ponte dei Greci (*map p. 404, A1*) is named after the Greeks who settled in this area in the 15th century after the fall of Constantinople and subsequent invasion of Greece by the Turks. Together with the Jewish community, this became the largest foreign settlement in the Renaissance city, and by the 16th century it numbered around 6,000 members. Venice represented the most important centre of Greek culture in the west, and the community is still very active. Houses were built in the area for the Greek inhabitants, as well as a hospital, archive and cemetery.

At the end of the 15th century the Greeks were given permission to found the *scuola* and Greek Orthodox church on the canal here, in a charming courtyard planted with trees. Beside them is the Greek College, named after its 17th-century founder, Girolamo Flangini, and now the seat of the Hellenic Institute of Byzantine and post-Byzantine Studies. This building and the decorative wall of the court, as well as the *scuola* itself (dating from 1678), are typical of the numerous 'minor' interventions in the townscape by the great Venetian architect Baldassare Longhena (architect of the Salute and Ca' Rezzonico).

SAN GIORGIO DEI GRECI

The **church of San Giorgio dei Greci** (*map p. 404, A1; open 9.30–12.30 & 2.30–5, Sun and holidays 9.30–1; closed Tues; entrance along Rio dei Greci, off Calle Madonna*) was the most important outside Greece for the Greek Orthodox rite. Its construction was begun in 1539 to a design by Sante Lombardo, member of the large family of sculptors and architects who were at work in Venice in the 15th and 16th centuries. The cupola and graceful leaning campanile were added later in the century. The iconostasis is decorated with late Byzantine works.

The Scuola di San Nicolò dei Greci houses a **Museum of Icons** (*map p. 404, A1; open 9–12.30 & 1.30–4.30, Sun and holidays 10–5*), opened in 1959 in a room once used as a hospital by the confraternity. The well-labelled collection is arranged chronologically. The first two Byzantine icons are particularly precious: a *Madonna and Child with Apostles and Saints*, and *Christ in Glory with the Twelve Apostles*, both from churches in Constantinople and dating from around 1350. They were donated to the Greek confraternity by an aristocratic Greek woman (Anna Palaeologina Notara), who had come to Venice just before the fall of Byzantium in 1453 and who remained here for the rest of her life (she died in 1507). The rest of the collection has been formed by donations over the centuries and is interesting above all for the icons produced in Venice by artists from Crete (the island was under Venetian dominion from 1210 until 1669), whose workshop was known as that of the '*madoneri di Rialto*'. They combined Byzantine traditions with Venetian elements, and the most skilled artists of this school, particularly active from the 16th–17th centuries, included Georgios Klontzas, Michael Damaskinos and Emmanuel Tzanfournaris, all of whom are represented here with signed works. The most famous member of this group, Domenicos Theotokopoulos, came to Venice from Crete in 1567 and was greatly struck by the work of Titian and Tintoretto. He moved to Spain, to flourish under the name of El Greco. There is also a small room with a display of vestments and liturgical objects, and a 14th-century illuminated manuscript, an exquisite Byzantine work.

On the other side of Rio dei Greci is Fondamenta dell'Osmarin, crossed by two pretty bridges. The first one, Ponte del Diavolo, was well reconstructed in 1983, and the second one, Ponte dei Carmini, dates from 1793. **Palazzo Priuli**, on the corner of Rio de l'Osmarin, probably dates from the late 14th century, and as Ruskin noted is 'a most important and beautiful early Gothic palace'. It is well preserved (now a hotel) and has a particularly attractive corner window with a balcony, although the frescoes on the façade by Palma Vecchio have totally disappeared. In contrast, another Gothic palace close by, with a superb courtyard, the Ca' Zorzi on Rio dei Greci, is now a luxury hotel.

Calle della Madonna and Salizzada dei Greci connect Rio dei Greci and Rio della Pietà. Here is the church of **Sant'Antonin** (*open by appointment on Fri afternoon or Sat morning; T: 041 241 3817 or enquire at the Museo Diocesano d'Arte Sacra; see p. 104*). Traditionally thought to have been founded in the 7th century, its 13th-century building was reconstructed in the 17th century, around the same time as the buildings for the Greek community close by, under the direction of Baldassare Longhena (although his façade was left unfinished). The campanile dates from the following century. Byron tells the story of the shooting of a circus elephant here in 1819, which had escaped from its cage and run amok in the streets before taking refuge in St Antonin: 'An Elephant went Mad here about two months ago—killed his keeper—knocked down a house—broke open a Church—dispersed all his assailants and was at last killed by a Shot in his *posteriore* from a field-piece brought from the *Arse*-nal.'

THE SCUOLA DI SAN GIORGIO DEGLI SCHIAVONI

Map p. 404, B1. Open Tues–Sat 9.15–1 & 2.45–6, Sun and holidays 9.15–1, Mon 2.45–6.
The Scuola di San Giorgio degli Schiavoni was founded in 1451 by the Dalmatians who came to live in the city (many of whom were sailors). The first (and closest) foreign territory to be conquered by the *Serenissima*, Dalmatia always enjoyed a special relationship with Venice, and its inhabitants are known to have rallied to the support of the Republic at its downfall at the hands of Napoleon. The façade of 1551 bears a relief of *St George and the Dragon* by Sansovino's pupil Pietro da Salò, and a 14th-century *Madonna and Child*.

The interior

A heavy red curtain hangs at the old-fashioned entrance to the dimly-lit interior, which is one of the most evocative places in the city, with an atmosphere that is redolent of old Venice. The walls of the famous little room are entirely decorated with a delightful series of paintings by Vittore Carpaccio (carried out between 1502 and 1508), relating to the lives of the three Dalmatian patron saints, Jerome, Tryphon and George, and bursting with detail, incident and symbolism.

VITTORE CARPACCIO

Carpaccio (1460–1525/6), the greatest Venetian narrative painter in the later 15th and early 16th centuries, produced his masterpiece for this *scuola*. He also worked for other *scuole* in the city, including that of Sant'Orsola (his nine paintings illustrating the *Legend of St Ursula* are now in the Gallerie dell'Accademia), and San Giovanni Evangelista (the *Miracle at the Rialto Bridge* or *Cure of a Lunatic by the Patriarch of Grado* is also now in the Accademia). Although influenced by the Bellini family (with whom he worked in the Doge's Palace on paintings subsequently lost in a fire), he had his own remarkable sense of colour and an eye for detail, and his works reflect an atmosphere of great calm. His famous painting of *Two Venetian Ladies* on a balcony is preserved in the Museo Correr. Carpaccio was the earliest Italian master of genre painting, and numerous details in his paintings give a particularly vivid picture of Venice and the Venetians at the end of the 15th century.

Left wall: The *Duel of St George and the Dragon* is justly one of Carpaccio's best-known paintings. It shows St George wounding the dragon with his lance. Scattered all around are the bones and severed limbs of the dragon's victims; snakes and lizards hiss and spit at the spectacle. The *Triumph of St George* follows, showing the blond-haired knight, his sword raised and holding the dragon by the princess's girdle, about to kill the beast. The king, queen and princess look on, while exotic musicians celebrate. Although the dragon appears defeated, the horses pull their heads back and shy away, obviously still nervous.

End wall: *St George Baptising the People of Silene* (the rescued king and princess kneel before St George, a white lurcher memorably in the foreground); and *The Miracle of St Tryphon* (the boy saint is freeing the daughter of the emperor from a demon, in the form of a basilisk).

Right wall: *Agony in the Garden*—Christ prays on the hillside, while the disciples lie stretched out and fast asleep—and the *Calling of St Matthew*. Another famous panel is the *Lion Led by St Jerome into the Monastery*, putting the terrified monks to flight, their habits streaming behind them, though the lion himself looks docile enough and bemused by all the fuss.

The *Funeral of St Jerome* is a touching depiction of the ceremony, with the lion throwing back his head in a final roar of grief. The last panel, the *Vision of St Augustine*, depicts the story of St Augustine writing a letter to St Jerome asking for his advice on a book he wanted to write about the saints in

Paradise. St Jerome's death occurred at the same time, and Augustine's studio was suddenly filled with light and he heard a voice reproaching him for daring to describe Paradise before his own death. Carpaccio shows us in great detail the inside of a monk's study, with its neatly arranged bookcase and scientific instruments, and a little white dog looking up at its master. The six-winged seraph in the painting's mosaic altar-niche is reminiscent of that in Bellini's *San Giobbe Altarpiece (see p. 147)*.

The *Madonna and Child* is attributed to Carpaccio's son, Benedetto.

Upper floor: The room was decorated in the 17th century and has a prettily carved and gilded wood ceiling incorporating paintings attributed to Andrea Vicentino, and a 16th-century carved wood altarpiece of *St George*.

Sacristy: The treasury of the guild (including a 15th-century processional Cross) is kept here (on the ground floor).

Also reached off the Rio Sant'Agostino is the huge deconsecrated church of **San Lorenzo** (*map p. 403, E4*), which has been closed for many years. The first church, on a basilican plan, was founded by the Particiaco doges in the 9th century. Marco Polo (1256–1324) was buried here, but his sarcophagus was lost when the church was rebuilt in 1592 by Simone Sorella.

SAN FRANCESCO DELLA VIGNA

Map p. 403, E3–F3. Open 8–12 & 3–7; coin-operated lights.
The name of this church recalls the vineyard bequeathed to the Franciscan order for a convent in 1253 by Marco Ziani, son of Doge Pietro Ziani. On this site, in 1534, Doge Andrea Gritti laid the foundation stone of the present church to be built by his friend Jacopo Sansovino. The humanist friar Francesco Zorzi was involved in the

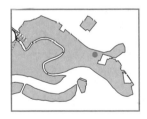

design, which is based on a complicated harmony of the progression of the number three.

THE CHURCH FAÇADE
In 1562 Giovanni Grimani, Patriarch of Aquileia (*see p. 271*), paid for the façade to be added by Palladio. His design was entirely innovative in church architecture, using the Classical elements of columns and pediments derived from ancient temples, which were to be employed with even greater success in his other two churches in Venice, San Giorgio Maggiore and the Redentore. Although the high relief and brightness of the Istrian stone demand our attention, it is difficult fully to appreciate the splendid design, since the church is sited in a rather cramped space. Above the door is one of the architect's typical Diocletian windows, which allows light into the nave. The medallion in the pediment bearing an eagle (symbol of Aquileia and of St John the Evangelist)

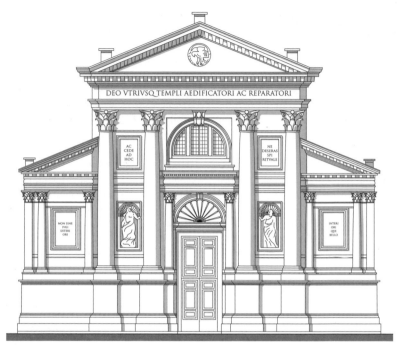

DEO VTRIVSQ_TEMPLI AEDIFICATORI AC REPARATORI

AC
CEDE
AD
HOC

NE
DESERAS
SPI
RITVALE

NON SINE
IVGI
EXTERI
ORI

INTERI
ORI
QVI
BELLO

SAN FRANCESCO DELLA VIGNA

and the inscriptions between the columns were ordered specifically by Grimani both to record the spiritual significance of the church and as a glorification of his own devotion. The two statues, *Moses* and *St Paul*, in contrasting dark bronze, added in 1592, stand out as the only colour on the façade. They are by Tiziano Aspetti, who is known principally for his works in this medium.

The bell-tower, which rises behind the east end (and is thus difficult to see close to), is one of the highest and slenderest in Venice, recalling that of St Mark's. It served as an aid to navigators in the northern lagoon during the days of the Republic, and its bells were tolled to announce meetings of the Great Council in the Doge's Palace. Built in 1581, but repeatedly struck by lightning, it has been carefully restored over the centuries.

THE CHURCH INTERIOR

The broad nave has five side chapels between Doric pilasters on either side and a long chancel (with the monks' choir behind the altar).

South transept: The most memorable work in the entire church is a ***Madonna and Child* (A)**, the only known work by Antonio da Negroponte, an artist about which nothing is known except that he was a friar and a native of the Greek island of Euboea (known as Negroponte under the Venetians). It is an exceptionally large painting with a charming Madonna in a rich brocade robe sitting on an intricately carved throne beneath a garland of fruit and in front of a dark wood of pomegranate trees, with a great variety of birds on the lawn at her feet. Painted around 1465, it represents one of the last great paintings in the florid Gothic style which had persisted in Venice under the influence of Antonio Vivarini. The *God the Father* in the lunette is by Benedetto Rusconi (Diana).

North transept: The Badoer-Giustiniani Chapel (B) belonged to the procurator Lorenzo Giustiniani and his brother Antonio and was designed in the 1530s by the architect of the church, Jacopo Sansovino. He decorated it with a series of very fine 15th-century sculpted reliefs by Pietro Lombardo and his two sons Antonio and Tullio, which had been removed from the earlier church where they were probably part of the choir screen. On the two side walls, rectangles bear reliefs of prophets and the four Evangelists, above which are scenes from the life of Christ. The same artists worked on the altarpiece.

A door leads out past a glass door through which you can see one of the two 15th-century **cloisters (C)**, still in very good condition.

Dolfin *Madonna* and Sacristy: In a peaceful little chapel **(D)** is a charming small painting of the *Madonna and*

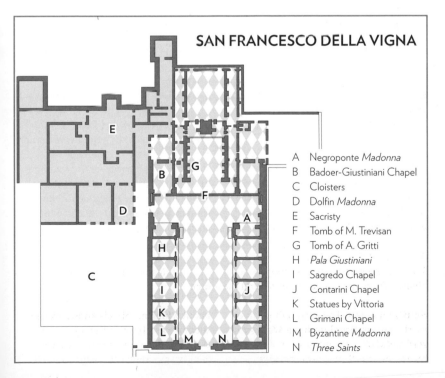

SAN FRANCESCO DELLA VIGNA

A   Negroponte *Madonna*
B   Badoer-Giustiniani Chapel
C   Cloisters
D   Dolfin *Madonna*
E   Sacristy
F   Tomb of M. Trevisan
G   Tomb of A. Gritti
H   *Pala Giustiniani*
I   Sagredo Chapel
J   Contarini Chapel
K   Statues by Vittoria
L   Grimani Chapel
M   Byzantine *Madonna*
N   *Three Saints*

Saints (*Sacra Conversazione*). Even though it is signed and dated 1507 by Giovanni Bellini, some scholars presume some of the figures were painted by assistants (and the donor, Giacomo Dolfin, is certainly repainted). The figure of the Madonna, with her beautiful blue and gold-lined cloak, and that of St Sebastian, who calls us into the scene, as well as the charming landscape, all appear to be by the master's hand. Sansovino's **sacristy (E)**, off the corridor here, survives intact.

Sanctuary: Beneath the crossing is the large pavement **tomb of Doge Marcantonio Trevisan (F)** who died in 1554 having been doge for just one year. (There is a polychrome relief of him over the sacristy door, showing him kneeling before the Crucifix holding the standard of the Republic. This seems to have been made the year after his death.) On the left wall is the **tomb of Doge Andrea Gritti (G)**, who founded the present church and built a *palazzo* in the *campo* for himself. The Palladian design of the funerary monument is in keeping with the architecture of the church, and it records with simple dignity this great doge—devoid of an effigy and with inscriptions now too dusty to read. Gritti was a cultivated man who could speak many languages, and although he was elected following success as a military commander, his rule was distinguished by diplomatic skills which allowed the Republic to enjoy many years of peace. He died, aged 84, in 1538. He also set up the symmetrical monument opposite to commemorate his ancestors.

Nave chapels: The fifth north chapel contains the *Pala Giustiniani* **(H)**, painted by Veronese for the Giustiniani brothers Lorenzo and Antonio (*see above*). It was the great painter's first Venetian commission (1551), showing the Virgin and Child and shepherds with St Catherine and St Anthony Abbot. The Virgin is placed to one side, recalling Titian's *Pala Pesaro* in the Frari. Even though the figure of St Catherine in the foreground, next to the long snout of St Anthony's black pig, is particularly graceful, this is clearly an early work: Veronese's skills progressed dramatically from here, and numerous later works are better painted and better composed.

The **Sagredo Chapel (I)** is beautifully decorated and still in excellent condition: it was begun in 1675 by Doge Niccolò Sagredo, but work was continued by his descendants in the late 17th and 18th centuries. Giovanni Gai carved the expressive bust of the doge, with his flowing hair, and that of his brother Alvise, who was Patriarch of Venice. The statue of the most illustrious member of the family, St Gerard Sagredo, is by Gai's contemporary Andrea Cominelli. St Gerard is known as the 'Apostle of Hungary' (where he is known as Gellért): he was influential in Christianising the Magyars and won the support of Hungary's saint-king, Stephen. In 1046, after Stephen's death, Gerard was seized by pagans and drowned in the Danube. The monochrome frescoes by Giambattista Tiepolo (including the four Evangelists and two medallions of the Virtues) and *trompe l'oeil* festoons fit well with the sombre sculpted decoration with its elaborate stucco garlands and angels flanking the Madonna in the lunette above the altar. The only colour is provided by the frescoes representing the *Apotheosis of St Gerard* in the cupola, by the Roman artist Girolamo Pellegrini (his only known work in Venice) and by the altar frontal in *pietre dure*.

Opposite is the **Contarini Chapel (J)**, commemorating two Contarini doges, Francesco and Alvise, both buried here (Alvise, who died in 1684, was the last doge of the Contarini, a family who had supplied the Republic with no fewer than eight doges since the 11th century). Here are two more busts by Giovanni Gai's father, Antonio, and the decorations of this chapel date from the 18th century except for the earlier altarpiece, a typical work by Palma Giovane.

The second north chapel **(K)** has three good statues of saints by Alessandro Vittoria. His *St Sebastian* recalls the pose of Michelangelo's *Dying Slave*, now in the Louvre. The first north chapel **(L)** was decorated for the Patriarch of Aquileia, Giovanni Grimani, as his burial place. In 1559 he recalled from Rome the Venetian artist Franco Battista (also known as Semolei), who carried out the paintings in the pretty vault, including the 'Angelic' and 'Human' Virtues. (Some years before, Semolei had also painted the altarpiece of the *Baptism of Christ* in the fifth south chapel in this church for another Patriarch of Aquileia, Daniele Barbaro.) Federico Zuccari, who also worked mostly in Rome, took over on Semolei's death and finished the vault and painted the altarpiece of the *Adoration of the Magi* (recently restored but badly damaged) and the *Resurrection of Lazarus* on the right. Since Grimani was absolved by the Inquisition in 1563 of accusations of heresy for his views on predestination and pardon, the imagery in the chapel, including the two bronze statues of *Justice* and *Temperance* by Tiziano Aspetti (1592), can be seen as allusions to the virtues of this cultivated churchman. who, as mentioned above, also paid for Palladio's façade (where there are two more statues by Aspetti).

West wall: To the right of the door as you face it, there is a very beautiful 13th-century Byzantine relief of the *Madonna and Child* **(M)**, known to have been brought to Venice from the East in 1341. The colourful triptych of *Three Saints* **(N)** (to the left of the door) is attributed to Antonio Vivarini.

From this remote corner of the city, you can either follow signs to the vaporetto landing-stage (Celestia) on the northern lagoon, or you can return south towards the Greek district via Santa Giustina, described below.

THE DISTRICT OF SANTA GIUSTINA

Take Calle San Francesco in front of the façade of San Francesco della Vigna to the Rio Sant'Agostino. Follow it left into Campo Santa Giustina, with the 18th-century Palazzo Gradenigo and the former church of Santa Giustina (*map p. 403, E3*). The façade of 1640 is a minor work by Longhena, although it was altered in the Neoclassical style by Giovanni Casoni in 1841, when it became a school for the education of sailors (the building is still used as a school). Ponte del Fontego leads into a *calle* which has some dilapidated but lovely old palaces and Salizzada Santa Giustina is brightened up with a few local shops. Some of the houses in this area, in *calli* which are exceptionally narrow, dark and dank, give a good idea of the hardships which face Venetian residents in their everyday life. In **Corte Nova** (*map p. 403, E4*), a typical old Venetian courtyard, with its well decorated with Gothic shields dating probably from the late 13th century and a café which retains its characteristic sign painted in red, there is a street chapel with an inscription recording that it was built to commemorate the local inhabitants' gratitude to the Madonna 'della Salute' for seeing them through a series of dangers, from the plagues in the 17th century to the air-raids in 1917–18. A passageway leads out to the *rio*, across which the *fondamenta* passes beneath a portico and brings you out on Fondamenta di San Giorgio degli Schiavoni.

CAMPO SANTA MARIA FORMOSA

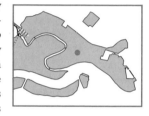

Campo Santa Maria Formosa (*map p. 402, C4*) is a lively place with a few market stalls, lying in an area abounding in canals. Behind the church, at the end of the *campo* bordered by a canal with four small bridges (mostly private), is the 16th-century Ca' Malipiero-Trevisan (no. 5250), attributed to Sante Lombardo. On the side opposite the church apse, Palazzo Vitturi (no. 5246) has Veneto-Byzantine decorations. Close by a plaque marks the lower house (no. 6129), which was the home of Sebastiano Venier, commander of the victorious fleet at the battle of Lepanto in 1571, and later doge. Palazzo Donà next door (no. 6125–26) has a pretty doorway and Gothic windows, and at the far end of the *campo*, the white marble Palazzo Priuli (now a hotel) is a classical work by Bartolomeo Monopola, dating from around 1580. The Renaissance well-head near the apse of the church bears a relief of the *Madonna della Misericordia*.

THE CHURCH OF SANTA MARIA FORMOSA
The name of the church (*open Mon–Sat 10–5; Chorus Pass; entrance at the north side door*) is derived from the tradition that the Madonna appeared to its founder, St Magnus (in the 7th century), in the form of a handsome (*formosa*) matron. It was rebuilt by Mauro Codussi in 1492 in an unusual Renaissance design, but only his dome can be seen from the exterior—the campanile and two façades were added later. The **main front at the west entrance**, dating from 1542, overlooks a canal and bears a statue on a sarcophagus which commemorates Vincenzo Cappello, Captain of the Venetian fleet, who had died the previous year (his place here is justified by the fact that the Cappello family had paid for the construction of the façade). Ruskin complained bitterly about the absence of religious elements, declaring that this façade marked the beginning of the period 'when Venetian churches were first built to the glory of man instead of the glory of God'. The other façade on the *campo* dates from 1604 and has three busts of other members of the family, and five 17th-century statues on the summit.

The Baroque campanile, designed by the parish priest Francesco Zucconi in 1678, has a grotesque mascaron at its foot. Local lore suggests the priest put it here to scare away the devil in case he tried to enter the bell-tower and ring the bells at the wrong time.

The interior
The exterior in no way prepares you for the symmetry of the beautiful interior, particularly pleasing since it is so full of light (it is lit by some 30 windows). The Greek-cross plan of the original church, derived from Byzantine models, was preserved by Codussi when he gave it this lovely Renaissance form in the 15th century. Its complex design, which involves a most original spatial concept (and in which, interestingly, you can feel somewhat disorientated), includes double open arches between the chapels, and domes over the bays in the aisles. It is the earliest purely Renaissance church in Venice, and set a model which was to be followed by other 15th-century architects who chose a centralised plan for their churches (Codussi repeated the design in San Giovanni Crisostomo). It was slightly altered when the roof had to be rebuilt after it was destroyed by a bomb in the First World War.

The church contains two very lovely altarpieces in marble frames, commissioned for their present positions. In the first south chapel is a charming **triptych by Bartolomeo Vivarini** of the *Madonna della Misericordia*, the *Meeting at the Golden Gate* and *Birth of the Virgin* (signed and dated 1473). The artist's characteristic use of bright colours (in particular red) can be seen here, and the scene of the meeting of the elderly St Anne and Joachim is especially touching. Bartolomeo was a pupil of his more famous brother Antonio, whose son Alvise was another important Venetian artist, and they were all at work in the city at the same time as the Bellini family. In the south transept is the Chapel of the Bombardieri, really no more than a recess, which in 1509 was granted to the Scuola dei Bombardieri (bombadiers or artillery-men), who had their meeting hall close to the church. It contains a celebrated **altarpiece by Palma Vecchio**. In 1522 the *bombardieri* were wealthy enough to commission the great Venetian artist to paint the composite work showing saints and a *Pietà*, notable especially for the colourful and majestic figure of their patron saint St Barbara, in the centre, typical of the Giorgionesque style of Venetian beauty. Like Vivarini, Palma also makes ample use of wonderful shades of maroon and red. The marble frame was added by Giuseppe Torretti in 1719.

PALAZZO QUERINI-STAMPALIA

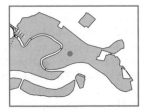

Map p. 402, C4. Open 10–6, closed Mon. Entrance in Campo Santa Maria Formosa near Ruga Giuffa.
The 16th-century Palazzo Querini-Stampalia is occupied by the Museo Querini-Stampalia and the Fondazione Scientifico Querini-Stampalia. The Querini were among the earliest settlers in Venice, and by the 13th century one of the city's five richest families. They acquired their second name, Stampalia, from the Greek

island of Astypalaia, where some members of the family chose to live after being exiled from Venice in the 14th century, for taking part in the Bajamonte Tiepolo conspiracy (*see p. 97*).

The collection of paintings was begun by the family in the 16th century, when they built the present palace, which was used from 1807–50 as the residence of the patriarchs of Venice. In 1869 Count Giovanni Querini bequeathed the palace and its art collection to the city.

GROUND FLOOR

In 1961–3 Carlo Scarpa reconstructed the ground floor of the palace. It is considered one of his most elegant and successful works and includes, at the former entrance, the wood and metal bridge across the *rio* from Campiello Querini. The atrium is also his, arranged on various levels and with water channels, as is a lecture hall and the little walled garden, in which water is again a prominent feature.

The rest of the ground floor was radically restored and reconstructed in the 1990s by Scarpa's pupil, the Swiss architect Mario Botta: his work included covering the medieval courtyard and installing a huge new staircase, interventions which permit one to forget, should one want to, that one is in a historic palace. The third floor was totally modernised for exhibitions and lectures with an auditorium, also designed by Botta, opened in 2009. The library has nearly 300,000 volumes and 1,300 manuscripts. It is well run and has long opening hours, so the palace is usually busy with students.

SECOND FLOOR: THE MUSEUM

The museum is displayed in the beautifully-kept period rooms on the *piano nobile*, once occupied by the Querini-Stampalia family.

The ***portego***, the characteristic large central hall, is decorated with stuccoes and frescoes by Jacopo and Vincenzo Guarana (1790), and has a colourful 19th-century Murano chandelier and seven 17th-century marble busts. A room off it displays three allegorical ceiling paintings by Sebastiano Ricci, removed from another room in the palace, and two allegorical paintings by Padovanino, between the windows.

In the room on the other side of the *portego* (on an easel designed by Scarpa) is the ***Presentation of Christ in the Temple***, a very fine work usually attributed to Giovanni Bellini (apparently a copy made c. 1469 of a painting by his brother-in-law Andrea Mantegna, now in Berlin). In the adjoining room are *Judith* by Vincenzo Catena, the *Coronation of the Virgin* by Catarino and Donato Veneziano (1372), and a *Sacra Conversazione* by Palma Vecchio. Palma's great-nephew Palma Giovane's homely self-portrait is displayed in the next room, together with other works by him. The lovely ceiling is by Guarana. Some 30 **genre scenes by Pietro Longhi** (one of the most interesting of which is *The Geography Lesson*) are displayed together in a room with 18th-century Venetian furniture and 16th- and 17th-century musical instruments. There is more good furniture in the next room, which is hung with portraits by Sebastiano Bombelli (1635–1719). The room with Pompeian-style furniture by Giuseppe Jappelli has two paintings by Matteo Stom and a clay model of Letizia Bonaparte (mother of Napoleon) made by Canova in 1804 for a statue now in Chatsworth. Nineteenth-century Sèvres porcelain and biscuit ware is charmingly displayed in the dining room, where the table is laid and there is also a sculpted head by Medardo Rosso.

In a room (and corridor) there is a selection of some of the 67 charming 18th-century **views of Venetian life by Gabriel Bella** which belong to the collection; the paintings provide a valuable document of the city at that period. A *studiolo* has three landscapes by Marco Ricci. The 18th-century bedroom has a tondo by Lorenzo di Credi, and in the Neoclassical boudoir there is an early portrait by Alessandro Longhi of Caterina Contarini-Querini.

The Red Drawing Room has a portrait of Andrea Querini by Bernardino Castelli, and the Green Drawing Room has four more large portraits of officials of the Republic, including (right of the door as you enter) Giambattista Tiepolo's splendid *Procurator Daniele IV Dolfin*. A room with 18th-century stuccoes by Giuseppe and Pietro Castelli contains the two masterpieces of the collection: a pair of **portraits by Palma Vecchio** of Francesco Querini and Paola Priuli-Querini, commissioned by the family to celebrate the couple's engagement, but not finished in time for their marriage in 1528 since the artist died in the same year. The couple are both dressed in black and rust-brown, and the unfinished state of the portrait of Paola is particularly interesting.

MUSEO DI PALAZZO GRIMANI

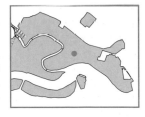

Map p. 103, D1. Entrance off Ruga Giuffa. Open 8.15–7.15, Mon 8.15–2, but subject to change; combined ticket available with the Gallerie dell'Accademia.

The opening to the public, after years of restoration, of this splendid huge palace has been one of the most important events in the city in the last few years. Both its architecture and its decorations are extremely interesting and unusual.

The monumental 16th-century land entrance off Ruga Giuffa, which may have been designed by Michele Sanmicheli, is surmounted by an aedicule, probably added in the 17th century to display three Classical Roman busts. The palace's 16th-century classical façade, with its water-gate in the same style as the land-entrance, is on Rio di San Severo: it can be seen by taking the next *calle* left (Calle di Mezzo) off Ruga Giuffa, and crossing a bridge to Fondamenta di San Severo. Since the palace was built to accommodate two families, it has an asymmetrical design (and another water-gate on Rio Santa Maria Formosa).

HISTORY OF THE BUILDING

The palace was begun around 1530 by Cardinal Domenico Grimani, son of Antonio (who was Doge from 1521–3), and work was continued in the 1560s and 1570s to enlarge the palace by Antonio's grandson Giovanni, Patriarch of Aquileia. It was once attributed to Michele Sanmicheli but more recently scholars have suggested that Jacopo Sansovino may have been involved, collaborating directly with Giovanni Grimani, who seems to have taken a great interest in the building work (using some of the land of its orchard for a new left wing) after he became the sole owner in 1558. It remained in the Grimani family up until the 19th century and became the property of the state in 1981.

THE GRIMANI FAMILY COLLECTIONS

Cardinal Domenico Grimani amassed a famous collection of Classical sculptures, part of which he donated to the Republic in 1523. The rest was kept in this palace until 1587, when some 200 pieces were arranged as a public gallery in the vestibule of the Libreria Marciana (this has been partly reconstructed; *see p. 80*). At the death of his grandson Giovanni in 1593, these Greek and Roman works were donated to the Republic and they formed one of the first museums of Classical antiquities in all Europe (they are still on public view, constituting the core of the collection of the Museo Archeologico; *see p. 79*). Domenico was an important collector in other fields, too: he purchased works by Hieronymus Bosch (on display here), Memling and Dürer; drawings by Leonardo; paintings by Raphael, Giorgione and Titian; and a breviary with 831 pages illuminated by Flemish artists in around 1500 (now known as the Grimani Breviary, and one of the most precious possessions of the Libreria Marciana). At the death of the last descendant of the family in 1865, all the works of art which remained in the palace were sold and dispersed.

TOUR OF THE PALACE

The very pleasing rectangular courtyard, with porticoes beneath an architrave, seems to have been modelled on the peristyle of an ancient Roman house. The monumental staircase, the grandest in a private palace in all Venice, has a barrel vault decorated with splendid white and gold stuccoes and painted grotesques by Federico Zuccari. Some of these are modelled on antique gems which formed part of the Grimani collections.

First floor

The rooms on the *piano nobile* which belonged to Giovanni Grimani were decorated for him with frescoes and stuccoes by Giovanni da Udine, Camillo Mantovano and Francesco Salviati. The ***portego* (A)** at the top of the stairs is more soberly decorated with stucco festoons between pilasters carved with leaves.

At one end opens the **Cameron d'Oro (B)**, where there are now plaster casts of some important Classical sculptures, recalling the marbles once exhibited here by the Grimani. The **Sala a Fogliami (C)** has a delightful ceiling covered with the thick foliage and branches of trees interspersed with fruits and birds, by Camillo Mantovano. Amongst the numerous plants the painter included maize and tobacco, recently arrived from north America. The fighting birds are said to be an allusion to Giovanni Grimani's tussles with the Inquisition on the subject of heresy (*see p. 267*). The two bronze busts displayed here of Hadrian and his wife Sabina (as Ceres) were made in the 16th century by Ludovico Lombardo, an artist from Ferrara.

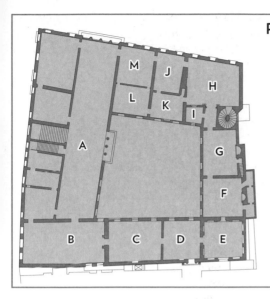

PALAZZO GRIMANI
(PIANO NOBILE)

A Portego
B Cameron d'Oro
C Sala a Fogliami
D Vestibule
E Tribuna
F Stanza da Letto
G Sala da Pranzo
H Sala di Doge Antonio
I Chapel
J Camerino di Apollo
K Camerino di Callisto
L Stanza di Psyche
M Bosch Room

Beyond a vestibule is the splendid **Tribuna (E)** designed by Giovanni Grimani to display some 130 masterpieces of the Classical statuary collection: it is very well lit from the ceiling and there are niches and shelves around the walls. It is now empty save for the *Ganymede and Eagle* (a second century Roman copy of a Hellenistic original), which has been returned from the Museo Archeologico and now again hangs from the centre of the ceiling as it did in the days of the Grimani.

The decorations of the **Stanza da Letto (F)** were added for the wedding of Giovanni Carlo Grimani and Virginia Chigi Albani, who came from a Roman patrician family, in 1791. On the ceiling is a copy of the famous ancient Roman fresco of a marriage scene which used to belong to the Aldobrandini (and is now in the Vatican Museums). At present the fresco of the female nude by Giorgione detached from the Fondaco dei Tedeschi (formerly exhibited in the Ca' d'Oro) is displayed here.

The delightful ceiling of the **Sala da Pranzo (G)** was also painted by Camillo Mantovano with fish and birds; in the centre is a painting of *St John the Baptist* by the 17th-century Venetian school. The tiled fireplace and marble floor here are also interesting.

The **Sala di Doge Antonio (H)**, and the little vestibule and **chapel (I)** adjoining, are all three decorated with exotic rare marbles in stucco frames. In a display case are terracotta statuettes by Camillo Rusconi and small bronzes including *St John the Baptist* by Jacopo Sansovino and *Mars* by Tiziano Aspetti. By the unusual fireplace is a bronze bust of Doge Antonio Grimani attributed to Andrea Briosco ('Il Riccio'). These rooms were used by the doge's descendant, the distinguished churchman Giovanni Grimani, who was buried in San Francesco della Vigna after he had paid for the façade of the church to be added by Palladio (*see p. 263*). Opposite the chapel, whose ceiling

PALAZZO GRIMANI
Detail of the stucco ceiling of the Camerino di Apollo.

bears an inscribed roundel with the motto 'Thou hast protected me, O Lord, in thy tabernacle, from the strife of tongues', you can see a little spiral staircase here derived from Palladian designs.

The ceilings of the **Camerino di Apollo (J)** and **Camerino di Callisto (K)** were decorated in the 1530s by Francesco Salviati, Giovanni da Udine and Lambert Sustris in stuccowork and fresco. A Classical marble head is displayed in the former, and two 16th-century paintings by Lo Schiavone in the latter. In the **Stanza di Psyche (L)** there is a large octagon hanging on the wall painted by Salviati, and on the window wall there are fragments of a charming painted frieze with birds and fish painted by Camillo Capelli (Mantovano), perhaps on a design by Giovanni da Udine. In the adjoining room, named after the famous painter **Hieronymus Bosch (M)**, there are four extraordinary panels painted by him around 1503 representing the *Fall of the Damned*, *Hell*, the *Ascension to Heaven* and *Paradise*. They formerly flanked a *Last Judgement*, but this was subsequently lost. The paintings were probably acquired in Antwerp in Bosch's lifetime by Cardinal Domenico Grimani, since they were already documented in his collection by 1521.

The last room, on the other side of the *portego*, frescoed in the 1560s, has a monumental fireplace, one of several very unusual chimneypieces in the palace. Other floors of the palace are used for exhibitions, and, at present, offices.

On the Fondamenta di San Severo (overlooked by the façade of Palazzo Grimani) are two Zorzi palaces: the Gothic **Palazzo Zorzi-Bon**, with two water-gates, and **Palazzo Zorzi**, by Mauro Codussi (c. 1480), with a beautiful façade on the water and three water-gates. The palace has been restored as the seat of BRESCE, the UNESCO Regional Bureau for Science and Culture in Europe, and the lovely courtyard can sometimes be visited on request. A bridge crosses the canal beside the palace, which has an entrance on the *salizzada* beneath a long balcony. The tiny Campiello del Tagliapietra has a fine Gothic well-head in good condition.

SAN LIO & SANTA MARIA DELLA FAVA

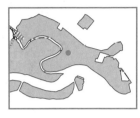

Fondamenta dei Preti leaves Campo Santa Maria Formosa by the west façade of the church (*map p. 402, C4*) and runs right along the canal across a bridge (note on the right the Roman tabernacle with a Latin inscription, set into the corner of a house) to the short Fondamenta del Dose, where at no. 5878 is the **house where Vivaldi lived** in 1722–30 and wrote the *Four Seasons*. Ponte del Paradiso, a 17th-century bridge, was well reconstructed in 1901. Here the *calle* has a fine overhead arch, the **Arco del Paradiso**, with a relief (on both faces) of the *Madonna* and a donor and the coats of arms of the Foscari and Mocenigo families. The *calle* preserves its wooden eaves for the whole of its length. The bridge, archway and *calle* were called 'Paradiso' because in former days they were at the centre of a district which would be illuminated by hundreds of lanterns every year on Good Friday.

SAN LIO

Map p. 402, C4. Open Mon–Fri 9–12; Sat 9–11.30 & 3.30–4.30.
The church is dedicated to Pope St Leo IX (1049–54), who was born in Alsace and is remembered for his reforms of the Roman curia: he is shown in glory surrounded by angels and the Cardinal Virtues in the ceiling painting by Gian Domenico Tiepolo. The beautiful domed Gussoni Chapel (right of the high altar) is thought to be an early work by Pietro Lombardo (possibly with the help of his son Tullio). It has exquisite sculptural details including a marble relief of the *Pietà* (with the extraordinary stylised body of Christ), decorative carving on all the pilasters, and four gilded tondi of the Evangelists in the ceiling. The unmarked tomb slab in the floor shows the purported resting place of Canaletto. Over the first north altar is a painting of *St James the Great* by Titian, one of his less known works, and next to it hangs a painted Byzantine *Madonna and Child*.

The organ (above the west door) bears paintings by the 18th-century Venetian school. High up at the end of the south wall (difficult to see) is a *Pietà*, attributed to Liberale da Verona, in an elaborate sculpted frame. On the left wall of the pretty sanctuary there is a large *Crucifixion* by Pietro Muttoni, which was an ex-voto for the plague of 1630. The silver high altar dates from the early 17th century, and the altarpiece of the *Deposition* above it is by Palma Giovane.

SANTA MARIA DELLA FAVA

Map p. 402, B4–C4. Open daily 8–11.30 & 4.30–7.30.
The church of Santa Maria della Fava (or Santa Maria della Consolazione) was begun in 1705 by Antonio Gaspari and completed by Giorgio Massari. In the interior, the

nave is decorated with statues in niches by Giuseppe Torretti, Canova's master, and the little high altar has exceptionally pretty marbles (the two angels on either side are by Morleiter). On the first altar on the south wall, Giambattista Tiepolo's *Education of the Virgin* is an early work (1732), and on the second altar on the north wall the very unusual painting in different tones of brown, the *Madonna Appearing to St Philip Neri*, is considered one of the best works by Giovanni Battista Piazzetta.

CAMPO DI SANTI GIOVANNI E PAOLO

Campo Santi Giovanni e Paolo (*map p. 402, C3*), although not spacious, is historically one of the most important *campi* in the city. Its simple houses, including a charming little old-fashioned café (Rosa Salva), are dominated by the flank of the Gothic brick church of the Dominican Order. Part of the original brick paving of the *campo* has been revealed close to the huge stained-glass window of the south transept. The exterior of the Gothic apse of

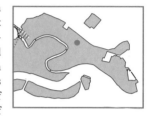

the church (seen from the *calle* behind) is particularly fine. The lovely 16th-century well-head is decorated with garlanded putti and is thought to be the work of a Tuscan sculptor. It was moved here from the courtyard of Palazzo Corner in 1823, when the well-shaft was sunk to provide water for public use. On a high pedestal, silhouetted against the sky, rises the superb bronze equestrian statue of the *condottiere* Colleoni by Verrocchio.

STATUE OF BARTOLOMEO COLLEONI

This splendid monument, a masterpiece of the Renaissance, was designed by the great Florentine sculptor Andrea Verrocchio. He made a full-scale model for it which he sent to Venice in 1481, but by the time of his death in 1488, the statue had still not been cast. In 1490 the casting was eventually entrusted to a Venetian, Alessandro Leopardi, who signed his name prominently on the horse's girth. Leopardi also designed the pedestal (later, in 1505, he was also commissioned to cast the three bronze pedestals for the flagstaffs in Piazza San Marco).

The horse, which owes much to Classical works including the Horses of St Mark's and the Marcus Aurelius monument in Rome, is particularly fine, and technically more advanced than the charger which supports Donatello's famous equestrian statue of another *condottiere*, Gattamelata, in Padua, since its front hoof is raised right off the ground, without the need for a support. The feeling of movement in the whole statue is further emphasised by the turn of the rider's body. Colleoni is portrayed as the embodiment of a great warrior, in an idealised portrait.

Colleoni (c. 1400–75), a native of Bergamo, was one of the most successful soldiers of fortune of his time. As a brilliant captain-general, he served both the Visconti and the Venetians at different periods, and he accumulated a huge personal fortune. When he died, he left a legacy to the Republic on condition that an equestrian monument be

SCUOLA GRANDE DI SAN MARCO
Stone lion by the Lombardo workshop.

erected in his honour in front of St Mark's. Since this would have been extremely out of place in Piazza San Marco (and against the Venetian constitution, which forbade the erection of monuments to individuals in the city's most important public space), after four years of discussion the *Signoria* decided they could interpret the will to mean the *campo* in front of the Scuola di San Marco instead. During the First World War the statue accompanied the Horses of St Mark's to Rome for safekeeping.

SCUOLA GRANDE DI SAN MARCO

The Scuola Grande di San Marco (*map p. 403, D3*), founded in 1261, was one of the six great philanthropic confraternities of the Republic. The *Scuola* moved to this site in 1437 and had to be rebuilt after a fire in 1485. The sumptuous façade was designed by Pietro Lombardo, assisted by Giovanni Buora (1489), but when half finished the brothers of the *Scuola* decided to engage Lombardo's chief rival, Mauro Codussi, to complete it (1495). It seems, however, that the Lombardo workshop continued to supply many of the sculptural elements to Codussi (including the statues of *St Mark*, *St John the Baptist*, and the angels and *Virtues* crowning the façade). The whole façade is an original work of great charm, where coloured marbles (the details of which were originally gilded) are used in a combination of styles. It is interesting to study the linear perspective of the reliefs in relation to the architecture of the building. When work was being carried out on the façade, the head of the *Scuola* was a rich jeweller named Domenico di Piero, who had a famous collection of superb gems; he is thought to have influenced the design.

The lower part has four panels with unusual false perspectives (as if they were windows) by the Lombardo. Guarding the doors are two lions in Istrian stone, boldly foreshortened; and two other reliefs, attributed to Pietro's son Tullio, illustrate scenes from the life of St Mark in Alexandria (healing the cobbler Anianus, and baptising him; *for the story, see p. 189*). It seems that the fictive architecture surrounding these reliefs may have been added later. The main portal by Giovanni Buora incorporates a relief by Bartolomeo Bon in the lunette, which survives from before the fire, depicting St Mark with the brethren of the *Scuola* (Bon also carved the statue of *Charity* above it).

The interior was first used as a hospital by the Austrians in 1809; since 1819 it has been occupied by the civic hospital of Venice, which extends all the way to the Fondamente Nuove on the lagoon (*for its chapel, San Lazzaro, see p. 286*). In typically Venetian good taste, and seemingly as a sign of respect for the magnificent architecture, there is no exterior indication that this is a busy hospital and the main door leads straight into the columned ground-floor hall of the *Scuola,* which has been remarkably well preserved (and is similar to those in the other main Venetian *scuole*).

THE VENETIAN *SCUOLE*

The *scuole* of Venice were lay confraternities dedicated to charitable works. Their members, elected mostly from the middle classes, attended to each other's needs and administered public charity throughout the city, as well as offering medical assistance and visiting prisoners. They were often associations of people in a particular trade or of a certain nationality. No priest or patrician could hold a position of responsibility in a *scuola*. The five most important, known as the *Scuole Grandi*, were those of San Marco, San Rocco, Santa Maria della Carità, the Misericordia and San Giovanni Evangelista (San Teodoro also became a *Scuola Grande* in the 16th century). There were probably as many as a hundred other *scuole* in the city. Many of them became rich through legacies and donations, and were an important source of patronage as they commissioned numerous works of art for their headquarters. The *scuole* held a particularly prestigious place in Venetian life from the 14th–16th centuries, and would take part in full regalia in all state ceremonies and celebrations.

THE CHURCH OF SANTI GIOVANNI E PAOLO

Map p. 403, D3. Open 9–6.30, Sun and holidays 12–6.30; small entrance fee.

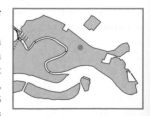

The church of Santi Giovanni e Paolo, shortened in Venetian dialect to 'San Zanipolo', is the largest in Venice. Founded by the Dominicans in 1234, the present building was begun around 1333, continued in 1373–85, and only consecrated in 1430. It is the burial place of 25 doges, and from the 15th century onwards the funerals of all doges were held here.

The façade was never finished; against it are the tombs of three doges including (second on the left) the donor of the site, Giacomo Tiepolo. The delicately carved main portal, attributed to Bartolomeo Bon (1460), incorporates six Greek marble columns from Torcello. It is flanked by Byzantine reliefs of the *Madonna* and *Angel Gabriel*. On the corner facing the *campo* is an interesting early relief of *Daniel in the Lion's Den*, of unknown provenance.

The vast light interior, suffused with a pink glow when the sun shines, is 101m long and 46m across the transepts. It has tall aisles separated from the nave by ten columns of Istrian stone blocks, slender arches and a beautiful luminous choir with a polygonal apse, lit by fine Gothic windows. The Baroque high altar, begun in 1619 (and attributed to Longhena) blends surprisingly well into the Gothic setting. Wooden tie-beams help to stabilise the structure of the building (an architectural feature of several Venetian churches). The organ was made in 1790 by Gaetano Callido.

Among the array of funerary monuments to doges and heroes of the Republic are some masterpieces of Renaissance sculpture by the Lombardo family, as well as earlier Gothic works.

(1) Monument to Doge Pietro Mocenigo: Pietro Lombardo's grand monument to this doge (d.1476) is undoubtedly his masterpiece. With the help of Tullio and Antonio, he here produced a superbly designed tomb which set a standard for later commemorative sculpture. Inside a triumphal arch flanked with niches containing statues of warriors, the doge, depicted as a general, stands in triumph on his sarcophagus, borne by three warriors representing the three ages of man. The sarcophagus has two reliefs of his most famous victories at Scutari, and Famagusta in Cyprus, and the inscription is a reminder that the monument was funded by war booty: *Ex hostium Manibus*—from the hands of my enemies. In the lower part are two reliefs, *Hercules and the Hydra* and *Hercules and the Nemean Lion*. The religious element is introduced only at the top of the monument with a relief of the *Marys at the Sepulchre*, and takes second place to the explicit intention to glorify the doge as a hero of the Republic.

THE LOMBARDO FAMILY OF SCULPTORS

Pietro Lombardo and his sons Tullio and Antonio carried out numerous sculptural commissions in Venice in the late 15th and early 16th centuries, when they were considered the most important sculptors at work here. Pietro, who was born in Lombardy and worked in Padua before coming to Venice around 1467, was of fundamental importance to the development of the Venetian Renaissance. His early work reveals the influence of Tuscan sculptors such as Antonio Rossellino and Desiderio da Settignano, but, with the help of his talented sons, he went on to produce works which are characterised by a clear Classicism even more pronounced than that of earlier Florentine masters of the Renaissance. In 1498 he succeeded Antonio Rizzo as *proto* of the Doge's Palace—a post he held until his death in 1515.

His son Tullio, who also carried out many commissions elsewhere in the Veneto, came to be considered the greatest marble sculptor of his time (his skills can be examined especially in his remarkable Classical double bust, preserved in the Ca' d'Oro). The younger son Antonio carried out important works in the Cappella Zen in St Mark's and in the Basilica of St Anthony in Padua. The family also worked together in Venice on the design and exquisite decoration of Santa Maria dei Miracoli, and in San Giobbe and the Frari. But it is here in Santi Giovanni e Paolo that their work can best be seen, in no fewer than five doges' tombs erected between 1467 and the end of the century: that of Pasquale Malipiero (d.1462), and those of Nicolò Marcello (elected 1473) and his four successors. Around the same time they were at work just outside the church on the lower façade of the Scuola Grande di San Marco.

(2) Monument to Doge Alvise Mocenigo: This enormous monument covers most of the west end of the church. It was begun by Giovanni Grapiglia, but not completed until the mid-17th century. It was under this doge (d. 1577) that Venice was victorious over the Ottomans at Lepanto.

(3) Monument to Doge Giovanni Mocenigo: This was the last monument to be designed for the church by Tullio

SANTI GIOVANNI E PAOLO

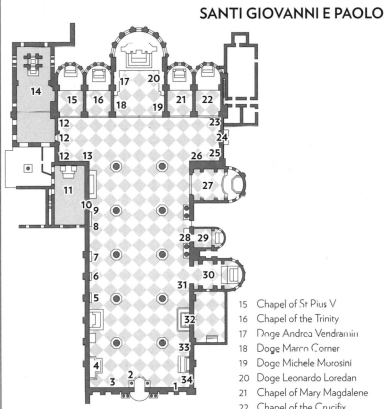

1   Doge Pietro Mocenigo
2   Doge Alvise Mocenigo
3   Doge Giovanni Mocenigo
4   *St Jerome*
5   Doge Nicolò Marcello
6   Doge Tommaso Mocenigo
7   Pompeo Giustiniani
8   Doge Michele Steno
9   Doge Pasquale Malipiero
10   Palma Giovane: *Allegory of Fame*
11   Sacristy
12   Venier tombs
13   Leonardo da Prato
14   Chapel of the Rosary

15   Chapel of St Pius V
16   Chapel of the Trinity
17   Doge Andrea Vendramin
18   Doge Marco Corner
19   Doge Michele Morosini
20   Doge Leonardo Loredan
21   Chapel of Mary Magdalene
22   Chapel of the Crucifix
23   *Christ between St Peter and St Andrew*
24   Stained-glass window
25   *The Charity of St Antoninus*
26   Nicolò Orsini
27   Chapel of St Dominic
28   Valier monument
29   Chapel of the Madonna della Pace
30   Chapel of the Scuola of the SS. Nome di Dio
31   Alvise Diedo
32   *St Vincent Ferrer*
33   Bragadin monument
34   Doge Ranier Zeno

Lombardo. The doge died in 1485. The very fine baptism reliefs (of Christ by St John, and of Anianus by St Mark) were clearly inspired by ancient Roman art.

(4) *St Jerome*: The signed statue on the altar here, of the hermit saint with his lion slumbering at his feet, is by Alessandro Vittoria.

(5) Monument to Doge Nicolò Marcello: Marcello reigned for just one year in 1474. His monument is a simple, well-proportioned work by Pietro Lombardo. The statues of the four Virtues are clearly based on ancient Roman originals.

(6) Tomb of Doge Tommaso Mocenigo: This sepulchre, in quite a different spirit from the Marcello monument by Pietro Lombardo, is in a transitional style between the Gothic and Renaissance by the Florentine sculptors who also worked on the façade of St Mark's, Pietro di Niccolò Lamberti and Giovanni di Martino da Fiesole. The doge, who died in 1423, lies beneath a 'fur-lined' canopy held back by two angels.

(7) Monument to Pompeo Giustiniani: This classical monument, with an equestrian statue in gilded wood, is to the *condottiere* known as '*Braccio di Ferro*' ('iron-arm'), a play on this simile for strength, but also because he had a prosthetic limb, having lost an arm in battle. He died in 1616.

(8) Tomb of Doge Michele Steno: Down on the level of the pavement, the doge (d. 1413) is portrayed in an alabaster effigy above his sarcophagus, which bears just two Crosses in quatrefoils. Ruskin considered this simple tomb the last to be fashioned in the pure Gothic style in Venice.

(9) Tomb of Doge Pasquale Malipiero: An early work by Pietro Lombardo, this is a masterpiece of delicate carving. The sarcophagus is protected by a baldacchino, and its design still shows the influence of Tuscan sculptors.

(10) Palma Giovane's *Allegory of Fame* is fitted around three busts (of the artist himself, of his great-uncle Palma Vecchio, and of Titian) above the sacristy entrance. Palma died in 1628; this is his monument.

(11) Sacristy: The 16th-century interior, with fine carved benches, has paintings by Alvise Vivarini (*Christ Carrying the Cross*; 1476) and Leandro Bassano (*Pope Honorius III Confirming the Rule of the Order of St Dominic*; 1606), and a ceiling painting by Marco Vecellio.

(12) Venier tombs: The two sumptuous Venier tombs, in the style of the Dalle Masegne brothers, are of Doge Antonio Venier (d. 1400) and his wife and daughter Agnese and Orsola. The bronze statue of Doge Sebastiano Venier (d. 1578), who commanded the fleet at Lepanto, is by Antonio dal Zotto (1907).

(13) Tomb of Leonardo da Prato: The tomb of this *condottiere* (d. 1511) bears a gilded wood equestrian statue attributed to Lorenzo Bregno or Antonio Minello.

(14) Chapel of the Rosary (*push-button*

light): This was erected at the end of the 16th century in memory of the Battle of Lepanto (fought on the feast day of the Madonna of the Rosary, 7th October), from the designs of Alessandro Vittoria. In 1867 it was gutted by fire. All its paintings were destroyed, including an important painting by Titian of *St Peter Martyr* (a copy of which, by Johann Carl Loth, can be seen on the second altar in the north aisle) and a *Madonna and Saints* by Giovanni Bellini, which had been placed here temporarily. The ceiling was redecorated with paintings by Paolo Veronese or his *bottega*, of the *Annunciation* (nearest the altar) *Assumption* (centre) and *Adoration of the Shepherds*, brought here from the ex-church of the Umiltà. In the choir is the *Adoration of the Magi*, certainly by the master's hand, and another autograph work is on the short wall opposite the altar: another *Adoration of the Shepherds*, in which the lamb and Christ Child seem blissfully unaware of the drama taking place around them. The wooden benches are finely carved by Giacomo Piazzetta (1698). In the choir is a splendid altar tabernacle in grey marbles with a gilded dome, attributed to Alessandro Vittoria or Girolamo Campagna; it encloses a terracotta *Madonna and Child* by Carlo Lorenzetti, which seems somewhat out of place here. On the walls are statues of prophets and sibyls, also by Alessandro Vittoria, and 18th-century marble reliefs.

(15) Chapel of St Pius V: On the right-hand wall is the hanging sarcophagus of Jacopo Cavalli, a captain of the Republic who had taken part (with Vettor Pisani; *see p. 336*) in the war against Genoa at Chioggia, when Venice came within an ace of destruction (the battle is depicted in the late 16th-century background). Cavalli died four years later, in 1384. His effigy, attributed to Paolo dalle Masegne, shows him in a suit of armour complete with helmet.

The hanging sarcophagus opposite commemorates Doge Giovanni Dolfin, who died of the plague in 1361, after a reign of only four years. His election had come while he was defending Treviso against the territorial ambitions of Louis the Great of Hungary. The request for his safe deliverance to Venice for his coronation was turned down by Louis, who instead boasted that he now held the doge captive. Dolfin nevertheless managed to escape, and was met in triumph by the Senate when he finally reached safety at the edge of the lagoon.

(16) Chapel of the Trinity: Here are a number of signed works by Leandro Bassano, including the altarpiece of the *Trinity*.

(17) Tomb of Doge Andrea Vendramin: A Renaissance masterpiece designed by Tullio Lombardo, with the help of his brother Antonio, and probably the most elaborate funerary monument in the city, complete with gilding. Similarly to the monument to Pietro Mocenigo (1), it takes the form of a Roman triumphal arch above the effigy of the doge, who died in 1478, surrounded by allegorical figures and warriors, all beautifully carved, some from Classical models, others in the late-Gothic style. The figure of Adam made for this tomb was sold to the Metropolitan Museum of New York in 1937. The monument was given pride of place here in the 19th century, when it was brought from the church of the Servi: the tomb of Giovanni Dolfin was moved at that time (*see 15*), but you can still see on the right of the monument faint traces of the frescoes by Guariento which used to surround it.

(18) Tomb of Doge Marco Corner: Ruskin found the tomb of this doge (d. 1368) much to his taste; it has a very beautiful central *Madonna*, signed by Nino Pisano.

(19) Tomb of Doge Michele Morosini: Ruskin felt that it was in the choir of Santi Giovanni e Paolo that one could see just how Venetian Gothic art deteriorated into a 'voluptuous and over-wrought' style which corrupted the simplicity of true Gothic. This monument, made less than 20 years after the previous tomb (the doge died in 1382), was for him a case in point and he complained about it bitterly, objecting to its elaborate tabernacle with statuettes in niches flanking the effigy of the doge as being too richly decorated and riddled with those 'Renaissance errors' that he was to spend much of his life denouncing. It has a mosaic *Crucifixion* probably by 15th-century Tuscan artists, and the carving is attributed to the Dalle Masegne workshop, run by the brothers Pier Paolo and Jacobello (and another Paolo, thought to be the son of Jacobello), who were very active in the city at the end of the 14th century.

(20) Tomb of Doge Leonardo Loredan: This in some ways bears out Ruskin's lament and illustrates how later Renaissance funerary sculpture became 'top heavy'. It is the work of the little-known artist Giovanni Grapiglia (who began the Mocenigo monument at the west end), but it incorporates good statues—that of the doge (in his *cornu* hat) signed by Girolamo Campagna, and allegorical figures by Danese Cattaneo. It commemorates one of the most important doges in the history of the Republic, an extremely able diplomat at a time when Venice had few allies (he died in 1521).

(21) Chapel of Mary Magdalene: The monument to Vettor Pisani is a modern reconstruction which incorporates the original framework and the statue. Pisani was the popular victor over the Genoese at the battle of Chioggia in 1380, decisive to the survival of the Republic. Also in this chapel is the sarcophagus of Marco Giustiniani della Bragora (d. 1346), and a plaque commemorating Marin Držić (d. 1567), the finest comic playwright of Ragusa (modern Dubrovnik), who died in Venice and is buried in the church.

(22) Chapel of the Crucifix: The effigy in armour on the 14th-century sarcophagus is thought to be Paolo Loredan, who took part in the conquest of Crete in 1365. Alessandro Vittoria made the two bronze statues for the *Crucifixion* group, and may also have designed the tomb of Edward, Duke of Windsor (d. 1574).

(23) *Christ between St Peter and St Andrew*: Painted in the early 16th century, this is one of the best works of Rocco Marconi.

(24) Stained-glass window: The beautiful glass in the great window was made in Murano in 1473 from cartoons by Bartolomeo Vivarini. Some of the panels are signed by Girolamo Mocetto, but it is also thought that the much better-known artist Cima da Conegliano was involved in the design.

(25) *The Charity of St Antoninus*: This extraordinary painting of Antonio Pieruzzi, a Dominican friar who became Archbishop of Florence, is one of the last works of Lorenzo Lotto (1542). It shows the saint enthroned receiving the counsel of two eccentric angels, which are flying rather dangerously close to him. The balcony is decorated with a lovely Turkish carpet (16th-century carpets of this type are known as 'Lotto carpets' since he depicted them in a number of his paintings). The saint's advisors are deeply involved in processing supplications from the poor people depicted at the bottom of the painting, some in attitudes of despair. We know that Lotto made studies of the poor in the city for this painting, and that he gave the Dominicans a discount on the price of the work in return for a place in the church cemetery (but sadly, he died in a monastery in Loreto, and his body was never returned here).

Lotto was one of the most idiosyncratic painters of the early 16th century. Not very successful during his lifetime, he was largely forgotten after his death until Bernard Berenson published a monograph on him in 1895. He worked in Treviso and Bergamo (where many of his paintings are now preserved) and then in Venice, where he also produced another important altarpiece for the church of the Carmini. One of his most striking portraits is in the Gallerie dell'Accademia.

(26) Equestrian monument to Nicolò Orsini: By Antonio Minello (formerly attributed to Lorenzo Bregno). Orsini died in 1509.

(27) Chapel of St Dominic: The six large bronze reliefs (1716–35) are by the Bolognese sculptor Giuseppe Mazza. The fine ceiling painting of *St Dominic in Glory* is by Giovanni Battista Piazzetta (1727).

(28) Valier monument: This splendid theatrical Baroque work, designed by Andrea Tirali (1708), records Bertucci Valier (doge in 1656) and his son Silvestro (doge in 1694). A few years later, Tirali designed the pavement which still survives in Piazza San Marco. In front of a huge yellow marble drape stand the figures of Bertucci flanked by his wife, Elisabetta Querini-Stampalia (the last doge's wife to be crowned as *dogaressa*), and Silvestro, by Giovanni Bonazza. Four colossal dark marble columns and more statues and reliefs complete the elaborate decorations. Ruskin must have been horrified.

(29) Chapel of the Madonna della Pace: The Byzantine *Madonna* here was brought to Venice in 1349, and (on the right wall) there is a *Flagellation* by Aliense.

(30) Chapel of the Scuola del Santissimo Nome di Dio: This was given its Baroque decoration, with a richly-ornamented ceiling, by Giambattista Lorenzetti around 1640. The altarpiece of *Mary Magdalene and St Louis of Toulouse at the foot of the Cross*, by Pietro Liberi, was painted some ten years later.

(31) Tomb of Alvise Diedo: This pavement tomb is a masterpiece of *niello* work (black inlay using silver, lead and copper) by the hand of Pietro Lombardo (Diedo died in 1466).

(32) Polyptych of St Vincent Ferrer (*push-button light on the left*): This is the most beautiful painting in the church, with a *Pietà* and *Annunciation* above. It is usually attributed, as a very early work, to Giovanni Bellini, with the possible help of assistants. The figure of St Christopher crossing a river is particularly remarkable. The predella appears to be by another hand. The superb gilded frame dates from c. 1523.

(33) Bragadin monument: Marcantonio Bragadin (d. 1571), the defender of Famagusta, flayed alive by the Turks, is recorded here with a bust above an urn.

(34) Tomb of Doge Ranier Zeno: This is the earliest doge's tomb in the church: Zeno died in 1268. It is without an inscription and is simply adorned with a Veneto-Byzantine relief of *Christ Enthroned in Glory* held aloft by two flying angels.

SAN LAZZARO DEI MENDICANTI & THE OSPEDALETTO

SAN LAZZARO DEI MENDICANTI
Map p. 403, D2. Open 8–12, but often in use for funerals.
Reached from the Fondamenta dei Mendicanti, this church was built by Vincenzo Scamozzi (1601–31), and is now used as the hospital chapel. The Ospedale of San Lazzaro dei Mendicanti was one of the four most important hospitals in Venice, transferred here from the island of San Lazzaro in 1595. It had been founded during the Crusades to help care for lepers, and later looked after 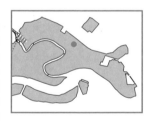 the city's destitute. Attached to the Mendicanti was an orphanage for girls. The church façade was completed by Giuseppe Sardi in 1673 (to a design by his father Antonio). Between the vestibule and the interior is the huge funerary monument in sumptuous marble of the procurator and admiral of the fleet Tommaso Alvise Mocenigo (d. 1654), also by Sardi, but carried out nearly 20 years earlier than the façade. It is one of the best Baroque monuments in Venice. On the side facing the church it has two Classical statues signed by Juste le Court, and reliefs of fortresses and battle scenes. Some of the sculptures here are attributed to an English artist named John Bushnell. This type of decoration was repeated by Sardi some 20 years later for another admiral (Antonio Barbaro), who commissioned him to erect a similar monument to commemorate his exploits on the façade of the church of Santa Maria del Giglio. Antonio and Giuseppe Sardi were also at work at this time at the Ospedaletto (*see below*).

The interesting architecture of the interior includes two singing galleries for the girls from the orphanage, where music was taught and performed. Venetian society would frequently come here to attend recitals when Baldassare Galuppi was choir-master (1740–51). The organ is by Callido (1772). The paintings include a delightful early work, *St Ursula and the Eleven Thousand Virgins* (*for the story, see p. 144*) by Jacopo Tintoretto, and a *Crucifixion with the Madonna and St John* by Paolo Veronese. On either side of the vestibule, the two large cloisters of the hospital of San Lazzaro can be seen, both planted with trees and also designed by Scamozzi.

MUSIC AT THE HOSPITALS OF VENICE

There were four main hospitals in Venice (the Ospedaletto, the Incurabili, the Mendicanti and the Pietà) where music was taught and performed. These institutions attained a remarkably high reputation in the 18th century, overshadowing even the music school of St Mark's. The Pietà had already achieved European fame for its music by the 17th century, through the choral and orchestral performances given by the orphans: the gifted *figlie di coro* were famed far beyond their cloisters, Vivaldi himself taught there, and sometimes even chose the instruments for his pupils. The hospitals were unique in that they were the only places in Italy where women were allowed to sing in church (although they were concealed behind grilles), and where they were even allowed to play instruments normally considered unsuitable for them (such as the oboe, bassoon, trumpet and horn). Some of the girls went on to become directors of the orchestra. In fact, the musical opportunities offered to orphan girls of talent often provided the greatest solace of their lives, as those who did not find husbands were often confined to the institution for the rest of their days. In his *Confessions*, published in 1782, Rousseau gives an account of the music that he heard:

'A kind of music far superior, in my opinion, to that of operas, and which in all Italy has not its equal, nor perhaps in the whole world, is that of the scuole....Amongst talents cultivated in these young girls, music is in the first rank. Every Sunday at the church of each of the four scuole, during vespers, motettos or anthems with full choruses, accompanied by a great orchestra, and composed and directed by the best masters in Italy, are sung in the galleries by girls only; not one of whom is more than twenty years of age. I have not an idea of anything so voluptuous and affecting as this music; the richness of the art, the exquisite taste of the vocal part, the excellence of the voices, the justness of the execution, everything in these delightful concerts concurs to produce an impression which certainly is not the mode, but from which I am of opinion no heart is secure...What vexed me was the iron grate, which suffered nothing to escape but sounds, and concealed from me the angels of which they were worthy. I talked of nothing else. One day I spoke of it at Le Blond's: "If you are so desirous," said he, "to see those little girls, it will be an easy matter to satisfy your wishes. I am one of the administrators of the house, I will give you a collation with them." I did not let him rest until he had fulfilled his promise. On entering the saloon, which contained these beauties I so much sighed to see, I felt a trembling of love which I had never before experienced. M. le Blond presented to me, one after the other, these celebrated female singers, of whom the names and voices were all with which I was acquainted. Come, Sophia,—she was horrid. Come, Cattina,—she had but one eye. Come, Bettina,—the small-pox had entirely disfigured her. Scarcely one of them was without some striking defect...I was almost in despair.*

> During the collation we endeavoured to excite them, and they soon became enlivened; ugliness does not exclude the graces, and I found they possessed them. I said to myself, they cannot sing in this manner without intelligence and sensibility, they must have both; in fine, my manner of seeing them changed to such a degree that I left the house almost in love with each of these ugly faces.'

OSPEDALETTO

Map p. 403, D3. Usually open Thur, Fri, Sat; April–Sept 4–7, Oct–March 3–6.
Beyond the south side of Santi Giovanni e Paolo the *salizzada* continues to the church of the Ospedaletto, otherwise known as Santa Maria dei Derelitti, with an extremely elaborate façade by the great architect Baldassare Longhena (1674).

The church and Sala della Musica were part of the Ospedaletto, one of the four great Venetian hospitals. Founded in 1528, it included a hospice and orphanage, and is still an old people's home. The Palladian **interior of the church** (1575) contains a very fine organ by Pietro Nacchini (1751) above Palladio's high altar flanked by the *Birth of the Virgin*, the *Visitation* and small paintings of the *Annunciation*, attributed to Antonio Molinari. The fine painted 18th-century spandrels high up along the walls include (between the second and third south altars) a *Sacrifice of Isaac* by Giambattista Tiepolo. The two apostles in the spandrels above the first north altar are also now attributed to Tiepolo, as his earliest known works (1715–16). The first altarpiece on the south side is by Johann Carl Loth.

The **Sala della Musica** is only open by previous appointment (*T: 041 271 9012, www.scalabovolo.org*). It is reached by a beautiful spiral oval staircase by Antonio and Giuseppe Sardi. The elegant little oval music room, with four doors and a pretty pavement in the Venetian style, was designed by Matteo Lucchesi in 1777. The girls' orphanage here had a very high musical reputation, particularly in the 18th century, when its last director was Domenico Cimarosa (1749–1801). The children sang behind the three screens (those at the far end are *trompe l'oeil*). The charming frescoes are by Jacopo Guarana, with *quadratura* by Agostino Mengozzi-Colonna. On the end wall the depiction of *Apollo and the Muses* includes portraits of some of the girls of the Ospedaletto with their master of music at a concert; the *Triumph of Music* is painted on the ceiling. It is sometimes possible to visit the charming gallery above, where the children sang. Concerts are still given here and in the church. The courtyard below was also designed by Longhena.

THE ARSENALE

Map pp. 404–405.
The vast Arsenale, the great shipyard constructed for the Venetian Republic's fleet, occupies a significant proportion of the entire area of the city, and was until the end of the 20th century used by the Italian Navy. Crenellated walls fortified by towers enclose huge monumental

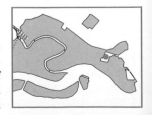

buildings, some of which are attributed to Jacopo Sansovino. The Corderia della Tana, where ropes were made, and the Artiglierie, where munitions were stored, now provide magnificent exhibition space during the Biennale art and architecture shows (*see p. 293*). The huge long warehouse of the former was rebuilt in 1583 by Antonio da Ponte. Another part of the Arsenale is used by the Istituto di Studi Militari Marittima, a centre for strategic naval studies. In the northern zone, a consortium for marine technology, research and development (called 'Thetis') operates, and some of the dry docks and wharves are used by Venice's water transport company (ACTV). There is also an operations room which monitors the tides.

An annual boat show (the *Salone Nautico*) is held in the Arsenale, and the Italian navy always opens their area to the public on 4th November. A huge hydraulic crane built in Newcastle-upon-Tyne in 1886 by William Armstrong and Charles Mitchell, and used by the Italian navy until the 1950s, still survives on the edge of the main basin, and is to be restored—appropriately enough—with the help of the (British) Venice in Peril Fund. At the time of writing, it had been announced that over half of the area of the Arsenale is to be made over to the municipality.

HISTORY OF THE ARSENALE

The Arsenale was founded in 1104. It was enlarged between the 14th and 16th centuries, and now occupies 32 hectares (80 acres). It gave its name (from the Arabic *darsina'a*, meaning workshop) to subsequent dockyards all over the world. Here the Republic's ships were overhauled and repaired, and from the end of the 15th century onwards shipbuilding was also concentrated here (it had formerly taken place in the numerous *squeri* which existed all over the city). Specialised workers made ropes and armaments and everything necessary to equip the warships and merchant galleys before they set sail. The workers, known as *arsenalotti*, held a privileged position in Venetian society, as well as enjoying advantageous working conditions. At the height of Venetian prosperity they numbered some 16,000 (out of a population of some 130,000). They had the honour of carrying the doge in triumph in the procession immediately following his election. For centuries the Arsenale remained the symbol of the economic and military power of the Venetian Republic.

Dante visited the Arsenale in 1306, and again in 1321 when he was sent as emissary to Venice from Ravenna. He described it in the *Inferno* (Canto XXI).

THE APPROACH TO THE ARSENALE ALONG THE WATERFRONT

At the far end of Riva degli Schiavoni, by the Arsenale vaporetto stop, the *riva* passes the **Ca' di Dio**, a pilgrim hospital founded in the 13th century for Crusaders. In 1545 Jacopo Sansovino added a hospice wing along the *rio* (seen from the bridge, with numerous chimney-stacks). Beyond it are the **Forni Pubblici** (1473), with an ornamental marble frieze. These were the bakeries of the Republic, which supplied ships as they set sail. The monumental Ponte dell'Arsenale, built in 1936, crosses the Arsenale canal to Campo San Biagio (with the Museo Navale; *described on p. 291*). Here a *fondamenta* skirts the **Arsenale Canal**. The Neoclassical guard-house was built in 1829 by Giovanni Casoni during the Austrian occupation. In Campo della Tana is the entrance to the Corderie and Artiglierie, open during Biennale exhibitions. The six big windows on the canal belong to the 16th-century Officina Remi, where oars (*remi*) were made and timber stored. It is now part of the Museo Navale and huge ships are displayed in it. The three vast halls still have their wooden roofs of 1546; they were large enough for the meetings of the Great Council to be held here for a time after the fire in the Doge's Palace in 1577.

At the end of the *fondamenta* you can cross the wooden bridge, which retains the form of previous bridges here, which up until 1938 were all drawbridges. The view embraces the oldest part of the Arsenale, with the archway opened in 1964 in its walls as an outlet onto the Fondamente Nuove.

On the other side of the bridge is the **land entrance to the Arsenale**, beside two massive towers (reconstructed in 1686) which protect the entrance from the lagoon. The great gateway, in the form of a triumphal arch, is one of the earliest Renaissance works in the city. It was begun in 1460 reusing Greek marble columns with Veneto-Byzantine capitals, by an unknown architect. The statue of *St Justina* above it is by Girolamo Campagna. The inscription was added in 1571 after the victory of Lepanto, and the court with its railings in the late 17th century. Beyond the door is a *Madonna and Child* signed by Jacopo Sansovino.

> ## THE LIONS OF THE ARSENALE
>
> The four ancient Greek lions guarding the entrance to the Arsenale are one of the most memorable sights of Venice, and their presence here is indicative of the extraordinary prestige of the Venetian Republic. The two largest, of colossal dimensions, were shipped from Piraeus by Admiral Francesco Morosini as spoils of war after his conquest of the Peloponnese (1687), and placed here in 1692 after he had been elected doge. The one sitting upright on the left (which gave the name of *Porta Leone—Aslan Liman—*to Piraeus) bears a (worn) Runic inscription carved in 1040 by Varangian guards sent from Byzantium to Athens to put down an insurrection; its fellow possibly stood on the road from Athens to Eleusis. The two smaller lions, one of them also brought to Venice by Morosini and the other added in 1716 in celebration of the reconquest of Corfu, may have come originally from the Lion Terrace at Delos.

SAN MARTINO

Map p. 404, C1–C2. Usually open 8.45–11.45 & 4.30–7, Sun 8–12.

From the Arsenale gateway a short *fondamenta* leads along the side canal to the *campo* in front of the church of San Martino, founded by 932. The façade was remodelled in 1897. The interior was rebuilt in 1553 by Jacopo Sansovino on a Greek-cross plan. The ceiling has 17th-century *quadratura*, and *St Martin in Glory* by Jacopo Guarana. The very fine Nacchini organ was modified by Gaetano Callido in 1799. On the organ case is a *Last Supper* by Girolamo da Santacroce (1549), who also painted the *Risen Christ* in the chapel to the right of the chancel.

Around the south door is a huge monument in coloured marbles to Doge Francesco Erizzo, dating from 1633, with the seated doge flanked by reliefs of trophies, and with an *Allegory of Faith* in the vault above painted by Jacopo Guarana. The doge's sombre black tomb-slab in the centre of the church bears the stark inscription stating that beneath it are the doge's bones. In the chancel are 18th-century frescoes by Fabio Canal and two paintings by Palma Giovane. On the left of the north door is an altar by Lorenzo Bregno, supported by four charming kneeling angels by Tullio Lombardo—the curly locks flowing down to their shoulders are characteristic of his works. The Crucifix was probably made in the mid-14th century, and there is a popular tradition that it was attached to the mast of a ship which took part in the Battle of Lepanto.

In the sacristy (*entered off the sanctuary*), the frescoed vault (with *quadratura*) by Antonio Zanchi was only rediscovered in 1960 (having been whitewashed in the 19th century). Zanchi also painted the altarpiece here, and the cupboards may have been designed by Baldassare Longhena. A Byzantine icon of the *Madonna and Child* (in an inappropriate bright red frame), a small 15th-century *Annunciation*, a 17th-century alabaster statuette of the *Immacolata* (with a ship beneath her feet), and three paintings of angels and a *Deposition* by Palma Giovane are all kept here.

Outside, the little **oratory** next door has a 15th-century relief of *St Martin and the Beggar* and some *barbacani*—the decorative wooden beams which support a projecting upper storey—which were once a characteristic feature of Venetian buildings. The porch on the north side has two Corinthian columns.

MUSEO STORICO NAVALE

Map p. 404, C2. Open 8.45–1 or 1.30 except Sun; the admission fee goes to support an institute dedicated to sailors' children.

The Museo Storico Navale, or Maritime Museum, is housed in the former Granary of the Republic. The exhibits are well arranged on four floors and the labelling (in English) is extremely good.

GROUND FLOOR

In Room 3 there is monument by Antonio Canova commemorating Angelo Emo (1731–92), last admiral of the Venetian Republic (he is buried in the church of San Biagio next door). Other highlights include cannon, one cast by Cosimo Cenni in 1643; models of the Fortezza di Sant'Andrea on the island of Le Vignole, and a fine display of arms with late 16th-century arquebuses, 18th-century muskets and blunderbusses, two cannon donated by the British to Garibaldi, 19th-century rifles, and 18th–19th-century swords. Exhibits from the Second World War period include a torpedo, invented in 1935, which destroyed 16 ships, as well as an electro-mechanical gunfire computer and diving gear for underwater assault operations. There are numerous boat models, including the *Michelangelo*, the last large ocean-going liner to be built in Italy (1962).

FIRST FLOOR

At the top of the stairs is a wooden sculpture of two Turks in chains, from the galley sailed by Francesco Morosini in 1684. The rooms display nautical instruments and

17th-century charts, models of the Arsenale, and models of boats, including one of an ancient trireme; 16th-century Venetian galleys; elaborate 17th-century carvings from a Venetian galley; and 18th-century boats, including a vessel built in the Arsenale by order of Napoleon, which carried 80 cannon. In a separate room is a model of the last *bucintoro* (1728), the gala ship used for the ceremonial marriage of Venice with the sea.

SECOND AND THIRD FLOORS

The displays here illustrate naval history, including navigational instruments, warships and torpedoes, as well as uniforms. There is a model of the Turkish caique that was used until 1920 by the Italian ambassador in Istanbul to cross the Bosphorus. The final rooms have exhibits on fishing and there is also an exhibition devoted to gondolas (including the wooden shelter, or *felze*, used to protect passengers in bad weather).

The **Padiglione delle Navi** in the Officina Remi, entered from the Arsenal canal (*described above*), is not usually open. It houses a miscellany of boats and part of Marconi's wrecked *Elettra*, recovered from the sea near Trieste, which was used for his first radio experiments.

Next to the museum stands the ex-naval church of **San Biagio** (*sometimes open to visitors, although closed to worship*). On the site of a 10th-century church, it was reconstructed in the 18th century. On the north altar there is an icon of St Spiridon painted in 1818 by a Greek artist named Karousos. The tomb of Angelo Emo, the last Captain of the Fleet, who died in Malta in 1792, has a good effigy by Giovanni Ferrari. The window over the high altar by Piero Modolo was made in 2010.

SANT'ELENA

Map p. 415. Served by vaporetti 1, 4.1 and 5.1.
The church of Sant'Elena stands in a very remote part of the city. It was founded in the early 13th century by the Augustinians and rebuilt in 1435 when the Olivetan Benedictines moved here. They abandoned the church in 1807, but it was re-opened in 1928 and now belongs to the municipality and is run by three friars of the commu- 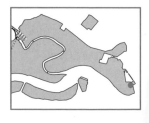 nity of the Servi di Maria. The dedication to St Helen dates from 112, when the relics of Constantine's mother were brought here from Constantinople. Over the doorway is a very beautiful and unusual sculptured group dating from around 1467 representing Admiral Vittorio Cappello kneeling before St Helen. The sculptor is unknown, but the work is usually attributed to Antonio Rizzo, or to Niccolò di Giovanni Fiorentino. The fine vaulted interior (*for admission, ring at the convent next door, which has a charming 15th-century cloister*) is typical of an abbey church, with a single nave and Gothic windows in the light chancel. The huge, unattractive triptych which serves as the high altarpiece was painted in 1958 and hides the Gothic apse. On the left wall is a *Marriage of St Catherine* signed by Bernardo da Brescia. The campanile dates from 1958.

The Canale di Sant'Elena ends on the waterfront near the landing-stage (Sant'Elena) of vaporetti nos 1, 4.2 and 5.2, which return to San Marco. The view encompasses many of the lagoon islands.

THE BIENNALE

The Biennale is Venice's famous biennial international contemporary art show, which has been held in odd years almost continuously since 1895. Since 1980 the Architecture Biennale has been held in even years. In the 1930s the art shows expanded their activities to include festivals of cinema, theatre, music (to which dance was added in 1999), and there are always numerous free collateral events throughout the city. In 2011 a record 89 countries were represented, including (for the first time) Saudi Arabia. 2013 saw the first participation of the Vatican City.

Today the Biennale is held in two venues only open when the shows are on (*from the summer to the autumn; combined entrance ticket*): in the Arsenale and the Giardini. They both have ticket offices. The entrance to the Arsenale exhibition halls is from Campo della Tana (*map p. 404, C2*), also reached off Via Garibaldi via Corte Nuova. The Giardini exhibition ground, reached from the Biennale (Giardini) No. 1 vaporetto stop, or approached from the Arsenale through the Giardini Garibaldi (*map p. 405, D3–E3*), is the original exhibition area and over the decades various nations built permanent pavilions here, clustered around the central Pavilion (formerly the Italian Pavilion, but since 2011 known simply as 'La Biennale'). The bookshop was built by James Stirling in 1991. The British pavilion, by Edwin Alfred Rickards, was one of the first to be built in the gardens (in 1909). The Hungarian pavilion is from the same year, with mosaics by the celebrated glass artist Miksa Róth showing Attila the Hun conquering Aquileia. The Swiss pavilion (1951) by Bruno Giacometti, brother of the sculptor, is next to the Venezuelan pavilion, by Carlo Scarpa (1954). The Netherlands pavilion is by the de Stijl architect Gerrit Rietveld (1954) and the Finnish pavilion is by the modernist Alvar Aalto (1956). The Australian pavilion was added by Philip Cox in 1988. The Austrian pavilion, in an enclosed addition to the park across Rio dei Giardini, is by Vienna Secessionist Josef Hoffmann (1934). In the last few decades exhibition space has been greatly increased with the adaptation of old industrial buildings in the Arsenale and on the Zattere, as well as interesting smaller spaces such as the cloister of San Gregorio in Dorsoduro and the Casa Tre Oci on the Giudecca, never before accessible to the public

A WALK THROUGH CASTELLO

This walk covers part of the extreme eastern end of the city, through a peaceful district where many Venetians still live. The solitary church of San Pietro di Castello, once the cathedral of Venice, preserves some interesting works of art.

ACROSS THE BRIDGE FROM RIVA SAN Biagio, the long, broad **Via Garibaldi** leads away from the waterfront. As the pavement shows, the street was created by filling in a canal. It was laid out by order of Napoleon in 1808. It is a lively street, with a miscellany of local shops and stalls, selling everything from clothes to food, and including (at no. 1311) the popular Bottegon, which boasts that it stocks over 20,000 household items—something very easy to believe once you penetrate its treasure-trove. The house at the beginning on the right (plaque) was the residence of the navigators John Cabot (1420–98) and his son Sebastian (1477–1537), who were the first to touch the American mainland and explore its coast, from Hudson's Bay to Florida.

Corte Nuova opens on the left, with two twin well-heads and with a view of the Arsenale buildings in the distance. The **church of San Francesco da Paola** (*usually open 8–12 & 4–7*) was founded in 1588 as a convent for the Minim Friars (the order founded by St Francesco da Paola) by the Neapolitan Carafa-Caracciolo family, since they were astonished to find no church dedicated to the patron saint of sailors when they visited the city. They commissioned the ceiling paintings from Giovanni Contarini, who included the family arms four times to commemorate its four most illustrious members. There is an interesting series of paintings around the top of the walls, added in the 18th century by leading artists including Gian Domenico Tiepolo (the second on the right, depicting the *Liberation of a Soul Possessed*). The church contains three paintings by Palma Giovane (the best of which is in the chapel to the right of the presbytery).

Opposite the church, at no. 1310, the Gothic portal of the **Ospedale de le Pute** survives, dating from c. 1375. It has sculptures of the *Redeemer*, and, below, *Sts Dominic, Andrew* and *Peter Martyr*, perhaps by a pupil of Filippo Calendario, who is thought also to have worked on the Doge's Palace. The hospice for girls was founded by Doge Marino Zorzi in 1311, and only the façade remains. It stood next to the church and convent of San Domenico, used after 1560 as a residence for officials of the Inquisition, but which was destroyed by Napoleon when he asked his favourite architect, Giovanni Antonio Selva, to lay out the public gardens here in 1808–12. They extend to the waterfront and adjoin the Biennale gardens. **Garibaldi's statue** by Augusto Benvenuti dates from 1885. The tepidarium glasshouse was restored in 2010 and there is a garden centre where plants are sold, and a pleasant café.

Via Garibaldi ends at the picturesque **Rio di Sant'Anna**, where a fruit and vegetable barge is moored. Number 1132 on the right is a Gothic house with

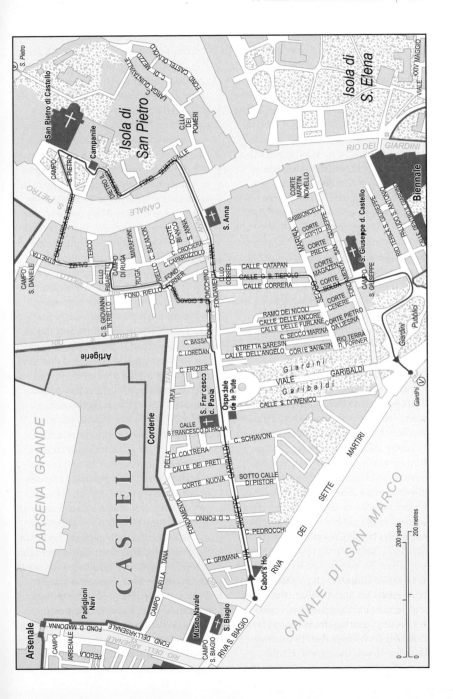

Byzantine roundels. The *fondamenta* on the left leads over a bridge to Calle San Gioacchino, which bears left at the end of the next bridge. As it turns the corner to the right, it passes (look up to the left) a mid-15th-century relief of the *Madonna and Child with Sts Peter and Paul,* and continues to the pretty **Rio Riello**, lined with the small houses that are typical of this area, with washing lines stretched across the canal.

Across the bridge, a *fondamenta* leads beneath a portico down the right side of the canal and, at the end, diverges right through **Campiello del Figaretto**, where there is a little votive chapel of 1842 (the wrought-iron doors were added in 1979). From here there is a good view of the white campanile of San Pietro di Castello.

From the adjoining Campo Ruga, with a 14th–15th-century well-head decorated with two amphorae, Salizzada Stretta leads left towards the Arsenale wall, and Calle Larga San Pietro diverges right for the fine wood and iron **bridge**, which leads over the wide Canale di San Pietro with its busy boatyards.

On the solitary Isola di San Pietro, formerly known as Olivolo, near the eastern limit of the city, the grass-grown Campo di San Pietro, with its line of plane trees and cluster of pretty houses, opens out before the church of **San Pietro di Castello** (*open Mon–Sat 10–5; Chorus Pass*). It was on this island that St Mark is said to have found shelter during a storm, and here it was that he had his dream, where the angel appeared to him and predicted that Venice would be his final resting place. Probably founded in the 7th century, this church was the cathedral of Venice from the 11th century until 1807, when St Mark's assumed the role.

The present church was built to a Palladian design of 1557 and the interior has Palladio's characteristic bright light. In the south aisle a venerable marble throne from Antioch is, incredibly enough, an Islamic work of the 13th century: the Arabic funerary stele is decorated with verses from the Koran. It may have been reworked when it came to Venice in the same century. The high altar, surmounted by rather too many statues, was designed by Longhena. On the right wall of the sanctuary is a large painting of *Doge Nicolò Contarini before the Blessed Lorenzo Giustinian during the Plague of 1630.* In the chapel to the left of the high altar is a dark wooden relief of the Crucifix with terminals in beaten copper (14th century). The Baroque Cappella Vendramin in the north aisle was designed by Longhena in the 1660s; it contains coloured marbles and reliefs by Michele Fabris Ongaro. The altarpiece of the *Madonna of the Carmelites* is by Luca Giordano. The Cappella Lando has some of the most interesting works in the church. Above the entrance is a painting by Veronese of *Sts John the Evangelist, Peter and Paul.* The altar-front is made from a pluteus which may date from the 9th century, and, in the pavement in front, there is an unusual Roman mosaic probably of the late 5th century: monochrome except for the delightful little dish of pomegranates in the centre. Above the altar is a mosaic (the pastel-coloured tesserae widely spaced) of a *Glory of Saints* by Arminio Zuccato (1580). Between two columns with lovely Veneto-Byzantine capitals (probably once part of the baptistery) is a striking half-figure of St Lorenzo Giustinian, made during his lifetime and attributed to Antonio Rizzo. His hooded eyes and beaky nose are instantly recognisable. Born in 1381, he retreated to the island of San Giorgio in Alga with a small group of followers at the age of 20 and in 1404 founded a congregation known as the '*Turchini*' from the blue colour of their habit. By all accounts he was a remarkable man who had a great influence on his contemporaries: in 1433 he became bishop of this church and in 1451, five years before his death, the first patriarch of Venice. He was canonised in 1690. On the west wall (above the side door) is the sarcophagus of the procurator Filippo Correr (d. 1417).

The isolated **campanile**, by Mauro Codussi, dates from 1482–8, crowned with an octagon (its dome was removed in 1670). This was the first bell-tower in the city to be faced with Istrian stone, and also served as a lighthouse. Its design appears to have taken its inspiration from the Pharos of Alexandria.

The **Calle dietro il Campaniel** (the '*calle* behind the campanile') soon rejoins Canale di San Pietro beside a fine (but damaged) Renaissance relief of the *Madonna and Child with St Peter*. Continue to a bridge, first built in 1910, which re-crosses the canal near several busy boat-repair yards. At its foot is the abandoned church of **Sant'Anna**, founded c. 1240 and rebuilt in the 17th century, next to a former naval hospital. Opposite, the canal is lined by a quaint row of old houses with typical chimney pots. Campiello Correr diverges left from Rio Sant'Anna to cross an area laid out with blocks of 19th-century tenement houses.

Beyond the more colourful Secco Marina, you can see the wall of the church of **San Giuseppe di Castello**

(*often closed*). The façade bears a relief of the *Adoration of the Magi* by Giulio del Moro. In the interior, the perspective ceiling dates from the 17th century. The huge monument to Doge Marino Grimani (d. 1605), was designed by Vincenzo Scamozzi, with two bronze reliefs by Girolamo Campagna. It is one of the grandest doge's tombs in the city, commissioned by the doge himself in 1601. His father, the procurator Giovanni Grimani (d. 1570), is commemorated in a monument in the sanctuary, which bears his portrait bust by Alessandro Vittoria. Over the high altar is an *Adoration of the Shepherds* by Veronese. The second north altar bears a curious relief of the Battle of Lepanto.

From Campo San Giuseppe, with its well-head of 1547 decorated with reliefs of Sts Anthony Abbbot, Augustine and Joseph, it is a short way through the public gardens out to the waterfront. Near the Biennale (Giardini) landing-stage, protected by four wooden piles in the water, is the **Monumento alla Partigiana** (1970), a moving monument to the women partisans of the Veneto killed in the Italian Resistance movement in the Second World War. Lying at the water's edge, her body lapped by the lagoon waters, is the bronze figure of a woman, her hands covering her face, her hair dishevelled. It is the best known work of Augusto Murer, an artist from Belluno (d. 1985). Originally, the sculpture was to have been on a floating pontoon, so it would rise and fall with the tide, but it was decided instead to place it firmly at the water's edge, to be covered by the water.

It is a short walk from here back to Giardini Garibaldi, where there is a pleasant café in the greenhouse.

SAN GIORGIO MAGGIORE

San Giorgio Maggiore

*This little island, lying across the water from Piazza San Marco, is famous
for its brilliant pink sunsets and for its church of San Giorgio, with paintings
by Tintoretto and a façade designed by Palladio.*

The small island of San Giorgio Maggiore, standing at the entrance to the city, across from the Bacino di San Marco and separated from the island of the Giudecca by a narrow channel, was given to the Benedictines in the 10th century and the convent became the most important in the lagoon. In 1951 the Giorgio Cini Foundation was established here.

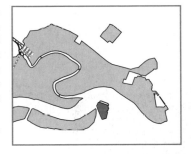

There are frequent *vaporetti* to the island (no. 2) from San Zaccaria or the Giudecca.

THE CHURCH OF SAN GIORGIO MAGGIORE

Map p. 404, A3. Open 9.30–dusk; Sun 9.30–10.40 & 12–dusk.

San Giorgio Maggiore is a masterpiece by Palladio, and one of the most conspicuous churches in Venice. The white façade, tall campanile, and brick main structure reflect the changing light of the lagoon, and are especially beautiful at sunset. The original church, dedicated to St George, was probably founded in the 10th century. In 1110 the body of St Stephen was brought to the church from Constantinople.

The present building was begun in 1565 by Palladio and is one of his most famous ecclesiastical works: it was completed after his death in the first years of the 17th century by Simone Sorella, who apparently finished the façade in 1610, almost certainly along the lines planned by Palladio. The front, with its four giant columns, is modelled on a temple portico, and was designed to produce its greatest effect when seen from a distance across the water (and this is the way it is, indeed, most often viewed). The campanile was rebuilt in 1791 and is similar to that of St Mark's. Everything else about the façade reflects Palladio's interest in mathematical proportion. The triangle formed by extrapolating (in imagination) the lateral cornices of the lower pediment reaches its apex at the base of the upper pediment.

WATERFRONT FAÇADE OF SAN GIORGIO MAGGIORE

INTERIOR OF SAN GIORGIO MAGGIORE

The church interior reveals Palladio's constant concern with illumination: the clean architectural lines are emphasised through painted stucco surfaces which cover the brick structures, and the use of numerous apertures for natural light. In the absence of superfluous decoration, this produces an effect of brilliant reflected whiteness. The numerous Classical columns are raised on pedestals, repeating the design of the façade. The cruciform ground plan has side aisles in the nave, but the transepts are unusually wide. Divided by the dome, lit by windows above its circular balcony, each ends in a semicircular exedra (the shape is well seen from the outside). The chancel is a separate rectangular space illuminated by its own natural light. The longitudinal plan of the building receives further emphasis by the exceptionally deep monks' choir, which is a detached feature at the extreme east end of the church.

The chancel is entered between two candelabra by Niccolò Roccatagliata (1598). The high altar, designed by Aliense, has a fine bronze group by Girolamo Campagna of the Saviour on a globe borne by the Evangelists, and two bronze angels by Pietro Boselli (1644). On the walls are two beautiful late works by Jacopo Tintoretto, painted in the final year of his life (1594). Even with the help of the coin-operated light they are unfortunately difficult to see in detail. The *Last Supper* (right wall) was the last of numerous paintings he produced of this subject, one which had fascinated him all his life. The row of disciples seems to take second place to the wonderful characteristic details of the food and the great variety of vessels, and the beautiful Venetian serving-girl kneeling in the foreground to unload a basket of sweetmeats for the banquet while a cat scrounges for a titbit. What is memorable above all is the disquieting presence of the ethereal spirits and angels which emerge from the dark background, perhaps harbingers of the death of this deeply religious painter. The *Shower of Manna* on the opposite wall is entirely different in atmosphere, seeming to portray a harmonious and joyous scene almost of domesticity. It is very different from Tintoretto's more dramatic rendering of the same subject on the ceiling of the Scuola di San Rocco.

In the monks' choir, the Baroque stalls and lectern are superb works made in the last decade of the 16th century by Albert van der Brulle and Gaspare Gatti, when the two small bronzes of *St George* and *St Stephen* on the balustrade were added by Niccolò Roccatagliata.

Other paintings in the church attributed to Tintoretto or his school include, on the north side: the *Resurrection*, with portraits of the Morosini family (left of the high altar), and the *Martyrdom of St Stephen* (north transept); and on the south side: the *Martyrdom of Sts Cosmas and Damian*, a well-composed painting (third south altar), and the *Coronation of the Virgin* (south transept). The church also contains painted altarpieces by Jacopo Bassano (*Adoration of the Shepherds*, on the first south altar) and Sebastiano Ricci, and a Venetian wooden Crucifix dating from around 1470.

On the west wall is a monument by Alessandro Vittoria to Doge Leonardo Donà (d. 1612), who was a friend of Galileo.

THE CAMPANILE

A corridor leads to the lift for the campanile (*open as the church*). The original angel which crowned the campanile until 1993 is displayed here: it was replaced with a bronze copy after it was damaged by lightning.

From the summit there is one of the best views in Venice. The long island of the Giudecca can be seen on the right. Ahead is the lagoon with the islands of La Grazia and San Clemente and, just to the right, Sacca Sessola. In the distance a tower marks the island of Spirito Santo. To the left is the spit of the Lido and Malamocco, with the island of San Lazzaro degli Armeni on the extreme left and Lazzaretto Vecchio nearer the Lido.

Looking east you can see the little port of this island, with the Lido straight ahead (and the island of San Lazzaro degli Armeni on the right). Beyond the Giardini is the brick tower of Sant'Elena and further left the white tower of San Pietro di Castello and part of the Arsenale. To the north there is a good view of St Mark's and the Doge's Palace. Straight across the water is the façade of the Pietà, with the tall campanile of San Francesco della Vigna and the end of the island of Murano visible behind. Farther left the huge church of Santi Giovanni e Paolo can be seen, with the campanile of the Gesuiti conspicuous to the left of that.

THE GIORGIO CINI FOUNDATION

Extremely interesting guided visits are offered at weekends on the hour from 10–5; otherwise by appointment (segreteria@civitatrevenezie.it). The important library of some 300,000 volumes is open to scholars: www.cini.it, T: 041 220 1215.

The island of San Giorgio Maggiore was given to the Benedictines in 982 by Giovanni Morosini. The monastery was rebuilt in 1223, and again in 1433 when Cosimo de' Medici was given hospitality here during his brief exile from Florence by his rivals, the Albizi family. At this time Cosimo's Florentine architect, Michelozzo, built the first library (damaged by fire and then replaced in the 17th century). In 1799, after the pope (Pius VI) had died in exile in France and the French had occupied Rome, Venice was chosen as the most suitable place to hold the next Conclave. The numerous cardinals were housed here in the monastery, and they took five long months in 1800 to elect Barnaba Chiaramonti, who became Pope Pius VII, aged only 58. His solemn coronation was held in the church of San Giorgio Maggiore.

There are still some six Benedictines who live in part of the monastery and officiate in the church. The rest of the monastery is now occupied by the Giorgio Cini Foundation.

THE GIORGIO CINI FOUNDATION

After many years' use as barracks, the monumental buildings of the monastery was restored in 1951–6 by Vittorio Cini (1884–1977), patron of the arts, collector, philanthropist and politician, as the Giorgio Cini Foundation, set up as a memorial to his son, who was killed in an air crash in 1949. The Foundation has become a prestigious research institute devoted to the study of the history of art (there is a library of some 800,000 photographs), history, literature, theatre, music and Oriental studies, and outstanding art exhibitions as well as conferences are held here. In the last decade or so, the buildings have been renovated and the Centro Internazionale di Studi della Civiltà Veneziana 'Vittore Branca' opened here. In 2012 Tiziano Terzani's library of Far Eastern works was donated to the Foundation.

The magnificent **first cloister** was designed by Palladio (1579). The **second cloister**, with its four cypresses, is by Giovanni Buora and his son Andrea (1516–40). Off it, and preceded by an anteroom with elaborate hand-basins, is the handsome **refectory**, another splendid space designed by Palladio (1560; now used as a conference hall). A remarkably good facsimile photographic reproduction of Veronese's *Marriage at Cana* has been installed on the end wall, from which it was removed by Napoleon (it now hangs in the Louvre), and at the same time the floor was remade in wood.

From the first cloister, a superb double staircase by Longhena (1643–5), very well lit, leads up to the **library** wing between the two cloisters designed by Baldassare Longhena, which contains 17th-century woodwork and ceiling paintings.

Closing the far wing of the second cloister, and extending for 128m behind the church, is the former dormitory corridor (56 monks' cells open off it, now used as offices) called the **Manica Lunga** ('Long Wing'), which was begun when Michelozzo was staying in the convent and was completed by Giovanni Buora (1494–1513). In

2009 it was turned into a magnificent second library space by the architect Michele De Lucchi, with shelving for some 100,000 books.

From here there is access to a roof terrace which overlooks a green **maze** in boxwood (with a handrail in braille), which was designed in memory of Jorge Luis Borges (who made his last visit to the Cini Foundation in 1984), inaugurated in 2011 and modelled on a similar garden designed by his friend Randoll Coate (1909–2005) in Argentina, inspired by Borges' short story *The Garden of Forking Paths*. Beyond are residences for visiting scholars and the 'Orti', which are used for performances and concerts.

THE PORT

The two Istrian-stone lighthouses were designed by Giuseppe Mezzani in 1810–11. Here you can see the pretty gabled façade (with a relief of *St George* by Giovanni Battista Bregno; 1508) of the Manica Lunga of the former monastery (*described above*). Beyond, a hall of the monastery was converted in 2012 into Le Stanze del Vetro, a study centre and exhibition space devoted to 20th-century Venetian glass.

GIUDECCA
View across the Giudecca Canal through the balustrade of Ponte Lungo.

The Giudecca

*The island of the Giudecca, mainly residential in character,
is known for the splendid Palladian church of the Redentore and
for the famous Hotel Cipriani.*

The island of the Giudecca lies across the wide Giudecca Canal, facing Dorsoduro. It was originally called Spinalunga, probably because of its elongated shape, but perhaps because thorn bushes used to grow here. Its present name could come from the fact that Jews (*Giudei*) established a colony here at the end of the 13th century, but it is more likely that it comes from *giudicato* (*zudecà*) or judgment, because in the 9th century allotments of land were conceded (by a judge) to families 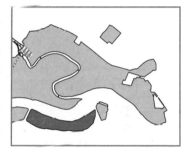 who were allowed to return to Venice from exile. Later on, grand villas and pleasure-gardens were built here by the aristocracy, and it is known that Michelangelo stayed here in 1529.

The Giudecca is home to many local families, and has an atmosphere all its own. Its most important building is Palladio's church of the Redentore, with a superb façade and bright white interior. The rest of the island is worth exploring, although some of the gardens, churches, and industrial buildings have now been abandoned. There are wonderful views from the *fondamenta* along the Giudecca Canal, always busy with boats, but the southern edge of the island is mostly inaccessible.

Boat services
The Giudecca has three landing-stages: Palanca, Redentore and Zitelle. Vaporetto no. 2 stops at all of these (from San Zaccaria via the island of San Giorgio Maggiore), or from the railway station, Piazzale Roma, Sacca Fisola and San Basilio and the Zattere in the other direction. Vaporetto 4.2 also serves the Giudecca from San Zaccaria, and vaporetto 4.1 from the railway station, Piazzale Roma, Santa Marta and Sacca Fisola (for full details, see pp. 348–9). At night, there is a ferry service to the Zattere (landing-stage near Santa Maria della Visitazione), and this is also usually guaranteed in fog, during acqua alta or vaporetto strikes.

THE REDENTORE

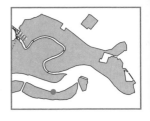

Map p. 402, C3. Open Mon–Sat 10–5; Chorus Pass.
The Franciscan church of the Redeemer (Redentore) is the most complete and perhaps the most successful of Palladio's churches (1577–92), finished by Antonio da Ponte after Palladio's death in 1580. The very fine exterior includes a handsome façade on the Giudecca Canal (carefully designed to have its maximum effect when approached across the water) and a lovely dome crowned by a statue of the Redeemer, and two little turreted spires. Its façade is a development of that of San Francesco della Vigna, which Palladio had designed some ten years earlier.

The church was built in thanksgiving for the deliverance of Venice from the plague in 1575–7 which left some 46,000 dead (25–30 percent of the population). The doge vowed to visit the church annually across a bridge of boats which united the Zattere with the Giudecca. The feast of the Redentore (third Sunday in July) remains one of the most popular Venetian festivals, and a pontoon bridge is still usually constructed for the occasion. There are now some 20 Franciscan friars in the monastery attached to the church.

ANDREA PALLADIO

The architect Andrea di Pietro della Gondola (1508–80)—by all accounts a pleasant, devout and modest man—was nicknamed Palladio, after Pallas Athene, the Greek goddess of wisdom. He was born in Padua and settled in Vicenza in 1523. His distinctive Classical style of architecture, with its harmonious proportions and bright illumination, was later imitated in domestic architecture all over the world, and he influenced both Vincenzo Scamozzi and Inigo Jones. His *Quattro Libri*, or *Four Books of Architecture*, became a manual for later architects, especially in England and the United States. In the engraved illustrations for this treatise, Palladio noted the significant dimensions of his buildings, linking together their plan, section and elevation in a series of proportional relationships. The seemingly easy elegance that distinguishes Palladio's designs was, in fact, the result of these careful calculations. In applying these systems of numerical progression, which were often associated with contemporary musical harmonic theory, to the spatial relationships of a building, Palladio succeeded in creating the pleasing visual harmonies that characterise his architecture.

After designing numerous country villas in the Veneto (on which he collaborated with Scamozzi) and rebuilding Vicenza, he planned the two conspicuous churches of San Giorgio Maggiore and the Redentore in Venice towards the end of his life. He also built the delightful suburban Villa Malcontenta on the Brenta Canal, just before it enters the Venetian lagoon.

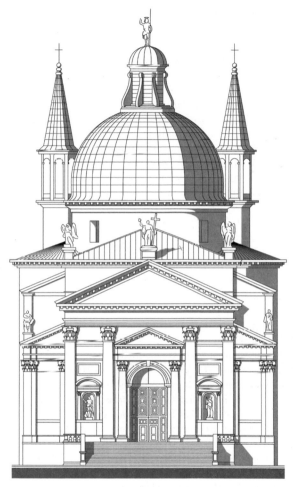

WATERFRONT FAÇADE OF THE REDENTORE

INTERIOR OF THE REDENTORE

The wonderful interior is characteristic of Palladio's churches, always brightly lit by natural light. Its superb, clean architectural lines include elements derived from ancient Roman buildings, notably the Diocletian windows in each side chapel, above the cornice of the nave, and in the apse. The huge, centrally-planned chancel (designed specifically to provide ample room for the clergy who would attend the sumptuous church ceremonies held here) is separated from the nave by a high archway, and from the monks' choir beyond by a lovely semicircular screen of columns. Each area of the church receives its own particular illumination. The dome is especially beautiful.

On the Baroque high altar (by Giuseppe Mazza) are fine (but very un-Palladian) bronzes by Campagna of the Crucifix, St Francis and St Mark, with the *Risen Christ* placed high up in the dome. The altarpieces in the church are by painters from Venice and the Veneto, including Francesco Bassano (*Nativity* and *Resurrection*) and Palma Giovane (*Deposition*).

In the charming little Sacristy (*opened on request; entrance from the south side of the church*), with a ticking clock and lined with wooden cupboards, is a *Madonna* by Alvise Vivarini, dressed in red and accompanied by two angel musicians, in a gold frame surrounded by reliquaries. Under glass domes is a series of realistic wax heads (19th century): they were all made from one mould, but the features, including glass eyes made in Murano, were altered to create supposed portraits of Franciscan Capuchin saints of the 16th and 17th centuries. The other interesting paintings here are on the entrance wall (all labelled), including a *Baptism of Christ* by Veronese, and Madonnas by Rocco Marconi and Lazzaro Bastiani.

THE ZITELLE & EASTERN GIUDECCA

THE ZITELLE

Map p. 413, F2. Only open at 11am on Sun for a service.
Near the eastern point of the island, on the Giudecca Canal, is the church of Le Zitelle. It was designed c. 1570 by Palladio but built after his death in 1582–6. The interior follows the typical Palladian formula, brightly lit with a dome and on a central plan. The high altarpiece of the *Presentation of the Virgin in the Temple* is by Francesco Bassano. On the left altar is a *Madonna* by Aliense, and

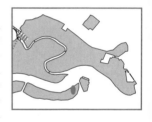

on the right altar, *Prayer in the Garden* by Palma Giovane. Around the upper part of the walls are mid-17th-century paintings. The statue of the *Madonna and Child* is by Giovanni Maria Morleiter.

THE EASTERN TIP OF THE ISLAND

Two wings of a **hospice** (part of it now the Bauer Palladio hotel) stand next to the Zitelle church. It was originally founded in 1561 for young girls, who were taught the art of lace-making. Next to the convent, the **Antichi Granai**, the old grain warehouses (*map p. 413, F2*), have been restored as exhibition space. To the left, the peaceful *fondamenta* continues up to the land entrance of the famous **Hotel Cipriani**, perhaps the most exclusive and invisible of Venice's luxury hotels, usually approached by water (its restaurant, 'Cip's', is on the waterfront here). The *fondamenta* ends by two pine trees at the headquarters of the customs police, whose grey launches are usually moored here.

To the right of the Zitelle is the very pretty neo-Gothic **Casa Tre Oci** (or Casa di Maria) with three large windows and an elaborate brick façade, the pattern of which was inspired by the Doge's Palace. It was built by a painter called Mario de Maria as his

REDENTORE
Wax head of a Capuchin sister.

studio in 1910–13 and is still in excellent condition. Its interesting interior is open for art exhibitions and during the Biennale, and it has lovely views.

Calle Michelangelo leads away from the waterfront through a stark modern district near a disappointing housing development built in 2005, with tiny dwellings, and past a new apartment building, to the other side of the island (one of the few points where this bank is accessible from land, since there is no *fondamenta* on this side). The *calle* ends beside the **Villa Heriott** (*map p. 413, F3*), a mock-Gothic building dating from 1929 and now owned by the *comune* (and in very good condition, with a garden on the lagoon). From here there is a view of the island of La Grazia. To the left, beyond the school and library, is the garden of the Hotel Cipriani (*see above*).

THE GARDEN OF EDEN

Fondamenta della Croce leads along the Giudecca Canal past warehouses and the Venice Youth Hostel—which must have the best position of all Italy's student hostels. Next to it, a large red edifice has been restored to house part of the State Archives. On the left, the huge church of **Santa Croce** (*map p. 413, D3*), rebuilt in 1508–11 and now part of an institution for the elderly and under-privileged, with a garden, can be seen.

Across the canal, a *calle* leads inland past a house with a handsome lion's mask above the bell and out onto the pretty Rio della Croce, lined with quaint old houses with boats moored alongside. A bizarre small bridge, made partly of wood and partly of iron, leads over the *rio* to a cypress which marks the entrance to the walled **'Garden**

of Eden' (*no admission*), which was created between 1884 and 1900 by the wealthy Englishman Frederic Eden and his wife Caroline, advised by the great garden designer Gertrude Jekyll, who was Caroline's younger sister. Caroline was a society hostess who also supported the English hospital in Venice and a sailors' home. On the six-acre site of an artichoke bed and abandoned orchard, their garden here became one of the largest and finest private gardens in Venice, famous for its vine pergolas and madonna lilies, paths bordered by box, with tubs of oranges and lemons decorating its paved courts and pools, and pasture for a small herd of fourteen cows. Eden's diary, *A Garden in Venice*, published in 1903, describes the work they did on it. Frederic, who was an invalid, died in 1916 and Caroline returned to England in 1920. The garden was later owned by Princess Aspasia of Greece, until 1972. From 1979 to 2000 it was owned by the Austrian artist Friedensreich Hundertwasser. Best known for his eccentric 'Hundertwasserhaus' in Vienna, he was deeply committed to conservationism and the green movement. He considered Functionalist architects to be 'irresponsible vandals', and set himself up as the prophet of organic architecture, striving in his work to bring man and nature closer together (even to the extent of having vegetation sprouting from the walls of his buildings). It was his firm belief that nature should be unrestrained, and so this garden became a wilderness. He died in 2000, leaving the property to the Viennese charity Gemeinnützige Stiftung.

FROM SANT'EUFEMIA TO MULINO STUCKY

Ponte Lungo (*map p. 412, B3*) is a long iron bridge constructed in 1895. There are ingenious small lifts for the disabled at either end. The canal is filled with fishing boats. On Fondamenta San Giacomo there is a plaque set up in 1995 in memory of heroes of the Resistance movement in the Second World War. On the other side of the bridge, a brief detour inland (via Calle delle Erbe and Rio della Palada) leads through an area traditionally inhabited by fishermen.

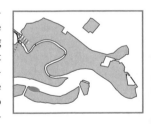

The *fondamenta* from Ponte Piccolo as far as Sant'Eufemia has almost all the island's local shops, as well as simple cafés and *trattorie*, including the Osteria ae Botti, much frequented by locals. It is particularly lively around the Palanca landing-stage. Calle del Forno leads into **Corte dei Cordami** (*map p. 412, A3*), with terraced houses built in the 17th century.

The church of **Sant'Eufemia** (*map p. 412, A2; open 8–12 & 3–7, Sun and holidays only 8–12*) founded in the 9th century, has a 16th-century Doric portico. On the exterior is an old relief of the *Crucifixion*, and a 16th-century lunette above the entrance with the *Madonna and Child with Sts Roch and Euphemia*. The Rococo interior has pretty stuccoes and paintings, some in grisaille. The Veneto-Byzantine capitals survive. The most precious work of art is a charming painting of *St Roch and the Angel* (with a *Madonna and Child* in the lunette above), signed by Bartolomeo Vivarini (1480).

On the Rio di Sant'Eufemia is the **former church of Santi Cosma e Damiano** (or San Cosmo), built at the beginning of the 16th century next to a monastery of a closed order of Benedictine nuns founded in 1481. In the 18th century the monastery owned important works of art but these were later sold, and the buildings were first used as a barracks, then as a hospital, and later as a factory. They were restored in 2004 as housing, workshops for artisans, exhibition rooms, studios for young artists, and space for archives of the Venetian composer Luigi Nono. The church, now used as office space and an 'incubator' for new businesses, has an *Annunciation* (c. 1540) on the triumphal arch attributed to the Florentine Mannerist painter Francesco Salviati, and in the spandrels of the dome the four Evangelists by his pupil Giuseppe Porta. The frescoes on the dome, drum, apse and side lunettes were added in 1672 by Girolamo Pellegrini.

THE FORTUNY BUILDING AND MULINO STUCKY

A bridge leads across to a pleasant waterfront with lawns and a few trees with benches in front of some handsome apartments. At the end is the large brick **Fortuny building**, where the famous Fortuny fabrics are still produced; their shop (*map p. 408, B4; open Mon–Fri 10–1 & 2–6*) is at no. 805. A bridge leads over to the huge brick **Mulino Stucky**, built in 1895 by the German architect Ernst Wullekopf as a flour mill complete with silos: when it was completed in 1920 it was considered the most modern such building in Italy. It still bears the name of its owner, Giovanni Stucky, who was part-Swiss and part-Venetian. Its neo-Gothic style is unusual for Italy, reminiscent of northern European industrial architecture. The mill ceased to function as such in the 1950s, and after a long and complicated restoration, leaving the magnificent exterior almost exactly as it was, it now contains some 100 apartments and the huge 'Hilton Molino Stucky Venice' hotel.

Inland, on the site of a former cement works, a rather stark housing project by Gino Valle was completed in 1986.

A long bridge connects the Giudecca to the island of **Sacca Fisola**, a 20th-century residential district: the houses built in 1982–9 in the Fregnan area are particularly successful.

LIDO
The beach in the early morning.

The Islands of the Lagoon

No visit to Venice is complete without a trip across the lagoon, since this is the only way to understand the city's extraordinary setting. The long sand-bars which protect the lagoon from the open sea, stretching all the way from the Lido to Pellestrina, with their sea wall and beaches a few metres from the settlements facing the lagoon in the other direction, are wonderful places to walk. All the islands are closed to cars, with the exception of the Lido. The most evocative island is that of Torcello, whose cathedral is one of the most memorable sights in all Italy.

SAN MICHELE

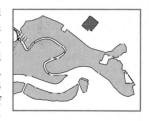

The walled island of San Michele, with its church and former monastery, is also Venice's cemetery. The church is in a site extremely vulnerable to flooding, so the paving in front of it is protected by metal breakwaters, and the boat now stops outside the cemetery wall. In 1212, hermits of the Camaldolese Order, founded in 1025 by the monk Romuald and following the strict rule of St Benedict, settled here. Their monastery was consecrated on the island in 1221, and in 1392 Abbot Paolo Venier renovated the buildings. San Michele became famous as a centre of learning, and the cartographer Fra' Mauro, whose celebrated map of the world can be seen in the Libreria Marciana (*see p. 80*), was a monk here (1433–59). The monastery was suppressed by Napoleon in 1810 and the property confiscated, although a small Franciscan community of friars lived here up until just a few years ago.

Getting there
Vaporetti 4.2 and 4.1 every 20mins to Cimitero (services continue to Murano). No. 4.2 arrives at Cimitero via the Cannaregio Canal and Fondamente Nuove; no. 4.1 comes via San Zaccaria and Fondamente Nuove. For full details, see pp. 348–9.

THE CEMETERY
Map p. 415. Open all day 7.30–dusk. Roman numerals refer to the signposted sections.
In the early 19th century, when burials in the city itself had ceased because of the risk of contagion, the island of San Cristoforo della Pace, next to San Michele, was turned into

Venice's cemetery. Once it was full, the canal between San Cristoforo and San Michele was filled in and in 1871 a new cemetery was designed on San Michele, in neo-Gothic style, by Annibale Forcellini, and it was planted with magnificent cypresses. In 1998, British architect David Chipperfield won an international competition to enlarge it.

Near the west wall (VII) lies the writer Baron Corvo (Frederick Rolfe; d. 1913; *see p. 188*). The Protestant enclosure (Reparto Evangelico, for Anglicans, Lutherans and Waldensians; XV) is on the far left. Amongst those buried here are the Russian poet Joseph Brodsky (1940–96); Sir Ashley Clarke (1903–94), British Ambassador to Italy from 1953–62 and founder of the Venice in Peril Fund; the poet Ezra Pound (1885–1972; *see p. 182*); the historian Rawdon Brown (1806–83; *see p. 197*), and G.P.R. James (1801–60), whose numerous historical romances are now forgotten, but who at the end of his life also served as British consul, first in Richmond, Virginia and then in Venice.

In the adjacent Orthodox enclosure, Sergei Diaghilev (1872–1929; *see p. 329*), famous for his direction of the Ballets Russes, lies near his composer protégé Igor Stravinsky (1882–1971), who died in New York but asked to be interred here.

THE CHURCH OF SAN MICHELE IN ISOLA

Usually open 8.30–12. Entrance by a side door from the cemetery.
This elegant and well-sited church was Mauro Codussi's earliest Renaissance work in Venice, and the first Venetian church façade to be built in Istrian stone (1469–78). The bright white surface, which reflects the water, has smooth-cut stones and plain classical features above. The lovely doorway has a 15th-century statue of the *Madonna and Child*. The little domed building to the left is the Cappella Emiliana, built some 50 years later. The campanile dates from 1460. The handsome 15th-century cloister of the former monastery has a gateway on the waterfront surrounded by a Gothic carving of *St Michael and the Dragon*.

In the interior, the vestibule is separated from the rest of the church by the monks' choir, decorated with marble carving on the pilasters. In front of the west door, a marble lozenge in the floor marks the **burial place of Fra' Paolo Sarpi** (*see p. 236*). Around the west door is a monument to Cardinal Giovanni Dolfin (d. 1622) with a **bust by Bernini**. The rest of the monument is by Bernini's father, Pietro. The wooden sculptures of the *Crucifix between the Madonna and St John* date from the 16th century, and, beneath the monks' choir with its intarsia stalls, is a stone statue of *St Jerome* by Juste le Court. The sacristy has an unusual ceiling—a painted vault in perspective. On the north wall of the church is an exquisitely carved Renaissance tablet (1501).

At the beginning of the north side is the entrance, through a domed vestibule, to the charming Renaissance **Cappella Emiliana**, built in 1528–43 by Guglielmo dei Grigi ('Il Bergamasco'). Ruskin rather grumpily described it as a 'summer house'. Hexagonal in form, it is beautifully designed, with fine polychrome marble inlay and reliefs by Giovanni Antonio da Carona. Restoration of the chapel, complicated by the need for desalination and damp-proofing, was completed in 2006, financed by the Venice in Peril Fund. The Istrian stone cupola, the weight of which had compromised its foundations, had to be radically restored and the rest of the stone re-pointed and the marble floor relaid.

MURANO

The pleasant island of Murano (*maps pp. 316 and 416*) has about 4,600 inhabitants and is much visited for its numerous glass factories, in many of which the art of glass-blowing can be watched and objects in glass purchased. First settled by refugees from Altinum (on the mainland to the north) fleeing the barbarian invasions, Murano had a considerable degree of independence from Venice as early as 1000, with its own governor, laws and mint. Since 1292 it has been the centre of the Venetian glass industry and in 1441–50 it was the seat of an important school of painters, headed by Antonio Vivarini and Giovanni d'Alemagna. At the beginning of the 16th century it is estimated that there were as many as 50,000 inhabitants, and Venetian noblemen built villas here.

Getting there
The circular vaporetto services nos. 4.1 and 4.2 serve the island every 20mins from the Fondamente Nuove (map p. 404, C1). On Murano, boats call at the landing-stages of Colonna, Faro, Navagero, Museo, Da Mula and Venier. Boats for Mazzorbo and Burano (with the ferry for Torcello) leave from the Faro landing-stage.

ALONG RIO DEI VETRAI
From the landing-stage of Colonna (*map p. 316, A4–B4*), named after a column with a pretty base, the *fondamenta* along Rio dei Vetrai (Canal of the Glassmakers) passes numerous glass factories (all of which welcome visitors). Palazzo Contarini (no. 27–29) houses the museum and **showroom of Barovier**, one of the oldest glass-making dynasties on the island (*guided tours of the museum Mon–Fri 10–12 & 2–5; T: 041 739049, barovier.com*). The name of Ponte Santa Chiara recalls the church and convent which once stood here. On the opposite side of the canal is a small 14th-century house with an overhanging upper storey above a portico. **Ponte Ballarin** (with a lion on its arch) marks the centre of the island; proclamations were read here beside the column with the symbolic lion.

The wide Calle Bressagio leads to the **Glass School** (Scuola del Vetro) on Calle Briati (*open to visitors on weekdays; T: 041 273 7711, abatezanetti.it*). It was founded in 1862 by Abbot Vincenzo Zanetti.

The houses diminish in size on the last stretch of the Rio dei Vetrai, as it bends left. To the right of Ponte San Pietro Martire opens Campo Santo Stefano, with a bell-tower on the site of a church demolished in the 19th century.

SAN PIETRO MARTIRE
Map p. 316, B3. Usually open all day.
This Dominican foundation is dedicated to St Peter Martyr, the first man to die in the Dominican cause. The Gothic church was partly rebuilt in 1511 and restored in the 20th century. On the left of the façade, one side of the cloister survives, along with a well dated 1346.

The pretty interior is hung with chandeliers: these, together with the attractive dossals and confessionals, were made on the island at the beginning of the 20th century. Above the nave arches are quaint 16th-century frescoes of Dominican saints. On the south side, the lovely ***Madonna with Angels and Saints*** (and Doge Agostino Barbarigo) is signed and dated 1488 by Giovanni Bellini. It was commissioned by the doge, who is represented kneeling before the Madonna to receive the blessing of Christ. St Mark is at his shoulder and his coat of arms is prominently displayed at the base of the Madonna's throne. The birds have a symbolic significance: the heron represents

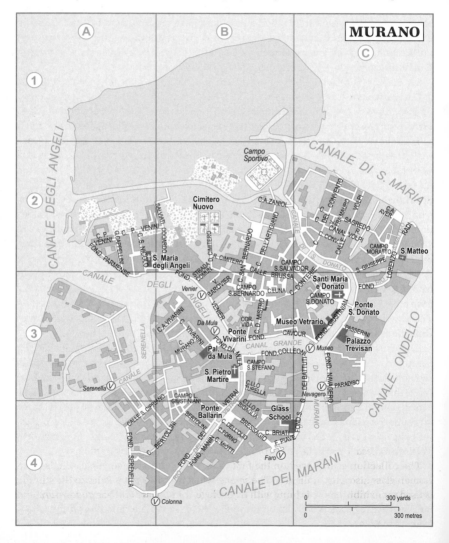

long life and the peacock eternal life. Barbarigo left the painting to the convent of Santa Maria degli Angeli on Murano—where two of his daughters were nuns—with the express wish that they pray before it for the salvation of his soul.

In a side chapel is the funerary monument of Giovanni Battista Ballarin, Grand Chancellor of the Republic, who died in 1666 in the war with Cyprus. The two interesting bas-reliefs show where he was imprisoned by the Turks, and his liberation from prison. The altarpieces on this side of the church are *St Nicholas and Saints* (by Palma Giovane) and the *Baptism of Christ* (attributed as a late work to Tintoretto).

In the sanctuary are large paintings of the *Marriage at Cana* and the *Multiplication of the Loaves and Fishes* by Bartolomeo Letterini (1721–3). In the Gothic chapel to the left, there is a good collection of 16th–17th-century paintings, including works by Bernardino Licinio, Giovanni Contarini, Domenico Tintoretto and Gregorio Lazzarini. The Renaissance altar has a beautiful relief of the *Pietà* dated 1495.

On the north wall of the church there are two works, both in very poor condition, by Veronese (*St Jerome* and *St Agatha in Prison*), as well as a huge *Deposition*, a very fine work by Giuseppe Salviati; and an altar decorated with charming, luminous little 18th-century tondi of the Rosary. There is a pretty red marble font on the west wall.

The **Parish Museum** is beautifully kept and includes the church sacristy, which has very well-carved panelling (1652–6), excellently preserved, by Pietro Morando, as well as 18th-century church silver, reliquaries, vestments and lanterns.

From the church, Fondamenta dei Vetrai continues past a **pharmacy** with a ceiling painting by Francesco Fontebasso (1750–60; *shown on request*). Ponte Vivarini crosses the main Canale degli Angeli near **Palazzo da Mula** (*map p. 316, B3*), one of the few grand palaces to have survived in Murano. It is partly Veneto-Byzantine but was largely restored in the 16th century.

MUSEO VETRARIO (GLASS MUSEUM)
Map p. 316, C3. Open 10–4 or 5, except Wed.

The Glass Museum has been housed in Palazzo Giustinian since 1861, when the collection was begun by Abbot Vincenzo Zanetti, founder of the Glass School (*see above*). It contains an excellent display of glass, from the Roman period to the 19th century.

The palace, built in the 15th century, was transformed by the Giustinian family in the 17th century, and in the 19th became the Town Hall. Beneath the loggia is a 14th-century well-head with a rim worn from use, a damaged 10th–11th-century Byzantine sarcophagus, and stone fragments mostly dating from the 14th century. In the little walled garden are three 15th-century well-heads, one decorated with the Lion of St Mark '*in moleca*' ('crab-like', in a crouching position, protected by its wings).

The collection is displayed on the first floor. It includes archaeological finds, with Roman glass also from Dalmatia. The *salone*, which survives from Palazzo Giustinian, is used for exhibitions. It is hung with three huge chandeliers and has *quadratura* and an allegorical ceiling fresco of the *Triumph of St Lorenzo Giustinian* (*see pp. 296–7*) by Francesco Zugno.

.The earliest Murano glass to survive dates from the 15th century and includes the famous dark blue Barovier marriage cup (1470–80). There is a little hanging lamp of a type which often appears in Venetian paintings of the late 15th century (for instance Giovanni Bellini's altarpiece in San Zaccaria, or Carpaccio's *Presentation of Christ in the Temple* in the Gallerie dell'Accademia). There is also enamelled and decorated glass from the Renaissance period. The 16th- and 17th-century glass includes crystal ware and filigree glass. Eighteenth-century glass includes examples from the Piratti workshops (showing the influence of Bohemian masters) and an intricate centrepiece, reproducing an Italianate garden, acquired from Palazzo Morosini in 1894.

VENETIAN GLASS

The ancient Romans, who had learned glass technology from their provinces in the East, had an important glass production centre at Aquileia. In the period after the collapse of the Roman Empire, when many of Aquileia's inhabitants took refuge in the Venetian islands, remnants of the tradition must have moved with them. Fifth-century Christian art was the first to use glass extensively for the decoration of buildings, combining the art of mosaic—until then executed almost solely in stone tesserae on floors—and using the much lighter material of glass, thereby enabling its application to walls and ceilings. Demand for this from the earliest Christian foundations in the Venetian lagoon and on the mainland nearby must have kept the industry alive through the second half of the first millennium. The taking of Constantinople in 1204 added new impetus and new techniques, as Venice availed herself of the ancient expertise and refinement of the glass-makers of the Byzantine capital and its hinterland. The industry grew rapidly in Venice and achieved European dominance: by 1291 it was important enough to the city's economy for it to be felt necessary to pass a law concentrating all the city's glass manufacturing in the enforced security of the island of Murano, ostensibly as a fire precaution, but more pragmatically for fear that the skills and secrets of the master glass-workers might be learnt by outside competitors. The glass-makers were forbidden, on pain of death, to leave the island without the express permission of the Republic's council; although greatly privileged and often ennobled, they became, in effect, prisoners of the state. Murano's dominance of the European fine glass market was further secured by its mastery of the technique of using manganese dioxide for producing clear, transparent glass—an old and more complex technology which had been lost since Antiquity. Glass objects could now have the appearance of artefacts cut from rare and precious rock-crystal: for this reason, we still refer to 'crystal' glass today as a term for heavier, cut glass. There was also a growing market in clear glass for windows, since Venice, unlike other cities, was able to build unfortified houses without central courtyards, whose rooms needed and could afford large expanses of window. Later still, there was demand for high-quality mirrors and lenses, which—after Galileo's visit to Venice to demonstrate his telescope—were keenly sought by the Republic's merchant and military navies. Most of all, though, Murano distinguished itself throughout the 15th and 16th centuries by its virtuoso and intricate designs for tableware, lamps and vases in delicately coloured and often exaggeratedly worked glass, inspired by, and to some extent intended to replace, the designs of silverwork.

Sober at first, the designs become increasingly more flamboyant towards the middle of the 17th century. but competition, first from France and then from Bohemia in the 17th and 18th centuries, and the political demise of the Serene Republic, caused a severe dip in the fortunes of Venetian glass.

The industry was revived at the end of the 19th century under the impulse of Antonio Salviati (with the help of Henry Layard; *see p. 179*) and others, and since then there has been a resurgence in glass-making as art on the island. The name of one of the most celebrated 15th-century masters, Angelo Barovier, who is cited by Filarete in his *Treatise on Architecture* (1464), is carried through in unbroken tradition by the Barovier descendants, whose business still flourishes (*see p. 315*). Today Murano is most widely known for the designs of its blown glass in translucent colour and intricate modelling, which manifestly follows in a long tradition from its ancient Roman predecessors. Always prized for its lightness, by comparison with French or English glass, and famous for its signature effects of *craquelure,* and *reticello* (in which threads of opaque white are used to form complex patterns of lines within the glass), Murano glass is now undergoing a renaissance, acquiring new terrain in the world of modern art, as sculpture, colour-collage and even fashion design.   N.McG.

Opposite the Museo Vetrario is **Palazzo Trevisan**, attributed to Palladio. It contains frescoed landscapes by Veronese, the only works by him left in Venice in a private building, and reliefs by Alessandro Vittoria. Sadly, it is not open to the public.

SANTI MARIA E DONATO
Map p. 316, C3. Open all day 8–7.
The splendid Veneto-Byzantine basilica of Santi Maria e Donato stands on the former main square of the island (the War Memorial is on the site of the Town Hall, and the well-head in Istrian stone dates from the late 13th century, with a relief of the Lion of St Mark dating from 1302). Facing the canal, once the entrance to Murano from the lagoon, is the basilica's magnificent apse, beautifully decorated in an unusual and intricate design with two tiers of arches on twin marble columns, the upper arcade forming a balcony, and the lower arcade blind. It bears fine dog-tooth mouldings, carved and inlaid zigzag friezes and carved Byzantine panels.

The church was founded in the 7th century by several wealthy families from the mainland settlement of Altinum. The present church was rebuilt around 1141 after the body of St Donatus, Bishop of Euroia in Epirus in the 4th century, had been brought here in 1125 from the Ionian island of Cephalonia, together with bones supposed to be those of the dragon he killed (four of these relics still hang behind the Baroque altar). In the early 18th century the wealthy Marco Giustinian became bishop and set to work on the church, destroying many of its most beautiful possessions in the vain belief that he was improving things.

The simple façade was formerly preceded by the baptistery (destroyed by Giustinian in 1719). It bears a late 14th-century marble relief of St Donatus and a devotee, and

MURANO
Apse mosaic of the Virgin (12th century).

two worn carved pilasters, good 2nd-century Veneto-Roman works. Above the door into the church is a lunette by Lazzaro Bastiani (1484) of the *Madonna and Child with Saints,* and the donor (the canon of the church, Giovanni degli Angeli) .

In the beautifully proportioned interior, with an early 15th-century ship's-keel roof, the columns of the nave with Corinthian capitals (dating from the late Roman period to the 6th century) support stilted arches. The splendid **mosaic pavement** in opus sectile and opus tessellatum bears an inscription in the centre of the nave with the date 1141. In 1977 the entire pavement was taken up, restored and relaid on a concrete base, but it is now again in poor condition.

The most beautiful work of art in the church is the 12th-century **apse mosaic of the Virgin**, shown on a gold ground, without a Child and with her hands raised in prayer. Beneath are 15th-century frescoes of the Evangelists. The Byzantine-style pulpit survives from the 6th century, and the stoup is placed on a carved pillar (7th–8th century). A finely carved 9th-century sarcophagus in Greek marble, discovered in the 1979 restoration, now serves as the high altar. In the sanctuary is a mid-14th-century polyptych with the *Dormition of the Virgin.* A large ancona of St Donatus in low relief, dated 1310 and commissioned by the *podestà* of Murano, Donato Memo, who is shown with his wife, kneeling, has been removed to the Museum of Diocesan Art behind the Doge's Palace. The unusual square **Roman sarcophagus from Altinum** (2nd century), with an inscription identifying it as the tomb of a Roman councillor called Lucus Acilius, is now used as the baptismal font (it has been given a modern glass top).

SANTA MARIA DEGLI ANGELI

The church of Santa Maria degli Angeli is in a remote part of the island (*map p. 316, A2; closed for restoration at the time of writing*). Over the gate into the churchyard, planted with trees, is a beautiful bas-relief of the *Annunciation*. The interior has a ceiling with panels painted by Pier Maria Pennacchi (c. 1520), and a high altarpiece of the *Annunciation* by Pordenone.

MAZZORBO

Map pp. 323 and 416. See Burano directions overleaf for boat services.

The boat from Murano to Mazzorbo passes close to **San Giacomo in Palude**, a walled island abandoned in 1964, with a little shrine on the waterfront. The boat skirts **Madonna del Monte**, another abandoned island which has a roofless building, and its dependent islet, where an ammunition factory operated until the Second World War. Beyond, the canal forks left and the boat soon enters the pretty canal of Mazzorbo, lined with a few houses and a boatyard.

Near the landing-stage, beyond the Trattoria alla Maddalena, is a campanile, behind an old churchyard wall which belonged to the destroyed convent of Santa Maria Valverde and now surrounds a kitchen garden beside Ristorante Venissa. (*for details of the restaurants, see p. 365*). At the other end of Fondamenta Santa Caterina is the **church of Santa Caterina** (1283–9), with its pretty campanile. Above the door is a 14th-century bas-relief of the *Mystical Marriage of St Catherine*. The beautiful Gothic interior has a ship's-keel roof, a 14th-century bas-relief of the *Madonna and Child* and a high altarpiece by Giuseppe Salviati.

A long bridge connects Mazzorbo to Burano near a little settlement where low-cost houses were built in 1979–86 by Giancarlo de Carlo, a well-known Italian architect who taught at Venice University, and carried out much work in Urbino and elsewhere. Mazzorbo has just one grocery shop.

BURANO

Burano (*map pp. 323 and 416*) almost resembles a toy village with its tiny little houses brightly painted in a great variety of colours, and miniature canals and *calli*. Its inhabitants are mostly fishermen and almost all the shops sell lace: curiously enough, some of the shops open early to sell groceries to the islanders, and then turn into lace shops in time for the arrival of the first tourists around 9.30. The total population of Burano, together with Mazzorbo and Torcello, is just over 3,000.

Getting there

Vaporetto no. 12 from Fondamente Nuove (map p. 402, C1) c. every 30mins via Murano (Faro) and Mazzorbo. Journey time c. 40mins. The trip, for the cost of a single vaporetto ride, is memorable and this is by far the best way of getting to Burano and Torcello: you should avoid the private excursion launches, which are much more expensive and only allow a brief visit to Torcello. If possible, plan to spend at least half a day on the trip as Torcello is the most beautiful place in the Venetian lagoon. For places to eat, see pp. 364 and 365.

There is just one wide main street in Burano, with nearly all the shops and restaurants on it, so it is usually very lively. It is named after Baldassare Galuppi (1706–85), known as '*Il Buranello*', the organist and composer of operatic and sacred music, who was born here. He was music master at the Ospedale dei Mendicanti (1740–51) and later at the Incurabili (1768–76), and Maestro di Cappella at St Mark's. He wrote music for works by Goldoni and collaborated with him at several theatres in Venice. Robert Browning celebrated him in verse ('A Toccata of Galuppi's'). He is commemorated in a bronze half-figure (1989) in the piazza outside the parish church of San Martino. Here, the only well on the island has a relief of the Lion of St Mark with one paw in the sea and one on the *terraferma*.

THE CHURCH OF SAN MARTINO

Map p. 323, B5. Open 7.30–12 & 3–6.

The traditional foundation date of the church is 959, and it was reconstructed several times up until 1645. In the north aisle is a splendid painting of the *Crucifixion* by Giambattista Tiepolo, commissioned by a pharmacist in 1722 (whose portrait, in an oval frame, is included in the painting). Christ is shown 'victorious' on the Cross, while one of the thieves (his nude figure superbly portrayed) lies rigid on the ground and the other writhes with pain on his cross. The Marys support the fainting Madonna, who has a deathly pallor, and the whole scene takes place beneath a threatening sky. The two (Venetian) bystanders are splendidly dressed: one, rather portly, in a grey and black striped costume and the other on horseback.

On the left wall of the sanctuary, the painting of *St Mark Enthroned with Four Saints* is by Girolamo da Santacroce. At the end of the south aisle are three charming small paintings by Giovanni Mansueti. They illustrate the *Marriage of the Virgin*, the *Nativity* and the *Flight into Egypt*, and possibly once decorated a singing gallery. The seated figure on the left in the *Nativity* is probably the donor of all three paintings. The *Flight into Egypt* is full of charming naturalistic details with numerous animals, and all three works show the influence of Jacopo Bellini. A 19th-century Russian icon is also hung here.

MUSEO DEL MERLETTO (LACE MUSEUM)

Map p. 323, B5. Open 10–5 or 6, except Mon.

Opposite the church is the former Scuola del Merletto, or lace-making school, now a lace museum. Burano was for long celebrated as the centre of Venetian lace-making,

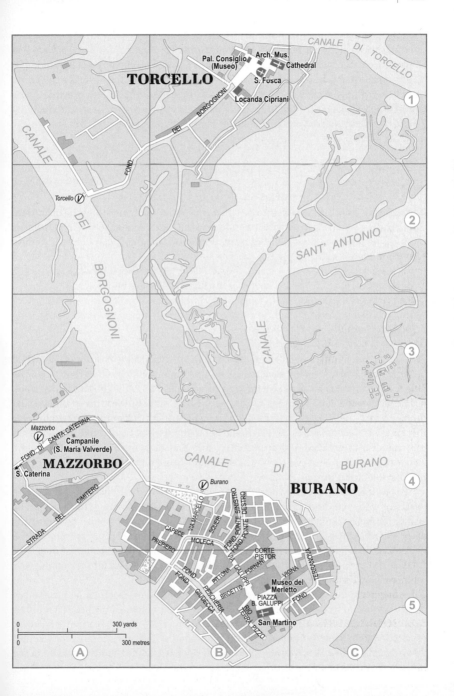

TORCELLO

CANALE DI TORCELLO

Pal. Consiglio
(Museo)

Arch. Mus.
Cathedral

S. Fosca

Locanda Cipriani

BORGOGNONI

FOND. DEI

CANALE DEI BORGOGNONI

Torcello (V)

SANT' ANTONIO

CANALE

Mazzorbo (V)

FOND. DI SANTA CATERINA

Campanile
(S. Maria Valverde)

MAZZORBO

S. Caterina

STRADA DEL CIMITERO

CANALE DI BURANO

(V) Burano

BURANO

VIA MARCELLO

CAPECE

PREPIERO

MOLECA

SQUERI

FOND. PONTE SINISTRO

FOND. PONTE DESTRO

PITTONA

FOND. PESCHERIA

FOND. GIUDECCA

BROETTO

VIA GALUPPI

FOND. FORNARI

CORTE
PISTOR

VIGNA

FOND. TERRANOVA

Museo del
Merletto

PIAZZA
B. GALUPPI

RIO TERRA PIZZO

San Martino

0   300 yards

0   300 metres

A   B   C

1
2
3
4
5

but the industry declined in the 18th century. In 1871–2, when the lagoon was frozen over and the fishermen were out of work, the home industry of lace-making was reintroduced. Lace was first made in Venice in the late 15th century, and spread to France, and in particular Flanders, in later centuries. The museum has a fine collection of lace (beautifully displayed chronologically from the 16th to the 20th centuries), and from Tues to Fri ladies from Burano still meet here to practise their art (although the school has not taken students since 1991).

TORCELLO

Torcello (*map pp. 323 and 416*), inhabited before Venice itself, is the most beautiful and evocative place in the lagoon, with a wonderful cathedral. Though now only consisting of a small and remote group of houses, it still preserves some lovely relics of its days of splendour.

Getting there
Vaporetto no. 9 from Burano in 5mins every half-hour. Torcello has a number of restaurants, but it is also a beautiful place to picnic (it has no shops, so you should bring food with you).

A short stretch of a Roman pathway dating from the 2nd century AD was unearthed at Torcello recently, proving that the island was already inhabited at that time. The people of Altinum, an ancient coastal settlement sacked by Attila the Hun in 452, took temporary shelter here from his hordes and from Lombard invaders in the 5th and 6th centuries, and Bishop Paul moved the bishopric of Altinum to Torcello in 639, bringing with him the relics of St Heliodorus, Altinum's first bishop (still preserved in the cathedral). The foundation stone of the cathedral, dedicated by Bishop Paul in the same year, survives. Torcello remained the island stronghold of the people of Altinum up until the 13th century.

At one time the island is said to have had 20,000 inhabitants and was a thriving centre of wool manufacturing, but it had started to decline by the 15th century. The rivalry of Venice compounded by malaria—due to the marshes formed by the silting up of the river Sile—brought about its downfall. In the 17th century the population had already dwindled to a few hundred; in the 1950s it had 270 inhabitants, and in the 1970s just 70: it now has only a handful. However, during the day for most of the year it is populated by tourist groups.

From the landing-stage a charming brick path follows the peaceful canal, crossed by a picturesque old stone bridge without a parapet, to the centre of the little island. The canal ends at the renowned Locanda Cipriani (*see p. 365*). Just beyond it is an open space surrounded by the famous group of monuments. There is a combined ticket for all of them, but they all have slightly different opening times: details are given in the individual entries below.

TORCELLO CATHEDRAL

Map p. 323, B1. Open March–Oct 10.30–5.30; winter 10–4.30. The crypt and sacristy can only be seen on guided tours.

This superb Byzantine basilica is one of the most beautiful churches in Venice, famous for its mosaics. Dedicated to the Assumption of the Virgin, it was founded in 639 and is a Veneto-Byzantine building derived from the Ravenna-type basilicas. Altered in 864, it was rebuilt in 1008 by Bishop Orso Orseolo (son of Doge Pietro II Orseolo). In front of the façade are remains of the circular baptistery, which was built as a separate building in the late 7th or early 8th century, and joined to the basilica in the 11th (the foundations of the perimeter wall and bases of the columns are visible). The hinged stone slabs, installed in the 11th century to provide shutters for its windows, can still be seen *in situ* on its right flank.

The interior

The dignified and cool-aisled interior has 18 slender marble columns with well-carved capitals, and an atmosphere all its own. It is one of the highest achievements of Christian architecture. The stilted arches of the colonnades were rebuilt in the 12th century, and the vaulting is secured by wooden tie-beams. The superb pavement has a mosaic design in black, red and white marble. In the nave are two altars with gilded and painted wood tabernacles. The splendid Byzantine mosaics were beautifully restored in 1977–84.

Apse: While at St Mark's the apse position is given to Christ Pantocrator, the cathedral of Torcello adheres to the usual rules of Byzantine iconography, showing the Mother of God. Depicted on a bright gold ground, this mosaic figure of the Virgin is one of the most striking ever produced in Byzantine art. We know that Greek craftsmen worked on the mosaics here, and this remarkable icon has no equal even in Constantinople itself. It is derived from a typical Byzantine image with Mary, as Mother of God (Theotokos), holding the Christ Child in her left arm and gesturing towards him, symbolising divine protection. Beneath are the Apostles (mid-11th century), and on the outer arch, the *Annunciation*, added in the second half of the 12th century.

East end: The iconostasis consists of four large marble plutei (11th century), elaborately carved with late Byzantine designs, and above the columns (with finely carved Corinthian capitals) are 15th-century local paintings of the Virgin and Apostles. Higher up is a wooden Gothic Crucifix. The choir has lovely marble panels (7th century) in the apse, beneath which fragments of very early frescoed decoration have been revealed. In the centre of the brick benches reserved for the clergy, steps lead to the bishop's throne. Below the high altar is a pagan sarcophagus (3rd century) which contains the relics of St Heliodorus. On the left, set into the wall, is the foundation stone of the church, which has somehow survived intact from 639.

Crypt: Reached down steps behind the apse, the crypt is thought to date from the 9th century. It is waterlogged at its lowest point.

North side: The marble pulpit and ambo on the north side are made up from fragments from the earliest church. In front of the north apse is the pavement tomb of Nicola Morosini, a bishop of Torcello, who died in 1305.

South apse: Here are more ancient mosaics: *Christ in Benediction with Saints and Angels*, and a delightful vault decoration of four angels with the mystic Lamb (11th century, possibly replacing an 8th- or even 7th-century mosaic), reminiscent of the mosaics in Ravenna. On the right wall of this chapel is a tiny 8th-century tabernacle, decorated with two dolphins.

West wall: A famous and intricate Byzantine mosaic of the *Last Judgement* covers the west wall: it dates from the late 11th century, although the three upper registers were heavily restored in the 19th. At the very top are Christ on the Cross between the Virgin and St John the Evangelist. Below is the *Descent into Limbo*, with the huge figures of Christ and the archangels Michael and Gabriel on either side. The scene below shows a much smaller, stylised figure of Christ in Glory between the Virgin and St John the Baptist, with serried ranks of the apostles and saints on either side. Beneath can be seen the preparations for the Last Judgement, with the throne being set up and the angels awakening the dead by blowing their trumpets. The lower register shows a number of scenes: in the centre above the lunette with the *Virgin Orans*, the Archangel Michael and the Devil are weighing souls, and on the left is a crowd of the Blessed in Paradise (with the clergy conspicuously in the lead and the ladies very much in the rear) above Abraham in a garden receiving their souls, close to the Madonna standing beside the Good Thief, St Peter and an angel at the door of Paradise. In contrast, on the other side of the church door, are gruesome scenes of Hell against a background of fire, with two angels shovelling sinners towards the black devil surrounded by busy demons and monsters, and various compartments of the Devil's kingdom, one showing disembodied heads and limbs, one with worms at work on skulls, and one area almost totally black, where one can only begin to imagine what is going on.

Near the west door is a stoup carved with strange animals.

The campanile

The tall, square, detached campanile (11th–12th century) is a striking landmark in the lagoon and has a wonderful peal of bells which ring out across the water. The tower is ascended by a brick ramp, with a few steps (*though at the time of writing, closed indefinitely*). From the bell-chamber at the top there is a wonderful view of Torcello and of the entire lagoon and, on a clear day, of the mainland and Alps in the distance.

CHURCH OF SANTA FOSCA

The church of Santa Fosca, a few steps from the cathedral, was built to house the body of St Fosca, brought to the island before 1011. The remarkable Byzantine design, on a Greek-cross plan, probably survives from the 11th-century building, although it has been drastically restored. It is surrounded by an octagonal portico on three sides (probably added in the 12th century). In the bare interior, the beautiful marble columns have Byzantine capitals and support a circular drum, which once probably carried a dome. This may have been destroyed in an earthquake, and it has been replaced by a low conical wooden roof.

MUSEO PROVINCIALE DI TORCELLO
Map p. 323, B1. Open 10.30–5; winter 10–4.30. Closed Mon and national holidays.
The old Palazzo del Consiglio houses the little museum of Torcello, which contains archaeological material and an interesting collection of objects from demolished churches on the island (which at one time numbered at least ten).

Mosaic fragments include late 12th-century works from the cathedral: the head of a (beardless) Christ and two angels formerly in the tympanum above the triumphal arch, and two pieces from the *Last Judgement*. The two heads of archangels come from a church in Ravenna and are sometimes dated as early as 545 or 546. They found their way here after Frederick William IV of Prussia had the entire apse of the Ravenna church detached and moved to Venice for restoration. Most of it ended up in the Bode Museum in Berlin, but other fragments exist in London (V&A) and in St Petersburg (Hermitage).

A 6th-century stoup has a Greek inscription: 'Take this water with joy since the voice of God is on the waters' (*Isaiah 12:3* and *Psalm 29:3*). There is also a medieval lance with astrological symbols and a runic inscription, thought to be an allusion to an ancient north German divinity. Among the architectural fragments are several plutei and a 10th-century well-head. The very precious **Pala d'Oro** in gilded silver, newly restored, consists of only 13 fragments since the other 29 plaquettes were stolen in 1806. However, they are of exquisite workmanship, dating from the 13th or 14th century and showing the Madonna sitting on a very unusual throne in the shape of a lyre, and two archangels, two prophets and six saints, all identified by engraved inscriptions, and two symbols of the Evangelists. Formerly decorated with precious stones and enamels, it used to be above the iconostasis in the cathedral (as the painting of 1845 shows).

On the upper floor there is material from the suppressed churches on the island, including the beautifully carved tomb of St Fosca. Also here are an 11th-century Latin Cross in marble; *St Christopher*, an early 15th-century Venetian painting; ten small wooden panels (from a ceiling decoration) with biblical scenes attributed to Bonifacio Bembo of Cremona (15th century); 16th-century paintings from the organ of Sant'Antonio; a case of 16th-century majolica found in recent excavations on the island; medallions, bronzes and doges' seals.

ARCHAEOLOGICAL MUSEUM
Exhibits are well displayed in the former Palazzo dell'Archivio. In the open loggia are some fine Roman sculptural fragments. The top floor has material from prehistory to the 6th century AD, including altars, funerary cippi, statues from the late Empire

(from Torcello and Altinum), small Roman bronzes and Etruscan ceramics. On the grass outside you can sit in an ancient stone seat known as **Attila's Chair**, which has survived here over the centuries and has thankfully never been swept up into a museum.

SAN FRANCESCO DEL DESERTO

The island of San Francesco (*map p. 416*) lies to the south of Burano in a remote part of the lagoon, identified by its clump of cypresses. It is said to have been a retreat of St Francis in 1220. In 1233, when it was known as the Isola delle Due Vigne, it was donated to the Franciscans by Jacopo Michiel. It took on its present name when it became a 'desert', after it was abandoned in the early 15th century. The church was built in 1460 on the site of an earlier foundation, and has two cloisters. The buildings and gardens are kept almost too immaculate by the six friars who still live here. Recent excavations have shown that it was settled in the 5th century AD, but was submerged by the waters of the lagoon at the end of the same century and only re-emerged at the beginning of the following century.

Getting there
The island is open to visitors daily except Mon 9–11 & 3–5 (T: 041 528 6863). It can be reached from Burano only by hiring a boat (ask locally or telephone Massimiliano on 347 992 2959, or 041 730238; www.lagunafla.it). The journey takes about 20mins.

THE LIDO

The Lido (*map pp. 416 and 330–31*) is a long narrow island (about 12km) between the lagoon and the Adriatic Sea. The first bathing establishments were opened here in 1857 and by the beginning of the 20th century it had become the most fashionable seaside resort in Italy. The name Lido was subsequently adopted by numerous seaside resorts all over the world. The Adriatic sea-front consists of a group of luxurious hotels and villas bordering the fine sandy beach, which is divided up into sections, each belonging to a particular hotel or bathing area, with deckchairs, beach huts and attendants (beach huts can often be hired by the day). At the extreme northern and southern ends of the island there are public beaches.

The rest of the northern part of the island has become a pleasant residential district, with fine trees and numerous gardens, crossed by several canals. The houses, mostly only a few storeys high, are spaciously laid out. The atmosphere on the Lido is very different from that in the city as it does not have many canals, and cars and buses are the means of transport (although bicycles can sometimes be hired by the vaporetto landing-stage). Today the Lido has a total of 17,200 inhabitants.

Getting there
*To reach the Lido, vaporetto no. 1 (every 10mins) from San Zaccaria in c. 15mins via
Arsenale, Biennale (Giardini) and Sant'Elena; or no. 5.1 (every 20mins) from Ferrovia
and Piazzale Roma via the Zattere and San Zaccaria. No. 5.2 makes the return trip.
For full details, see pp. 348–9. In summer there are usually more services including no.
8 from the Zattere and the Giudecca.*

*On the Lido ACTV buses (vaporetto tickets valid) A, B and C depart from the
vaporetto landing stage at Piazzale Santa Maria Elisabetta for San Nicolò, and (in the
other direction) for Malamocco and Alberoni.*

The landing-stage of Santa Maria Elisabetta (SME), where the vaporetto terminates,
is named after the church of 1627. Buses to all destinations pass through here. The
Gran Viale Santa Maria Elisabetta, the main street crossing the widest part of the
island, leads from here past numerous hotels and shops, to Piazzale Bucintoro on the
seafront. From there, Lungomare d'Annunzio leads left to the public beaches of San
Nicolò, while to the right Lungomare Marconi (with its numerous beach huts and
private beaches) leads past the grand hotels.

ALONG LUNGOMARE MARCONI: THE GRAND HOTELS
A little way west of Piazzale Bucintoro is the **Grand Hotel des Bains** (*map p. 330, C2*),
built by Francesco Marsich in 1905. Shortly after it opened in 1909, Diaghilev, Nijinsky
and Leon Bakst all stayed here, spending much time with Gabriele d'Annunzio
and Isadora Duncan. Nijinsky's widow suggested that it was while the friends sat at
Florian's watching the criss-cross movements of the pigeons and crowds in Piazza
San Marco that the great dancer first thought of turning to choreography. Diaghilev
and Nijinsky returned to Venice in 1916 for a charity performance of *tableaux vivants*
after Italian masters, organised by Mrs William K. Vanderbilt to help the inhabitants
of the Lido who had become homeless after a flood. Nijinsky played the part of one of
Carpaccio's gondoliers. The hotel also provided the setting for Thomas Mann's *Death
in Venice* (1913). The opera of the same name written by Benjamin Britten and the film
by Luchino Visconti (1973) were both based on this celebrated example of a refined
novel of the Age of Decadence. At the time of writing, the Des Bains was closed for
restoration partly as a hotel and partly as apartments.

Further south are the **Casinò** and the **Palazzo del Cinema**, both built in 1936–8 by
Eugenio Miozzi in streamlined Fascist style. The Palazzo del Cinema was modified in
1952 and there are long-term plan to rebuild it. The international Venice Film Festival
is usually held here in summer. Just beyond, and in a totally different spirit, is the
Hotel Excelsior (*map p. 330, A2*), an elaborate building in Moorish style by Giovanni
Sardi (1898–1908), with its private beach on one side and its landing-stage on the
other, on a canal used by the hotel launches and the Casinò boat.

THE CEMETERIES OF THE LIDO
The road on the lagoon side goes past the conspicuous **Tempio Votivo** (or Santa Maria
della Vittoria; *map p. 330, C1*), a domed war memorial begun by Giuseppe Torres in

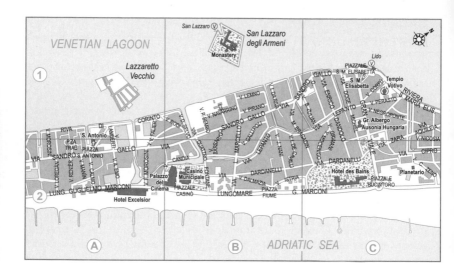

1925. Nearly 1km further on, Via Cipro leads to the **Catholic Cemetery** (*map above right, E1*). Some 18th-century tombstones from the old Protestant Cemetery (in use from 1684–1810 but obliterated in the 1930s when the airport was extended) have recently been set up in a corner of the newest part of this cemetery. These include the tombstone of the collector and art dealer John Murray, who was appointed British Resident in Venice in 1754. In 1766 he left to take up the post of Ambassador to Constantinople. When he was granted leave to return to Venice, he was put in quarantine on the island of Lazzaretto Nuovo, and died there of a fever in 1775. The singer Catherine Tofts, the first wife of Consul Smith (*see opposite*), is also buried here. As his second wife, Smith married John Murray's sister, Elizabeth.

Nearby is the **New Jewish Cemetery**, in use from 1774 onwards. Numerous older tombstones formerly in the Old Jewish Cemetery have been restored and set up here, in a corner by the gate.

On the main road, beside a row of seven cypresses, a small gate (signposted) precedes the **Old Jewish Cemetery** (*open Sun morning, guided tours at 2.30; T: 041 715359*). The Jewish community was granted this land (which belonged to the Benedictine convent of San Nicolò) as a burial ground in 1386, the earliest recorded presence of the Jews in Venice. In use up until the 18th century, the cemetery had to be enlarged over the years, and it grew to cover an area more than six times its present size. However, from the 17th century onwards it was encroached upon by military installations set up in this strategic part of the lagoon. In the 19th century, what remained of the old cemetery was cleared and the site 'arranged' with the tombstones placed haphazardly in rows, and the enclosure wall was built and the memorial obelisk erected, according to Romantic concepts. It was fondly described by both Byron and Shelley, and Niccolò Tommaseo (*see p. 113*). At the end of the 20th century many tombstones were salvaged from below ground and carefully re-erected or set up around the walls. They number

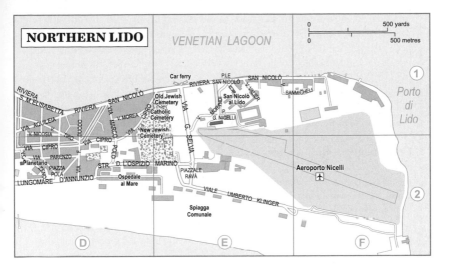

over a thousand, many of them decorated with beautifully-carved Hebrew symbols and family emblems. The fourteen 17th-century tombstones in the unusual form of columns decorated with Samson and the lion belong to a family from Cividale del Friuli.

VENICE'S CONSUL SMITH

Joseph Smith (1682–1770) first came to Venice around 1700 and remained here for the rest of his life. Antonio Visentini, architect, painter and engraver, carried out renovations for him at his palace on the Grand Canal (Palazzo Mangilli Valmarana) and also at the villa he purchased in 1731 on the *terraferma*. The two men collaborated on a 'guide' to Venice's most important buildings (*Admiranda Urbis Venetae*, now in the British Museum), with 488 plans and architectural elevations. After Smith's appointment as British Consul in the early 1740s, he was always known in the city as Consul Smith. He was the devoted patron of Canaletto (*see p. 173*) and also promoted other Venetian artists, including Sebastiano Ricci and his nephew Marco, and Rosalba Carriera. In the 1730s Smith set up as a publisher in Venice: his Pasquali Press became one of the most important in the city, and his bookshop in Campo San Bartolomeo was a place where foreign works could also be found. He is also known to have befriended the playwright Carlo Goldoni, who dedicated to him *Il Filosofo Inglese*, written for the Carnival of 1754.

But Smith is best remembered as a collector: apart from his outstanding collection of works by contemporary artists, his interests ranged from paintings by Giovanni Bellini to the Dutch and Flemish schools including Vermeer and Rembrandt, and he acquired several hundred drawings (many of them from the great Venetian collector Zaccaria Sagredo), including works by Raphael and the Carracci, and watercolours. Other highlights of his collection included books, Renaissance illuminated manuscripts, coins and medals. When he retired from the consulship and found himself in financial straits, in the decade before his death, he sold his collections to the young King George III: they are preserved today in the British Royal Collections and in the British Library, and constitute some of their most precious holdings.

In 1717, Smith married the beautiful Catherine Tofts, who had become famous as a singer in the Drury Lane and Haymarket theatres before coming to Venice in 1711. Their son died as a child and she predeceased Smith in 1756 and is buried on the Lido. The following year Smith, already aged 80, married Elizabeth Murray, sister of the collector and art dealer John Murray. In 1777, after the death of both Smith and her brother, Elizabeth sold the palace on the Grand Canal and returned to England. Smith was buried next to Catherine on the Lido, in a grave which Goethe took pains to find: '*I found the grave of the noble Consul Smith and his first wife. To him I am indebted for my copy of Palladio and I expressed my gratitude over his unconsecrated tomb. And not only unconsecrated, but half buried. The Lido has the aspect of an enormous dune; the sand is blown this way and that, piled up, smothering everything. It won't be long before the monument is entirely lost from view.*' Goethe's prediction did not come to pass. The tombstone was removed from the Lido and is now fixed to the north wall of the Anglican church on Campo San Vio.

SAN NICOLÒ AL LIDO
Map p. 331, E1. Usually open 9–12 & 4–7. Reached by Bus C from the vaporetto landing-stage at Piazzale Santa Maria Elisabetta.
Past the huge Tiro a Segno, erected in 1883–6 as a firing range, the main Riviera di San Nicolò leads to a pretty bridge over an inlet, at the end of which can be seen the **Lido airport**, opened after the First World War and enlarged in 1934. It is now used only for private planes, but a delightful annual air show with bi-planes is usually held here in the autumn. A short way beyond is the church of **San Nicolò al Lido**, founded in 1044. Its strategic position near the main entrance to the lagoon meant that the monastery attached to the church was used by the doge for the official reception of visitors. The emperor Barbarossa stayed here before his meeting with Pope Alexander III in St Mark's in 1177, and elaborate celebrations were held in honour of Henry III, King of France, in 1574. Domenico Selvo was elected doge here in 1071, while St Mark's basilica was being completed. Above the door of the church is a monument to Doge Domenico Contarini, the founder. The interior has an interesting narrow choir with huge capitals. In the sanctuary is a 14th-century wooden Crucifix and a high altar in *pietre dure*. At the west end are three bells cast in 1528, which rang out from the bell-tower after the victory of Lepanto, as well as a stone Cross dating from the 10th–11th century and fragments of polychrome mosaic with two eagles from the 11th-century basilica. The choir stalls, in excellent condition, were finely carved by Giovanni da Crema in 1635.

On the right of the church, a paved lane leads down to the entrance (flanked by two 11th-century capitals) of the **former Franciscan monastery**. The present buildings date from the 16th century and are now used by the European Inter-University Centre for Human Rights and Democratisation. There is a very grand staircase off the lovely cloister dating from 1530, with a well (the wrought iron work dates from 1710). In the north walk behind three doors (*opened on Thur from 3.30 to 5, but usually unlocked on* *request*) can be seen remains of the south aisle of the first 11th-century church, with its ancient arcade of five venerable Corinthian capitals with palmettes, and a very unusual Byzantine **monochrome mosaic floor** with a geometric and floral design, the earliest so far found in the lagoon apart from that of St Mark's.

Outside the church there is a view of the green island of La Certosa and, facing the Lido on the island of Le Vignole, the Fortezza di Sant'Andrea (*see p. 341*).

On the other side of the church stands the **Palazzetto del Consiglio dei Dieci** (1520). From it the road continues past 16th-century military buildings to the northern tip of the island which overlooks the Porto di Lido, the main entrance to the lagoon and always strongly defended (at one time it was closed by chains to bar entry to enemy ships). The Palazzo del Consiglio dei Dieci was the residence of those responsible for overseeing the Lido's defences as well as for choreographing the annual ceremony of the *Sensa*, the marriage of Venice with the sea.

THE *FESTA DELLA SENSA*

It was here in the Porto di Lido channel that the doge performed the annual ceremony of the marriage with the sea, when he threw his ring to his watery 'bride'. By the 16th century this was one of the most important and elaborate state occasions, but it has complicated and confused origins. According to tradition, in 1177 Pope Alexander III gave Doge Sebastiano Ziani a golden ring and the right to 'wed' the sea with it, in gratitude for his support against the emperor Frederick Barbarossa and his part in the reconciliation which took place between emperor and pope in St Mark's on Ascension Day in that year. Another tradition dates the gesture to Doge Pietro II Orseolo, the victor in 1000 over Slav pirates in Dalmatia, who is supposed to have blessed the sea here on Ascension Day every year. The legend of St Mark also incorporates an episode with a ring, when St Mark is said to have persuaded an old fisherman to placate a storm at the mouth of the lagoon by overturning a boatload of demons and afterwards present St Mark's ring to the doge.

Whatever its origins, the ritual, symbolising the Republic's dominion over the ocean, took place every year on Ascension Day, when the doge was rowed out in the *Bucintoro* in a procession of thousands of boats, also welcoming on board the Patriarch of Venice. They then attended Mass at San Nicolò, and a state banquet was held. The ceremony also coincided with the first evening in the year when Venetian ships were able to set sail again after the winter months in port. The *Festa della Sensa* is still celebrated on the first Sunday after Ascension Day, but nowadays, sadly, the mayor has to take the place of the doge.

MALAMOCCO

Map p. 416. Buses A, B and 11 (*they continue to Pellestrina and Chioggia*).
Malamocco, now a quiet village, was the ancient Metamauco, one of the first places to be inhabited in the lagoon by people from Heraclea to the northeast, which had been an important episcopal and administrative centre in the 7th–8th centuries. Metamauco became the seat of the lagoon government in the 8th century. It was the scene of the famous defeat of Pepin, son of Charlemagne, who had laid siege to the city

in 810. Submerged by a tidal wave c. 1107, the settlement was moved from the Adriatic seafront to this side of the island.

The little settlement centres on just two pedestrian streets, the wide Rio Terà and the parallel narrow Calle della Merceria, off which the side *calli* have herring-bone paving, and one of them has a quaint little wayside shrine honouring the Madonna. The **church of Santa Maria Assunta** (*usually only open at weekends*) has a large ex-voto painting by Gerolamo Forabosco in the sanctuary. On the right wall of the nave is an *Assumption* (1735) by Giulia Lama (born in Venice in 1681). On the first altar on the left side is a Crucifix, probably carved in northern Europe in the 12th or 13th century. A polychrome wood statue of the *Madonna and Child* (to be restored) is regally clothed on the second Sunday in July for a festival. In the sacristy (*shown on request*) is a very rare altar frontal with two horizontal panels showing the *Dormition of the Virgin* and statuettes of saints (early 15th century). The campanile is modelled on that of St Mark's. In the *campo* outside the church, with its two wells which retain their lions of St Mark, is a 15th-century palace, once the 'Residenza della Deputazione Comunale', which bears another high relief of the Venetian lion.

Rio Terà and Calle della Merceria meet at Piazza delle Erbe, where an arch precedes a brick bridge across a *rio*. Follow the road to the left as far as the wood bridge on the right, across which a path leads to the sea in less than 10mins, past remains of the old moated fort (now overgrown). The sea wall has a paved walkway. For many years Malamocco was the home of the writer and cartoonist Hugo Pratt (1927–95), who came from a Venetian family and is best remembered as creator of Corto Maltese.

ALBERONI

Alberoni is a little bathing resort on the southernmost tip of the island. The Lido golf course (18 holes) is entered through the tunnel of an old fortress. It is adjoined by a protected area run by the World Wildlife Fund, which is open daily and where fine walks can be taken (*entrance on the Strada de' Bagni by the beach buildings where the bus terminates in summer: at other times the stop is before, on Via di Ca' Rossa, just after the bus turns away from the lagoon*). The road continues to the end of the promontory (Alberoni Rocchetta) where there is a ferry (used by bus no. 11) for Pellestrina.

PELLESTRINA

The thin island of Pellestrina (10km long, and only a few hundred metres wide; *map p. 416*) is separated from the sea by a wall known as the *Murazzi*, a remarkable work of engineering, undertaken in 1744–82 by an engineer from Brescia called Bernardino Zendrini following a project drawn up in 1716 by the cosmographer Vincenzo Coronelli. This great sea wall, which extends for the entire length of the island, was formerly some 20km long running all the way from the Porto di Lido as far as Sottomarina. It was built of irregular blocks of Istrian stone and marble, and was later reinforced in places by huge blocks of concrete. Sections of it are very well preserved and at intervals there are little flights of steps protected by ropes to the walkway along the top. There are numerous inscriptions recording the dates of the various stages in its construction and stones indicating distances. Since 1967 huge quantities of sand have been dredged from the sea and a fence erected to protect the seaward side of the wall.

Getting there

Bus no. 11 c. every 30mins from Piazzale Santa Maria Elisabetta on the Lido (map p. 330, C1). It runs down to Alberoni, where it drives onto the ferry to Pellestrina.

The island is mostly well preserved and interesting for the colourful architecture of the two settlements of San Pietro in Volta and Pellestrina itself, which both face the lagoon. The houses, most of them in good repair (although the weather-proof doors, porches and windows detract from their appearance), are often connected with low porticoes, between the narrow *calli* and small *campi*. Despite the remoteness of the area, there is an air of well-being and the island does not appear to be suffering from depopulation, although the market gardens on which the local economy was partly based have now been abandoned. Many of the inhabitants are fishermen who work both in the lagoon (often at night) and the open sea, and their numerous fishing boats line the shore. The total number of inhabitants of San Pietro in Volta and Pellestrina is just over 4,000. The few shops are mostly in private houses without signs. Hardly any tourists come to this island, which is particularly peaceful (the only disturbing elements being the cars). In the last few years the *fondamente* along the lagoon have been carefully restored and the low wall slightly raised against flooding.

SAN PIETRO IN VOLTA

San Pietro in Volta is the first settlement (*request stop of bus no. 11, about 2km from the Porto di Malamocco*). From the bus stop, follow the lane which leads towards the lagoon along a moat which once surrounded a fortress, now in total ruin, where fishing boats are usually moored and nets spread out to dry. The road along the waterfront passes a house (no. 428) where Pope Pius VII sheltered from a violent storm in the year 1800. A passageway then leads past a bright red house in Art Nouveau style, near a water-tower. Beyond a little *campo* with pine trees and a public green used to hang out washing, are the post office, library, medical centre and kindergarten. The church of San Pietro was founded in the 10th century but was rebuilt in 1777–1813. It has a fine organ decorated with sculptures. The house beside the church has a bas-relief of *St Peter*. Nearby, slightly inland, a monument records the 1966 flood which miraculously reached only the ground floors of the houses, so that the island escaped serious damage. Near another mooring for boats, at no. 276, is a good seafood restaurant (Da Nane). The waterfront becomes even more picturesque, and, next to a café, a charming little yellow house which used to be a bakery is built out over the pavement.

PELLESTRINA

Pellestrina (*map p. 416*) is strung out for nearly 3km along the narrow sand-bar. The local industry of lace-making is disappearing, but most of the inhabitants are still fishermen. The settlement is divided into four districts: Scarpa, Zennari, Vianello and Busetto, named after local families sent from Chioggia to settle the island after the sea battle with Genoa in 1381. The descendants of many of those families still live here. A huge shipyard right on the lagoon adjoins the **district of Scarpa**, where there is a tiny votive chapel with a pretty campanile (1862). The wider lane here is one of a series on the island called '*carizzada*' (each of them numbered): these were built from the lagoon to the seafront during the construction of the Murazzi: they were just wide enough for a cart (*carro*; hence '*carizzada*') to pass with its load of heavy stones. The church of Sant'Antonio was founded in 1612 but enlarged a century later. The third south altar by Baldassare Longhena has an altarpiece by a 16th-century painter called Lorenzino di Tiziano (he also painted a scene of the *Battle of Chioggia* in Santi Giovanni e Paolo).

Beyond a playing field is the **district of Zennari**, with some bigger houses set back from the lagoon, with a well, school and water-tower. The Town Hall is in the **district of Vianello**, together with the octagonal church of San Vito, rebuilt by Andrea Tirali in 1723 in honour of the lovely 17th-century *Madonna and Child* on the high altar, of Spanish origin. As the ex-votos in the sanctuary show, this is greatly venerated since it is associated with a miracle in a chapel on this site in 1716, when the Turkish fleet was defeated at Corfu, and since 1923 the church has been named the '*Madonna dell'Apparizione*'. The large frescoes of four prophets on the vault and over the sanctuary date from 1950–52. In a side *calle* there is a little tabernacle with miniature antique columns and a bas-relief of the standing *Madonna and Child*, a rare survival.

The last district, the **district of Busetto**, has a few shops and a bar and the very long church of Ognissanti, founded in the 12th century and rebuilt and extended in the 16th and 17th centuries. It contains a huge reliquary.

At the south end of the island is the cemetery and no. 11 bus terminus, next to the landing-stage for the no. 11 vaporetto to Chioggia.

CHIOGGIA

Chioggia (*map p. 416*), one of the main fishing ports on the Adriatic with some 51,000 inhabitants, lies at the southern extremity of the Venetian lagoon, connected to the islands of Pellestrina and the Lido by vaporetto and bus, and to the mainland by a bridge. Its unusual urban structure—dating from the late 14th century—survives, with numerous straight, narrow *calli* very close to each other on either side of the Corso del Popolo and Canale Vena.

Chioggia's history has been interwoven with that of Venice since it was first settled by inhabitants of Este, Monselice and Padua in the 5th–7th centuries. Always loyal to Venice, Chioggia was destroyed by the Genoese in 1380; but the Venetians under Vettor Pisani succeeded in shutting the Genoese fleet in the harbour immediately afterwards. Genoa's subsequent surrender marked the end of the struggle between the two rival maritime powers. The Chioggia saltworks, first developed in the 12th century, were the most important in the lagoon and survived until the 20th century.

Getting there

Chioggia can be reached from the mainland in c. 1hr by bus no. 25 from Piazzale Roma (via Mestre), but the approach from the Lido, outlined below, is much more interesting. Bus no. 11 operates c. every 30mins from Piazzale Santa Maria Elisabetta (map p. 330, C1). It runs down to Alberoni, where it drives onto the ferry to Pellestrina. It then drives the length of Pellestrina to the landing-stage of vaporetto no. 11 to Chioggia (most vaporetti connect with the bus; otherwise services run every hour).

The crossing takes 25mins across the Chioggia channel. The whole journey takes c. 90mins. It is highly recommended.

The *vaporetti* dock on the quay in Piazzetta Vigo, at the beginning of Corso del Popolo, the lovely wide main street of Chioggia, which at certain times of day is crowded for the *passeggiata*. A beautiful grey-veined Greek marble column (lovingly patched up) stands on a later base, and has a diminutive lion of St Mark on the top. You have two choices: to explore the Corso first, with its churches and museums; or to take a detour to the church of San Domenico, which houses the last known painting by Carpaccio.

SAN DOMENICO

From the vaporetto dock in Piazzetta Vigo, a lovely bridge (1685) guarded by lions leads over Canale della Vena, beyond which a *calle* leads to another bridge over Canale di San Domenico (used by the fishing fleet) to the church of San Domenico (*open 9–12 & 3–5.30*). In the interior, on either side of the west door, are large historical canvases by Pietro Damini (1617–19). The first south altarpiece, *Three Saints*, is signed by Andrea Vicentino, who also painted the *Martyrdom of St Peter* on the altar opposite. Beyond the second altar, *St Paul* is the **last known work by Carpaccio** (signed and dated 1520). On the right and left of the choir arch, *Deposition and Saints* by Leandro Bassano and *Christ Crucified and Saints*, attributed to Tintoretto. On the high altar is a huge wooden Crucifix thought to date from the 15th century or earlier.

CORSO DEL POPOLO

The Corso has a medley of houses, many of them with balconies. Some way down on the left is the brick Veneto-Byzantine **Torre dell'Orologio**, which contains a little museum (*open on Sun and holidays*) arranged on its six floors. The clock dates from 1384 and there is a wonderful view from the top. It belongs to the **church of Sant'Andrea**, its white façade rebuilt in 1743. In the interior, the second south altar has a polychrome wood statuette of *St Nicholas* (16th century), and in the apse is a small oval painting of *St Andrew* by the local painter Antonio Marinetti, known as 'Il Chioggiotto'.

The low red building of the **Granaio**, set back from the Corso, was probably first built in 1322 (it preserves part of its old portico with stone columns and a carved wood architrave), but was restored in 1864. The little tabernacle houses a *Madonna and Child* relief by Jacopo Sansovino (the standing Child embracing the Madonna). Behind it there is a **fish market**, on the pretty Canale della Vena.

The large white **Town Hall** is a fine 19th-century building. The flagstaff is supported by three marble giants (1713). In the little piazza is the church of the Santissima Trinità, rebuilt by Andrea Tirali (1703). It now houses a **Pinacoteca** (*open Thur 10–12.30 or 1; Fri, Sat and Sun 5–8; June–Aug Sat and Sun 8.30–10.30pm*). The two paintings at the entrance with episodes from the life of St Nicholas (c. 1618) are by Pietro Damini and Andrea Vicentino. On the north altar is the *Presentation in the Temple* by Matteo Ponzone. The beautiful 16th-century oratory behind the high altar has a very fine ceiling with paintings by Paolo Piazza, Palma Giovane and others in elaborate gilded frames. On the walls are delightful statues of saints in niches, and gilded angels above the windows carrying Instruments of the Passion. The sacristy has a ceiling of 1689.

The police station occupies the early 16th-century **Loggia dei Bandi**, with its portico of six Ionic columns. The Post Office is housed in a building which used to be the Monte di Pietà pawnbroker's, built in 1839. Behind the war memorial is the church of **San Giacomo**, with a ceiling fresco of *St James*, with remarkable perspective, by Il Chioggiotto. On the high altar, a 15th-century Venetian *Pietà* is much venerated as the *Madonna della Navicella* (there are ex-votos all over the church).

Further on, also on the left, is the pretty pastel-coloured family **mansion of the painter Rosalba Carriera** (born here in 1675), later occupied by the playwright Goldoni (plaque). The 15th-century church of **San Pieretto** (*to reopen after restoration*) contains a venerated 16th-century wooden Crucifix and an ancient well-head serves as the altar. Opposite is the little church of **San Francesco**, with its bell-tower attached to the façade. It dates from 1743 and has a ceiling with stuccoes by Giacomo Gaspari and paintings by Michele Schiavoni. The statue of the *Immacolata* is by Pietro Baratta.

THE DUOMO AND MUSEO DIOCESANO

Near the far end of the Corso stands the **duomo**, beside its very tall domed campanile (1347). The portal has a lunette of the *Madonna and Child* and a long inscription dating from the 10th century. The white interior of the church (*open 7–12 & 4–5.30*) was reconstructed by Longhena in 1624. On the right of the sanctuary is a Baroque chapel with marbles and stucco work by Giacomo Gaspari and two oval paintings and a vault fresco by Michelangelo Schiavone. The chapel to the left of the sanctuary contains six fine paintings by Giovanni Battista Cignaroli, Gaspare Diziani, Tiepolo (*Torture of Two Martyrs*), Piazzetta (attributed) and Pietro Liberi. The sacristy was decorated in the 1590s with paintings of episodes in the history of Chioggia by Andrea Vicentino, Alvise dal Friso, Pietro Malombra and Benedetto Caliari. On the north side is an 18th-century statue of *St Agnes* signed by Antonio Bonazza. The marble baptistery contains three good statues of *Virtues* by Alvise Tagliapietra. The organ is by Callido.

Flanking the duomo is a canal with a pretty marble balustrade decorated with 18th-century statues, by a little garden in front of the red bishop's palace, dating from 1737. A short way along the *fondamenta* is the entrance to the **Museo Diocesano** (*open Thur 10–1, Fri and holidays 5–8; June–Aug Thur 10–1, Sat and Sun 8.30–10.30pm*), arranged around a cloister which was purpose-built for it in 1999, with capitals by the American artist Peter Rockwell. It is beautifully arranged with labelling also in English. In the first section is a remarkable group of Byzantine reliquaries in the form of ex-votos: a cranium, two feet and a hand, dating from before 1321. The paintings and sculpture (displayed in another wing) include a polyptych by the workshop of Paolo

Veneziano with a wooden relief of *St Martin and the Beggar*, arbitrarily recomposed; a lovely polyptych of the *Madonna with Four Saints* by Paolo Veneziano; a *Madonna and Child* by Cima da Conegliano (in need of restoration); and *St Barbara* by Giovanni Bellini (the lower part is not original). The large painted Crucifix with five saints at the foot of the Cross, from the church of Sant'Andrea, was commissioned from Palma Vecchio but documents record that the payment was paid to another artist, Giovanni Buonconsiglio, in 1523. Wooden panels with the *Mysteries of the Rosary* are attributed to the circle of Andrea Brustolon. Another section is to be opened dedicated to the drawings and paintings of Aristide Naccari, born in Chioggia in 1848.

MUSEO CIVICO DELLA LAGUNA SUD

The Corso ends at the foot of a bridge by the Torre di Santa Maria (or Porta Garibaldi), the old entrance to the town. The ex-church of San Francesco fuori le Mura, on the other side of the roundabout, houses the Museo Civico della Laguna Sud, the museum of the southern lagoon (*open Tues–Sat 9–1, Thur–Sat also 3–6; Sun and holidays 3–6*).

On the ground floor is archaeological material, including amphorae (1st–6th-centuries AD) found offshore between Malamocco and Sottomarina. There are displays on sea defences and changes in the coastline, as well as on the geology of the lagoon. Stairs lead up past a room with exhibits relating to Cristoforo Sabbadino, born in Chioggia in 1489, who was the hydraulic engineer of the Venetian Republic (the famous navigator John Cabot was also born in Chioggia, in 1425).

On the top floor is a sweet little 15th-century triptych of *Justice Enthroned between Sts Felice and Fortunato* in a lovely frame, by Ercole del Fiore (adopted son of Jacobello del Fiore). The same saints appear in the other painting exhibited here, dating from 1381, of *Christ in Majesty*. The rest of this floor, beneath the splendid wooden roof of the former church, is dedicated to boat-building, including models of boats. There are some good early 20th-century photographs of fishing and ship-building.

SAN SERVOLO & SAN LAZZARO DEGLI ARMENI

Getting there
The small ACTV motorboat no. 20 from Riva degli Schiavoni (San Zaccaria/ Monumento) runs at least every 40mins to San Servolo (in 10mins) and San Lazzaro degli Armeni (a few minutes more). Check the timetable to see which boat coincides with the opening times of San Lazzaro (daily 3.20–5). Visitors are also welcome to attend the service on Sunday at 11 in Armenian (again, check the vaporetto time).

SAN SERVOLO
The walled island of San Servolo (*map p. 416*) is the site of one of the oldest and most important Benedictine monasteries in the lagoon, founded in the 9th century and dedicated to a Roman soldier martyred at the time of Diocletian. The buildings were transformed in the 18th century by Temanza and were later used as a psychiatric

hospital. The island is now used by Venice International University, a department of the Accademia di Belle Arti, and the Fondazione San Servolo, a research institute on social and cultural marginalisation. It is also a conference centre with a simple restaurant and café. A few palm trees and agave grow here and the garden is well kept. The 18th-century church and pharmacy, and the museum dedicated to the grim history of psychiatric hospitals, can be visited by prior appointment (*T: 041 524 0119*).

SAN LAZZARO DEGLI ARMENI

The island of San Lazzaro degli Armeni, just off the Lido (*map pp. 330 and 416*), is distinguished by its tall campanile amidst cypresses and pine trees, crowned by an oriental cupola. Formerly the property of the Benedictines, it was used from 1182 as a leper colony. After a period of abandon, it was given to the Armenians in 1717 as the seat of an Armenian Catholic monastery, founded by Peter of Manug, called Mekhitar ('the Consoler'). The island has increased in size fourfold since the 18th century, and is beautifully kept by the present community of some 16 Mekhitarian Fathers, all of whom are Armenian. At the entrance is a 14th-century Armenian memorial Cross beside a plaque commemorating Lord Byron.

> ### BYRON IN VENICE
>
> When in 1816 his wife left him and he was threatened with bankruptcy, George Gordon, Lord Byron, settled on this island for a few weeks, admiring the monks as 'the priesthood of an oppressed and a noble nation'. He studied Armenian and even helped publish an Armenian-English dictionary and grammar. The self-styled 'broken dandy' was to stay in Venice on and off for the next few years at Palazzo Mocenigo on the Grand Canal (*see p. 131*), during which time he took daily rides on the Lido and would often enjoy a swim in the lagoon and in the canals. His epic swim from the Lido to the Grand Canal was commemorated until the 1960s in an annual race, '*Il Byron*', over the same course (but after the War only as far as the Giudecca). It was in Venice in 1819 that Byron met Contessa Teresa Guiccioli, his 'last attachment', at a reception given by the society hostess Marina Benzon. His devoted gondolier followed him to Greece in 1824, and attended him on his deathbed at Missolonghi.

The island is a centre of Armenian culture. It used to be celebrated for its polyglot printing press, established here in 1789. Since 1994 it has confined its activity to printing material for the Armenian Congregation and now operates at Mira, although the original presses have been kept on the island.

The monastery is shown on a guided tour, also in English (*entrance fee*). In the attractive cloister are some archaeological fragments. The church has 18th- and 19th-century decorations, and stained glass made in Innsbruck in 1901. In the refectory, where the fathers eat in silence while the Bible is read in classical Armenian, is a *Last Supper* by Pietro Novelli (1788). On the stairs are paintings by Palma Giovane and ceiling frescoes by Francesco Zugno. In the library vestibule is a fine ceiling painting of *Peace and Justice* by Tiepolo, and a delightful small collection of antiquities. The library, which houses about a quarter of the 170,000 volumes owned by the monastery in 18th-century carved pearwood cupboards with their original Murano glass, has more frescoes by Zugno. The typical Venetian mosaic floor survives. The plaster sculpture of Napoleon's son as the young St John the Baptist is by Canova. Another room has ancient bronzes, Armenian books, porcelain and textiles. Steps lead down to Byron's room, where his portrait hangs. Here is displayed an extraordinarily well-preserved mummy of the 7th century BC, complete with its rare cover of glass and paste beads, donated to the monastery in 1825, and a rare 14th-century Indian throne.

A walkway leads across to the Library Rotunda, built in 1967 to house the collection of some 4,000 Armenian manuscripts. Some of these are displayed, including the oldest known Armenian document (862), and an evangelistery by Sarkis Pizak (1331), the first book printed in Armenian (in Venice in 1512).

LA CERTOSA, LE VIGNOLE, LAZZARETTO NUOVO & SANT'ERASMO

Getting there

La Certosa (a request stop between Bacini and San Pietro) is served by vaporetto no. 4.2 and 4.1 between Fondamente Nuove and San Zaccaria. For Le Vignole, Lazzaretto Nuovo and Sant'Erasmo, take vaporetto no. 13 (about every hour) from Fondamente Nuove via Murano (Faro). Lazzaretto Nuovo is a request stop. There are three landing-stages on Sant'Erasmo: Capannone, Chiesa and Punta Vela. The whole trip as far as Punta Vela takes c. 1hr.

LA CERTOSA

The island of La Certosa (*map p. 416*) used to be occupied by an explosives factory until it was abandoned in 1968. It is now a public park. However, half of the island's 20 hectares were severely damaged by a tornado in 2012 and since some 1,000 trees were fatally damaged, there is a project to install a power plant here fuelled by wood.

LE VIGNOLE

After leaving the lighthouse of Murano, the boat runs straight across the lagoon to the secluded island of Le Vignole (*map p. 416*), with a handful of houses, a few *trattorie* open in summer, and no cars. Most of the market gardens have now been abandoned, although some artichoke beds are still cultivated (and the interesting system of irrigation channels, with small locks to regulate the water, survives in places). Much of the island is now a wilderness, fenced off and inaccessible. A grassy path leads from the landing-stage to a group of pine trees and a public water pump outside the little chapel—with a miniature campanile—of Sant'Eurosia, whose pretty bust is above the door. A service is held here on holidays at 9.30 by the priest from Sant'Erasmo. On the extreme southern tip of Le Vignole is the **Fortezza di Sant'Andrea**, the masterpiece of Michele Sanmicheli (1543), the architect and engineer appointed in 1534 to examine the lagoon defences. The Council of Ten finally gave their assent to the construction of a fortress here, guarding the Porto di Lido, despite the fact that Venice was renowned for the absence of heavily fortified buildings. It was one of the most important works of military architecture of its time, and a remarkable technical achievement since its foundations had to be laid on the lagoon bed. At present it is not accessible by land.

LAZZARETTO NUOVO

The Sant'Erasmo boat skirts the shore of Le Vignole and passes mud flats and marshes (known as *barene*). Boats call on request at Lazzaretto Nuovo (*map p. 416*). Visitors are met here and shown the island from April–Oct on Sat and Sun. You can travel by scheduled vaporetto, or book a different time by appointment (*T: 041 244 4011 or info@lazzarettonuovo.com*). An excellent system has been installed on the landing-stage by which you can activate a 'traffic light' to call the ACTV boats to return in either direction (for Sant'Erasmo or for Venice).

The island was first used as a quarantine hospital in 1468, for ships arriving from the East, and was called Lazzaretto Nuovo to distinguish it from the Lazzaretto Vecchio (*see p. 343*), which was already functioning as a plague hospital. It continued to be used as such for a number of centuries, and in the 19th century was occupied by the Austrians and used as an arms deposit. The island was abandoned by the military in 1975, and restoration and excavations began here in the late 1980s with the cooperation of volunteers of a local branch of the Archeoclub d'Italia, who still look after the island.

In the centre of the island is the **Tezon Grande**, one of the largest public buildings in Venice, more than 100m long, although internally it is divided in half. This was used to decontaminate ships' merchandise (the goods were then fumigated outside, using rosemary and juniper). The arches were blocked up when it was later used as a military store, but the splendid wood roof has been restored. On the walls are some interesting inscriptions made by sailors in the 16th century. The original brick herring-bone pavement survives (the Austrians inserted a wood floor above it, as can be seen from the raised stone blocks). Part of the building is now used as a deposit for archaeological finds made in the lagoon (*open to scholars*), and there are long-term plans to use the building as a museum dedicated to the plague or to the natural history of the lagoon.

Some 200–300 sailors could be housed here in small cells built against the perimeter wall, each with their own kitchen, fireplace and courtyard. They were demolished by the Austrians, but the floors of some of them have been excavated. Gunpowder and ammunition from the ships anchored here was stored in two little edifices, formerly with pyramidal roofs but altered in the 19th century (one of them has been restored as a museum, which contains finds from excavations, including prehistoric flints, Greek and Roman coins, and ceramics from later centuries).

Two well-heads survive, one still proudly decorated with the lion of St Mark. Excavations have also revealed remains of a church (it is known that the Benedictines had a settlement here in the 12th century) and a cemetery.

A path outside the walls leads right round the island in about half an hour—from it there is a very good view of the lagoon and its islands, and you can see its typical vegetation and wildlife (which includes herons, cormorants, swamp hawks, kingfishers and egrets). A sea dyke has been constructed on the west side of the island in an attempt to protect it from *acqua alta*, and a pilot project has been carried out close to the landing-stage which demonstrates that water can be purified by plant biology.

SANT'ERASMO

Sant'Erasmo (*map p. 416*) is a tongue of land formed by sediment from the sea, which became important to the defence of the lagoon. Artichokes and asparagus are cultivated here. The inhabitants (about 800) use vespas or little vespa vans (called *ape*—'bees' rather than 'wasps') to get about. It is an exceptionally peaceful place, with narrow surfaced roads, very few fences, and a scattering of holiday houses. The vegetation includes aster, laurel, blackthorn and tamarisk. White herons—some of them almost tame—abound at certain times of the year.

A road (built by the Austrians to connect the defences with the island of Lazzaretto Nuovo) leads straight from the Capannone landing-stage to the other side of the island and the **Torre Massimiliana** (*open at weekends in the summer, or by appointment; T: 041 523 0642*), a low circular fort built in 1813 and occupied by Daniele Manin in 1848. It has been heavily restored. A small exhibition attempts to illustrate its history. Close by there is a landing-stage for private boats and a (rather ramshackle) *trattoria*-cum-café known as 'I Tedeschi', which is open all year and has lots of tables outside.

After the landing-stage of Capannone, the boat follows a channel between the low wall which protects the island and the marshes: the main settlement is at the next landing-stage, Chiesa (with a church and a shop), which can also be reached on foot (a pleasant walk) from Capannone. The Ca' Vignotto restaurant (*see p. 365*) is about 500m from here, on the other side of the island.

THE MINOR ISLANDS

A number of small islands, originally monasteries, were also used during the Republic as isolation hospitals for plague victims, or as quarantine stations. One of these was the **Lazzaretto Vecchio** (*map pp. 330 and 416; no access*), where there was a pilgrims' hospice in the 12th century. In 1423 it was taken over by the Augustinian monastery of St Mary of Nazareth and became the first-known permanent isolation hospital in Europe. The name Lazzaretto (a corruption of 'Nazareth', with a secondary etymology from Lazarus, patron saint of lepers) was subsequently adopted for all leper hospitals.

There was a quarantine station for overseas visitors to the city on the island of **San Clemente** (*map p. 416*) until it became the home of a large Camaldolensian monastery in 1645 (its church, with a fine interior, has survived from that time). It was used as a hospital in the 20th century and then occupied by a luxury hotel which closed down in 2012 (though at the time of writing, there were bids to reopen it).

On the island of **Santo Spirito** there was another famous monastery, destroyed in 1656. **Sacca Sessola** was occupied by a hospital until 1980. Later these islands (*map p. 416*) were often used as military deposits or ammunition factories, but most of them were abandoned in the 1960s.

PRACTICAL
INFORMATION

Planning your Trip

WHEN TO GO

Venice is only relatively empty of tourists in late November, early December and January. This is the best time to see the major sights, even though the weather can be cold and wet, and thick sea mists may shroud the city for days at a time. During the most crowded seasons—Easter, September, October, Christmas and New Year, and at Carnival (ten days around the beginning of February, before Lent)—Venice often more than doubles its population; but even so it is usually possible to escape the crowds, which tend to congregate around Piazza San Marco and the Rialto Bridge. In July and August the city is thronged during the day, but many tourists do not stay overnight.

The climate of Venice is conditioned by its position on the sea. Although it is subject to cold spells in winter and oppressive heat on some summer days, there is almost always a refreshing breeze. As everywhere in Italy, Venice is crowded with Italian school parties from March until early May.

WEBSITES ON VENICE

Provincial Tourist Office (APT):	www.turismovenezia.it
Comune of Venice:	www.comune.venezia.it
ACTV transport system:	www.actv.it, www.hellovenezia.it
Biennale:	www.labiennale.org
Car parks:	www.asmvenezia.it
Hotel booking service:	www.veneziasi.it

For *acqua alta* warnings, see p. 370.

DISABLED TRAVELLERS

All new public buildings are obliged to provide disabled access and facilities, and most museums and galleries make provision for the disabled. Wheelchairs can be wheeled straight onto *vaporetti* (but not the *motoscafi*). The comfortable and rarely crowded Vaporetto dell'Arte has a special concessionary ticket for the disabled (*see www.hellovenezia.it*) although at present it does not operate in winter. The greatest obstacles are the bridges. Itineraries that work for wheelchair-bound visitors are shown at: www.veniceconnected.com and www.comune.venezia.it (città per tutti, accessible Venice). At certain times of the year the temporary wooden ramps which are set up beside some bridges for marathon events are left in place (especially on the Riva degli Schiavoni).

ARRIVING IN VENICE

BY AIR

From Venice airport: The best way of reaching Venice by water from the airport (Marco Polo; 9km north of the city; *www.veniceairport.it*) is by the Alilaguna motorboat service (*www.alilaguna.it*; large yellow boats) which runs every 15–30mins depending on the time of day and the route chosen. Tickets available in the arrivals hall or on line from www.venicelink.com. The two most direct services are the *linea arancio* (orange line) via the Cannaregio Canal and Grand Canal to the Rialto and San Marco (in 1hr 15min) or the *linea blu* (blue line) via Murano and the Lido to San Marco and the Zattere. However, there is quite a walk at the airport to the (signposted) Alilaguna landing-stage. Water taxis are moored closer to the arrivals hall: they are usually much more expensive, but you can book a return shared water-taxi for a minimum of 2 people on www.venicelink.com for a greatly reduced rate.

A less pleasant (but cheaper and faster) approach to the city is by road on the frequent shuttle bus service run by ATVO (blue coaches; www.atvo.it) which takes just 20min. to reach Piazzale Roma where there are 24-hour vaporetto services to all destinations. Tickets can be purchased online or at automatic machines in the baggage reclaim or a desk in the arrivals hall or on board. There is also an ACTV bus to Piazzale Roma, which has services about every 15mins (*see www.actv.it or www.hellovenezia.it*).

From Treviso airport: Treviso's Canova Airport is 30km from Venice. Regular buses run by ATVO or Barzi leave from outside the airport (tickets from the desks in the arrivals hall) to Mestre and Venice (journey time 40mins). ATVO buses go to Piazzale Roma. Barzi services terminate at Tronchetto, from where it is a couple of minutes' ride on the 'People Mover' shuttle train to Piazzale Roma, or you can take vaporetto 2 (*for its route, see p. 348*).

BY TRAIN

The railway station—Venezia Santa Lucia—is right on the Grand Canal, and water-taxis, *vaporetti* and *motoscafi* all operate from the quay outside. Some trains terminate at Venezia Mestre on the mainland, connected by frequent services to Santa Lucia in 5mins. The Santa Lucia left luggage office is open 24hrs a day.

BY CAR

Venice is connected to the mainland by a causeway (Ponte della Libertà) and you have to leave your car at one of the garages or open-air car parks (unless you are going on to the Lido, in which case you board the car ferry at Tronchetto). Parking space is very limited. At the most crowded times of year, signs on the motorway approaches indicate the space available.

Car parks

Piazzale Roma: The multi-storey garages here are the closest to the centre of Venice. There is a landing-stage (served by vaporetto nos 1, 2 and 5.2, and an all-night service) on the Grand Canal, and a taxi-stand. The garage at the end of the bridge is the Autorimessa Comunale di Venezia (municipal car park; open 24hrs), used almost exclusively by Venetian residents (*www.asmvenezia.it, T: 041 272 7211*). Other garages here charge considerably more. It is forbidden to park outside in Piazzale Roma; cars are towed away by the police to Via Torino, Mestre.

Tronchetto: Garage parking for 3,500 cars (open 24hrs; *T: 041 520 7555*). There is a rail shuttle service ('People Mover') from here to Piazzale Roma (*7am–11pm; Sun and holidays 8.30am–9pm; fare payable at the machines*) and it is also served by vaporetto no. 2 and an all-night service.

Other: Open-air car parks on the edge of the lagoon (cheaper than the garages) at San Giuliano (*connected April–Oct by vaporetto 21 to the Fondamente Nuove in c. 25mins; see www.asmvenezia.it or T: 041 532 2632, 340 703 8574*) and at Fusina (*connected April–Oct by vaporetto 16 to the Zattere in c. 25mins; see www.terminalfusina.it or T: 041 547 0160*). If the car parks are full, cars have to be left on the mainland in Mestre or Marghera, both connected by frequent bus and train services to Venice. One of the cheapest car parks is in front of Venice Mestre station (frequent trains to Venice Santa Lucia). There are also car parks on the far (east) side of the lagoon at Punta Sabbioni, Treporti and Cavallino. These are much further away but are sometimes less full. They are also connected to Venice by *vaporetti.*

INFORMATION OFFICES AND HOTEL BOOKING OFFICES

The official Venice tourist office, the Azienda di Promozione Turistica della Provincia di Venezia (APT; *T: 041 529 8711; www.turismovenezia.it*) has information offices at the Venice Pavilion, Giardinetti Reali (*map p. 407, D3; open daily 9–2.30; T: 041 529 8730*); and nearby, just off Piazza San Marco, close to the entrance to the Museo Correr (*map p. 407, D2; open 9–7*). Smaller branches at the railway station, Piazzale Roma car park, and the airport.

Hotel booking facilities of the Associazione Veneziana Albergatori (AVA) are available at the airport and railway station as well as the Autorimessa Comunale garage at Piazzale Roma (*www.veneziasi.it; T: 041 522 2264 from abroad; last-minute booking in Italy, T: 19 917 3309*).

GETTING AROUND

WATER-BUSES (VAPORETTI AND MOTOSCAFI)

ACTV (Azienda del Consorzio Trasporti Veneziano) runs an excellent service. Transport information: www.actv.it, and hellovenezia.it, recorded schedules on T: 041 2424. Tickets can be bought at tobacconists (*tabacchi*), newsagents and most landing-stages. Tickets must be validated at the reader machines on the landing-stages before each journey. If you board without a ticket, you can buy one from the conductor (for an extra charge). A single ticket lasts one hour (but only for journeys in the same direction).

IMOB tickets. Since single tickets are expensive, it is always best to buy an IMOB card, which gives unlimited travel on all the lines valid for a certain period (from 12hrs up to 7 days; various tariffs available): choose the one which coincides with the length of your stay. These also have to be validated at the reader machines on the landing-stages before each journey.
Student and youth fares. Visitors under 29 with a Rolling Venice card (*see p. 376*) are entitled to a cheap ACTV ticket which allows unlimited use of the system for 72hrs, and is sold at the manned landing-stages.

The *vaporetti* (nos 1 and 2) which serve the centre of the city can carry up to 220 people. *Motoscafi* are smaller and quicker (nos 4.1, 4.2, 5.1 and 5.2). They make circular routes of the city and carry around 130 people. Most of the services run at frequent intervals (every 10mins). Timetables are kept up-to-date on the ACTV websites and are usually available on request, free of charge, at the manned landing-stages. All services stick to a rigid timetable and are extremely reliable (electronic notices supply schedule information at the landing-stages). Some of the services (including no. 5.2) are suspended or modified during fog, although the Giudecca ferry, and the services to the Lido and between Fondamente Nuove and Murano are kept open whatever the weather conditions (using radar). *Motoscafi* nos 4.1, 4.2, 5.1 and 5.2 can be suspended during *acqua alta*.

Vaporetto routes serving the Grand Canal and Giudecca

1 (every 10mins): Runs slowly up and down the Grand Canal stopping at landing stages on both banks: Piazzale Roma–Ferrovia (railway station)–Riva de Biasio–S. Marcuola–S. Stae–Ca' d'Oro–Rialto Mercato–Rialto–S. Silvestro–S. Angelo–S. Tomà–Ca' Rezzonico–Accademia–S. Maria del Giglio–S. Maria della Salute–S. Marco–S. Zaccaria–Arsenale–Biennale (Giardini)–S. Elena–Lido.

2 (about every 10mins; route subject to variation according to the time of year): S. Zaccaria–S. Giorgio Maggiore–Zitelle–Redentore–Palanca–Zattere–S. Basilio–Sacca Fisola–Tronchetto–Piazzale Roma–Ferrovia (Scalzi)–S. Marcuola–Rialto–S. Tomà–S. Samuele–Accademia–San Marco. It follows the same route on the return journey.

N: Routes 1 and 2 are substituted at night by this service, which runs every 20mins: San Zaccaria–S. Giorgio Maggiore–Zitelle–Redentore–Palanca–Zattere–Palanca–S. Basilio–Sacca Fisola–Tronchetto–Piazzale Roma–Ferrovia–S. Marcuola–S. Stae–Ca' d'Oro–Rialto–S. Tomà–S. Samuele–Accademia–S. Marco–S. Zaccaria–Biennale (Giardini)–Lido. It follows the same route on the return journey.

Traghetto: The ferry across the Giudecca Canal from Zattere to Giudecca (Palanca) comes into operation at certain times of day.

Circular motoscafo routes for the Giudecca, Fondamente Nuove, Murano, Lido

4.1 (every 20mins, anti-clockwise): Murano (Museo, Da Mula, Venier, Serenella, Colonna stops)–Cimitero–Fondamente Nuove–Madonna dell'Orto–S. Alvise–Cannaregio Canal (Crea and Guglie stops)–Ferrovia– Piazzale Roma–S. Marta–

Sacca Fisola–Palanca–Redentore–Zitelle–S. Zaccaria–Arsenale–Biennale (Giardini)–S. Elena–Isola di Certosa (request stop)–S. Pietro di Castello–Bacini–Celestia–Ospedale–Fondamente Nuove–Cimitero–Murano (Colonna, Faro, Navagero, Museo, Da Mula and Venier stops).

4.2 (every 20mins, clockwise): Murano (Venier, Da Mula, Museo, Navagero, Faro and Colonna stops)–Cimitero–Fondamente Nuove–Ospedale–Celestia–Bacini–S. Pietro di Castello–Isola di Certosa (request stop)–S. Elena–Biennale (Giardini)–Arsenale–S. Zaccaria–Zitelle–Redentore–Palanca–Sacca Fisola–S. Marta–Piazzale Roma–Ferrovia–Cannaregio Canal (Guglie and Crea stops)–S. Alvise–Madonna dell'Orto–Fondamente Nuove–Cimitero–Murano (Colonna, Serenella, Venier, Da Mula and Museo stops).

5.1 (every 20mins, anti-clockwise): Lido–S. Pietro di Castello–Bacini–Celestia–Ospedale–Fondamente Nuove–Madonna dell'Orto–S. Alvise–Cannaregio Canal (Tre Archi and Guglie stops)–Riva de Biasio–Ferrovia–Piazzale Roma–S. Marta–Zattere–S. Zaccaria–Biennale (Giardini)–S. Elena–Lido.

5.2 (every 20mins, clockwise): Lido–S. Elena–Biennale (Giardini)–S. Zaccaria–Zattere–S. Marta–Piazzale Roma–Ferrovia–Riva de Biasio–Cannaregio Canal (Guglie and Tre Archi stops)–S. Alvise–Madonna dell'Orto–Fondamente Nuove–Ospedale–Celestia–Bacini–S. Pietro di Castello–Lido.

6 (every 20mins but at certain periods only on weekdays): Piazzale Roma–S. Marta–S. Basilio–Zattere–Giardini–S. Elena–Lido. Same route on return journey.

7 (every 20mins) from S. Zaccaria to Murano (Navagero, Faro and Colonna).

Lagoon services

9: every half-hour between Burano and Torcello.

11: (c. every hour, with bus connections for part of the journey). The service connects the Lido, Pellestrina and Chioggia, calling at Lido–Alberoni–Santa Maria del Mare–Pellestrina–Chioggia. The trip takes about 1.5 hrs.

12: serves the northern lagoon (and is the quickest approach to Burano, where the ferry, No. 9, for Torcello operates; it takes just over 40mins to Burano, an hour to Treporti, and 1hr 10mins to Punta Sabbioni) and runs about every half hour from Fondamente Nuove: Fondamente Nuove–Murano (Faro)–Mazzorbo–Burano–Treporti–Punta Sabbioni.

13: (c. every hour): Fondamente Nuove–Murano (Faro)–Vignole–S. Erasmo (Capannone)–Lazzaretto Nuovo (on request)–S. Erasmo (Chiesa and Punta Vela)–Treporti.

Car ferry (no. 17; c. every hour) from Tronchetto non-stop via the Giudecca Canal to the Lido in 30mins (the boat docks near S. Nicolò, north of S.M. Elisabetta.)

20: (service by small motorboat) S. Zaccaria–San Servolo–Isola di San Lazzaro degli Armeni.

Summer services

There are frequent variations in summer services. No. 2 is extended to the Lido, and there are also services (nos 8 and 10) from the Zattere and Giudecca via the Biennale

(Giardini) to the Lido. There is normally a direct service from Tronchetto to San Marco via the Grand Canal, and from the station via the Giudecca to San Zaccaria. The latest services and timetables have to be checked on the spot.

Vaporetto dell'Arte
A special summer service providing a leisurely tour: it is not cheap but is especially suitable for the disabled and elderly. You are supplied with an audio guide and you can get on and off as you like. It starts at the railway station and makes six stops on the Grand Canal before terminating at San Giorgio Maggiore (it continues to the Biennale when shows are in progress). See www.vaporettoarte.com.

WATER-TAXIS AND TAXIS
Water-taxis (motor-boats) charge by distance, and tariffs are officially fixed. However, it is always wise to establish the fare before hiring a taxi. Taxi-stands are on the quays in front of the station (*T: 041 716286*), Piazzale Roma (*T: 041 716922*), Rialto (*T: 041 723112*), San Marco (*T: 041 522 2303*), the Lido (*T: 041 522 2303*) and the airport (*T: 041 541 5084*). For taxicabs (cars) on the mainland: *T: 041 936137*.

GONDOLAS AND *TRAGHETTI*
The famous gondolas of Venice still decorate her canals and manage to keep majestically afloat amidst the many other boats needed to keep the city functioning. Indeed, they proudly take precedence in the busy traffic on the Grand Canal. The gondolier stands above and behind the passenger, and it is fascinating to watch how skilfully he navigates his vessel. They are, however, now used almost exclusively by tourists, except for the excellent gondola ferries (*traghetti*) across the Grand Canal (*see below*). Gondola customers are supplied with luxurious cushioned armchairs and travelling rugs, and the cost of the memorable, leisurely trip is understandably high. To hire one, it is best to agree the fare at the start of the journey. They can be hired for 40-min periods and the tariffs are fixed (*information from APT offices, or T: 041 528 5075*), with a night surcharge after 6pm. There are gondola stands at the railway station, Piazzale Roma, San Marco, Riva degli Schiavoni, Frari and Rialto, among other places.

Gondola ferries or *traghetti* cross the Grand Canal in several places providing a quick and easy means of getting from one side to the other. They are a cheap and delightful way to travel, and provide the opportunity to board a gondola for those who cannot afford to hire one. The fare is slightly higher for tourists than for residents; the requisite coins are traditionally placed on the boat's gunwale. Each is manned by two gondoliers, and passengers often stand for the short journey. There have been gondola ferries across the Grand Canal for centuries, and up until the 16th century each ferry had its own guild. Today the gondoliers, all of whom own their boat, take it in turns to man the ferries to ensure some sort of stable income. Traghetto routes are usually marked by green signs on the waterfront, and yellow signs in the nearest *calle*. They go either straight (*diretto*) or diagonally (*trasversale*). They normally operate from 6 or 8am–6 or 7pm including holidays, but some of them close at lunch time. Services are suspended in bad weather. Routes are marked on the maps at the back of this book.

Accommodation

HOTELS IN VENICE & THE LAGOON

There are hundreds of places to stay in Venice. It is always a good idea to book ahead. If you have to cancel the booking, you should do so at least 72hrs in advance, but each establishment has its own cancellation policy which you should check when making a reservation.

In addition to its famous luxury-class hotels, Venice also has a number of good middle-range hotels in some of the city's historic small palaces. Rooms in Venetian hotels tend to be particularly small because of the way the city is built. At the other end of the scale, a number of convents or former convents have been transformed into excellent hostel-type accommodation (usually listed on turismovenezia.it under *case per ferie*). Here the rooms are very simple but they often have their own modern bathrooms.

Dorsoduro has perhaps the best choice of moderately-priced hotels away from the most crowded areas. The hotels near Piazzale Roma and the station are good value, but in a much less attractive part of town. A selection of places to stay, mostly hotels and hostels, listed according to location and price range, is given below. Most of them have also been chosen because they are in particularly attractive and peaceful positions. Prices are a guideline only for a double room in high season:

€€€€	€900 and over
€€€	€350–900
€€	€150–300
€	€150 or under

BLUE GUIDES RECOMMENDED

Hotels, restaurants and cafés that are particularly good choices in their category—in terms of location, charm, value for money or the quality of the experience they provide—carry the Blue Guides Recommended sign: ■. These have been selected by our authors, editors or contributors as places they have particularly enjoyed and would be happy to recommend to others. We only recommend establishments that we have visited. To keep our entries up to date, reader feedback is essential: please do not hesitate to contact us (www.blueguides.com) with any views, corrections or suggestions.

HOTELS IN CANNAREGIO

€€€ **Boscolo Grand Hotel dei Dogi**. *3500 Cannaregio (Fondamenta Madonna dell'Orto), T: 041 220 8111, boscolohotels.com. 70 rooms. Map p. 401, E2.* In a peaceful and picturesque area with a walled, shady garden with fine trees. The rooms are pleasantly furnished, although the bathrooms are a little bit small. There are seven particularly grand rooms (more expensive) with high ceilings and chandeliers, and two 'presidential suites' at the bottom of the garden on the lagoon. The restaurant is tastefully decorated. The service could be more friendly.

€€ **Locanda ai Santi Apostoli**. ▪ *4391 Cannaregio (Strada Nuova), T: 041 099 6916, locandasantiapostoli.com. 11 rooms. Map p. 402, B3.* A charming little hotel on the third floor of Palazzo Bianchi-Michiel dal Brusà on the Grand Canal, with an inconspicuous entrance on the busy Strada Nuova (you ring the bell to enter the pretty courtyard and ancient columned *androne* with its well-head and water-gate). The rooms (reached by the old staircase or a lift), with wooden ceilings and Venetian marble floors, are particularly spacious, prettily decorated with colourful matching fabrics, and have excellent bathrooms. They have views over the roofs and are especially quiet. The two splendid rooms on the Grand Canal, each with three windows (including a corner window which provides a magnificent view straight down the Grand Canal) are the best (but a bit more expensive). The *portego* has comfortable chairs by the windows overlooking the Grand Canal and Rialto markets. It has very recently changed hands but it still seems to have preserved its friendly atmosphere, so that it will hopefully remain one of the best hotels in its category.

HOTELS IN CASTELLO

€€€€ **Danieli**. *4196 Castello (Riva degli Schiavoni), T: 041 522 6480, starwoodhotels.com/luxury. 200 rooms. Map p. 407, F2.* One of the most famous hotels in Venice, frequented since the 19th century, it occupies a neo-Gothic palace and its modern extension (built in 1948), a few steps from the Doge's Palace. Now owned by the Starwood hotel group, the best and most expensive rooms overlook the lagoon. There is an elegant bar. The luxury-class restaurant and bar on the roof has a superlative view. Between 3.30 and 6.30pm this bar is open to the public, and is a splendid place to relax with a bird's eye view of the city. Extremely professional and friendly service.

€€€ **Londra Palace**. *4171 Castello (Riva degli Schiavoni), T: 041 520 0533, londrapalace.com. 53 rooms. Map p. 407, F2.* Comfortable hotel right on the waterfront in a prime location. Good, friendly service. Comfortable rooms. Unusually for Venice, it was purpose-built as a hotel and the rooms are of a good size.

€€€ **Metropole**. ▪ *4149 Castello (Riva degli Schiavoni, next to the Pietà), T: 041 520 5044, hotelmetropole.com. 63 rooms.*

Map p. 404, A2. An old-established hotel, very well renovated. Its small restaurant retains its good name. It has a lovely little garden, nice bar, and a series of intimate reception rooms on the ground floor, where there is an eclectic collection (from Crucifixes to nut crackers) displayed in old showcases. The bedrooms are beautifully furnished and include three more expensive suites, two with *altane* and one with a small roof terrace. Water-gate on the side canal. No groups. Rates are reduced off season. Excellent service.

€€ **La Residenza**. ■ *3608 Castello (Campo Bandiera e Moro), T: 041 528*

5315, venicelaresidenza.com. 18 rooms. Map p. 404, B1. A small, family-run hotel in a lovely old Gothic palace in the peaceful *campo* beside the church of San Giovanni in Bragora. It has a splendid old frescoed *portego* on the *piano nobile* decorated with recently restored stuccoes and supplied with a piano and comfortable chairs, where breakfast is served. The pleasant rooms, some of them overlooking the *campo* and with parquet have spacious, light, modernised bathrooms. No groups. Cheaper rates Jan–March, July and Aug, and Nov–Christmas.

HOTELS IN DORSODURO

€€ **Accademia Villa Maravege**. *1058 Dorsoduro (Fondamenta Bollani), T: 041 521 0188, pensioneaccademia.it. 30 rooms. Map p. 409, D3*. An old-established hotel, which has for long been a favourite place to stay with the British and Americans. In an old palace with a *portego* hung with chandeliers, and spacious reception rooms, its special feature is its secluded courtyard (where breakfast is served in warm weather), with a little terrace close to the Grand Canal, and its garden at the back (where four of the most expensive rooms are situated). The rooms have marble Venetian floors or parquet, but some of them are extremely small, and the bathrooms are not large. Sometimes closed in Jan. Book well in advance. The service is sometimes not as friendly as it might be.

€€ **American Dinesen**. *628 Fondamenta Bragadin, T: 041 520 4048, hotelamerican.com. 35 rooms. Map p. 409, E3*. In an excellent quiet position on the lovely Rio di San Vio. The palace was rebuilt as a hotel in 1925 by Duilio Torres. The rooms, all with balconies, are on three floors: those overlooking the *rio* are slightly more expensive. There is a little (shared) terrace on the first floor.

€€ **La Calcina**. *780 Dorsoduro (Zattere), T: 041 520 6466, lacalcina.com. 29 rooms. Map p. 409, E4*. In a delightful position on the Zattere overlooking the Giudecca Canal. Ruskin stayed here in 1877. The rooms on the waterfront are more expensive. Parquet floors and modernised bathrooms. The restaurant has tables on the terrace built out onto the water. No groups. The cheapest rates are on weekdays for part of Jan and Feb and from late Nov–21 Dec. It has apartments for rent nearby (daily rates).

€€ **Locanda San Barnaba**. ■ *2785 Dorsoduro (Calle del Traghetto), T: 041 241 1233, locanda-sanbarnaba.com. 13 rooms. Map p. 409, D2*. A delightful little hotel in a 16th-century palace, a few steps from the Ca' Rezzonico vaporetto stop. The rooms are simply furnished with parquet floors (no lift). Some of those off the *portego* on the *piano nobile* have 18th-century ceiling frescoes, and the ones on the top floor have a little terrace. There is a pretty garden courtyard (where breakfast is served in warm weather) and a charming little bar and breakfast room. The family who lived here up until the last war still run it and give it its extremely cordial and attentive atmosphere.

€€ **Messner**. *216 Dorsoduro (Fondamenta di Ca' Bala), T: 041 522 7443, hotelmessner.it. 13 rooms. Map p. 409, F3*. First opened in 1942 and renovated over the years. It is on Rio delle Fornace, one of the prettiest and most peaceful canals in Dorsoduro. It has a tiny garden. Cordial service. It has two *dépendences* on the same canal.

€€ **San Sebastiano**. *2542 Fondamenta San Sebastiano, T: 041 523 1233, hotelsansebastiano.com. 17 rooms. Map p. 408, B2*. Opened in 2007, this is an attractive little hotel in a secluded position almost in front of the church of San Sebastiano. The rooms, some overlooking the *rio* and some the garden, are all very different, and the furnishing is kept to a minimum. Its most important feature is its beautiful little walled garden decorated with fountains and statues. No groups.

€€ **Seguso**. *779 Dorsoduro (Zattere), T: 041 528 6858, pensioneseguso.it. 36 rooms. Map p. 409, E4*. Old-established *pensione* in an historic house on the Zattere overlooking the Giudecca Canal. Run by the same family for many years, it retains a decidedly old-world atmosphere, with all its furnishings intact. The bedrooms are simply furnished, with marble floors. Some of the rooms lack a bathroom, but never more than two rooms have to share facilities. There are a couple of tables on the *rio* outside where you can sit and watch the world go by. No groups.

€€ **Tiziano**. ■ *1873 Dorsoduro (Calle Riello), T: 041 275 0071, hoteltizianovenezia.com. 14 rooms. Map p. 408, A2*. A charming hotel in a small palace in a very peaceful position far away from the crowds, at the extreme western end of Dorsoduro. The rooms (three of them single) have pleasant wood ceilings and marble floors, and painted furniture, although the bathrooms are rather small. Most of the rooms are on the front, where the window-boxes are always full of flowers, but two of them, which are particularly spacious, overlook the canal. The nearest vaporetto stop is San Basilio on the Giudecca Canal.

HOTELS ON THE GIUDECCA

€€€€ **Cipriani**. *Giudecca 10, T: 041 520 7744, hotelcipriani.com. 104 rooms. Map p. 413, F2*. In a secluded part of the city (private motor-boat service), this luxury-class hotel has long been favoured by the rich and famous. It has a large swimming pool, a tennis court, and is surrounded by lovely gardens. It was founded by Giuseppe Cipriani of Harry's Bar fame. Open from end March–Nov, with a small *dépendence* in the handsome Palazzo Vendramin, open all year. The luxury-class restaurant 'Cip's' overlooks the Giudecca Canal.

HOTELS IN SAN MARCO

€€€€ **Gritti Palace**. ■ *2467 San Marco (Campo S. Maria Zobenigo), T: 041 794611, hotelgrittivenice.com. 90 rooms. Map p. 406, C3.* A famous old-established hotel in a 16th-century palace at the beginning of the Grand Canal, furnished with great taste in Venetian style. Less grand than the Danieli, although also owned by the Starwood group, it is one of the smaller luxury-class hotels in the city, in a quiet position near San Marco, with a particularly friendly atmosphere. One of the loveliest rooms is no. 310 on the corner, with a superlative view of the Grand Canal. Terrace restaurant and a renowned foyer bar. John and Effie Ruskin stayed here in 1851. It was renovated in 2012.

€€€ **Europa & Regina**. *2159 San Marco (Corte Barozzi, off Calle Larga XXII Marzo), T: 041 240 0001, westineuroparegnavenice.com. 192 rooms. Map p. 407, D3.* In three palaces (including the 17th-century Palazzo Tiepolo) on the Grand Canal opposite the church of Santa Maria della Salute. The most attractive and largest rooms are those with cool marble floors and Neoclassical furniture, others are much simpler and carpeted. Owned by the Westin hotel group, it has friendly and efficient staff, and most of its clients are American or Japanese. Approached on foot through a very secluded *campo*. Luxury-class restaurant.

€€€ **Kette**. ■ *2053 San Marco (Piscina S. Moisè), T: 041 520 7766, hotelkette. com. 61 rooms. Map p. 406, C2.* In a very peaceful position in a side *calle* which ends on a small canal, but also extremely central. Well run with a very friendly atmosphere. The spacious rooms, on five floors, are pleasantly furnished, with good bathrooms, and overlook either the front or the small canal.

€€ **Flora**. *2283a San Marco (Calle dei Bergamaschi), T: 041 520 5844, hotelflora.it. 40 rooms. Map p. 406, C3.* A hotel in a quiet position with an extremely friendly atmosphere, lovely little garden and comfortable reception rooms. The bedrooms, all very different (no. 23 on the second floor is particularly pleasant), are well furnished, although a little old fashioned and very slightly shabby. Some of the bathrooms are small. No groups. Recently opened close by and run by the same family are the **Alloggi Novecento** (*2683 Calle del Dose, off Campo San Maurizio, T: 041 241 3765, novecento.biz; 9 rooms*), in the *affittacamere* category, furnished in Oriental style inspired by Mariano Fortuny.

HOTELS IN SANTA CROCE

€€€ **San Cassiano** (Ca' Favretto). ■ *2232 Santa Croce (Calle della Rosa), T: 041 524 1768, sancassiano.it. 36 rooms. Map p. 411, E1.* Entered from a narrow and dark *calle* between Ca' Pesaro and the church of San Cassiano, this occupies a spacious old palace on the Grand Canal with a lovely ground floor, splendidly furnished with tapestries and chandeliers. The rooms on the floors above (there is no lift) have high ceilings, some rather too heavily furnished (the best are the seven on the Grand Canal). There is a tiny terrace on the waterfront and a little entrance court with tables outside. A number of other pleasant reception rooms. No groups.

HOTELS IN THE LAGOON

Lido

€€€ **Excelsior**. *Lungomare Marconi 41, T: 041 526 0201, hotelexcelsiorvenezia. com. Map p. 330, A2*. One of the Lido's most famous hotels, right on the beach with private bathing huts, swimming pool, terrace restaurant. Elegant yet relaxed.

€€ **Quattro Fontane**. *Via Quattro Fontane 16, T: 041 526 0227, quattrofontane.com. 60 rooms. Map p. 330, B2.* A pleasant place to stay with a good restaurant.

€€€ **Villa Mabapa**. *Riviera San Nicolò 16, T: 041 526 0590, villamabapa.com, 61 rooms. Map p. 331, E1*. Owned by the Best Western group. A convenient place to stay if travelling with children as it has a large garden and is a short walk from the beach.

Lido Malamocco

€€ **Residenza Ca' del Borgo**, *Piazza delle Erbe 8, T: 041 770749, cadelborgo. com, 7 rooms; closed Jan*. In a delightful small Venetian *palazzo* in this very peaceful village. It has a lovely garden with swimming pool and tennis court and is a few minutes' walk from the open sea. Furnished with great taste and excellently run. Under the same management close by is another place, €€ **Ca' Alberti** (*Piazza Chiesa 3. T: 041 770749, cadelborgo.com, 13 rooms*), in a handsome small *palazzo* with very pleasant rooms. Both highly recommended, the former particularly for families.

Murano

€€ **Hotel Conterie**. *Ramo de le Conterie 8, T: 941 527 5003, locandaconterie.com, 12 rooms. Map p. 316, C3*. A simple hotel, family-run in a quiet position, with a little patio.

San Servolo

€ **Isola di San Servolo**. *sanservolo. provincia.venezia.it*. Pleasant, basic accommodation is sometimes available on this island, which has a university and conference centre, supplied with a café and simple restaurant. Vaporetto no. 20 from San Zaccaria (at least every 40mins); journey time 10mins.

Torcello

€€€ **Locanda Cipriani**. *T: 041 730 150, locandacipriani.com, 6 rooms. Map p. 323, B1*. Opened by Giuseppe Cipriani in 1935 and now run by his grandson. Its guests have included Ernest Hemingway, Charlie Chaplin, and the British royal family. A few steps from the wonderful basilica of Torcello this is one of the most delightful and peaceful places to stay, especially in winter (but closed in Jan). It is famous for its luxury class restaurant (half-board terms available) and has a lovely garden.

HOSTELS & CHEAPER ACCOMMODATION

€ **Casa Cardinal Piazza**. *3539a Cannaregio (Fondamenta G. Contarini), T: 041 721388, info@casacardinalpiazza. org. 24 rooms. Map p. 401, F2.* A convent in the splendid Palazzo Contarini-Minelli, in a very peaceful area with a large garden, close to the Madonna dell'Orto vaporetto stop. Run also as a conference centre and as a home for retired priests. All the rooms have bathrooms. Breakfast is available, and there is a little bar, but otherwise the restaurant is reserved for groups. Curfew at 11pm.

€ **Casa Querini**. ■ *4388 Castello (Campo San Giovanni Nuovo), T: 041 241 1294, locandaquerini.com. 6 rooms. Map p. 407, E1.* A simple hotel in a central but extremely quiet position. Run by a friendly lady, the spacious, air-conditioned rooms, well furnished and with high wooden ceilings, overlook a quiet *campo* and are kept spotless. In summer you can sit outside in the *campo* for breakfast.

€ **Centro Culturale Don Orione Artigianelli**. *909a Dorsoduro (Campo Sant'Agnese), T: 041 522 4077, donorione-venezia.it. 76 rooms. Map p. 409, E3.* A 'religious guest house'. Most of the rooms (single, double and triple, all with bathrooms) overlook the two somewhat severe cloisters. In a lovely position in Dorsoduro just off the Zattere. Very peaceful and friendly atmosphere. Breakfast available.

€ **Domus Ciliota**. *2976 San Marco (Calle delle Muneghe, off Calle de le Botteghe), T: 041 520 4888, ciliota.it. 60 rooms. Map p. 406, B2.* Formerly an Augustinian monastery, in a very quiet position close to Campo Santo Stefano. All of the rooms (single and double) have bathrooms: the most pleasant are those on the upper floors overlooking the cloister. Breakfast is available. No curfew. (Since it is also used as accommodation for university students, it is easiest to find rooms here from mid-July through August, but there is also limited space at other times.)

€ **Istituto Canossiano**. *1323 Dorsoduro (Fondamenta degli Eremite), T: 041 240 9711, romite323.com. 64 rooms. Map p. 408, C2.* This convent is situated on one of the prettiest and most peaceful canals in the Dorsoduro district. Since it also offers accommodation to university students, less than 30 places are available during the academic year (it is much easier to find a room in summer). All rooms (whether single, double or triple) have bathrooms, and some have facilities for the disabled. Most of the rooms are on the interior courtyard, and those on the third floor are the most pleasant. No breakfast. Curfew at midnight unless you make prior arrangements.

€ **Kosher House Giardino dei Melograni**. *2878 Cannaregio (Campo del Ghetto Nuovo), T: 041 822 6131, pardesrimonim.net. 14 rooms. Map p. 400, C2.* In the heart of the Ghetto, this used to be an old people's home for the elderly Jewish residents of the city. The simple rooms (with good views) have been renovated, and there is a café in the garden of pomegranates. Without pretension but very pleasant. Close to Venice's only certified kosher restaurant (*see p. 360*).

€ **Locanda al Leon**. ■ *4270 Castello (Calle Albanesi), T: 041 277 0393, hotelalleon.com. 6 rooms. Map p. 407, E2.* In a very central location, just off Campo San Filippo e Giacomo in a family house. Opened in 1998, it has a delightful atmosphere, and is particularly popular with Americans. The door on the street leads straight into a pretty little hall with the staircase. All the rooms (including a family room which sleeps four) are simply furnished with great taste and have bathrooms with showers, and overlook the *campo, campiello* or *calle.*

€ **Santa Maria della Pietà**. *3702 Calle della Pietà (beside the Pietà church on the Riva degli Schiavoni), T: 041 244 3639, pietavenezia.org. Map p. 404, A2.* A hostel opened in 2000 on the top floor of the building which houses the institute for the care of children run by the Pietà. Simple bedrooms off a pleasant *androne* with a terrace.

€ **Venice Youth Hostel** (Ostello per la Gioventù). *Giudecca 86 (Fondamenta Zitelle), T: 041 523 8211, vehostel@tin.it. 260 beds. Map p. 413, E2.* In a splendid position on the Giudecca Canal. Closed last two weeks in Jan. Book in advance in writing.

€ **Villa Rosa**. ■ *389 Cannaregio (Calle Misericordia), T: 041 716569, villarosahotel.com. 34 rooms. Map p. 400, B3.* A pleasant little hotel in an attractive house with a walled courtyard where you can sit or have breakfast in the summer. Although very close to the station and off the busy Lista di Spagna, it is in a surprisingly peaceful position. The rooms, most of them well lit and renovated, with air conditioning, are all very different, but the best are those on the upper floors with views over the roofs and balconies. One single room, and a number of family rooms also available. Friendly atmosphere and good value.

APARTMENTS TO RENT

There are a number of companies offering apartments in Venice, of varying sizes and specifications. See, for example, trulyvenice.com and palazzofoscarini.com.

Where to Eat

A selection of a few restaurants—divided into four categories according to price per person for dinner (bottled wine excluded)—is given below. Those in the lower categories are almost invariably the best value, particularly those in the €€ range, but they can be crowded and are usually much less comfortable than the *trattorie* and restaurants in the higher price ranges.

The listing below has been compiled first and foremost for the quality of the cooking— in all categories and with prices which match—and those in quiet, sometimes out-of-the-way, spots have usually been preferred. Blue Guide recommended restaurants are marked: ■. (*For information on Blue Guides Recommended, see p. 351.*)

€€€€	€80 a head or over
€€€	€60–80 a head
€€	€40–50 a head
€	€30 a head, or less

RESTAURANTS IN VENICE & THE LAGOON

RESTAURANTS IN CANNAREGIO

€€ **Alla Vedova**. ■ *3912 Calle del Pistor, directly across the Strada Nuova from Calle di Ca' d'Oro, T: 041 528 5324. Closed Thur and Sun lunch. Map p. 402, A2.* This has been an excellent place to eat cheaply for many years, and has a delightful atmosphere—used by the Venetians both as a *bacaro* for a quick drink with excellent *cicchetti* at the counter, and as a *trattoria*, where you can also order a plate of *cicchetti*, or one of the 5 or 6 first courses and 5 or 6 second courses, all of them extremely good (usually including *spaghetti alle vongole, fritto misto di pesce* and *polpette* (meat balls). Very reasonably priced. Professional, friendly service.

€€ **Antica Mola**. *2800 Fondamenta degli Ormesini, T: 041 717492, just by the Ghetto Nuovo bridge. Closed Wed. Map p. 401, D2.* A very simple *trattoria* frequented mostly by Venetians. It is particularly pleasant in summer when tables are put outside on the canal front. The *antipasto laguna* is substantial enough to have as a main course. Down-to-earth menu, mostly fish, and reasonably priced.

€€€ **Fiaschetteria Toscana**. *5719 Salizzada San Giovanni Crisostomo, T: 041 528 5281. Closed Tues all day, and Wed lunch. Map p. 402, B3*. One of Venice's oldest and best-known restaurants which was opened at the end of the 19th century by a family from Tuscany. Since 1956 it has been run by the Busatto family and the menu includes both fish and meat dishes. The desserts are excellent.

€€ **Hosteria del Ghetto**. *2878 Campo del Ghetto Nuovo, T: 338 797 7305. Map p. 400, C2*. Opened in 2011 by the Jewish community, this is the only certified kosher restaurant in Venice, and serves traditional Venetian food.

€€ **Trattoria dalla Marisa**. *652 Fondamenta di San Giobbe, T: 041 720211. Always open for lunch, but closed Mon, Wed, and Sun for dinner, and closed over the Christmas period. Map p. 400, B2*. A typical *trattoria* frequented by Venetians, where you are served extremely large helpings. Particularly good meat dishes, including *tagliatelle all'anatra* (with duck). Tables outside on the *fondamenta* in good weather.

RESTAURANTS IN CASTELLO

€€€€ **Al Covo**. *3968 Campiello della Pescaria, off Riva degli Schiavoni near San Giovanni in Bragora, T: 041 522 3812. Closed Wed and Thur. Map p. 404, B2*. Run by a professional chef, Cesare Benelli, and his charming wife Diane. It has a few tables outside in the quiet little *campiello*. Excellent fresh fish exclusively from the lagoon or the Adriatic, and seasonal locally-grown vegetables. Very imaginative menu with specialities including raw, fried and grilled fish, shellfish, home-made pasta, and also meat dishes. Home-made desserts by Diane.

€€€ **Corte Sconta**. *3886 Calle del Pestrin, T: 041 522 7024. Closed Sun and Mon. Map p. 404, B1*. Very inconspicuous in a narrow *calle*, a few steps from San Giovanni in Bragora, off Calle del Forno, which runs into the Riva degli Schiavoni. Famous amongst Venetians for its good fish and its hors-d'oeuvres, the unassuming, old-style exterior, which retains its old red painted sign, belies the up-to-date excellence within. Garden in summer.

€€ **Il Giardinetto**. *4928 Salizzada Zorzi (Ruga Giuffa), T: 041 528 5332. Closed Thur. Map p. 403, D4*. Typical family-run Venetian *trattoria* which is good value. Fish is usually the best choice and is reasonably priced. Frequented also by Venetians, as it is tucked away rather off the beaten track.

€€ **Il Nuovo Galeon**. *1308 Via Garibaldi, T: 041 520 4656. Closed Tues. Map p. 405, D2*. Characteristic *trattoria* serving traditional Venetian food.

€€€ **L'Osteria di Santa Marina**. *5911 Campo Santa Marina, T: 041 528 5239. Closed Sun and Mon lunch. Map p. 402, C3*. A traditional Venetian *trattoria* with good food. Comfortable interior. Besides *à la carte*, it offers several different fixed menus, with particularly interesting dishes such as *mantecato d'orzo al nero di seppia, su crema di zucca e scampi* (puréed barley with squid in their ink, with pumpkin and scampi sauce). Also specialises in raw fish.

€€€ **Da Remigio**. ■ *3416 Salizzada dei Greci, T: 041 523 0089. Closed Mon evening and Tues. Map p. 404, B1*. Run by a delightful family, with excellent fish, caught locally. Specialities include raw fish soaked in grapefruit juice. On a busy *calle*, frequented by Venetians, with a bustling (sometimes almost too noisy) atmosphere.

RESTAURANTS IN DORSODURO

€€€ **Ai Gondolieri**. *366 Fondamenta Ospedaletto (very close to the Peggy Guggenheim Collection), T: 041 528 6396. Closed Tues. Map p. 409, E3.* A very pleasant place to have a reasonably-priced meal. The little old-world interior retains its quaint furnishings. Specialises in meat and vegetables, rather than fish, but serves good risotto

€€ **Al Vecio Marangon**. *1220 Campiello Cento Pietre (behind the Toletta bookshop), T: 041 523 5768. Closed Wed. Map p. 409, D2.* The name comes from the carpenter's shop which used to be here (Signor Oscar's worktable has been retained). Typical Venetian dishes, good *cicchetti*, and an unexpectedly wide selection of Italian wines.

€€ **Casin dei Nobili**. *2756 Sottoportego del Casin dei Nobili (just out of Campo San Barnaba), T: 041 241 1841. Closed Thur. Map p. 409, D2.* Run by a group of young people, the food is good, with an imaginative menu and the prices fair. You are sometimes asked to wait if you order one of the excellent desserts, since they are cooked specially. It is also popular as a pizzeria. There is plenty of space so you can almost always find a place and it is open until late. Tables in the garden court in summer (which is covered over in winter). The service is fast and efficient.

€€ **Do Torri**. *3408 Campo Santa Margherita, T: 041 522 0686, info@ osteriadotorri.it. Map p. 408, C2.* Very pleasant, lively place for a glass of wine and dish of mixed appetisers or a full

meal. Friendly service. Also owns the pizzeria next door.

€€ **L'Incontro**. *3062 Rio Terrà Canal, Campo Santa Margherita, T: 041 522 2404. Closed Mon and Tues morning. Map p. 408, C2.* Run by Sardinians, this offers particularly good meat, cooked in the traditional Sardinian way. On request there is gluten-free pasta and breadsticks. It has two small rooms, but in warm weather it has tables outside on the wide *rio terrà*. Conveniently placed in the centre of the lovely district of Dorsoduro. It offers a lunch menu.

€€€ **Oniga**. *Campo San Barnaba, T: 041 522 4410. Closed Tues. Map p. 409, D2.* A sound choice—though perhaps a tiny bit pretentious. It has a comfortable interior, and tables also outside in the *campo*.

€€€ **Pane e Vino**. *Campo Angelo Raffaele, Dorsoduro, T: 041 523 7456. Closed Wed. Map p. 408, B2.* In a delightful position away from the crowds, behind the church of Sant'Angelo Raffaele. Reasonably priced and nicely run, with a warm interior and tables out in the *campo*. *Cicchetti* served at lunch time, as well as more substantial dishes (the first courses are particularly good). A popular place to eat for Venetians, its *clientèle* includes staff and students from the nearby university architecture faculty.

€€ **Quattro Feri**. *2754 Calle Lunga San Barnaba, T: 041 520 6978. Closed Sun. Map p. 408, C2.* A small popular *trattoria*, often with a rather chaotic atmosphere, and you are sometimes asked to share a table. Efficiently run by a vociferous jolly lady. The fish is usually good and the first courses are sound, including *schie con polenta*.

RESTAURANTS ON THE GIUDECCA

€€€ **Altanella**. *Calle delle Erbe, T: 041 522 7780. Closed Tues evening and Wed. Map p. 412, B3*. In a very inconspicuous position halfway down a dark narrow *calle* which leads away from the waterfront at Ponte Lungo. An old-established family-run restaurant with a devoted *clientèle*, mostly foreigners. It can be stuffy in the winter, so it is at its best in the summer, when you can eat outside on the simple terrace on a side canal. Specialities include *polenta al nero di seppia* (polenta with cuttlefish cooked in their ink), *bigoli in salsa* (thick spaghetti with an onion and anchovy sauce), bean soup, and the white grappa with raisins served at the end of the meal. Nowadays it is sadly not always quite up to standard.

€€€ **I Figli delle Stelle**. *70 Zitelle, T: 041 523 0004. Restricted opening in winter; phone to check. Map p. 413, E2*. In a superb position on the Giudecca Canal with a full view from the tables outside on the *fondamenta* of the Punta della Dogana and San Marco across the water. With simple modern décor, it also has a pleasant living room where you can have a drink. The menu has dishes from Puglia as well as Venetian specialities, featuring both fish and meat.

RESTAURANTS IN SAN MARCO

€€€ **A Beccafico**. *2801 Campo Santo Stefano, T: 041 527 4879. Map p. 406, B2*. Excellent fish and a great variety of Sicilian dishes. Very efficiently run by Tunisians, who also serve halal dishes for Muslims. *Le delizie del padrino*, listed under the *antipasti*, is a meal in itself, with a great variety of fish, served hot and cold, cooked and raw. Mussels are lightly cooked and enclosed in a case of bread so that you can enjoy them to the full. Occupying the former local post office, the one large room now has bright white walls and minimalist décor.

€€€€ **Harry's Bar**. *Calle Vallaresso, T: 041 528 5777. Map p. 407, D3*. The most renowned restaurant and cocktail bar in Venice, opened by the Cipriani in the 1920s and still frequented by all the celebrities who come to town. Even though it has no view and is rather small, this does not deter its famous and wealthy customers who, one suspects, come here above all to enjoy each others' company in its intimate atmosphere. The prices are what one would expect from such a famous establishment, and the food is not necessarily its strongest point, although the *scampi alla termidor* are usually good. The raw meat dish called *carpaccio* was invented here, as was the Bellini cocktail. A favourite dessert is the vanilla ice cream with chocolate sauce.

€€€€ **Quadri**. *120 Piazza San Marco, T: 041 528 9299. Map p. 407, D2*. Above the famous café of the same name (*see p. 71*), this was opened in 1844. With just two extremely elegant rooms hung with chandeliers overlooking the Piazza, it has for long been considered one of the best luxury-class places to eat in Venice. The charming old-fashioned atmosphere and highly professional service recalls the very best French restaurants. The Venetians criticise its prices, but there is also a set menu. €€€ **Vini da Arturo**. *3656 Calle degli Assassini, between Calle della Mandola and Campo San Fantin, T: 041 528 6974. No credit cards. Map p. 406, C2.* A tiny restaurant (booking essential) but extremely good. One of the few restaurants in Venice which does not specialise in fish, it is especially renowned for its excellent vegetables, imaginatively cooked, and meat dishes.

RESTAURANTS IN SAN POLO

€€€ **Alla Madonna**. *594 Calle della Madonna, T: 041 522 3824 (but no reservations). Closed Wed. Map p. 411, F3.* Off Riva del Vin, very near the Rialto. According to some, this famous old *trattoria* still serves the best fish in the city, and it has a faithful local and foreign *clientèle*. Its size (it can serve up to 250 people at a time) and its numerous rooms mean that it can be chaotically busy, and so it is sometimes difficult to enjoy your meal in peace. However, the service is professional and the atmosphere is that of old Venice. €€€ **Da Ignazio**. *2759 Calle Saoneri, T: 041 523 4852. Closed Mon. Map p. 411, D3.* An institution, run since 1951 by Ada, now helped by her son Fiorenzo. Typical Venetian cuisine superbly prepared. Garden in summer. €€€ **Antiche Carampane**. ■ *1911 Rio Terrà Rampani, T: 041 524 0165. Closed Sun and Mon. Map p. 411, E2.* Tucked away in a very quiet spot near Campo Sant'Aponal (the nearest vaporetto stop is San Silvestro). Its takes its name from the former Ca' Rampana brothel (*see p. 207*), and this theme is used in the restaurant logo. Opened some 25 years ago by the same cordial family who still runs it, this is a very small restaurant with a simple little interior, and tables outside in summer on the narrow *calle*. Popular and well-known for the excellence of its food, including fish served in a great variety of ways—as an hors-d'oeuvre, with pasta, baked, or fried—as well as meat dishes including Angus steaks, and an excellent wine list. Home-made desserts (excellent *sgroppino*) and sweet white wine served with Venetian biscuits. €€ **Osteria Antico Dolo**. *778 Ruga Vecchia S. Giovanni Elemosinario (opposite the end of Sottoportego and Calle dei Cinque), T: 041 522 6546. Map p. 411, E2.* Good *cicchetti* are served as hors-d'oeuvres, and other dishes include *zuppa di fagioli* (bean soup), *minestra di trippa* (tripe) and polenta. Simple but not as cheap as you might expect. €€€€ **Osteria Da Fiore**. ■ *2202 Calle del Scaleter, T: 041 721308. Closed Sun and Mon. Map p. 411, D2.* In a very narrow out-of-the-way calle by Ponte Bernardo, still with its old red and yellow sign. A tiny terrace on the canal, just large enough for a table for two, has a view of the superb Gothic Ca' Bernardo. Run by Mara and Maurizio Martin, this is considered by many to be the best restaurant in Venice in its class. The menu consists exclusively of fish and vegetables. It can serve just 50, and the interior, devoid of all fussy decoration, has a club atmosphere (with one table filling a room all on its own).

RESTAURANTS IN SANTA CROCE

€€ **Antica Besseta**. *1395 Salizzada de Cà Zusto (or Salizada Zusto), T: 041 721687, 041 524 0428. Closed all day Tues and Wed at lunch. Map p. 410, C1.* In a peaceful, out of the way *salizzada* near Campo San Giacomo dell'Orio, this is one of the most characteristic places to eat in Venice since it has retained its original furnishings and wood counter (its name comes from the lady who used to be behind it selling wine by the glass as well as lending money for interest).

€€€ **Vecio Fritolin**. *2262 Calle della Regina, at the end of Sottoportego de Siora Bettina, T: 041 522 2881. Open midday–11pm. Closed Mon. Map p. 411, E2.* A traditional small restaurant serving good fresh fish (they are proud not to own a freezer). It is said that in the old days the fried fish was served together with forks chained to the counter. Today it is much frequented by visitors.

RESTAURANTS IN THE LAGOON

Burano
€€€ **Trattoria al Gatto Nero da Ruggero**. *Fondamenta Giudecca 88, T: 041 730120. Map p. 323, B5.* Has a good reputation.

Chioggia
€€€ **El Gato**. *Campo S. Andrea, T: 041 401806.*
€€€ **Garibaldi**. *1924 Viale San Marco, T: 041 554 0042.* This restaurant is in fact in Sottomarina, east of Chioggia (*see map on p. 416*). It is reached from Corso del Popolo by Calle San Giacomo and the bridges across Isola dell'Unione.
€€ **Vecio Foghero**. *Via Scopici 91, T: 041 404679.* Off Corso del Popolo, opposite the church of Sant'Andrea. Also a pizzeria.

Le Vignole
€€ **All'Oasi**. *T: 041 520 4207. Open May–Sept.*

Lido and Malamocco
€€ **La Favorita**. *Via Francesco Duodo 33 (near the Jewish cemetery), T: 041 526 1626. Map p. 331, D1.*
€€ **Gran Viale**. *Santa Maria Elisabetta 10, T: 041 526 0322. Map p. 330, C1.*
€€€ **Quattro Fontane**. Attached to the hotel of the same name (*see p. 356*). Simple place, large outdoor garden.
€€ **La Rotonda**. *Via Sandro Gallo 173, T: 041 526 9279. Closed Mon. Map p. 330, A2.* Good local place. Simple menu of pasta and seafood, excellent pizzas.
€€ **Trattoria Scarso**. *T: 041 770834, closed Tues.* By the public gardens overlooking the lagoon in Malamocco. A pleasant, family-run fish restaurant with a large garden.
€€ **Valentino**. *Via Sandro Gallo 81, T: 041 526 0128, closed Wed. Map p. 330, B1.* Spacious outdoor terrace in summer. Traditional Venetian menu, good desserts, leisurely service.

€ Trattoria Al Ponte di Borgo. *Calle delle Mercerie 27, T. 041 770090, closed Mon.* In Malamocco. At the end of the street, almost in Piazza delle Erbe; an excellent little place to eat fresh fish as a snack or a full meal.

Mazzorbo
€€–€€€ Trattoria alla Maddalena. *T: 041 730151, closed Thur. Map p. 323, A4.* A simple, lively little restaurant on the waterfront by the landing-stage, which serves fish and game. Well known for its duck (roasted or served with *fettuccine*).
€€€€ Venissa, *Fondamenta S. Caterina 3, T: 041 527 2281, venissa.it. Closed Mon. Map p. 323, A4.* An elegant oasis, inconspicuously signed. Chef Antonia is known for her inventive taste combinations, such as mango with rucola, or parmesan cheese ice cream. The sommelier is a master: he will find a wine to match each course. Also has rooms.

Murano
€€ Ai Vetrai. *Fondamenta Manin 29, T: 041 739293. Map p. 316, B4.* A very reasonably priced *trattoria* and, as the name suggests, popular with glassblowers, who arrive for lunch in their leather aprons. Very good value set menu at lunch time.
€€ Trattoria Busa alla Torre da Lele. *Campo Santo Stefano 3, T: 041 739662,*

Map p. 316, B3. No closing day. Lele, the proprietor, is a well-known character and will entertain you with stories about the lagoon, as well as the celebrities he has welcomed here in the past. He produces traditional dishes based on fish caught locally.
€€€ Trattoria ai Frati. *Fondamenta Venier 4, T: 041 736694. Map p. 316, B3.* Lovely terrace on the canal.

Pellestrina
€€€ Da Celeste. *Calle Vianelli 625, T: 041 967043.* With tables outside overlooking the lagoon. Famous for its sunset views. Good food.

Sant'Erasmo
€ Ca'Vignotto. *Via Forti 71, T: 041 244 4000. Agriturismo* with a set menu. Many Venetians come here on the feast of San Martino (11 Nov) to eat goose.

San Pietro in Volta
€€€ Da Nane Canton. ■ Famous in Venice for its fish. The *pasticcio di pesce* is an excellent dish. Tables outside in summer.

Torcello
€€€€ Locanda Cipriani. ■ *T: 041 730150, closed Jan. Map p. 323, B1.* Elegant but not fussy or intimidating. Good food. Lovely garden in summer overlooking Santa Fosca.

BACARI, CAFÉS & BARS

BACARI
Osterie, or *bácari* as they are known in Venice, are cheap eating places which sell wine by the glass and good simple food (usually crowded and often less comfortable than normal *trattorie*). Many of these are open only at lunch time and closed at weekends.

Da Mario. *Fondamenta della Malvasia (Rio Malatin), near Santa Maria del Giglio, San Marco, Open 12–2.30 & 7.30–9.30. Map p. 406, C3*. Outside it vaunts its old red-painted sign, and the cosy interior is crammed full of every kind of decoration. In the hands of the efficient *padrona*, Anna Lisa Masiero, with a character all her own, this is a very popular traditional eating place. Apart from the simple genuine food, you will eat in the company of Venetians from all walks of life: the *clientèle* changes dramatically from the earliest customers at 12 (a notice in the window declares that for the first hour only *operai*, in other words, workmen who only get a one-hour lunch break between 12 and 1, will be served) to the businessmen who arrive around 1.30. You have the impression that the prices are thought up on the spot according to sympathy, and that only a happy few are allowed to choose their meal by a visit to the kitchen. However, 'tourists' are offered an excellent set menu (which includes fish).

Do Mori. ■ *Off Ruga Vecchia S. Giovanni Elemosinario, between 429 Sottoportego dei Do Mori and the parallel Ramo Prima Gallazza, with an entrance* on each, San Polo, T: 041 522 5401. Open 8.30am–7.45pm except Sun. Map p. 411, E2. A tiny *bacaro* without tables, but with one or two seats at a counter, and the ceiling hung with pewter pots. Although just a few steps from the busy Rialto markets, it is in a quiet corner. This is a favourite place for Venetians to have an aperitif before lunch or dinner, and it is one of the most genuine such places left in the city. Good wine sold by the glass from large demijohns, and a wide selection of excellent *cicchetti*.

Osteria ai Canottieri. *690 Fondamenta San Giobbe, Cannaregio, T: 041 717999. Closed Sun and Mon. Map p. 400, A2*. A straightforward little restaurant, with tables outside on the canal in summer.

Gislon. *Calle della Bissa, near Campo San Bartolomeo, 5424 San Marco. T: 041 522 3569. Map p. 407, D1*. Venice's most famous *rosticceria*, specialities include fish risotto, cuttlefish and *baccalà* (salt cod).

Schiavi (or Vini al Bottegon). ■ *Rio San Trovaso, Dorsoduro. T: 041 523 0034. Closed Sun afternoon. Map p. 409, D3*. Known simply as 'Il Bottegon', this is one of the most typical of all the Venetian *bacari* (*described on p. 160*).

FOOD FOR PICNICS

Bars sell ready-made sandwiches (*tramezzini*), which can be very good: one of the best places to find them is the **Bar dei Nomboli** (*2717c Rio Terrà dei Nomboli, San Polo; map p. 411, D3*). Sandwiches (*panini*) can also be made up on request at grocery shops. There are excellent food markets open in the mornings (except Sun) at the Rialto and in Rio Terrà San Leonardo (Cannaregio; *map p. 401, D3*). See also the short list of markets and supermarkets on pp. 375–6.

CAFÉS AND BARS

Visitors are often surprised at the Italian habit of standing up to drink or take a coffee and eat a snack. It is worth knowing that you will be charged considerably more (at least double) if you choose to sit down and be given waiter service. If you stand, the rule is that you place your order and pay the cashier first, then show the receipt to the barman, who will give you your order. If you sit down, you pay afterwards.

The two most famous cafés in the city are **Florian** and **Quadri** in Piazza San Marco, with tables outside and orchestras—you are charged a great deal extra for your magnificent surroundings. They are described on pp. 71 and 72. **Caffè del Doge** near the Rialto Market (*609 Calle dei Cinque, off Ruga Vecchia di San Giovanni Elemosinario; map p. 411, F2*) serves a great variety of excellent coffee.

Harry's Bar (*map p. 407, D3*) is the most celebrated cocktail bar, but the **Danieli and Gritti hotels** (*map p. 407, F2 and p. 406, C3*) also have foyer bars, renowned for their cocktails, décor and atmosphere. There are number of wine bars around town offering *vini sfusi*, wines by the glass.

CAKE SHOPS & TEAROOMS

Many Venetians consider **Tonolo**, on the corner of Calle dei Preti and Calle San Pantalon (Dorsoduro; *map p. 409, D1*) the best *pasticceria* in the city. At **Colussi** in Calle Lunga San Barnaba (Dorsoduro; *map p. 408, C2*) delicious cakes and biscuits are still made on the spot by 'Nonno' Colussi, but it has very erratic opening hours and can be closed for long periods. Another old-established cake shop is **Bonifacio** (*4237 Calle degli Albanesi, off Salizzada San Provolo, between St Mark's and San Zaccaria; map p. 407, E2*). **Rosa Salva** sells good cakes in its three shops, in Merceria San Salvador (*5020 San Marco; map p. 407, D1*), Calle Fiubera (*951 San Marco; map p. 407, D2*) and Campo Santi Giovanni e Paolo (*Castello; map p. 402, C3*) and they also run the pleasant café in Palazzo Franchetti (at the foot of the Accademia Bridge on the Dorsoduro side) where you can also have a light lunch. Also good are **Dal Cò** (*Calle dei Fabbri, San Marco; map p. 407, D2*); **Canonica** (*Campo Santi Filippo e Giacomo, Castello; map p. 407, E2*); **Rizzardini** (*Campiello dei Meloni, San Polo; map p. 411, E3*); **Didovich** in Campo Santa Marina (*Castello; map p. 402, C3*); and **Boscolo** in Campiello dell'Anconetta, near San Marcuola (*Cannaregio; map p. 401, D3*). There is a good *pasticceria* called **Rio Marin** (*784 Fondamenta Rio Marin; map p. 410, B2*) which has tables outside on the canal in good weather. **Tearoom Caffè Orientale** (*888 Rio Marin; open 12–9pm except Thur; map p. 410, C2*) is a delightful place to stop and have something simple to eat and drink. Francesco and Elena produce vegetarian and vegan dishes, and very good desserts (apple pie and chocolate cake), as well as scones. Good tea and drinks, both alcoholic and soft. **Tea Room Beatrice** (*2727 Calle Lunga San Barnaba; open 3–10pm; map p. 408, C2*) is a cosy place furnished in Oriental style in an inner courtyard.

S. Alvise

Madonna
dell' Orto

2

4 Jewish Mus.

5

CANNAREGIO

CANALE DI CANNAREGIO

GRAND

S. Stae

1

Ca' Pesaro

Ca' d'Oro

CANAL

Santa Lucia
Station

31

SANTA CROCE

S. Giacomo
dell'Orio

32

30

28

SAN POLO

29

26

Rialto
Bridge

S. Polo

Frari

27

S. Salva

GRAND

CANAL

25

15

Ca' Rezzonico

16

SAN MARCO

Carmini

19 17

S. Stefano

La Fenice

22

18 **DORSODURO**

14

13

Gallerie dell'
Accademia

Peggy Guggenheim
12 Collection

Salute

Gesuati

CANAL

CANALE

Mulino
Stucky

DELLA

GIU

20

Redentore

GIUDECCA

1	Alla Vedova	12	Ai Gondolieri	23	Harry's Bar
2	Antica Mola	13	Vecio Marangon	24	Quadri
3	Fiaschetteria Toscana	14	Casin dei Nobili	25	Vini da Arturo
4	Hosteria del Ghetto	15	Do Torri	26	Alla Madonna
5	Trattoria Marisa	16	L'Incontro	27	Da Ignazio
6	Al Covo	17	Oniga	28	Antiche Carampane
7	Corte Sconta	18	Pane e Vino	29	Antico Dolo
8	Il Giardinetto	19	Quattro Feri	30	Da Fiore
9	Il Nuovo Galeon	20	Altanella	31	Antica Besseta
10	Santa Maria	21	I Figli delle Stelle	32	Vecio Fritolin
11	Da Remigio	22	A Beccafico		

FONDAMENTE NUOVE
Santi Giovanni e Paolo
S. Francesco d. Vigna
S. Maria Formosa
CASTELLO
DARSENA GRANDE
St Mark's Basilica
S. Zaccaria
S. Giovanni in Bragora
Arsenale
S. Pietro di Castello
ISOLA DI SAN PIETRO
Doge's Palace
CANALE DI SAN MARCO
Giardini Pubblici
Biennale
San Giorgio Maggiore
ISOLA DI S. GIORGIO MAGGIORE
10
8
11
7
6
9

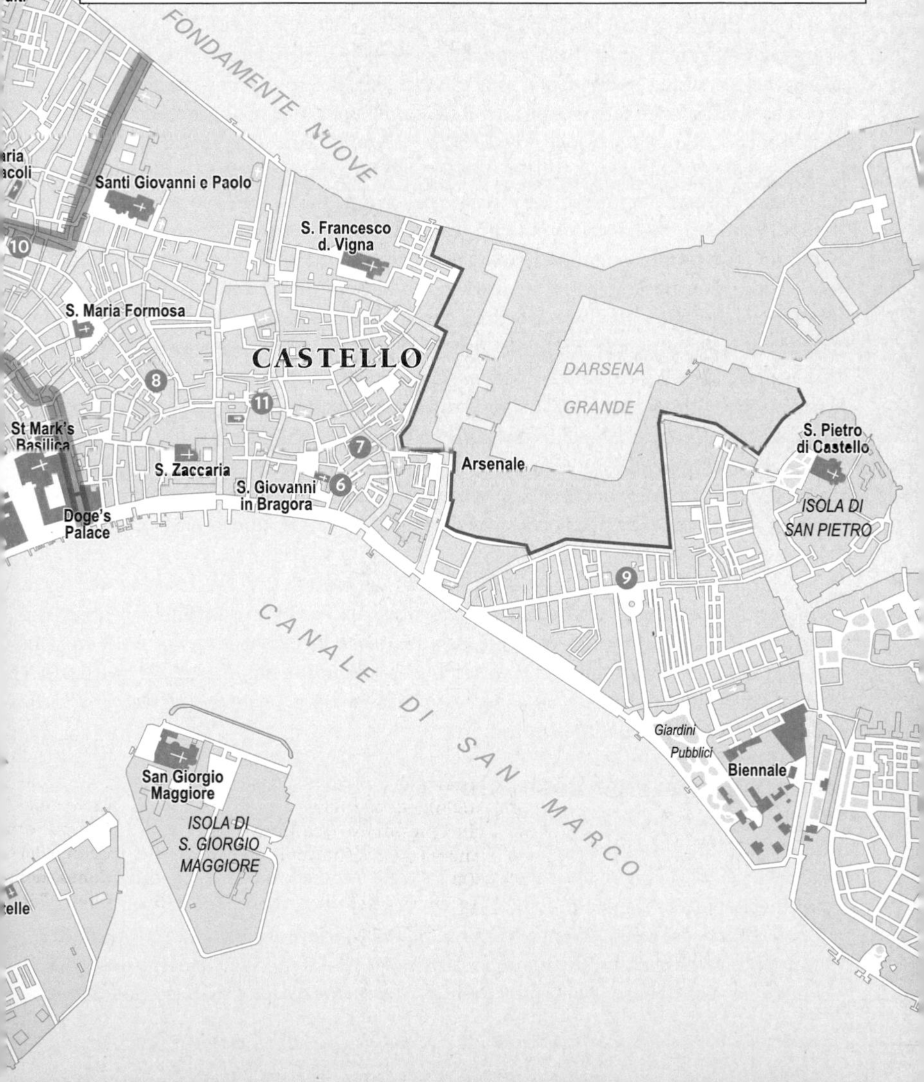

General Information

ACQUA ALTA

Acqua alta, a high tide which floods parts of the city when above 110cm, usually occurs many times throughout the year (especially between Sept and April), but the frequency of these tides varies greatly from year to year. They are caused by the position of the moon as well as adverse atmospheric conditions including strong sirocco winds. (*For more on the ecology of the lagoon, and the Mo.S.E. project to protect the city, see pp. 34–5.*)

A siren used to be sounded from the top of the campanile of San Marco when an *acqua alta* was imminent, but this has now been replaced by the even more eerie sound of digital acoustic signals: a prolonged sound at the same pitch announces a high tide of 110cm; two sounds on an increasing scale signify that the tide will be over 120cm; three sounds on an increasing scale that it will be over 130cm, and four sounds on an increasing scale announce an exceptionally high tide of 140cm, when nearly 60 percent of the city will be flooded (but this thankfully occurs very rarely). The flood tide usually lasts 2 or 3 hours, and *passarelle* or duck-boards are laid out in Piazza San Marco, by the landing-stages and in some of the *calli*. This raised thoroughfare throughout the city totals over 4km, and can usually provide a dry route from Piazzale Roma and the railway station to Piazza San Marco. However, it is not possible to get about the city on these occasions without wellington boots. A map showing the *calli* which do not normally get flooded, and those where the duckboards are set up, is available at www.actv.it.

For information there is an automatic call centre (*T: 041 241 1996, or see www. comune.venezia.it/maree*) which also provides an accurate weather forecast and warnings of *acqua alta* (and you can also ask to be forewarned by an SMS on your mobile phone). Some of the ACTV water-buses (including nos 4.1, 4.2, 5.1 and 5.2) are suspended or diverted during an *acqua alta* because they are unable to pass below the road and rail bridges near the station.

CHURCHES AND RELIGIOUS SERVICES

Opening times have been given in the text and were correct at the time of writing, though they are always subject to change. The association called Chorus provides access to the following 16 churches with a single admission ticket (or, much cheaper, combined ticket for them all):

Santa Maria del Giglio, Santo Stefano, Santa Maria Formosa, Santa Maria dei Miracoli, San Giovanni Elemosinario, the Frari, San Polo, San Giacomo dell'Orio, San Stae, Sant'Alvise, Madonna dell'Orto, San Pietro di Castello, Redentore,

Gesuati, San Sebastiano and San Giobbe.
These are usually open Mon–Sat 10–5 except for the Frari, which has longer opening hours (details are given in the main text).

Some other churches are kept open free of charge at different times by an association called Imago. These are:

San Trovaso, the Carmini, San Giovanni in Bragora, San Salvatore and San Moisè.

Lights (coin-operated) are installed in some churches to illuminate altarpieces. As a result it is essential to carry a great deal of change (if you run out, the sacristan or custodian can usually help). Some churches now ask that sightseers do not enter during a service, but normally visitors not in a tour group may do so, provided you are silent and do not approach the altar in use. If you are wearing shorts or have bare shoulders, you can sometimes be stopped from entering. Churches in Venice are very often not orientated. In the text, the terms north and south refer to the liturgical north (left) and south (right), with the high altar taken to be at the 'east' end.

Religious services

Roman Catholic: On Sun and, in the principal churches, often on weekdays, Mass is celebrated from the early morning up to midday and from 5.30–7pm. High Mass, with music, is held in St Mark's at 10am on Sun. At 11am Gregorian chant is sung at San Giorgio Maggiore. Mass in English is also held at San Giuliano (*map p. 407, E1*). On saints' days Mass and vespers with music are celebrated in the churches dedicated to the saints concerned. On the Feast of St Mark (25th April), special services are held and the Pala d'Oro is exposed on the high altar (also displayed at Christmas and Easter). For the Feasts of the Redentore (3rd Sun in July) and of Santa Maria della Salute (21st Nov), see p. 372.

Anglican: St George's (Dorsoduro; *map p. 406, B3*). Services on Sun at 10.30. See *stgeorgesvenice.com* for details.

Lutheran: Campo Santi Apostoli (Cannaregio; *map p. 402, B3, T: 041 524 2040*).

Greek Orthodox: Ponte dei Greci (Castello; *map p. 404, A1, T: 041 522 5446*).

Waldensian, Evangelical and Methodist: 5170 Calle Lunga Santa Maria Formosa (Castello; *map p. 403, D4, T: 041 522 7549*).

Synagogues: Scuola Spagnola and Scuola Levantina, Ghetto Vecchio (*map p. 400, C2, T: 041 715012*).

EMERGENCIES

For all emergencies, T: 113: the switchboard will coordinate the help you need.

First aid services (*Pronto Soccorso*) are available at hospitals, railway stations and airports. The most central hospital is Ospedale Civile, Santi Giovanni e Paolo, in the old *Scuola Grande* (*map p. 403, D3; T: 041 529 4111*). First aid services are available.

Ambulance service, T: 118.

Fire brigade, T: 115

Lost property: For the municipal police office, *T: 041 522 4576*. For the railway lost property, *T: 041 785 238*; and for objects lost on ACTV water-buses, *T: 041 272 2179*.

FESTIVALS

The **Venice Carnival** was famous throughout the Republic, when it lasted from 26th December to the first day of Lent. Parties and pageants were organised by special societies, and it was a time when the authority of Church and State was ignored and the masked inhabitants enjoyed a period of freedom and anarchy. In the 20th century the spirit of Carnival died out, but since 1980 the week or ten days in February before Lent has been celebrated by ever-increasing numbers, and it has become the most crowded (and expensive) time of year. The city is invaded by merry-makers in fancy dress and masks, and numerous theatrical and musical events take place, both indoors and out. On some days during Carnival week the city more than doubles its population. The festivities end on Shrove Tuesday, when a huge ball is usually held in Piazza San Marco. For details, see carnivale.venezia.it.

The *Vogalonga* (literally 'long row') takes place on a Sun in May. First held in 1975, it has become a very popular Venetian event. It is open to anyone prepared to row from the mouth of the Giudecca Canal around the east end of Venice (Sant'Elena) up past Murano, through the Mazzorbo canal, around Burano, past San Francesco del Deserto and back down past the islands of Sant' Erasmo and Le Vignole, through the main canal of Murano, and back to Venice via the Cannaregio Canal and the Grand Canal to the Punta della Dogana; a course of 32km. Any type or size of boat may participate, with any number of oarsmen in each boat. Rowing crews from London and Oxford also take part. A small participation fee is paid on enrolment. The departure is at 9am (best seen from the Zattere or Riva degli Schiavoni and the Giardini) and the first boats usually arrive back in the city at 11 or 11.30am (seen from the Cannaregio Canal and the Grand Canal). It is a non-competitive course, and the last oarsmen usually return around 3pm. Normally, some 1,500 boats and over 5,000 people take part in the event in a remarkable variety of boats, some of them elaborately decorated. For details, see vogalonga.net.

On the *Festa del Redentore* (on the Sat before the 3rd Sun in July) a bridge of boats is constructed across the Giudecca Canal; its vigil is celebrated with aquatic concerts and splendid fireworks (best seen from the Giudecca, the Zattere, or from a boat). Motor-boats are excluded from the Bacino di San Marco after 9pm.

The *Festa della Sensa* takes place on the Sun after Ascension Day (usually in May). This was celebrated throughout the Republic, when the Doge ceremonially cast a ring into the lagoon at San Nicolò al Lido (*see p. 333*) symbolising the marriage of Venice with the sea. For the occasion, the doge was transported in the elaborate *Bucintoro*. It is now celebrated by the Mayor and Patriarch and other Venetian authorities. They depart from the Bacino di San Marco and proceed to San Nicolò al Lido.

The *Regata Storica* (first Sun in Sept) starts with a procession on the Grand Canal of the historic *bissone*, boats of a unique shape with their high prows richly decorated. This is followed by the most famous of the Venetian regattas with four different races, culminating in that of the two-oar *gondolini*, rowed by expert Venetian oarsmen. Other regattas are held from June–Sept in the lagoon near Sant'Erasmo, Murano, Pellestrina and Burano.

The *Festa della Salute* (21st Nov) is celebrated by a bridge of boats across the

Grand Canal at the Punta della Dogana. All are welcome to join in the procession across the bridge, taking a lighted candle to the church of the Salute, to give thanks for deliverance from plague.

MUSEUMS
Museum opening times vary and often change without warning; those given in the text should therefore be accepted with reserve (check the website or telephone to check times). A current list of opening times is always available at the APT (tourist information) offices. Ticket offices close one hour before the museum. Opening hours for Sundays apply also to public holidays (*giorni festivi*). State museums are usually closed on Mondays, and other museums in Venice often on Tuesdays.

The **Venice Card**, valid for 7 days, allows free entrance to the ten civic museums of Venice (including the Doge's Palace, where you can thus avoid the queue), the Palazzo Querini-Stampalia, and the Jewish Museum in the Ghetto, as well as the 16 churches opened by Chorus, and reductions on some other museum entrances. There is also a combined ticket for the museums in Piazza San Marco (Doge's Palace and Museo Correr) and another ticket which allows you free entrance to all the civic museums of Venice.

EU citizens under 18 and over 65 are entitled to free admission to state museums and monuments in Italy (on production of an identity card proving your age). EU students between the ages of 18 and 26 are also entitled to a reduction (usually 50%) to state museums, and some other museums have special student tickets.

OPENING HOURS
Shops are normally open from 8 or 9am–1pm & 3 or 3.30pm–7.30 or 8pm, although they are allowed to adopt whatever opening hours they wish. Most of the year, some food shops are closed on Wed afternoon (in July and August they are closed on Sat afternoon), although many of them only close on Sun. Clothes shops, hairdressers, etc. are usually closed on Mon morning.

ORGANISATIONS FOR THE SAFEGUARDING/RESTORATION OF VENICE
The Association of International Private Committees for the Safeguarding of Venice (www.comitatiprivativenezia.org) operates in conjunction with the UNESCO Regional Bureau for Science and Culture in Europe (BRESCE), at Palazzo Zorzi (*4930 Castello, T: 041 520 7050*). Among the 30 members are the Associazione Amici dei Musei e Monumenti Veneziani and the Venice in Peril Fund (*www.veniceinperil.org*). The two North American organisations are Save Venice Inc., based in New York (*www. savevenice.org*) and Venetian Heritage Inc. (*www.venetianheritage.org*). The Venice Foundation at Ca' Lupelli (*3144 Dorsoduro*; adjoining Ca' Rezzonico) also does a great deal to help restore Venice's monuments.

PHARMACIES
Pharmacies or chemists (*farmacie*) are identified by their street signs, which show a luminous green cross. They are usually open Mon–Fri 9am–1pm & 4–7.30 or 8pm.

Those open 24hrs a day and at weekends are listed on the door of every pharmacy. See also www.farmacistivenezia.it and search '*farmacie di turno*'.

PORTERS

Porters in Venice are distinguished by their hats (with *portabagaglio* on the badge) and are available in various parts of the city to help with heavy luggage (they will also accompany you on *vaporetti*). Although tariffs are fixed, you should establish the price for each piece of luggage before hiring a porter.

PUBLIC HOLIDAYS

The main holidays in Italy, when offices, shops and schools are closed, are as follows:

1st January	New Year's Day
25th April	Liberation Day and the Festival of St Mark
Easter Monday	
1st May	Labour Day
2nd June	Festa della Repubblica
15th August	Assumption
1st November	All Saints' Day
8th December	Immaculate Conception
Christmas Day	
26th December	St Stephen

In Venice the *Festa della Salute* (21st Nov) is a public holiday, and also usually the festival of the Redentore (third weekend in July). There is usually no public transport on 1st May and the afternoon of Christmas Day.

SHOPPING

Venetian glass: Glass is sold in numerous glass factories and shops on the island of Murano and all over Venice, but you should always check that these have the Murano registered trademark which guarantees its quality. Shops specialising in glass in Venice itself include Paolorossi in Campo San Zaccaria (*map p. 404, A2*) and Venini in Piazzetta Giovanni XXIII (*map p. 407, E2*), which is one of the best-known shops for the sale of precious glass. Exquisitely made glass animals are sold at Amadi (*2747 Calle Saoneri; map p. 411, D3*) and Vittorio Costantini (*Calle del Fumo; map p. 402, C2*). Lovely glass pearls can be found at Gianni Moretti at San Moisè (*map p 407, D2*). Filippo Gambardella at Napé (*683 Calle della Chiesa; map p. 409, E3*) and Giordana Naccari at L'Angolo Del Passato (*Campiello dei Squellini; map p. 409, D2*) are both antique glass dealers. Marina and Susanna Sent in Campo San Vio (*map p. 409, E3*) make interesting glass jewellery. At no. 1045 Fondamenta Cannaregio (*map p. 400, B2*) the Fornace Angelo Orsoni, founded in the 19th century, still produces glass mosaic and Venetian enamel.

Fabrics: The three most famous manufacturers in Venice, founded in the 19th century and still producing wonderful fabrics, textiles and silks, are Luigi Bevilacqua (*1320*

Campiello della Cornare, Santa Croce, reached from the Riva de Biasio vaporetto stop; map p. 410, C1), Rubelli at Palazzo Corner-Spinelli (*3877 San Marco, at the Sant'Angelo vaporetto landing-stage; map p. 406, B1*) and Fortuny on the Giudecca (*no. 805 on the canal front next to the Mulino Stucky; map p. 408, B4*). Venetian Studium (*2403 Calle Larga XXII Marzo; map p. 406, C3*), also sells lovely fabrics.

Fashion: Very original shoes are handmade by Giovanna Zanella in her shop in Castello (*5641 Calle Carminati, near San Lio; map p. 402, C3*) and designer scarves and jewellery are produced at Gualti (*3111 Rio Terrà Canal in Dorsoduro; map p. 408, C2*). Zazù (*2750 Calle dei Saoneri; map p. 411, D3*), run by Federica Zamboni, has interesting clothes inspired by Indian art, some of them designed by Federica herself. Hibiscus at 1060 Calle de l'Ogio, or Calle dell'Olio (*the continuation of Ruga Vecchia San Giovanni which leads into Campo Sant'Aponal; map p. 411, E3*) sells clothes, accessories and jewellery made in Venice, all with a very distinctive style.

Models of boats: These and other nautical curiosities, plus modelling kits, are made by Gilberto Penzo (*2681 Calle 2 dei Saoneri; map p. 411, D3*), and another interesting shop is Anticlea Antiquariato (*4719 Calle San Provolo; map p. 407, F2*).

Bookshops: Among the best stocked are Goldoni (*Calle dei Fabbri, 4742 San Marco; map p. 407, D1*); Alla Toletta, also with a large selection of discount books (*1213 Calle della Toletta; map p. 409, D3*); and Studium, just off Piazza San Marco (*337 Calle Canonica; map p. 407, E2*). Filippi, near Santa Maria Formosa (*5763 Calle del Paradiso; map p. 402, C4*) and in Calle Casselleria (*5284 Castello; map p. 402, C4*) specialises in books on Venice. Marco Polo is an excellent travel bookshop (*5469 Salizzada San Lio; map p. 402, C4*). Another good place for books on Venice (as well as second-hand books and prints) is Lineadacqua (*3717 Calle della Mandola; map p. 406, C2*). The bookshop in the Ghetto Museum specialises in Judaica. Damocle Edizioni (*1311 Calle del Perdon; map p. 411, E3*) is a small independent publisher which produces handsome volumes, also with English texts.

Paper: Fine hand-made paper and stationery is sold at Alberto Valese-Ebrù (*Campo Santo Stefano, 3471 San Marco; map p. 406, B2*) and Gianni Basso, an excellent artisan printer, has his printing works in Calle del Fumo, off Calle Larga dei Botteri, near the vaporetto stops on the Fondamente Nuove (*map p. 402, C2*). Paolo Olbi in Calle della Mandola (*map p. 406, C2*) is a Venetian artisan who makes fine traditional stationery, photo albums, diaries, etc.

Open-air markets: The most important and best-value food market in Venice is the Rialto market, which sells a superb variety of produce every morning except Sun. The vegetables include asparagus and artichokes from the island of Sant'Erasmo, and there is a wonderful display of fresh fish in the large fish market. Bakers and grocers in the vicinity of the market are much favoured by the Venetians. There is a small daily produce market (and a few fish stalls) in Campo Santa Margherita (Dorsoduro; *map p. 408, C2*) open in the mornings. In Rio Terrà San Leonardo (Cannaregio; *map p. 401, D3*) there is a large street market on weekdays. Another small local market is in Castello at the end of Via Garibaldi (*map p. 405, E2*). Fruit and vegetable vendors often sell their wares from barges moored in the canals. There is one at Campo San Barnaba (*map p. 409, D2*) and another at Rio Sant'Anna (*map p. 405, E2*).

There are some small **supermarkets** in various parts of Venice, including Billa on Strada Nuova (*map p. 402, A2*) and at the further end of Fondamenta delle Zattere (*map p. 408, B3*), which is open late and also all day on Sun. There is another handy supermarket in Campo Santa Margherita (*map p. 408, C2*).

STUDENTS AND YOUNG VISITORS

Visitors between the ages of 14 and 29 can buy a Rolling Venice Card (valid up to the end of the year of issue) at the vaporetto landing-stages or APT tourist information offices, which entitles you to a reduced 72-hr ticket for the ACTV transport service, as well as discounts in certain shops and museums. It also gives access to the university canteen in Palazzo Badoer, Calle del Magazen, 2840 San Polo (closed in Aug). For student reductions in museums, see p. 373.

TELEPHONES

Telephone numbers in Italy require the area code, whether you are making a local call or a call from outside Venice. The Venice area code is 041.

Dialling UK from Italy (00 44) + number.

Dialling US from Italy (001) + number.

THEATRES

Venice has an extremely active programme of concerts throughout the year. The Fenice is one of the most famous opera houses in the world (*see p. 118*) and it also has an important concert season. The other important theatre for music is the Malibran. Prose performances are given at the Teatro Goldoni. Two very small but active theatres, with interesting experimental performances, are the Teatro alle Fondamente Nuove and the Teatro alla Vogaria in Dorsoduro. Concerts are also held in numerous churches all over Venice, and organ recitals also at the Salute and the Frari. Chamber concerts are held at the Conservatorio in Palazzo Pisani in Campo Santo Stefano in spring and summer. Concerts of French Romantic music are held frequently at the Palazzetto Bru Zane. For information about what's on, see wall posters and the monthly *Un Ospite di Venezia* (*A Guest in Venice*) available free at the tourist information offices and at hotels.

TIPPING

Tipping is less widespread in Italy than in North America. Most prices in restaurants include service: always check whether this has been added to the bill before leaving a tip. It is customary to leave a euro or two on the table to convey appreciation. Even taxi-drivers rarely expect more than a euro added to the charge (which officially includes service). In hotels, porters who show you to your room and help with your luggage, or find you a taxi, usually expect a euro or two.

Glossary

Albergo, small room used for committee meetings on the upper floor of a *scuola*

Altana (pl. *altane*), wodden roof terrace

Ambo (pl. *ambones*), pulpit in a Christian basilica; two pulpits on opposite sides of a church from which the gospel and epistle were read

Ancona, retable or large altarpiece (painted or sculpted) in an architectural frame

Androne, principal ground-floor hall behind the water entrance of a Venetian palace

Architrave, the lowest part of an entablature, the horizontal frame over a door

Archivolt, moulded architrave carried round an arch

Atlantes (or *telamones*), male figures used as supporting columns

Atrium, forecourt, usually part of a Byzantine church or a classical Roman house

Attic, topmost storey of a classical building, hiding the spring of the roof

Baldacchino, canopy supported by columns, usually over an altar

Bardiglio, marble streaked with blue and white

Basilica, originally a Roman building used for public administration; in Christian architecture, an aisled church with a clerestory and apse

Bas-relief, sculpture in low relief

Bottega, the studio of an artist; or the pupils who worked under his direction

Bozzetto, sketch, often used to describe a small model for a piece of sculpture

Campanile (pl. *campanili*) bell-tower, often detached from the building to which it belongs

Ca' (*casa*), Venetian term for palace (or important residence)

Calle (pl. *calli*) narrow Venetian street

Campiello, small Venetian piazza

Campo (pl. *campi*), Venetian term for piazza (or square)

Chiaroscuro, distribution of light and shade, apart from colour, in a painting

Ciborium, casket or tabernacle containing the Host (Communion bread)

Cipollino, greyish marble with streaks of white or green

Cippus (pl. *cippae*), sepulchral monument in the form of an altar

Cloisonné, type of enamel decoration, where areas of colour are partitioned by narrow strips of metal

Condottiere, captain-general of a city militia; soldier of fortune at the head of an army

Corbel, a projecting block, usually of stone, to support a beam or other roof structure

Cornu (or *berretta*), peaked doge's beret in red velvet, worn over a white linen skull cap

Corte, courtyard

Diocletian window, also known as a thermal window, the term refers to a (usually large) semicircular window derived from those used in ancient

Roman public baths (notably those of Diocletian). A characteristic feature of Palladian architecture

Diptych, painting or ivory tablet in two sections

Dossal, altarpiece

Duomo, cathedral

Exedra, semi-circular recess

Ex-voto, tablet or small painting expressing gratitude to a saint

Fondaco (*fontego*), trading post

Fondamenta (pl. *fondamente*), street alongside a canal

Forno (pl. *forni*), bakery

Fruttarol, greengrocer, hence 'Calle del Fruttarol', of which Venice has many

Greek cross, cross with vertical and transverse arms of equal length

Herm, quadrangular pillar decreasing in girth towards the ground, surmounted by a head

Iconostasis, high balustrade hung with icons of saints, separating the sanctuary of a Byzantine church from the nave

Intarsia, inlay of wood, marble or metal

Latin cross, cross where the vertical arm is longer than the transverse arm

Liagò, upper-floor loggia which protrudes from a Venetian palace façade

Lista, a lane which led up to an ambassador's palace

Loggia, covered upper-floor gallery

Lunette, semi-circular space in a vault or above a window or doorway, often decorated with a painting or relief

Magazen (*magazzino*), warehouse

Merceria, market

Matroneum, gallery reserved for women in early Christian churches

Monstrance, a vessel for displaying the Host (Communion bread)

Narthex, vestibule of a Christian basilica

Niello, a black inlay into stone, using silver, lead, copper, sulphur and borax

Ogee, of an arch, shaped in a double curve, convex above and concave below

Opus alexandrinum, mosaic design of black and red geometric figures on a white ground

Opus sectile, mosaic or paving of thin slabs of coloured marble cut in geometrical shapes

Palazzo, palace; any dignified and important building

Pali, wood piles used as foundations for buildings in Venice; and the mooring posts in front of palaces showing the livery colours of their proprietors

Pantocrator, in Byzantine iconography the Almighty, the ruler of the Universe

Paten, flat dish on which the Host (Communion bread) is placed

Patera (pl. *paterae*), small circular carved ornament (often Byzantine), used as a decorative feature

Pavonazzetto, yellow marble blotched with blue

Pax, sacred object used by a priest for the blessing of peace, and offered for the kiss of the faithful, usually circular, engraved, enamelled or painted in a rich gold or silver frame

Pendentive, one of four concave spandrels formed when a dome attaches to quadrilateral walls; often they are decorated with images of the Evangelists

Piano nobile, the main floor of a house, where the grandest apartments are to be found

Pier, a square or compound pillar used as a support in architecture

Pietà, group of the Virgin, sometimes with saints and angels, mourning the dead Christ

Pietre dure, hard or semi-precious stones, cut and inlaid to decorate cabinets, table-tops, etc.

Piscina, place where a basin of water connected to a canal formerly existed

Pistor, a baker, hence 'Calle del Pistor', of which Venice has several

Pluteus (pl. *plutei*), marble panel, usually decorated; a series of them are often used to form a parapet to precede the altar of a church

Polyptych, painting or panel divided into multiple sections

Porphyry, an extremely hard purplish rock quarried in Egypt, often used for sculpture by the Romans

Portego, the central hall of a Venetian house, usually running the whole depth of the building

Predella, small painting or panel attached below a large altarpiece

Pronaos, vestibule in front of the inner room of a temple

Proto, 'protomagister', chief architect

Pulvin, cushion-shaped block between the capital and the arch surmounting it

Putto (pl. *putti*), sculpted or painted figure, usually nude, of a baby boy

Quadratura (pl. *quadrature*) painted architectural perspectives

Quatrefoil, four-lobed cusp (on an arch)

Ramo, offshoot of a canal

Reredos, decorated screen rising behind an altar

Rio terrà, street along the course of a filled-in rio

Riva, wharf

Rood-screen, a screen below the Rood or Crucifix, dividing the nave from the chancel in a church

Ruga, street

Rustication, denotes the grooves or channels cut at the joints between huge blocks of facing masonry (ashlar) on grand buildings

Sacca, stretch of water where canals meet

Salizzada, name given to the first paved streets of Venice in the 17th century; now simply denotes a paved street

Sandalo, flat-bottomed Venetian rowing boat, used on the lagoon

Scuola (pl. *scuole*), lay confraternity, dedicated to charitable works

Sestiere (pl. *sestieri*), district of Venice

Situla, a water-bucket, for ceremonial use

Soffit, underside (or intrados) of an arch

Sottoportico, Venetian term for a street which passes beneath a building, or a street entered under arches

Spandrel, surface between two arches in an arcade or the triangular space on either side of an arch

Spezier, spicer or apothecary, hence 'Calle del Spezier', of which Venice has a number

Stilted arch, round arch that rises vertically (on a 'stilt') before it springs

Stoup, vessel for Holy Water, usually near the entrance of a church

Stylobate, basement of a columned temple or other building

Telamones, see Atlantes

Tessera, small cube of marble, glass, etc. used in mosaic work

Tondo (pl. *tondi*), roundel

Transenna, open grille or screen, usually of marble, in an early Christian church

Trefoil, three-lobed cusp (on an arch)

Tricuspid, having three points or cusps

Triptych, painting or tablet in three sections

Vera da pozzo, well-head

Verde antico, dark green marble from Thessaly, Greece

Virgin orans, Byzantine style of depicting the Madonna, with her two arms raised in supplication

Volute, tightly curled spiral scroll

The Doges of Venice

1.	697–717	Paoluccio Anafesto
2.	717–726	Marcello Tegalliano
3.	726–737	Orso Ipato
	737–742	*Interregnum*
4.	742–755	Teodato Ipato
5.	755–756	Galla Gaulo
6.	756–764	Domenico Monegario
7.	764–775	Maurizio Galbaio
8.	787–804	Giovanni Galbaio
9.	804–811	Obelario d. Antenori
10.	811–827	Agnello Particiaco
11.	827–829	Giustiniano Particiaco
12.	829–836	Giovanni Particiaco I
13.	836–864	Pietro Tradonico
14.	864–881	Orso Particiaco I
15.	881–887	Giovanni Particiaco II
16.	887	Pietro Candiano I
17.	888–912	Pietro Tribuno
18.	912–932	Orso Particiaco II
19.	932–939	Pietro Candiano II
20.	939–942	Pietro Particiaco
21.	942–959	Pietro Candiano III
22.	959–976	Pietro Candiano IV
23.	976–978	Pietro Orseolo I
24.	978–979	Vitale Candiano
25.	979–991	Tribuno Memmo
26.	991–1008	Pietro Orseolo II
27.	1008–1026	Otto (Orso) Orseolo
28.	1026–1032	Pietro Centranico
29.	1032–1043	Domenico Flabanico
30.	1043–1071	Domenico Contarini
31.	1071–1084	Domenico Selvo
32.	1084–1096	Vitale Falier
33.	1096–1102	Vitale Michiel I
34.	1102–1118	Ordelafo Falier
35.	1118–1130	Domenico Michiel
36.	1130–1148	Pietro Polani
37.	1148–1156	Domenico Morosini
38.	1156–1172	Vitale Michiel II
39.	1172–1178	Sebastiano Ziani
40.	1178–1192	Orio Mastropiero
41.	1192–1205	Enrico Dandolo
42.	1205–1229	Pietro Ziani
43.	1229–1249	Giacomo Tiepolo
44.	1249–1253	Marin Morosini
45.	1253–1268	Ranier Zeno
46.	1268–1275	Lorenzo Tiepolo
47.	1275–1280	Jacopo Contarini
48.	1280–1289	Giovanni Dandolo
49.	1289–1311	Pietro Gradenigo
50.	1311–1312	Marino Zorzi
51.	1312–1328	Giovanni Soranzo
52.	1329–1339	Francesco Dandolo
53.	1339–1342	Bartolomeo Gradenigo
54.	1343–1354	Andrea Dandolo
55.	1354–1355	Marin Falier
56.	1355–1356	Giovanni Gradenigo
57.	1356–1361	Giovanni Dolfin
58.	1361–1365	Lorenzo Celsi
59.	1365–1368	Marco Corner
60.	1368–1382	Andrea Contarini
61.	1382	Michele Morosini
62.	1382–1400	Antonio Venier
63.	1400–1413	Michele Steno
64.	1414–1423	Tommaso Mocenigo
65.	1423–1457	Francesco Foscari
66.	1457–1462	Pasquale Malipiero
67.	1462–1471	Cristoforo Moro
68.	1471–1473	Nicolò Tron
69.	1473–1474	Nicolò Marcello

70.	1474–1476	Pietro Mocenigo
71.	1476–1478	Andrea Vendramin
72.	1478–1485	Giovanni Mocenigo
73.	1485–1486	Marco Barbarigo
74.	1486–1501	Agostino Barbarigo
75.	1501–1521	Leonardo Loredan
76.	1521–1523	Antonio Grimani
77.	1523–1538	Andrea Gritti
78.	1539–1545	Pietro Lando
79.	1545–1553	Francesco Donà
80.	1553–1554	Marcantonio Trevisan
81.	1554–1556	Francesco Venier
82.	1556–1559	Lorenzo Priuli
83.	1559–1567	Girolamo Priuli
84.	1567–1570	Pietro Loredan
85.	1570–1577	Alvise Mocenigo I
86.	1577–1578	Sebastiano Venier
87.	1578–1585	Nicolò da Ponte
88.	1585–1595	Pasquale Cicogna
89.	1595–1605	Marino Grimani
90.	1606–1612	Leonardo Donà
91.	1612–1615	Marcantonio Memmo
92.	1615–1618	Giovanni Bembo
93.	1618	Nicolò Donà
94.	1618–1623	Antonio Priuli
95.	1623–1624	Francesco Contarini
96.	1625–1629	Giovanni Corner I
97.	1630–1631	Nicolò Contarini
98.	1631–1646	Francesco Erizzo
99.	1646–1655	Francesco Molin
100.	1655–1656	Carlo Contarini
101.	1656	Francesco Corner
102.	1656–1658	Bertucci Valier
103.	1658–1659	Giovanni Pesaro
104.	1659–1675	Domenico Contarini
105.	1675–1676	Nicolò Sagredo
106.	1676–1684	Alvise Contarini
107.	1684–1688	Marcantonio Giustinian
108.	1688–1694	Francesco Morosini
109.	1694–1700	Silvestro Valier
110.	1700–1709	Alvise Mocenigo II
111.	1709–1722	Giovanni Corner II
112.	1722–1732	Alvise Mocenigo III
113.	1732–1735	Carlo Ruzzini
114.	1735–1741	Alvise Pisani
115.	1741–1752	Pietro Grimani
116.	1752–1762	Francesco Loredan
117.	1762–1763	Marco Foscarini
118.	1763–1778	Alvise Mocenigo IV
119.	1779–1789	Paolo Renier
120.	1789–1797	Lodovico Manin

Index

Explanatory or more detailed references (where there are many), or references to places where an artist's work is best represented, are given in bold. Numbers in italics are picture references.

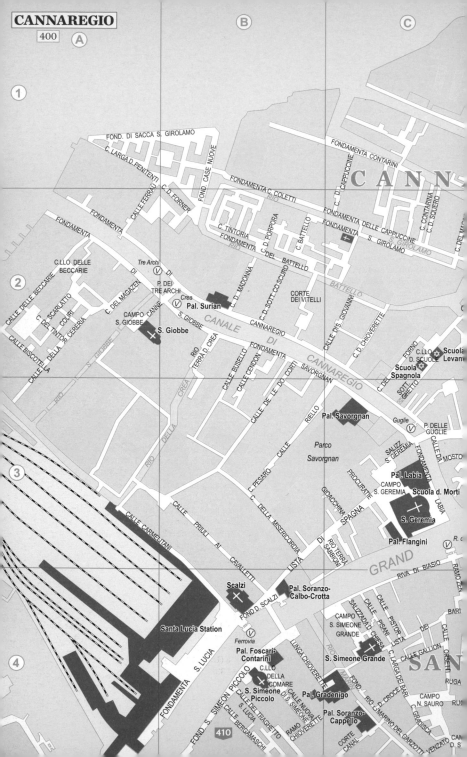

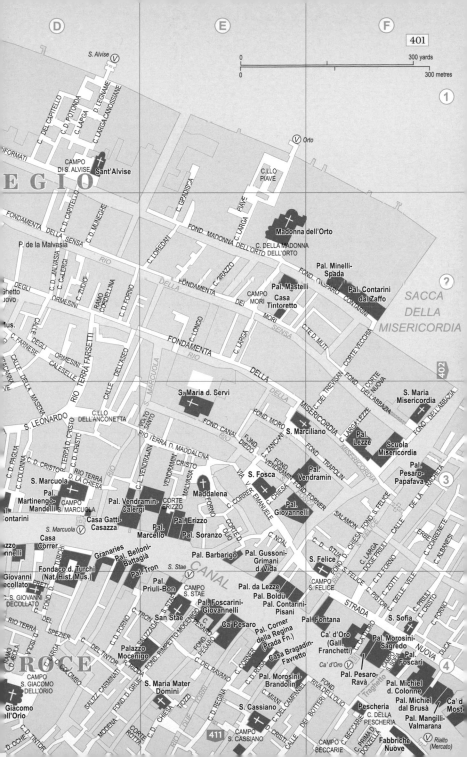

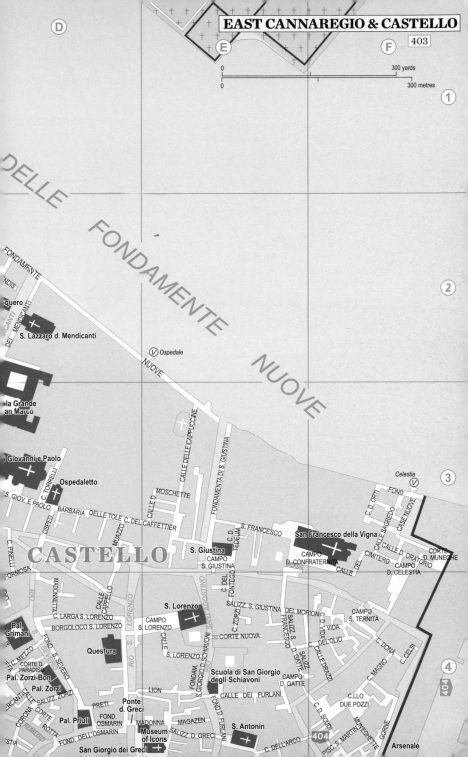

D   **E**   **F**

0   300 yards

0   300 metres

1

DELLE FONDAMENTE NUOVE

2

S. Lazzaro d. Mendicanti

quero

Ospedale

NUOVE

la Grande an Marco

Giovanni e Paolo

Ospedaletto

S. GIOV. E PAOLO

C. TORRELLI

CALLE DELLE CAPPUCCINE

MOSCHETTE

FONDAMENTA DI S. GIUSTINA

Celestia

3

FOND.

C. D. ORTI

CALLE SAGREDO

CASE NUOVE

BARBARIA DELLE TOLE C. DEL CAFFETTIER

MIAZZO

CALLE D

S. FRANCESCO

San Francesco della Vigna

CALLE D'ORATORIO

CORTE D. MUNEGHE

CASTELLO

S. Giustina

CAMPO S. GIUSTINA

C. DEL TEDEUM

CAMPO D. CONFRATERNITA

CIMITERO

CAMPO D. CELESTIA

CALLE DEI

C. PINELLI

FORMOSA

MADDONNETTA

C. LARGA S. LORENZO

CALLE CAPPELLO

RIO S. LORENZO

S. Lorenzo

CAMPO S. LORENZO

CALLE

C. DEL FONTEGO

SALIZZ. S. GIUSTINA

DEL MORION

C. ZORZI

CALLE DRAZZI

SALIZZ. S. FRANCESCO

C.D. VIDA

CAMPO S. TERNITÀ

C. DELL'OLIO

C. DONÀ

C. CELSI

C. MAGNO

Pal. Grimani

FOND. S. SEVERO

RIO S. SEVERO

Questura

BORGOLOCO S. LORENZO

CALLE S. LORENZO

CORTE NUOVA

FOND. S. GIORGIO D. SCHIAVONI SAN

SALIZZ. S. GATTE

C.D. VIDA

404

4

C. MEZZO

CORTE D. PARADISO

Pal. Zorzi-Bon

Pal. Zorzi

LION

Scuola di San Giorgio degli Schiavoni

CAMPO D. GATTE

C.LLO DUE POZZI

MERCANTILE

CORONA CORTE

SALIZZ. ZORZI

PRETI

Ponte d. Greci

FONDAM. S. GIORGIO D. SCHIAVONI

CALLE DEI FURLANI

C. D. SCUDI

C. DELL'ARCO

MUNEGHETTE

GORNE

ROTTA

Pal. Priuli

FOND. OSMARIN

MADONNA

FOND. FURLANI

S. Antonin

PISC. S. MARTIN

404

Arsenale

STIA

REMEDIO

FOND. DELL'OSMARIN

Museum of Icons

SALIZZ. D. GRECI

MAGAZEN

San Giorgio dei Greci

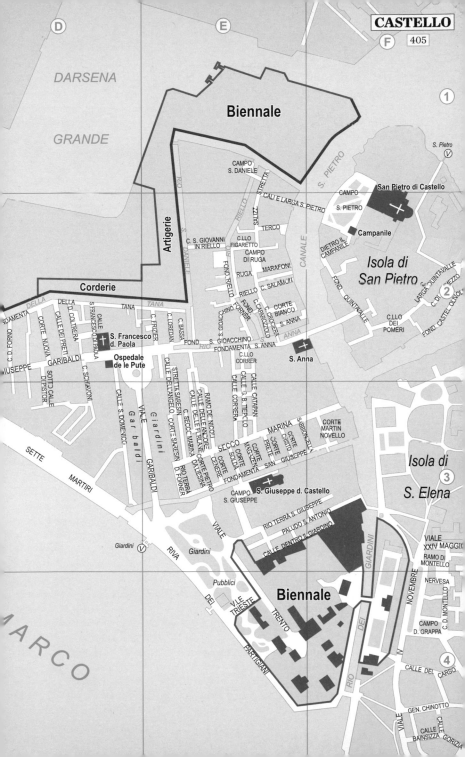

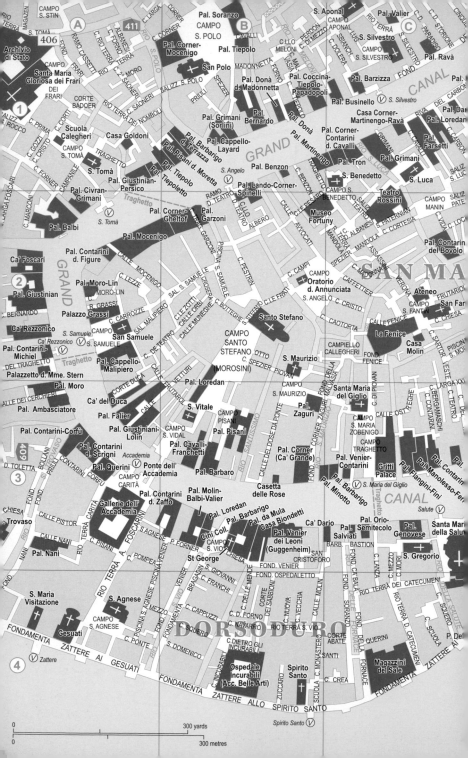

Bridge
SAL.PIO X
S. Bartolomeo
C. D. ZOCCO
CAMPO S. LIO
San Lio
C. BISSA
C. MARTINENGO
C. D. DOSE
402
FOND. PRETI
CAMPO SANTA MARIA FORMOSA
C. LUNGA S. M. FORMOSA
C. LIBRO
MADDALENA
CAPP.
407
CALLE
LORENZO

C. GALEAZZA
C. STAGNERI
MERCERIA DUE APRILE
CAMPO S. LIO
VELE
NAVE
C. D. VOLTO
SALIZZ.
C. PARADISO
C. DEGLI
C. Larga S. LORENZO
BORGOLOCO S. LORENZO

IIfin-
MAZZINI
MERCERIA
Santa Maria della Fava
CAMPO FAVA
RAMO MALVASIA
CALLE S. ANTONIO
C. M. NUOVO
Santa Maria Formosa
RUGA GIUFFA
FOND. D. SEVERO
Questura
RIO DI S. LORENZO
1

C. DEI MONTI
San Salvatore
MERCERIA
ACQUE DI MEZZO
Ridotto Venier
PISC. ZULIAN
CAMPO D. GUERRA
CASELLERIA
BANDE
Pal. Querini-Stampala
C. MEZZO
CORTE D. PARADISO
Pal. Zorzi-Bon
Pal. Zorzi

S. Salvador
M.S. ZULIAN
C. DEI PIGNOL
San Giuliano
CAMPO
QUERINI
C. REMEDIO REMEDIO
C. D. CORONA CORTE ROTTA
Pal. Priuli
PRETI FOND. OSMARIN

Croce d. Armeni
RAMO C. GALLO
S. C. GALLO
C. FIUBERA
SPADARIA
S. MARCO
C. CANONICA
S. Giovanni Nuovo
C. FIGHER
C. DELLA CHIESA
C. FIGHER
SAGRESTIA
FOND. DELL'OSMARIN
Museum of Icons

Torre d'Orologio
PTTA GIOVANNI XXIII
Pal. Patriarcale
Mus. Diocesan Art
RUGA GIUFFA
CAMPO SS. FILIPPO E GIACOMO
SALIZZ. PROVOLO
CAMPO S. PROVOLO
San Zaccaria

PIAZZA SAN MARCO
Procuratie Vecchie
Campanile
St Mark's Basilica
Bridge of Sighs
Hotel Danieli
CAMPO S. ZACCARIA

Museo Correr
Museo Archeologico
Doge's Palace
Prisons
Ponte d. Vin
DEGLI
SCHIAVONI

Procuratie Nuove
PIAZZETTA S. MARCO
Zecca
Libreria Marciana
P. DELLA PAGLIA
RIVA
S. Zaccaria

Ridotto
ASCENSION
Giardini Reali
404

Pal. Giustinian
C. BAROZZI
C. 13 MARTIRI
Cap. Porto
Harry's Bar
San Marco

al. Treves Bonfili

BACINO DI S. MARCO

3

D. DOGANA ALLA SALUTE
François Pinault Fn.
Punta della Dogana

ario cale

CAMPO S. GIORGIO
S. Giorgio
San Giorgio Maggiore
4

Cini Foundation

Isola di San Giorgio Maggiore

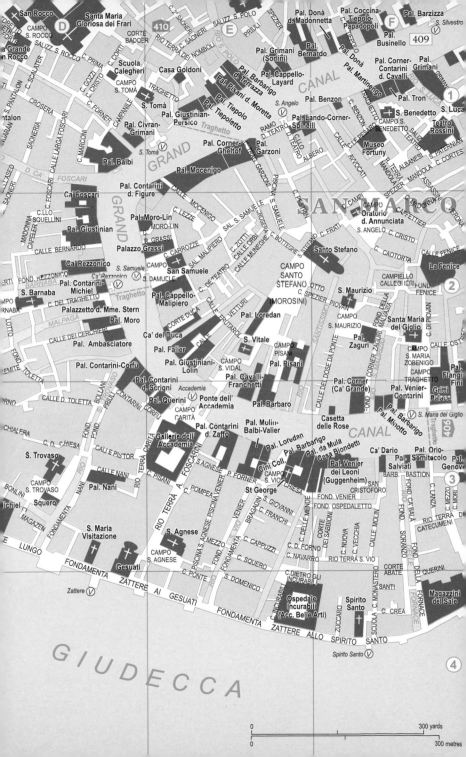

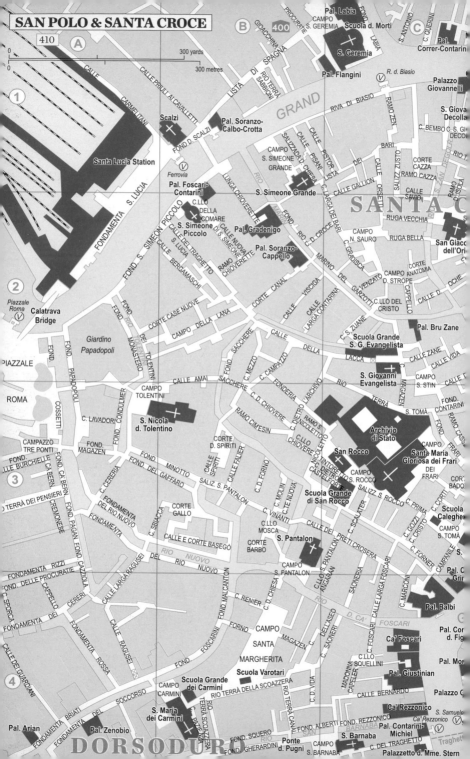

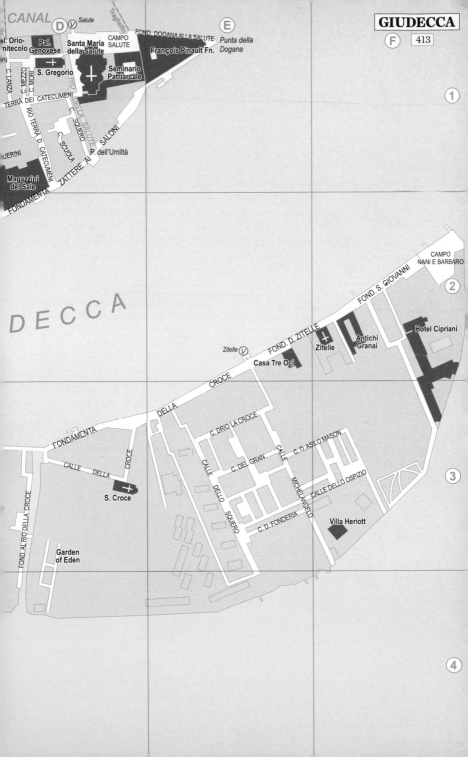

CANAL

GIUDECCA

F 413

D V Salute

Traghetto

FOND. DOGANA ALLA SALUTE

E Punta della Dogana

al. Orio-
nitecolo

Pal.
Genovese

Santa Maria
della Salute

CAMPO
SALUTE

François Pinault Fn.

S. Gregorio

Seminario
Patriarcale

C. MEZZO

C. MORI

C. LANZA

TERRA DEI CATECUMENI

RIO TERRA D. CATECUMENI

RIO DELLA SALUTE

C. SQUERO

C. SCUOLA

SALONI

P. dell'Umiltà

UERINI

ZATTERE AI SALONI

Magazzini
del Sale

FONDAMENTA

1

DECCA

CAMPO
NANI E BARBARO

2

FOND. S. GIOVANNI

Hotel Cipriani

Zitelle V

FOND. D. ZITELLE

Zitelle

Antichi
Granai

Casa Tre Oci

CROCE

DELLA

C. DRIO LA CROCE

C. D. ASILO MASON

FONDAMENTA

CALLE

C. DEL GRAN

CALLE

CROCE

CALLE DELLA

MICHELANGELO

CALLE DELLO OSPIZIO

3

S. Croce

CALLE DELLO SQUERO

C. D. FONDERIA

Villa Heriott

FOND. AL RIO DELLA CROCE

Garden
of Eden

4

414

pp. 400-01

pp. 410-11

pp. 408-09

pp. 406-07

pp. 412-13

S. Alvise

Madonna dell' Orto

Jewish Mus.

CANNAREGIO

I Ges

Santa Lucia Station

S. Stae

Ca' d'Oro

SANTA CROCE

Ca' Pesaro

S. Ma d. Mira

S. Giacomo dell'Orio

People Mover

SAN POLO

Rialto Bridge

S. Polo

Santa Maria Gloriosa dei Frari

S. Salvatore

Ca' Rezzonico

SAN MARCO

St. Ma Basil

Carmini

S. Stefano

La Fenice

Museo Correr

DORSODURO

Gallerie dell' Accademia

Peggy Guggenheim Collection

Salute

Gesuati

CANALE

Mulino Stucky

GIUDECCA

DELLA

Zit

Redentore

GIUDECCA

CANALE DI CANNAREGIO

GRAND CANAL

CANAL

GRAND CANAL

CANAL

CAN